ENLIGHTENMENTS

Encounters between Critical Theory
and Contemporary French Thought

Harry Kunneman
Hent de Vries
(eds.)

ENLIGHTENMENTS

Encounters between Critical Theory
and Contemporary French Thought

Kok Pharos Publishing House
Kampen — The Netherlands

This book is published with the financial assistance of the University for Humanist Studies and the Goethe Institute.

CIP-GEGEVENS KONINKLIJKE BIBLIOTHEEK, DEN HAAG

Enlightenments

Enlightenments : Encounters between Critical Theory and Contemporary French Thought / Harry Kunneman & Hent de Vries (eds.). — Kampen : Kok Pharos Teksten in het Engels, Duits en Frans. — Met bio- en bibliogr., index.
ISBN 90-390-0041-7
NUGI 619/631
Trefw.: Franfurter Schule / kritische theorie / deconstructie.

© 1993, Kok Pharos Publishing House,
P.O. Box 130, 8260 AC Kampen, The Netherlands
Cover Design By Rob Lucas
© Photo on cover: Pol Bury, 'Manhattan'
ISBN 90 390 0041 7
NUGI 619/631

Table of Contents

1. Introduction

HENT DE VRIES & HARRY KUNNEMAN

What should be the premises and forms of dialogue between those who, in contemporary debate, align themselves with the tradition of Western, Critical Theory (with or without 'pragmatic turn') and those who are more inspired by that other 'shift of paradigm' within philosophy, literary theory and psychoanalysis commonly — and undoubtedly insufficiently — defined as Post-Structuralism? This volume collects the papers presented at a recent international symposium at the newly founded *University for Humanist Studies* in Utrecht devoted to this question.

The debate between these quite different but also related positions which, we believe, cannot be reduced to the well-publicized controversy among so-called 'modernists' and 'postmodernists,' is one of the liveliest discussions of our time. However, the timely and topical significance of this Germano-Franco-Anglo-American (rather than merely 'Continental') dispute has also exerted an unmistakably negative influence on the intellectual and academic level of the debate: excessive polarization and journalistic simplification have all too often come to dominate the scene and snuffed out, in advance, the possibility of its being opened up to something more than a caricaturing exchange of views from two sides of a supposedly fixed borderline. Against this background, the symposium aimed to raise certain preliminary questions that could help generate a reconsideration of the 'ethics' and 'politics' of this discussion. Central to this task was the attempt to address certain prolegomena of this debate in a way that would neither be marred by precipitate conclusions and mutual exclusions nor be paralyzed by a simple re-enactment of what, regardless of all the raising of voices, is by now an all-too-familiar *dialogue de sourds*. To this end, contributions were invited from scholars whose work would not only guarantee international diversity and scholarly rigor but also, if possible, provide an awareness and explicit articulation of the possible structural limits of their own 'position.' By bringing together the work of theorists who demonstrate in what sense one could thus attempt to occupy both sides of the line of demarcation taken to divide post-Frankfurt-School-Critical-Theory and the most innovative readings that characterize recent French thought (indeed, *after* Structuralism), the present collection of essays offers a representative, if not exhaustive, overview of the current state of the debate. More specifically, the texts collected here also testify to the undiminished importance of at least one central question that continues to haunt us, as J. Derrida, perhaps, would write, 'here, at this very moment, in the situation where 'we' happen to find ourselves.'

What, then, is this question which, for the sake of clarity, can be said to run as a guiding thread through most of the essays assembled here? In what is to follow, we would like to suggest that it is the problem (or the problematization, for that matter) of *the possibility and the impossibility of a new or renewed 'Enlightenment,'* or to be more precise, of new and ever renewed 'Enlightenment*s*.' To be sure, throughout this volume the concept and the historical phenomenon of 'Enlightenment' is not simply described, re-affirmed or denied, let alone overcome, sublated or parodied. Rather, this phenomenon is analyzed and discussed, not only in view of a purported (formal) 'unity in the diversity of its voices' that J. Habermas discerns in the different forms in which modern reason manifests itself, but also in light of an internal division or 'performative tension' (to be described in more detail) that prevents us from ascribing a stable identity to its very concept and practice.

This is not to say that all of the contributions presented here address, let alone defend or criticize, 'Enlightenment' directly (provided this would be possible). But they all seem, in some way, to measure the distance between, on the one hand, the metaphysical, onto-theological, logocentric and traditionally humanist premises of 18th-century *Aufklärung*, based on the predominance of theoretical reflection and constative utterances (even in places where the primacy of practical reason is advocated), and, on the other hand, a certain 'performativity' (if that is the right word) that can be said to *precede* and *engage* all philosophical discourse reflecting 'clarity' and devoted to 'enlightened' praxis. The constative utterances that, traditionally, have sought to convey the identity of 'Enlightenment' fail to specify the ways in which its meaning is produced and transformed by a certain — linguistic and, perhaps, no longer simply linguistic — force that does not have its referent outside itself but is each time a new, singular occurence. For reasons explored by quite a few of the contributors to this book, this 'performativity,' which is also a certain 'normativity' (the normative, J.F. Lyotard writes in *Le différend*, 'resembles' a performative), is no longer describable in terms of speech acts originating in subjective intentions, nor does it exhaust itself in intersubjective deliberation or communication. Rather, this 'performativity' should be understood as the mark of 'forces,' of bodily desires, of gender, of power relations, theatricality and rhetoric as well as of the 'better argument,' whose 'success' and 'sincerity' is never absolutely guaranteed by any conventional context or rule and for which no appropriate idiom is ever readily at hand. Most of the essays assembled here could be read as attempts to find (or invent) a more adequate, proper or pertinent language for this 'inevitable contingency,' which, paradoxically, seems to elude not only the very concept of truth as *adaequatio* but also, more interestingly, the Heideggerian understanding of truth as historicity, epochality and *Ereignis* or propriation. And yet, even if no discourse of semantics, no fundamental ontology, hermeneutics or 'thought of Being' would be able to determine this 'performativity,' it does not thereby necessarily become a mere pragmatic, empirical or accidental moment. For this 'gesturing' of language and action 'is,' for all its indeterminacy, also characterized by a *'necessary contingency,'* which, instead of inaugurating the infamous 'anything goes,' obeys a 'logic' of its own, a 'logic' which demands to be clarified, even though, paradoxically, every such clarification would have to account for the fact that no clarification escapes the 'performative moment' that it seeks to elucidate. Not only should this 'logic' make it clear how the arguments that convince us of a 'necessary contingency' are linked up with a certain affirmation of the differences that would mark a 'liberal' culture as well as a democratic society. It should, A. Wellmer argues in his opening essay, also underscore that this contingency will always be accompanied by equally necessary *'idealizations,'* not the least of which is the acquiescence (a *sich verlassen* or *vertrauen*) to the gift of language, i.e. to the fact that our language, at least for a moment, can seem *'in Ordnung.'* And yet, such 'necessary idealizations' — which often take the form of more specific validity claims that transcend a given (for instance, 'our') context, language-game or life-form — always remain vulnerable to reflective revisions and therefore marked by the inevitable contingencies that they, inevitably, seek to escape. And it is only by acknowledging (and living) this paradox that we could hope to circumvent the unappealing choice between metaphysical objectivism or absolutism, on the one hand, and relativism or scepticism, on the other.

It is here, then, in the interpretation of the *necessary interplay of* '*contingencies*' and '*idealizations*,' that the most telling divergences between the essays presented here manifest themselves. Most of them start out from the presupposition that, at least at first sight, there is an insurmountable difference between, *on the one hand*, those who hold that philosophy and social theory should offer a theoretical (and falsifiable) account of rationality, which systematically reconstructs the universal conditions of possibility of intersubjectively valid argumentation — thereby aiming, it is claimed, at an indubitable, linguistic, foundation of critique and social justice — and those who, *on the other hand*, insist that any such descriptive and normative general theory is ultimately dependent on empirical, bodily and textual tropes inextricably bound up with all speech, cognition and action and thus *foreclosing all generalization and formalization.*

According to the latter hypothesis, any 'idea' of, say, responsibility and justice that could pretend to be genuine and compelling would have to take these elusive constitutive 'elements' into account as precisely the *quasi*-transcendental (or 'performative') conditions of their possibility as much as of their impossibility. For, if most particularly ethico-political criteria or norms rely on certain features of experience or gestures (rather than acts) of language which are not merely rhetorical or poetic (let alone aesthetic or a question of style), but retain a trace of the literary, the fictional and the fabulous (thereby giving yet another meaning to the prefix *quasi* in the formulation *quasi*-transcendental), then these criteria and norms are characterized by an inalienable asymmetry and are never able to present 'themselves' 'as such,' that is to say, in their purity. As a consequence, responsibility and justice (to name just two of the most heavily debated notions) would remain forever irrecuperable by any, however hypothetical or fallibilistic, rational reconstruction. And if this were the case, all ethico-political speech acts (if this designation is still appropriate here, where precisely the primacy of speech and action are in question) would disseminate themselves through the infinite (yet, 'in themselves,' radically finite) displacements of an instable, 'deconstructive' 'practice' or 'reading' — words to be used with much caution — incomparable to anything presented so far in the name of linguistics, hermeneutics and socio-psychological analysis.

On this view, the compelling character of moral 'obligation' would no longer be reducible to any determinate, explicit set of empirical regulations or transcendental categories that would leave no room for doubt and criticism as to what the 'origin' or 'meaning'

10

of this obligation might be. Nor would conformity to a general rule or formal procedure be enough to justify or 'ground' a responsible politics. For the very tribunal of reason to which these modes of justification refer would in itself be 'groundless' and marked by a certain 'performativity' contaminating its ideality, transparency and intelligibility, not in the least because, as Derrida has shown, every order of legality — the purported foundation of truth and justice — is always already itself, in turn, 'founded,' 'instituted' or 'postulated' by an 'act,' which, for obvious reasons, is neither simply just nor unjust, legal nor illegal. And this 'foundational act' would obey an even more disruptive 'performative' logic than that of singular ethico-political decisions, which are never without some 'reference' to existing rules of law, even though this 'reference' demands a kind of (reflective) judgment that must operate without recourse to unequivocal criteria of application or preestablished rules of linkage.

In his essay on the paradoxical ethics of pure prescription in Lyotard's *Le différend*, J.Rogozinsky retraces all the intricacies of such an ethics by demonstrating how it involves an account of obligation that is forced to situate itself uneasily between the ones developed by Kant, Kierkegaard and Levinas. Strictly speaking, the 'ethics of the *différend*' would be 'unjustified and unjustifiable' and, because of that heteronomy, be less the continuation or rejuvenation of Kant's idea of *Aufklärung* than a relapse in *Schwärmerei*. And yet, the 'ethics of the *différend*' would remain at a distance from any metaphysical and ethico-religious (read: Kierkegaardian or Levinasian) interpretation of this fundamentally unfounded obligation. In its affirmation of the irreducibility of the language (or the 'feeling') of obligation to other genres of discourse, specifically the regimen of cognative, constative phrases, the 'ethics of the *différend*' would thus reveal the 'blind spot' or the 'limit' of every Enlightenment that wishes to judge prescriptives in light of a principle of 'universality' itself modelled on the structure of theoretical reason.

Whatever the accuracy of the description of the controversy mentioned at the outset, it should come as no surprise, that most of the contributions to this volume, while continuing to spell out their different points of departure or theoretical aims, continue to make the case for the acknowledgment of some remarkable intersections, if not convergences. They suggest that, in the final analysis, both supposedly divergent conceptions of the task of thinking are forced

11

— by the very logic of their argument as well as by the very figures of thought and speech they invoke — to pay attention to the necessary interplay between, on the one hand, the discourse of philosophy and its inherent idealizations, and, on the other, certain — necessarily contingent — practices of 'reading' and 'linking,' of 'acting' and 'the body.' Both conceptions sketched above would thus, with more or less rigor, explore the interrelationships between what could be roughly called a universal pragmatics and a local pragmatics. In the last resort, they would *both* seem to be guided by a "new, very new *Aufklärung*," to use Derrida's intriguing formulation in the "Afterword" to *Limited Inc*, which was taken as the motto of this symposium. They would both seem to deal in differing ways with an *irreducibly normative* notion by means of which a *decentering mode of 'critique'* comes into view.

Seen in this light, every attempt at 'getting as clear as possible' about the boundaries between and the margins of Critical Theory and recent French thought is indeed marked, as G. Bennington argues, not so much by "a straightforward and honest 'enlightenment'-style ambition towards a clarity and illumination which could ideally (though perhaps not empirically) be achieved," as by "the sense that such an effort would quite rapidly come up against its own limit." The limit-concept of the 'border' or 'frontier' makes this clear. For the very attempt to determine this (or any other) line of demarcation terminologically would already presuppose that one knows that — and how — borderlines can be drawn. Not to think about this paradox — which, again, is that of 'necessary contingency' — would be the most significant characteristic of the 'dogmatism' of Enlightenment. And, to the extent that deconstruction affirms this paradox and any Habermasian position, whether unwittingly or not, relies on it, there is, Bennington surmises, perhaps "no 'debate' to be had here."

And, indeed, even in Habermas' *Der philosophische Diskurs der Moderne*, a book not particularly famous for its transgressive impetus with regard to the said borderlines, passages are to be found that refer to this problematic. Here, it is claimed that we need 'idealizations' precisely because convictions are shaped in and have to prove their mettle in a medium which is never 'pure.'

This does not imply, of course, that there are no real antagonisms or even *différends* between, say, the 'critical' and the 'deconstructive' approach or between the 'agonistic' struggle of 'phrases' and the 'negotiations' urged by 'pragrammatology' or, for that matter, between all these 'positions' and the insights prompted by a more psychoanalytic approach. But the most telling divergences between these conceptions or practices might very well not reside where we often assume they do. It might well be that these differences signal at least as much a difference in emphasis, accent or tone as a divergence in 'methods' followed or 'positions' taken. If this is the case, the question becomes whether (and to what extent) these differences can be 'retrieved' by 'discourse,' analyzed in their different constituents or overdeterminations and shared, if not in the harmony or symphony of a future consensus that would ultimately silence them in a secular *eschaton*, then at least in a 'composition' in which many voices would be allowed to make themselves heard and to 'enlighten' each other.

Enlightenments, we believe, could be the provisional title that indicates what is at stake in — and between — the following contributions. And this for at least three reasons. First and most obviously, because of the reference of this term to the historical 'sign' of the "good, old *Aufklärung*" (to cite Derrida once more), for instance in the recurrent references to the three critiques of Kant as well as to his political writings. For that *Aufklärung*, certain central concepts, such as reason, rationality, autonomy, universal rights, progress and emancipation formed a tightly knit network that was supposed to enable a free transfer from cognition to normative validity and aesthetic judgment and vice versa. And it is precisely this assumption that is disputed by most of the contributors to this volume, from whatever side or whatever end of the spectrum they speak. They all testify to the fact that this — illusory — homogeneity and transparency *obfuscates* the situated, and in this sense contingent, character of Enlightenment and loses sight of the aforementioned 'performative' moment of its foundation, its appellation, intervention and transformation. Most significant for the diverse notions of Enlightenment alluded to in the papers collected here, is the fact that they all exhibit an awareness of the complexities involved in this 'performativity,' which is described in different or even incommensurable terms. Due to this 'performativity,' tied to the bodily roots of rationality, to the *différends* between phrases and genres of discourse or to the so-called iterability of linguistic or other marks in general, the traditional modern (read: Kantian) dividing lines between cognition and practical or aesthetic valuation are themselves, in turn, divided. And, it is precisely this partition that could

13

be held responsible for an intriguing new disturbance and a new vigilance in the very 'idea,' 'task' and 'institution' of Enlightenment, one that would, perhaps, no longer be determined by the so-called dialectic of Enlightenment.[1] From now on, constative, prescriptive and so-called figurative speech acts have lost their purported isolation in separate realms and are forced to play in an unstable field with shifting boundaries, made possible and impossible by linguistic and other marks, troubled and empowered by bodily desires, allowing 'Enlightenment' to take place in the plural only.

Whereas the traditional-modern notion of Enlightenment — before and after the paradigm shift from so-called *Subjektphilosophie* to the reconstruction of the quasi-transcendental conditions of possibility of communicative action — seemed to be structured by a certain formal unity, the new Enlightenment(s) learn(s) to see or read this 'unity' as a 'phantom' and 'ideal' (or 'idealization') which is always already doubled and split. In its very 'performativity' it would not coincide with itself. On this view, there would no longer be just *one* Enlightenment; in its very 'idea,' procedures or 'practices,' Enlightenment would always already have lost its homogeneous, one-dimensional and unilateral character. *Aufklärung* would cease to be a question of linguistic communication only. And, what is more important, it would no longer be associated with the questioning attitude of transcendental inquiry, whether in its critical, juridical form that typifies the Kantian tribunal of reason or in the hermeneutic form it takes in the Heideggerean analytic of *Dasein*.

What, then, could Enlightenment mean for a kind of thinking that interrogates the metaphysical, onto-theological premises of classical conceptions of reason and patiently but irresistibly moves beyond the confines of formal rationality, without, therefore, becoming irrational? Does the respect for the 'performative appeal' that 'motivates' and 'institutes' reason not entrap thought in the paralyzing dilemma of silence and betrayal? And which political model would correspond to this analysis, exemplify it or, rather, *sign* it? Could the said 'performativity' ever be concretized, if not descriptively or phenomenologically then at least through a certain

---

1. For the ambiguities and intermediary 'position' of Horkheimers and Adorno's *Dialektik der Aufklärung* vis à vis the questions outlined here, cf. the contributions to Harry Kunneman and Hent de Vries, eds., *Die Aktualität der 'Dialektik der Aufklärung'. Zwischen Moderne und Postmoderne* (Frankfurt/M, New York: Campus Verlag, 1989).

14

practice? It is not difficult to see why a general answer to this question is so difficult and, perhaps, impossible.

The 'working hypothesis' of the symposium should therefore not create the illusion of being an argumentative exchange of viewpoints that is oriented toward the elimination of the borderlines mentioned earlier, let alone toward the erection of new barriers. On the contrary, if, as we think (and hope), there are *encounters* in (or as a result of) this volume, they will have been possible only in the plural, in the emphatic sense of the word, that is to say, by creating a new division with (or within) every partial and provisional 'consensus,' thus keeping open the possibility of an other 'agreement.'

Several contributions explore this possibility. Thus, L. Nagl's essay pursues the question of whether or to what extent deconstruction and Habermas' discourse theory can *complement each other*, whereas H.J. Adriaanse suggests that if there is any intersection possible at all between the universal pragmatic and deconstructive conception of Enlightenment it will be a *Schnittpunkt im Unendlichen*. Along different lines W. van Reijen considers a *juxtaposition* (as opposed to a synthesis) of discourse theory, Lyotard's 'ontology of phrases' and Rorty's transformation of pragmatism, whereas H. Kunneman, finally, engages in the project of *stretching* Habermas while subjecting him simultaneously to a quasi-deconstructive interrogation. On several pivotal points the theory of communicative action is thus shown to refer to extralinguistic resources that it can neither include in nor exclude from its conceptual framework, but which somehow contribute to its very motivation and mobility. This could be said specifically of the gestural expression of the body, of the caress, of silences, in short, of non-discursive 'acts' of 'linking,' which would have to be *incorporated* in a more general 'theory' of 'communication.'

Because these four confrontations do not exhaust the full range of possible encounters, the interpretation of the subtitle of this volume ('Encounters between Critical Theory and Contemporary French Thought') should, perhaps, be pushed even a little further. For some of the essays assembled here (like the ones contributed by Bennington and Rogozinsky) go so far as to situate themselves de facto *in between* these heterogeneous theoretical fields, often in their most crucial passages. Thereby, they open up the possibility of yet another encounter that is no longer guided by an ideal of confrontation, mediation or *Horizontverschmelzung*.

Enlightenments, then, could, secondly, be the index of a multilateral and multi-dimensional *ethics of discussion* that responds to the 'obsolescence' of this dialectical or hermeneutic ideal. Indeed, one of the central problems discussed throughout this volume regards the exchanges — in other words, the enlightenments — between the different assessments of the way in which this absence of indubitable criteria, middle terms or overlapping horizons should be addressed. Again, the notion of 'performativity' introduced above might help us to formulate what is at issue here. For it is remarkable that the debate on the Enlightenment as an historical and socio-political category can be described in terms of the increasing attention paid to the ways in which this discussion itself is embedded in contexts of argumentation, contexts whose boundaries are only relatively stable and are constantly being transformed. What, then, does this observation imply for the evaluation of philosophical argument or, for that matter, of all other relevant forms of discussion?

One way of engaging this question can be found in R. Gasché's careful analysis of Heidegger's introduction of the notion of 'confrontation' (*Auseinandersetzung*), particularly in the Nietzsche lectures. *Auseinandersetzung*, Gasché shows, stands for a non-polemical dialogue between philosophies, a dialogue which also entails an authentic and oriented critique. As such, it neither fits the 18th-century conception of critique as being a 'fixing' of 'standards,' nor is it comparable to the 'systematic mapping' that exhausts itself in drawing borders and lines of demarcation according to an ideal of pure (mathematical) intelligibility that is expected to bring reason into its own. Rather, *Auseinandersetzung* presupposes a responsiveness to the *Befremdung* of otherness or 'the Other,' which is affirmed in its very constitutive role as the condition of thought proper.

Starting out from a different horizon, S. Weber concretizes another *Auseinandersetzung*, namely the one between Walter Benjamin and Carl Schmitt. Weber shows their writings to be marked by a similar "methodological extremism," one that opens yet another perspective on the question of "what is involved in thinking the irreducibility of the norm," that is to say, in thinking its independency from any generality. Both Schmitt's theory of decision (especially of the sovereign's privilege in determining the *Ausnahmezustand* that is supposed to endanger the very existence of the state) and Benjamin's analysis of the historicality of the German *Trauerspiel* adopt a language of interruption and suspension that is not so much a negation of the present order of things but the affirmation of its being dependent on a certain transcendence exceeding and grounding the juridical realm. However, their secularization of theological concepts into political categories also reveals some striking differences. These differences, Weber demonstrates, reveal the profound distinction between a theory of authentic, ultimate and punctual decidability, on the one hand, and a staging of infinite revision and displacement, on the other.

This reading helps to prepare the ground for the third connotation of 'Enlightenments' that interests us here and that marks quite a few of the following essays. For, last but not least, the title *Enlightenments* also has a remarkable *quasi-theological* connotation. It could focus our attention on the, perhaps, unexpected "solidarity with metaphysics in the moment of its downfall," to cite the well-known phrase with which Adorno concludes his *Negative Dialektik* and that seems to have left its mark in several contributions to this book.

Not only are the different conceptions of Enlightenment, for instance of Habermas and Derrida, found to be ultimately dependent upon an irreducible (finite) *infinity* which manifests itself in incomparable, perhaps incommensurable, ways, as H.J. Adriaanse argues. At times it would also seem as if the discourse on formal (or procedural) rationality is brought back to or at least confronted with a pure attentiveness irreducible to any of its categories, precisely because the latter are always already traversed and unsettled by *Aufmerksamkeit*. R. Nägele analyzes this logic of disturbance by recalling Walter Benjamin's citation from Malebranche, according to whom this attentiveness would be the "natural prayer of the soul." This citation and the context in which it occurs — a reading of Kafka's 'dialectical *Aufklärung*' — reveal, Nägele suggests, that the demarcations ascribed to modern Enlightenment, such as the *Gattungsunterschied* between philosophy and literature, but also the borderlines drawn between the West and the East as well as between these two, on the one hand, and the tradition of Haggadah and Halacha, on the other, are subverted. And yet, the result of this subversion is hardly that of 'postmodern anarchy,' but, on the contrary, the exploration of another *Aufmerksamkeit*, one which is no longer intimidated by the 'modern' opposition of seriousness and play (or *Witz*), of the profane (or the natural) and the theological. This *Aufmerksamkeit* is intimately connected with a turn to writing, more precisely, to the reading or decipherment of a convoluted *Schrift*.

E. Weber, in her contribution, could be said to focus in on

precisely such a reading in her analysis of a 'text' of Derrida (or, more precisely, a "text running through several texts"), which she, with reference to a famous figure used by Adorno, describes as a "micrology of tears." Tears, whether written or wept, would mark that "situation of utterances," in which the 'self' is affected prior to its very constitution and that therefore cannot enter a historical narrative, let alone an autobiography. Weber explores how being affected in this way, in an immemorial time, is intensely connected, in Derrida's 'text,' with the 'experience' of the 'already-being-there' of a language that gives us our names and makes us speak and write. In Derrida's 'text,' she goes on to explain, this 'experience' is also an 'experience' of a circumcision that marks at once the universality of being inscribed into language and a certain — Jewish — singularity. This simultaneity characterizes the language of tears as it echoes, with a *Nachträglichkeit* that resists analysis, "a call sent out priori to any empirical language," like the Hebrew letter *aleph* that opens up the ten commandments and of which it could be said, following Scholem, that, although it denotes nothing in itself, it is nonetheless the passage to all articulate language. As the very origin of names and tears, it would, in Derrida's 'text,' resemble — or, more precisely, 'mix' with — what, in the langague of the tradition, is callled the 'name of God.'

H. de Vries in his contribution retraces yet another intriguing ellipsis and reinscription of theological figures, particularly in Derrida's recent rereadings of the work of Kant. This time the focus is on the so-called 'apocalytic tone' and 'angelic' structure of a discourse on 'vigilance' that can be said to displace its traditional, onto-theological predecessors. This 'lucid vigil' is read as the uneffaceable 'remainder,' not only of the deconstruction of the Kantian project of Enlightenment, but also of its irrational counterparts. It is this 'remainder' that explains why, according to Derrida, we can never simply 'forgo the *Aufklärung*.' Following the exposition of this *Leitmotif*, de Vries endeavors to demonstrate that the relation between this ellipsis of Enlightenment, on the one hand, and the demands of institutionalized, theoretical, academic discourse, on the other, are, in Derrida's writings — again — described elliptically, in yet another meaning of the word. For, it is argued, Derrida sees in this relation a polarity that, like an ellipse with two foci, precludes every possibility for discourse to close itself off in a 'uni-focal' (and univocal) dialectical, hermeneutic and, for that matter, vicious circle.

Enlightenment, then, would no longer be thinkable and practicable when defined in terms of a teleological and anthropocentric process, whatever its postulated ideal beginnings and whatever its conceivable end. Consequently, the *'humanisms'* that still pervade the Enlightenments that interest us here could certainly no longer be simply based on the premises of a metaphysical anthropology, even if the latter takes the form of a more radical thought of the essence of *humanitas*, as in Heidegger, or chooses to be responsive only to the 'humanism of the *other man*,' as Levinas urges in his famous phrase. To understand this, it is not enough to point to the aforementioned reception and reinscription of religious tropes long forgotten or deemed obsolete and 'immigrated into profanity.' More important is, perhaps, the fact that these Enlightenments go one step further by displacing the answer to (as well as the very form of) the question 'who comes after subject?'

B. Hanssen demonstrates how Derrida's most recent readings of Heidegger, in particular, unsettle the humanist axiomatics that overdetermines the very point of departure of fundamental ontology as formulated in *Sein und Zeit*. She explains that the interrogation of the questioning attitude that serves to justify the primacy of *Dasein* not only reiterates the longstanding deconstructive (and Nietzschean) *Leitmotif* of affirmation but also reinscribes Heidegger's later notion of the *Zusage* of language. In the trace of this notion, a different 'idea' of responsibility would become thinkable and urgent, one that no longer needs to exclude 'the animal' or 'the living in general' and, Hanssen concludes, "passes through a consideration for the infra-human," *without* therefore "calling upon itself the specter of inhumanity." On this reading, Derrida's interrogation of the margins of the human could be said to align itself more easily with Adorno than with Heidegger.

It is along these different and divided lines, then, that unanticipated Enlightenments come into sight, that is to say, *demands for more clarity from within and beyond, opposed to or virtually independent of 'the' 'project' of modernity*. These Enlightenments are explored systematically throughout this book, in theoretical discussions regarding the status of both ethico-political obligation and of the institution of the law (and decision), as they are found in the work of Benjamin, Habermas, Putnam, Rorty, Foucault, Deleuze, Lyotard, Derrida, de Man, Lacan and Lefort. But they are also put to test in analyses of concrete problems of democracy and human rights, feminism and the body. It is this combination of theoretical discussion and concrete analysis which reflects the intertwinement of cognitive and normative issues that characterizes all the conceptions of the task of thinking brought together here. For indeed, if Enlightenment — because of (or in view of) its essential, intrinsic multiplicity — can no longer be grounded in (or move in the direction of) one place or topic, then the distinction between its 'idea' and its purported 'concretization' or 'application,' also undermines itself. This does not imply, of course, that concrete issues lose their significance and urgency. On the contrary, if Enlightenment can no longer be restricted to critical (read: transcendental) inquiry, if it is no longer only or primarily a question of linguistic communication, then attention to its peculiar 'performativity' and embodiment becomes all the more important. Every genuine theorizing would have to recognize and affirm that it partakes in the very 'impurity' traditionally associated with practical questions as well as in the inevitable precipitation of decisions demanded here and now.

Seen against this background, the decision to regroup the essays under two major headings, for all its arbitrariness, does not entail a logical or, for that matter, chronological order of things. For, whereas the contributions gathered around the title *The Ethics of Discussion: Formal Pragmatics, Pragrammatology and the Differend* interrogate the 'theoretical' features and difficulties of three different approaches to 'Enlightenment' and, in the very subtleness of their performance, bear witness to the ethico-political implications of theorizing itself, the essays assembled under the rubric *Figures of Politics: Problems of Democracy, Human Rights and Feminism*, while putting more emphasis on 'material' topics, could also be read as further explorations of the pertinence of the analyses begun in the first part of this book.

This continuity is clearly manifested in the contribution by Ph. van Haute on Lefort, Derrida and the 'paradoxical' status of human rights, where it is argued that, in spite of some remarkable differences, Lefort's interpretation and defense of human rights can be read as articulating some major aspects of the 'deconstructive' view of the 'foundation' of the law. It is also manifest in the contributions directed at and inspired by feminist philosophy and psychoanalysis.

H. Nagl-Docekal's programmatic essay gives an overview of the different ways in which, up to the present day, philosophy has reproduced a gender-biased frame of thought. Against this background, she explores the prolegomena of what could be called a 'feminist transformation' of philosophy, which would be marked by different phases and thematic concerns.

This transformation is analyzed in further detail by R. Braidotti. She centers her contribution around the crisis of "the old forms of subjectivity," which, as she argues, instead of being a mere philosophical and ethico-political predicament, offers an opportunity for feminists to invent an alternative language and to 're-figure' the subject. Drawing on the work of Gilles Deleuze and Donna Haraway, Braidotti discusses the nature of the subject's embodiment and, more specifically, the recently introduced theme of the 'cyborg' as being a new possible figuration for feminist subjectivity.

By contrast, H. Geyer-Ryan, in her essay 'Unreal Presences,' raises doubts as to whether the insistence on a certain figurality, specifically in the language of 'literature' and 'allegory,' does not lead precisely to a forgetfulness and to disfigurations of the body, most often the female body. She argues that an ambiguous example of this can be found in the (later) work of Walter Benjamin, but she specifically takes Paul de Man to task for the way in which in his readings allegory is used. Critical thought (and, for that matter, praxis), she suggests, would not be able to do without 'real presences,' which do not necessarily have to take the form of traditional, religious or metaphysical 'postulates of transcendence,' as in G. Steiner's latest work.

The last two contributions both refer, albeit it from quite different angles, to the work of J. Lacan. P. Dews investigates the no-man's-land between Lacan and the Frankfurt School. Dews argues that a reconsideration of the early phases of Lacan's thinking, especially his *Les complexes familiaux*, could be of help in modifying the dichotomy within present day feminist theory between those forms of psychoanalytic inquiry that appear relatively 'remote' from socio-historical reality, on the one hand, and those studies, inspired by recent Frankfurt School thought, which have shifted their emphasis on "the complex internal structure of subjectivity," in favour of a preoccupation with an interrogation of "the normative structures of *inter*-subjectivity," on the other.

Finally, T. Brennan broadens this use of Lacan's work by raising yet another problem. Starting from an argument developed in some feminist writings on psychoanalysis, she explores the idea that psychological fantasies can be at the same time transhistorical and influenced by changing socio-historical circumstances. More specifically, she focuses on the desires 'encapsulated' in consumer goods — especially the desire for instant gratification and the desire to be waited upon and thus to control — as reflections of such an

21

underlying transhistorical fantasy. This fantasy is further specified in terms of the fantasies about the mother's body described by M. Klein. Building upon the implications of Lacan's theory of a paranoid social psychosis and an 'ego's era,' Brennan suggests that it is the transhistorical fantasy of controlling the mother's body, which in our time is played out with great social force in the production of commodities and the "spoiling of living nature" that is intrinsically connected with this production. There would be no reason, Brennan continues, why this process could never be reversed. At least up to a certain point, such a reversal is possible, even though it is not clear where the energy needed for it would come from.

It is here, then, that one could locate the greatest practical challenges of more than one contribution to this book, namely in the endeavor to engage in preparatory clarifications, or Enlightenments, that could open up discourse (and, for that matter, discursive practices) for interminable advents of 'the other.' These advents would have the 'performative' character ascribed above to the 'necessary contingencies' and 'idealizations' and could, perhaps, be seen as instances of precisely the '*Schatten von Differenz*,' which, as Habermas maintains, accompany the 'fragile' and 'transitorial' 'unity' of an, indeed, always already 'broken intersubjectivity.' It would only be this 'performative' character of the advents that would circumvent the latter's subjugation to an idealistic fallacy suffocating all singularity, and, one might add, forclosing — or prejudging — the testimony of the *Arrive-t-il*? This testimony, Lyotard suggests, recalls the void that engraves itself between phrases and genres of discourse and makes their very occurence possible. The void cannot be filled up and even — or especially — the appeal to new, different 'Enlightenments' would stand under this restriction and therefore re-affirm the 'contingency' of its very 'idealization.'

PART I:

THE ETHICS OF DISCUSSION:

FORMAL PRAGMATICS,

PRAGRAMMATOLOGY

AND THE DIFFEREND

2. Wahrheit, Kontingenz, Moderne

ALBRECHT WELLMER

I.

Wenn wir kommunizieren, etwas vortragen oder schreiben, erheben wir unvermeidlicherweise Wahrheitsansprüche oder — da vielleicht nicht jeder im Falle von moralischen oder ästhetischen Geltungsansprüchen von "Wahrheit" reden möchte — *Geltungsansprüche* verschiedener Art. Ich habe gerade selbst einen Geltungsanspruch erhoben. Wenn ich aber ernsthaft einen Geltungsanspruch erhebe, dann erwarte ich, daß jede/r andere gute Gründe hätte mir zuzustimmen, vorausgesetzt sie/er versteht, was ich gesagt habe und hat genügend Kenntnisse, Kompetenz und Urteilskraft etc. In diesem Sinn unterstelle ich, daß der von mir erhobene Geltungsanspruch ein guter Kandidat für ein intersubjektives Einverständnis ist, das auf guten Gründen beruht. Wenn aber jemand mit guten Gründen Einwände gegen das erhebt, was ich behaupte, dann müßte ich meinen Geltungsanspruch zurücknehmen oder zumindest zugeben, daß Zweifel daran angebracht sind. All dies scheint ziemlich trivial; aber wie wir wissen, sind es solche Trivialitäten, die im Zentrum der interessantesten philosophischen Kontroversen stehen. Wenn man beginnt darüber nachzudenken, was ein gutes Argument oder eine überzeugende Erfahrungsevidenz ist oder wenn man sich überlegt, aufgrund welcher Kriterien wir entscheiden können, was ein gutes Argument oder eine überzeugende Evidenz ist, dann verliert man leicht den Boden unter den Füßen; vor allem, wenn man sich klarmacht, wie schwer es sein kann, in solchen Dingen Einverständnis zu erzielen. Man könnte etwa die folgende Frage stellen: Angenommen, es gibt einen unauflösbaren Dissens bezüglich der Möglichkeit, Wahrheitsansprüche zu begründen, bezüglich der Standards der Argumentation oder der Überzeugungskraft von Erfahrungsevidenzen — etwa zwischen Mitgliedern verschiedener sprachlicher, wissenschaftlicher oder kultureller "communities" —, dürfen wir dann gleichwohl unterstellen, daß es — irgendwo — die *richtigen* Standards oder Kriterien, d.h. eine *objektive* Wahrheit mit Bezug auf die entsprechenden Probleme gibt? Oder sollten wir annehmen, daß Wahrheit immer "relativ" ist auf bestimmte Kulturen, Sprachen, Gesellschaften oder sogar Personen? Die zweite Alternative, der Relativismus, scheint inkonsistent, während die erste, der Wahrheits-"Absolutismus", metaphysische Annahmen zu implizieren scheint. Ich möchte dies die "Antinomie der Wahrheit" nennen. Während der letzten Jahrzehnte sind beträchtliche philosophische Anstrengungen darauf gerichtet gewesen, diese Antinomie der Wahrheit aufzulösen: auf der einen Seite durch Versuche zu zeigen, daß der Absolutismus keine Metaphysik impliziert, auf der anderen durch entsprechende Versuche zu zeigen, daß die Kritik am Absolutismus nicht zwangsläufig zum Relativismus führt. Wichtige Vertreter der ersten Argumentationsstrategie sind H. Putnam, K.O. Apel und J. Habermas; der vielleicht wichtigste Vertreter der zweiten Position ist R. Rorty. Ich will an dieser Stelle nicht auf Derridas Position eingehen, derzufolge Wahrheit ein hoffnungslos metaphysischer Begriff *ist*, wobei es aber für Derrida keinen direkten Weg aus der Metaphysik gibt, da wir offensichtlich nicht ohne den Wahrheitsbegriff auskommen können. Demgegenüber stimmen die zuerst genannten Philosophen darin überein, daß der Wahrheitsbegriff sehr wohl in einem nichtmetaphysischen *und* nichtrelativistischen Sinn verstanden werden kann. Freilich erheben Putnam, Apel und Habermas gegen Rorty den Vorwurf des Relativismus, während Rorty seinen Kritikern vorwirft, Metaphysiker zu bleiben. Diese interessante Konstellation zeigt, wie ich glaube, einmal mehr, daß die Antinomie der Wahrheit sich nicht so einfach auflösen läßt.

Im folgenden werde ich meine eigene Auflösung der Antinomie vorschlagen, und zwar auf dem Wege einer Kritik an der Art, in der die Alternativen durch Putnam, Apel und Habermas einerseits, und Rorty andererseits formuliert worden sind. Wenn man Putnam, Apel und Habermas in einem Atemzug nennt, läuft man natürlich Gefahr, die erheblichen Differenzen zwischen ihren philosophischen Positionen zu verwischen. Es läßt sich aber behaupten, daß ihnen eine bestimmte begriffliche Strategie gemeinsam ist, die darin besteht, Wahrheit in Begriffen einer "notwendigen Idealisierung" zu explizieren. Hierin liegt der Kern ihrer Kontroverse mit Rorty. Die nachfolgende Argumentation ist ein Versuch, diese Kontroverse neu zu beschreiben.

Putnam hat Wahrheit als rationale Akzeptierbarkeit unter erkenntnismäßig idealen Bedingungen[1] erklärt; Habermas erläutert Wahrheit als Gehalt eines rationalen Konsenses unter Bedingungen einer idealen Sprechsituation.[2] Apel schließlich hat zu Recht darauf hingewiesen, daß Putnams und Habermas' Erläuterungen des Wahrheitsbegriffs komplementär sind; denn einerseits muß die Idee erkenntnismäßig idealer Bedingungen sich auf eine Gemeinschaft von Sprechern beziehen, wenn sie nicht leer oder metaphysisch werden soll, andererseits kann eine ideale Kommunikationsstruktur allein keine ausreichende Garantie für Wahrheit sein: es muß darüber hinaus sichergestellt sein, daß die Beteiligten in einer solchen Kommunikationssituation über die relevanten Argumente und Erfahrungen tatsächlich verfügen. Deshalb hat Apel versucht, Putnams und Habermas' Vorstellungen zu *kombinieren* und Wahrheit als letztgültigen Konsens einer idealen Kommunikationsgemeinschaft zu explizieren. In dieser Auffassung wird das Konsensprinzip der Wahrheit mit einem Peirceschen Konvergenzprinzip verknüpft, das nicht nur auf naturwissenschaftliche Erkenntnis, sondern auch auf moralische und hermeneutische Wahrheitsansprüche bezogen wird.[3] Charakteristisch für alle drei Versuche, Wahrheit als rationale Akzeptierbarkeit unter idealen Bedingungen zu explizieren, ist folgendes: die Idealisierungen, auf die die Klärung des Wahrheitsbegriffs angewiesen zu sein scheint, müssen schon auf der Ebene alltäglicher Kommunikation beziehungsweise des argumentativen Diskurses als wirksam unterstellt werden, und zwar als "notwendige Präsuppositionen".

1. Putnam, Hilary: *Vernunft, Wahrheit, Geschichte*. Frankfurt (Suhrkamp) 1982. S. 83. Siehe auch Anm. 2.
2. Ursprünglich in: "Wahrheitstheorien". In: Fahrenbach, Helmut (Hrsg.): *Wirklichkeit und Reflexion*. Pfullingen (Neske) 1973. Wiederabgedruckt in: Habermas, Jürgen: *Vorstudien und Ergänzungen zur Theorie des kommunikativen Handelns*. Frankfurt (Suhrkamp) 1984. Vgl. insbesondere S. 174-183. Ich werde im folgenden unterscheiden zwischen einer "starken" und einer "schwachen" Interpretation der Idee "notwendiger Idealisierungen". Habermas hat ursprünglich einer starken Interpretation dieser Idee zugeneigt; ich glaube, daß er heute mehr oder weniger mit der schwachen Interpretation übereinstimmt, die ich hier verteidigen werde. Ähnliches gilt im übrigen für Hilary Putnam. Vgl. etwa sein Vorwort zu: *Realism with a Human Face*. Cambridge Mass. und London (Harvard Univ. Press.) 1990. S. viii. Putnam betont hier ausdrücklich, daß er eine (in meinem Sinne) "starke" Interpretation seiner Idealisierungsidee niemals vertreten hat.
3. Vgl. insbes. Apel, Karl-Otto: "Fallibilismus, Konsensustheorie der Wahrheit und Letztbegründung". In: *Philosophie und Begründung*. (Hrsg. vom Forum für Philosophie Bad Homburg). Frankfurt (Suhrkamp) 1986, Abschnitt IV.1 (S. 139-150) und IV.3 (S. 151-163). Vgl. auch unten Anm. 5.

Die Idee notwendiger Idealisierungen, die im Wahrheitsbegriff impliziert sind, soll die Unterscheidung zwischen rationaler Akzeptierbarkeit (oder dem rationalen Konsens) hier und jetzt und der rationalen Akzeptierbarkeit (oder dem rationalen Konsens) *überhaupt* sicherstellen. Es handelt sich also um die Differenz zwischen Wahrheit überhaupt (Wahrheit im absoluten Sinn) und dem, wovon wir auf der Grundlage von Argumenten, Kriterien und Evidenzen, über die wir hier und jetzt verfügen, glauben, daß es wahr ist (oder darin übereinstimmen, daß es wahr ist). Nun denke ich, daß sehr wohl eine *gewisse* Unterscheidung dieser Art zur logischen Grammatik unseres Wahrheitsbegriffs gehört. Einerseits nämlich können wir Wahrheitsansprüche nur auf der Grundlage derjenigen Argumente und Evidenzen rechtfertigen, über die *wir* jeweils verfügen, und andererseits können sich unsere Argumente und Evidenzen im Prinzip immer als ungenügend herausstellen, so daß wir also immer gezwungen sein können, unsere Wahrheitsansprüche zu revidieren: Der Wahrheitsbegriff impliziert eine notwendige Beziehung zu möglichen Argumenten oder Evidenzen, auf welche Wahrheitsansprüche sich gründen können, *und* er impliziert einen Überschuß über alle Argumente und Erfahrungsgründe, über die eine bestimmte Sprachgemeinschaft zu einer bestimmten Zeit verfügt.

Es ist die Interpretation eben dieser Differenz zwischen Wahrheit und rationaler Akzeptierbarkeit durch Putnam, Apel und Habermas, welche Rorty zurückweist.[4] Mit anderen Worten, Rorty weist die Vorstellung von im Wahrheitsbegriff implizierten "notwendigen Idealisierungen" zurück und er kritisiert darüber hinaus die These, daß wir notwendigerweise eine Art "Konvergenz" in unserer Suche nach der Wahrheit annehmen müssen. Was den zweiten Einwand betrifft, hat Rorty meiner Meinung nach recht. Ich glaube jedoch, daß wir nur durch eine Reformulierung seines ersten Einwands über die schlechte Alternative "Objektivismus" versus "Relativismus" hinauskommen können, die genau das bezeichnet, was ich die "Antinomie der Wahrheit" genannt habe.

Ich möchte im folgenden zeigen, daß die Idee "notwendiger Idealisierungen", die im Erheben von Wahrheitsansprüchen impliziert

---

4. Rorty, Richard: "Solidarität oder Objektivität?". In: Rorty: *Solidarität oder Objektivität?* Stuttgart (Reclam) 1988 und "Pragmatismus, Davidson und der Wahrheitsbegriff". In: Picardi, Eva und Joachim Schulte (Hrsg.): *Die Wahrheit der Interpretation.* Frankfurt (Suhrkamp) 1990.

sind, auf zwei verschiedene Weisen verstanden werden kann: in einem starken oder "totalisierenden" und in einem schwachen oder "lokalisierenden" Sinn. Wenn man die Idee in einem starken Sinne versteht, wird sie "metaphysisch" (wobei das Wort "metaphysisch" im Sinne Derridas zu verstehen ist); wenn man sie in ihrem schwachen Sinn versteht, wird sie unproblematisch und — wie ich versuchen werde zu zeigen — nicht nur immun gegenüber Rortys Einwänden, sondern zugleich ein Schlüssel zu einer Auflösung der Antinomie, welche Rortys "ethnozentrischer" Auflösung überlegen wäre.

Als erstes Beispiel wähle ich Putnams Idealisierungsthese. Wenn man den Begriff "erkenntnismäßig idealer Bedingungen" vor dem Hintergrund einer präsupponierten *Konvergenz* in der Suche nach Wahrheit versteht, dann, so scheint mir, müssen hiermit Erkenntnisbedingungen gemeint sein, unter denen die *volle* und *ganze* Wahrheit zugänglich wäre. Selbst wenn man den Begriff nur im Sinne einer regulativen Idee verstünde, wäre es doch die Idee eines absoluten Wissens, d.h. aber die Idee einer Sicht der Welt gleichsam vom Standpunkt Gottes. Nun hat Apel meiner Meinung nach völlig recht darauf zu bestehen, daß die im Wahrheitsbegriff implizierte regulative Idee — wenn denn eine impliziert ist — nicht nur als epistemische, d.h. als eine auf den Fortschritt der wissenschaftlichen Erkenntnis bezogene Idee verstanden werden darf.[5] Wenn man nämlich die verschiedenen Dimensionen von Wahrheit oder Geltung berücksichtigt, wenn man zudem berücksichtigt, daß Wahrheit immer auf eine Sprachgemeinschaft und die Möglichkeit eines rationalen Konsenses in einer solchen Sprachgemeinschaft bezogen ist, dann muß sich die im Wahrheitsbegriff implizierte regulative Idee auf ideale epistemische, moralische und kommunikative Bedingungen gleichermaßen beziehen. Die regulative Idee, die im Wahrheitsbegriff impliziert ist, wird so zur Idee eines letzten Konsenses in einer idealen Kommunikationsgemeinschaft. Hier wird die Idee der vollständigen, der "absoluten" Wahrheit mit der einer moralisch vollkommenen Ordnung und der einer vollkommen transparenten Kommunikationssituation verknüpft. Diese

5. Vgl. z.B.: Apel, Karl-Otto: "Szientismus oder transzendentale Hermeneutik? Zur Frage nach dem Subjekt der Zeicheninterpretation in der Semiotik des Pragmatismus". In: Ders. *Transformation der Philosophie. Bd. II: Das Apriori der Kommunikationsgemeinschaft.* Frankfurt (Suhrkamp) 1973. S. 215 ff. Ebenda: "Das Apriori der Kommunikationsgemeinschaft", S. 429 ff.

Idee einer idealen Kommunikationsgemeinschaft ist aber genau in Derridas Sinn metaphysisch, denn wenn man alle ihre Konsequenzen ausbuchstabiert, wird sie zur Idee einer Kommunikationsgemeinschaft, die "dem Spiel und der Ordnung des Zeichens"[6] entkommen wäre; zur Idee eines Zustands vollkommener Transparenz, absoluten Wissens und moralischer Vollkommenheit — kurz: einer Kommunikationssituation, die die Zwänge, die Opazität, die Fragilität, die Temporalität und die Materialität endlicher menschlicher Kommunikationsformen hinter sich gelassen hätte. Derrida hat zu Recht darauf hingewiesen, daß in solchen Idealisierungen die Bedingungen der Möglichkeit dessen, was idealisiert wird, negiert werden. Ideale Kommunikation wäre Kommunikation jenseits der Bedingungen der "différance" — um mit Derrida zu sprechen —, und deshalb Kommunikation außerhalb und jenseits der Bedingungen der Möglichkeit von Kommmunikation. Insoweit die Idee der idealen Kommunikationsgemeinschaft jedoch die Negation der Bedingungen endlicher menschlicher Kommunikation einschließt, impliziert sie die Negation der naturhaften und historischen Bedingungen menschlichen Lebens, der endlichen menschlichen Existenz. Ich denke, Nietzsche hat als erster darauf hingewiesen, daß solche Ideen am Ende ununterscheidbar werden von der des Nirwanas; ideale Kommunikation wäre der Tod der Kommunikation. Die Idee einer idealen Kommunikationsgemeinschaft bleibt selbst dann paradoxal, wenn sie nur als regulative Idee verstanden wird, der in der Welt nie etwas Wirkliches entsprechen kann; denn es gehört zum Sinn dieser Idee, daß sie uns darauf verpflichtet, auf ihre Realisierung hinzuarbeiten. Das Paradoxe daran ist, daß wir darauf verpflichtet wären, die Realisierung eines Ideals anzustreben, dessen Realisierung das Ende der menschlichen Geschichte wäre. Das Ziel ist das Ende; diese paradoxale Struktur bringt zum Ausdruck, daß Apels Erklärung der Wahrheit immer noch metaphysisch ist.

Nebenbei sei bemerkt, daß Derrida, soweit es um die im Wahrheitsbegriff implizierten notwendigen Idealisierungen geht, durchaus mit Apel übereinstimmt. Im Unterschied zu Apel betont er jedoch den metaphysischen Charakter dieser Idealisierungen. Wo Apel ein letztes Fundament unserer Verpflichtung auf (DIE) Wahrheit sieht, sieht Derrida eine (vorerst) unvermeidliche metaphysische, eine

---

6. Derrida, Jacques: "Die Struktur, das Zeichen und das Spiel im Diskurs der Wissenschaften vom Menschen". In: *Die Schrift und die Differenz*. Frankfurt (Suhrkamp) 1976. S. 441.

logozentrische Vergiftung selbst unserer Alltagssprache; dies war der Grund seiner Wendung von der Transzendentalphilosophie zur Dekonstruktion. Auch diese Alternative finde ich nicht überzeugend. Deshalb werde ich eine andere Lektüre jener "notwendigen Idealisierungen" vorschlagen, welche nach Putnam, Apel und Habermas im Begriff der Wahrheit, bzw. in der wahrheitsorientierten Kommunikation, impliziert sind.

Ich will wieder mit Putnam beginnen. Wenn die Idee erkenntnismäßig idealer Bedingungen nicht in jenem totalisierenden futurischen Sinn verstanden werden kann, den ich oben nahegelegt habe, dann bleibt als einzig akzeptable Lesart die folgende: Immer wenn wir Wahrheitsansprüche auf der Grundlage guter Argumente und überzeugender Evidenzen erheben, dann *unterstellen* wir die hier und jetzt gegebenen Erkenntnisbedingungen im folgenden Sinn als ideal: Wir unterstellen, daß in Zukunft keine neuen Argumente oder Evidenzen auftauchen werden, die unseren Wahrheitsanspruch in Frage stellen würden. Das heißt aber nichts anderes als zu sagen, daß wir unseren Wahrheitsanspruch für gut begründet, unsere Argumente für wirklich gut, unsere Evidenzen für zwingend halten. Wollte man dies eine Idealisierung nennen, so wäre es gleichsam eine "performative" Idealisierung; d.h. eine Idealisierung, die sich wesentlich darin zeigt, daß wir uns darauf *verlassen*, daß unsere Gründe und Evidenzen gut oder überzeugend sind. Und sich darauf verlassen, daß Gründe gut und Evidenzen überzeugend sind, heißt die Möglichkeit auszuschließen, daß sie sich im Lauf der Zeit als problematisch herausstellen könnten. Sobald wir aber auf unsere Praxis wahrheitsorientierter Kommunikation und Argumentation *reflektieren*, müssen wir natürlich einräumen, daß wir nie die Möglichkeit ausschließen können, daß neue Argumente oder neue Erfahrungen uns zwingen könnten, Wahrheitsansprüche zu revidieren. Dieses reflexive Bewußtsein der Fallibilität unserer Wahrheitsansprüche könnte auch als Bewußtsein dessen verstanden werden, daß sich die Erkenntnisbedingungen, die wir jeweils für ideal halten, am Ende als nicht ideal herausstellen könnten. Wenn wir weiterhin auf die verschiedenen Möglichkeiten reflektieren, hinsichtlich derer unsere Wahrheitsansprüche in Frage gestellt werden können, dann können wir nun auch zwischen verschiedenen Aspekten der im Erheben von Wahrheitsansprüchen implizierten "Idealisierungen" unterscheiden. Was wir sagen, kann z.B. als unklar, vage oder konfus kritisiert werden; die entsprechende "Idealisierung" besteht darin, daß wir uns darauf verlassen, daß unsere Sprache klar, verständlich, "transparent" ist. Oder es könnte unser ganzes Vokabular, eine Theorie, ein Sprachspiel, einige unserer grundlegenden begrifflichen Unterscheidungen in Frage gestellt werden; die dieser Kritik entsprechende "Idealisierung" bestünde in unserem Vertrauen darauf, daß die Sprache, die wir sprechen, "in Ordnung" ist so wie sie ist. Wenn wir die "notwendigen Idealisierungen" in diesem *performativen* Sinn verstehen, dann implizieren sie durchaus keinen totalisierenden Vorgriff auf eine zukünftige Realisierung oder Approximation idealer Wissens- oder Kommunikationsbedingungen. Ich möchte vielmehr behaupten, daß die totalisierenden Vorstellungen einer idealen Grenze des Wissens oder der Kommunikation nur Resultat einer objektivistischen Fehldeutung von Idealisierungen ist, welche wesentlich performativ sind. Die Frage ist natürlich, ob man überhaupt von Idealisierungen sprechen sollte. Denn eben dieser Begriff der Idealisierung scheint einen idealen Maßstab oder einen idealen Grenzwert nahezulegen und genau an dieser Stelle entstehen die Verwirrungen, auf die ich oben hingewiesen habe. Ich möchte die gerade aufgeworfene Frage diskutieren, indem ich auf die "pragmatischen" Idealisierungen eingehe, auf die sich Apel und Habermas konzentiert haben, d.h. Idealisierungen, die die intersubjektive Struktur der Kommunikation und/oder des argumentativen Diskurses betreffen.

Ich konzentriere mich auf Habermas' Begriff der idealen Sprechsituation, den ich als bekannt voraussetze. Die Idee der Wahrheit kann nach Habermas nicht von der eines rationalen Konsenses getrennt werden, wobei ein Konsens rational wäre, wenn er unter Bedingungen einer idealen Sprechsituation zustande käme.[7] Nun habe ich bereits Apels These erwähnt, daß der rationale Konsens in Habermas' Sinn keine *hinreichende* Bedingung für Wahrheit sein kann. Deshalb werde ich Habermas' Idee nur im Sinne einer notwendigen Idealisierung diskutieren, die in jeder ernsthaften Argumention involviert ist. Auf diese Idee läßt sich nun übertragen, was ich früher über Putnams Begriff erkenntnismäßig idealer Bedingungen gesagt habe: Wenn wir nämlich einen Konsens erzielen, von dem wir glauben, daß er auf guten Gründen beruht, dann gehen wir natürlich davon aus, daß keine Argumente unterdrückt worden sind bzw. kein Diskursteilnehmer daran gehindert wurde, relevante Gegenargumente vorzubringen. Auch hier handelt es sich um eine performative Idealisierung, die sich prinzipiell immer als falsch

7. Vgl. jedoch oben Anm. 2.

herausstellen kann, weil wir retrospektiv externe oder interne Zwänge entdecken können, die einige — oder alle — Sprecher daran hinderten zu sagen, was sie unter anderen Umständen hätten sagen können. Auch diese Idealisierung würden wir mißverstehen, wenn wir sie als Antizipation einer idealen Kommunikationssituation (Apels falsche Lesart) oder wenn wir sie als ideale Norm rationaler Argumentation verstünden, die als "Maßstab" verwendet werden könnte, um die Rationalität von Konsensen gleichsam von außen zu "messen". Es gibt jedoch eine wichtige Differenz zwischen Putnams und Habermas' Idealisierungsbegriff: In Diskurssituationen Argumente zu unterdrücken heißt Menschen zu unterdrücken. Daher stellt die Idealisierung, die nach Habermas in der Argumentationspraxis impliziert ist, eine Art Brücke zwischen Rationalitätsforderungen und moralischen Forderungen dar. Sie birgt ein normatives Potential in sich, das sich im Zusammenhang zwischen der modernen Idee der Demokratie und der eines öffentlichen Raumes politischer und moralischer Diskurse *zeigt*. Auch wenn es — entgegen dem, was Habermas immer angenommen hat — keinen *direkten* Zusammenhang zwischen universalpragmatischen Strukturen der Kommunikation und einer universalistischen Idee von Demokratie und Menschenrechten gibt, sind die Ideen der Wahrheit und der rationalen Argumentation ersichtlich auf vielfältige Weise mit den demokratischen und liberalen Ideen der Moderne verknüpft. Wie dem auch sei, an genau dieser Stelle läßt sich zeigen, weshalb der Begriff der "Idealisierung" als solcher irreführend ist: Wenn man diesen Begriff auf Strukturen der Kommunikation oder Argumentation bezieht, so wird er fast unvermeidlich eine *ideale* Struktur bezeichnen, die wir als normativen Maßstab zur Beurteilung realer Kommunikationsstrukturen verwenden und von der wir hoffen können, sie zu einem zukünftigen Zeitpunkt der Geschichte — zumindest annähernd — in der Welt zu realisieren. Die Idee einer solchen idealen Struktur von Intersubjektivität macht jedoch keinen Sinn. Dies erst verleiht den Einwänden Nietzsches, Derridas und Rortys gegen die idealisierenden Konstruktionen der Philosophie wirkliches Gewicht. Wenn man aber die performativen Präsuppositionen des Redens und Argumentierens in terms von "notwendigen Idealisierungen" interpretiert, hat man den scheinbar unschuldigen Schritt in Richtung einer Objektivierung jener Präsuppositionen schon getan. Auch Derrida noch macht jenen Schritt — freilich nur um zu zeigen, daß jene Idealisierungen ebenso notwendig wie unmöglich sind. *Gegen* Derrida, Apel, Putnam und Habermas möchte ich — vielleicht etwas paradox — behaupten, daß jene Idealisierungen in der Tat *notwendig*, daß sie aber genaugenommen keine *Idealisierungen* sind.

II.

Im Lichte meiner schwachen Verteidigung dessen, was ich die "Strategie der Idealisierungen" nennen möchte, werde ich jetzt einige von Rortys "ethnozentrischen" Thesen diskutieren. Offensichtlich bringt mich meine schwache und sozusagen kontextualistische Verteidigung der "Idealisierungsstrategien" zumindest in mancher Hinsicht in die Nähe von Rortys Ethnozentrismus. Ich glaube aber, daß Kontingenz etwas weniger Dramatisches ist, als Rorty uns glauben machen will. Ich möchte dies durch einige Überlegungen zu Rortys These über die "Kontingenz einer liberalen Gesellschaft"[8] und, allgemeiner gesprochen, durch Überlegungen über den Zusammenhang von Kontingenz und Moderne zeigen.

Ich habe oben unterschieden zwischen jenen performativen Präsuppositionen, die dem entsprechen, was manche Philosophen "notwendige Idealisierungen" genannt haben, einerseits und unserem reflexiven Bewußtsein der Fallibilität all unserer Geltungsansprüche (einschließlich unserer Diskurspräsuppositionen) andererseits. Ich vermute, daß Rorty mir darin zustimmen würde, daß dieses reflexive Bewußtsein der Fallibilität ein Moment dessen ist, was er als moderne liberale Kultur beschrieben hat. Dieses Fallibilitätsbewußtsein ist eng mit der von Rorty beschriebenen "Anerkennung von Kontingenz" verbunden — der Kontingenz unserer Sprache, unserer Weltorientierung, unserer Kultur, unserer Institutionen. Es scheint offensichtlich, daß eine solche Anerkennung von Kontingenz Folgen für unseren Umgang mit Geltungsansprüchen aller Art hat. Insbesondere wird sie auf die performative Dimension des Redens und Argumentierens selbst zurückwirken. Wenn uns der Weg zur Letztbegründung ebenso versperrt ist wie die Hoffnung auf eine letzte Versöhnung verwehrt — und hierin sieht Rorty zu Recht die Konsequenzen der "Anerkennung von Kontingenz" —, dann verlieren alle Formen von Dogmatismus und Fundamentalismus ihre Grundlage. Darüber hinaus werden wir in Kontroversen, in denen es keine intersubjektiv zwingenden Argumente oder Evi-

8. Rorty, Richard: *Kontingenz, Ironie und Solidarität*. Frankfurt (Suhrkamp) 1989. Kapitel 3: Die Kontingenz des Gemeinwesens, S. 84 ff.

denzen gibt — man denke an bestimmte moralische Konflikte, an Gerichtsentscheidungen, den Golfkrieg, historische Erklärungen — nicht immer davon ausgehen können, daß es im jeweiligen Fall eine absolute Wahrheit *gibt*: irgendwo am Ende der Geschichte, aus der Sicht Gottes, im letzten Konsens. Wenn wir aber nicht länger davon ausgehen können, daß eine absolute Wahrheit in jedem Falle existiert — auch wenn wir uns ihrer vielleicht hier und jetzt noch nicht sicher sein können —, und zwar deshalb nicht, weil diese Unterstellung durch kritische Reflexion auf die Bedingungen der Möglichkeit wahrheitsorientierten Redens und Argumentierens destruiert wurde (nämlich durch die Anerkennung von Kontingenz), dann muß dies Konsequenzen für unseren Umgang mit kontroversen Problemen der oben genannten Art haben: z.B. ein Mehr an Toleranz, die Bereitschaft, Überzeugungen zu revidieren, die Bereitschaft, mit Pluralitäten zu leben, die Bereitschaft, nach neuen Beschreibungen oder Interpretationen alter Probleme zu suchen, oder die Bereitschaft, auf das zu hören, was andere zu sagen haben. Wenn die Anerkennung von Kontingenz schließlich die Anerkennung impliziert, daß "endliche, sterbliche, zufällig existierende menschliche Wesen" den Sinn ihres Lebens aus nichs anderem herleiten können als aus "anderen endlichen, sterblichen, zufällig existierenden menschlichen Wesen"[9], dann muß jeder Versuch, theologisch, metaphysisch oder szientifisch inspirierte Sinnentwürfe gesellschaftlich verbindlich zu machen, als zutiefst diskreditiert erscheinen. Wenn aber die Anerkennung von Kontingenz, d.h. die Destruktion der Metaphysik — einschließlich der metaphysischen Residuen mancher moderner Verständnisse von Rationalität — die Destruktion der intellektuellen Grundlagen von Dogmatismus, Fundamentalismus, Intoleranz und Fanatismus impliziert, dann gibt es einen tiefen und interessanten Zusammenhang zwischen den Argumenten für Kontingenz und denen für eine liberale Kultur. Diesen Zusammenhang möche ich im folgenden untersuchen.

Zunächst einmal ist offensichtlich, daß die Kritik des Fundamentalismus und der Metaphysik, die zur Anerkennung von Kontingenz führt, sich auch auf unser Verständnis der demokratischen und liberalen Prinzipien der Moderne auswirken muß. Wir können nämlich nicht länger davon ausgehen, daß es einen Archimedischen Punkt — beispielsweise die Idee der Vernunft — gibt, in dem jene

9. Rorty, op. cit. S. 86. (Übersetzung geändert).

Prinzipien fest verankert wären. Insofern könnte man Rorty zuge-
stehen, daß die einzige Möglichkeit, die Prinzipien, Praktiken und
Institutionen einer liberalen Gesellschaft zu "rechtfertigen", darin
besteht, unsere tiefsten Überzeugungen, moralischen Orientierun-
gen und begrifflichen Unterscheidungen in möglichst kohärenter
Weise zu rekonstruieren. Diese Art von Rekonstruktion wird immer in einem gewissen Sinne zirkulär sein, da sie nicht von einem
Punkt aus durchgeführt werden kann, der jenseits der politischen
und moralischen "Grammatik" unserer eigenen Kultur läge; in
diesem Sinne wird die Rechtfertigung "ethnozentrisch" bleiben.
Das soll heißen — und dies ist, was Rorty betonen möchte —, daß
die Sprache, die politische und moralische Grammatik, die Praktiken und Institutionen einer Kultur nicht als ganze (und gleichsam
von außen) gerechtfertigt werden können, da das "Rechtfertigungs-
spiel" jeweils nur *innerhalb* eines bestimmten Sprachspiels einen
klaren Sinn hat, nicht aber im Hinblick auf ein Sprachspiel als
ganzes.

Obwohl diese These in einem *bestimmten* Sinn offensichtlich zutrifft — wenn wir nämlich anerkennen, daß es keinen Archimedischen Punkt außerhalb unserer eigenen Sprache oder Kultur gibt —,
ist durchaus nicht klar, was sie tatsächlich impliziert. Zunächst
scheint klar zu sein, daß wir ein Sprachspiel, ein Ensemble von
Praktiken, Institutionen, Prinzipien oder begrifflichen Unterscheidungen nur dadurch "rechtfertigen" können, daß wir sie *von innen*
her zu klären, zu rekonstruieren oder kohärent zu machen versuchen. Dies gilt selbst für die Mathematik, denn niemand könnte den
Witz der mathematischen Praxis, den Sinn mathematischer Begriffe
oder die Kraft bestimmter Argumente oder Beweise verstehen, der
nicht in diese Praxis einsozialisiert worden wäre. Analoges gilt
offenbar dann, wenn es um die Rechtfertigung eines Ensembles von
politischen Prinzipien, Praktiken und Institutionen wie jener einer
demokratischen und liberalen Tradition geht. In diesem Fall ist das
Problem der "Sozialisation" sogar noch dramatischer als in dem der
Mathematik, da das praktische Wissen, das zum Verstehen der
Prinzipien, Institutionen und Praktiken einer liberalen Kultur gehört, "habits of the heart" einschließt, d.h. moralische Urteile,
emotionale Reaktionen und eine Verflechtung von moralischen
Urteilen mit emotionalen Reaktionen und Interpretationsmustern.
Auch hier kann eine interne Klärung oder Rekonstruktion der
politischen "Grammatik" einer liberalen Kultur unmöglich eine
Rechtfertigung der Prinzipien und Praktiken jener Kultur für dieje-

nigen sein, die nicht in einem gewissen Sinn in diese Praktiken schon einsozialisiert worden sind.

Die Frage ist, ob all dies heißt, daß demokratische und liberale Prinzipien nur *ein* mögliches politisch-moralisches "Sprachspiel" unter anderen festlegen, vielleicht mit der Besonderheit, daß *unsere* moralischen Prinzipien uns zur Respektierung der Andersheit anderer Kulturen nötigen, während dies umgekehrt nicht der Fall zu sein braucht. Diese Frage ist äußerst komplex und ich denke, daß sie nicht mit einem einfachen "ja" oder "nein" beantwortet werden kann; ich glaube aber, daß ein *qualifiziertes* "nein" sich rechtfertigen läßt — und mit Rechtfertigung meine ich jetzt keine Rechtfertigung bloß *für uns*, sondern eben Rechtfertigung, *Punkt*. Ich möchte dies erläutern, indem ich nach und nach das Bild vervollständige, das ich eben skizziert habe.

Zunächst einmal sollte klar sein, daß die internen "Rekonstruktionen", "Klärungen" und "Rechtfertigungen", von denen ich gesprochen habe, durchaus voneinander abweichen können. Interne Rekonstruktionen liberaler und demokratischer Prinzipien können konservativ oder radikal sein, und zwischen "radikalen" — d.h. kritischen — Rekonstruktionen liberaler Prinzipien und der kommunitaristischen Kritik daran gibt es vielleicht keine klare Grenze. Hieran zeigt sich, daß die Art von Kultur, auf die wir uns hier beziehen, kein abgeschlossenes Sprachspiel ist, sondern eines, das sich auf der Grundlage seiner eigenen Prinzipien auf sich selbst kritisch und verändernd beziehen kann. Wenn ich im folgenden von liberalen und demokratischen Prinzipien spreche, dann denke ich immer *auch* an dieses kritische Potential, das den entsprechenden Institutionen und Praktiken als Spannung zwischen dem was ist und dem, was sein sollte, immanent ist. Ich habe mein Verständnis liberaler und demokratischer Prinzipien an anderer Stelle erläutert.[10] Hier sollte der Hinweis genügen, daß ich diese Prinzipien wesentlich als *gegen* soziale Ungerechtigkeit, Diskriminierung von Minderheiten, Sexismus, Kulturimperialismus oder -"hegemonismus", Manipulation der Öffentlichkeit oder soziale Gewalt (social violence) gerichtet verstehe; d.h. ich verstehe diese Prinzipien — wie wohl auch Rorty — nicht als Rechtfertigung des status quo in unseren Gesellschaften. Dabei gehe ich davon aus, daß es gute

---

10. Wellmer, Albrecht: "Models of Freedom in the Modern World". In: *The Philosophical Forum*. Vol.XXI, nr. 1-2, Herbst/Winter 1989/90.

Argumente — d.h. unserer Kultur immanente Argumente — gibt, diese Prinzipien in einem *kritischen* Sinn zu verstehen.

Mein zweiter Argumentationsschritt — ein Schritt, den ich in meiner kurzen Überlegung zu den verschiedenen Möglichkeiten, die politische Grammatik einer liberalen Kultur zu rekonstruieren, schon vorbereitet habe —, betrifft die Abstraktion, die der Unterscheidung zwischen *unserer* Sprache (oder Kultur) und *ihrer* Sprache (oder Kultur) zugrunde liegt. Diese Abstraktion besitzt eine suggestive Kraft, die sie zugleich äußerst irreführend macht. Es stimmt natürlich, daß ich meine Sprache — beziehungsweise die mit ihr verbundenen Praktiken — nicht jemandem gegenüber rechtfertigen kann, der ein völlig anderes Sprachspiel "spielt": Es gibt keine Meta-Normen, keine Metasprache, in bezug auf die einer von uns den anderen überzeugen könnte. Das ist so einleuchtend wie trivial. Die eigentlich *interessanten* Fälle sind jedoch offensichtlich nicht diejenigen, in denen jemand ein Ensemble von sprachlichen und außersprachlichen Praktiken gegenüber dem Angehörigen einer anderen Kultur zu rechtfertigen versucht (eine ziemlich künstliche, um nicht zu sagen absurde Idee), sondern jene Fälle, in denen verschiedene, sich teilweise überlappende Vokabulare miteinander konfrontiert sind, und vor allem Fälle, in denen neue Vokabulare in der Auseinandersetzung mit alten Problemen entstehen (und mit der Sprache, in der diese Probleme bisher formuliert wurden). Nun würde ich aber behaupten, daß jede interessante Argumentationssituation Elemente einer solchen Konstellation enthält. Denn sogar in unserer eigenen Sprache können wir für gewöhnlich einzelne Argumente nicht isolieren, und je interessanter und bedeutsamer Argumente sind, desto weniger entsprechen Argumentationen einem formalen Begriff von Rationalität, d.h. einem Modell deduktiver Ableitung. In unsere gewöhnliche Argumentationspraxis sind immer schon holistische, innovative und "Differenz"-Momente eingelassen: Wir müssen beim Argumentieren häufig erst den Kontext erzeugen, durch den Argumente die Kraft gewinnen, die sie haben können; Argumentationen schließen oft den Versuch ein, ein altes Problem oder eine vertraute Situation in einem neuen Licht erscheinen zu lassen. Demzufolge ist ein "holistisches" Element von Neubeschreibungen und Innovationen Bestandteil der interessanteren Formen unserer gewöhnlichen Argumentationspraxis. Es ist weiterhin so, daß das Sprechen einer "gemeinsamen Sprache" — wenn damit nicht nur die elementarsten Formen linguistischer Übereinstimmung gemeint sind — oft nicht der Ausgangspunkt einer Argumentation ist, sondern — wenn alles gut geht — deren Resultat. Man könnte dies das "Differenz"-Moment unserer alltäglichen Argumentationspraxis nennen. Deshalb würden wir die Pointe dieser Praxis verfehlen, wenn wir sie in terms eines gemeinsamen Systems von starren Regeln und Kriterien interpretierten, das semantisch abgeschlossen ist. Nur wenn wir die Reichweite rationaler Argumente im Sinne eines solchen starren Regelsystems interpretierten, könnte die Unterscheidung zwischen Begründungen *"innerhalb"* einer Sprache und der Begründung einer Sprache *von außen* gleichbedeutend werden mit der Unterscheidung zwischen einem Bereich möglicher Argumente und einem Bereich, in dem keine Argumente mehr möglich sind. Die interessantesten Fälle liegen jedoch gleichsam zwischen diesen Extremen. Daß diese interessanten Fälle überhaupt möglich sind, hängt natürlich damit zusammen, daß wir immer versuchen können, die Dinge aus der Perspektive anderer zu sehen, daß wir uns mit neuen Vokabularen oder Sichtweisen vertraut machen können, daß wir gelegentlich zwei Sprachen gleichzeitig sprechen und daß wir versuchen können herauszufinden, ob ein neues Vokabular oder eine neue Beschreibung alte Erfahrungen erhellen oder unsere alten Probleme lösen kann. Dieses "Ausprobieren" mag Zeit beanspruchen; Argumentationen beziehen sich immer auf einen Kontext von Erfahrung, Praxis und Reflexion zurück; neue Argumente können zu neuen Erfahrungen führen, genauso wie neue Erfahrungen uns neuen Argumenten zugänglich machen oder unser Verständnis bekannter Argumente verändern können.

Wenn dies alles — annähernd — richtig ist, dann kann Rationalität — in einem relevanten Sinne des Wortes — nicht an der Grenze geschlossener Sprachspiele enden (denn so etwas gibt es nicht); dann aber ist die "ethnozentrische" Kontextualität jeder Argumentation durchaus mit dem Erheben von kontexttranszendierenden Geltungsansprüchen zu vereinbaren, d.h. von Geltungsansprüchen, die den — lokalen oder kulturellen — Kontext transzendieren, in dem sie erhoben werden und in dem sie allein gerechtfertigt werden können. Es macht also durchaus Sinn zu sagen, daß die der Argumentation immanenten performativen Präsuppositionen sich nicht nur auf den lokalen Kontext beziehen, in welchem Wahrheitsansprüche jeweils erhoben werden, und daß Geltungsansprüche jeden partikularen Kontext transzendieren. In genau diesem Sinn würde ich Habermas' Beschreibung der Dialektik von Kontextimmanenz und Kontexttranszendenz zustimmen, einer Dialektik, die in der Praxis geltungsorientierten Sprechens und geltungsorientierter Argumentation wirksam ist.[11] Es ist genau das richtige Verständnis dieser Dialektik, welches uns den Wahrheitsgehalt jener "Idealisierungsstrategien" zugänglich macht, die ich anfangs diskutiert habe.

Wenn wir das Vorangehende auf Rortys These zur Kontingenz einer liberalen Gesellschaft beziehen, dann wird diese Kontingenz in einem neuen Licht erscheinen; und zwar wird sie weniger dramatisch erscheinen, als Rorty sie darstellt, da eine liberale Kultur — noch weniger als andere Kulturen — als ein geschlossenes Sprachspiel verstanden werden kann. Diese Kultur hat — in der zeitlichen Vertikale betrachtet — eine Geschichte und — in der zeitlichen Horizontale — ein Außen. In bezug auf beide Dimensionen der "Andersheit" — die uns beide in einem jeweils bestimmten Sinne zugänglich sind — gibt es eine ganze Reihe guter und interessanter Argumente für demokratische und liberale Prinzipien und Institutionen: man denke an die Geschichte der modernen Revolutionen, die Arbeiten von Kant, Tocqueville, Mill oder Paine, die "Federalist Papers", an die Erfahrungen von Totalitarismus, Nationalismus, Rassismus, Antisemitismus oder von religiösem und politischem Fundamentalismus. Weitere Argumente lassen sich aus einer internen und kritischen Rekonstruktion der Werte, Prinzipien und Selbstinterpretationen gegenwärtiger liberaler Gesellschaften gewinnen. Wenn wir nur die Idee einer Letztbegründung demokratischer und liberaler Prinzipen aufgeben, d.h. einer Begründung, die nicht schon Gebrauch machen würde von der Grammatik einer demokratischen und liberalen Politik, und wenn wir — historische und andere — Erfahrungen in der Argumentation zulassen, dann zeigt sich uns ein dichtes Netzwerk von Argumenten zur Begründung und kritischen Weiterentwicklung demokratisch-liberaler Prinzipien und Institutionen. Diese Argumente werden zwar kaum einen fanatischen Nationalisten oder religiösen Fundamentalisten überzeugen; aber die Tatsche allein, daß meine Argumente nicht jeden überzeugen, muß nicht bedeuten, daß sie keine guten Argumente sind — diese Trivialität sollte man, wie ich meine, nicht vergessen, selbst wenn es einen enormen Unterschied macht, ob man sie selbstkritisch versteht oder nicht.

11. Vgl. Habermas, Jürgen: "Die Einheit der Vernunft in der Vielfalt ihrer Stimmen". In: Ders. *Nachmetaphysisches Denken*. Frankfurt (Suhrkamp) 1988. Siehe insbes. S. 174-179.

Es ist ein Kennzeichen demokratisch-liberaler Gesellschaften —
solange es in ihnen noch eine irgend lebendige politische Kultur gibt
—, daß eine öffentliche Diskussion über die Interpretation von
Verfassungsprinzipien — z.B. über den Sinn von Grundrechten,
über zivilen Ungehorsam oder über das richtige Verhältnis zwischen individuellen Freiheiten und sozialer Gerechtigkeit — ein
zentraler Bestandteil der politischen Kultur ist. Es scheint eine
Eigentümlichkeit demokratischer und liberaler Prinzipien und Institutionen zu sein, daß sie nur am Leben erhalten werden können,
wenn sie im Medium des öffentlichen Diskurses und der politischen
Auseinandersetzung immer wieder neu interpretiert und definiert
werden. D.h. eine liberale Kultur zeichnet sich dadurch aus, daß der
öffentliche Diskurs über die Grundprinzipien dieser Kultur eine
konstitutive Rolle für den politischen Prozeß selbst gewinnt. Liberale Prinzipien sind gewissermaßen selbstreflexiv: Indem sie allen
Bürgern gleiche Rechte und Freiheiten garantieren, garantieren sie
ihnen zugleich gleiche Rechte und Freiheiten mit Bezug auf die
Teilnahme an jenem öffentlichen Diskurs, in dem immer wieder
ausgehandelt werden muß, was der Inhalt dieser gleichen Rechte
und Freiheiten sein soll. Nun scheint es mir aber ziemlich offensichtlich, daß es einen nicht-kontingenten Zusammenhang zwischen dieser Selbstreflexivität liberaler Prinzipen, d.h. der konstitu-
tiven Rolle des öffentlichen Diskurses für demokratisch-liberale
Gesellschaften einerseits und der "Anerkennung von Kontingenz"
in Rortys Sinn andererseits gibt.

Rorty selbst macht auf diesen Zusammenhang mit der interessanten — und wie ich glaube richtigen — Bemerkung aufmerksam, daß
die "destruktiven" Konsequenzen der fortschreitenden Aufklärung, insbesondere jene, die zur "Anerkennung von Kontingenz"
geführt haben, das Projekt einer demokratisch-liberalen Gesellschaft nicht etwa unterminieren, sondern es im Gegenteil auf eine
tragfähigere Grundlage stellen.[12] Insbesondere behauptet Rorty,
daß das Scheitern aller Versuche, Letztbegründungen zu finden —
einschließlich der Letztbegründung einer liberalen Gesellschaft —
für die liberalen Institutionen spricht und nicht gegen sie. Aus
dieser These folgt aber, daß es Argumente für demokratische und
liberale Prinzipien und Institutionen gibt, die *nicht* in irgendeinem
interessanten Sinn des Wortes ethnozentrisch sind. Denn offensichtlich kann die Kontingenzthese *nicht* so verstanden werden, als
träfe sie nur auf eine moderne liberale Kultur zu; vielmehr handelt

12. Vgl. Rorty, Richard: loc. cit. S. 102 ff.

es sich um eine philosophische These, die die Bedingungen der Möglichkeit einer Begründung von Wahrheitsansprüchen *überhaupt* betrifft.[13] Während die Anerkennung von Kontingenz jedoch zutiefst subversive Folgen für jede Kultur haben muß, die religiös fundiert oder um eine mythologische oder auch "szientifische" Weltsicht zentriert ist, verwandeln sich ihre subversiven Folgen hinsichtlich aller Versuche einer Letztbegründung in *zusätzliche* Argumente für die demokratischen und liberalen Prinzipien der Moderne. Vielleicht könnte man von einer *negativen* Rechtfertigung jener Prinzipien sprechen. Diese negative Rechtfertigung wird freilich keine *Letzt*begründung sein. Eher wird sie eine *negative* Rechtfertigung in *dem* Sinne sein, daß sie die intellektuellen Grundlagen von Dogmatismus, Fundamentalismus, Autoritarismus sowie von moralischer und rechtlicher Ungleichheit zerstört; sowie dadurch, daß sie ineins damit demokratische und liberale Institutionen als die einzigen auszeichnet, in denen die Anerkennung von Kontingenz mit einer zwanglosen öffentlichen Reproduktion von Legitimität vereinbar ist. Für diese These gibt es eine Reihe von Gründen, von denen ich im folgenden drei wichtige hervorheben möchte.

(1) Jene Prinzipien sind — wenn man sie universalistisch versteht (und so *sollte* man sie verstehen, pace Rorty) — die einzigen, die mit

---

13. Diese Behauptung hat eine gewisse Affinität zu Apels These, wonach das Fallibilismusprinzip nicht als selbstbezüglich verstanden werden darf. ("Fallibilismus, Konsenstheorie der Wahrheit und Letztbegründung", loc. cit. S.178-184). Ich glaube jedoch nicht, daß das Fallibilismusprinzip oder auch die "Anerkennung von Kontingenz" zu den notwendigen Präsuppositionen der Argumentation als solcher gehört. D.h. meine These ist weniger anspruchsvoll als diejenige Apels: Was ich sagen will, ist, daß die Kontingenzthese, wenn man sie ernstnimmt, nur so verstanden werden kann, daß sie für alle möglichen "Sprachspiele" gilt und deshalb nicht nur mit fundamentalistischen Selbstinterpretationen unserer eigenen Kultur unvereinbar ist, sondern ebenso mit entsprechenden Selbstinterpretationen anderer Kulturen. Dann gibt es aber offenbar Argumente, die man nicht sinnvoll gebrauchen kann, ohne einen *universalen* Geltungsanspruch zu erheben, d.h. einen Geltungsanspruch, dessen Anwendungsbereich nicht nach Belieben "ethnozentrisch" eingeschränkt werden kann. Wenn daher aus der "Anerkennung von Kontingenz" gute Argumente für eine liberale Kultur folgen, dann gibt es Argumente für eine liberale Kultur, die nicht ethnozentrisch in irgendeinem interessanten Sinne des Wortes sind — selbst wenn man zugesteht, daß bestimmte Argumente nur kontingenterweise zu einem gewissen Zeitpunkt verfügbar sein und verstanden werden können. Wenn dies aber zutrifft, werden liberale und demokratische Prinzipien viel weniger kontingent erscheinen, als Rorty annimmt.

der Anerkennung irreduzibler Andersheit — in Hinsicht auf Überzeugungen, Lebensformen, Formen von Identität — vereinbar sind und die es — zumindest begrifflich — erlauben, gleiche Rechte mit der Respektierung von Andersheit und Differenz zusammenzudenken. In diesem Sinne setzt selbst eine "Politik der Differenz" (politics of difference) den moralischen Universalismus voraus, der den demokratischen und liberalen Prinzipien der Moderne zugrunde liegt.

(2) Da jene Prinzipien in dem oben genannten Sinn selbstreflexiv sind, verlangen sie die Institutionalisierung eines öffentlichen Raumes — oder eines Raums von öffentlichen Räumen —, in welchem der genaue Gehalt jener Prinzipien, ihre Anwendung und Institutionalisierung immer wieder im Medium politischer und kultureller Diskurse bestimmt und neubestimmt werden muß, wodurch er zugleich eine Sache des öffentlichen Interesses werden kann. Ein solcher "kommunaler" Raum öffentlicher Freiheit scheint aber das einzig mögliche Substitut für jene Formen substantiell begründeter sozialer Solidarität zu sein, die das Charakteristikum traditionaler Gesellschaften waren; d.h. das einzig mögliche Substitut, wenn einmal die traditionalen Grundlagen sozialer Solidarität durch eine Aufklärung zerstört worden sind, die am Ende zur "Anerkennung von Kontingenz" geführt hat.

(3) Die demokratischen und liberalen Prinzipien sind in einem gewissen Sinn *Meta*-Prinzipien. Nach der Zerstörung der substantiellen Grundlagen von traditionalen Formen gesellschaftlicher Solidarität definieren diese Prinzipien nicht einfach einen neuen substantiellen Konsens, der beispielsweise einen religiösen Konsens ersetzen würde. Sie bezeichnen vielmehr eine Möglichkeit des gewaltfreien Umgangs mit unauflösbaren Dissensen in substantiellen Fragen und somit eine Möglichkeit, Konsens und Solidarität auf einer abstrakteren Ebene wiederherzustellen, gleichsam einen "prozeduralen" anstelle eines "substantiellen" Konsenses. Ich gebe zu, daß diese Unterscheidung eine relative und irreführende ist, da z.B. die "Prozedur" des Dialogs keine Prozedur im eigentlichen Sinne des Wortes ist und da der "prozedurale" Wert des Dialogs mit den substantiellen Werten der Freiheit, Solidarität und Gerechtigkeit zusammenhängt. Was mir vorschwebt, ist ein dynamisches Ineinandergreifen von formalen Prozeduren und Institutionen einerseits und informeller politischer Diskurse und einer informellen politischen Praxis andererseits; ein Ineinandergreifen, durch

welches jene substantiellen Werte ebenso öffentliche Angelegenheiten wie öffentliche *Projekte* werden können. In diesem Sinn ist das, was ich im Gegensatz zu einem "substantiellen" einen "prozeduralen" Konsens genannt habe, das Charakteristikum einer Gesellschaft, die ihre Legitimität nur reproduzieren kann, indem sie sich beständig im Medium politischer und kultureller Diskurse transformiert und verändert.

Während die Anerkennung von Kontingenz — wie ich zu zeigen versucht habe — neue Argumente für demokratische und liberale Prinzipien und die um sie zentrierten Institutionen schafft, bleibt sie dennoch eine Anerkennung von *Kontingenz*. Die *nicht* eliminierbare Kontingenz verweist jedoch nicht auf einen Mangel an guten Argumenten für liberale und demokratische Prinzipien, sie bezeichnet vielmehr das Moment der Kontingenz in allen Versuchen, diese Prinzipien erfolgreich zu institutionalisieren, am Leben zu erhalten und in eine Form demokratischer "Sittlichkeit"[14] zu übersetzen. Im übrigen können demokratische und liberale Gesellschaften infolge sozialer Spannungen oder ökologischer Zerstörungen, rassistischer oder ethnischer Konflikte, infolge der Zunahme von Gewalt, ökonomischer Krisen oder der Konsequenzen eines ökonomischen Imperialismus zusammenbrechen oder sich auflösen. Wenn dies einträte, würde sich auch die moralische Substanz demokratischer und liberaler Praktiken und Institutionen auflösen. Hier endet die Kraft guter Argumente: Argumente können nur zeigen, warum wir vernünftigerweise nicht wollen können, daß dies eintritt.

14. Ich glaube, es hat nichts Paradoxes an sich, wenn wir die formalen Prinzipien und prozeduralen Werte, die ich oben erwähnt habe (in dem Sinne, in dem ich sie erklärt habe), als die "Substanz" einer modernen Form "substantieller Sittlichkeit" verstehen. Obwohl *spezifische* Traditionen, Geschichten und Projekte immer eine wichtige Rolle für die Konstitution individueller und kollektiver *Identität* spielen werden, können diese besonderen Grundlagen von Identität nicht den substantiellen Kern einer demokratischen und liberalen Form von Sittlichkeit bilden. Insoweit nämlich eine solche Form von Sittlichkeit die Respektierung von Differenz und "Andersheit" fordert, verlangt sie zugleich eine reflexive Distanz zu jeder partikularen Tradition, Geschichte und zu jedem partikularen Projekt. D.h. sie fordert die *Anerkennung von Kontingenz*. (Vgl. auch: Wellmer, Albrecht: "Models of Freedom in the Modern World", loc. cit.)

3. The Frontier: between Kant and Hegel

GEOFFREY BENNINGTON

The paper I'm going to read is really no more than a series of fragments and summaries of analysis and commentary which form part of some work in progress, linked to a three-year seminar I have been running at Sussex under the aegis of the Collège international de philosophie. One of the reasons for proposing the general title 'frontiers' for the seminar was a vague sense of a need to keep things open, and according to what is only an apparent paradox — and which in fact is perhaps really all I shall be arguing — frontiers, far from simply enclosing and encircling and limiting, seemed to promise opening, and a certain *lack of definition* that seems potentially productive. Keeping the theme of the seminar open and vague was important to me not just because it was desirable for it to be able to accommodate the interests of DPhil students working on a broad range of topics, but because three years seemed a luxuriously long time in which to work, and a time I was anxious not to circumscribe too limitatively. Attempting to 'thematise' frontiers (though we might already suspect that there is something about frontiers that will evade thematisation) seemed a good way to prevent, or postpone, any *particular* frontier from enclosing the work before it got started. Working on 'the' frontier (in general) promised the possibility of not having to work within any particular frontier. Frontiers may limit and enclose, but *the* frontier, whatever sense we might be able to give to that general singular, seemed rather to open. Naturally enough, one of the things I hoped to be able to think about was why this enabling situation might be so.

Frontiers is in itself a vague enough term: I didn't want to predetermine its relationship with a cluster of other terms in the same semantic field or region or territory — being on the frontier for three years also seemed to involve thinking about being at the border, on the edge, at the limit, in the margin, on the boundary, on the barrier or the barricade or maybe even sitting on the fence: and perhaps especially about being in the no-man's land (or on the frontier, border, edge, limit margin, boundary, barrier, barricade or fence) *between* these various non-synonymous concepts or terms.

45

One, perhaps parodically philosophical way (deconstruction being in part describable as parodically philosophical) of going about dealing with this situation would involve, precisely, attempting to fix the meaning or 'grammar' (in Wittgenstein's sense) of these various terms as carefully and precisely as possible. And it does of course, as should go without saying, seem important to get as clear as possible about concepts and their differences. But in this case, at least, that 'getting as clear as possible' marks less a straight-forward and honest 'enlightenment'-style ambition towards a clarity and illumination which could ideally (though perhaps not empirically) be achieved, than the sense that such an effort would quite rapidly come up against its *own* limit (or frontier, or boundary, or barrier, etc.), in that any attempt to fix such concepts or terms would involve drawing frontiers or boundaries or edges between them, and would thus seem to presuppose what is at issue in thinking about frontiers, boundaries and edges. It would no doubt be nice to fix the frontiers of the concept of the frontier, but hard to see how this could be done without somehow assuming that we know in advance what frontiers are, and therefore slipping into dogmatism in the very effort to avoid it. It seems to me that this dogmatism is the dogmatism of enlightenment itself. The concept or term 'frontier' seems to share with terms or concepts such as 'difference' the feature (which can't be simply a *conceptual* feature) of saying something about what it is to be a term or concept at all: and this seems to give it an ambiguous privilege which I follow Derrida and Rodolphe Gasché in terming 'quasi-transcendental,' in the awareness that that term names a problem to be further explored. And of course the term 'term,' which I've been using to avoid or inflect what may already seem too philosophical in the term 'concept,' cannot escape this complication: the term 'term' means a boundary, border or frontier of territory (a term can be a stone or post, carved with the image of Jupiter terminus, god of boundaries).

It seems unsurprising, then, to find that the sort of philosophy which demands rigorous fixing of concepts (and I don't imagine for a moment that any thinking can be simply indifferent to such a demand) should resort almost inevitably to an analogical language of territory and frontier when it attempts to conceptualise that conceptual fixing, that assigning of terms to its terms. Frege most famously goes in for this,[1] and Wittgenstein equally famously contests this necessity, typically enough by pursuing Frege's analogy or 'picture' (which Frege has said "may be used only with caution," and to which he himself could not accord conceptual status — Frege's passage is, on its own terms, a non-conceptual description of what a concept is or must be, but it's hard to see how he could give an account of the conceptuality of concepts without stepping outside strict conceptuality, over the frontier of the concept in general, in order to do so).[2]

I'm not going to go into these texts in detail here. We would find in them a complex association of frontiers and boundary-lines with signposts and pointing across those frontiers, that would lead us quite rapidly on to Heidegger (the first two examples of signs given in § 17 of *Being and Time* are of signposts and boundary-stones),

1. "The concept must have a sharp boundary. If we represent concepts in extension by areas on a plane, this is admittedly a picture that may be used only with caution, but here it can do us good service. To a concept without sharp boundary there would correspond an area that had not a sharp boundary-line all round, but in places just vaguely faded away into the background. This would not really be an area at all; and likewise a concept that is not sharply defined is wrongly termed a concept. Such quasi-conceptual constructions cannot be recognized as concepts by logic; it is impossible to lay down precise laws for them. The law of excluded middle is really just another form of the requirement that the concept should have a sharp boundary. Any object that you choose to take either falls under the concept or does not fall under it; tertium non datur. E.g. would the sentence 'any square root of 9 is odd' have a comprehensible sense at all if square root of 9 were not a concept with a sharp boundary? Has the question "Are we still Christians?" really got a sense, if it is indeterminate whom the predicate 'Christian' can truly be ascribed to, and who must be refused it?" (*Grundgesetze der Arithmetik*, Vol. 2, 56: *Translations from the Philosophical Writings of Gottlob Frege*, ed. Black and Geach, Third Edition [Oxford: Blackwell, 1980], p. 139).
2. "One might say that the concept 'game' is a concept with blurred edges. — 'But is a blurred concept a concept at all?' — Is an indistinct photograph a picture of a person at all? Is it even always an advantage to replace an indistinct picture by a sharp one? Isn't the indistinct one often exactly what we need? Frege compares a concept to an area and says that an area with vague boundaries cannot be called an area at all. This presumably means that we cannot do anything with it. [You'll remember that Frege actually complains about an impossibility of laying down the law for it, which may not be quite the same as saying that we cannot do anything with it: this inaccuracy in Wittgenstein seems far from trivial]- But is it senseless to say: 'Stand roughly there'? Suppose that I were standing with someone in a city square and said that. As I say it I do not draw any kind of boundary, but perhaps point with my hand — as if I were indicating a particular spot." Or again, a little earlier: "I can give the concept 'number' rigid limits in this way, that is, use the word 'number' for a rigidly limited concept, but I can also use it so that the extension of the concept is not closed by a frontier. And this is how we do use the word 'game.' For how is the concept of a game bounded? What still

and then to Lyotard and Derrida and their difficult disagreement over the status of decitic terms in Husserl.

More surprisingly, perhaps, we should have to take account of arguments in Derrida's 'Afterword' to *Limited Inc*, around the status of conceptual boundaries, which we have just seen Wittgenstein suggest need not be rigid or precise. Searle accuses Derrida of hanging on to the Fregean assumption (which Searle rather sarcastically associates with logical positivism) of a need for rigid distinctions, and Derrida retorts, surprisingly no doubt for many of his readers, that he does indeed think that concepts must have sharp boundaries.

But any attempt to address the general question of conceptual boundaries or frontiers, to which we have been led almost immediately by the specific question of the concept of the frontier, would almost inevitably lead quite rapidly to Kant. Kant's philosophy in general is of course all about drawing frontiers and establishing the legality of territories. In the 'Introduction' to the third *Critique*, for example, there is a famous use of the spatial analogy in the distinction between conceptual fields, territories and

counts as a game and what no longer does? Can you give a boundary? No. You can draw one; for none has so far been drawn. (But that never troubled you before when you used the word 'game.') 'But then the use of the word is unregulated, the 'game' we play with it is unregulated.' — It is not everywhere circumscribed by rules; but no more are there any rules for how high one throws the ball in tennis, or how hard; yet tennis is a game for all that and has rules too." (§ 68) And, finally for now: "If I tell someone 'Stand roughly here' — may not this explanation work perfectly? And cannot every other one fail too? But isn't it an inexact explanation? — Yes; why shouldn't we call it 'inexact'? Only let us understand what 'inexact' means. For it does not mean 'unusable.' And let us consider what we call an 'exact' explanation in contrast with this one. Perhaps something like drawing a chalk line round an area? Here it strikes us at once that the line has breadth. So a colour-edge would be more exact. But has this exactness still got a function here: isn't the engine idling? And remember too that we have not yet defined what is to count as overstepping this exact boundary; how, with what instruments, it is to be established. And so on." (§ 88)

realms.[3] There is, too, the passage from the end of the transcendental analytic on leaving the well-charted island of the understanding for the stormy seas of Reason.[4]

There is much at stake in this language of boundaries, mapping and possession of territory. We should need to follow it not only in Kant, but in Lyotard's recent readings of Kant (and notably perhaps, in *Le différend*, his extension of Kant's island analogy to that of the archipelago of discursive genres: there's the suspicion of a residual naturalism here which may be troublesome). Hegel's critique of Kant, for example, is crucially concerned to undermine the legitimacy of this boundary-language, seeing it as the culprit for the diremption in Kant between understanding and Reason and eventually between the concept and the law. Both in the *Phenomenology* and in the *Greater Logic*, there are powerful arguments against this Kantian set-up. We might hasard a guess that insofar as the philosophy loosely entitled 'post-structuralism' or maybe 'post-modernism' might usefully be thought of as a non-Hegelian questioning of Kantian frontiers (and I suspect that the term 'quasi-transcendental' gestures in this direction), then working with the quasi-concept of the frontier might help our understanding of what this involves.

This general problem of conceptual boundaries (or frontiers, or edges, or limits) may seem, in classical fashion, to be preliminary to

3. "Concepts, so far as they are referred to objects apart from the question of whether knowledge of them is possible or not, have their field [*feld*], which is determined simply by the relation in which their Object stands to our faculty of cognition in general. — The part of this field in which knowledge is possible for us, is a territory (*territorium*) for these concepts and the requisite cognitive faculty. The part of the territory over which they exercise legislative authority is the realm (*ditio*) of these concepts, and their appropriate cognitive faculty. Empirical concepts have, therefore, their territory, doubtless, in nature as the complex of all sensible objects, but they have no realm (only a dwelling-place, *domicilium*), for, although they are formed according to law, they are not themselves legislative, but the rules founded on them are empirical, and consequently contingent." Kant, *The Critique of Judgement*, tr. James Creed Meredith (Oxford: Clarendon, 1928), p. 12.
4. "We have now not merely explored the territory of pure understanding, and carefully surveyed every part of it, but have also measured its extent, and assigned to everything in it its rightful place. This domain is an island, enclosed by nature itself within unalterable limits [presumably it is because it is 'enclosed by nature' that Kant uses the example of an island, i.e. a territory with a so-called natural boundary]. It is the land of truth — enchanting name! — surrounded by a wide and stormy ocean, the native home of illusion, where many a fog bank and many a swiftly melting iceberg give the deceptive appearance of farther shores, deluding the adventurous seafarer ever anew with empty hopes, and engaging him in

any investigation at all of our problem. It looks as though we ought to clarify the conceptual frontiers of the concept of frontier before we try to clarify problems with 'real' frontiers. I want to resist that implication, and at least postpone that clarification. I suggest this partly for 'pragmatic' reasons, but partly in the spirit of the deconstructive argument against the possibility of absolutely justifiable starting-points. According to the *Grammatology*, and implicitly throughout Derrida's work, we must start "somewhere where we are, in a text already...," and move on following our noses to see where we might be going. This also implies that it is in principle impossible for the sorts of question I have been raising to be settled as a simple methodological preliminary to the real business at hand. Wittgenstein says at the beginning of the 'Lecture on Ethics' that the problem resides in the fact that "The listener is unable to see both the road he is being led to take and the goal to which it leads" (in this case — but in fact in general — this is as true of the speaker as of the listener): here that necessary contingency (I take it that deconstruction is in part describable as a philosophy of the 'necessity of contingency,' though it would require almost infinite care to separate a deconstructive reading of that expression from a Hegelian reading)[5] pushes me to return rather more literally to Wittgenstein's and Kant's language of spaces and areas with or without frontiers — in other words, to a language of territory. The preliminary claim is that it is impossible to clarify the conceptual status of the frontier without working through its political status: or, to put it in a slightly more sloganising form, that there is an irreducible conceptual politics of the frontier. The guiding hypothesis of what I'm trying to do, so far as 'Kant' and the 'Enlightenment' are concerned, is that there is at the very least an uneasy relationship between the desire to establish sharp conceptual frontiers on the one hand, and on the other to abolish political frontiers through cosmopolitanism, and, as far as Hegel is concerned, that the negotiation of these

enterprises which he can never abandon and yet is unable to carry to completion. Before we venture on this sea, to explore it in all directions and to obtain assurance whether there be any ground for such hopes, it will be well to begin by casting a glance upon the map of the land which we are about to leave, and to enquire, first, whether we cannot in any case be satisfied with what it contains — are not, indeed, under compulsion to be satisfied, inasmuch as there may be no other territory upon which we can settle; and, secondly, by what title we possess even this domain, and can consider ourselves as secured against all opposing claims." Kant, *The Critique of Pure Reason*, tr. Norman Kemp Smith (London: Macmillan, 1929), p. 257 [A235-6: B294-5].

5. This is the task of a sub-sequence from the seminar.

problems, though immeasurably more sophisticated, founders on a point that it is difficult not to describe as dogmatic.

The more general, 'deconstructive' point of this is probably less to attempt to do 'political philosophy' than to argue for an essential complication of any frontier between regions called the 'political' and the 'philosophical:' and this complication ought to be sufficient to prevent any falling into trivial readings of sloganising propositions such as "everything is political," or "philosophy is the politics of truth," and so on. It ought also to complicate what is to my mind the entirely unsatisfactory formulation, in the programme of this conference, of 'post-structuralist' thought as to do with "those who insist on the fact that thought should rather concentrate on the contingent poetical and rhetorical dimensions" of texts (I do not accept this formulation *at all*, though I regret that in what follows there will be no time to dwell on the properly textual complexity of Kant and Hegel), and operate something like a pre-emptive cross-border strike at the supposedly alternative position, "which systematically reconstructs the universal conditions of the possibility of an intersubjectively valid argumentation."

The suspicion that guides this 'political' approach to the frontier is that political philosophy has tended to begin with an attempt to deduce, found, or describe the *polis*, to circumscribe it, draw a frontier around it to separate it from, say, an anterior and exterior 'state of nature.' Once these questions have been more or less successfully negotiated — but I'll be trying to suggest, obliquely, that they never can be —, the question arises of the relationship between the state in question (in its generic singularity — we might wonder naively, or empirically, what 'the State,' the habitual object of political philosophy, can possibly be) and other states the existence of which suddenly becomes obvious.

Marx says that exchange begins "accidentally" at the frontiers of "natural communities." Is the frontier of a natural community a natural frontier? A working hypothesis I'd like to suggest (it's quite a commonplace one) is that there are no natural frontiers: but an apparently paradoxical (and perhaps less commonplace) corollary of this quite banal hypothesis would seem to be that *all frontiers are natural*. For if all frontiers are non-natural inscriptions, then in some sense all frontiers are frontiers of nature, marking off nature, drawn against a nature on the other side. This situation seems to go with many traditional descriptions of the formation of the polis out of a so-called state of nature. By means thought of in a variety of ways, politics emerges from nature, possibly naturally, but comes

51

into its own by drawing a frontier against the nature from which it has come. It may be, as in Aristotle, that the *polis* is thought to be itself in some sense natural, or maybe what is *most* natural, but this does not seem to alter the fundamental setup.

This can be seen in Kant quite clearly: for Kant, it is nature (herself) which pushes man out of the 'state of nature' into political organisation, as part of its teleological purpose of promoting the highest possible development of man's faculties. Kant disrupts any arcadian reading of the state of nature by stressing that this development involves a measure of strife.

But we should be as careful of jumping at too rapid a reading of nature's desire for discord as at too arcadian a reading. For Kant, nature does not want discord in any absolute sense:

> Man wishes to live comfortably and pleasantly, but nature intends that he should abandon idleness and inactive self-sufficiency and plunge instead into labour and hardships, so that he may by his own adroitness find means of liberating himself from them in turn. The natural impulses which make this possible, the sources of the very unsociableness and continual resistance which cause so many evils, at the same time encourage man towards new exertions of his powers and thus seem to indicate the design of a wise creator — not, as it might seem, the hand of a malicious spirit who had meddled in the creator's glorious work or spoiled it out of envy.[6]

This means that nature must be thought of as already violent, and therefore, I suspect, no longer quite nature at all (you'll have guessed that, if it's true, the argument about frontiers being of nature but not natural would entail the claim that nature is not natural). It is not so much that nature wishes violence, as Kant has just said, but that nature is already and essentially violent.

It's important to be clear about the status of this discord or "violence." It may be, says Kant, that the state of nature is *in fact* peaceful, or in fact violent. But because nothing is to stop it being violent, *it is therefore violent*, even if, empirically, it is in fact absolutely peaceful (there's already a valuable hint in this reasoning about the asymmetrical status of the terms in oppositions such as peacefulness and violence or peace and war: potential violence is *already* violence, which is why the only peace worth its name would be perpetual peace). This transcendental argument is put most clearly in the 'Perpetual Peace' essay: "A state of peace among men

---

6. "Idea for a Universal History with a Cosmopolitan Purpose," in: *Kant's Political Writings*, ed. H. Reiss, tr. B. Nisbet (Cambridge: CUP, 1970), p. 45.

living together is not the same as the state of nature, which is rather a state of war. For even if it does not involve active hostilities, it involves a constant threat of war breaking out."[7]

I think it is possible to show in fact that nature here is never a thinkable state at all, but a name for the suspended crossing of its own frontier. The fiction of a 'state of nature' in philosophers as diverse as Hobbes, Spinoza, Montesquieu, Rousseau and Kant seems to be such that it is not in fact a state at all, but a frontier always already crossed. My hypothesis is that this reasonably constant fictional basis for political philosophy is in fact a retrospective projection (if I can say that) of a supposedly *secondary* state of nature, which is that which returns at the frontier of the *polis*. Although only Aristotle appears fully aware of this complication — in that in the *Politics* he tells a story about how the polis comes about as a result of a process of association which begins with the unsustainability of the state of nature for an isolated individual, but then claims a natural priority for the *polis* even though it comes last in the order of the narrative he tells — my suggestion is that this reversal is generalisable, and that the implication of this is that the nature with which to start political stories is not the unfindable nature which supposedly preceded the formation of political groupings, but the nature which returns at the frontiers between political groupings once they are formed. The frontier is *haunted* by nature, and therefore violence. The frontier just is where nature returns — but nature just is what returns at the frontier, already a ghost.

We seemed, then, to have crossed the frontier from nature to right and politics by founding the State, but that frontier returns when the 'literal' question of the state's frontiers is raised. The frontier surrounding the lawfully constituted polis in its generic singularity and autonomy, the frontier which marked the separation from the state of nature (even if that separation is naturally inspired, even if, as I have suggested, that frontier is more natural than nature), this frontier immediately also marks the return of nature or the return to nature, in the relation between states, as soon as its outer edge is taken into account.

This situation causes some trouble — and it is worth saying immediately that the reason for focussing on Kant in the discussion of this problem is that he seems to face that difficulty rather more explicitly than most. This problem posed by the return of nature at the frontier seems intractable, and it seems to me that its foreclosure

7. *Kant's Political Writings*, p. 98.

in political thought is a generalised foreclosure (indeed a foreclosure which defines political thought at least in its traditional form), which must in principle have left traces that we ought to be able to locate. It is to be expected that these traces will not only have to do with the question of the frontier as a theme for political thinking, but will themselves repeat that question by drawing frontiers of various sorts within the texts we are reading.

If it is true that political thought builds its polis *out of* nature (with the ambiguity that that implies — nature as the material from which the polis is built, and nature as the state left behind through the building of the *polis: à partir de la nature*) only to find nature returning to haunt it at its frontier, then it is reasonable to suppose that *this* nature, the one that returns in an apparently secondary position, is in fact the real or primary problem. This parodically Aristotelian reversal (in Aristotle's deduction what came last in the natural process was really first) implies, with Aristotle, that the *really* first natural thing is not the *apparently* first natural thing (i.e. individuals unable to subsist in nature without forming associations), but also suggests, against Aristotle, that no more is it the apparently last natural thing turning out to be really the first (the State as the telos and therefore the nature of the natural progress of associations and associations of associations), but the stage just beyond the last stage, the stage *after the last*, which ought, then, to turn out to be also the stage before the first. Aristotle claims that the State, which comes last in the story he tells about associations, is really first: I am suggesting that what is *really* first must be the quasi-natural state of nature *between* states. Before the state, which is before the individual, are relations between states, which do not yet exist. These formulations are paradoxical enough to undermine terms such as 'first' and 'last,' and what temporality they involve we can at present only guess at. Our whole problem henceforth will be to make some sense of this difficult idea, and of its apparent *necessity*.

The general sense, in tune with a broadly 'Enlightenment' reading, is, I imagine, that Kant solves these problems by projecting an Idea of Perpetual Peace as the teleological principle whereby this returning nature and violence can be overcome. Once mankind has abandoned the supposedly primary state of nature and formed lawful groupings, the frontier clashes of these groups spread them out across the surface of the earth, until its spherical form (which seems to have an almost transcendental status in Kant's argument here, which itself bears some investigation in light of the first

54

Walt,

Pizzonia, Domenico

Doubletree

1715

later tonight
or tomorrow
morning

Antinomy of the Transcendental Dialectic) forces them to meet up again and form frontiers: the argument is that the inevitable and intolerable violence of those frontiers must be overcome by the attempted realisation of perpetual peace. This straightforward view of Kant certainly seems encouraged by the text of 'Universal History from a Cosmopolitan Point of View,' which, despite many complexities in the argument which I cannot go into here, ends up projecting a happy cosmopolitan state beyond current violence, and it looks as though that cosmopolitan state is the promise of the removal of frontiers to allow everyone to be, precisely, a 'citizen of the world,' and to that extent the promise of the overcoming of nature as violence, the final realisation of the political as something like the community of free rational beings which guides the ethical writings. And this would support Kant's claim that there can be no incompatibility of morality and politics. It is quite easy to show that this end of politics would be the end of politics (Kant's cosmopolitan situation is one which he explicitly imagines would maintain itself *automatically*:[8] the perpetual peace which would accompany that existence would be by definition undisturbable, otherwise it would not be perpetual, and therefore not really peace).[9] The suspicion that this has a broader implication for philosophy as a whole is one I'll just indicate by referring to Heidegger's suggestion in *Kant and the Problem of Metaphysics* that the three questions around which Kant claims "all the interests of my reason combine" (in the 'Canon of Pure Reason' near the end of the First Critique), viz, "What can I know?," "What ought I to do?" and "What may I hope?" (A805; B833), that these questions define man not as a natural being but as, precisely, a "citizen of the world," that they define the object of philosophy "in weltbürgerlicher Absicht" and to that extent define the field of true philosophy.

My suggestion is that, in spite of its title, the 'Perpetual Peace' essay of 1796 seriously complicates this set-up, and, by extension, the whole organisation of Kant's philosophy. In it, Kant is acutely

8. *Kant's Political Writings*, p. 48.
9. This "the end of x is the end of x" formulation seems to me to be broadly applicable, at least to 'Enlightenment' thought and its offshoots. It seems clear, for example, that on a Habermasian view of communication, its end is its end. This (suppressed) mortal effect of teleological thinking is presumably the opening whereby appeals to the excellence of communication and rational argumentation can so easily become intolerant and exclusionary. Again, the confrontation of this type of analysis of Enlightenment with Hegel's version of it in the *Phenomenology* is part of work in progress.

aware that the perspective of perpetual peace can always be a perspective of death (the text opens on a slightly uneasy joke about an inn called the 'Perpetual Peace' which has a sign depicting a graveyard, and the image returns several times in the course of the essay). This is a more complex text than I suspect has been recognized, and I won't have time to do it justice here. But through a variety of apparently contradictory arguments, according to which a frontierless world state is presented as 1) desirable but impracticable, as 2) a contradiction in terms, and as 3) undesirable but perhaps all too possible in the form of a "soulless despotism" which would necessarily revert to anarchy and the sort of natural violence we started from, Kant in fact, against all his explicit statements, draws back from the very notion of cosmopolitan perpetual peace, even as a regulative Idea, and formulates instead an ideal in terms of a federation of states in which frontiers are very definitely preserved in what he calls a "healthy rivalry," and are still associated with the dispersive force of nature, now seen "wisely" to separate the nations through linguistic and religious differences. Perpetual peace turns out to be possible only as the perpetual postponement of its own perpetuity.

This means that Hegel is no doubt right when he says that Kant's conception of perpetual peace remains "infected with contingency" (*Philosophy of Right*, § 333, remark). What Hegel means is that Kant has failed to secure any necessity for his desired progress towards perpetual peace, and this is because in the sort of confederation of states that is Kant's mitigated aim, there is nothing to prevent any one state unilaterally breaking the terms of the agreement and committing an act of violence on the others. To the extent that Kant maintains frontiers, and we have seen that he decides he must to prevent the worse violence that would result from any attempt at their straightforward abolition, then he maintains contingency. The frontier just is the place of contingency, where states touch on one another, the place, as we have seen, where natural violence, or nature as violence, returns to haunt the political organisation that was in principle set up to escape from precisely that natural violence, or at least the 'original' of which this is the ghost. And this situation appears to be precisely that seen by Hegel, for whom contingency, and violence, are precisely the domain of nature, and the passage through it a necessary part of spirit's coming to knowledge of itself, in philosophy, as absolute.

Hegel also, of course, builds in to his description of the state the necessity that there be this violence on the frontier. He insists throughout his work, from the early 'German Constitution' text to the late *Philosophy of Right*, via the *Natural Law* essay, that states must defend themselves actually (and not just declare their intention to do so) if they are to be worthy of being considered as states. Whereas in Kant, in his explicit arguments at least, war and peace were asymmetrical concepts insofar as peace was only worth its name if it was perpetual peace (any other notion of peace in fact being already warfare simply as threat of war), in Hegel peace is only worth its name if it is *not* perpetual peace, in other words only if it is already troubled by the promise of war as actual defence of the state on its frontier. Hegel makes an eloquent point in the *Natural Law* essay about the healthy ethical aspects of war which prevents the state stagnating and rotting, and is pleased enough with it to quote it again in the *Philosophy of Right* (§ 324). This does not, however, mean that Hegel is in any straightforward sense recommending war as such, or implying that a permanent state of warfare among states is a desirable state of affairs. This is not simplistic warmongering. But any possibility of peace is never a prospect of perpetual peace, as that would imply the quiescent death of the restless negativity of Spirit and a return to the mere *an sich* of matter. We seem to reach something remarkably like the result of *our* reading of Kant, i.e. peace as a sort of rhythmic oscillation of war-and-peace.

The problem this poses for Hegel is none other than that of contingency in general, which we have said is *the* problem of the frontier. States, which are the ethical totality in Hegel (or rather, 'the' State is the ethical totality: the whole problem being, of course, that Hegel recognises that states are constitutively and originarily plural, so there is necessarily more than one ethical totality) — states are only states to the extent that they are perpetually not-quite-established as frontiered units, but perpetually defending themselves by paradoxically exposing the values of civil society to destruction along frontiers that have never quite formed but which can never quite be abolished, and which are nonetheless the measure of the State's statehood.

It is precisely here that we must pause and draw a frontier in Hegel's text, in spite of Hegel. Insofar as the frontier is the place of contingency (and Hegel does nothing to deny this, except of course in general to affirm the dialectical identity of the contingent and the necessary, but that is just what is in question here), then Hegel is committed to its sublation. We have seen that that sublation cannot take the form of an immediate cosmopolitanism, for reasons that are not essentially different from those that Kant comes to see, almost in spite of himself. Hegel can, of course, allow himself to entertain contingency to a much greater extent than almost any other philosophy, and this is no doubt the reason for the immense power of the speculative dialectic, but he must nonetheless demonstrate its sublation into necessity. At the end of the International Right section of the *Philosophy of Right*, Hegel happily and almost complacently recognises that with the frontier-clashes between states (which is, remember, the only sense we can give to the identity of states, their not-yet and already-no-longer identity as self-dissolution) we have reached what he calls "the highest point of external contingency" (but contingency could scarcely be other than external for Hegel).

Here is § 340, ending and summarising the whole section on International Right and preparing the transition to the section on Universal History: first the recognition of the apparently almost uncontrollable degree of contingency we have reached at this point:

In their relations among themselves, because they are determined as particular, there is to be found [*fällt*: there befalls, precipitates out, linked of course to the case (*fall*), but also to *Zufälligkeit*, contingency] the most mobile play of the inner particularity of passions, interests, talents and virtues, violence, injustice and vice, of external contingency in the greatest dimensions of its appearance [my emphasis] — a play in which the ethical totality itself, the independence of the state, is exposed to contingency.

But we know of course that this cannot be so in reality, i.e. in the life of the Spirit, and that this has always already limited the degree of possible contingency, making possible the apparent recklessness and high drama of Hegel's descriptions. If we didn't know Hegel better, we might feel that things would get stuck here, in a situation which is directly comparable to the one we ended up with in Kant, and which, if this were really the end of the *Philosophy of Right*, would retrospectively remove the justification for Hegel's complaint about the contingency remaining in Kant's version of perpetual peace — and indeed have much greater retrospective effects than that. So the second part of the paragraph starts reeling it back in:

The principles of the spirits of peoples (*Volksgeister*) are essentially limited [*beschränkte*, enclosed by a frontier, precisely] by the particularity in which they have their objective reality and their self-consciousness as existing individuals, and their destinies and actions in their relations one with another are the phenomenal manifestation of the dialectic of these spirits as finite, out of which dialectic universal spirit, the World-Spirit, as

58

unlimited [*unbeschränkt*, frontierless] is brought forth [or 'brings itself forth,' *sich hervorbringt*] and it is it which exercises on them [i.e. on the finite particularities that the various states are] its Right — and its Right is the highest of all — in world- history as world-tribunal [*in der Weltgeschichte, als dem Weltgerichte*]. (§ 340)

This world-tribunal must clearly be situated on a level different from that of the states themselves — everything we have seen shows that it cannot be thought of as a sort of United Nations Organisation or cosmopolitan agency. From the point of view of world-spirit, the apparently contingent and violent play of the particular interests and passions of the various states (which we have consistently been able to link to the notion of a state of nature as it returns to haunt the polis at its frontier) is indeed seen to be on the side of nature, as it were, insofar as nature in Hegel is the necessary self-alienation of Spirit as part of the hetero-tautological movement of its own return to itself as absolute knowledge through philosophy. World history cannot be left to the apparent blind necessity/contingency of warfare dictated by particular passions:

Universal history is, furthermore, not the simple judgement of force, i.e. the abstract and irrational necessity of a blind fate [*eines blinden Schicksals*], but, as it is in and for itself Reason, and as the being-for-itself in spirit is a knowledge, it is, from the concept of its liberty alone, the necessary development of the moments of reason, and with it its self-consciousness and its liberty — the interpretation and actualisation of universal spirit. (§ 342)

But this moment in the *Philosophy of Right*, which is the moment of transition to history 'itself' (the final section of the book being essentially a summary of the *Philosophy of History*), is dogmatic and non-dialectical. Hegel accurately describes, more explicitly and more precisely than does Kant, precisely the sort of violent quasi-natural dispersion of states that we have suggested just is (inter-)national politics. But he attempts to resolve that situation by a violent temporal re-serialisation of what is a violently plural spatial dispersion. The dialectic *does violence to violence* in the attempt to sublate it, in contingently attempting to determine contingency as necessity. It can in fact be shown that the whole of the *Philosophy of History* remains 'infected' by this contingency, by this violence done to violence, by this contingent dealing with contingency. This problem has very little to do with any supposedly "contingent poetical and rhetorical dimension" which is supposed to be the domain of post-structuralism.

The frontier is indeed contingency. But does not a reading of Kant and Hegel such as that I have sketched out transform that contingency into a necessary contingency, to be affirmed? If, as goes without saying, the state of nature is indeed a state of intolerable violence, and if, as Kant shows rather in spite of himself, and as Hegel says clearly, cosmopolitan perpetual peace would return first of all to the worst despotism and then to a new state of nature, do we not have to affirm the political as the space (which is doubtless not a territory, still less a realm, and perhaps not even a field, according to the classification from the Introduction to the third *Critique*, but in fact the space of the frontier itself, the spacing of the frontier) as the space of this "contingency" which will never sublate into any necessity other than that of its contingency? From this point of view, we shall say that the concept of "frontier" cannot be a concept like another concept (which will imply that in fact there is never a concept like another, to the extent that the concept of 'concept' must presuppose an understanding of the frontier), but that the work of this quasi-concept of the frontier in the texts of Kant and Hegel inscribes a frontier in their textual system, so that, whereas the concept of dog does not bark and the concept of sugar is not sweet, *the 'concept' of frontier is a frontier*, and cannot to that extent remain the concept that it is.

If we can show on the basis of these texts that frontiers can never be absolutely established (which would come down to having only an inside, absolute immanence) nor entirely abolished (which would come to the same thing) nor even speculatively sublated, then we should have to re-read all the "literal" and "metaphorical" (but this opposition is no longer strictly pertinent here) frontiers in Kant and Hegel (for example) as the figure of a non-figurable absolute alterity that any enlightenment of any sort necessarily presupposes, and which provides as much the conditions of impossibility of, for example "an intersubjectively valid argumentation" as its conditions of possibility (these conditions, as always in deconstruction, in fact being the same conditions, this sameness defining the quasi-transcendental). There is no 'debate' to be had here, insofar as deconstruction affirms this quasi-transcendental, and any Habermasian position must presuppose it. I hope and trust, to that extent, that we shall not reach agreement. Let not the end of our discussion be the end of discussion.

60

4. Habermas and Derrida on Reflexivity

LUDWIG NAGL

My paper re-examines some aspects of Habermas' reading (and rejection) of Derrida. It is inspired by Rodolphe Gasché's analysis of 'deconstruction' which refines Derrida studies considerably. Gasché focuses on "the criticism of the notion of reflexivity."[1] By following him in this, I hope that my juxtaposition of two theories as divergent as Habermas' and Derrida's will bring to the fore not only well-known differences but also unexpected parallels between an (intersubjectivity- and consensus-oriented) critique of *Subjekt-philosophie* and the 'deconstructive' attempt to "question reflec-tion's unthought." (TM 6)

1) A common starting point: The end of Philosophy (with a capital P). Both Habermas and Derrida share the view that *traditional* philosophy has come to an end. For Habermas this awareness is deeply embedded in all thought after Hegel: "The discourse of modernity which we are still conducting down to our day," he writes, "is marked by the consciousness that philosophy is over."[2] During the last century the great (and negatively inverted) narrative that philosophy has come to an end had been spelled out in many forms. "To be sure," Habermas writes, "the destruction or over-coming of metaphysics by Nietzsche and Heidegger meant some-thing other than the sublation of metaphysics [Bruno Bauer had in mind], and the farewell to philosophy by Wittgenstein and Adorno meant something other than the realization of philosophy" Marx envisaged (PDM 52). Today "the situation of consciousness," so Habermas, "still remains the one brought about by the Young Hegelians when they distanced themselves from Hegel and philo-sophy in general." (PDM 53)

Whoever criticizes philosophy's claim for aprioricity and ulti-mate foundation — and thus tries to avoid (in the famous phrase of William James) "Philosophy with a capital P" — sees the aporias

1. Rodolphe Gasché, *The Tain of the Mirror*. Derrida and the Philosophy of Reflection (Harvard University Press, 1986) (= TM), p. 5.
2. Jürgen Habermas, *The Philosophical Discourse of Modernity*. Twelve Lectures (MIT Press, 1987) (= PDM), p. 51.

and *Holzwege* of modernity that disfigure the project of enlightenment as the outcome of its constitutive 'principle of subjectivity.'
Or, as Habermas writes: "Agreement exists about the fact that the
authoritarian traits of a narrow-minded enlightenment are embedded in the principle of self-consciousness... That is to say the
self-relating subjectivity purchases self-consciousness only at the
price of objectivating internal and external nature... it renders itself
at once opaque and dependent in the very acts that are supposed to
secure self-knowledge and autonomy. This limitation, built in the
structure of the relation-to-self, remains unconscious in the process
of becoming conscious. From this springs the tendency towards
self-glorification and illusionment, that is, toward absolutizing a
given level of reflection and emancipation." (PDM 55)

The modern 'quest for certainty' — the Cartesian 'relation-to-
self' as a foundational, 'auto'-constitutive relation — has various
'blind spots.' Habermas thinks (not unlike Derrida) that a *reflection*
which aims at a complete *'présence-à-soi'* (at 'total self-transparency') leads to dichotomizations that stubbornly resist 'reconcilia-
tion.' His criticism of the reflective self goes beyond Hegel's critical
investigation of *Reflexionsphilosophie*, in claiming that Hegel's 'absolute dialectic' (which turns reflection upon itself and thus tries to
come to grips with its unthought, with the split between a 'subjective subject-object' and an 'objective subject-object') remains
tied to an 'inflated' principle of 'monological' subjectivity.

Such a critique of dialectical self-transparency can be expressed in
various ways, however: Derrida focuses on a different trait, the
(romantic) thought-figure of a 'return to an origin.' For Hegel the
shortcoming of *Reflexionsphilosophie* was its inability to reflect
itself in such a way that a regrounding of its opposed moments in a
presupposed *totality* could take place. *Post*-Hegelian thinkers are
convinced, however, that Hegel's own *Begriffsbewegung* solves
"the problem of a self-reassurance of modernity...*too well*," as
Habermas once ironically put it (PDM 42). Dialectical totalizations
which aim at an *'identity* of identity and nonidentity' follow a 'logic
of *Aufhebung'* that both Derrida[3] and Habermas[4] reject. But if the
idea to make reflection 'self-transparent' has to be abandoned since
the thought figure of *Einholen* — of a mediated return to an origin
— rests on the dubious notion of self-*Vergegenwärtigung* (as Derrida points out), how then can the disturbing 'shadow' of reflexivity

---

3. f.in J. Derrida, *Positions* (University of Chicago Press, 1981) (= P) p. 95.
4. f.i. in PDM 42.

(which gives rise to a destructive 'dialectic of enlightenment') be dissolved? This question troubles most contemporary philosophers who want "to find a way out of the Philosophy of 'the Subject'" (PDM 294). Derrida and Habermas both address it (and at the same time doubt that their respective answers to the challenge of our post-Hegelian thought constellation has the necessary degree of sophistication). For Habermas, Derrida's experiments to 'deconstruct' metaphysics, and thus to subvert the division between thought and unthought, are tied to a self-defeating concept of critique (which tends to collapse into a new version of negative theology).[5] Derrida, in contrast, sees 'everyday language' (which according to Habermas entails the possibility of a non-absolute 'reflection of reflection') not as an 'innocent and neutral' remedy at all: For him, ordinary language is the very *Inbegriff* of "the language of Western metaphysics."[6] Is it thus plausible to assume that — in spite of this mutual negative assessment — non-trivial parallels do exist in Habermas's and Derrida's attempts to philosophize 'after Philosophy'?[7]

2) *Habermas's communicative option: Two notions of reflexivity.* Let us first consider how discourse theory tries to overcome the limits of 'Subjektphilosophie.' According to Habermas, "the objectifying attitude in which the knowing subject regards itself as it would entities in the external world is no longer *privileged* [in communicative action]. Fundamental to the paradigm of mutual understanding is, rather, the performative attitude of participants in interaction, who coordinate their plans for action by coming to an understanding about something in the world." (PDM 296) Thus ego is able to relate "to himself as a participant in an interaction from the perspective of alter." Habermas insists that communicatively structured forms of self-reflection have a thoroughly new quality; discourse theory avoids the idea of a *présence-à-soi* that accompanies 'transcendental reflexivity:' "And indeed," so Habermas, "this *reflection* undertaken from the perspective of the partici-

---

5. PDM 161-210.
6. P 19 (Interview with J. Kristeva).
7. Richard Bernstein, in his article "An Allegory of Modernity/Postmodernity," *The New Constellation*, 1991, p. 199-229, recently suggested to interpret the controversy between Habermas and Derrida as a 'force-field,' i.e. 'as a juxtaposed rather than an integrated cluster of changing elements that resist reduction to a common denominator.' Only together 'they show the tangled intertwined strands of the 'modern/postmodern' *Stimmung*' (p. 225).

pant escapes the kind of objectification inevitable from the *reflexively* applied perspective of the observer." (PDM 297)

Thus, in Habermas' view, a sound and non-speculative notion of reflection is conceivable that dissolves the first of Foucault's three doubles (which — according to *The Order of Things* — insistently accompany modernity): the strict separation, i.e., between the 'transcendental' and the 'empirical.' (PDM 298) "The first person," so Habermas, "who turns back upon himself in a performative attitude from the angle of vision of the second person, can *recapitulate* the acts it just carried out. In place of *reflectively* objectified knowledge — the knowledge proper to self-consciousness — we have a recapitulating reconstruction of knowledge already employed." (PDM 297) This 'reconstruction' circumvents not only the aporetical forth and back between the empirical and transcendental 'moments' of a (monological) self-thematisation. It also makes possible a methodically carried out self-critique that does not get trapped in Foucault's second double ('conscious'/'unconscious'), according to which "the thought of subject philosophy oscillates back and forth between heroic exertions bent on *reflexively* transforming what is in-itself into what is for-itself, and the recognition of an opaque background that stubbornly escapes the transparency of self-consciousness." (PDM 298)

Within the communicative paradigm of mutual understanding these two aspects of self-reflection [self-consciousness and -unconsciousness] "are no longer incompatible," because all dialogically constructed self-critique is related to the (limiting but alterable) totality of a presupposed (and *prereflective*) 'lifeworld.' Thus the patient work of reflective learning is carried out in a manner which avoids both, the illusion of 'self-transparency' and the complementary illusion of a total intransparency of the self: On the one hand, "the dissolution of hypostatizations, of self-engendered objective illusions, is due to the experience of *reflection*. But its liberating force is directed toward *single* illusions: It *cannot make transparent the totality* of a course of life in the process of individuation or of a collective way of life." (PDM 300) (Emphasis added L.N.)

Discourse theory thus tries to re-conceptualize reflexivity and reason "in a more modest fashion" (PDM 43). It thereby seeks to avoid not only (monological) *Reflexionsphilosophie* but also Hegel's absolute dialectic, and the various post-Hegelian 'aggrandizements' of 'the Subject' (Nietzsche's neo-metaphysics of a 'will to power' f.i.). The intersubjective reconstruction of reflexivity (which is spelled out in speech-act theoretical terms) thus forms the core of

Habermas's communication theory: Reflective 'communication about communication' deals with the unthought in a piecemeal form, without totally penetrating or once an for all unmasking it. If we seriously intend to enlighten enlightenment about its short-comings, the patient work of our mutual learning processes seems more promising to Habermas than a radical 'deconstruction' of reason.

But is it really plausible that an intersubjective reconstruction of 'reflection' dissolves all the fundamental aporias of (monological) subjectivity? And: Is Habermas's core concept of communication fully explored by speech act theory (which entails a rigid conception of meaning-identity)? Or can discourse theory still learn something from experimental practices like Derrida's which try to avoid the philosophical concept of reflexivity altogether and instead investi-gate its 'supplements,' since they assume — as M. Frank says — that "the paradigm of reflection (of a speculative return to the point of departure)... does not stand up to the experience of an unlimited economy of semantic oppositions?"[8] But then how to deal with the suspicion that the supplements of reflection ('dissemination of meaning,' 're-marquer,' 'différance') — which supposedly subvert *Subjektphilosophie* — tacitly presuppose what they publicly de-nounce, subjectivity (in its radical form of arbitrariness).[9] Thus the plan to 'stretch' discourse theory with the help of Derrida would not sound all too promising! Maybe deconstruction deconstructs distorted images of reflexivity only: Hegel's 'overwhelming' ver-sion of reason (PDM 42), f.i., and, on a more trivial level, the paradoxical notion of reflection as 'mirroring'? Derrida's critique of reflection's 'présence-à-soi' presupposes, it seems, elements or trac-es of an optical image of reflexivity (which, by the way, already infested Husserl's epistemology). Such optical metaphors have their origin in the captivating notion of 'mirroring' which R. Gasché characterizes as follows: "Reflection is the structure and the process of an operation that, in addition to designating the action of a mirror reproducing an object, implies that mirror's mirroring itself, by which process the mirror is made to see itself." (TM 17) If analyzed in some detail, this mirror metaphor of reflexivity turns out to be full of dubious implications, however. Neither can a mirror image show, why a mirror mirrors itself; we usually avoid to examine the

8. M. Frank, *What is Neostructuralism?* (University of Minnesota Press, 1989), p. 427.
9. See Ch. Taylor, *Sources of the Self* (Cambridge University Press, 1989), p. 488.

65

literal meaning of this claim by actually imagining, not that the mirror mirrors itself, but that it mirrors — and is mirrored in — another mirror! But if we are willing, for the sake of the argument, to grant that a mirror could 'mirror itself,' even this would not explain the miracle how a mirror — as a result of 'mirroring itself' — could become aware of itself: it never actually happens to empirical mirrors, as far as we know, or, for that matter, to photographs which — by means of mechanical reproduction — quasi-reflective-ly 'depict themselves.' It is hard to see how the adding of temporal indices (like 'presence' and 'delay') to the extremely dubious and misleading 'optical' metaphor of reflection could help rendering it more intelligible. How deeply, we thus have to ask, is Derrida's subversion of reflection and subjectivity infested by this paradox-ical image of a 'mirror,' the 'tain' (or 'tainlessness') of which decon-struction wants to make visible in pointing out the various dis-seminative supplements of reflexivity?

3) *Deconstructivism, a new 'Ursprungsphilosophie'?* Habermas interprets Derrida's project to unmask Reason as logo- ethno- and phallocentrism as a post-Heideggerian version of a "Philosophy of Origin." (PDM 161) In Derrida's thought, so Habermas, "the achewriting takes on the role of a subjectless generator of structures that... are without any author" (PDM 180). This shift in the project to ground (and unground) reason does not warrant, however, that Derrida can do without recourse to central thought figures of modernity: in spite of his manifold attempts to circumvent 'the logic of constitution,' the movement which his thinking performs when it encircles the differance between phonemes and that which sets them in operation ('an archewriting not itself present') has to be read, so Habermas, in terms of a neo-metaphysics of 'foundation.' This remains true even if Derrida's image of 'origin' — under the spell of Nietzsche — gets an inverted and negative twist: "In the metaphor of the archewriting and its trace," so Habermas, "we see ...the Dionysian motif of the God making his promised presence all the more palpable to the sons and daughters of the West by means of his poignant absence," and he concludes, quoting Derrida: "But the movement of the trace is necessarily occulted, it produces itself as occultation. When the other announces itself as such, it presents itself in the dissimulation of itself." (PDM 181)

Is Habermas's attempt to read deconstruction as a negative ver-sion of *Ursprungsphilosophie* fair, however? How deeply is Derri-da's project tied to arguments which center around a logic of 'constitution'? The strength and significance of such a linkage was denied recently by Richard Rorty[10] and Heinz Kimmerle.[11] Habermas could find support for his interpretation of deconstruction, however, in the texts of early Derrida. As Gasché pointed out, *Of Grammatology* indeed "speaks of the relation between the infrastructures and that which they are infrastructures of in terms of constitution and production, thus meeting all the requirements of traditional philosophizing." But at the same time, so Gasché, "Derrida's book as a whole consists of a critique of the philosophical concept of origin, and thus of the idea of a linear genesis." (TM 157) And in *Speech and Phenomena* Derrida says that "the very concept of constitution must itself be deconstructed."

This does not fit well into Habermas's picture of a "new Ursprungsphilosophie." As far as I see, the difference between his and Derrida's project lie somewhere else. Although Habermas, like Derrida, opposes 'foundationalism,' it is the double-bind of Derrida's strategy (his attempt to ground *and* unground transcendentality in 'différance') which remains alien to Habermas' thought. He suspects that the indirect language of deconstruction (with its evasions, subversions and *Zurücknahmen*) dissolves into a rhetorical web of 'performative contradictions.' Thus the positive sense of a modest, speech-act theoretical re-interpretation of reflection is missed. What, however, is — in more detail — the organizing idea of Derrida's project? We try to approach it in two steps, by looking at it historico-genetically and by examining aspects of Derrida's methodology.

4) Derrida's move away from classical forms of reflection. Derrida points out that the way for deconstruction was paved by phenomenology. Husserl's conception of *Abbau* already contains motifs of a *nonreflective* method of transcendental investigation (TM 109-111) Although 'dismantling' seems often to be just "another name for phenomenological reduction" (TM 109) it entails nevertheless, as Gasché shows, significant differences: *Abbau* rests on a complexly structured form of retrogression which is not a mere product of transcendental reflexivity, since it "is at once mediated and nonreflective" (TM 111).

10. R. Rorty, in: "Is Derrida a transcendental philosopher?," *Essays on Heidegger and others. Philosophical Papers*, Vol 2 (Cambridge University Press, 1991), p. 119-128.
11. H. Kimmerle, in: "Ist Derridas Denken Ursprungsphilosophie?," *Die Frage nach dem Subjekt*, Hg. v. M. Frank, G. Raulet, W.v. Reijen, p. 267-282; and "Gadamer, Derrida und kein Ende," *Allgemeine Zeitschrift für Philosophie*, 16/3, 1991, p. 59-69.

The move away from reflection becomes prominent in Heidegger's notion of *Destruktion* (*Sein und Zeit*): In contrast to Husserl who brackets the natural attitude toward the world "in order to focus on the transcendental subjectivity that constitutes it," retrogression for Heidegger becomes "a means of regaining the original metaphysical experience of Being" (TM 112). *Destruktion* is thus the necessary correlate of a process of 'phenomenological construction.' Only *durch kritischen Abbau* can the concealment of *Sein* be dissolved. Gasché shows how Heidegger in *Schritt zurück*, *Andenken* and *Besinnung* avoids the terminology of reflection through "a fundamental shift from a subjective transcendental perspective toward the question of Being as the transcendental question par excellence, giving *transcendental* a historically new meaning." (TM 114)

Derrida wants to go one step further. Although Heidegger's break with metaphysics presupposes a "more radical concept of time," it repeats involuntarily, so Derrida, traditional figures of thought: "The extraordinary trembling to which classical ontology is subjected...still remains within the grammar and lexicon of metaphysics," he writes in *Ousia and Gramme*. *Deconstruction* tries to be nonreflexive in a much more radical way than *Destruktion* ever envisaged: Although it still seeks the "ultimate foundation" of concepts (so Derrida in *Of Grammatology*), it claims at the same time that their rationality "no longer issues from a logos." To ground concepts is to unground them. Derrida is quick in emphasizing, however, that this post-reflective activity "inaugurates...not the demolition but the de-sedimentation...of all the significations that have their source in that of the logos."[12]

(5) *Deconstructive methodology*. How can such a radical (or maybe radically paradox) project be carried out, however? Gasché explains Derrida's method as follows (TM 174-6): "Deconstruction *starts* with an interrogation of a variety of contradictions and aporias in the discourse of philosophy. These are not contradictions and aporias proper, however, since the discourse of philosophy accommodates them without difficulty." Everyday modes of reflectivity (critique on a basic level 1) can handle such inner-philosophical tensions. But "in addition to these contradictions and aporias, which pertain to the formation of concepts and to the development of philosophical arguments, deconstruction addresses many other dis-

12. J. Derrida, *Of Grammatology* (Baltimore/London, 1974), p. 10.

cursive and conceptual inequalities that have never before been questioned by philosophy."

The method of deconstruction thus raises a very strong claim, indeed; if we want to overcome metaphysics, we have to scrutinize — in a manner which has some analogy with psychoanalysis — the fragile and cracking (but nevertheless unalterably rigid) language game of 'Philosophy.' Philosophical thought has a solid (and solidly defective) structure, which cannot be reached by regular reflection. Deconstruction is a sort of non- and extra-reflective *Durcharbeiten* of unconscious material. This leaves two questions open, however: first why 'Philosophy' is understood in this manner, i.e. as nothing but a compact (but nevertheless cracking) language game with a pattern of fixed conscious (and supplementary unconscious) rules? And secondly, from which pre-or post-reflective source the deconstructive enterprise draws its strength when neither 'the subject' nor 'reflexivity' can be its *movens* any longer? Before we deal with these questions we return to Gasché's characterization of Derrida's method, however: The 'unthought of philosophy' which deconstruction wants to unsettle (as well as to unlock) is approached as follows: "All these aporias, differences of levels, inequalities of developments, and disparities characteristic of the discourse of philosophy, yet which do not seem to disturb the logic of philosophy, also contribute to the establishment of that logic. All the gestures of philosophy — reflection and transcendentalization, all the themes of philosophy, but primarily those of subjectivity, transcendentality, freedom, origin, truth, presence, and the proper — are impossible without the differences and discrepancies that permeate philosophical texts. Yet these same disparities also limit the scope of these gestures and of the purity and coherence of the philosophical concepts or themes." (TM 174)

When philosophy is characterized in such a way, it is not seen as a complex and liberating interplay of language and (reflective) metalanguage, but is read as a closed discourse system with 'significant' limits. It is assumed that we are unable to modify, alter or improve the defective language game of philosophy, even if we become aware of its shortcomings. The best thing we can do is to make its — unavoidably 'constitutive' — fissures and cracks and its peculiar compromises visible through deconstructive readings. Or, as Gasché says: "Deconstruction is an attempt to account for these various and essentially heterogeneous aporias and discursive inequalities with what I have called infrastructures. These minimal structures are both the grounds of possibilities of the canonical philosophical

69

gestures and themes *and their ungrounds*, that is, that which makes them impossible." (TM 175)

But how can this 'transcendental double-bind' which turns around the ambivalence of 'limit' — that conditions of possibility are at the same time conditions of impossibility — ever be rendered intelligible? "Deconstruction," so Gasché, "does not merely destroy metaphysical concepts; it shows how these concepts and themes draw their possiblity from that which ultimately makes them impossible. The infrastructures achieve this double task." (TM 175). These grounding/ungrounding conditions of possibility/impossibility (like 'différance,' f.i.) are articulated in deconstruction, i.e., their outlines can be pointed out in various ways (i.a. as 'arche-trace' and 'supplementarity'). Thus the question reoccurs whether these 'infrastructures,' as Gasché calls them, are altogether beyond reflexivity: since they are results of a process of enlightenment about the closures of metaphysics, they could also seem to be the outcome of reflection in a Habermasian sense. Maybe the liberating potential of reflexivity vanishes only if we emphatically misconceive reflection as identity-bound, as we do in concepts of 'absolute speculation' (where re-flection is thought to perform the impossible movement of a complete 'return to itself') or in trivial 'mirror metaphors' of reflexivity (which keep reoccurring — directly or in inverted mode — not only in deconstruction but also in Lacan's and Rorty's grandiose narratives about the genesis of individuality)?

Derrida does not belief, however, in a communicative rehabilitation of reflexivity of the type which Habermas suggests: to direct the deconstructive impulse exclusively against *speculative* interpretations of reflection is not satisfactory, since Derrida wants to demonstrate that logos, *Herrschaftswissen*, dominates *all* forms of presentistic speech. The infrastructures which ground and unground ordinary and philosophical discourse are thus not part of the game of basic, level 1-reflection: they are operative on a meta-level (which is inaccessible — in principle — to Philosophy). Thus all pre-deconstructive systems of thought are seen as unalterable patterns of arguments (plus supplements): "Since philosophy has grown out of these infrastructures... it cannot dominate [them] with either its gestures or its themes." (TM 175) Infrastructures can neither reflexively intervene into the closed discourse of Philosophy, nor are they — in the classical sense of Hegel's dialectic — 'reflective in themselves.' As in negative theology, "the infrastructures are in a dissymmetrical and heterogeneous relation to what they make possible."

Deconstruction thus is, as Gasché points out, "in essence *a heterology*," that is, an experimental exploration of the Otherness of the Other. Its method is torn between two extremes, however, since it aims at rigid argumentation/presentation and — at the same time — at the displacement of it. Gasché expresses this ambivalent wish in the following way: "Deconstruction both conserves the immanence of philosophical argumentation and concept formation while simultaneously opening it up to that which structurally disorganizes it." (TM 175) This practice is said to follow a logic of inversion and adaptation: "As in Hegel's speculative thinking, where "dialectic has been separated from proof," and where thus "the notion of philosophical demonstration has been lost," deconstruction, by reinscribing philosophical argumentation, radically displaces it." (TM 175)

If Hegel's 'speculative' ambitions are criticized, however — which both Derrida and Habermas do — the question arises whether an inversion and displacement of Hegel's idea — that concepts develop in a form of self-movement — and its substitution through the notion of a radically heterogeneous, self-less dissemination of meanings, retains any sense of plausibility?

(6) Problems. At that point our suspicion might grow that, maybe, we can render intelligible the complex interplay between established philosophical argumentation and its limits only, if we deflate reflective speculation as well as de-reflective deconstruction and start to carefully analyze the traces of non-identity which we can find in communicative interaction. Such a move does not force us to reject, however, a 'transcendental' analysis of Derrida like Gasché's[13], which demonstrates quite brilliantly the ambivalent motifs at the center of Derrida's thought and their historico-genetical background. With the help of Gasché the question can be posed clearly, how plausible Derrida's concatenation of divergent post-reflective advances and practices is. If deconstruction, however, has to 'conserve the immanence of philosophical argumentation,' as Derrida claims, this probably will affect all experiments which aim at the subversive dissolution of argumentation. If meanings turn out to be unstable in this process, and hermeneutical 'objectivism' is thus shattered, deconstructions, nevertheless, become plausible only, if their content can be rearticulated (in principle) *in propositional form*. As Rorty pointed out, 'subpropositional' claims like, f.i., Hegel's talk of a *Bewegung des Begriffs* and Derrida's assertion that

13. R. Rorty, *Philosophical Papers*, Vol 2, p. 119-128.

"concepts and discursive totalities are already cracked and fissured by necessary contradictions and heterogeneities," can hardly pass as arguments.[14] They will count as *erschlichen* as long as their plausibility is not demonstrated in a propositional manner. Argumentation, this is the central thought of Habermas, is not just one more language game, which we can play for a while, as a starting point for rhetorical disseminations f.i, and then put aside again, since, in the end, there is no divinatory *Spezialwissen* that could serve as a functioning 'supplement' to discourse. Even if we intend to subvert *some* of our practices of argumentation (those f.i. which are structurally infested by the hierarchical asymmetry between men and women), we find no *locus* beyond discourse, but continue — even in our attempts to alter meanings — to participate in a communicative structure which includes the possible recourse to the 'forceless force' of the better argument. Unlike Derrida Habermas thus rejects the idea of a disseminative floatation of meanings and defends the *Unhintergehbarkeit* of argumentation in all philosophical and metaphilosophical writing.

(7) The subject, constituted by the other(s). Habermas and Derrida agree in another non-marginal respect, however. Both hold that the subject, which classical philosophy understood as a self-sufficient *locus* of reflection, is not originary, but 'produced:' it is the result of the constitutive activities of others (or, respectively, of *its* other). Habermas tries to show that the ego develops in processes of socialization (which he analyzes with the help of Durkheim's and Mead's theories of intersubjectivity). And Derrida thinks of the (transcendental) subject as 'presupposing,' as a 'non autos,' since it depends in its significant self-relation on 'differance': 'Self-presence' presupposes its other (like the voice presupposes its 'incarnation' or 'writing').

(8) Against 'Identitätszwang.' And there is another affinity between Habermas and Derrida. Both have learned from Adorno that the ultimate integration of negativity, difference (and freedom) into 'speculative reflection' is untenable. Habermas's *Theory of Communicative Action* marks a shift away from the thought figures of 'self-transparency' and 'monologicity' toward the acknowledgment of alterity and resistance. Communicative reflexion does not circle in itself. The participants of a discourse have 'heterological' stature for each other; they make unpredictable and unexpected contributions to, and are invited to criticize, any actual mode of empirical

14. Ibid., p. 124.

72

consensus. The validity of meaning is not 'given,' it is not a matter of mere re-presentation and unalterable rule following, but has to be produced and defended discursively: this entails the possibility of subversive moves against all kinds of interim agreements. To speak with (and to write about) each other does not only activate mutual acknowledgment, it also implies the negation and falsification of theories and the discursive re-examination of intentions and value judgments; at no given *empirical point in time* communication thus terminates in an unchallengeable super-identity (in 'The Consensus' with a capital C; or in an abstract unity where all otherness of the other is integrated once and for all into a rock-solid meaning-identity). Consensus thus is no empirical fact for Habermas, it has the status of a (necessary) regulative ideal. This implies that empirical agreements — in case they occur — remain open to falsification. As John Rawls pointed out recently[15] — ongoing disagreement between different persons about truth and validity is not a matter of bad intentions but the unavoidable result of the finite stature of or 'burdened reason.' It keeps re-occurring even under the strong hypothetical condition that all the participants of an empirical discourse are well-meaning and reasonable. No absolute closure can take place in empirical communication, if it is guided (as the search for truth and goodness is) by the 'ideal' of a consensuos rationality. Alterity (and individual 'meaning perspectivism') continue to stimulate (and to trouble) all interim unities.

Derrida — and other post-modern authors like Lyotard — charge, however, that discourse re-enacts the problematic traits of Plato's *symploke*, of a unity i.e., which plaits together opposites that are at war with one another in a way that in the end implies exclusion. Gasché outlines this Platonic metaphor as follows: In the process of unification, *symploke* "leaves a variety of other possible relations unreckoned. Or rather, they become violently excluded..." (TM 96). Is this repression of alterity in the service of unity characteristic also of discourse theory? If we stay at the surface level of Habermas's concept of communication this could seem to be the case, since all empirical discourses suffer from temporal and spatial limitations and from the actual non-representation of relevant interests. The strong heterological impulse, however, which forms the core of discourse theory rules out any final closure: Nobody can 'in the long run' be legitimately excluded from processes of discursive

15. J. Rawls, "The Domain of the Political and Overlapping Consensus," *New York Law Review*, 64/2, 1989, p. 233-255.

enlightenment: "In Aufklärungsprozessen gibt es nur Teilnehmer." All false unity will be reopened and deconstructed, since in the ongoing process of meaning formation every participant is a nucleus of otherness. 'Interests' — as expressions of an inexhaustible potential for the creation of new self-images and desires — are plural and can be articulated best by those concerned.

(9) *Discourse and non-identity*. That there is a quiet emphasis on non-identity at the core of Habermas's theory is not as well known as Derrida's insistence on (and rhetorical experimentation with) alterity and differance. Since Habermas often emphasizes the normative aspects of consensus which presuppose a (non-totalizing) version of unity (a prerequisite of, by the way, even Derrida's extreme articulation of différance), the heterological structure of his communication paradigm is frequently overlooked.

Derrida, like Habermas, aims at new and open forms of 'syntheses' that are neither transcendental nor speculative, neither 'monological' nor 'absolute.' His search for these synthetic 'infrastructures' cannot be read as a search for deeper and more profound 'grounds,' however: Derrida does not crave for an origin which is more fundamental than Heidegger's *Sein*, he does not try to rehabilitate *Ursprungsphilosophie* as Habermas criticizes. The sort of syntheses which his heterology tries to articulate (archetrace, différance, supplementarity) has a crucial status in logical terms, however. Gasché explains that "these 'syntheses'... 'account' for structurally nontotalizable arrangements of heterogeneous elements, with the result that the system of predicates that they form is also essentially incomplete." (TM 100) Due to this, the otherness which they try to express is not 'domesticated': it is not merely a *bestimmte Negation* of *R*eason that terminates in a new *T*ruth of philosophy. Derrida's open syntheses seek to avoid all definite shape. They nevertheless raise a tremendous (truth?) claim, as we learn from Gasché: "Thought... would in this manner become able, perhaps for the first time [! L.N.], to think something other than itself, something other than itself in its other, or itself in itself." (TM 101) Derrida's syntheses claim to break the spell of reflection, its totalizing unity: a spell which is at least as old as Hegel's early conception of love, according to which *Vereinigung*, synthesis, (in a paradigmatic movement of reflective totalization) was determined as "im Andern *bei sich* sein."[16] (Emphasis L.N.)

16. G.W.F. Hegel, *Werke in zwanzig Bänden*, Vol.1, Frühe Schriften (Frankfurt, 1971), p. 239-254.

But are the (potentially uncompletable) synthetic infrastructures which Derrida introduces in his deconstructive experimentation paradoxical, as Derrida claims, only by logocentristic standards, or do they turn out to be — at closer inspection — unthinkable altogether? Is an alterity which is characterized as a 'negativity without negativity' more than an excessively radicalized and de-differentiated version of Kant's (non-totalizable) *Grenzbegriff*, of his (non)concept of a *Ding an sich* at the border of *Vernunft* (which Hegel, the grandfather of our sophisticated and deeply puzzling notions of speculative reflection, in a grandiose gesture, sought to compliment out of philosophy as the mere 'caput mortuum of reflection,' thus giving rise to the totalizing project of an 'absolute dialect')? Even worse: isn't it plausible to think that Derrida's experiments, his *Randgänge* at the border of 'logos,' his plays and *Verschiebungen* 'situated on the margin of what can be meaningfully totalized,' *fall back* behind Kant's uncompromising logic of alterity, Kant's claims, i.e., not only in *Critique of Pure Reason* that the 'X' of a (preconstituted) reality, but also in *Groundwork of the Metaphysics of Morals* that the X of our and the others consciences cannot be reached by any material conceptualization? Are Derrida's experiments of deconstruction positioned *only seemingly* on the fringe of our 'constituted logos,' since all his examples of a non-totalizable alterity quickly get predicated — in a kind of *Fröhliche Wissenschaft* — by puzzling sequels of meaning shifts, *Zurücknahmen* and annulments? How convincing is Derrida's attempt to have it both ways, rigorously and *fröhlich*?

(9) Conclusion: Toward a fuller articulation of the heterological motifs of discourse theory. In spite of the fact that the project of deconstruction leaves many questions unanswered, various things can be learned from Derrida's experiments: The heterological depth-structure of speech and writing is not fully spelled out, it seems, in the standard presentation of discourse theory. Habermas gets more and more aware of this shortcoming, and recently tends to stress aspects of alterity and non-identity. In his 1991 paper on Peirce, f.i., he criticizes semiotic theory "weil sie jenes Moment Zweitheit vernachlässigt, das uns in der Kommunikation als Widerspruch und Differenz, als der Eigensinn des *anderen* Individuums entgegentritt."[17] Any exploration of the heterological presuppositions (i.e., of the non-regulated, rule-*producing*, aesthetically

---

17. J. Habermas, in: "Charles S. Peirce über Kommunikation," *Texte und Kontexte* (Frankfurt, 1991), p. 32.

charged sources) of communication seems to be closely linked, however, to a non-classical (post-egological) analysis of individuality. It is doubtful whether discourse theory really — as Habermas's remark on Peirce suggests — sufficiently accounts for the heterogeneity of the other and for the non-domesticated sources of the self. As Manfred Frank pointed out, the *Theory of Communicative Action* has considerable shortcomings with regard to a full exploration of individuality (the individuality of *ego* as well as of *alter*).[18] Habermas, it seems, gets more and more aware of the difficulties which occur when we try to speak of the other, as the closing passage of a recent interview suggests where he writes: "Das Nicht-Identische wäre durch die Versehrbarkeit seiner Integrität geradezu definiert, wenn es sich denn definieren ließe. Es ist ein Deckname für jenen emphatischen Begriff des Individuellen, der uns bisher nur in religiöser Sprache überliefert ist."[19] Since theological images have lost their force, however, their content has to "immigrate into profanity" (as Habermas concludes, quoting Adorno). Thus the question arises, how much a modern, discourse theoretical reconstruction of reflexivity, which tries to carefully analyze and reconstruct the communicative structures of theoretical and practical argumentation, can learn from the advanced and (in themselves oftentimes excessive) aesthetic and rhetorical experiments of deconstruction, in order to make possible the "immigration of the experience of the 'emphatically individual' " — of which Adorno has spoken — into our post-religious language. Can an aesthetically charged heterology (which resists *Identitätszwang* and focuses on individual expressivity) become a *complementum* of discourse theory?

---

18. See M. Frank, *Selbstbewußtsein und Selbsterkenntnis* (Stuttgart, 1991), p. 410-477.
19. J. Habermas, "Was Theorien leisten können — und was nicht," in: *Vergangenheit als Zukunft* (Zürich, 1990), p. 158.

5. Stretching Habermas

HARRY KUNNEMAN

1. *Introduction*

As acknowledged champion of present-day Critical Theory and principal defender of the 'project of Enlightenment,' Jürgen Habermas has attracted lots of critical, even hostile attention from philosophers affiliated to postmodern thinking. This hostility is certainly understandable, if only as a retaliation in kind to Habermas own, markedly aggressive reading of postmodern texts. But it also has important philosophical and political reasons. Especially Habermas' quasi-transcendental conceptual strategy meets with deep suspicion from the side of postmodern and feminist philosophers. His efforts to develop universally valid rational reconstructions, demonstrating the unity of reason and the reconciliatory powers situated in the deepstructure of speech, are not only brushed aside as remnants of an outdated philosophical project, but are also widely criticized as inherently oppressive. This kind of critique has in turn induced exasperated comments from the side of Habermas: "Noch immer gilt der moralische Universalismus als Feind des Individualismus, nicht als dessen Ermöglichung. Noch immer gilt die Zuschreibung identischer Bedeutungen als Verletzung metaphorischer Vieldeutigkeit, nicht als deren Bedingung. Noch immer gilt die Einheit der Vernunft als Repression, nicht als Quelle der Vielfalt ihrer Stimme."[1]

As transpires from this quotation, Habermas not only feels misunderstood as to the intentions underlying his quasi-transcendental strategy, but also with regard to its normative and political significance. Similar feelings are to be found however on the other side of the fence, due to Habermas' apparent inability to understand and endorse the normative and political significance of postmodern analyses. I think these feelings merit serious consideration. Not only because they are justified up to a point — on both sides of the fence — but also because they point, paradoxically, towards the

---

1. Cf. J. Habermas, *Nachmetaphysisches Denken* (Frankfurt a.M.: Suhrkamp, 1988), p. 180.

proximity of the normative intuitions underlying the work of for instance Foucault, Lyotard and Irigaray on the one hand, and of Habermas and Wellmer on the other. One of the principle barriers obstructing such an understanding seems to be erected by Habermas himself, namely the claim that his own quasi-transcendental conceptual strategy provides the indispensable basis for the necessary continuation of the 'project of Modernity.' I will try to remove this barrier 'from within,' by focussing on the tension existing in Habermas' work between two different strains or motives of thought, one immediately visible and dominant, the other much more hidden. On the one hand his philosophical efforts are propelled by the idea that rational reconstructions of the reconciliatory potential situated in the deep structure of speech are necessary to safeguard the actual manifestation of this potential both in the (social) sciences and in the political realm. On the other hand, there are places to be found in his work where he seems to imply that this reconciliatory potential is *not*, or at least not exclusively, dependent on the rational deep structure of speech. Pursuing the latter strain of thought could have led him to acknowledge the possibility and reality of different resources for and different articulations of 'the project of Enlightenment,' which are not only to be found on the level of intellectual discourse, but also in quite different, especially bodily registers of human existence. Due to his anxiety with regard to the chances for the practical actualisation of this reconciliatory potential, Habermas is led to overburden his rational reconstructions with exclusive pretentions and to overstate the importance of his project of Enlightenment. If the existence and importance of different resources for and different articulations of this project could be demonstrated, this need to overburden rational reconstructions with exclusive pretentions could be alleviated, thus paving the way for more constructive forms of dialogue between postmodern thinkers and those philosophers, who - like myself - are impressed and inspired by the heuristic power and the political importance of Habermas' communicative paradigm, but who do not wish for that reason to be shut off from the vital insights contained in present day postmodern thought.

2. *The intentions*

Even a rather superficial reading of Habermas' principal writings, soon reveals that his quasi-transcendental conceptual strategy is not motivated by some sort of philosophical 'Wille zur Macht,' but is inspired by the same deeply felt concern for the non-identical characteristic of Adorno's philosophy. In fact the normative inspiration underlying Habermas' rational reconstructions could very well be summed up with the quote from Adorno, cited in chapter four of the *Theorie des kommunikativen Handelns*: "Der versöhnte Zustand annektierte nicht mit philosophischem Imperialismus das Fremde, sondern hätte sein Glück daran, daß es in der gewährten Nähe das Ferne und Verschiedene bleibt, jenseits des Heterogenen wie des Eigenen."[2] According to Habermas Modernity has to ensure itself of its own potential for non-violent forms of communication. In principle it can live up to this task by taking the normative potential of its own rationality seriously. This potential not only manifests itself in the inner dynamic of modern science, propeling the sciences time and again beyond "die Erzeugung technisch verwertbaren Wissens," but also comes to light in the universalistic foundations of law and morality "die in den Institutionen der Verfassungsstaaten, in Formen demokratischer Willensbildung, in individualistischen Mustern der Identitätsbildung auch eine (wie immer verzerrte und unvollkommene) Verkörperung gefunden haben."[3] Habermas' rational reconstructions are thus motivated by the wish to safeguard the normative space for individuation, difference and plurality, presupposed as a matter of course by postmodern and feminist philosophers alike. "Je mehr Diskurs, um so mehr Widerspruch und Differenz... Je abstrakter das Einverständnis, um so vielfaltiger die Dissense, mit denen wir gewaltlos leben können."[4] The rational reconstruction of the deep structure of communicative action should bring to light "die Idee einer unversehrten Intersubjektivität, die eine zwanglose Verständigung der Individuen im Umgang miteinander ebenso ermöglichen würde wie die Identität eines sich zwanglos mit sich selbst verständigenden Individuums." The endeavour to anchor the notion of 'zwanglose Verständigung' in the deep structure of speech thus has an unmistakably practical and political background, as can be elucidated further by means of the 'black diagnosis' of Western civilisation formulated by Horkheimer and Adorno in their *Dialektik der Aufklärung*. According to Habermas, this diagnosis indicates that

2. Cf. J. Habermas, *Theorie des kommunikativen Handelns*, 1 (Frankfurt a.M.: Suhrkamp, 1981), p. 523. The quote is taken from Th.W. Adorno, *Gesammelte Schriften*, 6 (Frankfurt a.M., 1973), p. 192.
3. J. Habermas, 1981, p. 138.
4. Cf. J. Habermas, *Nachmetaphysisches Denken* (Frankfurt a.M.: Suhrkamp, 1988), p. 180.

they failed to lay the normative foundations for their critical theory of society deep enough so as not to be threatened by the decomposition of civic culture "wie sie sich damals in Deutschland vor aller Augen vollzogen hat."[5] Habermas' efforts to construct deeply seated normative foundations for his own critical theory of society are strongly motivated by the wish not to succumb to the 'hemmungslose Vernunftskepsis'[6] to which Adorno and Horkheimer fell a prey in his eyes. The unwavering belief in the possibility of 'Verständigung,' not as a subjective preference, but as a structurally given and rationally reconstructable possibility of social interaction, is itself of prime political importance as a defence against all the contingencies threatening it.

3. Contingency

Contrary to popular misunderstandings on this point, Habermas exhibits a clear consciousness of the context-boundedness and contingency of his own philosophical enterprise: "…die kommunikative Vernunft setzt fast alles kontingent, selbst die Entstehungsbedingungen ihres eigenen sprachlichen Mediums."[7] And indeed, apart from the origin of language, there are several other places to be found in his work where Habermas stresses "die geschichtlich-gesellschaftliche Situierung der Vernunft" and points out the empirical, contingent conditions under which his reconstruction of communicative action has to prove its mettle. In the first place, he is well aware of the influence and even dominance of conflicts, power and exclusion on the level of everyday communicative action. Take for example the following quote from his essay on discourse-ethics: "…praktische Diskurse, wie alle Argumentationen, (gleichen) den von Überschwemmung bedrohten Inseln im Meer einer Praxis, in dem das Muster der konsensuellen Beilegung von Handlungskonflikten keineswegs dominiert. Die Mittel der Verständigung werden durch Instrumente der Gewalt immer wieder verdrängt."[8] In his *Theorie des kommunikativen Handelns* this judgement is specified

---

5. Cf. J. Habermas, *Der philosophische Diskurs der Moderne* (Frankfurt a.M.: Suhrkamp, 1985), p. 156.
6. Ibidem.
7. Cf. J. Habermas, *Nachmetaphysisches Denken* (Frankfurt a.M.: Suhrkamp, 1988), p. 179
8. Cf. J. Habermas, "Diskursethik, Notizen zu einem Begründungsprogramm," in: idem, *Moralbewußtsein und kommunikatives Handeln* (Frankfurt a.M.: Suhrkamp, 1983), p. 116.

further in terms of the rationalisation and the colonisation of the lifeworld. Foregoing all technicalities we could say that in the rationalised lifeworld the difference between communicative and strategic action has become a matter of course and all ideologies have become criticisable in terms of the notion of symmetrical communication underlying this difference. As a result of the colonisation of the lifeworld however, the room for communicative action which has potentially become available is at the same time severely restricted. According to Habermas this can not only be inferred from the influence of money and power in the lifeworld, but also from the symptoms manifesting themselves on the level of culture, institutions and the personality. To topp it all, the mechanisms involved in the colonisation of the lifeworld remain more or less hidden from everyday consciousness because of its fragmentation: it is cut off from the results of the learning processes taking place in the different 'Expertenkulturen': "An die Stelle des falschen tritt heute das fragmentierte Bewußtsein, das der Aufklärung über den Mechanismus der Verdinglichung vorbeugt."[9] Thus, Habermas has not only provided an analysis of the structural influence of power on the level of everyday communicative action, but has also pointed out that, due to the fragmentation of everyday consciousness, the chances for his own critical analysis to find recognition are not that good.

Seen against this background it is clear that Habermas is not unaware of the 'geschichtlich-gesellschaftliche Situierung der Vernunft,' even to the point where he clearly states that there is no guarantee at all that the reconciliatory powers of communicative reason, as brought to light in his own analysis, will be able to shift the balance. But it is precisely the fact that communicative reason is enveloped and threatened by contingencies which obliges us to ensure ourself that it will not drown in 'the sea of contingencies:' "Die kommunikative Vernunft ist gewiß eine schwankende Schale - aber sie ertrinkt nicht im Meer der Kontingenzen, auch nicht wenn das Erzittern auf hoher See der einzige Modus ist, in der sie Kontingenzen 'bewältigt.'"[10]

4. *Two motives*

Here we have before us the first strain of thought or the first motive

9. J. Habermas, *Theorie des kommunikativen Handelns*, 2, p. 522.
10. Ibidem, p. 185.

referred to above, which could be designated as the Titanic-Ark, or 'Titark' motive for short. The vessel of communicative reason is thought to contain all the resources for non-violent forms of communication available to mankind, and thus to contain the emancipatory potential of the project of modernity as a whole. Precisely for this reason this vessel has to be unsinkable and has to be construed as a Titanic.

Alongside this first motive however, a second much more hidden motive or strain of thought is to be found in Habermas' work which up to a point contradicts the 'Titark-motive,' because it refers to the importance and even indispensability of non-linguistic, extra-discursive sources of non-violent, symmetrical communication. A first indication of this second motive is to be found in the context of the methodological justification of rational reconstructions. This context is of special significance, because the rational reconstructions of universal human competences, and especially of communicative competence, provide so to speak the ribs supporting the hull of Habermas' Titark.

The cognitive status of these reconstructions is justified trough an intriguing mix of ideas taken from Kant, Chomsky, Piaget and Kohlberg. Rational reconstructions are Kantian in so far as they aim to identify the general and unavoidable presuppositions, the constitutive structures, involved in the relations between human subjects and the world and between subjects themselves. They are Chomskyan, in so far as these structures are not analysed with reference to a transcendental subject, but are pictured as competences of mature individuals, identifiable as deep structures underlying actual performances and reconstructable in the form of a 'know that' implicitly underlying the 'know how' of competently acting subjects. In the third place, these reconstructions are modelled after the paradigm of Piaget in so far as they are analysed both horizontally, under abstraction of their development, and vertically, according to the inner logic of their genesis. Moreover, in a decidedly un-Kantian move, these reconstructions are thought of as 'empirically' falsifiable, along the lines developed by Kohlberg in his research on moral development. The rational reconstructions of universal competences developed by philosophers and social scientists should be used as input for empirical research in which these reconstructions are confronted with the intuitions of competent actors. If the reconstructions are not recognised by them as a valid explication of their 'know how,' their intuitively mastered competence, then these reconstructions have to be reconsidered and reformulated to reach a better match with the intuitions of competent actors.[11]

The second motive dimly appears here in the form of the pivotal role accorded to the intuitions of competent speakers in the justification of rational reconstructions. For the whole procedure not to be completely circular, these intuitions cannot and should not be interpreted beforehand according to the fundamental categories of the theoretical perspective which is put to test, but should be accorded an independent status. Of course, Habermas postulates in his *Theorie des kommunikativen Handelns* that the evolution of mankind has to be understood as the progressive linguistic assimilation of the pre-linguistic, 'instinctual' material going into the process of hominisation, up to the point where 'everything that can be meant can be said' and individuation is becoming dependent upon processes of 'diskursive Willensbildung.' However, this vertical reconstruction of the evolution of mankind is logically dependent upon the horizontal reconstruction of the deep structure of communicative action and thus cannot be presupposed when testing this reconstruction against the 'intuitions' of competent speakers. So here we get a first glimpse of 'something in there,' which is not necessarily part of the deep structure of speech, but which does somehow partake in its normative core, because it is able to recognise, to intuit it.

More light is shed on this second strain of thought by Habermas' reflections on the inherent limitations of his discourse ethics. In his discussion of the relation between 'Moralität und Sittlichkeit,' Habermas has pointed out that universalistic morals cannot stand on their own feet, but have to be complemented by corresponding and responsive life forms: "Universalistische Morale sind auf Lebensformen angewiesen, die ihrerseits so weit 'rationalisiert' sind, daß sie die kluge Applikation allgemeiner moralischer Einsichten ermöglichen und Motivationen für die Umsetzung von Einsichten in moralisches Handeln fördern."[12] In a later publication he has added that the gap between moral judgements on the one hand and actions in accordance with these judgements on the other, is situated on the

11. Cf. J. Habermas, "Was heisst Universalpragmatik?" in: K.O. Apel (Hrg.), *Sprachpragmatik und Philosophie* (Frankfurt a.M.: Suhrkamp, 1976), p. 183 ff.; J. Habermas, "Interpretatieve sociale wetenschap versus radicale hermeneutiek," in: *Kennis & Methode*, 1981, 1, p. 4-24, reprinted as "Rekonstruktive versus verstehende Sozialwissenschaften", in: *Moralbewußtsein und kommunikatives Handeln* (Frankfurt a.M.: Suhrkamp, 1983), p. 29-53.
12. J. Habermas, "Diskursethik," in: J. Habermas, 1983, p. 119.

'output-side' of practical discourses. The problem is repeated however on the input-side: "Vom Diskurs selbst können die Bedingungen nicht erfüllt werden, die notwendig sind damit alle jeweils Betroffenen für eine regelrechte Teilnahme an praktischen Diskursen instandgesetzt werden." In many cases not only the necessary institutional arrangements are lacking, but also "die Sozialisationsprozesse, in denen die erforderlichen Dispositionen und Fähigkeiten zur Teilnahme an moralischen Argumentationen erworben werden."[13]

These are interesting statements. A new 'actor' has appeared on the stage, in the form of *motives* harboured by concrete actors not only for entering discourses, but also for putting into practice conclusions reached therein. Here, moral universalism does not appear as the condition for individuality, but specific motives of individuals are presented as the condition for moral universalism. The animals cannot be supposed to be on the Titark allready. They are in need of their own motives to embark. These cannot be thought of as contingent themselves, because in that case the fate of the Titark would be completely dependent on contingent motives of individuals. Nor do these motives partake directly in the deep structure of communicative reason, because this structure is situated on the level of speech acts, not on the level of individual motives. Of course, these motives are shaped also within the medium of language, since, according to Habermas the whole personality, even the possibility to say 'I', is dependent upon the performative structure of linguistic communication. However, the motives Habermas is referring to cannot be completely determined by their linguistic ancestry, otherwise all individuals would be motivated as a matter of course to partake in practical discourses and practice their conclusions; quod non. The problem here is that this discrepancy and possible motives for overcoming it can neither be deemed contingent, because then the realisation of the deep structure of language would be completely contingent, nor can they be interpreted solely in terms of the deep structure of language, because then the discrepancy would be incomprehensible. So it would seem that here we have another place before us where Habermas nolens volens presupposes the existence of resources for non-violent, symmetrical

13. Cf. J. Habermas, "Moralität und Sittlichkeit. Treffen Hegels Einwände gegen Kant auch die Diskursethik zu?" in: W. Kuhlmann (Hrg.), *Moralität und Sittlichkeit* (Frankfurt a.M.: Suhrkamp, 1986), p. 30.

interaction which appear to be independent up to a point from the deep structure of language.

This second strain of thought also comes to the fore in the context of Habermas' well known analysis of the possible significance of present day philosophy as "Platzhalter und Interpret."[14] Philosophy has to step down from its high throne and limit itself to a position as 'placekeeper' for rationality within the social sciences, a much more modest position according to Habermas - although not quite that modest in view of the great influence exerted by the social sciences in modern societies. In the present context the second task he reserves for philosophy is of much more interest: helping to bridge the gap between the different groups of experts in the fields of art, morality and the sciences on the one hand and the domain of everyday communicative praxis on the other. The different 'Expertenkulturen' corresponding to the three domains of rational learning processes distinguished by Habermas, have not only attained independence with regard to each other, but first and foremost with regard to the domain of everyday communicative action. In this domain claims to truth, righteousness and authenticity are necessarily and unavoidably intertwined. According to Habermas, this interdependence and interpenetration should also manifest itself on the level of culture: "In der kommunikativen Alltagspraxis müssen kognitive Deutungen, moralische Erwartungen, Expressionen und Bewertungen einander ohnehin durchdringen. Die Verständigungsprozesse der Lebenswelt bedürfen deshalb einer kulturellen Überlieferung auf ganzer Breite, nicht nur der Segnungen von Wissenschaft und Technik. So könnte die Philosophie ihren bezug zur Totalität in einer der Lebenswelt zugewandten Interpretenrolle aktualisieren. Sie könnte mindestens dabei helfen, das stillgestellte Zusammenspiel des Kognitiv-instrumentellen mit dem Moralischpraktischen und dem Ästhetisch-Expressiven wie eine Mobile das sich hartnäckig verhakt hat, wieder in Bewegung zu setzen."[15]

Two things are of special interest in this passage. In the first place the fact that Habermas refers to the interpenetration of cognition, morality and expressivity on the level of culture not as a matter of course but as a desideratum. The processes of 'Verständigung'

14. Cf. J. Habermas, "Die Philosophie als Platzhalter und Interpret," in: idem, *Moralbewußtsein und kommunikatives Handeln* (Frankfurt a.M.: Suhrkamp, 1983), p. 9-28.
15. Ibidem, p. 26.

taking place in the lifeworld are in need of a cultural tradition which is not limited to (social) scientific knowledge, but which integrates this knowledge to a certain extent with moral insights and aesthetic-expressive elements. Within the framework of Habermas' theory of rationality, this need for interpenetration and even integration takes on a special urgency, because according to this theory the development of modern rationality is characterised by a centrifugal movement, in which the three domains of rationality, by way of the restless development of their own inner logic, necessarily move away from each other. Following Max Weber, Habermas states that the rationalisation process does not show any *inherent* integrating tendencies. Of course, contrary to Weber, Habermas holds fast to the formal unity of reason, manifesting itself in the structural similitude of the procedures of rational argumentation with regard to truth, righteousness and authenticity. But this procedural unity only provides for the possibility of 'Übergänge' between the different discourses, it certainly does not provide for their interpenetration, let alone their integration. At this point then Habermas accords to philosophy not only the task of assisting in the transfer of the specialised insights gained in the different expert cultures to the realm of everyday communicative action, but also the task of furthering the unity of reason on the level of culture, thus contributing to a new balance between the "auseinandergetretene Momente der Vernunft in der kommunikativen Alltagspraxis."[16]

Interesting and stimulating as this suggestion might be, it is not very convincing. In the first place, philosophy itself has developed into a highly specialised expert culture, struggling with 'Vermittlungsprobleme' of its own, as anybody who has ever tried to explain, say, Habermas' theory of communicative action or Lacan's analysis of the mirror stage to a lay public can easily confirm. Moreover, within philosophy itself the differentiation between the various expert cultures in the domains of cognition, morality and aesthetics is repeated in the form of the multiple divisions between the philosophical experts in these fields. Moreover, where Habermas rightfully stresses the structural similitude between philosophy and the (social) sciences as forms of argumentative discourse, it is not al all clear on what rational basis philosophy could escape the 'centrifugal,' differentiating tendency which, according to his own analysis, is characteristic of rational argumentation. Against this background I think a special significance has to be attached to his

16. Ibidem.

formulation that philosophy 'could at least *help*' to get the entangled mobile of modern rationality to move freely. This formulation implies that there have to be other forces at work here, which could be assisted and supplemented by philosophy. These forces, however, cannot in turn be reduced to the rational deep structure of language, since the only 'acting force' left within the analytical framework presented by Habermas is everyday communicative action itself. This does indeed exhibit a 'centripetal' integrating movement in its permanent interpenetration of the different validity claims, but the *rationality* of this interpenetration is completely dependent upon argumentation, and argumentation leads us away again from the level of everyday communicative action into the expert cultures and their centrifugal specialisation.

So I conclude that here we have a third place before us where Habermas' own analysis refers to sources of non-violent, symmetrical interaction, serving as resources for rational communicative action not situated in the deep structure of language but stemming from elsewhere, thus escaping the categorical framework of his rational reconstruction. Formulated in terms of the metaphor of the 'Titark,' we could say that Habermas inadvertently refers here to the existence of animals which are not in need of the vessel of communicative reason in order to be saved from drowning in the sea of contingencies, but instead posses their own, extralinguistic survival kits.

So far I have tried to elucidate the tension between the 'Titarc-motive' and the second, more hidden motive by focussing on places in Habermas' work where he inadvertently seems to refer to extra-linguistic sources of non-violent, symmetrical interaction. In conclusion of this paragraph I would like to supplement these 'positive' examples with a 'negative' example, by focussing on one of the places in his work where the absence of this second motive and the complete dominance of the first contribute to a conspicious blind spot in his analysis. This blind spot is to be found in his consensus-theory of truth, more specifically in his analysis of the different levels of argumentation which have to be opened to the participants in a discourse in order to be able to reach a rational consensus.[17]

The nature of this blind spot can be elucidated by means of Lyotard's analysis of the 'differend.' One of the most important

---

17. Cf. J. Habermas, "Wahrheitstheorien," in: idem, *Vorstudien und Ergänzungen zur Theorie des kommunikativen Handelns*, (Frankfurt a. Main: Suhrkamp, 1984), p. 127-187.

differences between Lyotards analysis of interaction and Habermas' analysis of communication - which in some respects show surprising similarities[18] - concerns the explicit inclusion by Lyotard of non-discursive acts as forms of linking, as phrases. One cannot nòt link, he says, linking is unavoidable, for remaining silent in answer to a phrase is also a form of linking. Lyotard is especially interested in silences as signs of a 'differend,' as signs of a situation in which something that wants to be put into words cannot be articulated discursively and is assimilated to the inner logic of discourses in which it is not allowed to try and speak for itself. The possibility of such a 'differend' points to an important blind spot in Habermas' analysis of rational discourse. According to this analysis, *remaining silent* - for example on the third level of argumentation in a 'Diskurs' where the possible introduction of alternative presuppositions is at stake - implies in the last analysis that one is unable to contest the arguments of the other party in a fundamental way, and thus, at least for the time being, acknowledges their superiority. So, where Lyotard's analysis would urge us to heed silences as possible signs of a 'differend,' Habermas' analysis of rational discourse simply does not provide the conceptual means to adequately analyse this situation.

5. *The 'communicative' potential of the body*

According to Rosi Braidotti and other feminist philosophers, the whole debate on the meaning of Enlightenment and the crisis of the rational subject confronts us with the urgent need to rethink 'the bodily roots of the thinking process' and even more so the bodily roots of communication and social interaction: "One cannot ask the question of the crisis of modernity without raising the issue of sexual difference, or of gender."[19] Following the lead of contemporary feminist philosophers and their efforts to rethink the embodied nature of subjectivity, one could venture to suggest that the aforementioned tension in Habermas' work could be alleviated by taking into account the 'communicative' potential of the body, which is systematically disregarded by Habermas. "Könnten wir nicht auf das Modell der Rede Bezug nehmen, wären wir nicht imstande,

---

18. Cf. H. Kunneman, *Der Wahrheitstrichter. Habermas und die Postmoderne* (Frankfurt a. Main: Campus, 1991), esp. p. 304-314.
19. Cf. R. Braidotti, *Patterns of Dissonance* (Cambridge 1991), p. 8 and p. 276.

auch nur in einem ersten Schritt zu analysieren, was es heißt, daß sich zwei Subjekte miteinder verständigen." This formulation of the hard core of his theory of communicative action has to be read in conjunction with Habermas' reinterpretation of Freud. In a discussion with Joel Whitebook he has stated that the essential difference with Freud "consists only in replacing 'drive energies' with 'interpreted needs' and describing 'instinctual vicissitudes' from the perspective of identity formation and processes of interaction. In this communication-theoretical reading, inner nature is in no way vaporised into culturalistic haze...it does not entail the elimination of inner nature as an extralinguistic referent."[20] Taken together these two pillars of Habermas' theory of communicative action indeed do not imply the elimination of inner nature as an extralinguistic referent, but they most certainly do entail the elimination of the body as a relatively autonomous field and independent source of symmetrical interaction. I do not want to explore the complicated background of this elimination of the body from Habermas' work here, a background involving inter alia the experience of fascism and Habermas' ambiguous relationship with Adorno. Instead I would like to point out that essential elements of symmetrical interaction, exclusively situated by Habermas in the deep structure of 'sprachliche Verständigung,' do have non-trivial parallels at the level of touching and caressing bodies.

Habermas' most impressive and essential intuition with regard to the proces of 'Verständigung,' has to do with the peculiar nature of reasons and with the concomittant difference between empirical, or contingent action-coordination and rational action-coordination by way of validity claims. "Die Anmeldung eines Geltungsanspruches ist nicht Ausdruck eines kontingenten Willens... Geltungsansprüche sind intern mit Gründe verknüpft."[21] The strange and according to Habermas unique characteristic of reasons is, that they break down as soon as their addressee gets the impression that they are used as empirical means of influencing the interaction. Arguments can only count as such as long as their addressee is convinced of the fact that she is left free to say yes or no to them on the basis of her own appreciation and evaluation of their mening and value.

20. Cf. J. Habermas, "Questions and counterquestions," in: R. Bernstein (ed.), *Habermas and modernity* (Cambridge, 1985), p. 213.
21. Cf. J. Habermas, *Theorie des kommunikativen Handelns*, 2, p. 405.

This is an essential insight, but it can be demonstrated I think that this whole interactive structure is not limited to communicative action by means of speech acts, but has a complete and probably even more deeply seated equivalent on the level of touching and communicating bodies. I think the interactive logic of the caress and the embrace show the same inner anticipation and acceptance of the possible no of the other as validity claims do. It seems as if Habermas, and so many others with him, can only think of touching and interacting bodies under the sign of libido and sex, essentially involving empirical forms of action coordination, such as 'bringing about' a climax. In this way however one foregoes the whole range of bodily experiences and forms of action coordination constituting the fragile domain of bodily intimacy. Here for example a persons caress can only count as such between two individuals if it is freely recognised by the other, that is to say: solely on the basis of the recipient's appreciation of its meaning and value. A caress and the intimacy connected with it cannot be brought about by empirical means. Just like arguments, caresses and embraces break down as soon as their addressee is under the impression that they are used as empirical means of influencing the interaction.

6. *Conclusion*

At this point I think an essential limitation of Habermas' theory of communicative action comes to light. If this symmetry in the interactive deep structure of validity claims and bodily intimacy could be made more plausible, the conclusion would follow that 'Verständigung' brought about by linguistic means as analysed so impressively by Habermas, is only one, be it a very important form of symmetrical, non-violent interaction. My analysis of the two motives manifesting themselves in Habermas' work seems to suggest that this form cannot stand on its own, but has to be reinforced and supplemented by other sources of non-violent interaction. This would mean, then, that we would have to develop a new, more general concept of 'communication,' with the help of which the own contribution of both language and the body to symmetrical non-violent forms of interaction could be made understandable. Such a more general concept of communication could benefit from the efforts of feminist philosophers such as Jessica Benjamin and others to reinterpret and reappropriate psychoanalytical theory, for instance by revalorising the relationship between mothers and daughters and bringing to light the inner relationship between reciprocity and the female pattern of differentiation from the mother's body.[22]

In this way the vessel of communicative reason would no longer have to serve as an Ark and thus would no longer have to be constructed as a Titanic. If the need to overburden rational reconstructions with exclusive pretentions could be overcome, Enlightenment might be thought of as dependent upon a plurality of 'projects' and upon different sources, each characterised by their own modes of articulation, both linguistic and extralinguistic.

22. Cf. f.e. J. Benjamin, "A desire of one's own" in: *Feminst Studies/Critical Studies*, ed. T. de Lauretis (Bloomington, 1986), p. 78-99.

6. Vers une éthique du différend

J. ROGOZINSKI

Liminaire

Note sur l'éthique du Differend
"L'ordre reçu par Abraham de sacrifier son fils est-il plus intelligible qu'une circulaire administrant la rafle, le convoi, la concentration, la mort lente et la mort rapide? N'est-ce pas une affaire d'idiolecte? Abraham entend: *Qu' Isaac meure, c'est ma loi*, et il obéit. Le Seigneur en cet instant ne parle qu'à Abraham, et Abraham n'est responsable que devant le Seigneur. Comme la réalité, sinon du Seigneur, au moins de la phrase qui lui est imputée, ne peut pas être établie, comment savoir qu'Abraham n'est pas un paranoïaque sujet à des poussées homicides (infanticides) ? Ou un simulateur?
La question n'est même pas celle de l'obéissance, mais celle de l'obligation. La question est de savoir si, quand on entend quelque chose qui peut ressembler à un appel, on est tenu d'être tenu par lui. On pourra lui résister ou y répondre, mais il aura fallu d'abord l'accueillir comme un appel (…).
Mais la demande qui harcèle le président Schreber, celle qui accable Abraham, celle qui galvanise les SS sont toutes différentes!-(…) du moins ces diverses autorités ne prescrivent pas les mêmes actes! On peut les reconnaître à ce qu'elles ordonnent de faire! — Je ne dis pas que le contenu de la loi soit indifférent, mais il ne permet pas de distinguer la bonne autorité de l'imposture." (J.F. Lyotard, *Le Différend* § 162-164)

L'éthique du *Différend*, celle que ce livre esquisse comme en filigrane, pourrait se définir comme une éthique de l'obligation — ou de la prescription — *pure*. Ethique paradoxale qui se radicalise jusqu'à atteindre sa limite, que désigne cette référence (inhabituelle chez Lyotard) à Kierkegaard, au nom d'Abraham. Obligation pure, d'abord en ce sens que le genre éthique — comme *tout* genre de discours — reste intraduisible dans un autre genre; que le régime de phrases qui le compose (phrases prescriptives) demeure — comme *tout* régime de phrase — hétérogène, incommensurable aux autres régimes, et notamment aux cognitives et aux descriptives qui composent le discours de la connaissance théorique.[1]
De ce que "la phrase éthique est intraduisible dans la phrase

---

1. cf. *Le différend*, Minuit, 1984, §178-179, p.187.

cognitive", il s'ensuit que "la phrase prescriptive pure n'est pas légitimée, et pas légitimable", sauf à disparaître comme obligation. L'ordre donné à Abraham de prendre son fils pour le sacrifier en holocauste sur la montagne de Moria vaut comme prescription pure, dans la mesure où il ne se fonde sur aucune thèse préalable, pas même sur la croyance que "ce que Dieu prescrit est juste"; où il demeure donc privé de tout légitimation ou, comme l'écrit Kierkegaard, "absurde". L'éthique du *Différend* peut ainsi s'autoriser de Kant, de l'impossibilité, alléguée par la deuxième *Critique*, de "déduire" la Loi morale à partir de la liberté, ou d'une autre instance plus "originaire".

Cependant, cette référence à Kant s'avère provisoire: au moins sur le plan de l'éthique, le "moment kantien" du *Différend* cède la place à une problématique très différente, qui se réfère à Lévinas. Et tout le problème va consister à enchaîner, à articuler ces deux perspectives peut-être incompatibles. A l'éthique kantienne de l'autonomie, morale d'*Aufklärer*, victime d'une "apparence transcendantale pratique" qui efface la dissymétrie entre destinateur et destinataire, transforme la "communauté d'otages" en "communauté de constituants"[2], qui impose ainsi à l'éthique les règles de la légitimation cognitive (celles du consensus et de la commutabilité des partenaires), s'oppose l'exigence lévinassienne "qu'on ne peut phraser l'éthique qu'éthiquement, c'est-à-dire comme obligé". Si le genre éthique n'admet pour règle "que l'obligation sans condition", si son enjeu est "le désintéressement parfait du moi, le dessaisissement de la volonté"[3], l'éthique du *Différend* impliquera une *hétéronomie* radicale, et purement *formelle* — définie uniquement par l'instanciation sur la position du destinataire, la situation de l'être-obligé —, impossible donc à intégrer ou à phraser dans une perspective kantienne, qui ne conçoit d'hétéronomie que "matérielle" comme l'état d'une volonté "pathologiquement affectée" par les inclinations sensibles et le désir du bonheur. Entre le point de vue de Kant (celui de l'*Aufklärer*, pour qui l'éthique de Lévinas contresignerait une rechute dans la *Schwärmerei*, dans la morale théologique, le "mysticisme de la raison pratique") et celui de Lévinas (qui voit dans l'affirmation kantienne de l'autonomie l'un des sommets du "narcissisme" égologique de la philosophie occidentale, de sa ré-

---

2. op.cit. p.183-184
3. p. 172, 189, etc. — cf. l'ensemble de la 'notice Lévinas'.

duction de l'Autre au Même, de son oubli de l'Infini)[4], le différend paraît irréductible.

Du moins, à passer ainsi de Kant à Lévinas, le *Différend* aurait-il résolu la question de la légitimation de l'obligation? Pour Lévinas, en effet, cette question — critique ou "transcendantale" — ne se pose même pas: car la révélation de l'infini dans l'épiphanie du Visage est *toujours* légitime, fondée sur sa "franchise" originaire, sur l'univocité ou "l'authenticité absolue" de son "expression": sur son "évidence qui rend possible l'évidence comme la véracité divine qui soutient la rationalisme cartésien".[5] Ce qui laisse en suspens la question de l'origine de l'inauthencité ou de l'équivocité lorsqu'elle m'advient *de l'Autre*, et interdit à Lévinas de constituer une "typique", un "schématisme pratique" permettant de *s'orienter* éthiquement dans les rapports concrets avec autrui.

Pourtant, à la différence de Lévinas, le *Différend* reste sur ce point fidèle à l'enseignement de Kant, se refuse à légitimer *par principe* l'obligation éthique en l'enracinant dans une "authenticité" ou une "évidence" métaphysique. En enchaînant immédiatement son moment kantien — impossibilité de déduire ou d'authentifier l'obligation — et son moment lévinassien — hétéronomie radicale de l'obligation —, le *Différend* se trouve en présence d'une aporie très remarquable. La situation éthique consisterait en effet en une soumission inconditionnée à une prescription obligeante, venue du Dehors et de l'Autre, privée de tout fondement et de toute évidence, de tout critère de jugement permettant de justifier l'obligation, de "distinguer la bonne autorité de l'imposture", de faire le partage entre l'ordre donné à Abraham et le délire d'un fou, ou une circulaire d'Eichmann. Le "quasi-fait de l'obligation", écrit Lyotard, se donne à l'obligé "comme un signe", "sous la forme du sentiment. L'obligé a une présomption sentimentale qu'il y a une autorité qui l'oblige".[6] Mais, précisément parce qu'il accompagne toujours *toute* obligation, ce sentiment ne permet pas de distinguer les différents modes d'obligation. Qu'il n'y ait pas de sentiments "faux" ou "trompeurs" — l'amour de transfert, Freud le souligne, est un *véritable* amour, tout comme celui que Swann éprouve pour Odette

---

4. cf. entre autres *La philosophie et l'idée de l'infini*, in *En découvrant l'existence avec Husserl et Heidegger*, Vrin, 1967, p.165-167.
5. *Totalité et infini*, M. Nijhoff, rééd. 1984, p.176-179.
6. *Le différend*, p.178.

— signifie aussi que le sentiment n'a aucun rapport à la vérité, aucun pouvoir de décèlement ou de discernement, ne saura jamais empêcher le psychotique de prendre son délire pour la voix de Dieu, ni Swann de gâcher sa vie pour une femme "qui n'était même pas son genre".

L'éthique du *Différend* (du livre portant ce titre) nous apparaît ainsi comme une éthique du différend. Non pas seulement au sens où elle prescrirait de "faire accueil" aux différends, de tenter de les surmonter, de les transformer en litiges en inventant de nouveaux idiomes pour les phraser, ce qui est d'ailleurs l'une des "prescriptions" de base et l'une des principales difficultés du *Différend*.[7] Mais aussi en ceci que la situation éthique elle-même, celle de l'être-obligé, implique déjà *comme telle* un différend (ce qui n'est pas le cas de tous les genres de discours, ni de toute instanciation dans un univers de phrase): qu'elle présuppose une dissymétrie, une hétérogénéité irréductible entre les positions du destinateur et celle du destinataire de l'obligation. Entre la phrase du destinateur appelé 'Dieu' — "Prends ton fils..." — et la phrase silencieuse où l'obligé fait allégeance, cette quasi-phrase qu'est le silence d'Abraham. Car l'affect du destinataire, l'angoisse d'Abraham dont parle Kierkegaard, ne trouve pas de phrase pour se dire dans une langue commune, où le différend serait compris et la dissymétrie enfin aplanie. Que serait d'ailleurs ce méta-discours commun à l'obligé et au destinateur de l'obligation, au fini et à l'infini? Quelle réponse saurait, en phrasant l'affect, se rendre commensurable la folie meurtrière, absurde, de l'Appel? Plusieurs "réponses" pourraient être imaginées, plus ou moins comiques dans leurs tentatives dérisoires de combler l'écart, d'effacer le scandale de l'obligation. Celle, par exemple, d'un Abraham théologien: "Seigneur, merci pour cette épreuve qui m'aidera à affermir ma foi". Ou encore celle, spéculative, d'un Abraham hégélien: "Esprit Absolu, j'ai compris ta ruse: tu m'éprouves *pour* que je te prouve ma foi, et je sais que, au terme de cette dialectique, tu me restitueras ce que je feins de te sacrifier". Sans oublier celle, plus cocasse, d'un Abraham tenant de l'"action communicationnelle", revendiquant hautement son droit à rétablir "l'égalité des chances discursives", à parvenir par une argumentation rationnelle à un "consensus" avec Dieu, et dénonçant comme une "contradiction

7. Sur ce point, nous nous permettons de renvoyer à notre étude *Lyotard, le différend, la présence*, in *Témoigner du différend*, Osiris, 1989, p.61-79, trad. en anglais in *L'esprit créateur* XXX-1,1991.

performative" le refus de Dieu de s'y soumettre.[8] A quoi Kier-kegaard, ou plutôt "Johannes de Silentio", auteur pseudonyme de *Crainte et tremblement*, oppose le silence d'Abraham, son angoisse muette devant l'indétermination radicale de l'Appel.

Autant le dire: l'éthique du *Différend* ne s'inscrit pas dans le projet prétendûment "inachevé" de la modernité, n'appartient pas à l'*Aufklärung* -fût-ce à une très problématique "Idée neuve de l'*Aufklärung*" — dont elle révèle au contraire une limite, le *point-aveugle* des Lumières. Dès lors, comment peut-elle encore s'autoriser de Kant, d'une philosophie qui se réclame de l'autonomie du Sujet, de son autonomie pratique *et théorique — sapere aude!* — comme de la devise des Lumières? A l'angoisse d'Abraham, nous le verrons, Kant avait tenté de répondre, en phrasant son silence, en proposant un méta-critère universel de légitimation des prescriptives qui n'est autre que le critére *de* l'universalité, la règle prescrivant d'universaliser les maximes pour juger de leur conformité à la forme d'une législation universelle (impératif catégorique). Règle irrecevable pour une éthique de l'obligation pure, pour autant qu'elle soumet les prescriptives à un critère *théorique* ou logique, valable à la rigueur pour les cognitives, la forme de l'universalité n'étant selon l'*Analytique transcendantale* qu'une "fonction logique de l'entendement dans les jugements". Ce qui atteste d'un abandon du "primat de la raison pratique" et de sa démarcation fondamentale d'avec la raison théorique; ou encore, comme l'écrivait naguère Lyotard, d'un "retour du dénotatif" au sein du "jeu de langage" prescriptif.[9] Sans doute faut-il y voir une *résistance* de la pensée kantienne, un recul angoissé devant la folie de l'Appel, l'*in-fondé* de la prescription pure. "La loi kantienne, écrit encore Lyotard, ne dit pas ce qu'il faut faire, elle est vide comme le désert du Sinaï (…), elle veut seulement que tu veuilles quelque chose par pur respect pour elle. C'est là où la clause kantienne du "comme si universalisable" vient sauvegarder la volonté de la folie".[10]

---

8. C'est ainsi que Manfred Frank, commentant l'analyse de la "dissymétrie éthique" et du paradoxe d'Abraham dans *Le différend*, déclare ceci: "Que l'obligation introduise une "dissymétrie" essentielle dans la relation intersubjective ne peut être relevé que d'un point de une critique (…) (celui) d'une morale qui interdise la production d'effets d'inégalité des chances"… *Dissension et consensus selon Lyotard et Habermas*, in *Cahier de Philosophie* n°5, 1988, p.181-182.
9. *Logique de Lévinas*, in *Textes pour E. Lévinas*, J.M. Place, 1980, p.134.
10. *Anamnèse*, in *Hors-Cadre* n°9, 1991, p.112.

Ouverture d'une instance d'obligation pure et vide, aussitôt recouverte par une résistance affolée, par l'ambiguïté d'une "typique du jugement pratique" ("agis comme si"...) dont le type, le quasi-schème symbolique, impose à la Loi de liberté la *Gesetzmässigkeit*, la forme-de-légalité d'une loi de nature (universalité). Dans l'éthique du *Différend*, le "moment kantien" se trouve ainsi situé et dépassé. Selon un geste qui en répète d'autres, qui poursuit à sa manière ces aventures de pensée où l'éthique kantienne de la Loi se voit destituée, divisée d'avec elle-même, "suspendue". Ce qui ne reviendrait peut-être qu'à en retrouver la vérité cachée. Tout comme le "suspens" kierkegaardien de la Loi éthique, ou l'énigmatique scène narrative que lui monte l'écriture kafkaïenne, l'éthique de la prescription pure esquissée par le *Différend* ne prendrait ses distances avec la "morale kantienne" qu'en renouant avec son paradoxe fondateur, en éprouvant à nouveau l'ouverture initiale de la Loi. C'est l'enracinement d'un tel geste — qui sous-tend l'éthique du *Différend* — dans le paradoxe de l'éthique kantienne que nous voudrions maintenant, en délaissant la pensée de Lyotard, tenter d'analyser.

Le paradoxe de l'éthique

"Devant la Loi se dresse le gardien de la porte. Un homme de la campagne se présente et demande à entrer dans la Loi. Mais le gardien dit que pour l'instant il ne peut pas lui accorder l'entrée. L'homme réfléchit, puis demand s'il sera permis d'entrer plus tard. "C'est possible dit le gardien, mais pas maintenant'..."[11] Ainsi commence l'apologue que l'abbé, à la fin du *Procès*, raconte à Joseph K. pour lui faire comprendre qu'il "se méprend sur la Justice'. Le récit est censé illustrer une "illusion" (*Täuschung*), celle de "l'homme de la campagne" qui croit que la Loi doit être "accessible à tous et toujours" et qui, devant le refus du gardien, devant cet interdit qui est ajournement, promesse, reste captif du seuil tout au long de sa vie; jusqu'au moment où, sur le point de mourir, il demande au gardien comment il se fait, "si chacun désire tant approcher la Loi", qu'il n'y ait eu que lui qui ait demandé à entrer — et s'attire cette réponse: "Ici nul autre que toi n'avait le droit d'entrer, car cette porte t'était destinée (*bestimmt*) à toi seul. Maintenant je m'en vais et je ferme la porte". Sentence énigmatique qui conclut l'apologue. Elle sera suivie d'une longue discussion entre

11. Kafka, *Le Procès*, trad. Lortholary, Garnier-Flammarion, 1983, p. 256-257.

Joseph K. et l'abbé, sur la question de savoir si le gardien a ou non trompé l'homme, et s'il a lui-même été trompé; à moins — hypothèse la plus inquiétante — que douter du gardien "revienne à douter de la Loi", et que l'on n'ait pas à tenir pour vrai son dire, "mais seulement à le tenir pour nécessaire"-"Triste opinion, répond K.: elle érigerait le mensonge en loi universelle". La méprise sur la Loi ne serait le fait ni de l'homme ni du gardien, mais de la Loi elle-même — son "mensonge', l'illusion de la Loi, l'illusion qu'il y ait la Loi. Nuit noire du doute, moment du nihilisme, qui semble clôre le débat. Le dernier mot revient pourtant à l'abbé, en ce *finale* du *Procès* où il revèle à K. sa méprise: "La Justice ne te veut rien, elle t'accueille quand tu viens et te laisse quand tu t'en vas".

On n'aura pas la prétention de tenter un "commentaire philosophique" d'un texte dont la densité limpide défie tout commentaire, d'autant qu'il nous prévient ironiquement de la vanité d'une telle tentative: "Il ne faut pas, déclare l'abbé, que tu tiennes trop grand compte des gloses. L'Ecriture est immuable et les gloses n'expriment le plus souvent que le désespoir des glossateurs". Encore moins s'agirait-il de réduire l'apologue kafkaïen à une "explication" avec Kant, bien que plusieurs allusions — au "devoir" et à la "dignité" du gardien, à la "libre décision" de se soumettre à la Loi, et surtout au mensonge "érigé en loi universelle" — indiquent que ce texte peut *aussi* se lire ainsi. Mais l'on peut tenter de repérer ce qui, dans le récit de Kafka, retrouve le chemin de la question kantienne, la mauvaise posture de la pensée, l'énigme de la Loi. Car c'est bien du Passage qu'il s'agit, de l'exigence kantienne de "faire le pas" vers la Loi, vers une Loi qui se retire et *se garde* — dont la pensée, disait Kant, doit se faire *Selbsthalterin*, "gardienne de ses propres lois'. Retrait de la Loi, qui ouvre l'espace de la re-présentation, des "gardiens", schèmes ou symboles, qui figurent à distance la sans-figure de la Loi, avec le risque toujours présent d'une défiguration, imposture ou mensonge du gardien, ou même de la Loi qu'il représente. C'est le préjugé de l'homme, sa présomption naïve, qu'il croit possible de forcer cette garde, de "pénétrer dans la Loi" pour la dévoiler, la posséder, pour se faire le Sujet de la Loi. Il se la représente en effet comme *universelle*, "accessible à tous et toujours": loi intemporelle de la raison, valable pour tous les êtres raisonnables, et comme loi d'*autonomie* — c'est, dira l'abbé, "par une libre décision volontaire", qu'il s'est "lié à la Loi". La naïveté de l'homme est celle de la "morale kantienne", et son histoire pourrait assez bien illustrer la critique hégélienne de cette morale: de l'in-détermination, de la cruauté d'une Loi transcendante, des déplace-ments-équivoques d'une conscience-morale progessant à l'infini vers un idéal inaccessible. L'apologue décrit de cette manière le retrait de la Loi, en le figurant à la fois sur un plan temporel, comme promesse dont l'accomplissement est indéfiniment différé — "c'est possible, dit le gardien, mais pas maintenant" — et d'un point de vue spatial, en ce cauchemar d'un mortel étirement de l'espace, d'une prolifération sans fin des gardes de la Loi — "de salle en salle, il y a des gardiens de plus en plus puissants...".

Pourtant, rien n'est plus étranger à la parabole de Kafka que la prétention hégélienne d'abroger la Loi en la relevant dans la volonté du Sujet. C'est, nous l'avons vu, au nom d'un véritable universel, d'une autonomie absolue que s'effectue le dépassement de la vision morale du monde. Ce que révèle le gardien à l'homme est au contraire la *singularité* de la Loi, sa destination singulière, l'envoi "destiné à toi seul" d'une loi qui n'en demeure pas moins *la* Loi, celle "que chacun désire approcher", anonyme et universelle. Révé-lation paradoxale de la Loi comme appel singulier qui n'advient pas à l'homme dans la libre décision du Sujet autonome, mais en son extrême dépossession, son dessaisissement: c'est alors seulement, à la veille de mourir, qu'il aperçoit dans les ténèbres la "glorieuse lueur" qui passe par la porte de la Loi. On aurait donc tort de croire que son attente ait été vaine, ou (comme se l'imagine Joseph K.) que le gardien lui ait donné le "message libérateur" lorsqu'il était "trop tard". Car la Loi se donne, s'est toujours déjà donnée en vérité à celui qui la désire et l'attend. La méprise sur la Loi consiste à penser qu'elle pourrait se présenter au terme de l'attente, qu'il serait pos-sible de l'atteindre en passant au-delà du garde et du seuil — sans comprendre que la porte "ouverte comme toujours" est déjà l'Ou-vert de la Loi; que la promesse du gardien n'est pas la marque de l'Interdit, mais l'appel du Possible; que son "seuil" est le *limen*, le lieu ou l'instant *sublime* de sa donation. Que son retrait n'est pas la transcendance métaphysique d'une Idée ou d'un idéal inaccessible, ni celle d'une norme morale qui accuse et condamne, sans doute parce qu'elle est la Loi même de l'existence, l'existence comme Loi, qui "ne veut rien", mais saisit chaque existant quand il vient au monde et le laisse quand il s'en va.

Expérience paradoxale d'un retrait de la Loi dans sa destina-tion singulière: lui feront écho d'autres paradoxes, d'autres aventures de la pensée. Qu'elles mettent en scène la folle division de la Loi[12], ou l'épreuve d'une obligation singulière au-delà de toute loi, celles-ci ont en commun avec Kafka de s'expliquer avec Kant, de se déterminer plus ou moins directement contre une certaine doxa kantienne définissant le principe suprême de devoir comme loi morale universelle. Pourtant, à explorer les paradoxes de l'éthique et les limites ou les défaillances de la Loi, peut-être se retrouvent-elles plus proches qu'elles ne le croient de Kant, du versant le plus paradoxal de sa pensée. C'est Kant lui-même qui désigne le geste constitutif de son éthique comme *paradoxe*: comme ce "paradoxe de la méthode dans une critique de la raison pratique" qui qualifie le renversement du rapport entre le Bien et la Loi "à savoir que le concept du bien et du mal ne doit pas être déterminé antérieurement à la Loi morale (à laquelle, en apparence, il devrait pourtant même servir de fondement) mais seulement (comme il arrive ici) après cette Loi et par elle"[13]. Au renversement "copernicien" du rapport entre la connaissance et l'objet opéré par la première *Critique*, succède ainsi une *révolution copernicienne de l'éthique*. Comme le remarque Deleuze, c'est seulement à la suite de ce geste kantien qu'il devient possible de parler de *la Loi*, sans aucune spécification: la "Loi morale" de Kant est cette pure forme de la Loi, dont "l'objet se dérobe essentiellement", que l'on a toujours déjà transgressée sans même savoir ce qu'elle commande, si bien que les deux pôles de l'expérience moderne de la Loi — Sade ou Masoch, révolte ironique ou soumission perverse-prennent tous les deux appui sur la position kantienne pour la subvertir[14].

Le renversement effectué dans la deuxième *Critique* peut être dit para-doxal en ce qu'il brise avec une évidence première de la doxa, de ce sens commun moral dont Kant lui-même aura mis longtemps à se défaire. Dans le *Canon de la raison pure*, les "lois morales" étaient subordonnées à l'impératif de réaliser le Souverain Bien, demeuraient en ce sens des lois *du* Bien, lois "pathologiques" soumises au désir de bonheur et à la crainte. A peu près contemporaine du *Canon*, la *Leçon sur l'éthique* était encore plus explicite, en posant que "la nécessité morale consiste dans la bonté (*Bonität*) absolue de

12. Ainsi Blanchot, dans *la folie du jour*.
13. I. Kant, *Oeuvres* (Gallimard-Pléiade, 1980-84), *Critique de la raison pratique* (CRp), *Fondements de la métaphysique des moeurs* (FM), *La religion dans les limites de la simple raison* (Religion), CRp, 2, p. 684 (Vrin p. 76)
14. cf. Deleuze, *Présentation de Sacher-Masoch*, 1967, rééd. 10/18, 1973, pp. 81-90.

l'action"[15], distinguée de la "bonté hypothétique" qu'expriment les impératifs pragmatiques. Or, dans cette même *Leçon*, Kant allait se trouver confronté à la définition classique de l'impératif moral proposée par Wolff et Baumgarten: *fac bonum*. A la question de savoir *ce qu'est* le bien à faire, remarque-t-il, cet impératif ne donne aucune réponse déterminée et, puisque le bien n'est ici rien d'autre que ce que l'impératif prescrit d'accomplir, "ce principe *vague* est également un principe *tautologique*" où s'énonce simplement qu' "il est bien de faire ce qui est bien", que "je dois faire ce que je dois faire"[16]. C'est l'ensemble des principes moraux de la Tradition, du "juste milieu" d'Aristote au "principe de perfection" de Wolff qui se réduisent selon lui à cette "tautologie de la raison pure", "non-philosophique et vide". Mise en question qui ne peut manquer d'atteindre sa propre conception de l'impératif moral comme impératif de bonté, l'obliger à reconsidérer la relation du Bien et de la Loi. L'inconsistance tautologique des morales traditionnelles ne pourra être évitée qu'en cessant de faire du Bien le principe et la fin de l'obligation éthique, en reconnaissant que l'impératif catégorique ne prescrit pas d'agir bien, mais d'agir par devoir, c'est-à-dire selon la Loi. De là le paradoxe de la *Critique*: que le Bien n'est plus au fondement de la Loi, que c'est elle au contraire qui rend possible le Bien, qui permet de déterminer objectivement les concepts de bien et de mal.

A l'appui de sa thèse, la *Critique* avance une réfutation par l'absurde: s'il en allait autrement, si la Loi se fondait sur un concept préalable du bien, celui-ci — en l'absence de toute intuition intellectuelle d'un Bien supra-sensible — se ramènerait au bien-être sensible, au bonheur: il ne pourrait être "que le concept de quelque chose dont l'existence promet du plaisir", et "c'est à l'expérience seule qu'il appartient de décider ce qui est immédiatement bon ou mauvais"[17]. L'opposition éthique du bien et du mal se dilue alors dans la différence psychologique — incertaine et fluctuante — du plaisir et du déplaisir, privant l'éthique de tout critère objectif de jugement. Ainsi, le dogmatisme d'une morale ordonnée au Bien se renverse-t-il nécessairement en empirisme pratique, en nihilisme. On voit que l'argumentation repose entièrement sur cette thèse fondamentale: que le "principe du bonheur" est incapable de don-

15. *Vorlesung über Ethik*, éd.Menzer, Pan Verlag R. Heise, 1921, p. 18-22.
16. id. p. 28-32.
17. CRp, p. 678 (p. 71-72).

ner une loi objective à notre volonté, que la Loi doit se poser au-delà du principe du bonheur. La *Critique* aurait percé à jour "le fondement de tous les errements (*Verirrungen*) des philosophes quant au principe suprême de la morale"[18]: au lieu de partir de la pure forme de la Loi, ils "cherchaient un objet de la volonté pour en faire la matière et le fondement de la Loi", et "qu'ils placent cet objet de plaisir (*Gegenstand der Lust*) qui était censé fournir le concept suprême du Bien dans le bonheur, dans la perfection, dans le sentiment moral ou dans la volonté de Dieu, leur principe était toujours hétéronome et ils devaient inévitablement buter sur des conditions empiriques pour établir une loi morale". Le fondement de toutes les doctrines morales "pré-coperniciennes", leur principe inconsistant qui les fait verser dans le nihilisme, est donc *l'hétéronomie*: soumission de la volonté à un "principe pratique matériel de détermination" extérieur à la pure forme du vouloir, et subordination *de la Loi elle-même* à une instance plus originaire dont elle serait dérivée[19]. A quoi s'oppose le principe éthique de *l'autonomie*, non seulement comme autonomie *de la volonté* se soumettant librement à une Loi qu'elle reconnaît comme sa forme et sa Loi, mais aussi, plus radicalement, comme "autonomie du principe de la moralité", autodonation originaire *de la Loi* dans le *factum*.

Aussi diverses soient-elles, les morales de la Tradition s'autorisent d'un geste unique, d'une même subordination de la Loi à un Principe "supérieur". Elles supposent toutes que la donation-de-Loi n'est pas auto-donation; que, pour reprendre les termes de Heidegger, ce n'est pas la Loi qui "donne aux lois le pouvoir d'être des lois". Peu importe en ce sens que l'instance hétéronome d'où procèdent les lois se présente comme Idée du Bien, Raison de Dieu, Volonté du Sujet humain, voire comme vérité de l'Être: seul compte, à ce niveau, cette décision fondatrice, ce geste violent par lequel le don de la Loi est arraché à la Loi, livré à une instance plus "originaire", un Hors-la-Loi qui s'arroge le pouvoir de faire-loi. Et peu importe que ce Principe, source ou "auteur" de la Loi, soit lié à la Loi qu'il édicte, voué à respecter une essence immuable du Bien et de la Loi — définie alors comme "loi éternelle" de Dieu ou de la Nature; ou qu'aucune détermination d'essence préalable n'entrave sa libre décision créatrice: qu'en posant la Loi, il la dépose et s'en

18. id. p. 685-686 (p. 77).
19. cf. la "table des principes matériels" (hétéronomes) qui fondent l'ensemble des doctrines morales traditionnelles depuis les Grecs, p. 656 (p. 54).

délie. On y verra autant de modes, certes dissemblables, d'un même assujettissement, d'une même défiguration de la Loi. Sous le règne de l'hétéronomie, c'est en effet le sens même de la "loi" qui s'en trouve perverti. Ce que l'on nomme "la Loi" se dit en plusieurs sens, selon les langues, les époques, les configurations de pensée où elle s'énonce. Considérons par exemple la définition classique de la *lex* par Thomas d'Aquin: "Une loi est une mesure des actes qui prescrit ou interdit d'agir. Le mot loi vient du verbe "lier", et en effet une loi établit une obligation dans l'ordre de l'action. Or, la règle et la mesure des actes humains est la raison (...). Par conséquent, la loi appartient à l'ordre de la raison"[20]. Il précise dans la *quaestio* suivante qu' "une loi n'est rien d'autre que ce que dicte la raison pratique du chef qui gouverne une communauté". L'univers étant régi par la raison divine, le principe ultime du monde "a donc le caractère d'une loi", laquelle se présente chez les créatures douées de raison comme "loi naturelle" leur permettant de distinguer le bien du mal. La "loi" se définit ainsi à la fois comme *prescription*, commandement ou consigne, et comme *lien* (toujours "synthétique" en ce sens): elle est *ob-ligation* ou *Fügung*, "injonction qui porte et qui lie".

De ces deux significations conjointes dans la conception classique de la "loi", la modernité n'en retient qu'une seule, en définissant la "loi naturelle" comme liaison nécessaire, rapport constant entre les phénomènes, et nous avons vu que cette compréhension mutilée de la "loi" pèsera lourdement sur la Critique, alors même que Kant s'efforce de penser la Loi de liberté dans sa différence d'avec les lois naturelles, en tant qu'appel, prescription impérative. Mais le concept classique de loi portait déjà lui-même les marques d'une altération essentielle. En rapprochant la *lex* du verbe *legere*, Thomas d'Aquin l'installait dans une certaine constellation de sens: celle du *legein* grec, du Logos. Pour la pensée la plus initiale, ce nom ne désignait pas encore la raison ni le discours, mais la liance qui recueille et rassemble, la "Pose recueillante" — *die lesende Lege*, dira Heidegger —, la dis-position, l'ordonnance du monde[21]. Pris en ce sens, le Logos est venue en présence, dé-cèlement — *alèthéia* — où ce qui se rassemble vient de soi-même à paraître, se montre

20. Saint Thomas d'Aquin, *Somme Théologique*, I-II, qu.91, ad.1.
21. cf. Heidegger, *Logos*, in *Essais et conférences*, Gallimard, 1958, rééd. 1978, pp. 249-278. Ainsi que son *Introduction à la métaphysique*, Gallimard, 1967, rééd. 1980, p. 134-143.

librement de soi-même dans sa déclosion: *phusis*. C'est faire violence à la liberté du Logos, à son auto-donation, que de demander *qui* dispose et ordonne, d'attribuer un "sujet" au *legein*. Lorsque l'on identifie la Loi au commandement d'un Souverain de l'univers, son auto-nomie originaire s'est perdue, la Loi se trouve dépossédée du pouvoir de faire-loi, de se donner d'elle-même comme Loi. Et peut-être cette dépossession s'accompagne-t-elle d'une autre violence; en effet, à faire fonds sur le terme latin (*lex*), on tire inexorablement le sens de la loi vers l'économie du *Logos* grec et, par suite, de la *ratio* entendue comme raisonnement et calcul, de sorte que toute loi paraît forcement "appartenir à la raison". Ce faisant, on oublie que, pour les Grecs, la "loi" n'avait rien à voir avec le *logos*, que le terme grec de *nomos* procéde d'une autre constellation de sens: car *nemein* signifie le *partage*, séparation et donation à la fois, le fait de répartir ce que l'on donne, d'assigner à chacun son dû. Ainsi le pâtre est-il *nomeus*, qui attribue à ses bêtes leur pâture, sans pourtant les enfermer dans la limite d'un enclos, en les laissant aller librement, en *nomades*[22]. Dans un espace illimité qui n'en est pas moins leur *èthos*, domaine ou demeure: de là provient le sens plus tardif, post-homérique, de *nomos* comme repaire, habitation, région, contrée. Loin de signifier la liaison, le rassemblement, la mise en ordre, le *nomos* grec évoque la partition, la dispersion, l'errance aventureuse, ou encore la mélodie, comme scansion, césure, partage rythmique des tons et des voix — et l'on devra se demander si, de ce nomos sauvage et nomade, un écho retentit encore dans l'appel de la Loi kantienne, violence sublime et césure de l'existence. On remarquera pourtant que, assez tôt, le sens de ce terme s'infléchit, qu'il va désigner, déjà chez Pindare, le "sujet" du *nemein*, la puissance qui distribue les parts et veille à la juste répartition, Némésis ou Zeus *némétôr*, et finalement la Puissance comme telle, le fait de dominer, d'être le maître — *panta némôn Zeus* dira Eschyle — comme si, là encore, la pensée ne pouvait se représenter le faire-loi de la Loi qu'en l'hypostasiant, en l'attribuant à un Principe plus haut que la Loi. Sans doute cette analyse exigerait-elle d'être approfondie, en tenant compte d'une autre langue, d'un troisième nom pout la Loi, qui pense cette fois sa donation comme transmission, enseignement, *Thora*. La subordination de la Loi à Celui qui l'édicte s'y impose en tout cas avec encore plus de force. En déterminant la Loi à partir du

---

22. Pour tout ce qui suit, cf. l'étude d'E. Laroche, *Histoire de la racine NEM- en grec ancien*, Klincksieck, 1949. Sur la notion d'un "nomos nomade", cf. aussi Deleuze, *Différence et répétition*, PUF, 1968, p. 54-55.

Bien, les morales de l'hétéronomie se plient donc à une décision plus initiale, répétée dans diverses traditions, qui dépossède la Loi de la puissance de donner loi.

C'est à cette *Verirrung*, cet égarement de toujours, que doit mettre fin la révolution copernicienne de l'éthique: en délivrant la Loi de son assujettissement aux diverses figures du "Bien", de sa "déduction" ou de sa fondation à partir des Principes suprêmes de chaque époque; en la révélant en son auto-donation originaire, son libre paraître de soi-même sans fondement ni sujet. Le paradoxe de la Critique consiste simplement à affirmer, à l'encontre de la Tradition, que *le don de la Loi appartient à la Loi*. Que ce n'est pas à un Principe hors-la-Loi, qu'il soit immanent ou transcendant, ontique ou ontologique, mais à la Loi elle-même qu'il revient de "donner aux lois le pouvoir d'être des lois". Sous ce nom de "Loi éthique", il ne faut pas se représenter un principe régional ontique, un précepte de moralité distinct des lois religieuses, juridiques, historiques ou psychologiques, mais ce qui décide de la *Gesetzmässigkeit* de ces lois, la pure forme de leur légalité, la Loi des lois, qui leur donne force de loi. *Sittengesetz*: non la devise d'une "éthique" particulière, mais le Nomos comme loi du *site*, de l'*èthos* qui est demeure pour l'existence — et le *site des lois*, leur assise ou leur Pose, la *Ge-setzung* qui les tient et les garde.

Le paradoxe de la Critique correspond ainsi au troisième pas de la pensée, au pas-en-avant où elle surmonte la mauvaise posture de l'éthique "en se faisant la gardienne de ses propres lois". C'est ici que pointe le litige, lorsqu'il s'agit de déterminer la signification de ce "pas", sa *situation* historiale. Faut-il, avec Heidegger, comprendre cette "garde" comme fondation métaphysique de la Loi à partir de la subjectivité? Le paradoxe de l'éthique kantienne, sa rupture avec la Tradition se ramènerait à un Passage entre deux époques de l'errance, simple charnière, *passation* des pouvoirs entre le Principe théologique de l'hétéronomie et le principe moderne de l'autonomie, et les équivoques de la problématique kantienne se réduiraient à un clivage historique, flottement ou hésitation dans le mouvement d'une transition nécessaire. Ou bien cette position kantienne de la Loi où elle se dégage de tout "point d'attache dans le ciel ou sur terre" signifie-t-elle qu'elle s'ex-pose, se libère de toute imposition d'un Principe métaphysique, qu'elle échappe à son ancienne allégeance au Ciel de la transcendance divine, sans se laisser réapproprier "sur la Terre", dans l'immanence du Sujet? Dans les ambiguïtés, les lignes de fracture de l'oeuvre, il faudrait repérer les traces de cette ex-position paradoxale de la Loi, de son retrait, de son excès transcendant les Principes fondateurs des époques... Sauf si c'était, chez Kant, la Loi elle-même qui se posait en Principe: si sa "suprématie" (*Obergewalt*) ne désignait la surpuissance d'un Fondement ontique, "universel" et "sacré" comme il siée, en régime d'onto-théologie, aux Seigneurs de l'étant. En posant que ce n'est plus le Bien qui fonde la Loi, mais la Loi qui fonde le Bien, le "paradoxe de la méthode" se contenterait d'inverser la préséance traditionnelle des Principes, sans affecter en rien la structure du rapport inversé, sans renoncer à la recherche d'un Premier Fondement, d'une "position ferme" qui supporte tout étant.

A ceci près que Kant n'écrit jamais que la Loi *fonde* le Bien, mais seulement qu'elle "détermine et rend possible" son concept. Ce sont les morales de l'hétéronomie qui recherchent "un matière et un fondement" pour la Loi. La difficulté consiste alors à comprendre la relation du "bien" à cette Loi qui n'en est ni le fondement, ni la cause, ni le sujet — à élucider le rapport (non-fondatif et non-causal: an-archique) de la Loi à la volonté du sujet, qu'elle détermine à l'action par une obligation inconditionnée sans pourtant s'imposer du dehors comme une force étrangère. Ce qui nous ramène au problème jamais vraiment résolu de la synthèse pratique comme lien a priori du vouloir et de la Loi. Il s'agit donc de penser la Loi à la fois en son *ex-position* — sa transcendance, son excès, qui interdit de la considérer comme une loi *de* la volonté — et en son immanence ou son inhérence *à* la volonté, excluant toute hétéronomie: de concevoir la transcendance immanente de la Loi comme *forme* du vouloir et *soutenance* du sujet. En d'autres termes, on devra se demander comment penser ensemble l'an-archie de la Loi et sa souveraineté (son *Obergewalt*), comment comprendre sa prévalence souveraine sur les Principes "matériels" sans la réduire à une prédominance historique et ontique dans la guerre des Principes. Plutôt que d'un "retrait" de la Loi (notion trop voisine du "retrait de l'être" heideggérien) ou de sa "transcendance" (trop proche de la transcendance métaphysique de "Dieu" ou d'un Bien supra-sensible), on préférera parler de son excès, de son outrance, de son *ex-position*. A entendre d'abord comme délivrance de la Loi, comme cette césure, ce retournement où elle s'affranchit de la tutelle du Bien, se pose *au-dehors* et au-delà des Principes d'époque et des Fondements suprêmes. A entendre ensuite comme monstration, révélation, au sens où l'on "expose" une oeuvre d'art, ou un révélateur à la lumière: la Loi s'y présente enfin en vérité, dégagée des hypostases qui la défiguraient, en préservant cependant sa part de secret, sans jamais s'offrir à découvert dans l'évidence d'un Savoir Absolu. On dira enfin qu'en ce mouvement même qui la soustrait à toute pré-détermination par les Principes et la Bien, elle *s'expose* au Danger, au risque de l'arbitraire, de l'indétermination. Situation exposée, mauvaise posture où se découvre l'insoutenable vacuité de la Loi, sans cesse menacée de retomber sous l'impire d'un Principe qui en comblerait le vide et en recouvrirait l'énigme.

L'*exposition* de la Loi ne se distingue donc pas de sa révélation dans le *factum*, de l'appel qui transit chaque existence et la rappelle à sa liberté. Si ce n'est qu'elle qualifie plus fortement encore un événement singulier, situable et repérable dans l'histoire, et qui ne se limite pas à cette révolution copernicienne de l'éthique où la *Critique* "expose" la conception kantienne de la Loi. L'exposition-révélation de la Loi coïncide avec cette phase inaugurale de notre modernité, où se dénoue le lien séculaire du pouvoir, du savoir et de la Loi, où celle-ci se "désincorpore", se dérobe à son ancrage dans le corps du monarque ou la volonté divine, faisant signe désormais vers un Autre sans figure, un foyer immaîtrisable et indéterminable, enjeu d'un questionnement sans fin. Avec la menace toujours présente de se laisser précipiter dans l'immanence, identifier aus "lois" de l'Histoire ou de la Nature, réapproprier à l'ordre de l'Homme ou de Peuple-Sujet, de la Classe ou de la Race, dont l'actualisation "efface la dimension de la Loi comme telle."[23] L'analogie classique entre "révolution copernicienne" et Révolution française, la mise en parallèle du régicide Robespierre et d'un Kant "décide" seraient moins naïves qu'il ne paraît: le geste critique kantien — ce double geste de dégagement de l'Apparence et d'ex-position de la Loi — et les révolutions démocratiques de la modernité seraient effectivement "contemporains", au sens où l'on dit en mathématiques que deux ensembles sont "contemporains" lorsqu'ils sont pénétrés par la même inconnue... Il y a en tout cas une solidarité profonde entre la délimitation de l'Apparence effectuée dans la *Dialectique transcendantale* et la révolution éthique de la deuxième *Critique*. Car l'hétéronomie est le règne de l'Apparence, l'usurpation des Principes qui prétendent faire loi à la place de la Loi: il fallait que soient

23. Sur l'expérience de la démocratie moderne comme 'désincorporation' de la Loi et épeuvre de l'indétermination, on renverra à l'ensemble de l'oeuvre de C.Lefort, tout particulièrement à *L'invention démocratique*, Fayard, 1981 et aux *Essais sur le politique*, Seuil, 1986.

défaites la consistance illusoire de "Dieu" et celle du Sujet pour que la Loi s'expose en vérité. Aussi son ex-position paradoxale poursuit-elle l'oeuvre de la *Dialectique*, en permettant de déterminer "Dieu" comme simple objet de croyance, "postulat de la raison pratique" et, plus radicalement, de le penser comme *hypostase de la Loi*, comme étant "la Loi elle-même personnifiée". Renversement de la morale théologique: si la Loi n'est plus la loi de Dieu, c'est Dieu qu'il faut considérer comme le "dieu" *de* la Loi (au sens où l'on parle des dieux du feu, de la guerre, de la mort ...) *der Grenzgott der Moral*.

Telle est la bonne nouvelle kantienne: *qu'il n'y a pas d'auteur de la Loi*, que "celui qui commande au moyen de la Loi" — le "législateur" (*Gesetzgeber*: celui qui (se) donne la Loi) — "n'est pas pour autant son auteur (*Urheber*), car alors la Loi serait contingente et arbitraire".[24] Pas d'auteur, de principe, de fondement, *pas de Sujet de la Loi*: on peut entendre cette thèse en un sens restreint, répéter à la suite de Kant que la morale théologique est hétéronomie, que Dieu n'est pas le "sujet" créateur de la Loi. Il est aussi possible de l'interpréter en un sens plus radical, en la tournant contre Kant lui-même, contre un aspect de sa pensée, cette morale humaniste du Sujet autonome qui déclare que "l'Homme est le sujet de la Loi morale".[25] Il se peut que d'être sujet *à* la Loi lui interdise de se poser en Sujet *de* la Loi; que la liberté de la Loi, son auto-donation originaire, la délivre de *tout* Sujet, sur la terre comme au ciel. Nous savons que Kant demande que la philosophie pratique ne soit "mélangée ni d'anthropologie ni de théologie"[26], refuse que l'on "dérive la réalité (de la Loi) de la *constitution particulière de la nature humaine*"[27]; qu'il distingue de la "disposition à l'*humanité*" de l'homme, la disposition à la *personnalité* comme aptitude au respect pour la Loi.[28] Si la Loi peut être définie comme "Loi de la raison pure pratique", cela ne veut surtout pas dire que la raison pratique soit une faculté de l'Homme et qu'elle "nous donne" la Loi, la produise ou la constitue, s'en fasse le Sujet. C'est bien plutôt la

---

24. *Doctrine du droit*, Introduction IV, 3, p. 475 -cf. aussi *Traité de pédagogie*, 3, p. 1199.
25. CRp., 2, p. 714 (Vrin p. 145).
26. FM, 2, p. 271 (D p. 110).
27. FM p. 290 (D p. 144). En ce sens, la pensée kantienne n'est pas un 'humanisme' (du moins si l'on entend, par ce terme, une anthropologie centrée sur l'*homo phaenomenon*).
28. cf. *Religion*, 3, p. 37-39.

raison pratique elle-même qui nous est révélée, nous est donnée par le fait de la Loi. Raison inhumaine, plus qu'humaine, qui n'est rien d'autre que notre disposition à accueillir la Loi. Une Loi qui n'est ni celle de Dieu, ni celle du Sujet ou de l'Homme, qui n'est pas la loi de la raison ou de la volonté humaine. Et encore moins la loi du bien: il est bien de faire ce que la Loi prescrit. Par ce terme de "bien", il faut entendre désormais "l'objet nécessaire de la faculté de désirer", ce que la Loi commande au désir avec une nécessité objective. Ainsi, nous ne savons plus ce qui est Bien: car tout bien n'est bien que d'après la Loi, et celle-ci ne prescrit aucune norme, aucune valeur, aucun idéal de vertu préexistant, dont la détermination précéderait la prescription impérative, lui imposerait d'avance un "contenu", soumettant à nouveau la Loi à l'autorité hétéronome de ce "bien". Si toute morale implique la préassignation d'un bien et d'un mal, de devoirs concrets et d'interdits, de vertus et de vices, il faut admettre que la philosophie pratique kantienne — la "partie pure de l'é-thique"[29] — ne se définit pas comme une doctrine morale[30]: que, en dépit des flottements terminologiques de Kant, la *Sittengesetz* n'est pas une "loi morale", ne se confond pas avec l'impératif d'une "conscience morale", la voix accusatrice du Tribunal intérieur. La méprise de Joseph K. repose précisément sur une conception à la fois *moraliste* et *judiciaire* de la Loi: il s'épuise à la recherche de son Juge caché, de la Faute secrète dont il se serait rendu coupable, sans comprendre que la Loi "ne lui veut rien". Que rien ni personne ne le condamne, si ce n'est sa propre obstination à se croire coupable.

Est-ce à dire qu'il n'y aurait plus ni bien, ni mal, plus de tort envers la Loi? que la *Critique* aurait, avant Nietzsche, délivré le vouloir de toute dette, rendu son "innocence" (*Unschuld*) au devenir? C'est au contraire l'unique *objet* de la Loi que de marquer la différence du bien et du mal, de la déterminer objectivement, comme l'opposition entre l'objet nécessaire du désir et l'objet d'une nécessaire "aversion"[31]. Et c'est précisément *parce qu*'elle rend possible leur opposition qu'elle ne lui appartient pas; qu'elle la précède — non d'une antériorité temporelle, mais d'une précession transcendantale —, qu'elle s'ex-pose *endeçà du bien et du mal*, dans une paradoxale neutralité: non comme la volonté d'un Sujet posant arbitrairement des "valeurs" (la Loi "ne veut rien", n'est pas une loi

---

29. FM p. 244-248 (D p. 77-83).
30. Même si l'on peut en dériver une morale en l'appliquant au donné anthropologi-que de la nature humaine, ce qui fera l'objet de la *Doctrine de la vertu*.
31. CRp p. 678 (p. 71).

de la Volonté, ne donne aucun contenu au bien et au mal), ni comme une instance in-différente qui surplomberait l'opposition éthique (la neutralité de la Loi exclut toute "indifférence" au bien et au mal)[32], mais comme la *condition* de cette opposition, comme l'O-rient du désir, le point=X qui permet au vouloir de se repérer, de s'orienter vers le bien et le mal, de se décider pour ou contre la Loi. La Loi n'est ni "bonne" ni "mauvaise", diffère des termes de la différence qu'elle constitue. L'ex-position de la Loi culmine en ce *paradoxe de l'instauration* où l'excès de la Loi sur le Bien, son absence de bonté, est requis afin de marquer ce qui est bien et le démarquer du mal, en cette "bifurcation des deux voies"[33], ce point de croisement qui est la croix (le *stauros*) de l'instauration éthique. S'il y a analogie entre Révolution française et révolution coperni-cienne, c'est sans doute en ce qu'elles se trouvent toutes deux confrontées à l'*écart absolu* de la Loi dans l'événement de son instauration, qui est la violence sublime de la liberté, la Terreur même — au sens où "la Terreur révolutionnaire se distingue de celle des tyrans" (du simple arbitraire de la volonté d'un despote) "parce qu'elle est supposée déterminer le principe de la distinction du bien et du mal", "qu'elle est la loi en acte, la loi qui tranche entre le bien et le mal, entre l'être et le néant", "en même temps qu'elle dissout pratiquement les critères de la culpabilité et les critères du juge-ment"[34]. Entre la Loi éthique kantienne et la "loi" de la Terreur jacobine, il ne s'agit pourtant que d'une analogie, d'une homologie de *rapports* entre deux événements dissemblables et, si nous voulons éviter l'amalgame, l'interprétation "terroriste" (hégélienne) de la Loi éthique, il faudra tenir compte de leur proximité comme de leur distance, et de cette ambiguïté du jugement de Kant sur la Révolu-tion française, où il salue avec enthousiasme le signe historique d'une avancée vers le Bien, et appréhende avec horreur l'indice du mal le plus radical.

Nous savons que Kant qualifie la voix de la Loi de "terrible" (*schrecklich*), et le respect pour la Loi est également présenté comme un sentiment "terrifiant" (*abschreckend*), source de "douleur" en tant qu'il nous "humilie", "anéantit notre arrogance"[35]. On peut se demander s'il ne confond pas deux modalités très différentes du

32. Le "rigorisme" kantien exclut tout "indifférentisme", cf. *Religion*, 3, p. 33.
33. FM, p. 259 (D p. 99).
34. C. Lefort, *Essais sur le politique*, pp. 75-109, notamment 90-91 et 99-103.
35. CRp p. 697-698, Ak V p. 73-74 (p. 90).

rapport à la Loi, la voix accusatrice de la conscience-morale dont l'injonction pourrait être *pathologique*, et le pur appel de la Loi. Kant lui-même met en garde contre le "moralisme despotique"[36], contre cette "vertu imaginaire (fantasmatique: *phantastisch*)" qui "jonche tous ses pas de devoirs comme autant de chausses-trappes"[37]. De ces "formes grimaçantes de la vertu" qui règnent par la crainte et "l'esclavage de l'âme", il va jusqu'à écrire qu'elles supposent toujours "une *haine* cachée de la Loi"[38]. Mais peut-être l'appel, qu'il soit ou non pathologique, est-il toujours "terrible", fait-il toujours violence à celui qu'il atteint.

La terreur de la Vertu et du Bien ne serait pas la pire: plus inquiétante que la tyrannie de la Morale, l'imposition despotique de tabous et de normes, est le vide de la Loi, son absence de fondement et de sens. Avoir conscience qu'il y a la Loi, qu'elle oblige de manière inconditionnée, sans savoir à quoi elle oblige, c'est là l'éprouver comme énigme, c'est-à-dire dans l'angoisse. Ce hiatus entre conscience-de-Loi et connaissance de la Loi, procède donc du paradoxe fondateur de l'éthique, de la précession de la Loi sur le Bien qui la prive de tout contenu déterminé, rend son appel proprement *insensé*.

C'est le même paradoxe que Kierkegaard nous fait découvrir dans le récit de la *Genèse*. Impossible à Adam de comprendre l'ordre divin, l'interdiction de goûter aux fruits de l'arbre de la connaissance du bien et du mal, puisque la "connaissance" qu'il implique, la compréhension de la faute, n'est possible qu'après sa transgression. Pour savoir ce qu'est le bien, il faut être dans le mal: pour pouvoir respecter la Loi, il faut l'avoir déjà transgressée. Lorsqu'Adam reçoit le commandement sans comprendre ce qu'il commande, s'éveille en lui la possibilité de la liberté, la liberté comme vertige du néant, pouvoir de choisir entre deux possibles vides, également privés de sens.[39] Cette "possibilité infinie de pouvoir" le livre à l'angoisse, qui est le vertige de la liberté exposée au néant de ses possibles. Avant toute faute, l'innocence s'est déjà perdue, car l'angoisse de l'innocence en appelle à la faute possible, à la transgression

36. Formule qui qualifie, dans le *Projet de paix perpétuelle*, la position des Jacobins — cf. 3, p. 368.
37. *Doctrine de la vertu*, Introduction XVII, 3, p. 694.
38. cf. *Anthropologie* § 88, 3, p. 1097 et *Religion*, 3, p. 35 note.
39. Kierkegaard, *Le concept de l'angoisse*, Gallimard, 1935, rééd. 1976, p. 46-49.

qui donnerait sens à l'Interdit. Ainsi l'angoisse est-elle la condition du péché — sans s'identifier au péché: elle conduit la liberté, jusqu'au bord du néant, où celle-ci, "plongeant dans son propre possible", s'effondre et se relève coupable. "C'est entre ces deux instants qu'est le saut qu'aucune science n'a expliqué ni ne peut expliquer".[40] Kierkegaard s'accorde en effet avec Kant pour reconnaître dans le choix du mal un acte de liberté, qui advient à nouveau en chaque existence par un "saut", une décision absolument singulière, irréductible à ses conditions, incompréhensible. Il distingue cependant plus rigoureusement que Kant les deux modes d'angoisse que partage le saut: l'angoisse primordiale d'avant la faute, où la liberté s'angoisse de rien, de sa pure puissance de commencer, et l'angoisse morale, le sentiment de culpabilité qui n'est plus la condition du péché mais sa conséquence. Avec la faute, une angoisse nouvelle est entrée dans le monde, dont l'objet "est maintenant une chose déterminée (...) puisque la différence entre le bien et le mal est posée *in concreto*, ce qui ôte à l'angoisse son ambiguïté"[41]. Lorsque Kant évoque l'angoisse indissociable du respect pour la Loi, "mélancolie", "terreur" ou "sombre exaltation de l'angoisse (*Angst*)", il ne parvient pas à distinguer ses deux visages, l'angoisse du Bien et l'angoisse du Rien, l'angoisse psychologique et morale devant la faute — réellement commise ou imaginaire — et l'angoisse originaire qui précède toute faute, angoisse éthique pure devant la Loi. Que la Loi comme telle puisse être source d'angoisse, non parce qu'elle accuse et condamne, mais parce qu'elle "ne veut rien", Kant ne peut l'envisager. C'était précisément cette angoisse du vide, cette "mélancolie" devant le flux héraclitéen des apparences, le jeu incertain et instable des sentiments et des formes, que la révélation initiale de la "Loi" lui avait permis d'apaiser. Il lui avait fallu de nombreuses années pour que ce "point d'appui" inébranlable lui apparaisse lui aussi en mauvaise posture, suspendu dans le vide et même alors l'évidence immédiate de la révélation vient recouvrir son énigme, l'empêche de saisir, derrière l'angoisse de la faute, l'angoisse originaire de la Loi.

Ce qui le rend sourd et aveugle à cette autre angoisse, cet autre paradoxe que Kierkegaard découvre dans l'histoire d'Abraham. "Paradoxe inaccessible à la pensée", qui redouble et aggrave le paradoxe d'Adam: c'est encore d'un appel insensé que surgit l'an-

40. id. p. 66.
41. id. p. 115.

goisse. Non du vide de sens, de l'*Unsinn*, mais cette fois de *Widersinn*, de "l'absurde": D'un commandement du Bien (de Dieu) qui ordonne le mal, "paradoxe inouï de la foi, capable de faire d'un crime un acte saint et agréable à Dieu". Ce n'est pas seulement le meurtre de son fils que Dieu exige d'Abraham, car Isaac est "l'enfant de la Promesse", l'unique garant de l'Alliance et du don de la Loi. En ordonnant l'holocauste, en reniant l'Election qui l'érigeait en Dieu — "tu seras Mon peuple, et Je serai ton Dieu" —, le Dieu d'Abraham renie cette Promesse *qu'Il est*, se renie lui-même comme Dieu. Le paradoxe d'Abraham présente donc la même structure formelle que le paradoxe d'Adam, énonce la même contradiction performative, la même *folie de la Loi*: à chaque fois, la Loi prescrit de transgresser la Loi, ne parvient à faire loi qu'en s'auto-détruisant comme Loi. Cette folie, pour Kierkegaard, ne saurait être le fait de la Loi éthique, mais seulement de la Foi. Il considère en effet la sphère de l'éthique — englobant la "morale kantienne" comme la *Sittlichkeit* hégélienne — comme le règne du *général*, d'une Loi universelle, "applicable à chacun", "à chaque instant", qui condamne comme mauvaise toute revendication par l'individu de son individualité[42]: de ce point de vue, Abraham n'est qu'un vulgaire criminel, et quiconque tenterait d'universaliser la maxime de son action ou simplement d'imiter son exemple ne serait lui-même qu'un meurtrier ou un fou. Mais Abraham est *aussi* Abraham, le chevalier de la Foi, et "c'est en cette contradiction que réside l'angoisse (...) sans laquelle Abraham n'est pas l'homme qu'il est".[43] L'acceptation du paradoxe demande donc de passer dans une autre sphère, où l'Individu est "placé au-dessus du général": de faire "dans l'épouvante" le saut de l'éthique au religieux.

Le paradoxe de la Foi naît d'un appel singulier, exigeant d'un individu singulier un acte contraire à toutes les lois, impossible à ériger en loi universelle. C'est la même affirmation de la singularité, d'une ouverture "qui t'était destinée à toi seul", avec la même menace d'un folie possible de l'Appel, que nous avions repérées dans l'apologue de Kafka. "Johannes de Silentio" et l'auteur de *Procès* ont en commun de s'opposer à Kant, à une certaine doxa kantienne définissant la Loi comme loi d'universalité, au nom d'un *impératif singulier*. A la différence de Kafka, le penseur religieux se refuse pourtant à désigner cet impératif comme celui de la Loi: ce

---

42. Kierkegaard, *Crainte et tremblement*, Aubier, 1984, p. 82-83.
43. id. p. 37.

qui, pour Abraham, fait loi et le livre à l'angoisse lui proviendrait d'une obligation au-delà de toute loi. Au moment où il tente de dépasser sa sphère, Kierkegaard entérine ainsi le principal préjugé de la "morale kantienne", l'assimilation de la Loi à la "forme d'une législation universelle", la certitude que l'impératif de la Loi ne prescrit que d'universaliser les maximes, ne peut prescrire que des actions universalisables et universellement communicables; que la Loi ne saurait donc se diviser ou s'opposer à elle-même, exiger une action contraire à "la Loi", qu'elle puisse commander le mal. Le nom d'Abraham indique ce point-limite de l'Impossible, cet excès de l'Appel sur la "loi d'universalité", voire cet excès de la Loi sur elle-même. Ce que explique l'horrreur qui saisit les tenants de l'éthique à la seule évocation de ce nom. *Medusenkopf*, "tête de Méduse", c'est le cri qu'arrache au jeune Hegel cette figure emblématique de l'abjection juive. Effroi partagé par Kant, qui revient à trois reprises sur le cas d'Abraham, pour le désavouer comme un exemple d'extrême *Schwärmerei*. Là où Hegel croira saisir *ce qu'est* la Loi, la vérité de la Loi judéo-kantienne en son arbitraire et sa folle cruauté, Kant croit repérer ce qu'elle *n'est pas*, ce qu'elle ne doit pas être. Car il doit y avoir un critère, un "signe négatif" permettant de distinguer l'authentique Appel de ses simulacres, sans quoi la raison serait "comme paralysée".[44] L'Idée de "Dieu" n'étant qu'une personnification de la Loi, un commandement divin qui ne serait pas universalisable ne saurait provenir de "Dieu", c'est-à-dire de la Loi, et "si ce qui lui est proposé (à l'homme) par l'intermédiaire de cette voix est contraire à la Loi morale, le phénomène peut bien lui sembler aussi majestueux que possible (...): il lui faut pourtant la tenir pour une illusion".[45] De là ce curieux dialogue avec Dieu imaginé par Kant, comme s'il fallait à tout prix recouvrir le silence d'Abraham et l'angoisse: "à cette prétendue voix divine, Abraham aurait dû répondre: 'Que je ne doive pas tuer mon bon fils, c'est parfaitement sûr (...) quand bien même cette voix tomberait, retentissante, du ciel (visible)"...[46]. Plus évidente que l'évidence sensible de l'appel est la certitude rationnelle de l'universalité de la Loi.

Soumission de l'Appel, de "Dieu", de la Loi elle-même à la forme logique de l'universalité. Telle est la parade de Kant, sa défense affolée contre une possible folie de la Loi, contre la "contradiction

44. *Religion*, 3, p. 108. -cf. aussi p. 225.
45. *Le conflit des facultés*, 3, p. 871-872.
46. id. p. 872 note.

absolue" qui constitue le paradoxe de la Foi. De ce paradoxe, il s'angoisse, se scandalise: l'éthique kantienne, l'ensemble de la sphère éthique est ce cri de scandale, ce recul angoissé devant l'ouverture d'un rapport au tout-Autre, à un "différent absolu et sans nul indice distinctif"[47], sans aucun Signe qui saurait faire la différence "entre le dieu et le pire des imposteurs", entre l'appel d'Abraham et le délire d'un fou. Cette "différence que ne se laisse pas fixer", que la raison ne peut que méconnaître, il nous faudrait la penser, au-delà du paradoxe d'Abraham, comme un retrait infini du dieu *dans* sa donation, une *kénose* où l'amant se dépouille de sa gloire, s'abaisse au point de "ne plus rien laisser soupçonner" de sa divinité, ce qui est le paradoxe absolu, l'insondable de l'amour.[48] La sphère de l'éthique trouve là sa limite, en cet appel insensé qui lui arrive du Dehors et de l'Autre, qui l'investit dans l'instant sans qu'elle puisse le comprendre: "le scandale reste donc en-dehors du paradoxe" — "tout ce qu'il dit du paradoxe, c'est de ce dernier qu'il le tient, quoique, profitant d'une illusion acoustique, il prétende l'avoir découvert lui-même" — "car, comme la vérité, le paradoxe aussi est *index sui et falsi* et le scandale, hors d'état de se comprendre lui-même, est compris du paradoxe"[49]. Compris: enveloppé, circonscrit comme "sphère de passage" dont "l'exigence négative infinie" fait faillite[50], mais aussi mis à nu, démasqué comme "illusion acoustique", simple déni, résistance de raison à l'excès du tout-Autre, et ainsi *destitué*. "Suspension" de la Loi qu'il ne faut surtout pas confondre avec une *Aufhebung* dialectique: autant que celle de Kant, l' "éthique" de Hegel participe d'un même aveuglement, appartient elle aussi aux "trois classes de sophistes" de la modernité qui esquivent le Saut, méconnaissent et altèrent le paradoxe du religieux.[51] Sous ce terme d'*éthique*, c'est la modernité toute entière, c'est toute la philosophie occidentale depuis Socrate qui se voit ici révoquée. La délimitation des trois sphères d'existence jouerait le même rôle dans la pensée de Kierkegaard que la doctrine des trois ordres chez Pascal: d'ouvrir l'horizon où la métaphysique pourrait être laissée à elle-même, traversée et désertée sans destruc-

---

47. Kierkegaard, *Riens philosophiques*, 1948 rééd. 1969, p. 105-108.
48. id. p. 70-85.
49. id. p. 105-108.
50. Kierkegaard, *Etapes sur le chemin de la vie*, Gallimard, 1948, p. 383-384. Sur la conception kierkegaardienne du 'stade éthique', cf. A. Clair, *Pseudonymie et paradoxe*, Vrin, 1976, p. 265-287.
51. id. p. 393-394.

tion, "comprise" comme résistance aveugle au Transcendant qui la "comprend" et l'excède.[52]

Tel est l'enjeu du paradoxe d'Abraham: conduire l'éthique, comme sphère d'existence et site de la pensée, jusqu'au Saut où elle va à sa perte. Pourtant, loin de s'y perdre sans retour, elle trouve dans sa destitution la chance d'une reprise, d'une répétition. On sait que Kierkegaard envisage la possibilité d'une "seconde éthique", d'une phase éthico-religieuse de l'éthique, où celle-ci échapperait à la domination de l'Universel, à l'immanence du Sujet Autonome, pour accueillir le paradoxe absolu. De cette "autre éthique", Kant se serait-il déjà approché? Même s'il est de nature très différente, s'il n'a rien à voir avec une révélation religieuse, c'est malgré tout d'un paradoxe que s'initie l'exposition kantienne de la Loi. En cet impératif qui commande une soumission inconditionnée à la Loi sans nous dire ce que la Loi commande, nous reconnaissions le paradoxe d'Adam décrit par le Vigile de Copenhague. Et si la Loi n'est plus la loi du Bien, si elle s'ex-pose endeçà du bien et du mal, il peut se faire qu'une telle Loi se présente, à l'encontre des valeurs et des normes du sens commun moral, en se dérobant à la prise du sujet qui croyait la comprendre, qu'elle lui apparaisse ainsi "hétéronome", "immorale", radicalement mauvaise, comme l'injonction folle d'une Loi hors-la-loi. Cela même qui nous saisit d'angoisse devant le paradoxe d'Abraham. A ce scandale, cette paralysie de la raison, Kant s'efforçait de trouver un remède: le "signe négatif" de l'universalisation, écartant comme illusoire et mauvaise toute prescription impossible à universaliser sans contradiction. Ce qui le condamne à recouvrir la singularité de l'Appel sous l'universalité de la Règle, à réduire la Loi éthique à une fonction logique de l'entendement. Or, rien ne prouve qu'une Loi pratique *pure*, qui ne se fonde sur aucun concept théorique, aucune règle logique, aucun Principe onto-logique, puisse être encore conçue comme loi d'universalité ou loi d'autonomie du Sujet: que ces détermination — "kantiennes", certes — ne fassent pas violence à l'essentielle indétermination de la Loi, à son exposition paradoxale qui la laisse sans point d'appui, suspendue dans le vide. Si rien ne détermine plus la Loi, ne la retient plus au bord de

---

52. cf. J.L. Marion, *Sur le prisme métaphysique de Descartes*, PUF, 1986, pp. 293-378 -notamment p. 377 sur la distinction entre la "destitution de la métaphysique" opérée par Pascal et la "déconstruction" heideggérienne-derridienne. Si l'analogie peut être soutenue, il faudrait dire que la référence à Kant et Hegel assure la même fonction chez Kierkegaard que la référence à Descartes chez Pascal: d'offrir une figure éminente de l'onto-théologie à sa destitution par la Charité ou la Foi.

son néant, tout repère vacille et, comme le pensait Hegel, la cruelle folie d'Abraham serait la vérité même de la Loi. C'est de son propre paradoxe que Kant s'angoisse et se scandalise: ce sont les ultimes conséquences de sa pensée de la Loi qu'il récuse comme *Schwärmerei* et illusion religieuse. En marquant la limite des morales de l'Universel et de l'Autonomie, la destitution kierkegaardienne n'atteindrait pas le foyer central de l'éthique kantienne, ne "suspendrait" pas la Loi éthique comme telle: elle permettrait au contraire, en révoquant ses représentations morales, de découvrir sa face la plus secrète, ce que Kant nomme parfois la "Loi des lois", le "noyau de la Loi".

Cette injonction singulière insensée, Kierkegaard refuse — comme s'il était victime lui aussi d'une sorte d'"illusion acoustique" — de la reconnaître comme celle de la Loi: non seulement parce qu'il accepte la détermination kantienne de la Loi par la forme logique de l'universalité, mais aussi parce qu'il se plie au tout-puissant préjugé qui dénie à la Loi le pouvoir de faire-loi, d'être la source originaire de l'archi-prescription, pour la subordonner à une instance plus haute, au-delà de toute loi. Dès lors, poussé à sa pointe extrême, le paradoxe se dénoue: pour le penseur religieux, le commandement absurde qui transit d'angoisse Abraham n'est plus l'impératif de la Loi, mais l'appel d'un Dieu de bonté et d'amour qui ne saurait vouloir le mal, qui se devait de restituer à Abraham ce fils dont il exigeait le sacrifice. "Double mouvement" d'une reprise où Abraham "s'est infiniment résigné à tout, pour tout ressaisir en vertu de l'absurde".[53] Cela, Abraham ne le savait pas, tandis qu'il gravissait la montagne de Moria et s'apprêtait à l'holocauste, sinon sa résignation infinie et sa foi n'auraient été que calcul, ruse dialectique. Mais *nous* le savons, nous sommes au fait de l'heureux dénouement. "Johannes de Silentio" lui-même, qui met en scène le paradoxe, ne s'identifie pas au Chevalier de la Foi, n'éprouve pas sa détresse; il réfléchit sur son cas à distance, depuis la certitude de la reprise et du salut. Car le penseur religieux est un penseur *chrétien*, pour qui le sacrifice d'Isaac préfigure la kénose du Christ et la gloire de la Résurrection.[54] N'est-ce pas, là encore, esquiver ou relever — d'une

---

53. Kierkegaard, *Crainte et tremblement*, p. 47, 57, etc. C'est là comme l'on sait, le motif central de *La répétition*.
54. "Voilà le rapport entre judaïsme et christianisme. Pour le christianisme, Isaac est réellement sacrifié -mais ensuite c'est l'éternité; dans le judaïsme, c'était seulement une épreuve; Abraham garde Isaac; mais alors tout demeure malgré tout essentiellement dans le cadre de cette vie", *Journal*, Gallimard, t.IV, p. 429.

"relève" non-dialectique… — l'insoutenable radicalité du paradoxe d'Abraham? Ce qui lève le paradoxe de la Loi, d'une loi qui apparaît *impliquée* dans le mal, est le paradoxe de l'Amour: du don surabondant et de la Grâce, par où la faute est rachetée et la Loi abolie. Aussi authentique soit-elle, aussi dénuée de calcul, la foi se présente ici à son tour comme une défense contre l'angoisse et le vertige du vide, incapable de supporter l'indétermination de l'Appel sans lui réassigner aussitôt une Origine transcendante et une destination.

C'est cette certitude consolante qui fait défaut à une éthique radicale, exposée à soutenir jusqu'au bout l'énigme de la Loi — d'une loi qui n'est plus celle d'un Dieu de bonté — sans aucun critère, aucun signe d'élection qui saurait authentifier l'orgine de l'Appel (est-ce vraiment de la Loi qu'il provient?), sa destination (est-ce bien à moi qu'il est adressé?) ou son sens (ai-je compris ce qu'il m'ordonne?). Impossible, donc, d'esquiver la rigueur de la Question par le saut dans la foi, où tout désespoir a disparu[55]. Aucun saut n'est possible, aucun dépassement de la Loi vers une instance plus originaire ou un principe plus haut — ni par relève, ni par déconstruction, ni par destitution — s'il n'est rien qui donne loi au-delà de la Loi. Rien d'autre que la Loi, même lorsqu'elle semble appeler à transgresser toute loi, à s'anéantir elle-même comme Loi. Rien que la Loi, qui n'est plus la loi d'un Autre, ni celle de Dieu, ni celle du Sujet, voire même de l'Être, qui n'est loi de rien d'autre qu'elle-même, qui est Loi de Rien, Loi de la Loi. Kant avait beau jeu d'ironiser sur les "principes vagues" des morales du Bien, qui se réduiraient à cette tautologie qu'"il est bien de faire ce qui est bien". En renversant le rapport de Bien et de la Loi, son éthique paradoxale n'aboutit elle aussi qu'à une pure tautologie: c'est la Loi de faire ce qu'ordonne la Loi. Plus "vague" encore, puisqu'elle supprime le dernier critère (le bonheur sensible) que préservaient les morales traditionnelles: plus démunie, plus dépourvue de repères que l'empirisme pratique, plus "nihiliste" que ce nihilisme éthique qu'elle devait surmonter… De ce que la Loi n'est rien, rien de déterminé ni rien d'étant, de ce qu'elle n'"est" peut-être *en rien*, le nihilisme conclut qu'il n'y a pas de Loi. Comment lui donner tort? Que subsiste-t-il ici de la Loi, sinon un simple mot, un "titre vide sans concept", le néant absolu d'un *Unding*: si ex-posée qu'elle se dé-pose et se perd dans le néant?

55. Sur la foi comme "état d'un moi où le désespoir est entièrement absent", cf. la conclusion de *La maladie mortelle (Traité du désespoir)* Gallimard, 1949, rééd. 1973, p. 248.

Le paradoxe de la Critique inaugure ainsi une *éthique négative* (au sens où l'on parle de "théologie négative"), privée de la consolation que dispensaient l'assurance du Bien et la promesse de la Foi. On se souvient de la question soulevée par la *Religion*: lorsqu'il "ne nous reste que la désolation (*Trostlosigkeit*)", comment "veiller à ce que cette désolation ne dégénère pas en un sauvage désespoir"? Que reste-t-il de la Loi au terme de son ex-position qui puisse sauver du désespoir? Rien sinon la Loi elle-même, le don de la Loi. Car la Loi se donne, se révèle à travers son exposition: celle-ci ne se réduit pas à une totale dé-position, à cet évidement, cet anéantissement de toute détermination dans la nuit du nihilisme, qui n'est que le "deuxième pas" de l'éthique, son *vernichtende Rückgang*, nécessaire pour dissiper les illusions de Bien, pour rabattre la prétention des Principes à faire loi à la place de la Loi. A l'extrême limite de la désolation, un retournement doit être possible, l'amorce d'un Passage, d'un "troisième pas", où la Loi se pose, se détermine *dans* son ex-position indéterminée, où le Rien de la Loi s'inverse en affirmation. Traversée de l'Apparence, dépassement du nihilisme dont nous savons qu'ils demandent de soutenir jusqu'au bout l'épreuve du néant. Toute la difficulté consiste alors à situer la Limite ou le point de non-retour, la césure de la révolution éthique. A repérer *jusqu'à quel point* il faut poursuivre l'annihilation: trop radicale, l'ex-position de la Loi la dé-poserait, la ferait sombrer sans retour dans l'abîme du non-sens; insuffisamment radicale, elle resterait un nihilisme 'incomplet', prisonnier des déterminations dogmatiques qu'il devait anéantir, et la Loi retomberait sous l'emprise d'un Principe du Bien. La révolution copernicienne de l'éthique suppose ainsi une double opération, de réduction ou de suspension de toute pré-assignation de la Loi aux Principes, d'in-détermination de ses déterminations onto-logiques et morales — mais aussi de détermination *de* cette indétermination, de réassignation d'une prescription impérative à partir de la Loi. Double geste de déconstruction-reconstruction, analogue à ce que Kierkegaard pointait dans le paradoxe d'Abraham comme un "double-mouvement", comme dessaisie infinie suivie d'une reprise où "tout est ressaisi en vertu de l'absurde". La révélation de la Loi nous commande elle aussi de traverser un point d'angoisse ou d'horreur, où vacille la certitude du Bien, où l'impératif de la Loi se présente comme Appel insensé, étranger aux normes et aux "lois" — pour découvrir sous la folie de l'Appel la vérité et le don de la Loi, la promesse d'une césure, d'un retournement qui délivre: de ce "choix nouveau du caractère intelligible" qui serait "comme une nouvelle naissance".

7. Towards an Ethics of 'Auseinandersetzung'

RODOLPHE GASCHÉ

In a process now all too predictable, critical and theoretical concepts such as 'critical theory,' or 'deconstruction,' are abandoned, long before their full potential has even begun to be tapped, in favor of seemingly new and more promising terms. *Auseinandersetzung* is one such notion now beginning to make its appearance in texts of literary and cultural criticism. As opposed to the alleged abstraction of critical theory and the obscurantism of deconstruction, *Auseinandersetzung* promises a more intimate and more engaged, if not more visceral relation to texts, works, or thoughts. In *Auseinandersetzung*, the critic comes face to face in a direct confrontation with the thought of an Other. Out of the ensuing clash of ideas, real and concrete issues come to word, while the debate itself mobilizes energies that themselves testify to the urgency and seriousness of the problems in question. Moreover, *Auseinandersetzung*, by virtue of its greater intimacy and engagement with texts or ideas, takes shape as a relation in which critical vigilance, paired with truly concrete concerns, guards against dogmatic positions and conclusions. In confrontation as *Auseinandersetzung*, opponents meet stripped of ideological masquerade. It is a debate that suggests honesty, responsibility, and a shared commitment to things that truly matter.

It is no secret that the term *Auseinandersetzung* is lifted from Heidegger. Returning to what this term implies and seeks to achieve in its original context, the following discussion of *Auseinandersetzung* intends not only to confront its current use with its strict definition, but also to set conditions for fruitfully putting this term to work. Indeed, recourse to *Auseinandersetzung* either as a refuge from concepts that have come under attack, or from unresolved difficulties adhering to these concepts, may serve to recontextualize and clarify the very nature of criticism and deconstruction. There is at least a chance that a sustained and informed confrontation with the Heideggerean concept in question could lead to a productive re-evaluation of the critical and deconstructive 'relation.' This debate, however, may show *Auseinandersetzung* to be more than a simple alternative to the relations in question. Located in an array of

121

positions from which to choose, *Auseinandersetzung* may be a privileged vantage point from which insight into the limits, promises, and achievements of critique and deconstruction may be gained. It is in view of such critical re-evaluation that the subsequent developments have been undertaken.

Auseinandersetzung is a term that, in the mid-thirties, abruptly appears in Heidegger's work, in particular, in his lectures on Nietzsche and in *An Introduction to Metaphysics*. From the outset, this word, devoid of any anterior philosophical meaning, indicating, in addition to its juridical meaning of partition, only the explication of something, a debate or dispute, functions as a terminus technicus. The Nietzsche lectures advance the term in question as *the* philosophical and hermeneutic mode of relating to the subject matter of a philosopher's thought. It serves to conceptualize the relation to that which, in a thinker's thought, resists access by its very nature, to any extraneous approach, namely, that which cannot "be determined anywhere else than from within itself." *Auseinandersetzung* is the exclusive relation to that which, in a thinker's thought, is "true philosophy,"[1] that is, to what in his thought obeys the law of thinking, thinking's own law. As such, it dictates a bracketting of anything that in thinking is of heteronomous origin, anything that would reveal concerns extrinsic to those of thinking itself.

In the "Author's Forward to all Volumes," Heidegger notes that the object of *Auseinandersetzung*, for which these lectures are to pave the way, is to be *the matter* (*die Sache*) of Nietzsche's thought. *Die Sache* is *der Streitfall*, Heidegger continues, showing that he has in mind the original germanic meaning of *die Sache* as legal matter, legal case, a case taken to court. *Auseinandersetzung* thus understands that which, in the thinking of a philosopher, is determined only from within itself, as a point in question, a case or conflict under dispute. More precisely, "the matter, the point in question, is in itself a confrontation (*Auseinandersetzung*)."[2] The philosophically autonomous core of a thinker's thought is *Auseinandersetzung* not only also because it must be construed or established through the proceedings of the debate, but also because having in itself the structure of debate, *the matter* itself invites the confrontational relation in which *the matter* is to be determined as

1. Martin Heidegger, *Nietzsche*, Vol. I: *The Will to Power as Art*; Vol. II: *The Eternal Recurrence of the Same*, trans. D.F. Krell (San Francisco: Harper, 1991).
2. p. XXXIX.

what it is. Being responsive to such a *matter* of thinking is neither talking *about* it, nor judging it *from outside*, but rather entering into a relation of *Auseinandersetzung* with it. Thinking, insofar as it is determined only from within itself, invites only one mode of responsible response, namely, one of *Auseinandersetzung* with the case in dispute.

The reason that Heidegger proposes in the first pages of "The Will to Power as Art" for the fact that such an *Auseinandersetzung* with Nietzsche's thought has not yet begun, that even its prerequisites are still to be established, reveals a decisive structural feature without which any debate with that which has the law in itself cannot take place. He writes: "Nietzsche's thought and speech are still too contemporary for us. He and we have not yet been sufficiently separated (*auseinandergesetzt*) in history; we lack the distance (*Abstand*) necessary for a sound appreciation of the thinker's strength."[3] From this we see that any debate of the kind in question requires a setting-apart, a distance, across which the thinker's strength may come into view and justice may be done to his specific achievements. As long as Nietzsche remains caught up in present day concerns, no glimpse of him as a true philosopher can be had. But the distance implicit to all *Auseinandersetzung* must also be seen as a function of the definition of *the matter* of thinking itself, i.e., as that which is determined solely from within itself. If what matters in thinking is thinking free from all heteronomy, then thinking itself is constitutive of the distance which allows any appreciating *Auseinandersetzung* to get off the ground. While confrontation assures that a thinker's thought be recognized in its true strength, such strong thought itself engenders the distance required to appreciate it. *Auseinandersetzung* debates that which in thinking is determined by itself alone, but it does so from a respectful distance, allowing such thought to unfold from itself and in itself.

Before further discussion of the complex structural features of the notion of *Auseinandersetzung* now beginning to emerge, let me first open the dictionaries. *Auseinander*, Grimm's *Deutsches Wörterbuch* tells us, is the result of drawing together in one word what remains separate in living speech while at the same time inverting the natural order of the words, that is, putting the preposition *aus* in *ein aus dem andern* ahead of the other words. This operation engenders what Grimm calls a hardened and motionless linguistic mass. If moreover, *auseinander* is connected to verbs implying an

3. p. 4.

idea of separation or dissection, "a variety of the most ponderous compounds arise."[4] *Auseinandersetzung* is one of them. This linguistic monster solidifies in one ponderous compound, what, by nature is discrete, distinct, and separate, and which can only be drawn together by neutralizing the sense of separation inherent to both *ein aus dem anderen* and *setzen*. In *Trübner's Deutsches Wörterbuch*, Coetze prefaces his presentation of the historical evolution of the meaning of the term by noting that it is a very weak verb in New High German and has no ground (*nirgends Boden hat*) in any of the dialects. According to Coetze's dictionary, the legal meaning of *auseinandersetzen*, referring to the partition of the common property of parties who have shared ownership, is historically primary. The verb later acquired the more general meaning of a "clarification of a legal matter, of awarding to each litigant what is properly his or her own," but was subsequently transposed by representatives of the Enlightenment, Johann Christian Gottsched, for instance, to the realm of literary representation where it acquires the meaning of "presenting in such a manner that all viewpoints are given due attention (*zu ihrem Recht kommen*)." The contemporary use of the word in the sense of explaining, examining, presenting, or laying out, Coetze adds, derives from this meaning of *auseinandersetzen*.[5] Finally, in *Handwörterbuch der deutschen Sprache*, from a purely semantic account of the term, Heyse determines that *auseinander* signifies "a development (*Entstehen*), a succession or consequence (*Folge*), of one thing from another, or a distancing (*Entfernung*) of one thing from another. Consequently, *auseinandersetzen properly* means, to set apart from one another; *improperly*, to elucidate or explain a representation to some one by dissolving it into its components; *sich über etwas auseinandersetzen*, is to annul or dissolve the community with others regarding a matter, to reach a settlement about such a matter (a heritage, for instance)." He concludes saying that *die Auseinandersetzung* can be taken in *all* the meanings of the verb.[6]

Yet, how are we to understand Heidegger's use of the term? Speaking of the necessity of an *Auseinandersetzung* with Nietzsche in the appendices to his 1941-42 lectures on "Nietzsche's Metaphysics," Heidegger writes: "We take the word *Auseinanderset-*

4. Jacob and Wilhelm Grimm, *Deutsches Wörterbuch* (Leipzig: Hirzel, 1854).
5. *Trübner's Deutsches Wörterbuch*, ed. Alfred Coetze (Berlin: de Gruyter, 1939).
6. J.C.A. Heyse, *Handwörterbuch der deutschen Sprache* (1833) (Hildesheim: Olms, 1968).

zung literally. We seek to posit his and our thought apart from and into a relation of opposition to one another (*ausser einander und in das Gegeneinander über zu setzen*); but in a thinking, and not in a comparative mode."[7] Heidegger's literal understanding of the term stresses the *separation* of the two kinds of thoughts, the *distance* thus created between them, as well as the relation of *adverseness* into which they come to stand, or rather, into which they are *set*, or posited. Consequently, the common meaning of *Auseinandersetzung* as debate and confrontation, explanation and exposition, ought not to incur on its philosophical meaning. Still, the literal (*wörtlich*) meaning of the term is not exhausted by the traits of separation, distance, adverseness, and furthermore, Heidegger makes it such a compound of traits that it literally ceases to be a word.

As shall become increasingly clear, Heidegger's valorization of the word derives from both the history *and* semantics of *Auseinandersetzung*. As a philosophical term, *Auseinandersetzung* is a term not to be found in the dictionaries, for it combines the semantically primary meaning of setting apart, or distancing, with the historically primary meaning of awarding each party what is properly its own. In other words, *Auseinandersetzung* is a formation that draws together in one intimate linguistic whole, meanings thoroughly alien to one another. The word, if it still is one, allows semantically and historically irreducible senses of *auseinandersetzen* to dwell together. Moreover, the different ways Heidegger writes the word — *Auseinandersetzung*, *Aus-einandersetzung*, *Aus-einander-set-zung* — suggest a complex synthesis in which multiple and different modes of separation and belonging-together cohabit. Finally it also means struggle, conflict, and is thus, as we shall see, a translation of *polemos*.

Yet, linguistic condensation is not the sole means by which Heidegger forges this new philosophical concept. He furthermore differentiates *Auseinandersetzung* from critique by determining it as genuine or authentic critique. He writes: "Confrontation (*Auseinandersetzung*) is genuine criticism. It is the supreme way, the only way, to a true estimation of a thinker. In confrontation we undertake to reflect on his thinking (*seinem Denken nachzudenken*) and to trace it in its effective force, not in its weaknesses. To what

---

7. Martin Heidegger, 1.*Nietzsches Metaphysik*. 2.*Einleitung in die Philosophie. Denken und Dichten*, *Gesamtausgabe*, Vol., 50 (Frankfurt am Main: Klostermann, 1990), 84.

purpose? In order that through the confrontation we ourselves may become free for the supreme exertion of thinking."[8]

As genuine critique, confrontation is not negative. In *Die Frage nach dem Ding*, he remarks that the common meaning of critique is "to find fault with, to check mistakes, to bring out deficiencies, and subsequently to reject something."[9] In the appendices to the original lectures on "The Will to Power as Art," (written between 1936-37, and published in Vol. 43 of the *Gesamtausgabe*) Heidegger is clear about this. We read: "*Auseinandersetzung ‡ Bemängelung*." Nor does it manifest itself as a polemic. But confrontation as genuine critique must also be distinguished from the meaning of critique that emerges in the second half of the 18th Century, particularly in the context of reflections on art and aesthetics, where it signifies "fixing standards, rules, where it means legislation, that is, an emphasis of the universal over the particular."[10] Finally, Heidegger's genuine critique has nothing in common with critique in the Kantian sense. From Heidegger's developments with respect to Kant's use of the term in *Die Frage nach dem Ding*, we can conclude that *Auseinandersetzung* is not identical with a systematic mapping, based on the model of intelligibility particular to modern mathematics, of the powers of pure reason. It is not the method by which reason comes to know itself, and through which it achieves its most intimate rationality.

What then is genuine critique? It is critique in the originary sense, Heidegger holds in *Die Frage nach dem Ding*. The established root of critique is *krinein*, commonly translated as 'to separate,' 'put asunder,' 'distinguish,' 'decide,' etc. In conformity with this originary meaning of the word *krinein*, concepts of criticism ranging from the common notion of criticism as estimation to its dialectical form based on determined negation, have consistently articulated a faith in the possibility of pure, if not absolute distinction. The critical operation thrives on the dream of a pure difference guaranteeing that the separated suffers no contamination by that from which it is cut off, and allowing the determination of essence to proceed in a realm free of all intrusions and within which decision is clear and without ambiguity. This is the philosophical meaning and thrust of

---

8. Heidegger, *Nietzsche*, pp. 4-5.
9. Martin Heidegger, *Die Frage nach dem Ding. Zu Kants Lehre von den transzendentalen Grundsätzen* (Tubingen: Niemeyer, 1975), 93.
10. Martin Heidegger, *Nietzsche: Der Wille zur Macht als Kunst, Gesamtausgabe*, Vol. 43 (Frankfurt am Main: Klostermann, 1985), 277 and 279.

critique established by the tradition out of the original meaning of *krinein*. But is it in this sense that we are to understand *Auseinandersetzung*? In *Die Frage nach dem Ding*, Heidegger too makes recourse to the original Greek word *krinein*. Yet, he translates it as follows: "'sondern,' 'absondern,' und so 'das Besondere herausheben,'" in English: to separate, to isolate, and *to thus bring out the particular*. From the beginning, Heidegger's translation subordinates separation to the end of bringing out the particular. However, before drawing out the consequences entailed by this translation for an understanding of 'confrontation,' we need to read in full this passage wherein Heidegger establishes the originary meaning of critique:

"Critique" comes from the Greek *krinein*; this means: 'to separate,' 'to isolate' and thus to 'bring out the particular.' Such contrasting (*Abheben*) against other (*gegen anderes*) arises from a lifting (*Hinaufheben*) to a new standing. The meaning of the word "critique" is not negative at all, on the contrary it means the most positive of the positive, namely the positing of that which in all positing (*Setzung*) must be presupposed (*im voraus angesetzt*) as what determines and decides. Critique is decision in such a positing sense. Only afterwards — since critique is separating and emphasis of the particular, the uncommon and at the same time of what gives the measure (*des Massgebenden*) — critique also becomes rejection of the common and the inappropriate.[11]

Critique in a genuine sense is thus neither negative nor determined by the goal of establishing an invulnerable limit. Rather than a severing of one thing from another in pure difference and free of all contamination, critique, in the authentic sense, serves to raise what is separated into its proper rank precisely by contrasting it to what it is separated from. Critique secures propriety and property as it locates its possibility in the other. Critique allows particularity to arise on both sides of the divide, indeed, it is the very condition through which something can come into its most proper own. In this sense critique is the same as *Auseinandersetzung*. In the operation of setting apart by setting against, the particular is posited as such for the first time. Genuine critique is thus what is most positive, since the very possibility of innermost propriety, which, however, is only what it is against what is on the other side of the divide, and vice versa, rests on the decision that it brings about.

11. Martin Heidegger, *An Introduction to Metaphysics*, trans. R. Manheim (New Haven: Yale University Press, 1959), 63.

Auseinandersetzung understood this way, is thus as much charac-terized by the setting apart as by the intimate interrelation of what occupies the respective sides of the division.

Before I analyze this complex economy of *Auseinandersetzung* occurring in one thinker's dialogue (*Zwiegespräch*) with the subject matter of another thinker's true philosophy — Nietzsche, in this case — it may be appropriate to recall that for Heidegger, in *An Introduction to Metaphysics*, *Auseinandersetzung* translates *pole-mos*. In the following, it will indeed be necessary, to demarcate *Auseinandersetzung* as *polemos* from the confrontation that charac-terizes the genuine dialogue of philosophies. *Polemos* is, of course, not just any war, struggle, or conflict, nor is it war, struggle, or conflict in general. It is also distinct from "mere polemics ... the machinations and intrigues of man within the realm of the given."[12] Rather, *polemos* — the reference, obviously, is to fragment 53 of Heraclitus — names "the original struggle, for it gives rise to the contenders as such; it is not a mere assault on something already there."[13] The *polemos* of fragment 53, Heidegger writes, "is a con-flict that prevailed prior to everything divine and human, not a war in the human sense. This conflict, as Heraclitus thought it, first caused the realm of being to separate into opposites (*lässt im Gege-neinander das Wesende allererst auseindertreten*); it first gave rise to position, order, and rank. In such separation (*Auseinandertreten*), cleavages, intervals, distances, and joints opened. In the conflict (*Auseinandersetzung*) a world comes into being."[14] In other words, *polemos*, seen not as "mere quarreling and wrangling but the con-flict of the conflicting (*der Streit des Streitbaren*), that sets the essential and the nonessential, the high and the low, in their limits and that makes them manifest,"[15] shows *Auseinandersetzung*, not only to be a separation that enables the particular to be what it is in contrast to what it is set against, but a unification as well. Heidegger remarks: "Conflict (*Auseinandersetzung*) does not split, much less destroy unity. It constitutes unity, it is a binding-together, *logos*. *Polemos* and *logos* are the same."[16] *Polemos* binds together in that it gathers in an intimate bond what stands in a relation of the highest antagonism. In this sense, *polemos* is the same as *Geist*, spirit, of

12. Martin Heidegger, *An Introduction to Metaphysics*, trans. R. Manheim (New Haven: Yale University Press, 1959), 63.
13. p. 62.
14. p. 62.
15. pp. 113-14.
16. p. 62.

which Heidegger writes in *Erläuterungen zu Hölderlins Dichtung*: "Spirit reigns as the sober but audacious *Aus-einandersetzung* which institutes everything present into the clearly distinct boundaries and arrangements of the present's presencing. Such *Auseinandersetzen* is essential thinking. The 'Spirit's' ownmost proper are the thoughts. Through them everything, because it is separated (*auseinandergesetzt*), belongs together. Spirit is unifying unity. This unity lets the being-together of everything real appear in its gathering."[17] Heidegger's comments in the appendices to Vol. 4 of the *Gesamtausgabe*, as to what he identifies as Hölderlinean guiding words — *Alles ist innig* — reveal intimacy (*Innigkeit*) as indeed the very criterion for what is in a mode of *Auseinandersetzung*. Heidegger remarks: "*Alles ist innig*. This means: One is appropriated into the Other (*Eines ist in das Andere vereignet*), yet in such a way that in this appropriation it remains in its own (*in seinem Eigenen bleibt*). More precisely, through this appropriation into the Other it acquires its ownness to begin with: gods and men, earth and sky. Intimacy does not signify a fusion and dissolution of differences. Intimacy names the belonging-together of what is alien to one another, the happening of *Befremdung* [of being taken (aback) by the Other, or alien] ..."[18] Setting apart is thus the condition under which *Befremdung* can occur, that is, a being-affected by the Other through which selfhood is granted to self. The being-appropriated into Other, by which One, or self, is always already disappropriated, is at the same time the very relation in which One, or self, acquires, through the Other, selfhood and Oneness. The proper and the Other here stand in a relation of mutual implication and disimplication. In *Auseinandersetzung* as *polemos* — and as *logos*, which is the same thing — a harmonious ringing takes place in which there is no priority, neither of the One nor of the Other. Indeed, One and the Other both presuppose *das Walten der Befremdung*.

Everything we still shall see shows *Auseinandersetzung* as genuine critique, as the 'method' of the dialogue between philo-

17. Martin Heidegger, *Erläuterungen zu Hölderlins Dichtung*, *Gesamtausgabe*, Vol. 4 (Frankfurt am Main: Klostermann, 1981), 60.
18. p. 196. In Heidegger's analysis in "Language" of Trakl's "A Winter Evening," intimacy becomes determined as the very middle from which the intimate "divides itself cleanly and remains separated." Intimacy here names the middle from which the extremes are held apart (*auseinander*) so that they are at one with each other (*zueinander einig*). Martin Heidegger, *Poetry, Language, Thought*, trans. A. Hofstadter (New York: Harper, 1971), 202-04.

sophies, to exhibit the same basic attitude as in the originary struggle, *polemos*. Still, differences obtain between *polemos* and genuine critique that prove significant for any evaluation of the ethics of *Auseinandersetzung*. If in the following I thus try to underline not only the parallels between the play of the proper and the Other in *polemos* and genuine critique, but also the differences, it is in order to circumscribe, with as much precision as possible, certain limits that haunt the dialogue between thinkers. Undoubtedly, *Auseinandersetzung* has a clear advantage over critique, for rather than putting separation to work as a means to exclude the Other, or non-proper, in *Auseinandersetzung*, separation, as the space from which *Befremdung* occurs, is the very condition by which not only justice is done to Other, but in which the constitution of propriety shows itself to be a function of the Other's (dis)appropriating address. Yet it seems that *Auseinandersetzung* is not identical to the harmonious interplay between the One and the Other, the harmony of differences in play characteristic to *polemos*. *Auseinandersetzung* is oriented. It follows a path and has a purpose. As the introductory pages to Heidegger's *Nietzsche* demonstrate, *Auseinandersetzung* with Nietzsche's thought seeks to determine to what extent the few thoughts that determine the whole of Nietzsche's thinking remain thought-worthy. Such evaluation, moreover, is not disinterested. If it is true that one must get on the way (*unterwegs*) to *die Sache* of Nietzsche's thinking, it is true too, that the debate with him — the *Auseinandersetzung* with the matter of Nietzsche the philosopher *comes from* somewhere and *goes somewhere*. Indeed, through confrontation with the Other, Heidegger's thought seeks to achieve an essential historicality for itself.[19]

Before addressing this question of *Auseinandersetzung's* orientation let us first see how as a struggle, a debate, or a confrontation, it adheres to the basic features of the original struggle of *polemos*. In the addendi to Vol. 43, Heidegger describes the *Zwiegespräch* between thinkers in the following way: "Only in *Auseinandersetzung* does creative interpretation become possible, an interpretation in which Nietzsche comes to stand with respect to himself into his strongest position (*auf sich selbst in seiner stärksten Stellung zum stehen kommt*)."[20] Only through *Auseinandersetzung* does Nietzsche, or the thought of any other great thinker, acquire a relation to itself which is, moreover, of the strongest kind. In

19. Heidegger, *Nietzsche*, p. XXXIX-XL.
20. Heidegger, *Nietzsche, Gesamtausgabe*, Vol. 43, pp. 275-76.

Beiträge, Heidegger notes that *"Aus-einandersetzung* with the great philosophies — as fundamental metaphysical positions within the history of the guiding question — must be structured in such a manner that each philosophy comes to stand essentially as a mountain among mountains, and thus brings to a stand what is most essential about it."[21] The confrontation in question allows the opponent to stand in what is greatest about him, to acquire his strongest properties. In addition, by reflecting on the opponent's thinking, on its effective force rather than on its weaknesses, he who confronts a thinker, becomes free as well "for the supreme exertion of thinking."[22] *Auseinandersetzung* is consequently a relation "in which the opponent is chosen, and in which we and he are brought into a position of confrontation, more precisely, into a struggle for the essential."[23] By being intended in a manner such that the opponent comes to stand in a relation of strength with respect to himself, and that he who confronts the opponent becomes thus capable of the supreme task of thinking, *Auseinandersetzung* virtually guarantees that rather than leading to antagonism, the struggle, free from extraneous concerns, will be solely for what is essential and deter-

21. Martin Heidegger, *Beiträge zur Philosophie, Gesamtausgabe,* Vol. 65 (Frankfurt am Main: Klostermann, 1989), 187.
22. Heidegger, *Nietzsche,* pp. 4-5. In the addendi to the lecture on "Nietzsche's Metaphysics," from 1941-42, as well as in the lecture "Introduction into Philosophy. Thinking and Poetry," from 1944-45, Heidegger conceives of *Auseinandersetzung* not only primarily as a confrontation with Nietzsche, but as well as a debate that secures "our thinking: that which is thought-worthy for us" (p. 84). He writes: *"Auseinandersetzen:"* Thinking confronts thinking (*Denken setzt sich mit dem Denken auseinander*). Only thus can one thinking encounter another. Only in this manner is there response (*Entgegnung*). In this manner alone, thinking frees itself from standing against one another in opposion (*aus dem Gegen der Gegnerschaft*) — into the belonging into the same." (p. 87). "In an *Auseinandersetzung* the thought that addresses us and our own thinking bring themselves into a relation of opposition. With this separation (*Auseinandertreten*) the distance perhaps occurs from which an appreciation matures of what constitutes one's own essentiality and the unattainable strength of the encountered thought. Genuine *Auseinandersetzung* does not track down weaknesses and mistakes, it does not criticize, rather it brings the historically encountered thinking before our thinking, and in the open of a decision which the encounter renders inevitable. Therefore we can meditate on the thought of Nietzsche, as well as on all other thinking, only through *Auseinandersetzung,* through which alone we are included into the fundamental feature (*Grundzug*) of historically encountered thought, in order to respond to it in a historical manner." (Martin Heidegger, *1. Nietzsches Metaphysik. 2. Einleitung in die Philosophie. Denken und Dichten.* (p. 98)
23. Heidegger, *Nietzsche, Gesamtausgabe,* Vol. 43, p. 276.

mined from within itself. Heidegger continues: "Such 'bringing the-opponent-into-position' requires the development of the most essential questions; the opponent must be unfolded from the innermost depth of his work to what is most extreme about him."[24] In short, an *Auseinandersetzung* begins only when the most essential questions are being raised, that is, when a confrontation with Nietzsche, for instance, "is at the same time conjoined to a confrontation in the realm of the grounding question of philosophy."[25] In other words, a confrontation requires not only that a thinker and his opponent come to stand in their strongest position with respect to themselves, but also that the struggle be over the most essential, that is, the most binding concern and thereby entail an essential intimacy between the opponents. In the addendi to vol. 43, Heidegger remarks that "the rigor of *Auseinandersetzung* is possible only when it is based on the most intimate affinity or relationship. It is possible only where there is a Yes to the essential."[26] Genuine critique binds together as much as it sets apart. In *Auseinandersetzung*, *logos* or *Geist* dominates as much as *polemos*, or *Streit*. In confrontation, the essential is fought for, and gained (*erstritten*) in opposition, and hence mutually. This essential, causing the opponents to coil into what they are in strength and most properly as they struggle over something that they share, is constitutive of confrontation in the strict sense, and suggests that ultimately it is not the opponents that truly matter in this conflict, but rather that for which the struggle is waged, since it is the struggle that assigns the places of the opponents. And yet, without the opponents' strife, nothing essential could occur. Is thus the *Auseinandersetzung* between dialoguing thinkers, or rather between one and the matter of the true philosophical thought of the Other, identical with the appropriating and disappropriating play of the proper and the Other that we have encountered with the originary struggle? Is it comparable to the harmonious constitution of One and Other in mutual *Befremdung* that we had seen to characterize *polemos*?

At this point, and before attempting an answer to the preceding question, we do not escape the issue of the range, or sweep, of *Auseinandersetzung*. As a relation in which thinkers, or rather the matter of their thought, comes to stand in what most powerfully characterizes them, and in which justice is done to the Other as

24. p. 276.
25. Heidegger, *Nietzsche*, p. 5.
26. Heidegger, *Nietzsche, Gesamtausgabe*, Vol. 43, p. 277.

Other, a question arises as to the specificity of *Auseinandersetzung*. Is it a relation valid for all dialogue, or a model with only one application, restricted to the dialogue with Nietzsche's thought alone? Is the very nature of Nietzsche's philosophical achievement such that any appropriate relation to it must have the form of *Auseinandersetzung*, and is this relation to Nietzsche unique? Although evidence points to a certain generalizability of *Auseinandersetzung* as the structure for all thinking dialogue, there seems to be a certain tension in Heidegger's writings, especially in those from the mid-thirties concerning this question. Undoubtedly, in *Beiträge*, he speaks at one point of Nietzsche's *Auseinandersetzung* with Schopenhauer;[27] in the lectures on "Thinking and Poetry" from 1944-45, he even seems to suggest an *Auseinandersetzung* with Hölderlin's poetry;[28] and more importantly, in the Seminar of 1968 at Le Thor he is said to have spoken of the necessity "to embark on an *Auseinandersetzung* with Hegel, in order for Hegel *to speak* to us."[29] But, is it not significant that in *Beiträge*, after having reviewed the different stages in the history of metaphysics in need of historical treatment — Leibniz, Kant, Schelling, Nietzsche — that only in the case of Nietzsche is such treatment called an *Auseinandersetzung*? He writes: "to venture the *Auseinandersetzung* with Nietzsche as him who is closest, and yet, to recognize that he is most remote from the question of Being."[30] Finally, what is the significance of the fact that Heidegger elaborates the concept of *Auseinandersetzung* itself exclusively in the Nietzsche lectures, and only with respect to his debate with the latter? In response to these questions, I would argue that *Auseinandersetzung* is primarily cut to size to fit the debate with Nietzsche, this thinker still too close to be engaged in a just dialogue, with respect to whom the distance across which his true philosophical contribution, his strongest self, can come into view, has yet to be attained. But, as we now shall see, there is certainly another reason that might hold the key to why confrontation is cut to shape to Nietzsche more than to any one else.

In the addendi to "The Will to Power as Art," Heidegger notes that the battle positions in a genuine *Auseinandersetzung* "must be

27. Heidegger, *Beiträge zur Philosophie*, p. 181.
28. Heidegger, *1. Nietzsches Metaphysik. 2. Einleitung in die Philosophie. Denken und Dichten*, p. 100.
29. Martin Heidegger, *Vier Seminare* (Frankfurt am Main: Klostermann, 1977), p. 24.
30. Heidegger, *Beiträge*, p. 176.

historical — Nietzsche's and ours, and this again in the perspective of the mountain range (*in der Richtung der Höhenzüge*) of the essential history of philosophy."[31] Indeed, *Auseinandersetzung* is a kind of debate that *comes from*, and is *waged from* and *for* what Heidegger calls in *Nietzsche*, but in particular in *Beiträge*, "*der andere Anfang*," the other beginning. Once that has been established, a definite limitation of *Auseinandersetzung* to the case of Nietzsche's thought will not fail to come into view. Nietzsche, we are told at the beginning of "The Will to Power as Art," proceeds within the vast orbit of the ancient guiding question (*Leitfrage*) of philosophy.[32] This guiding question which has been *the* question of the history of metaphysics, is the question constitutive of "the first beginning" (*der erste Anfang*), and consists of the question: "What is Being?" It is a question that inquires into the essence of beings in terms of existence, in terms of an *existing* essence. In what is to follow, it is essential to distinguish this guiding question from what Heidegger calls the grounding question (*Grundfrage*), the question "What is the truth of Being?" This question does not itself unfold in the history of philosophy as such, yet it inaugurates "the other beginning." Now, as Heidegger remarks, his lectures on Nietzsche intend "to elucidate the fundamental position within which Nietzsche unfolds the guiding question of Western thought and responds to it. Such elucidation is needed in order to prepare a confrontation (*Auseinandersetzung*) with Nietzsche. If in Nietzsche's thinking the prior tradition of Western thought is gathered and completed in a decisive respect, then the confrontation with Nietzsche becomes one with all Western thought hitherto."[33] As is well known, Heidegger's point in *Nietzsche*, is that Nietzsche completed the guiding question which he persisted to think, and thus has brought the whole of Western thought into a view that, presupposing a distance to this whole implicitly harbors an other beginning. Showing that Nietzsche has brought the first and, as Heidegger stresses, greatest beginning, to an end — and has thus become "a transition" — Heidegger has also brought his opponent into the position in which he stands to himself in his strongest relation. In the above mentioned addendi, he notes that to be a transition is "the highest that can be said of a thinker. A transition,

31. Heidegger, *Nietzsche, Gesamtausgabe*, Vol. 43, p. 276.
32. Heidegger, *Nietzsche*, p. 4.
33. p. 4.

that prepares transitions to the second beginning."[34] Moreover, in *Beiträge* Heidegger writes, "the transitional is the authentic struggle."[35] From this it follows that the true opponent, Nietzsche at his strongest, as transition and authentic struggle, is in himself *Auseinandersetzung*. In him, and for the first time, the first and the second beginning are at war. Thus, it would seem that the mode of dialogue called *Auseinandersetzung* must be restricted to Nietzsche, that is, to the only thinker who, by having completed the first beginning, is in virtual transition to the other beginning. *Auseinandersetzung* seems to be limited to a debate in the name of the other beginning. As Heidegger emphasizes, such a debate with Nietzsche has not yet begun because we are still too close to him. Any *Auseinandersetzung* requires that we be sufficiently set apart from Nietzsche. Indeed, what must come into view is that Nietzsche, bringing the first beginning to an end, has achieved a position of exteriority of some sort to it. As Heidegger remarks in *Beiträge*, in order to experience what began in and as that beginning, it is necessary "to occupy a distancing position (*Fernstellung*). For *without* this position of distance — and only the position in the *other* beginning is a sufficient one — we always remain too close to the beginning, and this in an incriminating (*verfänglich*) fashion … The position of distance with respect to the first beginning makes it possible to experience that there the question of truth (aletheia) remained necessarily unquestioned and that this nonoccurring has from the start made Western thinking 'metaphysical' thinking."[36] In short, then, *Auseinandersetzung* is strictly speaking a debate with a position characterized by distance (*Fernstellung*), namely, distance to the first beginning, and which as such is at least virtually in transition to the other beginning. *Auseinandersetzung* presupposes that the subject matter to be confronted has set itself *apart* from the first beginning, and that this distance is what unites the thinkers in opposition. *Auseinandersetzung* requires a distance to one's opponent that permits a sight of the extent to which the thinker has already taken a position of distance from the first beginning. However, since, according to Heidegger, Nietzsche occupies this privileged position in the history of Western thought of having brought himself in opposition to the whole of Western thought, while at the same time being furthest away from the grounding question, from

---

34. Heidegger, *Nietzsche, Gesamtausgabe*, Vol. 43, p. 278.
35. Heidegger, *Beiträge*, p. 179.
36. pp. 185-86.

the *Seinsfrage*, Nietzsche must be the opponent par excellence, the exemplary thinker whose matter, unlike that of any other thinker in the history of metaphysics, demands a confrontation in the mode of *Auseinandersetzung*.

The role of the other beginning constitutive to any appreciation of what Heidegger calls *Auseinandersetzung* clearly shows it as an oriented debate. Heidegger's contention that bringing the opponent into a position of strength is the condition by which he becomes free "for the supreme exertion of thinking," rings with ambiguity. *Auseinandersetzung* has the look of an unequal struggle in which justice is done to the Other for the mere benefit of the *explicit* development of the question that, while remote to Nietzsche, is Heidegger's opening question. But let us not come to a hasty conclusion. Indeed, as Heidegger would have it, what counts in this debate is not the person "Nietzsche," or "Heidegger" for that matter, but the essential Yes that both share, the Yes to the essential question. Moreover, the unfolding of that question in an *Auseinandersetzung* with a properly posited Nietzsche, could well be the unfolding of a kind of thought that, according to its very nature, while potentially harboring in itself the promise of an other beginning for all the voices that have made up the whole of the Western metaphysical tradition, the whole of the first beginning, is only to be gained in a biased struggle. To sustain such a point, I return to the question of the first and the other beginning.

The necessity of the other beginning, Heidegger reminds us in *Beiträge*, arises from the originary positing of the first beginning itself. More precisely, the first beginning does not only explain the necessity of the other beginning, but it necessarily sets the other beginning apart from and opposite to itself. (*Die Auseinanderandersetzung der Notwendigkeit des anderen Anfangs aus der ursprünglichen Setzung des ersten Anfangs*).[37] The first beginning is characterized by the experience and positing of the truth of beings (*die Wahrheit des Seienden*), yet since "what thus became disclosed in the first beginning, being as being, necessarily overpowers everything else, the question concerning truth as such is not asked here."[38] Indeed, the more extreme the forgetting of the question of truth becomes, the more imperiously metaphysics sets the space for another beginning apart from and opposite to itself. However, with the other beginning, only that which could not be questioned in the

37. p. 169.
38. p. 179.

first beginning — as a result of the sheer overpowering disclosure of being as being — is questioned: truth itself. By explicitly asking the question of the truth of being, the other beginning conceptualizes what in the first necessarily receded into oblivion in order for there to be a first beginning in the first place, but from which alone the first beginning draws its true meaning. In the confrontation with the first beginning, this first beginning — metaphysics in other words — is not denounced as error. No demarcation of the other beginning from the first can possibly be a turning down or belittling.[39] On the contrary, to cite Heidegger, "the leap into the other beginning is a return into the first and vice-versa. Yet return into the first beginning (the "*Wieder-holung*") is not a taking back into something past as if the latter could be made 'real' in the common sense. The return into the first beginning is precisely a distancing (*Entfernung*) from it."[40] In the *Auseinandersetzung*, the other beginning is only the repetition of the first beginning, yet in such manner that the explicit questioning of the forgotten question constitutive of the first beginning, leads to a deepening of it, and hence to its complete recasting. Heidegger writes: "The other beginning helps from a renewed originarity the first beginning to achieve the truth of its history and, consequently, its own most inalienable Otherness (*zu seiner unveräusserlichen eigensten Andersheit*), which becomes only fruitful in the historical dialogue of the thinkers."[41] In short, in the *Auseinandersetzung* between the first beginning and the other beginning and necessarily set forth by the first, the first beginning, by coming into its own, by achieving what it is most properly, and hence what is most inalienably other about it, becomes the greatest of the beginnings. In addition, only by having come to an end, by having in its most extreme position reached its own limits, is it possible, in the confrontational dialogue, for the first beginning to fulfill that greatness.

What, then, does this imply for the dialogue, the confrontation between Nietzsche and Heidegger? If the other beginning, from which the *Auseinandersetzung* takes place, is the condition under which Nietzsche's thought can be established in its greatest strength, in what is most proper to it, then an *Auseinandersetzung* is not only what does justice to Nietzsche's thought, but also takes place in a place necessarily called upon by that thought itself.

39. p. 178.
40. p. 185.
41. p. 187.

Hence, the unequal struggle at which we pointed, as well as the orientation of the confrontation toward enabling Heidegger to exert the supreme task of thinking, is demanded by *the matter* of Nietzsche's thought itself. For without it, the thought of the thinker cannot achieve what is most inalienably other about it, and hence also most inalienably proper to it. *The matter* of Nietzsche's thinking — in itself *Auseinandersetzung* — itself entails a certain injustice, or delay in justice, such that justice can be done to *the matter* in the first place.

Although Nietzsche's thought necessitates from within a certain injustice on Heidegger's part in order that it be recognized in its greatest strength, this necessary injustice, this limitation of justice to do justice, is at the same time the condition by which Heidegger will be able to exert the supreme task of thinking. The very specificity of Heidegger's philosophical achievement is a function of that interpretation called upon by Nietzsche's thought "itself." Consequently, what looked at first like an unequal relation by virtue of the historical nature of the battle positions now appears to have all the characteristics of the rather harmonious play of contestants in the originary struggle of the *polemos*. Undoubtedly, interpreting Nietzsche's thought from the perspective of the other beginning, restricts it to representing "only" — "an 'only' that is not a limitation, but the demand for something more originary"[42] — a completion of the first beginning. In that, however, Nietzsche's thought achieves a greatness it could not have had by itself in itself. For there is no such thing as a thought, even a thought exclusively determined from within itself, which is solely of itself, is only thought. The thought of the other beginning, by contrast, is a thought whose necessity has always been required by the first beginning. It is what it is "only" in so far as without it, the first beginning could never have been the greatest beginning. In the *Auseinandersetzung* between Nietzsche's thought and Heidegger's thinking, the necessity of the latter's thought is staged in view of the needs of the first. On the other hand, the thought of the other beginning requires that it be demarcated from what it must construe as the first beginning, and this demarcation reflects the thought of the other beginning into its own. In *Auseinandersetzung*, the bias is shared. One and the Other, the first beginning and the other beginning, Nietzsche and Heidegger, without priority, reflect each other into their own by calling

42. p. 175.

138

upon the respective Other's biased approach.[43] In such *Auseinandersetzung*, one thinker's thought and that of another play into, by playing against one another. This movement shares the allure of dialectics, but differs from it in the important respect in that in it the One and the Other, far from being poles destined for eventual supersession, constitute themselves as themselves to begin with. Their irreducible, inalienable difference from one another hinges upon the mutual call for disappropriation. More importantly, however, *Auseinandersetzung* differs from dialectics in what might be called, the *generalized biasing*, or *systematic slant* that characterizes its movements. As we have seen, only in view of the thought of the other beginning does Nietzsche achieve what is most inalienably proper to him, and conversely, Heidegger's own thought comes into its own only through its demarcation from a Nietzsche 'reductively' interpreted as having completed the first beginning. Unlike critique, *Auseinandersetzung* accords a necessary, a constitutive function to the Other. Yet, it is also clear from what we have developed so far, that the possibility of recognition itself of the Other and *Befremdung* of the One by the Other hinge on a presentation of the One and the Other from a special angle. *Auseinandersetzung*, and thus the existence of a One and an Other in the first place, is only possible on the condition of a slanted, slightly unjust understanding that does not see the One and the Other as being what it is solely in and out of itself. This injustice not only causes Nietzsche to appear in his greatest strength and hence as Other to begin with, but also makes Heidegger's "supreme exertion of thinking" *merely* the humble recasting of the first beginning. Consequently, one slant counterbalances the other. No dissymmetry prevails here, and hence, in *Auseinandersetzung*, the One and the Other merely secure their respective places by unseating one another in a movement of reciprocal reference, or *Befremdung*. Yet,

---

43. This is perhaps the point to anticipate a possible objection to the preceding developments. It might be argued that the confrontation between Heidegger and Nietzsche as we have outlined it, would correspond, at best, to Heidegger's treatment of Nietzsche in the lectures on "The Will to Power as Art," whereas in the later lectures, Nietzsche will become restricted to such a degree that it would be truly misleading to still characterize it in terms of an *Auseinandersetzung*. Yet, let us recall that the "Author's Forward," from 1961, prefaces "all Volumes." Indeed, is not the radically constricted Nietzsche of the later lectures — in which the completion of metaphysics becomes "reduced" to, or "substituted" by technology as the fulfillment of metaphysics, precisely the opponent at its strongest — 'unfolded from the innermost depth of his work to what is most extreme about him' — as required by all genuine *Auseinandersetzung*?

although this symmetric play between the One and the Other seems to reveal a definite limitation on the ability of *Auseinandersetzung* to take in the Other as Other, it also brings into view a clear limit on the extent to which propriety — the ownmost in its inalienable Otherness — may be attributed to an opponent in dialogue. It is in light of this essential limit without which there would not be any *Auseinandersetzung*, that the following remarks by Heidegger on the limits of greatness must be read. In the addendi to "The Will to Power as Art," Heidegger remarks that to valuate a thinker does not mean to overlook what he has not overcome. The fateful belongs to greatness, he notes.[44] While *Auseinandersetzung* is not a finding fault or scoring of mistakes, it is nonetheless "a fixing of limits." "Limits belong to greatness. They do not exist in order to be regarded as something faulty, for they are the border — of the other and the created," Heidegger writes.[45] Confrontation as genuine critique thus points out the *necessary* limits to greatness, limits that belong intimately, inalienably to thinking. If these limits become thematic,in *Auseinandersetzung*, "it is in order to take up the task once again and to know the necessity of the limits. The limits of all greatness — the moment of its birth."[46] The very Otherness of greatness calls for the repetition of a thinker's thought, demanding that *the matter* be taken up again, and in thinking its limits, be developed, or rather, be thought further.

44. Heidegger, *Nietzsche, Gesamtausgabe*, Vol. 43, p. 278.
45. p. 277.
46. p. 277.3

8. Taking Exception to Decision: Walter Benjamin and Carl Schmitt

SAMUEL WEBER

The short text that outlines the space in which this symposium is situated, concludes with the following question: Do not the two intellectual approaches, Critical Theory and Post-Structuralism, which have been invited to enter into a reasoned and if possible non-polemical dialogue with one another, both deal in differing ways with an *irreducibly normative* notion by means of which a *de-centering mode of critique* can be conceived? The following remarks do not provide a direct response to this question, but rather respond by asking yet another question: What is involved in thinking the irreducibility of the norm? Both Carl Schmitt and Walter Benjamin address this question, in ways that are related to one another and yet also quite divergent. Is there a norm that informs their relation? Or is it perhaps the question of the norm as such that both brings them together and drives them apart?

I.

...epigrammatisch [steht] über einem Kupfer, der eine Bühne darstellt, auf der links ein Possenreißer und rechts ein Fürst sich zeigen: Wann die Bühne nu wird leer/Gilt kein Narr und König mehr. (Ursprung, S. 133)[1]

In December, 1930, Walter Benjamin sends the following letter to Carl Schmitt:

"Sehr geehrter Herr Professor,

Sie erhalten dieser Tage vom Verlage mein Buch Ursprung des deutschen Trauerspiels. Mit diesen Zeilen möchte ich es Ihnen nicht nur ankündigen, sondern Ihnen auch meine Freude darüber aussprechen, daß ich es, auf Veranlassung von Herrn Albert Salomon, Ihnen zusenden darf. Sie werden sehr schnell bemerken, wieviel das Buch in seiner Darstellung der Lehre von der Souveränität im 17.

---

1. References to this work are to: Walter Benjamin, *Ursprung des deutschen Trauerspiels* (Frankfurt am Main: Suhrkamp, 1963).

Jahrhundert Ihnen verdankt. Vielleicht darf ich Ihnen darüber hinausgehend sagen, daß ich auch Ihren späteren Werken, vor allem der Diktatur eine Bestätigung meiner kunstphilosophischen Forschungsweisen durch Ihre staatsphilosophischen entnommen habe. Wenn Ihnen die Lektüre meines Buches dieses Gefühl verständlich erscheinen läßt, so ist die Absicht seiner Übersendung erfüllt.

Mit dem Ausdruck besonderer Hochschätzung
Ihr sehr ergebener
Walter Benjamin"[2]

This letter is not to be found in the two volumes of Benjamins *Correspondence*, published in 1966[3]: the esteem that Benjamin expressed for the eminent political thinker who, just a few years later, was to publish texts such as *Der Führer schützt das Recht* (1934) and *Die deutsche Rechtswissenschaft im Kampf gegen den jüdischen Geist* (1936) hardly fits the picture that Benjamin's two editors and former friends, Gershom Scholem and Theodor Adorno, intended to make known to a broad audience. As understandable as their decision to exclude this letter is, it nonetheless expresses a malaise that is related to the way in which the figure of Walter Benjamin tends to resist any attempt at univocal classification or straightforward evaluation. It is as though the fact that he had been able to admire and draw inspiration from the work of a Catholic conservative who was soon to become a conspicuous member of the Nazi party, could only muddy and *confuse* the meaning of an oeuvre that both Adorno and Scholem, whatever their other differences about it might be, agreed was of exemplary significance. It is as though the acknowledgement of a debt amounted to a moral contamination of Benjamin by Schmitt.

Such a malaise is palpable in the remark of Rolf Tiedemann, who is to be credited with publishing the letter to Schmitt in the critical apparatus he assembled for the edition of Benjamin's *Collected Writings* that he edited. The letter, he remarks, is *denkwürdig*, although he does not say just what sort of thoughts it might elicit or deserve (GS I/3, S. 887). One response that is often encountered in

---

2. Walter Benjamin, *Gesammelte Schriften*, vol. I/3, (Frankfurt am Main: Suhrkamp, 1980, S. 887).
3. Walter Benjamin, *Briefe*, edited by Gershom Scholem and Theodor W. Adorno, (Frankfurt am Main: Suhrkamp, 1966).

this context, traces Benjamin's interest in Schmitt back to the critique of liberal, parliamentary democracy shared by both. But this explanation, as evident and as accurate as it may be, hardly suffices to account either for the debt mentioned by Benjamin in his letter, or for the *manner* in which it manifests itself in his book. Rather, the work of Schmitt figures in that book for at least two related, but very distinct reasons. First of all, the play of mourning at work in the *Trauerspiel* and above all the character of its origin both imply a certain relationship to *history* and to *politics*.[4] Second, and more specifically, Benjamin encounters the question of sovereignty not simply as a theme of German Baroque theater, but as a methodological and theoretical problem: as we shall see, according to Benjamin every attempt to interpret the German Baroque risks to succumb to a certain *lack of sovereignty*. Let us examine just how these two factors help to explain Benjamin's recourse to Schmitt.

The German baroque mourning play has as its true object and substance historical life as represented by its age (51). But the relationship between *Trauerspiel* and history is far from a one-way street: if baroque theater is concerned primarily with history, this history is in turn construed as a kind of *Trauerspiel*. This is why Benjamin's formulation, here as elsewhere, must be read as rigorously as possible: the true object of baroque drama is not just historical life as such, but rather historical life *as represented* by its age (*das geschichtliche Leben wie es jene Epoche sich darstellte*). The primary representation and representative of history, however, in the baroque age is the sovereign: *Der Souverän repräsentiert die Geschichte. Er hält das historische Geschehen in der Hand wie ein Szepter* (54).

Benjamin's insistence on the historical subject-matter of the *Trauerspiel* thus leads him necessarily to the question of political sovereignty and its relation to history. But it is not merely the thematic aspect of his subject that leads Benjamin to examine the question of sovereignty, and hence to the theories of Schmitt. In his letter, Benjamin writes that he has found in Schmitt's works a confirmation of his own style of research, *meine[n] eigenen*

4. I have discussed the historicality of Benjamins notion of Ursprung, as elaborated in his epistemo-critical Preface to this book, in, "Genealogy of Modernity: History, Myth and Allegory in Benjamins *Origin of the German Mourning Play*," MLN, 106, 1991, esp. 467-474.

Forschungsweisen. Just what Benjamin might be referring to becomes clearer if we turn to the beginning of the first chapter of his book, dealing with *Trauerspiel* and Tragedy. Benjamin begins his study proper with a notion elaborated in the Epistemo-critical Preface: namely, that the conceptualization of a philosophical investigation such as that he proposes must be directed towards the extreme (*die notwendige Richtung aufs Extreme*).

In thus foregrounding the constitutive importance of a turn toward the extreme in the process of philosophical conceptualization, Benjamin places himself squarely in a tradition that goes back at least to Kierkegaard's essay on *Repetition*; but the text in which this mode of thinking probably impressed itself most profoundly upon Benjamin was Schmitt's *Politische Theologie*, the first chapter of which concludes by insisting on the significance of the extreme case:

> *Gerade eine Philosophie des konkreten Lebens darf sich vor der Ausnahme und vor dem extremen Falle nicht zurückziehen, sondern muß sich im höchsten Maße für ihn interessieren. Ihr kann die Ausnahme wichtiger sein als die Regel, nicht aus einer romantischen Ironie für das Paradoxe, sondern mit dem ganzen Ernst einer Einsicht, die tiefer geht als die klaren Generalisationen des durchschnittlich sich Wiederholenden. Die Ausnahme ist interessanter als der Normalfall. Das Normale beweist nichts, die Ausnahme beweist alles; sie bestätigt nicht nur die Regel, die Regel lebt überhaupt nur von der Ausnahme.*[5]

In the *Erkenntniskritische Vorrede* to the *Trauerspiel* book, where Benjamin seeks to elaborate the premises and implications of his reading of the German baroque theater as an idea, it is precisely to the extreme that he appeals in order to indicate just how the idea distinguishes itself from the subsumptive generality of the concept:

> *Als Gestaltung des Zusammenhanges, in dem das Einmalig-Extreme mit seinesgleichen steht, ist die Idee umschrieben. Daher ist es falsch, die allgemeinsten Verweisungen der Sprache als Begriffe zu verstehen, anstatt sie als Ideen zu erkennen. Das Allgemeine als ein Durchschnittliches darlegen zu wollen, ist verkehrt. Das Allgemeine ist die Idee. Das Empirische dagegen wird um so tiefer durchdrungen, je genauer es als ein Extremes eingesehen werden kann. Vom Extremen geht der Begriff aus. (16)*

What is characteristic of the *Einmalig-Extreme* is, as Schmitt explicitly states, that it is a borderline notion: it is situated at the extremity of what is familiar, identically repeatable, classifiable; it is the

---

5. Carl Schmitt, *Politische Theologie, Vier Kapitel zur Lehre von der Souveränität,* (Berlin: Duncker & Humblot, 1985, S. 22) (all references to this edition).

point at which the generally familiar is on the verge of passing into something else, the point at which it encounters the other, the exterior. To think the idea as a configuration of singular extremes (*Einmalig-Extreme*) is to construe its being as a function of that which it is not.

Such passages indicate how Benjamins mode of investigation, his *Forschungsweise* is indebted to that of Schmitt: both share a certain *methodological extremism* for which the formation of a concept is paradoxically but necessarily dependent upon a contact or an encounter with a singularity that exceeds or eludes the concept. This singular encounter takes place in and as the extreme and it is the readiness to engage in this encounter, according to Benjamin, that distinguishes philosophical history from art history, literary history or any other form of history that presupposes the givenness of a general concept under which the phenomena it addresses are to be subsumed:

Die philosophische Geschichte als die Wissenschaft vom Ursprung ist die Form, die da aus den entlegenen Extremen, den scheinbaren Exzessen der Entwicklung die Konfiguration der Idee als der durch die Möglichkeit eines sinnvollen Nebeneinanders solcher Gegensätze gekennzeichneten Totalität heraustreten läßt. Die Darstellung einer Idee kann unter keinen Umständen als geglückt betrachtet werden, solange virtuell der Kreis der in ihr möglichen Extreme nicht abgeschritten ist. Das Abschreiten bleibt virtuell. (31)

The circle of extremes can be traversed only potentially not only because the extremes themselves are never fully present or realized as such. Rather, they articulate themselves historically in terms of a split into a *Vor- und Nachgeschichte*. This pre- and post-history of the singular idea constitutes *die verkürzte und verdunkelte Figur der übrigen Ideenwelt* (32).

This figure is to be deciphered, *abzulesen*. And it is here, precisely, that Benjamin finds himself faced with a problem that seems to bear a particular relation to the German baroque and its interpretation:

Immer wieder begegnet in den improvisierten Versuchen, den Sinn dieser Epoche zu vergegenwärtigen, das bezeichnende Schwindelgefühl, in das der Anblick ihrer in Widersprüchen kreisenden Geistigkeit versetzt. [...] Nur eine von weither kommende, ja sich dem Anblick der Totalität zunächst versagende Betrachtung kann in einer gewissermaßen asketischen Schule den Geist zu der Festigung führen, die ihm erlaubt, im Anblick jenes Panoramas seiner selbst mächtig zu bleiben. (43-44)

145

In the baroque, the circle of potential extremes to be traversed in the staging of an idea has become an encirclement of contradictions and of antitheses from which there seems no escape, but only the giddiness, the vertigo that its spectacle elicits.

What sorts of contradictions and antitheses encircle the German baroque? Not the least of these appears to be a singular discrepancy between its artistic intentions and the aesthetic means at its disposal. And it is here that Benjamin encounters the problem of sovereignty in a guise that seems to be peculiar to the German theater of the time:

Das deutsche Drama der Gegenreformation hat niemals jene geschmeidige, jedem virtuosen Griff sich bietende Form gefunden, die Calderon dem spanischen gab. Gebildet hat es sich [...] in einer höchst gewalttätigen Anstrengung und dies allein würde besagen, daß kein souveräner Genius dieser Form das Gepräge gegeben hat. Dennoch liegt der Schwerpunkt aller barocken Trauerspiele in ihr. [...] Dieser Einsicht ist eine Vorbedingung der Forschung. (34)

What is modern, topical, *aktuell* about the baroque in general, and about the German baroque in particular, is thus tied on the one hand to a certain *lack* of sovereignty, to a certain incapacity of producing consummate artistic forms, and on the other, to an effort of the will that strives to compensate for this lack but which threatens instead to overwhelm all those who seek to interpret it:

Einer Literatur gegenüber, die durch den Aufwand ihrer Technik, die gleichförmige Fülle ihrer Produktionen und die Heftigkeit ihrer Wertbehauptungen Welt und Nachwelt gewissermaßen zum Schweigen zu bringen suchte, ist die Notwendigkeit der souveränen Haltung, wie Darstellung von der Idee von einer Form sie aufdringt, zu betonen. Die Gefahr, aus den Höhen des Erkennens in die ungeheuren Tiefen der Barockstimmung sich hinabstürzen zu lassen, bleibt selbst dann unverächtlich. (43)

The lack of sovereignty of the German baroque theater, as well as the power of its will seeking to compensate for that lack, render a sovereign attitude all the more imperative and all the more difficult for those who seek to interpret it. This is at least one explanation of why Benjamin is led to look for a confirmation of his style of research in the *Lehre* of Schmitt concerning, precisely, the question of sovereignty.[6]

6. Here the question should at least be raised in passing whether the vertigo that Benjamin identifies with the German baroque is not also, in part at least, a result of his own determination of the origin as a Strudel, a vortex or maelstrom that

146

II.

If the primary object of the German *Trauerspiel* is history as represented in the figure of the sovereign, the destiny of the ruler in the baroque theater manifests a regularity that suggests the inevitability of a natural occurrence:

Das ständig wiederholte Schauspiel fürstlicher Erhebung und des Falls [...] stand den Dichtern nicht sowohl als Moralität, denn als die in ihrer Beharrlichkeit wesenhafte, als die naturgemäße Seite des Geschichtsverlaufs vor Augen. (84)

History as a repetitive and ineluctable process of rise and fall is identified with the nature of a fallen creation without any discernible, representable possibility of either grace or salvation. It is the loss of an eschatological perspective that renders the baroque conception of history inauthentic and akin to a state of nature.

Such a conception or confusion of history with nature entails at least two fundamental consequences for a theater whose primary concern is, as we have seen, precisely the spectacle of this history. First, the loss of the eschatological dimension results in a radical transformation of the dramatic element of the theater, insofar as it had been tied to a narrative-teleological conception of history. The traditional Aristotelian analysis of the plot in terms of unity of action resulting from the exposition, development and resolution of conflict, is no longer applicable. History, as Benjamin puts it, wanders onto the stage (*Die Geschichte wandert in den Schauplatz*

reißt in seine Rhythmik das Entstehungsmaterial hinein (29). The rhythm of the origin is split between a tendency to restore and to reproduce (*Restauration, Wiederherstellung*) on the one hand, and a certain incompletion (*Unvollendetes, Unabgeschlossenes*) on the other. This split in the origin is what then articulates itself as the division into pre- and post-history. The lack of a center, fully present to itself, in the origin is perhaps the origin of that *Schwindelgefühl* that Benjamin associates with the Baroque in general, and its German variant in particular. It remains to be determined, however, whether this connection indicates that the Baroque is a particularly *originary* age, or rather whether the origin itself is not particularly *baroque*. Nor is there any guarantee that the answer to this question must conform to the schema of an either/or, a simple decision. We will return very briefly at the end of this paper to the relation between decision and rhythm as articulated in Benjamin's book.

147

hinein, 89). Second, the baroque naturalization of history profoundly affects the figure of the sovereign, primary exponent, we remember, of history. The naturalistic destiny of the prince does not merely imply the rise and fall of an individual figure, but more importantly, the *dislocation of sovereignty as such*. Out of this dislocation Benjamin develops what he calls *the typology and political anthropology* of the baroque. The reason that this typology must be elucidated at the outset is because it arises out of the articulation, or rather disarticulation of sovereignty, and hence of history, the primary object of the German baroque *Trauerspiel*.

Benjamin's reconstruction of the political anthropology of the baroque consists of three figures, of varying stature and status, and yet each of which unthinkable without the others. This trio embraces the tyrant, the martyr and the plotter (*der Intrigant*). It is the first and the last that will be of particular interest to us here.

The point of departure for this typology is, of course, the figure of the prince. It is here that Benjamin makes explicit reference to Carl Schmitt's theory of sovereignty. To grasp the significance of Benjamin's use of Schmitt, it will be helpful if we first review certain aspects of the latter's discussion of sovereignty, starting with the famous passage at the beginning of *Political Theology* in which the notion is first announced:

Souverän ist, wer über den Ausnahmezustand entscheidet.
Diese Definition kann dem Begriff der Souveränität als einem Grenzbegriff allein gerecht werden. Denn Grenzbegriff bedeutet nicht einen konfusen Begriff, wie in der unsaubern Terminologie populärer Literatur, sondern einen Begriff der äußersten Sphäre. (11)

Despite the apparent and seductive clarity of this definition, it leaves a number of problems unresolved, above all regarding the notion of the state of exception. First of all, the state of exception, Schmitt insists, is not simply equivalent, in German, to a state of emergency or of siege: not every danger or threat constitutes an *Ausnahmezustand* in Schmitt's sense, since not every exception *per se* represents a threat to the norm. The state of exception that constitutes the object and product of the sovereign decision is one that threatens or calls into question the existence and survival of the state itself as hitherto constituted. Sovereignty is constituted in the

148

power to decide upon or about the state of exception and thus in turn includes two moments: first, a decision *that* a state of exception exists, and second, the effective suspension of the state of law previously in force so that the state may meet and surmount the challenge of the exception. In thus deciding upon the state of exception, the sovereign also effectively determines the limits of the state. And it is this act of delimitation that constitutes political sovereignty according to Schmitt.

This is why the translation of *Ausnahmezustand* by state of exception is not quite accurate, or rather, why it obscures the delicate balance of similarity and distinction that determine the relationship of the State as *Staat* and the exception as *Zustand*. The *Ausnahmezustand* is a state in the sense of having a relatively determinate *status*; as a *Zustand*, it is

immer noch etwas anderes [...] als eine Anarchie und ein Chaos, [und daher] besteht im juristischen Sinne immer noch eine Ordnung, wenn auch keine Rechtsordnung. Die Existenz des Staates bewährt hier eine zweifellose Überlegenheit über die Geltung der Rechtsnorm. Die Entscheidung macht sich frei von jeder normativen Gebundenheit und wird im eigentlichen Sinne absolut. Im Ausnahmefall suspendiert der Staat das Recht, kraft eines Selbsterhaltungsrechtes, **wie man sagt**. (18-19, my emphasis)

The paradox or aporia of Schmitt's position is suggested here by the conclusion of the passage just quoted. For if the decision is as radically independent of the norm as Schmitt claims, it is difficult to see how the decision of the state to suspend its laws can be justified at all, since all justification involves precisely the appeal to a norm. This is why, in appealing to a *right* of self-preservation Schmitt acknowledges that the term is more *a way of speaking* than a rigorous concept: *Im Ausnahmefall suspendiert der Staat das Recht, kraft eines Selbsterhaltungsrechtes*, **wie man sagt**.

On the one hand, then, the sovereign decision marks the relationship of the order of the general: the law, the norm, the concept, to that which is radically heterogeneous to all such generality. In this sense, the decision as such is sovereign, i.e. independent of all possible derivation from or subsumption to a more general norm. It is a pure act, somewhat akin to the act of creation except that what it does is not so much to create as to interrupt and to suspend. If such interruption and suspension can never be predicted or determined in advance, it is nonetheless not arbitrary insofar as it is understood

149

to be necessary in order to preserve the state as the indispensable condition of all possible law and order.

And yet, precisely insofar as it is situated in this temporality of repetition and reproduction, the decision cannot be considered, Schmitt notwithstanding, to be entirely absolute. Rather, it constitutes itself in and as *a break with...*, an interruption or suspension *of... a norm*. In separating what belongs to the norm from what does not — and in this sense *every* authentic decision, as Schmitt asserts, has to do with an exception — the decision distinguishes itself from the simple negation of order, from chaos and anarchy as Schmitt writes, and can indeed lay claim to having some sort of legal status. The problem, however, is that such a claim can only be evaluated and judged *after the fact*, as it were, which is to say, from a point of view that is once again situated *within* a system of norms.

For Schmitt, this paradox is articulated as the fact that the State, which is the condition of all law and order, is itself constituted by a decision that is prior to and independent of all such considerations: *Die Autorität beweist, daß sie, um Recht zu schaffen, nicht Recht zu haben braucht.* (20) On the other hand, the non-legal or a-legal status of the sovereign and exceptional decision is justifiable and indeed, identifiable, only insofar as it provides the conditions for the reappropriation of the exception by the norm. The State thus has the first and the last word in Schmitt's theory of sovereignty.

This brings us to a second aspect of Schmitt's thought. Up to now, we have been considering it in terms of a relatively abstract, general and quasi-logical theory of decision; but Schmitt's thinking is also historical, as the very title of his book, *Political Theology*, suggests and as the following passage renders manifest:

Alle prägnanten Begriffe der modernen Staatslehre sind säkularisierte theologische Begriffe. Nicht nur ihrer historischen Entwicklung nach, weil sie aus der Theologie auf die Staatslehre übertragen wurden, indem zum Beispiel der allmächtige Gott zum omnipotenten Gesetzgeber wurde, sondern auch in ihrer systematischen Struktur, deren Erkenntnis notwendig ist für eine soziologische Betrachtung dieser Begriffe. Der Ausnahmezustand hat für die Jurisprudenz eine analoge Bedeutung wie das Wunder für die Theologie. Erst in dem Bewußtsein solcher analogen Stellung läßt sich die Entwicklung erkennen, welche die staatsphilosophischen Ideen in den letzten Jahrhunderten genommen haben. (49)

To be sure, in the analogy that Schmitt is here constructing, historical development is subordinated to systematic considerations. At the same time, it is only in a reflection or recall of the historical transfer or rather, transformation of theological categories into political ones, that the systematic structure of political discourse is fully revealed. The salient trait of that structure is, as we have already seen, its dependence upon a certain transcendence, upon that which exceeds its self-identity, upon an irreducible alterity and exteriority: just as the miracle in Augustinian doctrine both exceeds and explains the created world.

If historical reflection upon the development of political discourse reveals its theological origins and hence its dependence upon a certain transcendence, the actual historical development of political theory and of theology has moved in an opposite direction:

Zu dem Gottesbegriff des 17. und 18. Jahrhunderts gehört die Transzendenz Gottes gegenüber der Welt, wie eine Transzendenz des Souveräns gegenüber dem Staat zu seiner Staatsphilosophie gehört. Im 19. Jahrhundert wird in immer weiterer Ausdehnung alles von Immanenzvorstellungen beherrscht. (63)

To these representations of immanence belong the identification of ruler and ruled, and above all that of the State with the State of Law (the *Identität des Staates mit der Rechtsordnung*, 63). But if the development of modern thought has thus tended to efface the originary and constitutive relationship of the political to transcendence, in the name of notions of autonomy and self-identity, Schmitts own approach does not seem to be entirely free of such tendencies. This can be seen in the manner in which he conceives that consciousness of the analogy between political and theological categories, which for him is the key to authentically historical and systematical understanding.

For what emerges in Schmitt's discussion of the relation of politics and theology is that he construes the analogy between them above all in terms of identity, rather than in those of transformation or of alteration. For instance, he finds confirmation of his theological-political thesis in the position of Atger, for whom

der Monarch in der Staatslehre des 17. Jahrhunderts mit Gott identifiziert wird und im Staat die genau analoge Position hat, die dem Gott des kartesianischen Systems in der Welt zukommt... (60)

The method that Schmitt advances in *Political Theology*, which he calls the sociology of concepts, thus employs the notion of analogy in order to reduce difference to identity, as the following programmatic declaration clearly demonstrates:

Das metaphysische Bild, das sich ein bestimmtes Zeitalter von der Welt macht, hat dieselbe Struktur wie das, was ihr als Form ihrer politischen Organisation ohne weiteres einleuchtet. **Die Feststellung einer solchen Identität ist die Soziologie des Souveränitätsbegriffes.** (59-60, my emphasis)

One would be tempted to say that Schmitt's critique seeks to replace the *Immanenzvorstellungen* of modern political theory with *Identitätsvorstellungen* that seek to recall the heterogeneity of political concepts out of the oblivion into which they have fallen, but only succeed in once again reducing their alterity to the same: to *dieselbe Struktur* and to *die Feststellung einer [...] Identität.*

III.

With the ambivalence of Schmitt's approach to the political in mind, let us now turn to the manner in which the question of sovereignty emerges in Benjamin's study of the German baroque theater:

Der Souverän repräsentiert die Geschichte. Er hält das historische Geschehen in der Hand wie ein Szepter. Diese Auffassung ist alles andere als ein Privileg der Theatraliker. Staatsrechtliche Gedanken liegen ihr zugrunde. In einer letzten Auseinandersetzung mit den juristischen Lehren des Mittelalters bildete sich im siebzehnten Jahrhundert ein neuer Souveränitätsbegriff [...] Wenn der moderne Souveränitätsbegriff auf eine höchste, fürstliche Exekutivgewalt hinausläuft, entwickelt der barocke sich aus einer Diskussion des Ausnahmezustandes und macht zur wichtigsten Funktion des Fürsten, **den auszuschließen.** (54-55, my emphasis)

A note at the end of this passage refers to *Political Theology*. And yet, the very words which seem only to paraphrase Schmitt constitute in fact a slight but decisive modification of his theory. Schmitt, we remember, defines sovereignty as constituted by the power to make a decision that consists of two moments: first, the determination *that* a state of exception exists, and second, the effective suspension of the state of law with the end of preserving the state as such. For Schmitt, then the state of exception must be removed, *beseitigt*, done away with, but only *in each particular case*, never *as such*: that is precisely what Schmitt criticizes modern political theory for

152

trying to do, by excluding consideration of the state of exception from the determination of sovereignty.[7] Benjamin, by contrast, describes the task of the sovereign in the very terms that Schmitt rejects: the sovereign is charged with the task of excluding the state of exception, *den auszuschließen*. In short, that which is already exterior, the **Aus**-*nahmezustand*, is to be exteriorized once again, **aus**-*geschlossen*, and this applies not simply to the state of exception as an individual, determinate threat to the state — the position of Schmitt — but to the state of exception as such, that is, as that which transcends the state in general.

In short, the function assigned to the sovereign by the baroque, according to Benjamin, is that of *transcending transcendence* by making it immanent, an internal part of the state and of the world, of the state of the world. And the reason why the baroque is so attached to the state of the world Benjamin explains as follows:

Der religiöse Mensch des Barock hält an der Welt so fest, weil er mit ihr sich einem Katarakt entgegentreiben fühlt. Es gibt keine barocke Eschatologie; und eben darum einen Mechanismus, der alles Erdgeborne häuft und exaltiert, bevor es sich dem Ende überliefert. Das Jenseits wird entleert von alledem, worin auch nur der leiseste Atem von Welt webt und eine Fülle von Dingen, welche jeder Gestaltung sich zu entziehen pflegten, gewinnt das Barock ihm ab und fördert sie auf seinem Höhepunkt in drastischer Gestalt zu Tag, um einen letzten Himmel zu räumen und als Vakuum ihn in den Stand zu setzen, mit katastrophaler Gewalt dereinst die Erde in sich zu vernichten. (56)

What the Baroque rejects is any admission of the *limitation of immanence* and it does so by emptying transcendence of all possible representable content. Far from doing away with transcendence, however, such emptying only endows it with an all the more powerful force: that of the vacuum, of the absolute and unbounded other, which, since it is no longer representable, is also no longer localizable out there or as a beyond. The otherness that is no longer allowed to remain transcendent therefore reappears this side of the

---

7. *Aber ob der extreme Ausnahmefall wirklich aus der Welt geschafft werden kann oder nicht, das ist keine juristische Frage. Ob man das Vertrauen und die Hoffnung hat, er lasse sich tatsächlich beseitigen, hängt von philosophischen, insbesondere geschichtsphilosophischen oder metaphysischen Überzeugungen ab.(13)*

horizon, represented as a cataract, abyss or fall. Or, even more radically, such transcendence will be represented by, and as, *allegory*.

In this perspective, the function of the sovereign to exclude the state of exception conforms fully to the attempt of the German Baroque to exclude transcendence. But the very same desire to exclude transcendence also condemns the function of the sovereign to malfunction: for unlike the political-theological analogy of Schmitt, the baroque sovereign and particularly, the German baroque sovereign is defined precisely by his *difference* from God, just as baroque immanence sets itself up in contradistinction to theological transcendence. At the very point in time where the political sovereign successfully gains his independence vis-a-vis the Church, the difference between worldy power and that of the divine can no longer be igno The result, as Benjamin formulates it, turns out to be directly contrary to the conclusion of Schmitt:

Die Ebene des Schöpfungsstands, der Boden auf dem das Trauerspiel sich abrollt, bestimmt ganz unverkennbar auch den Souverän. So hoch er über Untertan und Staat auch thront, sein Rank ist in der Schöpfungswelt beschlossen, er ist der Herr der Kreaturen, aber er bleibt Kreatur. (79)

Schmitt, we recall, had construed the theological-political analogy in terms of a relationship of fundamental identity: The sovereign transcends the state as God transcends the creation. By contrast, Benjamin's notion of secularization stresses precisely the incommensurability of the change it entails. Such *incommensurability* becomes even more evident in the specific case of German baroque theater:

Die Abkehr von der Eschatologie der geistlichen Spiele kennzeichnet das neue Drama in ganz Europa; nichtsdestoweniger ist die besinnungslose Flucht in eine unbegnadete Natur spezifisch deutsch. (75)

The German baroque theater flees wildly to nature — which we remember is for it the other face of history — only to discover that there is no grace or consolation to be had there either. The undoing of the sovereign is the fact that in a creation left entirely to its own devices, without any other place to go, the state of exception has become the rule.[8]

---

8. See Alexander García-Düttmann, *Das Gedächtnis des Denkens: Versuch über Adorno und Heidegger*, (Frankfurt am Main: Suhrkamp, 1991, S. 211 ff).

The result is that the sovereign finds himself in a situation in which a decision is as imperative as it is impossible:

Die Antithese zwichen Herrschermacht und Herrschervermögen hat für das Trauerspiel zu einem eigenen, nur scheinbar genrehaften Zug geführt, dessen Beleuchtung einzig auf dem Grunde der Lehre von der Souveränität sich abhebt. Das ist die Entschlußunfähigkeit des Tyrannen. Der Fürst, bei dem die Entscheidung über den Ausnahmezustand ruht, erweist in der erstbesten Situation, daß ein Entschluß ihm fast unmöglich ist. (62)

The sovereign is incapable of taking a decision, because a decision, in the strict sense, is not possible in a world which leaves no place for heterogeneity: the inauthentic, natural history of the baroque allows for no interruption or radical suspension of its perennial interruptions. The sovereign reacts by seeking to gather all power and thus becomes a tyrant; and yet the more power he has, the more he demonstrates his incapacity to arrive at an effective decision. Faced with this situation, the tyrant can easily turn into a martyr. Both figures, Benjamin observes, are for the Baroque only two sides of the same coin, die *Janushäupter des Gekrönten, [...] die notwendig extremen Ausprägungen des fürstlichen Wesens* (60).

In emphasizing the dictatorial tendency of the sovereign, Benjamin follows Schmitt here practically to the letter.[9] And yet in so doing, he arrives at a result that is almost diammetrically opposed to that of Schmitt: the very notion of sovereignty itself is put radically into question. One extreme illustration of this is the figure of Herod, King of the Jews, *der als wahnwitziger Selbstherrscher ein Emblem der verstörten Schöpfung wurde* and as such also an exemplary illustration of the fate of the sovereign for the seventeenth century: *Der Gipfel der Kreatur, ausbrechend in der Raserei wie ein Vulkan und mit allem umliegenden Hofstaat sich selber vernichtend. [...] Er fällt als Opfer eines Mißverhältnisses der unbeschränkten hierarchischen Würde, mit welcher Gott ihn investiert, zum Stande seines armen Menschenwesens. (61-62)*

The key to the secularization of which the German baroque is the result, is thus for Benjamin not so much an analogy based on

---

9. *Die Theorie der Souveränität, für die der Sonderfall mit der Entfaltung diktatorischen Instanzen exemplarisch wird, drängt geradezu darauf, das Bild des Souveräns im Sinne des Tyrannen zu vollenden (60).*

proportion, and hence on identity, as a relation based on *dis-proportion*, on a *Mißverhältniß*.

The effects of this disproportion do not stop at the dismantling of the sovereign, who is split into an ultimately ineffective if bloody tyrant, and a no more productive martyr; neither does it come to rest at any of the compromises possible between these two poles, such as that represented by the stoic ostentation that often characterizes baroque representations of the prince. Rather, the splitting of the sovereign is accompanied by the emergence of a third figure, who stands in radical dissymmetry to the other two. That figure, who completes the baroque political anthropology and typology, is the plotter, the *Intrigant*: and it is he who turns out to hold the key to the fate of sovereignty in the German Baroque mourning play.

IV.

To understand what distinguishes the plotter from the two other figures in the baroque political typology it must be emphasized that the incapacity of the sovereign to decide involves the transformation not merely of an individual character-type, but of the manner in which history itself is represented in the *Trauerspiel*. And this in turn determines the way in which representation takes place. With the split of the sovereign into tyrant and martyr, what is dislocated is not just the unity of *a* character, but the unity of *character as such*. This disarticulation is of particular importance for baroque theater. If the Aristotelian theory of tragedy assigns primary importance to the unity and wholeness of action, and requires to this end consistency of character (*Poetics*, 1454a), it is precisely this consistency and unity that is undermined together with the status of the sovereign. Nothig however demonstrates the distance of the *Trauerspiel* from the Aristotelian theory of tragedy more than the fact that it is precisely this disarticulation of unity of the sovereign and hence, of the action that contributes to the peculiar *theatricality* of Baroque drama, as the following passage suggests:

So wie die Malerei der Manieristen Komposition in ruhiger Belichtung garnicht kennt, so stehen die theatralischen Figuren der Epoche **im grellen Scheine ihrer wechselnden Entschließung.** *In ihnen drängt sich nicht sowohl die Souveränität auf, welche die stoischen Redensarten zur Schau stellen, als die jähe Willkür eines jederzeit umschlagenden Affektsturms, in dem zumal Lohensteins Gestalten wie zerrißne, flatternde Fahnen sich bäumen. Auch sind sie Grecoschen in der Kleinheit des Kopfes, wenn diesen Ausdruck bildlich zu* *verstehen gestattet ist, nicht unähnlich. Denn nicht Gedanken, sondern schwankende physische Impulse bestimmen sie. (62, my emphasis)*

From this account it is clear that the dilemma of the sovereign in Baroque drama is also and above all that of the subject as such: it is no longer determined by its head — i.e. by its consciousness, its intentions — but by forces that are independent of it, that buffet and drive it from one extreme to another. A powerful dynamic is thus unleashed which, however, does not really go anywhere. Instead, like torn flags whipped about in the wind, the baroque figures are driven by tempestuous affects over which they have little control. What results is a rhythm of abrupt and unpredictable changes and shifts and it is this rhythm that determines the structure of the plot in the *Trauerspiel*. Moreover, since neither plot nor character are sufficiently unified or consistent enough to provide a comprehensive framework for the play, this framework must be sought elsewhere. That elsewhere turns out to be the theater itself, as stage. as artifice and as apparatus. This is implicit in the passage cited, which describes how the theatrical figures of the age appear *im grellen Scheine*, in the harsh glare of their changing resolve. The dismantling of decision, of a definitive, ultimate and absolute act, gives way to a different kind of *acting*: that which takes place on a stage lit up by spotlights: the phrase, *grellen Scheine*, which recurs frequently in Benjamins text, recalls the *Scheinwerfer* of the theater.

In the theatrical space thus opened by the dislocation of the action and of the subject, and in the confusion that results, the sovereignty of the tyrant is replaced by the *mastery* of the plotter:

Im Gegensatz zu einem zeitlichen und sprunghaften Verlauf, wie die Tragödie ihn vorstellt, spielt das Trauerspiel sich im Kontinuum des Raumes — choreographisch darf mans nennen — ab. Der Veranstalter seiner Verwicklung, der Vorläufer des Balletmeisters, ist der Intrigant. (94)

The discontinuous temporality of decision, here associated with tragedy, is replaced — i.e. resituated — within a continuum of space in which exceptional interruptions are no longer possible because they have become the rule. The regular nature of the interruption paradoxically becomes programmable and the programmer, or choreographer, is the intriguer. The etymology of the word: *in-trigare*, to con-found and confuse, is all the more appropriate in a world in which the clear-cut separation of the de-cision is no longer effective.

157

The intrigue or plot is thus designated by Benjamin as a *Verwicklung*: an embroglio or entanglement, but one which is organized. The baroque drama thus entails a plot that is based not upon a sovereign subject but upon a masterful organizer or promoter (*Veranstalter*). It is precisely the *calculating* nature of this mastery that fascinates the baroque audience:

Seine verworfnen Berechnungen erfüllen den Betrachter der Haupt- und Staatsaktionen mit um so größerem Interesse, als er in ihnen nicht allein die Beherrschung des politischen Getriebes, sondern ein anthropologisches, selbst physiologisches Wissen erkennt, das ihn passionierte. Der überlegne Intrigant ist ganz Verstand und Wille. (94)

The amoral calculatedness of the plotter contrasts radically with the attitudes of both the tyrant and the martyr. For only the intriguer confronts a state of the world in which the exception has become the rule, and therefore in which universal principles — and be it the principle of the interruption of principle qua decision — can no longer be counted upon. The intriguer exploits mechanisms of human action as the result of forces over which there can be no ultimate control, but which can therefore be made the subject of probabilistic calculations.

The contingency of such calculations turn the intrigue into something closer to a game or to the exhibition of a certain virtuosity, rather than to the expression of a cosmic strategy for the good of all or of the State. Thus, not only the subject-matter of the *Trauerspiel* — historical action — changes, but its dramaturgical structure as well. The plot is replaced by plotting: *Das Drama des Barock kennt die historische Aktivität nicht anders denn als verworfene Betriebsamkeit von Ränkeschmieden* (84). At the same time, however, the structure of the plot changes:

Vom sogenannten Gegenspiel der klassischen Tragödie ist sie durch Isolierung der Motive, Szenen, Typen unterschieden. [...] das Drama des Barock (liebt auch) den Gegenspielern in grelles Licht gestellte Sonderszenen einzuräumen, in denen Motivierung die geringste Rolle zu spielen pflegt. Die barocke Intrige vollzieht sich, man darf es sagen, wie ein Dekorationswechsel auf offener Bühne, so wenig ist die Illusion in ihr gemeint. (67-68)

The utter indifference to psychological or moral motivation, combined with the encapsulation of conflicting figures through *in grelles Licht gestellte Sonderszenen* precludes any sort of resolution in a totalizing *dénouement*. What interests the baroque is not so much the dramatic resolution of conflict as its representation through a mechanism that acknowledges and even flaunts its own theatricality. The buffeting of individual figures in the winds of passion finds its adequate representation in a staging that demonstrates its own artifices.

The privileged site and scene of such emphatically theatrical artifice is the *court*:

Das Bild des Schauplatzes, genau: des Hofes, wird Schlüssel des historischen Verstehens. Denn der Hof ist der innerste Schauplatz. [...] Im Hof erblickt das Trauerspiel den ewigen, natürlichen Dekor des Geschichtsverlaufes. (90)

The eternal, natural character attributed to the court in the baroque testifies to the situation of an historical period, in which

die Christenheit oder Europa aufgeteilt [ist] in eine Reihe von europäischen Christentümern, deren geschichtliche Aktionen nicht mehr in der Flucht des Heilsprozesses zu verlaufen beanspruchen. (72)

Thus, with the eschatological perspective blocked, the irreducible partiality and provinciality of the local court renders it the exemplary site and stage of a movement of history that has been reduced to conspiratorial plotting, the aim of which is the destabilization rather than the taking of power. This is why the structural dynamics of the plotter causes him to resemble comic figures or the fool rather than the prince who would be sovereign. If the plotter is most at home in the court, it is only insofar as he knows that there can be no proper home (*keine eigene Heimstätte*, 96) for him.

In this sense the plotter can be said to be the *Exponent des Schauplatzes* as that place in which no one, including the Sovereign, can be at home. Unlike the sovereign, however, the plotter knows that the court is a theater of actions that can never be totalized but only *staged* with more or less virtuosity. By thus heeding only the rules of the game without seeking to reach ultimate principles, the plotter *begins* where the sovereign hopes to end: with the ex-clusion of the state of exception. The state of exception is excluded as theater. What characterizes this theater is that in it, nothing can ever authentically take place, least of all the stage itself:

Im ganzen europäischen Trauerspiel ist [...] auch die Bühne nicht streng fixierbar, eigentlicher Ort, sondern dialektisch zerrissen auch sie. Gebunden an den Hofstaat bleibt sie Wanderbühne; uneigentlich vertreten ihre

Bretter die Erde als erschaffenen Schauplatz der Geschichte; sie zieht mit ihrem Hof von Stadt zu Stadt. (125)

If the stage of baroque theater is dialectically riven and thus inauthentic, what distinguishes the German baroque is the impossibility of a dialectical *Aufhebung* that would constitute a totality:

Nur die Intrige wäre vermögend gewesen, die Organisation der Szene zu jener allegorischen Totalität zu führen, mit welcher in dem Bilde der Apotheose ein von den Bildern des Verlaufes artverschiedenes sich erhebt und der Trauer Einsatz und Ausgang zugleich weist. (268)

But it is precisely the inability to reach such an apotheosis that characterizes the German baroque theater in contrast to its Spanish counterpart in Calderón. And yet if this limits its aesthetic value, it is also what gives it its distinctive historical-philosophical significance.

The theater of the German baroque diverges both from classical tragedy and from the Schmittian theory of sovereignty in that it leaves no place for anything resembling a *definitive decision*. Rather, it is precisely the absence of such a verdict and the possibility of unending appeal and revision that marks the *Trauerspiel*:
*Man darf wohl den Exkurs in das Juristische noch weitertreiben und im Sinne der mittelalterlichen Klageliteratur von dem Prozeß der Kreatur sprechen, deren Klage gegen den Tod **oder gegen wen sonst sie ergehen mag** am Ende des Trauerspiels halb nur bearbeitet zu den Akten gelegt wird. Die Wiederaufnahme ist im Trauerspiel angelegt... (148, my emphasis)*

Nothing could demonstrate more clearly the distance between this eternal revision and Schmitts notion of an absolute, and absolutely definitive and ultimate decision. Here as there, the question of decision, of its power and its status, is always tied to a certain determination of space. Whereas in Benjamin however this determination is revealed to be the errant stage of an inauthentic and unlocalizable place, for Schmitt decision can be situated in terms of an unequivocal *point*:
*Die rechtliche Kraft der Dezision ist etwas anderes als das Resultat der Begründung. Es wird nicht mit Hilfe einer Norm zugerechnet, sondern umgekehrt; **erst von einem Zurechnungspunkt aus** bestimmt sich, was eine Norm und was normative Richtigkeit ist. Von der Norm aus ergibt sich kein Zurechnungspunkt, sondern nur eine Qualität eines Inhaltes. (42-43, my emphasis)*

160

If Schmitt asserts here that the norm presupposes a point of ascription, a *Zurechnungspunkt* upon which one must *count*, but which the norm as such cannot provide, the unmistakeable implication is that decision alone does provide such a point. In his reinscription of Schmitt, Benjamin takes exception to this point, thereby revealing it to be a stage upon which anything can happen, even a miracle, but nothing definitively decided.

9. Die Aufmerksamkeit des Lesers: Aufklärung und Moderne

RAINER NÄGELE

Die Konstellation von Aufklärung und Moderne hat im deutschen Sprachbereich — und in Deutschland besonders — die politische Rhetorik mit einer eigentümlichen moralischen Tönung besetzt. Die Verwechslung von moralischer Entrüstung und Aufrüstung mit politischer Analyse ist mit der Geschichte der bürgerlichen Aufklärung in Deutschland stärker als in Frankreich und andern westeuropäischen Ländern verknüpft. Die liberale und linke politische Rhetorik, die darauf sich beruft, ist anfälliger denn je für die Abdankung politischer Anlyse zugunsten moralisierender Kurzschlüsse. Es ist dies freilich längst kein Privileg der deutschen Situation. Der politische Diskurs in den USA, die Reaktion der europäischen liberalen und linken Intelligenz auf den Golfkrieg sind alarmierende Symptome.

Umso mehr ist Vorsicht gegen allzu großzügige globale Diagnosen geboten. Umso mehr ist die Aufmerksamkeit fürs Detail, für die Besonderheit und auch, vielleicht vor allem sogar, die Absonderlichkeit angebracht. Das Folgende wird sich deshalb auf die bescheidenste und entschiedenste Weise auf einige wenige Texte konzentrieren, ja beinahe auf einen einzigen, und auch auf diesen nur stellenweise, einige Motive berührend: Benjamins Lektüre von Kafka.

So abgelegen von den einleitend evozierten politisch-moralischen Problemen eine solche Lektüre sich zu situieren scheint, vertraut sie umso mehr der aufschließenden Kraft einer Aufmerksamkeit fürs Detail, die Kafkas und Benjamins Texte in eine spezifische Konstellation mit der Tradition der Aufklärung stellt. Sie setzt sich ebenso dezidiert ab von jenen Projektemachern, die am lautesten Aufklärung und Moderne so für sich zurechtschneidern, daß von den Texten und Bildungen der Moderne nichts mehr übrigbleibt als das reine nicht einmal abstrahierte, sondern phantasierte Projekt. Wenn im "Philosophischen Diskurs der Moderne" bei Habermas bereits Nietzsche zum Eingangstor der Postmoderne erklärt wird, kann die Moderne nur noch als Projekt gegen sämtliche Texte und Bildungen ihrer Philosophie, Literatur, Malerei und Musik sich behaupten. Die *Zeit* der Moderne, skandiert von den Texten Nietzsches, Adornos, Benjamins, Heideggers, Batailles ist relegiert an die Unzeit einer Postmoderne, deren Post vor aller Moderne diese schon gestrichen hat.

Dabei gibt es wohl eine immanente Konstellation von Moderne und Aufklärung: nicht nur in Nietzsches Vorliebe für die französischen Aufklärungsphilosophen, nicht nur in Adornos dialektischem Rettungsversuch, nicht nur in Brechts insistierender Berufung auf Diderot und Lessing, nicht nur in Musils penibler Entfaltung und Verfaltung von Mystik und Ratio, nicht nur in der sexuellen Aufklärung (eine übrigens primäre Konnotation des Wortes im Deutschen) von Freud, Bataille und Lacan, sondern auch und vielleicht vor allem in den parabolischen Verschlingungen von Kafkas Texten und einer Lektüre wie derjenigen Benjamins, die sich nicht scheut, auf die Verfaltungen solcher Texte sich einzulassen.

Wenn Kafkas Texte, ein Urgestein der Moderne wenn irgendeines, bei Habermas nicht in der geringsten Spur sich zeigen, so wird er das wohl damit begründen, daß er sich an den philosophischen Diskurs der Moderne halte. Jedem Autor ist das Recht auf die Begrenzung seines Untersuchungsfeldes zuzugestehen, solange nicht die Sache selbst sie in Frage stellt. Wenn aber gerade der philosophische Diskurs der Moderne "sich vielfach mit dem ästhetischen" "berührt und überschneidet"[1], ist wohl die Frage berechtigt, wie weit eine solche Berührung und Überschneidung den Kern dieses Diskurses betrifft und verändert. In der Tat müßte ein Blick auf die philosophischen Texte von Kierkegaard und Nietzsche bis zu Adorno, Benjamin, Heidegger, Bataille, Blanchot und Derrida deutlich vor Augen bringen, wie sehr der philosophische Diskurs nicht nur berührt, sondern im Innersten betroffen ist von einer sprachlichen Seite, die, ohne aufs Ästhetische reduzierbar zu sein, den Status philosophischer Diskurse radikal verändert. In der simplistischen Alternative Philosophie oder Literatur ebnet Habermas die Frage ein und relegiert die kontaminierten Texte auf den Abfallhaufen der Postmoderne.

Ein Jahrzehnt vor Adornos und Horkheimers *Dialektik der Aufklärung* verweist Benjamin in seinen Notizen zum Kafka-Aufsatz auf "Die dialektische Aufklärung Kafkas", die an einer Behandlung des Verhältnisses von Vergessen und Erinnern "einen besonderen

---

1. J. Habermas, *Der philosophische Diskurs der Moderne* (Frankfurt a.M.: Suhrkamp, 1985), S.7.

Stützpunkt haben" müßte (II,1255).[2] Das Vergessen als Moment einer dialektischen Aufklärung ist zugleich eines der Motive der Moderne, das von Nietzsche über Freud, Proust, Kafka bis zu Heideggers philosophischer Arbeit an der Seinsvergessenheit keineswegs auf das negative und einfach zu beseitigende Komplement der Erinnerung reduzierbar ist. Das höchst komplizierte, vielleicht sogar konstitutive Verhältnis des Vergessens zum Erinnern zu entfalten, oder auch nur seine Irruptionen und Zäsuren zu markieren, würde auch eine Geschichte der Moderne erzählen.

Aber wie läßt sich über Vergessen erzählen anders als im Abbrechen des Erzählens? Und daß es mit dem Erzählen und dem Erzähler in der Moderne kritisch bestellt, ja vielleicht zu Ende sei, davon erzählen nicht wenige Texte der Moderne und auch Benjamin. Aber auch dem direkten philosophischen Zugriff und Begriff entzieht sich das Vergessen. Das Vergessen läßt sich nicht sagen. Wenn aber eine dialektische Aufklärung nach Benjamin am Verhältnis von Vergessen und Erinnern seine Stütze hat, kommt sie um das Vergessen nicht herum und damit auch nicht um das Problem seiner Darstellung.

Wie lassen sich Texte darstellen, denen das Vergessen wie ein Buckel aufsitzt? Indem man vom bucklichten Männlein erzählt, scheint Benjamins Antwort. Indem man erzählt?

"Es wird erzählt:", beginnt kategorisch der Kafka-Aufsatz (II,409). Wo denn, bei wem? Es wird erzählt bei Benjamin, es wird erzählt bei Kafka, es wird anonym erzählt. Es wird erzählt: Der Doppelpunkt öffnet die Tür zu vielen Geschichten. Jedes Kapitel des Aufsatzes beginnt mit einem Erzählen oder einem Bild. "Es wird erzählt: Potemkin litt an schweren mehr oder weniger regelmäßig wiederkehrenden Depressionen"; und die Erzählung geht ihren Gang zum rätselhaften Ende. "Es gibt ein Kinderbild von Kafka" (II,416), beginnt das zweite Kapitel und stellt die Gabe dieses Bildes, das gegeben ist von einem "Es" wie das Erzählen im allerersten Satz, in die Konfigurationen der Kafkaschen Erzählungen. Erzählen hat bei Benjamin viel mit Erfahrung zu tun. Und so beginnt das dritte Kapitel unter dem Titel vom "bucklicht Männlein", unter der Signatur des Vergessens also, mit einer Anekdote von einem großen Erzähler: "Knut Hamsun, so erfuhr man vor längerer Zeit, habe die Gepflogenheit..." (II,425). Was man so

---

2. Alle Benjaminzitate, wenn nicht anders vermerkt, nach: Walter Benjamin, *Gesammelte Schriften*, Hrsg. v. Rolf Tiedemann und Hermann Schweppenhäuser (Frankfurt a.M.: Suhrkamp, 1980).

erfuhr hat seinerseits mit einer merkwürdigen Art des Vergessens zu tun, daß nämlich, wie es scheint, der Erzähler gründlich vergessen konnte, was der Autor geschrieben hatte, und daß eben dies das Erzählen und eine Erfahrung möglich machte. Und so kehrt der Text im vierten und letzten Kapitel zum anonymen Erzählen zurück: "In einem chassidischen Dorf, so erzählt man..." (II,433).

In dieser Weise literarische Texte in der Form von Erzählungen darzustellen, müßte nach den Kategorien von Habermas eindeutig als "Einebnung des Gattungsunterschiedes zwischen Philosophie und Literatur", bzw. zwischen Kritik und Literatur als "Abschied von der Moderne" in die Nacht der Postmoderne verwiesen werden. Die akademische Kafka-Literatur hat denn auch bis vor kurzem, wenn überhaupt eher spröde auf diesen Aufsatz sich bezogen. Und wenn auch noch einzelne Sätze als Zitate brauchbar schienen, die Darstellungsweise als Ganze mochte man so ganz ernst nicht nehmen. Eben dies aber: wie ernst oder nicht ernst Texte zu nehmen sind und in welchem Sinne, war eines der Zentralthemen in den Gesprächen zwischen Brecht und Benjamin über Kafka.

Aber bleiben wir zunächst noch beim Erzählen und seinem Status als Darstellungsform eines kritischen Textes. Benjamins Erzählungen biedern sich nirgends mit dem selbstgefälligen Gestus 'kreativen' Schreibens an. Was sie erzählen, kommt immer schon von anderswoher: was schon erzählt wird, was man erfuhr, was man erzählt; und sie stellen den Leser vor Bilder, die "es gibt". Es kann dann freilich geschehen, wie im Kinderbild von Kafka, das es gibt, daß es sich in rätselhafter Weise in ein anderes Kinderbild von Benjamin, das es ebenfalls gibt, verwandelt wie die enigmatische Signatur Potemkins, dessen Federzug den Namen Schuwalkins schreibt.

Dieses gewissermaßen sekundäre Erzählen, das immer nur nacherzählt, rückt dennoch in weite Distanz zu allem, was sich etwas hinterhältig Sekundärliteratur nennt, um desto brutaler die sogenannte Primärliteratur in den Griff zu bekommen. Was in Benjamins Text erzählt wird, ist keineswegs sekundär in Bezug zu Kafkas Erzählungen, die ihrerseits, auch wenn sie es nicht immer explizit aussprechen, sich im Gestus eines Entzifferns aus alten Blättern darbieten. Was dort auf den alten Blättern erzählt und geschrieben steht, wird nirgends erzählt, weder von Kafka noch von Benjamin, und wird dennoch nur da, in diesen sekundären Nachschriften und Nacherzählungen, überhaupt erst geschrieben und erzählt worden sein.

165

Benjamins Erzählungen erklären desto weniger Kafkas Erzählungen als sie an dessen dialektischer Aufklärung teilhaben. Sie verhalten sich zu ihnen etwa so wie nach Benjamins Übersetzungstheorie die Sprachen sich zueinander verhalten: keine ist primär oder sekundär zur andern, aber alle beziehen sich auf die Sprache als ihr Zentrum. Auf dieses Zentrum sind Benjamins Erzählungen ausgerichtet, indem sie sich sozusagen zu Füßen von Kafkas Erzählungen niederschreiben. Das Zentrum, auf das sie sich und Kafkas Texte beziehen, erscheint in ihnen mehrfach als die "wolkige Stelle" (II,420; 1258; 1263). Diese Stelle bleibt wolkig. Keine Aufklärung durchdringt sie.[3] Was Benjamin Kafkas dialektische Aufklärung nennt, geschieht, wenn sie geschieht, an den Rändern dieser wolkigen Stelle als eine Art Blitz in der geladenen Spannung einer Triangulation zwischen den Texten und der wolkigen Stelle.

Was ist aber mit solchen Bildern gesagt? Wenig, ja nichts sobald man glaubt, man könne darin sich häuslich niederlassen. Wenn nach Benjamin das dialektische Bild als Moment einer Lesbarkeit als Blitz einschlägt, ist einige Vorsicht geboten. Schreiberfahrungen, die an der Schwelle der Moderne Spuren gelassen haben, wie die Hölderlins, verweisen nicht ohne Alarm auf Semeles Schicksal.

Nüchternheit ist das oberste Gebot der Lektüre. Je hinfälliger die Hierarchie von erklärendem Metatext und literarischer Bild- und Erzählsprache sich zeigt, desto genauer ist der Status spezifischer Texte zu vermessen.

Benjamins Kommentartext zu Kafka nähert sich nicht nur dessen Erzählgestus an, sondern nimmt auch dessen andere Seite, den immer schon eingeschriebenen Kommentar mit auf und kommentiert ihn. Um die wolkige Stelle herum lagert sich eine Form von Texten an, die weder im Erzählen noch im kritischen Diskurs ihre Erfüllung finden. Sie sind "Gegenstand zu Überlegungen, die kein Ende nehmen", die "aber sonderbarerweise auch dann kein Ende nehmen, wenn sie von Kafkas Sinngeschichten ausgehen" (II,420). Statt der Überlegung und ihrer Überlegenheit bleibt nur die schier unendliche

---

3. Das unterscheidet sie vom Erkenntnisoptimismus des 18. Jahrhunderts, dem die Auflösung aller wolkigen Stellen sicher scheint. Vgl. etwa Herder im Aufsatz 'Vom Erkennen und Empfinden': 'Jeder Irrtum muß eine Wolke sein, die sich einmal zertrennet, und jede auch fehlgeschlagne Übung in Entwirrung der Symbole des Weltalls muß der Seele eine neue Formel geben, die sie witzige und beßre.' J.G. Herder, *Werke*, Hrsg. v. Wolfgang Pross (Darmstadt: Wissenschaftliche Buchgesellschaft, 1987), II,557.

Entfaltung in die Auslegung, die bereits in Kafkas eigenen Texten ihren Anfang nimmt.

Es gibt nun eine literarische Textsorte, angesiedelt zwischen Literatur und Philosophie, die eine alte Tradition hat: die Parabel. Lange Zeit legitimer Bestand der Poetiken wie der Philosophie schien sie in der Neuzeit von beiden verfemt, bis sie in literarischen und philosophischen Texten der Moderne sich wieder zunehmend zu behaupten scheint. Von Kafkas Texten als Parabel zu sprechen, ist in der Literaturkritik längst gängig.

Aber sind diese Parabeln noch Parabeln, wenn sie wiederkehren in Schriften wie denen von Kafka (oder auch von Beckett oder Brecht), wenn sie, wie die Parabel "Vor dem Gesetz", sich selbst erzählend in jedem Sinne *vor* dem Gesetz ansiedeln, das zu exemplifizieren die alten Parabeln gesetzt waren? Es ist die Frage, die Benjamin sich stellt.[4]

Die Parabel bedarf der Explikation, wofür im Deutschen das Wort "entfalten" sich anbietet, und gibt sie manchmal selber mit. Eine solche Entfaltung der Parabel "Vor dem Gesetz" vermutet Benjamin im *Prozeß*, um aber sogleich das Wort "entfalten" auseinanderzufalten: Das Wort "entfalten" ist aber doppelsinnig. Entfaltet sich die Knospe zur Blüte, so entfaltet sich das aus Papier gekniffte Boot, das man Kindern zu machen beibringt, zum glatten Blatt. Und diese zweite Art der "Entfaltung" ist der Parabel eigentlich angemessen, des Lesers Vergnügen, sie zu glätten, so daß die Bedeutung auf der flachen Hand liegt. (II,420)

Es entspräche diese zweite und klassische Art der Parabel wohl auch einem klaren Ideal von Aufklärung, nicht nur weil sie am Ende "die Bedeutung auf der flachen Hand" anbieten kann, sondern weil sie diese Bedeutung aus dem Kinderspielzeug herausgeholt hat, und indem sie das Kinderspielzeug vernichtet hat, das unmündige Kind mit dem glatten Papier zum mündigen Erwachsenen erklärt. Wenn nun Kafkas Parabeln dagegen nach Benjamin im ersten Sinn sich entfalten, ergibt sich ein eigentümlich doppeldeutiges Phänomen. Diese Entfaltung der Blüte zur Knospe schreibt sie einerseits einem ästhetischen Dichtungsideal ein, das seit der Romantik die Autonomie des Ästhetischen mit Vorliebe in organischen Metaphern be-

---

4. Derrida nimmt sie wieder auf in seiner Lektüre dieses Textes. Die Grenzen, die das Gesetz einer nicht unvernünftigen Konvention einem Aufsatz setzen, verbieten eine Einbeziehung dieser Lektüre. Es mag aber auch im Rahmen unseres Argumentes nicht ohne Nutzen sein, die Frage in einem Text zu entfalten, der noch nicht so sehr, wie die Schriften Derridas, der Postmoderne zugeschrieben ist. Umso mehr tritt dann vielleicht auch Derridas Lektüre als rigorose Lektüre der Moderne hervor statt des mystischen Gemurmels eines Verrückten in der Dachkammer der Postmoderne, wohin Habermas ihn zu bannen sucht.

gründet. Sie erscheinen damit in einem wesentlicheren und ernsteren Sinne als 'wahre' Dichtung gegenüber den seit dem 18. Jahrhundert zunehmend marginalisierten didaktischen und allegorischen und rhetorischen Formen. Gleichzeit wären sie damit aber vom 'Ernst' der Philosophie und deren spezifischem Wahrheitsanspruch abgespalten.

Als "der Dichtung ähnlich" bezeichnet denn auch Benjamin die Kafkaschen Parabeln. Aber eben: nur ähnlich. Hier beginnt eine Differenz sich abzuzeichnen, die mit den Gattungsgrenzen gleichzeitig auch geo-historische ideologische Grenzen ins Spiel bringt und sprengt. Kafkas Texte sind "der Dichtung ähnlich". Aber:

Das hindert nicht, daß seine Stücke nicht gänzlich in die Prosaformen des Abendlandes eingehen und zur Lehre ähnlich wie die Haggadah zur Halacha stehen.

Kafkas Texte also fallen nicht nur aus den konventionellen Gattungsformen heraus, sondern auch aus den Grenzen des Abendlandes. Diese Grenzen aber sind konstitutiv für jene Art von Aufklärung, die Habermas der Moderne vorschreiben möchte. Die Mißachtung dieser Grenzen konstituiert bei Habermas die postmoderne Anarchie, die Loslösung der Moderne "von ihren neuzeitlich-europäischen Ursprüngen", die Unterbrechung eines geschichtlichen Zusammenhangs im Namen des "okzidentalen Rationalismus" und schließlich, in einer letzten rhetorischen Steigerung der Abschied vom "Horizont der abendländischen Vernunft".[5]

Das Projekt der Aufklärung als Projekt einer Rekonstruktion, die ihre Legitimation an lokalisierbare Ursprünge knüpft und in einer ausschließenden Genealogie sich behauptet, verwirft im Namen der Postmoderne eben jene Moderne, die in der Form der Konstruktion jeden Begriff der Rekonstruktion und deren Bedingungen in Ursprung und Genealogie auflöst.[6]

Unaufdringlich und doch insistierend verweist Benjamins Kafkalektüre immer wieder auf die Sprengung des abendländischen Horizontes, am frappierendsten da, wo auch Kafkas Texte gewissermaßen an der Urszene der Moderne teilhaben, wo diese als Moderne gegen ihren andern Begriff, die Antike, sich konstituiert. Diese Antike ist von der Renaissance bis zu Lukács ausschließlich die abendländische, d.h. griechisch-römische Antike. Sie ist, wie immer

---

5. Habermas, l.c, S.10f.
6. Zur Kritik der Rekonstruktion vgl. Benjamin V, S.587.

variiert, das dialektische Andere der Moderne, ihr Anderes, von dem sie sich abgrenzt und ihr Anderes als ihr Spiegelbild. Alles Andere, und das war schon beim jungen Hegel das jüdische Andere, wurde zum nicht-dialektischen und deshalb zu vernichtenden Andern.

Nun scheint es freilich, daß das neuzeitliche Drama der *querelle des anciens et des modernes* seine Dringlichkeit in der Moderne längst eingebüßt hat. Dennoch konstruiert Benjamin nicht nur seine Theorie der Moderne in der radikalen Trennung des Trauerspiels von der griechischen Tragödie, sondern gibt auch in seiner Baudelaire-Lektüre dem Motiv der Antike ein eigentümliches Gewicht.

Bei Kafka werden wohl die wenigsten Leser auf Anhieb an griechisch-römische Antike denken. Man muß schon etwas suchen, und wenn einem dann das "Schweigen der Sirenen" einfällt, oder die merkwürdig traurig-komische Traumszene von K.'s Kampf mit einem nackten griechischen Gott im *Schloß*, erscheint das alles in sehr weiter Ferne von den geläufigen abendländischen Familienromanen. Und dennoch will Benjamin gerade bei Kafka die griechische Antike vor dem Vergessen bewahren: "Unter den Ahnen, die Kafka in der Antike hat, den jüdischen und den chinesischen, auf die wir noch stoßen werden, ist dieser griechische nicht zu vergessen" (II,415). Diese Geste des Erinnerns und des Bewahrens des griechischen Ahnen Kafkas, Odysseus, der fast schon wieder zum *oudeis*, zum Niemand, geworden ist, ist eigentümlich doppeldeutig. Sie bewahrt, indem sie sanft, aber radikal verschiebt: wo die abendländische Vernunft auch bei Habermas nach Schema nur die griechische Antike kennt, erscheint sie bei Kafka in Benjamins Lektüre als eine, die auch noch dazu kommt zur jüdischen und chinesischen. Der Satz wischt den ganzen Horizont der abendländischen Vernunft wie Spinngewebe weg. Es ist verlockend, in den jüdischen und chinesischen Ahnen die Einführung einer orientalischen Vernunft in die okzidentale zu begrüßen, verfiele man damit nicht schon wieder in jene Szenarien, die das philosophische Unbewußte der abendländischen Vernunft ausmachen. Als Herausforderung meldet freilich unter dem Zeichen des Orientalischen etwas Anderes sich an in solchen Schwellentexten der Moderne wie Hölderlins "orientalischer" Übersetzung griechischer Tragödien und in Benjamins Lektüre von Hölderlins "Blödigkeit".

Was in Kafkas dialektischer Aufklärung aufgeht zwischen Morgen und Abend ist eine Textsorte, die weder der Philosophie noch der Dichtung im abendländischen Sinne sich zuschlagen läßt, und die dennoch ihren Anspruch stellt. Ein großer Teil der Gespräche zwischen Benjamin und Brecht über Kafka kreisen um diesen merkwürdigen Status der Kafkaschen Texte. Benjamin ist fasziniert von einer Brechtschen Parabel über mögliche Texttypen. Brecht geht "von der Fiktion aus, Konfuzius habe eine Tragödie oder Lenin einen Roman geschrieben. Man würde das als unstatthaft empfinden, so erklärt er, und als ein ihrer nicht würdiges Verhalten. [...] Konfuzius dürfte auch kein Stück von Euripides schreiben, man hätte das als unwürdig angesehen. Nicht aber sind das seine Gleichnisse. Kurz, all dies läuft auf die Unterscheidung zweier literarischer Typen hinaus: des Visionärs, welchem es ernst ist, auf der einen und des Besonnenen, dem es nicht ganz ernst ist, auf der andern Seite".[7] Dies ist der Punkt, wo Benjamin die Frage nach Kafkas Zugehörigkeit aufwirft und sie als unentscheidbar einstuft.

Aus der Sicht eines philosophischen Diskurses, der seines Status sich in klarer Abgrenzung sicher ist, muß eine solche Unentscheidbarkeit doppelt unernst erscheinen. Denn wenn schon poetische Texte vor der Instanz der Vernunft nicht ganz ernst zu nehmen sind, so verlieren Texte, die sich auch nicht mehr eindeutig auf die poetische Wahrheit berufen können, völlig ihren Grund.

Viel in dieser Argumentation hängt aber davon ab, daß man ohne weiteres die Vernunft für ernst und den Ernst für vernünftig hält. Das unterliegt einigem Zweifel, der auch bei Brecht und Benjamin sich andeutet. Nicht nur daß Brecht von sich selber sagen muß, "Ganz ernst ist es mir nicht. Ich denke ja auch zu viel an Artistisches"[8], auch Brechts Typologie vom "Visionär", dem es ernst ist, und dem "Besonnenen", dem es nicht ganz ernst ist, läßt an der Kongruenz von Vernunft und Ernst einige Zweifel aufkommen.

Dieser Zweifel erhält seine theoretische Entfaltung in der erst neulich wieder gefundenen zweiten Fassung von Benjamins Aufsatz über "Das Kunstwerk im Zeitalter seiner technischen Reproduzierbarkeit". Die alte Schillersche Entgegensetzung und Verschränkung vom Ernst des Lebens und dem Spiel der Kunst erscheint hier als Unterscheidung einer frühgeschichtlichen ersten Technik von unserer heutigen modernen Technik:

Die technische Großtat der ersten Technik ist gewissermaßen das Menschenopfer, die der zweiten liegt auf der Linie der fernlenkbaren Flugzeuge, die keine Bemannung brauchen. Das Ein für allemal gilt für die erste Technik (da geht es um die nie wiedergutzumachende Verfehlung oder den

7. *Benjamin über Kafka. Texte, Briefzeugnisse, Aufzeichnungen*, Hrsg. v. Hermann Schweppenhäuser (Frankfurt a.M.: Suhrkamp, 1981), S.149.
8. Ibid., S.149.

ewig stellvertretenden Opfertod). Das Einmal ist keinmal gilt für die zweite (sie hat es mit dem Experiment und seiner unermüdlichen Variierung der Versuchsanordnung zu tun). Der Ursprung der zweiten Technik ist da zu suchen, wo der Mensch zum ersten Mal und mit unbewußter List daran ging, Abstand von der Natur zu nehmen. Er liegt mit anderen Worten im Spiel. (VII,359)

Wenn es der ersten Technik todernst ist, weil die Situation todernst ist, so bindet eben dieser Totenernst sie auch an Opfer, Mythos und Magie. Vernunft würde erst da sich regen, wo Witz und List ihr Spiel treiben und zwar von einem Bereich aus, den Benjamin nicht anders als Freud dem Unbewußten zuerkennt.

Kafkas Version von der Sirenen-Episode, die auch bei Adorno und Horkheimer als Schlüsseltext der dialektischen Aufklärung erscheint, ist ausdrücklich in der Form einer Beweisführung eingeführt: "Beweis dessen, das auch unzulängliche, ja kindische Mittel zur Rettung dienen können".[9] Das Kindische (nicht das Kindliche) mit all seinen Konnotationen von Albernheit, Schabernack und unschuldiger Boshaftigkeit ist allgegenwärtig in Kafkas Geschichten. Es ist das, was aus den Bildungsromanen, wenn es erscheint, eliminiert wird wie Mignon und umso aufdringlicher in den Figuren der Gehilfen bei Kafka sich eindrängt. In dem Maße als sie aus den Geschichten des bürgerlichen Bildungsromans ausscheren, erscheinen sie als Figuren minimaler Hoffnung und verweisen gleichzeitig auf jenen surrealistischen Bild- und Leibraum, den Benjamin als den "Raum des politischen Handelns" (II,309) vom bürgerlichen Raum der moralischen Metapher scheidet. Es ist ein Raum voller Fehlleistungen, konstituiert "im Witz, in der Beschimpfung, im Mißverständnis" (II,309).

Es sind lauter Begriffe, die etwas windschief im philosophischen Diskurs innerhalb des abendländischen Horizontes stehen, wo der Wind immer schön von Osten nach Westen bläst. Windschief aber scheint in der Tat die Figur der Moderne, wie sie etwa in Charlie Chaplin verkörpert vor Brechts Augen tritt: "und da setzt er den Hut schief auf und geht nach hinten ab, ins Dunkle, schwankend wie ein auf den Kopf geschlagener, ganz schief, wie vom Wind umgeblasen, ganz windschief, wie kein Mensch geht".[10] Und wind-

9. Franz Kafka, *Sämtliche Erzählungen* (Frankfurt a.M.: Fischer Taschenbuch Verlag, 1983), S.304.
10. Bertolt Brecht, *Gesammelte Werke*, Werkausgabe Edition Suhrkamp (Frankfurt a.M.: Suhrkamp, 1967), 15,60.

schief sind nach Benjamin auch die Dinge bei Kafka: "Kafka dagegen stößt schon allenthalben auf das Gesetz; ja man kann sagen, daß
er sich die Stirn an ihm blutig stößt [...], aber es ist nirgends mehr
das Gesetz der Dingwelt, in der er lebt, und überhaupt keiner
Dingwelt. Es ist das Gesetz einer neuen Ordnung, zu der alle Dinge,
in denen es sich ausprägt, windschief stehen, das alle Dinge, alle
Menschen entstellt, an denen es in Erscheinung tritt" (II,1205). Und
auch bei Benjamin erscheint die Figur dieser windschiefen Ordnung
in der Verkörperung Chaplins:

Wie Chaplin Situationen gibt, in denen sich auf einmalige Art das Ausge-
stoßen- und Enterbtsein, ewiges Menschenweh, mit den besondersten
Umständen heutigen Daseins, dem Geldwesen, der Großstadt, der Polizei
u.s.w. verbindet, ist auch bei Kafka jede Begebenheit janushaft, ganz un-
vordenklich, geschichtslos und dann auch wieder von letzter, journalistist-
scher Aktualität. Von theologischen Zusammenhängen zu reden hätte
allenfalls der ein Recht, der dieser Doppelheit nachginge; gewiß nicht, wer
nur ans erste dieser beiden Elemente anschließt. Im übrigen setzt sich diese
Zweistöckigkeit genau so in seiner schriftstellerischen Haltung durch...
(II,1198)

Zweistöckigkeit ist nach Gilles Deleuze die Grundstruktur barok-
ker Architektur und Gedankenwelt.[11] Ihre Ausprägung in den Figuren der Moderne verwickelt diese in eine Formenwelt, die windschief in den gängigen Kulturgeschichten von der Renaissance in die
Moderne steht.

Benjamin liest die barocke Zweistöckigkeit von Ewigkeit und
Zeitlichkeit, von Seele und Körperlichkeit, von Transzendenz und
Immanenz in Chaplin und Kafka als Verbindung der Extreme von
ewigem Menschenweh und besondersten Umständen, von unvor-
denklich Geschichtslosem und letzter journalistischer Aktualität.
Daß diese Verbindung der Extreme sich aber als "Zweistöckigkeit"
darstellt, betont gleichzeitig ihre Trennung und Säkularisation im
Raum. Das eine ist nicht Ausdruck des andern, sondern wie Spleen
und Ideal treten sie in harter Fügung zusammen und auseinander.

Vor allem aber treten sie als Extreme in Erscheinung und damit in
jenen Formen, die die klassische Aufklärung tendentiell ausschließt: als das Theologische und das Natürliche. Nun scheint es,
daß gerade diese Ausschließung explizit auch Benjamins Lektüre-
prinzip ausmacht, wenn er schreibt: "Zwei Wege gibt es, Kafkas

---

11. Gilles Deleuze, *Le Pli. Leibniz et le Baroque* (Paris: Edition de Minuit, 1988), S.
    5ff.

Schriften grundsätzlich zu verfehlen. Die natürliche Auslegung ist der eine, die übernatürliche ist der andere" (II,425). Benjamins Lektüreverfahren ist aber gerade im Kafka-Essay nicht von der Ausschließung der beiden, sondern von deren harten Fügung geprägt.

Benjamins Verfahren ist markiert von dem eigentümlichen Akzent, den der Begriff einer "natürliche[n] Auslegung" annimmt. Hier setzt eine radikale Umfunktionierung der klassischen bürgerlichen Ästhetik ein, wie sie sich programmatisch in Lessings "Hamburgischer Dramaturgie" abzeichnet, wenn er gegen Märtyrerstükke und christliches Trauerspiel auf einem Theater besteht, wo alles, "aus den natürlichsten Ursachen entspringen muß".[12] Es ist diese Natürlichkeit, die Benjamin in ihrer moderneren Ausprägung in der Form einer sich psychoanalytisch gebärdenden Interpretation als von vornherein verfehlt betrachtet.

Wenn Benjamin gleichzeitig Freuds *Jenseits des Lustprinzips* als besten Proust-Kommentar preist und diesem Text auch in seinem Baudelaire-Aufsatz einen gewichtigen Platz einräumt, läßt sich vermuten, daß das Verdikt sich gegen eine bestimmte Domestizierung der Psychoanalyse in eine humanistische und humanisierte Natürlichkeit richtet. Dagegen spricht in Benjamins von barocken Texten mitgeprägten Lektüren eine Natürlichkeit, die im Begriff des Kreatürlichen in extremen Antinomien zum Geistigen und gleichzeitig in einer unvorgängigen Konjunktion mit dem Theologischen auftritt. Nicht im Ausdruck der menschlichen Gestalt und ihres Leibes, sondern in der Körperlichkeit des Subhumanen, Tierischen, Dinglichen oder auch "allzu" Menschlichen phänomenalisiert sich hier die Natur.[13] Und nur in der Konjunktion mit dieser kreatürlichen Natur, außerhalb ihrer humanistischen Domestizierung, wird auch die Theologie lesbar als das von der humanistischen Säkularisierung nicht Überwundene, sondern Verdrängte.

Im spitzen Winkel dieser Konjunktion, im Zwielicht ihrer Extre-

12. G.E. Lessing, *Werke* (München: Hanser, 1973), IV,239.
13. Wie fremd ein solches Denken in der Tradition der klassischen bürgerlichen Aufklärung ist, kommt unfreiwillig komisch in einem ZEIT-Interview mit dem rumänischen Schriftsteller Mircea Dinescu zum Ausdruck (amerikanische Ausgabe 16. August, 1991). Dinescu spricht da über die Auswirkungen der politischen Diktatur in Begriffen, die dem aufgeklärten ZEIT-Reporter offenbar böhmische Dörfer sind. Dinescu spricht von köperlichen Mutationen bei Stechmücken, Ratten und Menschen: '...Diese Mücken stechen auch im Winter, weil sie in unseren feuchten Kellern, wo aus durchgerosteten Heizungsrohren Wasser ausläuft, ganzjährig überleben.' Auf die wohl etwas ironisch intonierte Frage des Interviewers 'Und das sind rein rumänische Moskitos?', fährt er weiter:

me siedelt Benjamin Kafkas dialektische Aufklärung an. Sie findet in den Zwischenräumen statt, "im Treppenhaus, auf Gängen, im Flur",[14] wo Odradek sein Unwesen treibt, und wo "Die Wendung der traumhaften Schicht in die theologische Schicht" "an der Kommunikation der Wohnräume und Gerichtsräume" zur Darstellung kommt in der barocken Zweistöckigkeit der Moderne: als Wendung und Trope der Lektüre: Umkehr zur Schrift, heißt sie bei Benjamin.

Die Umkehr zur Schrift ist nicht einfach eine Rückkehr zum alten Topos der Welt als Buch. Als Umkehr ist sie auch ein Umstülpen der Dinge und der Theologie, im Umstülpen ihre Entleerung und Entzifferung als Schrift, als Schrieb.[15] Symptomatisch für fast alle Disskussionen über Postmoderne, Moderne und Aufklärung ist eine grundsätzliche Verweigerung zur Lektüre. Habermas erklärt das offen zum Prinzip, wo immer ein Text sich nicht der deklarativen Äußerung von Inhalten beugt. Terroristisch usurpieren Paraphrasen die Texte. Um die Inhalte zu retten, blendet diese Aufklärung die Augen gegen die Sichtbarkeit der Schrift.

Die Geschichte des Auges in der Aufklärung ist eine andere als die von Bataille erzählte und eine andere als die des lesenden Auges. Soweit es eine Geschichte der Übersichtlichkeit und Übrersichtigkeit ist, muß sie die Tropen des Obszönen ebenso ausblenden wie die physiognomsichen Züge des Buchstäblichen. Diese können dann höchsten noch mit der Postmoderne in die Dachkammer der neuen Unübersichtlichkeit weggesperrt werden. Wenn man dann dort doch, wie in Kafkas *Prozeß* die staubigen Gesetzbücher öffnet, kann es sein, daß man mit obszönen Blättern konfrontiert ist.

Es ist freilich niemals eine einfache Frage von Sehen oder Blindheit. Sichtbarkeit ist immer auch eine Frage ihrer Grenze. Diese erscheint in einer sehr bestimmten Prägung in Benjamins Kafka-Aufsatz: "Wenn Max Brod sagt: "Unabsehbar war die Welt der für

'Nein, wahrscheinlich gibt es die auch in Sofia und Moskau. Aber in den Kühlhäusern, wo Ceausescu die rationierten Lebensmittel gehortet hat, sind Ratten mit weißem Fell aufgetaucht: Polarratten in Bukarest. Ärzte erzählen, daß einfache Fleischwunden, die bei Menschen im Westen in drei Tagen verheilen, sich in Rumänien erst nach zehn Tagen schließen. Der ständige Mangel an Vitaminen und Mineralien hat sogar unsere Körper genetisch angegriffen.' — An diesem Punkt reißt offenbar der Geduldfaden des abendländischen ZEIT-Reporters, dem es um wichtigers, nämlich um den Kopf geht: 'Aber das Erbe der Diktatur', wirft er ein, 'lebt auch in den Köpfen fort'.

14. Kafka, *Sämtliche Erzählungen*, l.c., S.139.
15. Ein Begriff, den Norbert Haas entwickelt hat als das, was sich schreibt in der Aporie von Lesbarkeit und Unlesbarkeit.

ihn wichtigen Tatsachen", so war für Kafka sicher am unabsehbarsten der Gestus" (II,420). Der Gestus erscheint auch als die "wolkige Stelle": er ist die sichtbare physiognomische Darstellung im Raum, Zug einer Schrift, und als solcher gleichzeitig Stelle einer Grenze des Sichtbaren. Im Begriff des Unabsehbaren erscheint diese Grenze in einer bestimmten Differenz zu anderen Grenzsetzungen des Sichtbaren: zur Unsichtbarkeit und zur Unübersichtlichkeit. Das Unsichtbare gehorcht einer metaphysischen Ordnung und dem Prinzip der Metapher, das Unübersichtliche einer Ordnung der Totalität und Kontrolle. Von beiden unterscheidet das Unabsehbare sich, daß es weder kategorisch unsichtbar ist (obwohl die englische Übersetzung symptomatischerweise "invisible" setzt), noch je in gerundeter Übersicht zum Ende des Sichtbaren kommt. Es folgt metonymisch dem Zug der Schrift. Es ist also gerade nicht die Welt als Buch, sondern als Schrift, deren Zug und Züge sichtbar und unabsehbar sind. Die Überlegungen kommen an ihr zu keinem Ende.

Wenn nun dialektische Aufklärung bei Kafka, bei Benjamin heißt, den Zügen dieser Schrift zu folgen, was heißt dann Lesen? Es erfordert wohl zunächst ein gewisses Interesse für das, was sich schreibt im buchstäblichen Sinne als ein sich Verhalten im Inter-Esse, im Zwischensein dessen, was als Schrift sich darstellt: als irreduzible Materialität der Spur und ebenso irreduzible Spürbarkeit der Spur.

Wenn im Gleichnis — angefangen von der Gleichung des Signifikanten mit dem Signifkat bis zu den parabolischen Gleichnissen als Textformen — die Lesbarkeit der Schrift sich behauptet, kehren die Züge des Schriftbilds die so bedeutete und bedeutende Bilderschrift immer wieder in die Unlesbarkeit zurück. In dieser Doppelheit konstituiert sich nach Benjamin die spezifische Textform Kafkas in der Antinomie und Verschränkung zwischen gleichnishafter "Sprache der Unterweisung" und symbolischer (d.h. aber bei Benjamin: unlesbarer) "Geberdensprache" (II,1260).[16] "Während der Lehrgehalt von Kafkas Stücken in der Form der Parabeln zum Vorschein kommt, bekundet ihr symbolischer Gehalt sich im Gestus" (II,1255). Was hier als Symbol benannt ist, hat offenbar

16. Benjamins Emphase auf der Theatralik von Kafkas und Brechts Texten weist auf das besonder Paradox einer Episteme der Moderne hin, die im Paradox des Phänomens als das unabsehbar Sichtbare sich kristallisiert: die aufdringliche Geste des Zeigens in der theatralischen Gebärde zeigt zuerst und zuletzt auf ihre eigen Unlesbarkeit.

nichts mehr von Coleridges romantischer "translucency", sondern umgekehrt bekundet es sich als die dunkle, wolkige Stelle, wo die Lesbarkeit an ihre Grenze kommt. Daß diese sich im Begriff des Symbolischen darstellt, ist Indiz dafür, daß es keine Frage einer Reduktion auf 'reine' Materialität ist, sondern eben die Stelle einer Grenze, wie Freuds Nabel des Traums, wo dieser dem Unerkannten aufsitzt.

Es ist nun gerade diese Zwischenstellung von Kafkas Texten, ihre Darstellungsform, nicht irgendein Inhalt, die sie in Benjamins Augen nicht nur der Dichtung, sondern auch der Philosophie in einer ihrer strengsten Formen annähert: dem Traktat. Die Vorrede zum Trauerspielbuch stellt die Traktate gewissermaßen als Texte vor dem Gesetz vor: Sie sind nicht Lehre, sondern "Propädeutik", der "die unumschreibliche Wesenheit des Wahren vor Augen stand" (I,208). Nicht paraphrasierbare Inhalte, sondern "Darstellung ist der Ingebriff ihrer Methode" (I,208). Die Parabel "Vor dem Gesetz", wie sie im *Prozeß* steht, wird so für Benjamin gleichzeitig die Darstellung des Traktats: "Unnennbarkeit dieser Geschichte: titellos. Sie lebt als solche in der Dimension arabischer oder hebräischer Traktattitel" (II,1191). Die Formulierung knüpft an den Text "Innenarchitektur" in der *Einbahnstraße* an:

Der Traktat ist ein arabische Form. Sein Äußeres ist unabgesetzt und unauffällig, der Fassade arabischer Bauten entsprechend, deren Gliederung erst im Hofe anhebt. So ist auch die gegliederte Struktur des Traktats von außen nicht wahrnehmbar, sondern eröffnet sich nur von innen. Wenn Kapitel ihn bilden so sind sie nicht verbal überschrieben, sondern ziffernmäßig bezeichnet. Die Fläche seiner Deliberationen ist nicht malerisch belebt, vielmehr mit den Netzen des Ornaments, das sich bruchlos fortschlingt, bedeckt. In der ornamentalen Dichtigkeit dieser Darstellung entfällt der Unterschied von thematischen und exkursiven Ausführungen. (IV,111)

In seiner Bestimmtheit als "ziffernmäßig bezeichnet[e]" Form im Unterschied zum Verbalen und zum Malerischen stellt der Traktat sich als Schrift und Graphik dar.

Gegenüber der scheinbaren Eindeutigkeit verbaler Semantik und malerischer Bildlichkeit will Schrift gelesen sein. Lesen heißt zunächst: auflesen, sammeln; dann den Linien und Zügen ihrer Gleise folgend die Schrift nachbuchstabieren. Lesen als Nachbuchstabieren tritt an die Stelle der Selbstreflexion, wo diese vor der wolkigen Stelle versagt. Es ist die Stelle, wo unter andern Freud, Benjamin, Kafka sich und einander und durch einander in einer dialektischen Aufklärung treffen. "Beim Bau der Chinesischen Mauer" stellt dieses Nachbuchstabieren als die einzige Form einer kollektiven

Selbsterkenntnis sich ein: "Wir — ich rede hier wohl im Namen vieler — haben eigentlich erst im Nachbuchstabieren der Anordnungen der obersten Führerschaft uns selbst kennengelernt".[17] Benjamin zitiert die Stelle im Kafka-Aufsatz und kommentiert sie mit einer Stelle aus Metchnikoffs Werk über "Die Zilvilisation und die großen historischen Flüsse", deren Geo-Graphik "Resultat kunstvoll organisierter gemeinsamer Arbeit von ... Generationen" ist (II,421). Im Hintergrund steht hier auch Hölderlins Dichtung als immer wieder neu ansetzender Versuch, die Graphik der großen Flüsse, die auch an seiner Bio-Graphik mitgeschrieben haben, zu entziffern. Daß nicht nur die großen graphematischen Erscheinungen, die großen Schriften der Erde, des Himmels, der Kollektive und der Bücher, sondern schon die viel kleinere und bescheidenere schriftliche Einheit eines Aufsatzes z.B. Resultat einer Organisation ist, die als Ganzes und im Detail dem Schreibenden nie gegenwärtig war und ist, kann jede Schreiberfahrung nachvollziehen.

Kafka hat sich oft Gedanken gemacht zu diesem Phänomen auch unter dem Gesichtspunkt der Schwierigkeit zu enden.[18] "Die Schwierigkeit der Beendigung, selbst eines kleinen Aufsatzes" verlangt "vom Verfasser eine Selbstzufriedenheit und eine Verlorenheit in sich selbst", daß die Versuchung, vor dieser Konzentration und gleichzeitigen Verlorenheit auszureißen, den Schreib- wie den Leseakt fast immer zum Scheitern bringt. Der Schluß wird dann zur Verzweiflungstat von Schreibhänden, "die nicht nur arbeiten, sondern sich auch festhalten müssen".[19]

Unter der Gefahr, daß auch dieser Schluß eine solche Verzweiflungstat darstellt, sei es gestattet zum Ende die Aufmerksamkeit kurz auf diese merkwürdige Doppelhaltung des Schreibens und Lesens zu richten, die bei Kafka als "Selbstzufriedenheit" und "Verlorenheit in sich selbst" erscheint. Benjamin setzt die Aufmerksamkeit als eine Grundhaltung Kafkas ans Ende des Kapitels vom Vergessen und vom bucklichten Männlein: "Wenn Kafka nicht gebetet hat — was wir nicht wissen — so war ihm doch aufs höchste eigen, was Malebranche 'das natürliche Gebet der Seele' nennt — die Aufmerksamkeit" (II,432). Das Verhältnis der Aufmerksamkeit zu den von Kafka genannten Schreibbedingungen —

17. Kafka, *Sämtliche Erzählungen*, l.c., S.292.
18. Ausführlicher dazu R. Nägele, 'Schloß ohne Schluß: Kafka, Benjamin und kein Ende', in: Jürgen Söring (Hrsg.), *Die Kunst zu enden* (Frankfurt a.M./Bern/New York: Peter Lang, 1990), S. 163-186.
19. Franz Kafka, *Tagebücher 1910-1923* (New York: Schocken, 1949), S.156.

"Selbstzufriedenheit" und "Verlorenheit in sich selbst" — ist aber keineswegs einfach. Wenn Aufmerksamkeit als eine gewisse Konzentration und Sammlung in sich selbst aus der gesammelten Kraft des Selbstzufriedenen und in sich Eingefriedeten sich nährt, so nähert sie sich als Öffnung für das Andere, als eine Form der Andacht — wie das holländische Wort heißt — der Verlorenheit nicht nur in sich selbst sondern auch von sich selbst. Konzentration und Zerstreuung überschneiden sich in ihr und bringen sie zur Schwebe: schwebende Aufmerksamkeit.

Man darf wohl vermuten, daß in Kafkas Aufmerksamkeit Benjamin auch seine eigene Lese- und Schreiberfahrung anspricht und als Form einer dialektischen Aufklärung und auch einer politischen Praxis zur Darstellung bringt. Die politische Aufgabe für die Zukunft erscheint dann als Hingabe an die Vergangenheit in Kafkas Hingabe an die Überlieferung. Diese Hingabe ist sowohl Konzentration wie auch ein Sich-gehen-Lassen, ein Sich-Aufgeben an eine Aufgabe, ein Aussetzen des Willens. Benjamin mißt daran den historischen Abstand zwischen Kafka und Hofmannsthal, wenn er an Adorno schreibt: "Es bleibt eine Seite an Hofmannsthal unberührt, die mir am Herzen liegt. [...] Hofmannsthal hat sich von der Aufgabe abgekehrt, die im Chandosbriefe auftaucht. [...] Die Sprache, die Hofmannsthal sich entzogen hat, dürfte eben die sein, die um die gleiche Zeit Kafka gegeben wurde".[20]

Die Aufgabe, von der Hofmannsthal sich abkehrte, stellt Benjamin an zwei Hofmannsthalschen Figuren dar: die eine ist Crassus, im Chandosbrief, Crassus "mit seinen Tränen über eine Muräne"; die andere Julian im "Turm" als derjenige, "dem nichts als ein winziges Aussetzen des Willens, als ein einziger Moment der Hingabe fehlt, um des Höchsten teilhaftig zu werden".[21] Es fehlte Hofmannsthal gewissermaßen am Mut, der der *Mu*räne eine *Trä*ne gewidmet hätte.

Kafkas Gabe ist das Geschenk für eine Hingabe, in deren Aufmerksamkeit und Andacht er, "wie die Heiligen in ihre Gebete, alle Kreatur eingeschlossen hat". Das erfordert von jedem humanistischen Standpunkt aus auch eine abgründige Geistesabwesenheit und Zerstreutheit, wie Benjamin sie im Bild eines andern Graphikers der Moderne liest: "Ein bedeutender Zug des wirklichen Baudelaire — nämlich des seinem Werk verschriebenen — [...] ist die

20. Walter Benjamin, *Briefe*, Hrsg. v. Gershom Scholem und Theodor W. Adorno (Frankfurt a.M.: Suhrkamp, 1978), S.851f.
21. Ibid.3

Geistesabwesenheit" (I,572). Geistesabwesenheit und winziges Aussetzen des Willens können dann als Momente einer dialektischen Aufklärung verstanden werden, wenn man wie Benjamin und Freud davon ausgeht, daß das Verdrängen von uns ausgeht, das Drängen aber von der anderen Seite herkommt: "Vergessenheit ist das Behältnis, aus dem die unerschöpfliche Zwischenwelt in Kafkas Geschichten ans Licht drängt" (II,430).

Schreiben in diesem Sinne und Schreiben der Moderne im besondern wäre also immer auch ein Sich-Verschreiben in Selbstvergessenheit und Selbstverlorenheit, vielleicht auch immer schon ein "Sich-Verschrieben-Haben"; und Lesen hieße dann, den arabesken und nicht unbedingt abendländischen Zügen dieser Verschreibungen zu folgen. Aber das kann man niemandem vorschreiben, schon gar nicht im Ernst, höchstens mit dem raschelnden Gelächter Odradeks.

10. The Easily Stirred Tribe of Tears. A Text of Jacques Derrida

ELISABETH WEBER

I

"Oh, such a tear, (...)
That prowls inside the human breast, sets all
the fire bells of feeling ringing, cries Misery!
so that all of that tribe, the one easily stirred,
rushes out the eyes, and, gathered into seas,
weeps over the ruins of her soul."[1]

Why does Penthesilea weep?[2]
Why does she weep following the duel with Achilles that was no
duel; why does she weep even before she has recovered her senses,
even before she knows what she has done?

Who weeps within her? The lover, the warrior or one who needs
absence in order to "exist," the absence or confusion of mind? Is the
mourner already weeping in her even before she becomes conscious
of the loved one she has mutilated? Is it the abandoned one who
weeps?

For whom does she weep? The dead one, the beloved living one,
herself, the abandoned one? She weeps before she knows. But
perhaps another in her knows before she does and knows more.
Knows otherwise. Would it be she, the other one, who weeps? And
would it be because of her that the "easily stirred tribe" of tears
"rushes out"?

Penthesilea's weeping is directed at nobody. But still it is the first
sign announcing her return from a field that one could call, to

---

1. Heinrich von Kleist, *Penthesilea*, 24 th scene. (For this particular "close-reading"
   I have chosen to do my own translations of the Kleist passages, but haved
   consulted Martin Greenberg's *Heinrich von Kleist: Five Plays*, trans. and with an
   introduction by Martin Greenberg, New Haven & London: Yale University
   Press, 1988). (Translator's note)
2. Kleist's *Penthesilea*. As is well known, in one version of the Greek legend Achilles
   kills Penthesilea. In this regard it might be of interest to remember that Homer has
   his heros express their mourning, their pain, through tears. One of these weeping
   heros is Achilles.

180

borrow a term from Lacan, the field of "absolute destruction." It is not the field of battle, of violence, of destruction that was able to cause the "ruins of her soul." For that, another destruction, another violence was needed. She will not be able to find a way back from this other field; her tears mark a threshold that she will not have finally crossed over just as long as she remains unknowing. Beyond this threshold the tears run dry. Penthesilea says it expressis verbis when she sees the mutilated body of Achilles:[3]
"I don't want to know who slew the living man, in the presence of our ever sublime gods!

She's free as a bird to go wherever she wants
Who killed the man already dead is what I'm asking (...)
Who so mangled this young man, the very image of the gods, that life and decay will not argue possession of him; who so hacked him that pity has no tears for him, and love, undying love, like a whore, untrue even in death, must turn away from him:
I'll sacrifice her to my revenge."

It is not the dead man she wishes to avenge, but rather the mutilated dead man; she wants to avenge the impossibilty of weeping at the sight of Achilles, the impossibility of tears. For it is in the tears that the image that the one who weeps gives himself of the one wept for, is reflected. If this image is destroyed to the extent that the mirror no longer recognizes it, then it shatters. When the mirror, also called "Psyché,"[4] can no longer grasp the image, because it no longer resembles the loved one whatsoever, the tears dry up. The "easily stirred tribe" is paralysed. It is where love — of which it is said that it is "strong" or "powerful" like death — "must" turn away, that this tribe can no longer "rush out." For there is a violence behind the violence of death. In regard to this violence, the violence of the destruction of death, Penthesilea says that love, the love of eros, must turn away from. And where the love of eros *must* turn away, the tribe of tears can no longer be stirred.

At the threshold where the tears "rush out," neither does an experience find space and take place, nor does an address find its destination. There, where she weeps, Penthesilea lacks the self-presence or presence of mind necessary for an experience, and her weeping has no addressee, no goal, no purpose. But it is in this very

3. Kleist, *Penthesilea*, 24th scene.
4. Cf. Jacques Derrida, *Psyché. Inventions de l'autre*, Paris: Galilée 1987 pp. 10 and 31.

"non-address" of the tears that it is solely a question of "addressing myself only to you. To you uniquely, you, you, and you cannot stand it, you are afraid, you grow agitated, you flee, you seek to distract yourself."[5]

II

This sentence fragment from the *Carte Postale* opens up the text of Jacques Derrida announced in the title, that is to say, *one* of Jacques Derrida's texts. 'A text of Jacques Derrida' does not mean in this instance a text circumscribed by title, beginning, and end, but rather a text running through several texts, running throughout Derrida's writing, a text which could be described as a micrology of tears in Adorno's sense of micrology as "refuge from the totality,"[6] but also in the sense of a "pragrammatology," that always takes account of the "situation of the marks," of utterances, the place of the senders and addressees and so forth.[7]

Examined here will be a "situation of utterances," one marked by tears written or wept, and respectively, marked by a "recherche" of tears like that resonating in one of the most recent (and oldest) of Derrida's texts: "... à l'autobiographie je dois de dire que j'ai passé ma vie à enseigner pour enfin revenir à ce qui mêle au sang la prière et les larmes [...]."[8] "I owe it to autobiography to say that I have spent my entire life teaching, in order to finally return to that which mixes the prayer and the tears with the blood [...]."

The "recherche" of tears would therefore be the oldest one, but not just in the sense of a continuous and successive chronology, that decides between the most recent and the oldest. For the straight line of such a chronology is broken up by those experiences associated with tears. An example of such an event and the example par excellence in the cited text "Circonfession," of one which mixes the prayer and the tears with the blood (in Derrida's text the tears are,

5. Derrida, *The Post Card From Socrates to Freud and Beyond*, trans. Alan Bass (Chicago & London: The University of Chicago Press, 1987), 49.
6. Adorno, Theodor W., *Negative Dialektik*, Frankfurt am Main: Suhrkamp Verlag, 1966), 397.
7. Cf. Derrida, *Taking Chances: Derrida, Psychoanalysis, and Literature*. Joseph H. Smith and William Kerrigan, eds. (Baltimore and London: Johns Hopkins University Press, 1984), 27.
8. Jacques Derrida, "Circonfession," in *Jacques Derrida*, G. Bennington and J. Derrida (Paris: Seuil, 1991), 22.

significantly, those of another, namely the mother), is the un-rememberable event of circumcision: the event of a wound inflicted even prior to the possibility of remembering it, of interiorizing it. If such "interiorization" is, as is well known, the conditio sine qua non for the so-called "working through," or to use an Hegelian term, "labor of the negative," then here there is no "work," neither "labor of the negative," nor work of mourning. The wound has been inflicted upon one who hasn't had the slightest chance of preparing for it, defending against it, or reacting to it. It happened prior to the constitution of the "self," prior to the time of real-ization, and for just that reason no continual chronology, including that of a "working-through" can be valid.

But for Derrida "circumcision" also signifies a special experience within language: "Dès qu'on a un rapport poétique à la langue, c'est-à-dire aussi un rapport d'expérience à ce qui nous fait naître à la langue, de l'être-déjà-là de la langue, du fait que la langue nous précède, commande notre pensée, nous donne les noms, etc., cette expérience poétique de la langue est d'entrée de jeu une expérience de circoncision (coupure et appartenance, entrée originaire dans l'espace de la loi, alliance dissymétrique entre le fini et l'infini)." "Once one has a poetic relationship to language, that is, when one also has a relationship of experience to that which awakens us to language, an experience of the 'already being there' of language based on the fact that it precedes us, orders our thinking, gives us names, etc., — then this poetic experience of language is from the outset an experience of circumcision (incision and belonging, origi-nal entry into the space of law, dissymmetrical alliance between the finite and the infinite)."[9] Its determining feature of standing for both a singular and a universal becomes clear through its link with names. Does one ever, Derrida asks in "Schibboleth," "circumcise without circumcising a word? A name? And how can one circum-cise a name without doing something to the body? First of all to the body of the name which is recalled to its condition as word by the wound, to its condition as carnal mark, written, permeated, en-graved into a network of other marks, a mark both endowed with and deprived of singularity?"[10]

9. From a discussion between the author and J. Derrida which will appear in fall 1993 in a collection of discussions entitled: *Jüdisches Denken in Frankreich* (Frankfurt am Main: Jüdischer Verlag im Suhrkamp Verlag).
10. Derrida, 'Schibboleth pour Paul Celan', (Paris: Galilée, 1986), 98. The English translation (found in *Midrash and Literature*, Ed. Geoffrey H. Hartman and

Circumcision is thus simultaneously the mark of Jewish singularity *and* of the universality of being inscribed into language.

An experience in this sense that is both singular, specifically Jewish, as well as exemplary, is asserted in another text of the fate "that summons the Jew and places him between voice and cipher; and he weeps for the lost voice with tears as black as the trace of ink."[11] Nevertheless, the lost voice was never present; it can only be called lost in regard to the mode of a 'voice' that the people of Israel are said to have heard on the Sinai. From this voice, according to one of the different interpretations, the Israelites heard not so much the articulation of the ten commandments, in fact not even that of the first one, but rather only: "that 'aleph' with which in the Hebrew text of the Bible the first commandment begins, the 'aleph' of the word 'anokhi,' 'I.' [...] For in Hebrew the consonant aleph represents nothing more than the position taken by the larynx when a word begins with a vowel. Thus the 'aleph' may be said to denote the source of all articulate sound [...] To hear the 'aleph' is to hear next to nothing; it is the passage to all audible language [...]."[12]

In the first case the tears are those of another. They accompany a wound that belongs for the subject to time immemorial. In the second case they are more a dictation than an expression of the subject itself and aim toward a voice from time immemorial. The wound, the tears of the other one, for instance the mother, the voice whose loss dictates "tears as black as the trace of ink," writing, — all this took neither place nor time in the subject's present. To name these tears in the text, to go in search of them in the text, thus does not only mean to weep for a lost present even if the mourning for a lost presence can normally not be divorced from weeping. In both cases however, the text refers to a certain temporality into which an event intruded and convulsed the subject prior to the constitution of a present time. One might perhaps venture to suspect that this particular temporality lays hold of the weeping one as well. That is to say, that the period of time in the weeping one that extends momentarily from the present to that immemorial time of the

Sanford Budick, New Haven and London: Yale University Press, 1988, 340) is not identical with the French text, as the English version preceded the French.

11. Derrida, *Writing and Difference*, trans. Alan Bass (Chicago: The University of Chicago Press, 1978), 73.

12. Gershom Scholem, *On the Kabbalah and Its Symbolism*, trans. Ralph Manheim (New York: Schocken Books, 1969), 30. Manheim's translation has been very slightly modified.

wound, of the voice and of the tears of the other, allows an excess to break into the subject's presene.

Levinas describes this excess as absence of any refuge, as the impossibility of escape and thus the announcement of mortality: "In suffering there is an absence of any refuge. [...] Not in the instant of suffering where, backed against being, I still grasp it and am still the subject of suffering, but in the crying and sobbing toward which suffering is inverted. Where suffering attains its purity, where there is no longer anything between us and it, the supreme responsibility of this extreme assumption turns into supreme irresponsibility, into infancy. Sobbing is this, and precisely through this it announces death. To die is to return to this state of irresponsibility, to be the infantile shaking of sobbing."[13]

This excess marks the pain and the tears even when these are perhaps not necessarily or exclusively tears of pain. They are excessive because they respond to immemorial time before the voice, before the presence, and before the call is heard. Response to the tears before the tears; to the tears of the other. Tears would perhaps be the echo of a response to a call sent out prior to every empirical language. It is to that extent that they are *affirmative* even prior to the opposition of affirmation and negation. Their temporality however is one of "après-coup," of deferment. The tears always arrive "à contretemps," at the wrong time, or "Un-zeit" as Hamacher defines it: they arise at the "intersection of incompatible and unassimilable times and dimensions" which in turn "has neither a definable time nor dimension."[14]

Or, to borrow a term from Levinas, tears arise within a "time-lapse," within the leap in continual temporality that separates the event from the subject's presence. It has already occurred, it exhibits the structure of the trace, as Levinas and Derrida have defined it. The tears follow this trace.

13. Emmanuel Levinas, *Time and the Other*, trans. Richard A. Cohen (Pittsburgh: Duquesne University Press, 1987), 72. An echo of this excess is found with Adorno and Horkheimer, when they note that the wailing is "always exaggerated, however honest it may be, since the whole world seems to be enclosed in every plaintive note." Theodor W. Adorno and Max Horkheimer, *Dialectic of Enlightenment*, Trans. John Cumming, (New York: Continuum, 1990), 182.
14. Werner Hamacher, "Des contrées des temps," in: Zeit-Zeichen, ed. G. Tholen and M. Scholl (Weinheim: Acta Humaniora, 1990), 30.

III

Tears, or more exactly, the ability to weep, is considered by humanists, medical doctors, and psychologists, to be, like the laugh, one of the distinctive features of the human species.[15]

But at the same time, these tears which are supposed to be so exemplary for the human species are according to Hegel something 'neutral,' something indifferent.

For Hegel "an inner tear ('Zerrissenheit') within the suffering one, brought about through a 'negative,' is expressed in weeping, — pain. The tears are the critical eruption, — thus not simply the expression ('Äußerung'), but at the same time the elimination ('Entäußerung') of the pain; in the presence of significant mental suffering they thus benefit health just as pain which is not disbursed into tears can become harmful to health and life. In the tear, pain, — the feeling of that cutting antithesis that has forced its way into the heart —, turns to water, becomes neutral, indifferent, and the neutral material itself, into which the pain is transformed, is expelled by the soul from its corporeality. It is in this expulsion and in that embodiment that the cause of the beneficial effect of weeping is found."

Just prior to this, Hegel introduces his reflexions on laughing and weeping with the following sentence:
"Such an exteriorizing embodiment of the inner self is shown in *laughter*, but even more in *weeping*, in moaning and sobbing, and generally in the *voice* already before this voice is articulated, even before this voice becomes speech."[16]

For Hegel, tears are then on the one side adjacent to the voice, and in fact prior to its articulation, and on the other hand they act to neutralize, that is, to exteriorize a splitting contradiction which has forced its way into the heart, by embodying it. Tears are the physical expression (for example and par excellence) of pain. In that way they represent a threshold, perhaps a revolving mirror, bet-

---

15. Cf. for example P. Greenacre, "On the Development and Function of Tears," in: *The Psychoanalytic Study of the Child*, vol. XX, New York: 1966 p. 211-214, R.L. Sadoff, *Crying and Weeping in the Expression of Emotion*, University of California Los Angeles 1963, Arthur Schopenhauer, *The World as Will and Idea*, trans. by R.B. Haldane and J. Kemp, (London: Routledge & Kegan Paul Limited, 1948), 486.

16. Hegel, *Enzyklopädie der philosophischen Wissenschaften* III, ed. E. Moldenhauer and K.M. Michel, vol. 10, Frankfurt/M. 1986, p. 113-115 (Postscript to para. 401).

ween physis and 'psyché.' Tears give expression to an inner tearing ('Zerrissenheit'), they are provoked by this 'Zerrissenheit.' In English this seems to be reflected or rather occurs in the same spelling for tear ('die Träne'): and to tear ('zerreißen').

But what about when one commits a slip of the tongue, when one takes this instead of that, like Penthesilea who mistakes bites for kisses, "Bisse und Küsse," because they rhyme.[17] "It was a slip of the tongue, I swear it by Diana" ('Ich habe mich, bei Diana, bloß versprochen') she says.[18] Has she not also mistaken the tearing ('das Zerreißen') for the tears ('die Tränen')? the excess of revenge for the excess of love? Still, the word 'revenge' describes the situation only superficially if at all. Penthesilea expresses the deepest logic of her love, a logic which is interpreted by the Amazons as a sign of madness when, after having learned who killed Achilles, she sceptically asks: "I tore him to shreds. Or did it happen otherwise? Did I kiss him dead? Did I not kiss him? Really tore him to shreds?,"[19] and when she then justifies herself:

"As is often the case, with her arms wound around her beloved's neck, a woman says she loves him, oh, so much she's ready to *devour* him for love. But then, upon examining the word more closely, the poor fool finds she's had a bellyful of him already.
Well, my love, that was not my way.
You see: when I wound my arms around your neck
I did just that, word for word, devour you.
I wasn't so mad as it might seem."

What Penthesilea here expresses *consciously*, that is, in the mode of an overly sharp memory, is not simply the translation of reality into language, but above all the manner in which she actually translated language back into reality, literally, without the shadow or the flight of a blind spot, of a forgetting or of a repressing: not only could she "devour" the beloved one, she did it "word for word." Her tears, which she weeps prior to becoming so sharply conscious, give no expression to the split ('Zerrissenheit') in the Hegelian sense, whereby a pain would be expelled through its tears. Here, the tears tear the observer: "This sight tears the heart to shreds worse than knives! /

---

17. "So war es ein Versehen. Küsse, Bisse. Das reimt sich, und wer recht von Herzen liebt, kann schon das eine für das andere greifen." (425)
18. 'Sich versprechen' also has the meaning of 'to promise oneself.' Another possible translation might read: "I promised myself by Diana."
19. Kleist, p. 265, The responses of the Amazons were left out in the quotation.

She wipes away a tear." ('O Anblick, herzzerreißender, als Messer!/ Sie wischt sich eine Träne ab.') Instead of healing the tear, this tear announces an incurable one: it calls in the entire tribe so that it might weep for the ruins of her soul, to weep for an irrevocable tear. Would this mean that the tears wept for a lost unity? Are the ruins of her soul the opposite pole of a 'complete' soul?

Penthesilea has not only committed a slip of the tongue ('sich versprochen'), but also a mistake ('sich vergriffen'). She substitutes one word for another, then a word for a deed. This possibility, which in general is that of the metaphor and in particular that of madness, of splitting, or psychosis, provides sufficient information on the hypothetical unity, namely that it is illusory.

The possibility of doing something "word for word" implies the principal impossibility of ruling out that one can "mistake one for the other," bites for kisses, tears for tears. With Penthesilea the tears stir on the delicate line of this 'for,' on the delicate gap or tear along the metaphoricity. There, where kisses and bites, tear and tears actually converge, there namely, where Penthesilea (whose name by the way contains 'penthos,' the sorrow of mourning) lets them converge in-deed, and there where she consciously pronounces and affirms this equivalence, she weeps not and weeps no longer. The tears are only possible in the time interval and only in the spatial interval separating two words from each other and one word from what it names.

Freud also underscores this delicate tear of metaphoricity when he stresses that the "conscious presentation of the object" can be "split up into the presentation of the *word* and the presentation of the *thing*..."[20] While the presentation of the thing remains intact in repression without however being grasped in words (these succomb to the repression), there is, in the psychotic symptom, a predominance of the word relation over the thing relation. Based on the similarity or identity of words one can 'sich versprechen' when one 'sich verspricht' (meaning in German to 'commit a slip of the tongue' *and* to 'promise oneself') and thereby *make* real, word for word, the performative act of such a 'Versprechen' (slip *and* promise). That is the delicate tear ('Riß') in the subject that may more or less gape, but in any case extends through the subject.

If the word relation substantially outweighs the thing relation (a situation which for Freud often proceeds accompanied by a con-

20. Sigmund Freud, *The Standard Edition of the Complete Psychological Works*, ed. James Strachey (London: The Hogarth Press, 1963), VII, 201.

scious elucidation on the part of the subject which has "the value of an analysis,"[21] an elucidation conspicuous in Penthesilea), then the tear deepens within the subject, the split expands. Madness translates the extension of this tear, which now also affects the relation of the self to the outside world. Penthesilea's tears run dry as she crosses over that fragile line. Here, the tears mark the fragile borderline (and the question begs to be asked whether or to what extent they ever mark this borderline).

IV

But where does this delicate tear ('Riß') run, this tear that passes through the subject and can gape open in words, when the word is not a name, but rather a proper name? This question can be pursued through Derrida's reading of *Romeo and Juliet*, which begins, if not with a tear ('Riß'), then certainly with a dissociation which will continue by way of a proper name right up to the possible tear ('Riß'). Derrida's text, "L'aphorisme à contretemps," develops as a series of aphorisms: "Aphorism is the name. As its name shows, the aphorism separates, it marks the dissociation ('apo'), it terminates, limits, restrains ('orizô'). It concludes by dividing, it severs in order to end and to define. Aphorism is a name, but each name can assume the form of an aphorism."[22]

That is the case for the proper names Romeo and Juliet. If the "aphorism delivers us unprotected to the experience of the contretemps, to non-time,"[23] then *Romeo and Juliet* is the staging of this "non-time": "What Romeo and Juliet experience is the exemplary anachronism, the essential impossibility of an absolute synchronization."[24] On the other hand this very impossibility is the condition for their desire and for desire at all. "There is no time for desire without the aphorism. Desire does not take place without the aphorism."[25] *At the same time* however, it is also stated that "there is no aphorism without speech, without naming, without invoca-

21. Freud, p. 198.
22. Jacques Derrida, *Psyché*, p. 519. "Aphorisme est le nom. Comme son nom l'indique, l'aphorisme sépare, il marque la dissociation (apo), il termine, délimite, arrête (orizô). Il met fin en séparant, il sépare pour finir — et définir. Aphorime est un nom mais tout nom peut prendre figure d'aphorisme."
23. Derrida, p. 520
24. Derrida, p. 521
25. Derrida, p. 521, "Il n'y a pas de temps pour le désir sans l'aphorisme. Le désir n'a pas lieu sans l'aphorisme."

tion, even without a letter to be torn."[26] In other words, if Romeo and Juliet make Romeo's name responsible for the aphorism, that is, for the impossibility of synchronization, of a presence, then it is just this aphorism, which is Romeo's name, that provides a place for their love. And if Juliet designates Romeo's name as her enemy and implores not it, but rather Romeo himself "O be some other name," she still calls him, as Derrida stresses, "in his name." In this name "she calls him and asks him to no longer be named Romeo and begs him, Romeo, to renounce his name."[27]

"She declares war on 'Romeo,' on his name, in his name, she will win this war only with the death of Romeo himself. Himself? Who? Romeo. But 'Romeo' is not Romeo. Exactly. She wants the death of 'Romeo,' Romeo dies, 'Romeo' survives. She keeps him dead in his name. Who? Juliet, Romeo."[28]

When Juliet implores Romeo, himself, to be another name: "O be some other name," and asks him why he is Romeo, "wherefore art thou Romeo?" then she does so knowing, as Derrida shows, that his name, "as detachable and separable, as aphoristic as it may be, is his essence and not to be seperated from his being."[29]

Derrida recalls Juliet's incisive analysis of the proper name, which leads to her recognition of the "inhumanity or the non-human" of the name. This inhumanity or "non-humanity" consists of bearing a name that designates nothing of me, not even a piece of me, and yet "affects the being of the one who bears it."[30] It is exactly this name that Romeo would like to tear ('zerreißen'): "Had I it written, I would tear the word."

Because he has not written his name, but rather received it from his father, he can neither efface it nor tear it.[31] The dynamic of the

26. Derrida, p. 520: "il n'y a pas d'aphorisme sans langage, sans nomination, sans appellation, sans lettre même à déchirer."
27. Ibid., p. 526
28. Derrida, p. 527, "Elle déclare la guerre à "Roméo", à son nom, en son nom, elle ne gagnera cette guerre qu'à la mort de Roméo, lui-même. Lui-même? Qui? Roméo. Mais 'Roméo' n'est pas Roméo. Justement. Elle veut la mort de 'Roméo'. Roméo meurt, 'Roméo' survit. Elle le garde mort dans son nom. Qui? Juliette, Roméo."
29. Derrida, p. 528: "si détachable et si dissociable, si aphoristique soit-il, son nom est son essence. Inséparable de son être."
30. Derrida, p. 529: "cette inhumanité [du nom] qui consiste à affecter l'être même de qui le porte alors qu'il ne nomme rien de lui."
31. Derrida, p. 530.

proper name makes it impossible to sever the tie with the name "Romeo" even in the demand for the death of that name.[32] Romeo and Juliet are in love unto death with their names.

And because they cannot tear ('zerreißen') these names without tearing themselves, they bemoan these names, themselves, so much that they are spoken of as being drunk with their tears. After the murder of Juliet's cousin Tybalt, resulting in Romeo's banishment from Verona, the monk Lorenzo describes Romeo as lying "There on the ground, with his own tears made drunk," the nurse, reporting on Juliet, responds "Even so lies she, blubb'ring and weeping, weeping and blubb'ring," and further, "O, she says nothing, sir, but weeps and weeps [...] and then on Romeo cries ..." Romeo consequently begs the Franciscan, "O tell me, friar, tell me,/ in what part of this anatomy / Doth my name lodge? Tell me, and I may sack / The hateful mansion." But this very name will survive not only that part of the anatomy in which Romeo searches for it hoping to stab it, but rather will survive the life of this body in its entirety. Romeo and Juliet are torn by the impossibility of tearing a name. Their tears move along the impossible tear (Riß) that they want to execute on Romeo's name, word for word.

The impossibility of tearing a name, is the impossibility of retroactively making it 'uncalled': it was called and named even before the subject could answer.[33] In *this* respect the name has the same structure as the 'aleph', of which nothing was heard other than the fact *that* it was emitted. That is why the name is just as untearable as the 'aleph'. When Derrida writes in "Circonfession": "et je mêle ici le nom de Dieu à l'origine des larmes," "and here I mix the name of God with the origin of tears,"[34] then this sentence exceeds its autobiographic meaning. The name of God is the very aphorism itself — it is impossible to tear it. The origin of tears may therefore be located at the immemorial site of the calling out, of the name that calls out and cannot be obliterated by anything.

In this regard, the tears as well as the name have been *given*[35] to an immemorial childhood and to a child who is introduced to the reader in "Circonfession," perhaps long before the reader is aware of it: "... et ceux qui me lisent de là-haut, je me demande s'ils voient

---

32. Cf. Derrida, p. 527
33. A conceptual figure often used by Levinas as well.
34. Derrida, "Circonfession", p. 113.
35. Cf. Derrida, *Donner le temps* (Paris: Galilée, 1991)

mes larmes, aujourd'hui, celles de l'enfant dont on disait 'il pleure pour rien' …"[36]

… and those who read me from up above, I wonder if they see my tears, today, those of the child of whom one said "he is crying for nothing" …

Pleurer pour rien, to cry for nothing … — perhaps for the 'nothing' of a fragile border, of a delicate tear that runs through the subject, through his language, perhaps for the 'nothing' of a delicate cut that binds the name and the wound together in an absolute immemoriality, that binds by cutting.

At this "cutting point of incompatible, unassimilable times and dimensions," at this "non-time,"[37] it is thus not the 'I' that weeps. If another passage from Derrida's "Circonfession" reads:

"… c'est Dieu qui pleure en moi, qui tourne autour de moi, se réapproprie mes langages, en disperse le sens à tous vents …

… it ist God who weeps within me, who turns around me, reappropriates my languages and scatters their meaning to every wind …,"[38] then these tears bind the self-withdrawing site of the calling ('Ort des Anrufs') with the dissemination of language. The tension between calling and dissemination however, is just what defines the proper name and its "non-humanity," a "non-humanity" as the passage from Derrida just cited indicates, insofar as a speaker bears a name that names nothing of him, not the slightest part, yet "affects the very being of the one who bears it."

The question arises, whether the tears are possibly a privilege of man in the sense and to the extent that they attach themselves to that 'non-humanity' of the name. The name is simultaneously the strangest and most intimate. It makes it possible for one to imagine oneself as other, as stranger, and yet still perceive this name as one's own. By an exactly analogous movement Schopenhauer describes the impulse that induces weeping: "Weeping is by no ways a direct expression of pain, for it occurs where there is very little pain. In my opinion, indeed, we never weep directly on account of the pain we experience, but always merely on account of its repetition in reflection. […] in this very complex frame of mind, in which the directly felt suffering only comes to perception by a doubly circuitous route, imagined as the suffering of another, sympathized with as

36. Derrida, "Circonfession", p. 40
37. Hamacher, p. 31
38. Derrida, "Circonfession", p. 207

such, and then suddenly perceived again as directly our own, — in this complex frame of mind, I say, nature relieves itself through that remarkable physical convulsion."[39]

The "doubly circuitous route" removes the tears from the pain, whose expression and exteriorization were, for Hegel, represented by these tears. In the "very complex frame of mind," that occasions the weeping, reflections become interwoven: the revolving mirror, Psyché, revolves between the inward and the outward, feeling and expression; these reflections however are crossed by those originating from the turning between the self and the other. Above all however, the mirror turns so that the tears are always in the first instance those of the other, in a similar way that the name is first always that of the other.

In the tension between call and dissemination of language the doubly circuitous routes are in any case the rule. Along these doubly circuitous routes, it can never be ruled out that one word can be taken instead of another; that a name, in spite of and because of the impossibility of tearing it, should be torn: for the very reason that with calling and dissemination it is solely a question of "addressing myself only to you. To you uniquely, you, you, and you cannot stand it, you are afraid, you grow agitated, you flee, you seek to distract yourself." It is to this tension that the tears bear witness, to these "doubly circuitous routes" beyond all sentimentality, along that delicate tear that separates words from one another and a name from its bearer. But then the tears are no more and no less 'human' than a name; their humanity is that of the inhumanity or "non-humanity" of a proper name. They attest to the essential, exemplary anachronism between the weeper and himself, between the weeper and another. It is in this tension between absolutely unique address that addresses itself to you, solely to you, and an essential non-address, non-destination, "you flee …," that Derrida's text moves. Without shelter you try to distract yourself, above all because this text says, "je n'aime que les larmes, je n'aime et ne parle qu'à travers elles …," "I only love the tears, I only love and speak by way of them …"[40]

(Translated from the German by Steele Burrow.)

39. Arthur Schopenhauer, *The World as Will and Idea*, vol. I. trans. R.B. Haldane and J. Kemp, (London: Routledge & Kegan Paul Limited, 1948) Book 4, p. 486.
40. Derrida, "Circonfession", p. 95.

11. "The correct/just point of departure"
Deconstruction, Humanism, and the Call to Responsibility

BEATRICE HANSSEN

In *Of Spirit: Heidegger and the Question* (1987) Derrida pursues the thematics of spirit in Heidegger's writings, from its first appearance in quotation marks in § 10 of *Sein und Zeit*, through its phantom return in the writings of the thirties, to the eventual staging of *Geist* as the One, the flame, and *Versammlung*, in *Unterwegs zur Sprache*. In accordance with the Heideggerian figure of *Geflecht*, the study suggests that spirit could be regarded as a knot, in which four threads are gathered or interlaced. As a series of "unthoughts" in Heidegger's writings, these threads of what is said to have been "left hanging, uncertain, still in movement and therefore... *yet to come* in Heidegger's text,"[1] are the "question of the question," the issue of technology, the discourse of animality, and of epochality. As such, *Of Spirit* also assembles the threads of a series of Derrida's earlier writings, particularly the essays that constitute the *Geschlecht* cycle,[2] and it reintroduces, with a renewed force, Derrida's interrogation of Heidegger's ontologico-phenomenological *point of departure*.

In the course of the analysis, the first of these four threads gains a certain precedence, for what appears to focalize Derrida's reading of Heidegger — as indicated by the study's subtitle — is the deconstruction of the privilege of the question in Heidegger's writings, whose true form will prove to be that of a more originary answer, response, or *Zusage*. Parallel then to the analysis of the covert itinerary and teleology of spirit from the early writings to the

---

1. Jacques Derrida, *Of Spirit: Heidegger and the Question*, trans. Geoff Bennington and Rachel Bowlby (Chicago and London: University of Chicago Press, 1989), 8.
2. This cycle comprises the following articles: *Geschlecht I*: "*Geschlecht*: Différence sexuelle, différence ontologique," published in *Psyché: Inventions de l'autre* (Paris: Galilée, 1987); *Geschlecht II*: "La main de Heidegger (Geschlecht II)," in *Psyché*; *Geschlecht III*, but has not been published as such, is referred to in *Psyché*, 439ff., and focuses on Heidegger's Trakl reading, also addressed in chapter 9 of *Of Spirit*; *Geschlecht IV*: "L'Oreille de Heidegger: Philopolemologie (*Geschlecht IV*)," forthcoming. Part of *Geschlecht IV* has appeared under the title "La voix de l'ami," in *Cahier du Groupe de recherches sur la philosophie et le langage*, 12 (1990) 163-176.

writings of the fifties, *Of Spirit* also charts the vicissitudes of the thematics of questioning in Heidegger's thinking. Thus, the study first focuses on the existential analytic of *Sein und Zeit*, which finds its *Ansatz* or point of departure in the foundational question (*Fundamentalfrage*) — *die Frage nach dem Sinn vom Sein* — and the alleged exemplarity of *Dasein*; it then addresses the privileged position the question will acquire in the writings following the turn; to finally emphasize Heidegger's fundamental engagement with a more primordial starting point, apparent in *Unterwegs zur Sprache*.

Well beyond the limits of the Heidegger study, however, several of Derrida's latest writings have returned, with a marked persistence, to the disputable authority *Sein und Zeit* confers upon the question and a questioning *we*, as well as to the resonances of a covert humanism in the writings after the turn, despite Heidegger's attempt to shed a metaphysical humanism.[3] The interrogation of the ontologico-phenomenological point of departure that informs *Sein und Zeit* is central, for example, to an interview that Derrida conducted with Jean-Luc Nancy in 1988, entitled "Il faut bien manger ou le calcul du sujet."[4] In response to Nancy's inquiry about what or who is to come *after* the subject, Derrida defines the ethico-political task that awaits deconstruction as the endeavor to "seek a new (postdeconstructive) determination of the responsibility of the 'subject'" — a responsibility that can only be defined in relation to "the 'yes' or to the *Zusage* presupposed in every question."[5] At the same time, some cautionary remarks are issued with respect to the contemporary philosophical *doxa*, inasmuch as it holds that the classical, substantialist subject has been "liquidated," and, further, that its most radical critique is to be found in the existential analytic of *Sein und Zeit*. For, "whatever the force, the necessity, or the irreversibility of the Heideggerian gesture, *the point of departure* for the existential analytic remains tributary of precisely what it

---

3. Cf. Martin Heidegger, *Brief über den Humanismus* (Frankfurt a.M.: Vittorio Klostermann, 1981).
4. Jacques Derrida, "'Il faut bien manger' ou le calcul du sujet," *Cahiers Confrontation*, 20, Hiver 1989, 91-114. An English translation has appeared under the title "'Eating Well,' or the Calculation of the Subject: An Interview with Jacques Derrida," in: Eduardo Cadava, Peter Connor, Jean-Luc Nancy, eds., *Who comes after the subject* (New York: Routledge, 1991).
5. Derrida, "Eating Well," 105. On the issue of Heidegger's point of departure, see also John Sallis, "Flight of Spirit," Diacritics, Fall/Winter 1989, 25-37.

puts into question."[6] That is, "the chosen point of departure, the being exemplary for a reading of the meaning of Being is the being that *we* are, we *questioning* beings, we who, in that we are open to the question of Being and to the mode of being we are, have this relation of presence and proximity, this relation to ourselves that is lacking in everything that is not *Dasein*."[7] As such, Derrida's deconstructive project seeks to turn a Heideggerian principle against itself, namely, that "however provisional the analysis [is], it always and already demands the assurance of a correct point of departure, [*un point de départ juste*]"[8] — a phrase that serves to translate Heidegger's "Sicherung des rechten Ansatzes,"[9] in § 9 of *Sein und Zeit*.

If the French phrase *"un point de départ juste"* appears to be double-sided (*zweideutig*) in that *juste* can be translated as either "correct" or "just"/"righteous," then this ambiguity proves to be quite fortuitous, or aleatory. For, in a first moment, the two-sidedness of the word *juste* brings into play the relation between *justesse* and *justice*, and therewith the relation between a certain conception of truth, that is, truth as *adequation*, or the truth of theoretico-constative utterances, and, on the other hand, justice as a performative force, which is anterior to the theoretico-constative *"dispositive"*[10] — a distinction thematized in "Préjugés,"[11] *Limited Inc.*,[12] and "Force of Law." Second, the apparent duplicity of the phrase would seem to indicate that the Derridean attempt to gain a more appropriate starting point at once presents itself as a call for a responsible discourse, that is, a discourse *on* responsibility and justice, and on the attendant issue of violence. Indeed, the persistence of the thematics of the question expresses a pronounced ethico-political concern on the part of Derrida to redefine the issue of responsibility with regard to a more originary *yes*, which is "the unquestionable itself in any question," or "the unquestioned possi-

6. Derrida, "Eating Well," 104, italics added.
7. Derrida, "Eating Well," 104, modified translation.
8. Derrida, *Of Spirit*, 18.
9. Martin Heidegger, *Sein und Zeit* (Tübingen: Max Niemeyer Verlag, 1986), 43.
10. Jacques Derrida, "Force of Law: The 'Mystical Foundation of Authority,'" *Cardozo Law Review*, 11.5-6, 1990, 968.
11. Jacques Derrida, "Préjugés: devant la loi," in: *La Faculté de juger* (Paris: Minuit, 1985), 96.
12. Jacques Derrida, *Limited Inc.* (Paris: Galilée, 1990).

bility of the question."[13] I shall suggest that it is possibly in the displacement and "de-limitation" of the Heideggerian endeavor to find a more appropriate starting point, that one most readily can discern Derrida's concern with delineating the conditions of possibility of a postdeconstructive concept of responsibility, "before and in view of all possible autonomy of the who-subject."[14] For it is precisely to the degree that deconstruction thematizes a "relation to self," traversed by "*différance*, that is to say alterity, or trace,"[15] that it does not discard the so-called classical notions of ethical, political, and juridical responsibility, but all the more urgently asks for their reconsideration. Further, following the itinerary of the four guiding threads, deconstruction's continued probing of the Heideggerian starting point also expresses itself in an analysis of the *topos* of animality and the role of the existential-hermeneutical *als* (*le comme tel*) in the existential analytic, to interrogate what it variously defines as Heidegger's "profoundest metaphysical humanism,"[16] Heidegger's "anthropocentric or even humanist teleology,"[17] axiology, or onto-theology. In this respect, the endeavor to reformulate the notion of responsibility proves to be mediated through a rereading of Heidegger's *Brief über den Humanismus*, and thereby takes up again — from an admittedly different angle — some of the issues first raised in 1968 in "Les fins de l'homme." It is particularly the interrelation of these two deconstructive projects — Derrida's call to responsibility, with its renewed critique of humanism, and, further, the novel form his "anti-hermeneutical polemic" ("polémique anti-herméneutique"[18]) has taken — which I would like to subject to a closer scrutiny in what is to follow. I shall first address the lecture "Force of Law," then reexamine Derrida's current critique of Heidegger's humanism, to finally return to the interview "Il faut bien manger."

I. *This 'Other' Hermeneutical Circle*

The lecture "Force of Law: The 'Mystical Foundation of Author-

---

13. Derrida, *Of Spirit*, 10.
14. Derrida, "Eating Well," 100.
15. Derrida, "Eating Well," 100.
16. Derrida, *Of Spirit*, 12.
17. Derrida, *Of Spirit*, 55, 56.
18. Jean Greisch, "Mise en abîme et objeu. Ontologie et textualité," in: Jean Greisch, ed., *Le Texte comme objet philosophique* (Paris: Beauchesne, 1987), 261.

ity',", delivered at the Cardozo Law School in New York, responds to the injunction formulated by the conference organizers to clarify the question posed by the symposium's title: "Deconstruction and the Possibility of Justice."[19] In a chiastic turn the lecture inverses the relation of the terms to ask about justice as the very possibility of deconstruction. The significance of the lecture lies in the fact that it reformulates the task of deconstruction in ethico-political terms, as a response, that is, to the concepts of justice and responsibility. Further, "Force of Law" explicitly takes issue with certain charges leveled at deconstruction, according to which its thematization of the undecidability and incalculability inherent in all decision-making, would of necessity lead to a "quasi nihilism,"[20] and an effacement of the boundaries between justice and injustice. Against such an alleged *"neutralization"*[21] of the issue of justice, Derrida holds that deconstruction's investigation of "the limits of the human subject," particularly of the implied *we* that underpins the subject of law (*droit*), on the contrary leads to a radical "reinterpretation of its criteriology"[22] and an uncovering of its latent anthropocentric axiomatic.

In addressing the issue of justice and responsibility, the first part of "Force of Law" establishes a distinction between two notions of deconstruction: on the one hand, deconstruction as the performative movement or force of an "absolute" justice in *things themselves*, in history, and in the history of justice as law, right (*droit*), and, on the other hand, deconstruction as an *exercise*. Inasmuch as it is an exercise, not a methodology — a distinction already underscored in *Limited Inc.* — deconstruction is indebted by a double task, or marked by a double movement, namely, the historical responsibility to retain the memory of the very concept of responsibility, and, second, the transcendental-philosophical task to formalize what essentially defies formalization, *i.e.*, the logico-formal paradox or aporetic structure of justice. In conformity with other texts of Derrida's, such as those recently collected in *Du Droit à la philosophie*, the lecture calls for an interrogation of the institutional "stabilizations" of the concept of responsibility and a chain of

---

19. The proceedings of this 1989 conference have been published in the *Cardoza Law Review*, 11.5-6, 1990.
20. Derrida, "Force of Law," 953.
21. Derrida, "Force of Law," 954, italics added.
22. Derrida, "Force of Law," 953.

related deconstructible terms, e.g. the Kantian notion of "autono-my," or subjective "decision-making." The central aporia that in-habits justice is that of the dissymmetrical relation between two forms of justice: an absolute justice *in itself*, which is distinct from justice as right/*droit*. In a transposition or displacement of the Heideggerian figures of *die Gabe* and of *polemos*, absolute justice is presented as *le don*, as an incalculable, affirmative, infinite, and excessive force, which at once and of necessity is menaced by the violence of injustice, by the distributive, calculative justice of *droit* (law, right).

The second part of the Cardozo lecture provides an "anamnestic reading" of a 1921 essay by Walter Benjamin, "Zur Kritik der Gewalt." Partly written against the demise of liberal, parliamentary democracy that marked the Weimar Republic,[23] Benjamin's essay offers a critique of *Gewalt*, in its double meaning of "violence" and "institutional power." Much as in the earlier "Schicksal und Cha-rakter," the essay seeks to uncover the mythical foundations of law and to query the state's monopolization of violence through the law, in order to point to a Judaic conception of a *justice sans droit*,[24] that is, to a divine, thetic violence or decidability, manifested in the name of God.[25] But the Cardozo lecture to no small degree reads "Zur Kritik der Gewalt" against the messianic grain of the text. In accordance with *Margins of Philosophy*,[26] in which Derrida had already explicitly distinguished the quasi-concept *différance* from a Biblical, typological *arche*, his Benjamin reading deliberately tran-sliterates and displaces Benjamin's apparent messianic foundation-alism into the force of différance. Thus, the thetic, typological act of Genesis, "In the beginning was the word," is transformed into "In the beginning there will have been force,"[27] a phrase that would warrant an analysis of its temporal structure. At the center of Benjamin's essay then lies the "différantial" contamination of law-making and law-preserving violence, and of foundational and con-servational violence. In its critical analysis of the right to strike, of the symbolical, contractual nature of war and of peace, and of the spectral aspect of the police, whose privileges contradict the de-

23. Derrida, "Force of Law," 1014.
24. Derrida, "Force of Law," 1024.
25. Derrida, "Force of Law," 1022.
26. See the opening essay "Différance," in: *Margins of Philosophy* (Chicago: Uni-versity of Chicago Press, 1982).
27. Derrida, "Force of Law," 935.

mocratic separation of legislative and executive powers, "Zur Kritik der Gewalt" would expose an apparently contradictory structure of violence endemic to law/right. In place of the absolute thesis or foundation with which Benjamin's essay had ended, "Force of Law" uncovers the operations of a paradoxical law of iterability,[28] following which there is only originary repetition so that instaurational discourse calls for its own conservation or repetition. The phenomenological structure of this violence within the law is qualified as a *performative tautology*, that is, as the "*a priori* synthesis, which structures any foundation of the law upon which one performatively produces the conventions that guarantee the validity of the performative, thanks to which one gives oneself the means to decide between legal and illegal violence."[29]

But one must wonder further whether the discourse of auto-legitimation and auto-conservation that informs justice as *droit* might not amount to nothing less than the hermeneutical discourse, for throughout "Force of Law" a homology is set up between performative, foundational, juridical force and the force of interpretation. In its analysis of the mystical foundation of law, of the peculiar logic of readability-unreadability of instaurational discourse, and of the force of iterability according to which instaurational violence calls for its repetition, the Cardozo lecture continues the Derridean critique of the violence of the hermeneutical circle — already addressed in *Margins of Philosophy*,[30] *Dissemination*, *Schibboleth pour Paul Celan*, "Privilège,"[31] or the Derrida-Gadamer dispute[32] — specifically of what now is called "this other hermeneutical circle" ("cet autre cercle herméneutique").[33] For the foundation of a new state — a word to be taken in all its possible meanings, as "nation" but also as "states of interpretation"[34] — reproduces, reinstates *après coup* what it already had legitimized beforehand (*d'avance*). The temporal structure of this "other" hermeneutical circle, while

28. Derrida, "Force of Law," 1006, 1008.
29. Derrida, "Force of Law," 943.
30. See "Différance" in *Margins of Philosophy*, 12.
31. Derrida, *Du Droit à la Philosophie*, 63.
32. See also Greisch, *Le Texte*, 268.
33. Derrida, "Force of Law," 993.
34. Cf. Derrida's contribution "Some Statements and Truisms about Neo-logisms, Newisms, Postisms, Parasitisms, and other small Seismisms," to the collection of essays *The States of "Theory,"* ed. D. Carroll (New York: Columbia University Press, 1989).

in appearance that of the future perfect, in fact but dissimulates the temporality of the present/presence, to which Derrida opposes justice as the *a-venir*, as the *still to come*. Deconstruction then is beset by two temptations, for while, on the one hand, it is to be understood as a "general strike" that seeks to overthrow the States of Interpretation, or as a shortcircuiting of the hermeneutical *Gespräch*,[35] on the other hand, it does not relinquish itself to pure undecidability or incalculability, but on the contrary reflects on the aporetic dissymmetry between the incalculable gift and the calculability of certain given ethical, political, and grammatical rules.[36]

The "différantial" contamination that Derrida uncovers in Benjamin's critique of violence is in fact but the other side of the "différantial" imbrication of violence, the juridico-symbolical order, and language, and as such part of a theme that runs like a subtext of sorts through the entire lecture. One of the most important threads or "sheaves" of this relation concerns the distinction Derrida makes between the performative force of justice *in itself*, on the one hand, and the derivative performative and constative speech acts of instaurational juridical discourse, which, as thematized by speech act theory, would merely be reflective of a humanistic onto-theology. As Derrida observes in *Limited Inc.*, the "quasi-concepts"[37] of iterability, of the trace, or the mark, surpass the humanistic axiology of speech act theory, which remains informed by an oppositional dichotomy between "l'animal qui n'aurait pas le langage et l'homme, auteur de *speech acts* et capable d'un rapport à la loi, qu'il soit d'obéissance ou de transgression."[38] Similarly, in "Force of Law," in a passage questioning the classical delineation of the subject of law, Derrida indicates that justice *as right* implicitly assumes the Greek notion of man as *zoon logon echon*, for: "What we confusedly call 'animal,' the living thing as living and nothing else, is not a subject of the law or *droit*."[39]

35. Derrida, "Force of Law," 994.
36. See also Derrida, *Limited Inc.*, 277ff.
37. Derrida, *Limited Inc.*, 216, 231.
38. Derrida, *Limited Inc.*, 248.
39. Derrida, "Force of Law," 951, modified translation. From the very beginning, the "quasi-concepts" of the trace and writing were introduced as a fundamental critique of a metaphysical tradition ruled by the notion of *zoon logon echon*. One of the most explicit passages with respect to deconstruction's displacement of this tradition can be found in an interview that Derrida conducted with Eva Meyer: "Ich spreche nicht gerne vom sprechenden Wesen, weil man sehr schnell geneigt ist, es mit dem sprechenden Subjekt, dem sprechenden Menschen oder

II. *The Subject of Violence* — Dasein *as "Homo Humanus"*

The emphasis on an "anthropocentric teleology," characteristic of juridical violence also emerges, as noted at the outset, in Derrida's most recent readings of Heidegger, notably in the *Geschlecht* cycle and *Of Spirit*. And this anthropocentric oppositional logic is shown further not merely to inform Heidegger's existential analytic, according to which "[t]here is no animal *Dasein*" ["Il n'y a pas de *Dasein* animal"],[40] but also to resurface in the later works after the turn, in which the *Ansatz* or starting point has been placed higher, as when Heidegger, in the *Brief über den Humanismus*, states: "Gegen den Humanismus wird gedacht, weil er die *Humanitas* des Menschen nicht hoch genug ansetzt."[41] It is to these Derridean readings that I would now like to turn to examine to what extent Derrida's reformulation of the question of justice and responsibility hinges on a deconstruction of the metaphysical distinction between what traditionally counts as a subject, and the "infra-human"[42] or the "living in general" (*le vivant en général*).[43] I will primarily focus on two moments that occupy Derrida in his readings of the early Heidegger, namely, first, Heidegger's exlusionary gestures to the living in general, that is, his inability to thematize life (*das Leben*),

auch Gott zu übersetzen. Das würde das Tier ausschließen. Es gibt aber das Tier, es gibt Wege der Tiere, Spuren, Wildwechsel, *ein gespurtes Labyrinth*, und da sind wir nicht mehr im Heideggerschen Raum. Was unterscheidet zwischen dem Tier, das nicht spricht und also kein sprechendes Labyrinth zur Verfügung hat, und dem Menschen, dem sprechenden Tier, das darüber verfügt? Wenn man die Wege, die Spuren der Tiere in der Wüste z.B. betrachtet, sieht man sehr wohl, daß sie Orte haben, daß sie Verbindungen, Kehren, Umwege machen, *die Spur im Allgemeinen*. Es gibt ein 'Unterwegs' auch des Tieres, das labyrinthisch ist, und wenn man von Spur, Marke, Fährte spricht, statt von Rede, eröffnet man die Frage nach der *Verräumlichung* und befreit sie von ihren anthropotheologischen, anthropomorphen und theologischen Grenzen." "Labyrinth und Archi/Textur. Ein Gespräch mit Jacques Derrida," in Eva Meyer, *Architexturen* (Basel: Stroemfeld/Roter Stern, 1986). See also "Eating Well" 116-117.

40. Derrida, *Of Spirit*, 56.
41. Heidegger, *Brief über den Humanismus*, 21.
42. Derrida, "Eating Well," 116.
43. Derrida, "Eating Well," 108, 112. For the purposes of the present discussion the *topos* of the hand in "Geschlecht II" — as it bears on Heidegger's failure to thematize *Dasein*'s incarnation in *Sein und Zeit*, as well as on the theme of "giving" — will be bracketed. The topic has also been addressed by Didier Franck, *Heidegger et le problème de l'espace* (Paris: Minuit, 1986); Michel Haar, *Le chant de la terre: Heidegger et les assises de l'histoire de l'être* (Paris: l'Herne, 1985); and Jean-François Courtine, "Donner/Prendre: La Main," *Philosophie*, 17, Hiver 1987, 73-92.

the living in general (*das Lebewesen*), and the "infra-human," other than in a privative way gestures that are informed by what *Sein und Zeit* conceives to be the derivative nature of the "ontology of life." Within the context of fundamental ontology this means that Derrida's critique would seem to put into question nothing less than Heidegger's reduction of regional ontologies — specifically anthropology and biology — to fundamental ontology. The second moment involves Derrida's interrogation of the diacritical force accredited to the existential-hermeneutical *als*, as discussed in § 31 and § 33 of *Sein und Zeit* and in *Die Grundbegriffe der Metaphysik*. In order to capture the force of these moments and how they relate to what Derrida has called his "hesitation" and "disquiet" with respect to Heidegger's humanism, it will be necessary to briefly recall the argument of "Les fins de l'homme."

The complexity of the argument set forth in "Les fins de l'homme" — a lecture that, crucially, was held in the context of a symposium on philosophy and anthropology — derives from its multiple layers or frames, its constant reframings, which are held in suspension by the encompassing question of the *clôture* and *l'outre-clôture*[44] of metaphysics. Thus, at its core the lecture discusses the logic of sublation characteristic of Western metaphysics, epitomized in the equivocal semantic play of the concept *fin*, which brings together the meanings of death, *telos*, and eschatology. The lecture then shows this logic to be still operative in Heidegger's *Brief über den Humanismus*, for in its attempt to regain the essence of man and to surmount the metaphysical conceptions of *humanitas*, it still exposes an ontological repetition of the phenomenological metaphorical language of *proximity* in *Sein und Zeit*, as well as an allegiance to the teleological dimensions of the personal pronoun *we*. Next, and on a third level, so to speak, the lecture discusses the very disturbance (*ébranlement*) of such an economy of proximity — that is, an economy according to which man is the proper of Being — as well as its inevitable repercussions for contemporary French thought; to finally note that the latter's attempt to proclaim the end of man remains itself inscribed within the inner margins of metaphysics. The lecture ends with a quasi-allegorical, ironic passage in which the position of Derrida's own questioning *we* is held in suspension by two perilous temptations — figured by Nietzsche's higher man and the *Uebermensch* — which not only point to the very limits of

44. Jacques Derrida, *De la grammatologie* (Paris: Minuit, 1967), 25.

metaphysics, but also come to signal the two temptations of deconstruction: one, which inscribes itself within the economy of the "relève" of metaphysical language, the other, which seeks to incur a radical rupture with metaphysics and to gain a new field.

If the thematization of the privilege of the question, of the *we*, and of the proximity or presence to self of *Dasein* in "Les fins de l'homme" would seem to suggest a certain continuity in Derrida's current critique of Heidegger's humanism, there remains nevertheless an important difference, reflective of a distinct shift in perspective. For whereas "Les fins de l'homme" principally questions the coincidence of man's finitude with the eschatological and the teleological, and, further, questions the sublation of an anthropological humanism in Heidegger's ontological turn, Derrida's more recent critique, at least of *Sein und Zeit*, often would appear to find its own starting point at the problematic intersection of fundamental ontology and the other sciences or regional ontologies, such as anthropology or biology. This is not to say, however, that such an inquiry would amount to a falling back into the anthropological reception of Hegel, Husserl, and Heidegger, represented by Sartre or Kojève, and criticized in "Les fins de l'homme." Rather, in Derrida's work Heidegger's exclusionary gestures towards life and the concomitant demarcation (*Abgrenzung*) of *Dasein* from the living in general are first of all placed in a historical context; that is, in a first moment, they are granted a certain legitimacy inasmuch as they present a fundamental critique of the philosophy of life. Second, in *Of Spirit* Derrida suggests that the disappearance of the quotation marks around "spirit" in the writings of the thirties, with the attendant superimposition of a humanistic axiology onto the animal, might possibly be interpreted as the inevitable phantom return of spirit in the wake of an "ethico-political denunciation of biologism, racism, and naturalism."[45] Next the analysis also asks on formal-structural grounds about the status of the privative foundation of an ontology of life in the understanding of *Dasein*. The reference is to § 10 of *Sein und Zeit* — "Die Abgrenzung der Daseinsanalytik gegen Anthropologie, Psychologie und Biologie" — but also to § 42, where Heidegger, in a reduction of the biologico-ontic analysis of death to the ontological, reiterates that life can only be "fixated" ontologically in a privative orientation to *Dasein* ("in privativer Orientierung am Dasein ontologisch fixiert werden kann"). By contrast,

45. Derrida, *Of Spirit*, 56.

Derrida's recent writings explicitly question Heidegger's thanatology, for example in "Geschlecht II," in which Heidegger's comments on the animal's *Verenden* are queried, or in a note to chapter 6 in *Of Spirit*, where Derrida asks: "What is being-towards-death? What is death for a *Dasein* that is never defined *essentially* as a living thing? This is not a matter of opposing death to life, but of wondering what semantic content can be given to death in a discourse for which the relation to death, the experience of death, remains unrelated to the life of the living thing."[46]

One could say then that what is at stake in Derrida's critique of these reductive, exclusionary gestures, and of Heidegger's point of departure, is precisely Heidegger's method, his methodology, or his point of access to *die Sache*. Indeed, as noted in the 1929-1930 Freiburg lecture course, *Die Grundbegriffe der Metaphysik*[47] — a course extensively commented upon in *Of Spirit* — the word "method" is to be translated as *zugehen*, and thus engages the issue of gaining access to *die Sache* or *das sachliche Problem der Zugänglichkeit selbst*. The issue of "gaining access" finds a double inscription in Heidegger's seminar, for, first, one of the guiding threads of the course is the question of how to gain access to life and the living while avoiding the inadequate mode of substitution (*Versetzen*) of biology; and, second, it is the particular nature of accessibility to beings (*Zugänglichkeit zu...*), which is said to distinguish the mode of being (*Seinsmodus*) of the animal from that of man. Derrida takes up the issue in *Of Spirit* when he addresses the three theses of the seminar, following which the stone would be worldless, the animal poor in world (*weltarm*), and man formative of the

---

46. Derrida, *Of Spirit*, 120. Similar reconfigurations can be found in other recent French receptions of *Sein und Zeit*, such as the work of Michel Haar or Didier Franck, whose *Heidegger et le problème de l'espace* has probed the problem of *Dasein*'s incarnation. (cf. supra, note 43) Further, in an essay, "Being and the Living," published in the collection *Who comes after the subject*, Franck has argued on internal grounds that the physiological in fact precedes the existential in *Being and Time* and that Heidegger's inability in general to thematize what in the *Brief* is called the "abgründliche leibliche Verwandschaft" (*Brief über den Humanismus*, 17) between man and the animal is the price to be paid for an unconditional allegiance to ontological difference.
47. Martin Heidegger, *Die Grundbegriffe der Metaphysik: Welt—Endlichkeit—Einsamkeit, Gesamtausgabe*, Bd. 29/30 (Frankfurt a.M.: Klostermann, 1983).

world (*weltbildend*).[48] That is to say, contrary to man, the animal, while having access to beings, does not have access to beings *as* beings. Following the distinction introduced in *Sein und Zeit*, the seminar suggests that the privative nature of the animal not only implies that it is deprived of the derivative, apophantic *als* (the Greek particle *y*, the Latin *qua*, the French *comme tel*), which belongs to the proposition or *Aussagesatz*, but also, that it is denied the more originary hermeneutical *als*.[49] By contrast, in its progressive unveiling of the concept of world, the seminar comes to define man's world as a being-free (*Freisein*), as a pre-logical openness for beings as such (*das Seiende als solches*). Precisely this very mode of accessibility, the *comme tel* supposed to be characteristic of man,

48. In both *Of Spirit* and "Eating Well," Derrida underscores that Heidegger's remarks about the animal are not only "violent" and "awkward," but even "contradictory." (Derrida, "Eating Well," 111.) Indeed, while in the seminar Heidegger referred to the animal as *weltarm*, in the *Einführung in die Metaphysik* he would posit: "Das Tier hat keine Welt, auch keine Umwelt." According to Derrida, such a confounding of categories but underscores that within Heidegger's thinking the animal operates as a "principle of disorder or of limitation." (Derrida, "Eating Well," 111.)

49. Derrida also addresses the issue in "La voix de l'ami." As he observes, while especially § 33 of *Sein und Zeit* takes issue with the conception of *zoon logon echon* and seeks to point to a pre-Aristotelean and even pre-Platonic notion of *logos*, anterior to propositional logic, Aristotelian remainders nevertheless still inform the reference to the voice of the friend that every *Dasein* is said to carry with him, inasmuch as only a human "subject" is capable of friendship: "Le *Dasein* étant l'essence de l'homme, cela n'est donc pas contradictoire avec le propos aristotélicien selon lequel il n'y a d'amitié par excellence (de *prote philia* ou de *teleia philia*) qu'entre les hommes: ni entre les dieux et les hommes, ni entre l'animal et l'homme, ni entre les dieux, ni entre les animaux." (Derrida, "La voix de l'ami", 173) At the bottom of Heidegger's notion of friendship and the implicit opposition between the human and the nonhuman it propagates, lies again the hermeneutical *als* or *comme tel*: "La différence entre l'animal et le *Dasein* passe là encore par la possibilité du 'comme tel' (*als*) et de l'entendre ou du comprendre (*Verstehen*)... qu'il s'agisse de la main, des pieds, de l'oeil, du sexe et de l'oreille, la phénoménologie heideggerienne du corps du *Dasein*, dans ce qu'elle a de plus original et de plus nécessaire, suppose précisément le phénoménologique comme tel ou le 'comme tel' phénoménologique. La différence structurelle entre le *Dasein* et le non-*Dasein*, par exemple l'animal, c'est la différence entre un étant ouvert au 'comme tel' et un étant qui ne l'est pas, et de ce fait est 'weltarm,' pauvre en monde. Du coup la voix de l'amie, et par suite l'amitié en général, ne se donne à entendre que dans l'espace phénoménologique du 'comme tel.' Pas d'amitié hors d'un monde où le 'Verstehen' et la phénomólogie sont possibles. Et l'animal, si quelque chose de tel existait qui eût quelqu-'unité, n'aurait pas d'oreille. Une oreille capable d'écouter." (Derrida, "La voix de l'ami," 173)

will acquire a pivotal place in the interview with Nancy, in which Derrida calls for an-other, nonhumanistic kind of responsibility.

In the exchange with Nancy, Derrida responds to the question *"Who comes after the subject?"* by dissecting all the component parts of the question, and, again, by probing the very nature of questioning itself, so as to ask about the status of another, irreducible responsibility that takes the form of a more primordial answer or response. As such, the inquiry proves to be informed by previous discussions of the logic of a more originary *yes, yes* or *Zusage*,[50] to be found, above all, in a long footnote in *Of Spirit*. It is here that Derrida has commented most extensively on the essay "Das Wesen der Sprache,"[51] in which Heidegger revoked the status of the question as "the very piety of thinking" and redefined the proper of man as the *Zusage* to the *Zuspruch* of language. While one would have to analyze in more detail than is possible within the present context, the exact nature of Derrida's decisive displacement of this Heideggerian *topos* — for example, how it is linked to the analysis of the call (*Ruf*) in *Sein und Zeit* — what interests us here in particular is that the question of humanism and animality is again raised. Not only does Derrida's response to Nancy posit that the issue of "who comes *after*" is to be recast as what or who might *precede* the "subject," but it also presents an endeavor to think the *who* — in its capacity as an interrogative or relative pronoun — as one no longer determined by the metaphysical grammar of the calculating, stable, stabilized subject. As a "differing singularity" (*singularité différante*),[52] the dislocated *who* that deconstruction seeks to think is defined no longer by the *logos*, but traversed by the nonhuman mark, the trace, iterability, differance, "at work everywhere, which is to say, well beyond humanity (*bien au-delà de l'humanité*)."[53] Taking up again the topos of animality, of the living in general, and the call coming from the other, Derrida argues for another philosophical discourse, one able to account for a form of responsibility that not only lies "at the root of all ulterior responsibilities," but furthermore pre-cedes, pre-figures any "subject," be it a divine or a human one:

50. Derrida, "Eating Well," 100.
51. Martin Heidegger, *Unterwegs zur Sprache*, *Gesamtausgabe*, Bd. 12 (Frankfurt a.M.: Vittorio Klostermann, 1985).
52. Derrida, "Eating Well," 101.
53. Derrida, "Eating Well," 109.

A discourse thus restructured can try to situate in another way the question of what a human subject, a morality, a politics, the rights of a human subject are, can be, and should be. Still to come [à venir], this task is indeed far ahead of us. It requires passing through the great phenomenologico-ontological question of the *as such*, appearing as such, to the extent that it is held to distinguish, in the last analysis, the human subject or *Dasein* from every other form of relation to the self or to the other *as such*. For the experience of the opening of the *as such* in the onto-phenomenological sense, is maybe not only that of which the animal and the stone would be deprived, but it is that to which one cannot nor should submit the other in general, the *who* of the other which can never nor absolutely appear as such, without disappearing as the other.[54]

The passage at first sight appears to invoke the main points of criticism advanced in *Of Spirit*, were it not for the fact that the *comme tel* now no longer is defined in purely Heideggerian terms, as the privileged mode of access to "beings as such," but, in a second moment, comes to stand for a principle of foreclosure, one that forecloses the appearance of the other *as* other. Significantly, the call of the other *as* other can only be heard by an ethics and a politics that are able to account for *the living in general*, and thus have divested the "other" of the humanistic overtones still to be discerned in Heidegger's destruction of the metaphysical subject. Anything but the reinstitution of the notion of *bios* as the *arche* of a questionable philosophy of life, however, Derrida's inquiry of Heidegger's covert humanistic point of departure does not entail a falling back behind the position formulated in 1968 in "La Différance." It will be recalled that it was here that Derrida had introduced the non-concept or quasi-concept of "différance" in defiance of an ontological archeology, that is to say, of an absolute and absolutely "rightful" *point of departure* or *arche*.[55] Rather, "Eating Well" points to the animal as a "limit concept" and a "principle of disorder," one that serves to re-interpret and "de-limit" the entire apparatus of limits within which the West has inscribed its criteriology of the just and the unjust.[56] Its deconstruction brings to light a "metaphysico-

---

54. Derrida, "Eating Well," 109-110, modified translation.
55. "...there is nowhere to *begin* to trace the sheaf or the graphics of *différance*. For what is put into question is precisely the quest for a rightful beginning, an absolute point of departure, a principal responsibility. The problematic of writing is opened by putting into question the value *arkhe*." (Derrida, *Margins of Philosophy* 6-7.) On this issue, see also Geoffrey Bennington's contribution in this volume.
56. Derrida, "Force of Law," 953.

anthropocentric axiomatic" or a *carno-phallogocentrism*,[57] founded on carnivorous sacrifice, or the symbolic ingestion of the other, and linked to the violent institution of the human subject. In this expansion of the notion of the other to include the infra-human, Derrida locates his differences from Levinas. Indeed, distinct Levinasian overtones can be discerned, not only in Derrida's interpretation of the call, the trace, or the injunction to "learn-to-give-the-other-to-eat" that traverses the theme of "eating well," but Derrida also would seem to intimate as much when, in his analysis of the infinite excess and absolute dissymetry of justice, he pays tribute to Levinas' *Totality and Infinity*,[58] in which justice is said to be more primordial than ontological truth. Yet, to the extent that Levinas' Judaic humanism of the "other man" defines its concept of responsibility in terms of the commandment "Thou shalt not kill," to the exclusion of the injunction "Thou shalt not put to death the living in general,"[59] it is said to be also informed by a profound carno-phallogocentrism.[60]

Finally, inasmuch as Derrida's critique of humanism questions the boundaries of what counts as a subject, the limit of the *inhuman* — in its pejorative sense — also announces itself. But, while an ethics and politics of the "living in general" has to pass through a consideration for the infra-human, and while the trace, through which the

57. Derrida, "Eating Well," 113; see also Derrida, "Force of Law," 953.
58. Derrida, "Force of Law," 959.
59. Derrida, "Eating Well," 113.
60. Resonances of this debate can be found in a recent interview with Levinas, published under the title "The Paradox of Morality," in which Levinas is indirectly asked to respond to the Derridean question of animality. (Published in Robert Bernasconi and David Wood, eds., *The Provocation of Levinas: Rethinking the Other* [London and New York: Routledge, 1988]; also cited by John Llewelyn, *The Middle Voice of Ecological Conscience: A Chiasmic Reading of Responsibility in the Neighbourhood of Levinas, Heidegger and Others* [London: MacMillan, 1991] 49-67 and "Am I Obsessed by Bobby? (Humanism of the Other Animal)," in Robert Bernasconi and Simon Critchley, eds., *Re-Reading Levinas* [Bloomington and Indianapolis; Indiana University, 1991.] If the animal can at all be said to have a face, as Levinas at times would seem inclined to grant, this can only be so in analogy with the human face. For: "It is clear that, without considering animals as human beings, the ethical extends to all living beings. We do not want to make an animal suffer needlessly and so on. But the prototype of this is human ethics. Vegetarianism, for example, arises from the transference to animals of the idea of suffering." (*The Provocation of Levinas*, 172) Furthermore, it is in this interview that Levinas, in an unorthodox reading of *Sein und Zeit*, posits that Heidegger's notion of *Dasein* is still mired in a Darwinian vitalistic conception of life, expressed as "care for one's being." To

"subject" proves to be inscribed by différance, "operates well beyond humanity," such an openness to another responsibility does not call upon itself the specter of inhumanity. Rather, throughout Derrida's writings the analysis of animality as a "limit concept" remains indisputably linked to a sustained interrogation of the question of the monster, monstrosity, and *le pire*.[61] As such, Derrida's inquiry differs fundamentally from the isolated reference to the *inhuman*, in the sense of *Unmenschlichkeit*, that one finds in the *Brief über den Humanismus*, in which Heidegger had sought to counter the possible charge that his critique of a metaphysical humanism would amount to a thinking "[das sich] auf die Gegenseite des Humanen schlüge und das Inhumane befürworte, die Unmenschlichkeit verteidige und die Würde des Menschen herabsetze."[62] By contrast, Derrida's engagement with the limits of the human unmistakably places itself in another tradition, one that explicitly confronts the history of the inhuman. It is a tradition that runs from Adorno's injunction, that in the wake of the holocaust and the ineluctable belatedness of justice, the best one can hope for is to have lived like a *good animal*,[63] to the only image of the animal one possibly finds in Levinas' work, namely, that of the dog Bobby, "dernier kantien de l'Allemagne nazie."[64]

this, Levinas' metaphysical ethics opposes the moment of *rupture*, the advent of ethical man, as the one who radically separates himself from being and "the struggle for life." As Levinas observes: "You ask at what moment one becomes a face. I do not know at what moment the human appears, but what I want to emphasize is that the human *breaks with* pure being, which is always a persistence in being. This is my principal thesis. A being is something that is attached to being, to its own being. That is Darwin's idea. The being of animals is a struggle for life. A struggle for life without ethics. It is a question of might. Heidegger says at the beginning of *Being and Time* that *Dasein* is a being who in his being is concerned for this being itself. That's Darwin's idea: the living being struggles for life. The aim of being is being itself. However, with the appearance of the human — and this is my entire philosophy — there is something more important than my life, and that is the life of the other." (*The Provocation of Levinas*, 172) If Levinas' interpretation of *Sein und Zeit* as an existential version of Darwinism could be called a "misreading," in that the notion of *Dasein* was itself explicitly directed against vitalism, then such a "misreading" serves to reestablish Levinas" view that justice is anterior to or more primordial than any ontology.

61. For example, in *Of Spirit*, "Eating Well," "Geschlecht II."
62. Heidegger, *Brief über den Humanismus*, 21.
63. Theodor W. Adorno, *Negative Dialektik* (Frankfurt a.M.: Suhrkamp, 1975), 294.
64. Emmanuel Levinas, "Nom d'un chien ou le droit naturel" in *Difficile Liberté* (Paris: Algin Michel, 1976), 216.

12. Ellipses of Enlightenment: Derrida and Kant[1]

HENT DE VRIES

> *"A tone decides; and who shall decide*
> *if it is, or is not, part of discourse?"*[2]

In an intriguing and in his own words "very, very ambivalent"[3] essay, entitled *D'un ton apocalyptique adopté naguère en philosophie*,[4] Derrida sets the tone for the complex task that will occupy us here: to rethink, rewrite or, rather, reinscribe the premises, concept and institution of a historically overdetermined phenomenon called *Aufklärung*, while still somehow — perhaps, inevitably — continuing to subscribe to its very 'idea' or 'practice.' In so doing, Derrida's text, originally presented as a keynote address on the occasion of the first major conference devoted to his work in Cerisy-la-Salle in 1982, could be said to underscore — once more — the paradoxical nature of every attempt at deconstructing traditional and modern philosophemes such as those related to the 'problematic' of Enlightenment 'critique,' for example in the work of Kant. As we shall see, Derrida re-affirms this peculiar movement of displacement by maintaining that, in its very interrogation of a classical figure of thought, deconstruction derives its force precisely from the 'thing' it 'questions' (if that is still the right word). Deconstruction does not negate, denegate, let alone sublate, what it puts

1. The earliest version of this article was presented as a lecture at the University of California at Berkeley in November 1989 and again at Loyola University of Chicago in January 1991. The third part of the text is of a more recent date and formed the substance of my contribution to the symposium in Utrecht, December 1991, to which this volume is devoted.
2. J. Derrida, *Signéponge*, bilingual edition, transl. R. Rand (New York: Columbia University Press, 1984), 2 (translation modified).
3. "Jacques Derrida in Discussion with Christopher Norris," in: A.Papadakis, C.Cooke, A.Benjamin, *Deconstruction*, Omnibus Volume (New York 1989), pp. 71-75, 75.
4. J. Derrida, *D'un ton apocalyptique adopté naguère en philosophie* (Paris: Galilée, 1983), "Of an Apocalyptic Tone Recently Adopted in Philosophy," translated by J.P. Leavy, Jr., *Semeia*, 23, 1982, 63-96. Hereafter cited parenthetically in the main text with the page numbers of the translation followed by those of the original.

under erasure. For, in the never ending closure of metaphysics, its 'logic' is neither that of a dialectical progression nor that of a Heideggerian 'step back.'[5] Rather, as Derrida seems to suggest in the *D'un ton apocalyptique*, its receives its 'light' and 'vigilance' from an elliptical 'remainder' or 'remaining' (*restance*) of what it seeks to deconstruct. The summoning of the logocentric presuppositions of a given, historically and socially established form of Enlightenment could, Derrida tells us, only be *effective* or, what is more, *responsible* when advanced in the name of a new 'idea' or, rather, re-enactment of that very same institutional (and more-than-institutional) force. Enlightenment, then, would no longer coincide with 'itself,' nor be put to rest in an historical archive. It would be marked by an intrinsic duplicity — as we shall see, a non-speculative, spectral doubling — that is no longer describable in terms of the age-old philosophical dichotomy of mere appearence and essence.[6] And the *task* of 'thought,' a task which is a *necessity* as well, would be to articulate the doubling of this 'double bind' in view of a more subtle, more elliptical (and, perhaps, also more 'enlightened'?) *Aufklärung* than the one Kant and his followers, as well as his opponents, deemed possible or justifiable.

At least since the publication of *D'un ton apocalyptique*, then, there was no longer room for any sincere doubt: Derrida was "in favour"[7] of *Aufklärung*, of its critical and more-than-critical 'potential' or import. From now on, deconstruction would have to be understood in light of *Les Lumières* (and the plurale tantum is not without significance here) just as much as, conversely, Enlightenment, like the tradition of metaphysics of which it forms a moment, would have to be exposed to a reading bringing to light the deconstructibility of its very presuppositions, argumentative procedures and institutions. In this contribution, I will try to delineate some of the most compelling insights promised by this mutual illumination, both in the aforementioned essay on Kant and in some of Derrida's more recent, juridico-political writings. It will be argued that the form this illumination takes in these texts reveals a singular — elliptical — structure of 'an Enlightenment' divided in (and against)

---

5. Cf. M. Heidegger, *Identität und Differenz* (Pfullingen: Neske, 1978), 39 ff.
6. In philosophy, Derrida claims in the recent preface to *Du droit à la philosophie* (Paris: Galilée, 1990), 20-21, a certain essentialism or originarism, on the one hand, and a nominalistic pragmatism or conventionalism and contextualism, on the other, go hand in hand and presuppose each other. The 'thought' that Derrida prepares here and elsewhere seeks to escape this opposition.
7. "Jacques Derrida in Discussion with Christopher Norris," 75.

212

'itself' and for that reason given only *in the plural*. If there is to be
Enlightenment, Derrida tells us, it would be in the form of *ellipses*,
that is to say, in the form(s) of Enlightenment*s*. In what follows, I
shall attempt to describe the most significant features of this multiple appeal and the attention it provokes. First, by retracing some
of the steps of Derrida's reading of Kant in *D'un ton apocalyptique*
(I). Secondly, by focusing on his more general remarks on the
so-called apocalyptic genre of which Kant's essay turns out to be a
telling 'example' (II). It is here that it will become manifest that the
ellipsis of Enlightenment should be read, to begin with, as a non-
phenomenological (and non-reductionist) 'reduction' of *Aufklärung* to what is called a '*lucid vigil(ance)*.'[8] After having demonstrated how the urgency of this vigil haunts every ethico-political decision, I will circle back to the confrontation with the critique of pure
(practical) reason by recalling some of Derrida's observations with
respect the Kantian institutional politics spelled out in *Der Streit der
Fakultäten* (III). It is in this context that I will briefly allude to the
intriguing relation of the (first) ellipsis of Enlightenment to the
dominant interpretation of reason as formal discourse, as well as to
its institution, in particular in the modern university. I will argue
that this relation can, again, be described elliptically. This second
ellipsis (or, rather, ellipse) is less a rhetoric than a geometric figure,
even though it is impossible to draw a clear line of demarcation
between these two.

I

D'un ton apocalyptique develops its thesis, if there is one (or just
one), by way of a careful rereading of a relatively short polemical

---

8. The phenomenological *terminus technicus* 'reduction' should, of course, be used
with as much precaution as possible. Like the notion 'epoché' it implies a
movement 'in the name and in view' of a 'meaning' (cf. J. Derrida, *L'écriture et la
différence* [Paris: Seuil, 1967], 393-394) which is not identical with the vigilance
that will interest us here. Already in *La voix et la phénomène* (Paris: PUF, 1967),
3, Derrida insists that he is less concerned with the problem of whether or to what
extent the metaphysical tradition has imposed limits upon the vigilance of the
phenomenologist. What is at issue, he writes, is rather whether this vigilance is not
in its very "*phenomenological* form" determined by the metaphysics of presence.
This, of course, would be the place to spell out some of the similarities and
dissimilarities between Derrida's notion of vigilance and the argument set forth in
E. Levinas' article "De la conscience à la veille. A partir de Husserl," first
published in 1974 reprinted in his *De dieu qui vient à l'idée* (Paris: Vrin, 1982),
34-61.

text of Kant. In this essay, *Von einem neuerdings erhobenen vornehmen Ton in der Philosophie*, published in the *Berlinische Monatschrift* of 1796, Kant defends a formally defined idea of rationality against what he considers to be the obscurantist claims of enthusiastic or exalted mystagogues. More precisely, his charge is levelled at "die allerneueste deutsche Weisheit (...) *durchs Gefühl zu philosophieren* (nicht etwa, wie die um verschiedene Jahre ältere [i.e. Kant's own], *durch Philosophie* das sittliche *Gefühl* in Bewegung und *Kraft zu versetzen*."[9] These so-called *Schwärmer* had accused him of amputating a vital — *the* vital — part of reason. Kant, however, retorts the charge on his accusers. If ever there was an amputation of reason, it surely was on the part of this renewed Neoplatonic tradition, which appeals to something that can never become an object of experience and for that reason does not contribute to the progress of (theoretical) knowledge and is thought to present itself in a divination (*Ahnung*, 384, 386) or vision (*Anschauung, Vision*, 384, 394) of the supernatural and of the things as they are in themselves. For these purported modes of 'experience,' Kant argues, entail a dangerous transition or a leap (*Übersprung*) from concepts to what lies beyond them. And, in philosophy, this comes down to nothing less than a '*salto mortale.*' To operate with 'concepts' in this transcendent realm would at best offer a 'surrogate' (*Surrogat*) of knowledge: a 'mystic illumination' (*mystische Erleuchtung*, 386) which is not only the "death" of all genuine discursive thought but also a form of 'idolatry' in that it puts an end to all rational theology.[10] For, it is obvious (*leuchtet von selbst ein*), Kant writes, that to follow this secret path only leads to a derailment of thought resulting in a "*Verstimmung der Köpfe zur Schwärmerei*" (386) which is at odds with the less exalted illumination of ever vigilant critique (*Beleuchtung einer immer wachsamen Kritik*, 394).

It is the abuse of the art of a certain Plato or rather *Afterplato* which has ignited the spreading fire of these illuminati. But, ultimately it is no one less than Plato himself who must be held responsible. Especially the esoteric, unacademic Plato of the (apo-

---

9. I. Kant, *Werke in zehn Bänden*, Hrsg. von W. Weischedel (Darmstadt: Wissenschaftliche Buchgesellschaft, 1983), Bd. 5, 377-397, 390-391. Hereafter cited parenthetically in the text.
10. Cf. ibid., 391 note: "Die *Theophanie* macht (...) aus der Idee des Plato ein *Idol*, welches nicht anders als abergläubisch verehrt werden kann; wogegen die *Theologie*, die von Begriffen unsrer eigenen Vernunft ausgeht, ein *Ideal* aufstellt, welches uns Anbetung abzwingt, da es selbst aus den heiligsten von der Theologie unabhängigen Pflichten entspringt."

cryphal) letters, Kant surmises, has "zur Schwärmerei die Fackel angesteckt" (380 Remark).[11] It comes as no surprise then, that the pamphlet starts out by taking to task the polemical explanatory remarks with which one year earlier the *Gefühlsphilosoph* (389) Johann Georg Schlosser[12] had presented a new translation of Plato's letters to the general reading public. However, much more is at stake in Kant's vehement and satrical riposte. His main target is not so much this translation nor its translator but, more generally, the tendency of which, in his eyes, this publication is symptomatic. For Kant, this text illustrates once more the urgent need to defend the primacy of a restrictive, formal and discursive interpretation of the tribunal of reason over and against its dogmatic inflation and devaluation in light of merely subjective sentiment (*Gefühl*) and presentiment (*Vorempfindung*, 384, 386). At issue, therefore, is nothing less than the privilege of conceptual labor over an aesthetic mode of (re)presentation (*eine ästhetische Vorstellungsart*, 396). The exalted 'hyperphysics' (*Hyperphysik*) which accompanies the mystic illumination does not inquire into the formal principles and regulative ideas of practical reason but gives a confused 'theory' of the supernatural (of God and the human spirit) which is composed out of threads from different categorical realms in a manner which is hardly subtle (*nicht gar so fein*, 389 Remark). And instead of painstakingly justifying its propositions, this pseudo-philosophy takes recourse to a more elevated, immediate insight based on the affirmation of the seemingly indisputable 'fact' (*Faktum*) that philosophy has its 'tangible secrets' (*fühlbaren Geheimnisse*, 384). It is thus in a *philosophia arcani* (382) that the enthusiasts find the source of inspiration for their poetic talents as well as the resource for their social power. For, the 'overlordly' or 'superior' tone that is denounced here is also institutionally overdetermined. Kant argues that it not only rests on epistemological presuppositions which have become untenable in light of the critique of pure (practical) reason. He also fears that the insurgence of a cacophonic noise is politically fatal in that it destablizes the state and favors the private (i.e. subjective and thereby particular) interests of mystagogues and their initiated adepts. In his advocacy of a 'blind faith,' the mysta-

11. On Plato's letters, cf. also J. Derrida, *La carte postale, de Socrate à Freud et au-delà* (Paris: Flammarion, 1980), 92 ff.
12. Cf. J. van der Zande, *Bürger und Beamter. Johann Georg Schlosser 1739-1799* (Stuttgart, 1986) and the characterization of Schlosser as "antikritischer Philosoph" in Kant's "Verkündigung des nahen Abschlusses eines Traktats zum ewigen Frieden in der Philosophie," *Werke* Bd. 5, 405-416, 413-415.

gogue, whatever his popularity or populism, is 'despotic.' In his role of self-appointed guide he is a "Klubbist" (388) who, whether he knows and intends it or not, poses himself in opposition to the "people."[13]

What deserves our particular interest in Derrida's reconsideration of this debate is not only that it directs our attention to one of Kant's more unfamiliar texts and provides us with an even more unfamiliar reading of its unresolved tensions. What is more important is that Derrida focuses on the uncanny circumstance that in many respects this short essay sets the stage for the by now all-too-familiar contemporary controversy around the purported end of metaphysics and its transformation into a supposedly postmetaphysical form of thinking. This transformation, it has been argued, would continue an 'uncompleted project' of modernity by protecting the rigorously 'prosaic' character of its philosophical discourse, just as Kant did (cf. 397 Remark), against the permanent temptations of rhetorical devices and bodily desires. The positions taken by Kant and his alleged antagonists would thus show us in a mirror how the recourse to certain, supposedly unshakable, premises and arguments mimics and settles a much older conflict. In retrospect, Derrida suggests, the present debate might well prove to be nothing but a repetition and parody: "Not that today anybody can be recognized on this or that side, purely and simply, but ... it could be shown that today every slightly organized discourse is found or claims to be found on both sides, alternately or simultaneously, even if this emplacement exhausts nothing ... And this inadequation, always limited itself, no doubt indicates the thickest of difficulties. Each of us is the mystagogue *and* the *Aufklärer* of another." (78, 53). Both the call for Enlightenment and its alleged mystification might very well from *the very beginning of philosophy* have co-existed, struggled for our recognition or appealed to our vigilance. And as far as we know, they have always done so in the name of some original or ultimate 'unveiled' truth. Moreover, even

---

13. It is in precisely this sense, that his posture betrays a curious and paradoxical mixture of 'ressentiment' and veiled power. Kant writes: "So sind die Gleichmacher der politischen Verfassung nicht bloss diejenigen, welche, nach Rousseau, wollen, dass die Staatsbürger insgesamt einander gleichen, weil ein jeder *alles* ist; sondern auch diejenigen, welche wollen, dass alle einander gleichen, weil sie ausser Einem insgesamt *nichts* seien, und sind Monarchisten aus Neid: die bald den Plato, bald den Aristoteles auf den Thron erheben, um, bei dem Bewusstsein ihres eigenen Unvermögens, selbst zu denken, die verhasste Vergleichung mit andern zugleich Lebenden nicht auszustehen." (ibid., 383 note).

the deconstructive 'unmasking' of the true nature (or conditions of possibility) of this dialectic that marks philosophy from its very beginning to its purported end, would still, in a sense, contribute to its prolongation.

Throughout his reading, Derrida leaves no doubt that we cannot hope to find a solution to this conflict or overcome our dependence on the positions involved. There has always been and there will always be a desire to find, to uphold or to restore reason in its very purity and self-sameness. It has always been the dream of philosophical "allocution" as well as the language believed to purvey its truth, that it express an unambiguous meaning or attain an universal import by neutralizing all *tonal* differences or by making them *"inaudible"*: the tone, Derrida concludes, never passed for "essentially philosophic" (66, 18).[14] Conversely, there has always been a desire to let oneself be enticed by what — from a formal, rational viewpoint — is 'impure' or 'other.' And, indeed, more often than not this seduction has manifested itself in what Kant considers to be an illegitimate use of figural (re)presentations in the very determination of the essence of the moral law.

Yet, if Kant's critique is directed against an improper imitation of superior tone *in the philosophical discipline*[15] (rather than against true — social — superiority itself), then this implies that a confusion between two different voices has at least been possible. In order for the tone to feign, fake genuine superiority, the simulacrum must be sufficiently close to its purported original. The tone makes a difference which is therefore not simply that of 'thematic,' 'stylistic' or even 'rhetoric' distinction. Rather, Derrida surmises, it consists in an uncanny doubling which leaves us almost no room to discern what, if anything, came first and what was merely an echo.

Everything in Kant's text is centered around this problem of a recurrent temptation (*Verleitung*, 377) to drift away from a supposed original pretention of philosophical meaning(fulness). Eve-

---

14. In *Glas* Derrida had already noted the difficulty Hegel has in coming to terms with the resistence of the *Klingen* and the *Klang* against the concept (*Glas* [Paris: Galilée, 1974], 16, left col.). And it is no accident, that the polemical preface to the *Grundlinien der Philosophie des Rechts*, Hrsg. von J. Hoffmeister (Hamburg: Meiner, 1962), 5, decries at bottom a 'formless' back and forth of mere opinions characterized by a certain despicable "Ton."

15. As Derrida points out, the text in which Kant addresses (and, perhaps, also raises) an 'apocalyptic' tone in philosophy operates completely according to the protocols of academic and public debate formulated, two years later, in *Der Streit der Fakultäten*.

rything revolves around the possibility of a radical mis-conception of the task of philosophy with respect to the questions of what can be known, what should be done and what can be hoped for. On the one hand, Kant describes this derailment as a contamination due to a mere misapprehension. On the other hand, however, one can find passages where he seems to be forced to admit that the derailment accompanies philosophy from its first origin and, perhaps, even constitutes it from within.

Derrida elaborates on a hint Kant that gives in order to explain why, from the very beginning of philosophical thought, at an early date situated close to its origin, there was a flight from the labor of thought in mystification and speculation. Ever since it was possible to use the word 'philosophy' without a secure reference to its first context and proper sense, this deviation has been possible, and "no mystagogic speculation would have been credible or efficient, nothing or no one would have untuned ... in philosophy without this errance of the name far from the thing, and if the relation of the name philosophy to primordial sense had been assured against this very accident" (68, 25). Therefore this originary accident would haunt all philosophical discourse as a "continuous catastrophe" (73, 38-39), tied as it is to the structure of language as we know it. From now on, the hermeneutic 'seduction,' Kant seems to acknowledge, would seem to be inevitable. The souring of the proper tone (or, more precisely, of philosophy's atonality) would be given with the emergence and diffusion (and progress?) of rational discourse as such.

Chr. Norris suggests that "two different things" pervade the structure of Derrida's reading.[16] One the one hand, *D'un ton apocalyptique* appears to "side with Kant" and defend the 'lucid vigil' of the faculty of reason against the obscurantist claims of an immediate, mystagogic illumination or vision. On the other hand, however, Derrida's text at times also seems to change, if not to raise, its tone and thereby to reiterate, mimic or parody what Kant fears leads to a certain death of philosophy as such (and not just the death of a certain philosophy). On this reading, *D'un ton apocalyptique* would maintain that if philosophy (or 'thought') is to survive its own apparent end or closure, Kant's critique is both 'indispensable' and in need of being opened up. To bring out the force and the

16. "Jacques Derrida in Discussion with Christopher Norris," 75, cf. also: idem, "On Derrida's 'Apocalyptic Tone.' Textual Politics and the Principle of Reason," *Southern Review*, vol. 19, nr.1, 1986, 13-30.

218

weaknesses of Kant's critique would demand that one engage in a highly convoluted exchange of gestures and speak in more than one tongue. Instead of relying on a 'single' and ultimately 'monological' voice of practical reason that would dictate and orient a theoretical discourse that — in and for itself — is without tone, the 'Enlightenment' of (and the enlightenment with) this given, historically determined form of *Aufklärung*, would have to speak with many, different voices *at once*. Moreover, it would have to be shown that this multiplicity or variety and change of tone also takes place within one and the same discursive 'utterance,' within one and the same 'word,' within one and the same 'syllable,' in short, within one and the same 'mark.' But how could this occur? How precisely, does Derrida's reading, as is suggested here, do — at least — two things at once? How can it claim to be at once inside and outside the Kantian project? How can Derrida refuse to simply "take sides" with the parties involved but instead bring to light "the ancient interdependence of the antagonists or protagonists" (76, 45). How can one, by displacing the stages of Kant's de-mystification "come to the point of doing the contrary" of what Kant does or even ("preferably," Derrida writes) "something else" (68, 23)?

It is, Derrida notes, Kant's proposal to resolve the conflict (*"Aber, wozu nun aller dieser Streit ...?"*, 395) between argumentation and intuition or divination and to pave the way towards a possible future consensus, co-existence or even co-operation that indicates that we can hardly speak here of a real "antinomy" (78, 52), let alone a *différend*. For Kant concludes his essay by declaring the discrepancy — or lack of harmony — between philosophy's atonality and the increasing cacophony of voices ultematily null and void (*"ein Lärm um nichts"*), that is to say a controversy that because of the common aim of the parties involved is only in demand of mutual explication in order to bring the dissension to an end. It is, in other words a "Verunreinigung aus Missverstande, bei der es keiner Aussöhnung, sondern nur einer wechselseitigen Erklärung bedarf, um einen Vertrag, der die Eintracht fürs künftige noch inniglicher macht, zu schliessen" (395). Kant and his opponents, Derrida notes, have in common that they both exclude something as *"inadmissible"* (78, 52). In foregrounding a striking sexual metaphorics which Kant takes up from Schlosser and simply turns against him, Derrida first of all points to the fact that both parties express a desire to uncover, to denude or unveil truth *without castrating the logos*, i.e. without stripping reason of its 'phallus.' The debate between philosophy and its poetic seduction would thus be readable as a *phallogocentristic* debate centered around the anxious attempt to prevent or circumvent the emasculation (*Entmannung*, 389-390) of reason. On the one hand, there would be the emasculation of which Schlosser accuses Kant: a castration would occur whenever reason cuts from itself everything which exceeds the narrow bounds of formal reason. In this operation, reason would lose its substance and quasi-divine nature through a "metaphysical sublimation" and run the risk of becoming so thin or so 'delicate' (*feinnervig*) that it becomes impotent and unable to stand up against seduction of idolatry (*Laster*, 389-390). On the other hand, there would be the emasculation of reason of which Kant, in turn, suspects Schlosser. This castration would occur whenever reason permits itself to be enticed by subjective, intuitive or sensualistic devices and becomes caught up and lamed (*gelähmt*) in the metaphor of a — feminine — veil and therein forgets its own formidable power (*Stärke*, 390).

Kant criticizes in particular a *personification* which would compare the moral law to a veiled goddess, to the figure of Isis, who — as the "murderess of Osiris all of whose pieces she later recovers, except for the phallus" (79, 55) — reminds us by her very name of the castration complex that seems to haunt this text.[17] We should, Kant urges, not *personify* the law, which is transcendent, not only in relation to things but, in a sense, also *vis à vis persons*, who only deserve our respect "in sofar as they offer an *example* of the moral law," which, Kant holds, is "the only cause" of this respect.[18] For, the moral law is not based on the assumption of any unity of divine nature and human freedom that is said to be given in our deepest

---

17. Even though Kant does not establish an explicit link between the feared castration of reason and the sudden appearance of Isis, there is, Derrida suggests, a "tropical continuity" (75, 43) between these two citations. And for all the difficulties related to its very concept, it is precisely as a trope or "simulacrum" (76, 47), instead of as an anatomical, 'real' incision, that so-called castration affects a given symbolical order and threatens its 'phallus.' For a discussion of 'castration,' its 'concept' and 'metaphor,' cf. *La dissémination* (Paris: Seuil, 1972), 32, and *La vérité en peinture* (Paris: Flammarion, 1978), 136-138.
18. J. Derrida, "Préjugés — devant la loi," in: J.F. Lyotard, ed., *La faculté de juger* (Paris: Minuit, 1985), 87-139, 53, "Before the Law," transl. by A. Ronell and Chr. Roulston, in: Derrida, *Acts of Literature*, ed. by D. Attridge (New York, London: Routledge, 1992), 183-220, 190.

sentiments.[19] And the critique of pure (practical) reason excludes any possibility of an intellectual intuition of the ultimate, highest good. For Kant, on Derrida's reading, the moral law would therefore be "more in tune with the essence of the voice that hears/understands itself but neither touches nor sees itself, thus seeming to hide itself from every external intuition ... in its very transcendance the moral voice is nearer, and thus more auto-affective, more autonomous. Moral law then is more auditory, more audible than the mystagogic oracle still contaminated with feeling, illumination, or intuitive vision, contact" *(73, 37)*. The voice of practical reason would say "nothing of the describable" *(72, 35)* but only prescribe (itself) unconditionally, categorically. And yet, even though this is precisely the reason why it "gives rise to autonomy" *(72, 36)*, Kant must acknowledge that it expresses itself in a manner that, paradoxically, also rests upon a certain heteronomy. For it only speaks with authority, when "the law it dictates is as little flexible, as little subject to free interpretation as if it came from the completely other in me" (ibid.).

It is here then that the extremes of this debate meet and it comes as no surprise when, in the final paragraph of his essay, Kant reluctantly associates precisely the criticized seductive figure of the veiled Isis with his own understanding of the sublimity of the moral law: "Die verschleierte Göttin, vor der wir beiderseits unsere Knie beugen, ist das moralische Gesetz in uns, in seiner unverletzlichen Majestät. Wir vernehmen zwar ihre Stimme, und verstehen auch gar wohl ihr Gebot, sind aber beim anhören in Zweifel, ob sie von dem Menschen, aus der Machtvollkommenheit seiner eigenen Vernunft, oder ob sie von einem anderen, dessen Wesen ihm unbekannt ist, und welches zum Menschen durch diese seine eigene Vernunft spricht herkomme. Im Grunde täten wir vielleicht besser uns dieser Nachforschung gar zu überheben; da sie bloss spekulativ ist, und, was uns zu tun obliegt (objektiv) immer dasselbe bleibt, mag man

19. According to Jacobi, one of the authors with whom Kant polemizes in his essay (cf. H. Timm, "Die Bedeutung der Spinozabriefen Jacobis für die Entwicklung der idealistischen Religionsphilosophie," in: K. Hammacher, Hrsg., *Friedrich Heinrich Jacobi*, Philosoph und Literat der Goethezeit [Frankfurt/M, 1971], 68 n. 81), the inalienable awareness of freedom and moral consciousness, the synthetic character of our experience as well as the conviction that we are really affected not just by phenomena or mere appearances of things but by the *things as they are in themselves*, would be incomprehensible when philosophy would use *demonstration* and *mechanical reasoning* as its privileged method of inquiry. We would never be able to infer or to affirm the existence of the *ens realissimum*, i.e. God, because formal rational argument forbids the use of such categories as *cause* and *substance* outside the realm of the spatio-temporal world.

eines oder das andere Prinzip zum Grunde legen" (395). Therefore, in spite of the analogy, the identification of the moral law with a sensible, veiled, feminine figure - or, more precisely, her *body* - remains an aesthetic mode of (re)presentation even when it attributes no other characteristics to this law than those (already or separately) discovered by discursive and prosaic demonstration. This personification should be more in place if invoked only *after* the principles of morality have been laid bare in their purity. Only then could one use images from the senses, in short, an analogical presentation (*analogische Darstellung*, 396), in order to *encourage* rather than to *ground* moral conduct. By reversing this proper order, by deducing morality from sentiments or sensuous images, one would always be in danger of conflating the law with a mystic vision which, again, would come down to the demise — the death — of all (moral) philosophy in favor of mere arbitrary opinion: "Jene Göttin (...) *ahnen* zu können, würde ein Ausdruck sein, der nichts mehr bedeutete als: durch sein moralisches *Gefühl* zu Pflichtbegriffen geleitet werden, ehe man noch die Prinzipien wovon jenes abhängt, sich hat *deutlich* machen können; welche Ahnung eines Gesetzes, sobald es durch schulgerechte Behandlung in klare Einsicht übergeht, das eigentliche Geschäft der Philosophie ist, ohne welche jener Ausspruch der Vernunft die Stimme eines Orakels, welches allerlei Auslegungen ausgesetzt ist, sein würde." (396).[20]

20. Which does not exclude the possibility of Kant also writing, in the *Kritik der Urteilskraft*: "Vielleicht ist nie etwas Erhabeneres gesagt, oder ein Gedanke erhabener ausgedrückt worden, als in jener Aufschrift über dem Tempel der Isis (der Mutter Natur): 'Ich bin alles was da ist, was da war, und was da sein wird, und meinen Schleier hat kein Sterblicher aufgedeckt." (*Werke*, W.Weischedel, vol. 8, 417 note). These words are added to a passage that evokes the sublime (*erhabene*) feelings caused by the virtuous, intelligible character, feelings which are compared to the limitless prospect of a joyful future unattainable by any definite (*bestimmten*) concept. On the one hand, Kant leaves no doubt that this aesthetic idea is a representation of the imagination (*Einbildungskraft*) which simply supplements a given concept (*eine einem gegebenen Begriffe beigesellte Vorstellung*) and is bound up with an irrecuperable multitude of partial and freely deployed representations. The latter are said to surround the given concept with much that has to remain ineffable (*Unnennbares*) thus allowing the cognitive faculties to be experienced more vividly or quickened (*belebt*, ibid., 417) and thus bind the mere 'letter' of language to its 'spirit.' On the other hand, however, this logical and temporal order of conceptual thought and aesthetic imagination can apparently also be reversed. The said note explains approvingly that Segner, in his *Naturlehre* used the temple of Isis as an emblematic figure in order to inspire his pupil (*um seinen Lehrling, den er in diesen Tempel zu führen bereit war, vorher mit dem heiligen Schauer zu erfüllen, der das Gemüt zu feierlicher Aufmerksamkeit stimmen soll*' (ibid.). Derrida briefly refers to the

Kant claims that, unlike the sensible and singular voice of the oracle, the voice of (practical) reason, that is to say of moral law, does not (or should not) lend itself to any such mis-interpretation. It is only when this voice is mimicked and parodied, when it is mistaken for (or mixed with) a voice that does not speak to all of us in the same unequivocal way, but only through the veil of particular, sensible tropes, that it loses its proper tone and its 'true secret.' The very universality of the law forbids it from speaking a private language and from taking people aside. And yet, if the genuine *Geheimnis* thus has a certain intimacy or domesticity (as is suggested by the *heim* or *heimisch* that Derrida reads in the German *Geheimnis*), it is at the same time also transcendent, to the point of being *unheimlich*. For Kant, the sublimity of the moral law consists precisely in the fact that it speaks from a distant height.

On closer scrutiny, Derrida contends, this remains true for the *Schwärmer* as well. For although Kant at one point accuses the mystagogues of being "Kraftmänner, welche neuerdings mit Begeisterung eine Wahrheit verkündigen, die ihnen keine Mühe macht, weil sie diese Göttin beim Zipfel ihres Gewandes erhascht und sich ihr bemächtet zu haben vorgeben" (391 note), he is also aware of the fact that they do not and cannot penetrate her veil either. The most they can hope for is "der Göttin Weisheit so nahe zu kommen, dass man das *Rauschen* ihres Gewandes vernehmen kann" (389), but the veil itself cannot be lifted. The *Schwärmer* only make it so thin that they can divine (*ahnen*) a presence behind it. And since it remains unclear how thin the veil is made, Kant suspects them of leaving it ultimatily intact and thick enough so as to allow them to take the *phantom* (*Gespenst*) behind it for whatever they please. What thus seems to attract them in the figure of Isis makes its very appeal exclusively *in* the veil. It is the veil, Derrida concludes, which "unleashes what Freud calls *Bemächtigungstrieb*" (77, 48). This drive is therefore evoked by a relative absence or, rather, presence-absence, that the veil, playing *around* the body, symbolizes or allegorizes. As a consequence, the desire cannot conquer its 'object' without destroying its — fatal — attraction, that is, without liquidating what it strives for. It is constituted from within as that which excludes all vision and conceptual or poetical appropriation: "The mystagogues of modernity ... do not simply tell us what they see, touch, or feel. They have a *presentiment* of,

cited passage in "Economimesis," in: S. Agacinksi et al., *Mimesis: Des articulations* (Paris: Aubier-Flammarion, 1975), pp. 57-93, 73.

they anticipate, they approach, they smell out, they are men of imminence and the trace [sic]" (75, 43).[21]

What is excluded by both Kant and the *Schwärmer* is the *body* behind the veil. For Kant, the whole desire surrounding the feminine figure (whether that of her veil or her body) is always in danger of confusing the voice of reason, which is bestowed with a *univocal* meaning and thereby guarantees universality, with a sensible voice, which speaks — or, more precisely, seduces — in private. Moreover, this desire is in danger of conflating two distinctive 'feelings.' For, as Kant notes: "Diejenige Lust (oder Unlust), die notwendig *vor dem Gesetz* vorhergehen muss, damit die Tat geschehe, ist *pathologisch*; diejenige aber, *vor welcher*, damit diese geschehe, *das Gesetz* notwendig vorhergehen muss, ist *moralisch*." (384 Remark).

Since the apriorical form of the law has to preside over every concrete — in Kant's words, material — determination of the will (*Willensbestimmung*), all desire should always be summoned *before the law* that preceeds it. The righteous moral disposition (*Gesinnung*) would only obey the law in so far and as long as it neglects all motivational drives, whether they are inspired by an ideal of beatitude (*Glückseligkeit*) or by any other empirical interest. For these supplements to pure duty contaminate (*verunreinigen*) the categorical character of true obligation.[22]

21. To the extent that the mystagogues respect the veil and do not touch, let alone violate or incorporate, the *body* of the goddess behind the veil, they seem to observe the very same play of the veil that Derrida himself has analyzed in *Éperons*, in his reading of the styles of some of Nietzsche's most enigmatic fragments, where the 'truth' of 'woman' is precisely described in terms of a truth of this play which allows no *essential* truth at all. To what extent, then, does deconstruction repeat the gesture that Kant condemns in the *Schwärmer*?

22. Elsewhere, in "Préjugés - devant la loi," Derrida suggests that this condition of possibility of any critique of *pure* practical reason is, in a sense, also the impossible *par excellence*. Caught up in a so-called double bind, this fundamental presupposition that the law be pure *must* but *cannot* be sustained. Derrida makes this clear by relating the reading of a literary parable, namely Kafka's "Vor dem Gesetz," to a reconsideration of this major paradox or aporia of Kant's, and perhaps all, moral philosophy. Kafka's text, Derrida suggests, obliquely addresses the problem of the quasi-literary presentation and concealment of the law of pure practical reason, which in Kant's own words is the guardian ('*Aufbewahrerin*') and narrow gate ('*Pforte*') of moral conduct. And it is not difficult to see how also the dramatic scene of *Von einem neuerdings erhobenen vornehmen Ton in der Philosophie* prefigures some of the features of Kafka's parable. It is as if Schlosser, the one who presents himself as someone holding the key (or one of the many keys) to the gate of the law (the castle, the tabernacle), but also the one who closes it off, plays the role of a jealous

However, the very attempt to immunize reason against all seduction by preventing it from making a surreptitious slip from

guardian, whereas Kant forces himself in the position of the man of the country who thinks that the law should be equally accessible to all. What is at stake in this reading of Kant in light of Kafka — and, it should be noted, *vice versa* — is first of all the suggestion that the very *a priori* character of the *Sittengesetz* must be thought of as parasitic on the contingent, phenomenal world of tropes of language and figures of speech, that is to say, on all those 'impure' carriers of experience from which the Kantian notion of the law has to set itself apart in order to sustain its philosophical and non-empirical, intelligible or noumenal, character. The Kantian law, Derrida suggests, cannot proclaim its authority or articulate its prescriptions, in particular the categorical imperative, without a minimal 'narrative' wording. Its very first 'example' betrays it. This paradox or aporia appears at numerous places throughout Kant's work, some of which are analyzed in great length in *Glas*, in the notes to "Les fins de l'homme," in *Marges de la philosophie*, and in "Parergon," in *La vérité en peinture*. And all of these inquiries into the intersection of practical philosophy and literature could be said to prepare the elaboration of a 'narrative pragmatics' (a term Derrida uses, in 'Préjugés,' with reference to Lyotard's *Au Juste*). In the same vein, Derrida explains, in "Préjugés," how Kafka's "Vor dem Gesetz" succeeds in teasing out the intricacies of any discourse on morality, whether Kantian, Freudian or Heideggerian. It does so by evoking a certain 'literariness' in the heart or at the origin of practical reason as well as in the manner in which the moral law arouses respect. This narrativity would be revealed by Kant's most intriguing expressions such as his reference to a *typology* (*Typik* as opposed to the 'schematism') of practical reason (*Kritik der praktischen Vernunft* A, 119 ff.), to a *symbolic* presentation of the moral good, to the form of respect aimed at *examples* of the moral law and, finally, to the *as if* (*als ob*) in the second formulation of the categorical imperative ('Act as if the maxim of your act were by your will to turn into a universal law of nature') (cf. "Before the Law," 190, "Préjugés," 108). It is for this reason that Derrida writes that although the very "authority" and "rationality" of the law "seems alien to all fiction and imagination — even the transcendental imagination — it still seems *a priori* to shelter these parasites" (ibid.). Seen against this background, it would be difficult to decide whether Kafka's *récit* "proposes a powerful philosophic *ellipsis*" ("Before the Law," 191, "Préjugés," 109, my italics) or whether (the critique of) pure practical reason is ultimately dependent upon non-philosophical resources and retains an element of the fantastic, the fictional or the fabulous. To be sure, "Vor dem Gesetz" is hardly a systematic treatise in disguise, reconstructable at wish in a formal argument. And it is, perhaps, for this very reason that its narration (its *récit*) might be called *literary*. But the demarcation of philosophy and literature does not prevent the intermingling of the ethical and narrative 'regime' from having far-reaching implications. For, if it is characteristic of a specifically literary text that it gives us neither the criteria nor the strict methodological guidelines which could help us to get hold of its idea; if it is plausible, moreover, that we — as its addressees — *cannot avoid* deciding on its purported meaning, however 'unjust' or arbitrary such a step might be, then an intriguing problem arises. Derrida characterizes it in the following terms: what if the so-called law of literature and of reading would be *analogous* to the — often enigmatic and disturbing — way in the noumenal into the phenomenal — "a leap from concepts to the unthinkable or the irrepresentable" (72, 34) — also confronts thought with the danger of yet another eclipse or apocalypse. For,the defense of a neutrality of tone in philosophy, the pretention that philosophy could leave tonal differences behind, ultematily comes down to condemning it to a certain death. While Kant's purported 'progressivism' thus overcomes a certain 'dogmatic' as well as mystagogic 'metaphysics,' it does at the same time inaugurate another, more subtle, more formal and fundamental and transcendental 'eschatology.'[23] On what grounds, if any (the question of the 'ground' being precisely what is in question), does Derrida draw this conclusion?

which the moral law manifests itself: "what if the law [i.e. the moral law, HdV], without being itself transfixed by literature, shared the conditions of its possibility with the literary object?" (ibid.). What would the *quasi-literary constitution of all practical reason(ing)* teach us about the viability, the hermeneutics, the application and the possible deconstruction of a specific — for instance, Kantian — ethics? And what, conversely, would the parallellism between the two laws imply for the ethics of deconstruction itself? It is tempting to look for the 'hermeneutic key' to this problem and its possible solution in a fascinating passage which I, admittedly, quote out of context here. It reads: the *récit* and the law "appear together [before their common law, before the law of the law, HdV] and find themselves summoned one before the other" (ibid.). Can we infer from this formulation that the two (apparently extreme) positions, for which, in Derrida's text, the names of Kant and Kafka stand — in short, that of the unconditionality and purity of the (moral) law and that of its fictional or fabulous 'presentation' or 'manifestation' — are in truth nothing but *oscillating poles* which necessarily and incessantly refer to one another like the foci of an ellipse, to the extent that the first cannot be thought without the other, and *vice versa*? We will return to this question at the end of this essay. Here it suffices to recall that Derrida never conflates the 'spheres' of law and morality, on the hand, and the fictional or fabulous, on the other. Moral and legal principles and rules are "not things found in nature, but ... symbolic inventions, or conventions, institutions, that in their very normality as well as in their normativity, entail something of the fictional" (J. Derrida, *Limited Inc* [Evanston: Northwestern UP, 1988], 134, French edition, Présentation et traductions par E. Weber [Paris: Galilée, 1990], 243-244). That does not mean, however, Derrida goes on to explain, that they are "the same as novels," but that they are "not 'natural entities' and that they depend upon the same structural power that allows novelesque fictions ... to take place;" and this explains, Derrida concludes, "why literature and the study of literature have much to teach us about right and law" (ibid.).

23. For a critique of this 'conclusion,' cf. J. Simon, "Vornehme und apokalyptische Töne in der Philosophie," *Zeitschrift für philosophische Forschung*, 1986, 489-519.

II

One of the most thought-provoking aspects of Derrida's reading of this text is that it associates Kant's gesture of denunciation and unmasking the obscurantism of the *Schwärmer* with the quest for disclosure and uncovering that characterizes the *apocalyptic* tradition. Derrida claims that the denuding to which all critical, progressive discourses of modernity aspire, not unlike apocalyptics, presupposes a *vision of light* as well as a *spiritual enlightenment*. Conversely, the apocalyptic pathos often has a 'critical' intent *vis à vis* the existing order. Therefore, each of these two genres throws light — of quasi-divine human reason and of divine illumination respectively — on the other. Western tradition, Derrida contends, has been dominated by several and yet not-so-different programs that proclaim the final end of the paradigms that precede them: the end of God and of morals, of history and class struggle, of the subject and of Oedipus, of art and of the university. As a result of these revolutions and reversals, each new *Aufklärung*, even the one devoid of religious overtones, can be read as an eschatology that substitutes the others that preceded it. Even the proclamation of the "end of the end" with which one could be tempted to identify Derrida's own 'position,' would still partake in this chorus of apocalyptic tones and raise just one more voice in the same "concert" (81, 60). Who could claim to possess the "metalanguage" (ibid.) that would govern and organize all eschatologies? The supposition that there would be "just *one* fundamental *scene, one* great paradigm" (83, 67), which makes both these strategies possible, would still obey an 'onto-eschato-teleological' hermeneutics. This suggestion could therefore claim no other status than that of a self-defeating projection and performative contradiction or, in other words, a 'fiction' and 'fable.' It is no accident, then, that Derrida begins by saying that he will not only write *on* but also *with* an apocalyptic tone. (The first sentence reads: "*Je parlerai donc d'un ton apocalyptique en philosophie*"). As always, Derrida's text does not only explore a 'theme' but also a 'practice' of writing.

D'un ton apocalyptique listens to (and reiterates) the resounding of the *glas*, the 'death knell,' of apocalyptics and asks: what is it that remains of this genre, what of the critique, both of (pure) reason and of ideology in all its different Marxist, Nietzschean and Freudian forms? Are not the distinctions between these devices in the final analysis "measured as gaps or deviations in relation to the fundamental tonality of this [apocalyptic] *Stimmung* audible across so

227

many thematic variations? Haven't all the *différends* taken the form of a going-one-better in eschatological eloquence, each newcomer, more lucid than the other ...?" (80, 59). And if one can only refute one eschatology by appealing to another, more sophisticated one, would this not mean that 'eschatology' has come over us even before we have uttered a word? Seen in this light, every questioning, every destruction, every overcoming as well as every deconstruction would always already have responded to a call — a debt as well as a promise, an inspirational fire as well as an 'all-burning' 'flame' — that in 'itself' can never be questioned, but only *affirmed*, as a *fatality* but also as a *chance*. And what, if eschatology thus indeed "surprises us at the first word" (81, 63), is it that we can or should say and do?

Although Derrida does not discuss the question whether *all* past paradigms are *equally* arbitrary and mortal or even lethal, he re-marks in parentheses that *one* eschatology in particular, namely, the one that claimed that *morality* should (or could) be overcome, was the "most serious" of all these "naïvete[s]" (80, 59). It is this remarkable statement that introduces (and, at least in part, motiv-ates) the transformation of the Kantian idea of Enlightenment into an elliptical notion of unconditional lucid vigilance or guardedness, which exceeds or, rather, preceeds the false dilemma of formal reasoning and intellectual *illuminatio*, both of which, Derrida holds, mutilate and suffocate all responsible thought: "We cannot and we must not — this is a law and a destiny — forgo the *Aufklärung*. In other words, we cannot and we must not forgo what compels recognition as the enigmatic desire for vigilance, for the lucid vigil [*veille*], for clarification, for critique and truth, but for a truth that at the same time keeps within itself enough apocalyptic desire ... to demystify, or if you prefer, to deconstruct the apoca-lyptic discourse itself and with it everything that speculates on vision, the imminence of the end, theophany, parousia, the Last Judgement, and so on" (82, 64-65). Unlike Kant and his opponents, Derrida does not identify this summoning with any specific — or exclusively — ethico-political or religious obligation let alone with some aesthetic playfulness or gravity. The differing and deferral that characterizes this elusive 'law' and 'destiny' and that leaves its trace in each word and each act, is rooted neither in nature nor in culture nor in any noumenal realm. And yet, paradoxically, it entails an appeal that demands immediate response. In *D'un ton apocalyp-tique* this call is 'exemplified' with a citation of the *Viens!* (the 'Come!') that accompanies the opening of each of the seven seals in the *Revelation of John* (cf. 17:1 and *passim*). This text, Derrida stresses, could be read as the paradigm of the vigil that surrounds all known ends as well those that are still to come. Without ever being able to turn its (last) page, every '*Wake*,' anticipating, preparing or announcing an end, unwittingly re-cites John's *Revelation* or, Derrida clarifies, "at least the fundamental scene that already programs the Johannine document" (85, 71), its 'fable.'

Derrida assumes that a careful rereading of the *Revelation* — "before and beyond a narratology" (85, 72) — could retrace the aleatory character of the "narrative voice" (ibid.) in this text. For, according to the prologue of the *Apocalypse*, John cites the words of Jesus, which, in turn, have been transmitted to him by a third instance — a messenger or angel — and sends them to the seven communities or, more precisely, to their angels. As a result, Derrida concludes, we do no longer know "who addresses what to whom" (87, 77): too many voices occupy the "telephone line" (86, 75). Since this uncertainty, Derrida stresses, defines the apocalyptic or 'angelic' tonality — i.e. renders every determinate tone discordant — a crucial question imposes itself: "if the dispatches [*envois*] always refer to other dispatches without decidable destination, the destination remaining to come, then isn't this completely angelic structure, that of the Johannine Apocalypse, isn't it also the structure of every scene of writing in general? ... wouldn't the apocalyptic be a *transcendental condition* of all discourse, of all experience itself, of every mark or every trace? And the genre of writings called 'apocalyptic' in the strict sense, then, would be only an example, an *exemplary* revelation of this transcendental structure" (87, 77-78). To the extent that it reveals nothing determinate, the *Apocalypse* enlightens the structure of language, of all experience, in short, of "the mark in general: *that is, of the divisible dispatch [envoi] for which there is no self-presentation nor assured destination*" (87, 78).

It is tempting to recognize in these passages a reiteration and inversion of the project of transcendental, critical philosophy. Instead of the identical spatio-temporal structures of perception (*Anschauungsformen*) and the categories of understanding, Derrida would seem to argue that it is, on the contrary, the unstable differing and deferral of the *différance* of all marks in general which can be seen as the *quasi*-transcendental condition of possibility of all experience. A real appeal or event would only be possible on the basis of the — properly speaking impossible — 'experience' of the arbitrariness of the categories of all experience. Like Kant, Derrida would make it plausible that the claims of formal reason *and* the presenti-

229

ments of obscurantism ultimately obey one and the same law. To be sure, Derrida leaves no doubt that there *is* no *Archimedian* point beyond the Kantian principle of reason. Moreover, the principle of (this) reason — in its Leibnizschean formulation: *nihil est sine ratione* — 'is' not 'in itself' again or simply reason.[24] But this does not imply that responsible thought should stop here. For, without having had an 'idea' or, rather, presentiment of the *abyss* that surrounds decisions, and of all the risks involved, we would not be able to make a single new step, we would never be *open* or *vulnerable* for the *gift* and the *burden* of future possibilities. There would exist nothing but an universe of *causality*, everything would be *programmed*. Only if the other gives the law, could there be 'autonomy,' in Kant's sense. Instead of focusing on the rational foundation and explication of what can be known or done, one should therefore begin by re-thinking *heteronomical* unconditionality as the quasi-transcendental 'condition' of all rational thought or conduct. By definition, this unconditionality could be a *promise* as well as a *threat*, a *revelation* as well as an *apocalypse*: "Generalized *Verstimmung* is the possibility for the other tone, for the tone of another, to come at no matter what moment to interrupt a familiar tonality ... *Verstimmung* is called the derailment, the sudden change ... of tone ..., it is the disorder or the delerium of the destination (*Bestimmung*), but also the possibility of all emission or utterance. The unity of tone, if there was such, would certainly be the assurance of the destination, but also death, another apocalypse" (83-84, 67-68). Every attempt to de-mystify the apocalyptic genre would have to rely on this 'structure' and let itself be 'inspired' or diffused by a similar desire for more light. Every denunciation of false prophets would speak in the prophetic mode which it, in this form or another, for better or worse, seeks to overcome. There is, perhaps, nothing that could bring an end to this unending process of demystification, negation and denegation or denial.

To be sure, the proces of de-mystification, Derrida stresses, should and must be pushed "as far as possible" (89, 81) and this "task" is "interminable" since no inquiry would ever be able to "exhaust the overdeterminations and the indeterminations of the apocalyptic strategems" (ibid.). One should deploy or 'mobilize' all the empirical and hermeneutic resources one can think of here, whether socio-economical, psychoanalytic, linguistic, rhetoric or

24. Cf. *Du droit à la philosophie*, 470, 471.

pragmatic. For, a deconstruction — even when it, as Derrida notes, "does not come to a stop here" — could never succeed without this "second work" (83, transl. modified, 66). However, none of these modes of explanation and interpretation can ever reduce the "ethico-political motif or motivation" (of their targets as well as of themselves) to something "simple" (89, 81) or to a single 'cause.'[25] The most important 'reason' for this irreducibility or indetermination is not so much the finitude that characterizes every empirical and hermeneutic inquiry, but the "(perhaps) more essential" (90, 83) limit inscribed in advance in every attempt to demystify. It is the circumstance that every proclamation of ends always already *responds* to a 'Come' that calls it into being, without 'itself' ever becoming part of this revealment or advent of the event of being. And, it is the acknowledgement (or affirmation) of this internal margin — a pocket or 'invagination' of 'the other' in the very constitution of even the most autonomous thoughts, acts or gestures — which seems to mark the difference (as well as the *différend*) between deconstruction and the Kantian *Aufklärung*.[26]

No 'onto-eschato-theology' would ever be able to determine or to analyze this coming or to-come of the event. Only a "spectrography of the tone" (93, 92) could try to re-trace the 'writing' of this calling that does not let itself be represented as a thematic object or a rhetoric trope that would categorize its inscription and injunction.

25. Derrida points out that the apocalyptic genre cannot be judged in light of Kant's indictments only. More often than not, the apocalyptic genre has misled those in power, if only by multiplying detours in order to delude that other 'vigilance' called censorship. Derrida recalls that the apocalyptic genre flourished when the censorship in the Roman Empire was most intense. And, generally speaking, the apocalyptic tone could be considered as being the instance which at different times and places, whether in a political context or not, upsets an exclusive discourse or challenges a dominant idiom (cf. 89-90, 82-83).
26. And yet, Derrida points out that this is already clear from the very structure of the argument developed in the first preface of the *Kritik der reinen Vernunft*. There philosophy is called the guardian of a tribunal of reason that is to be instituted in response to an appeal (*Aufforderung*) that has already preceded it. The critique of pure reason and the architectonics, whose foundations it lays down, would be nothing but the 'modern' repetition or re-iteration of an age-old response to what is 'in truth' an immemorial call. This call would derive its force from this precedence or anteriority, from its being *before the law* of reason (cf. *Du droit à la philosophie*, 92-93). The responsible gesture of interrogating precisely that law could therefore no longer follow the method of a transcendental, whether Kantian or, for that matter, phenomenological and fundamental-ontological, questioning. And this for different reasons, not the least of which is that the *quasi*-transcendental structure of 'implication' uncovered here does not "fold itself back" to any "thetic" or "hypothetic" form of

Any such semantic, figural or pragmatic analysis would be off the mark. As a "citation without a past present" (ibid.), the 'Come' gives itself to be read in different 'narrations' or *récits* (in the *Revelation of John*, in the writings of Blanchot): 'Come' resounds as a "recitative and a song whose singularity remains at once absolute and absolutely divisible" (ibid.). No existing or possible ontology or grammar could ever decompose let alone synthesize this tone or answer what 'it' 'is.' For the question 'what is?,' Derrida explains, "belongs to a space ... opened [and traversed] by a 'come' come from the other" (93-94, 93). This tone then cannot but be *affirmed* and *re-affirmed*. In this respect, the 'Come' resembles the Heideggerian motif of the *Zusage*, which Derrida, in *De l'esprit* and elsewhere, reads as the "acquiescing to language," or simply as "the mark,"[27] presupposed by every questioning, be it that of fundamental ontology or that of (transcendental) critique. And yet, the 'vigil' provoked or entailed by this originary 'yes,' while 'itself' beyond any question (a "beyond of the question"), would be "anything but precritical."[28] For the 'beyond-question,' the 'gage' or 'en-gage' of language, of the mark, would always already offer 'itself' as split, as at least double(d), as a 'yes, yes.' The *affirmation* would never take a dogmatic, firm or closed, form.[29] To speak of *a* tone or of *tonality*, in general terms, would already be saying too much or, rather, not enough. Consequently, there could never be a 'first' or 'last' call.

But not only would the tone(s), 'in themselves,' be divided, the

presupposition (ibid., 34). The problematization (if that is still the right word) would consist of an 'interpretative' *act* that re-founds or invents. And in so doing, it would testify to a responsibility that is responsive to an 'obligation' which, Derrida suggests, does not yet (*pas encore*) let itself be determined by the Kantian critique of pure practical reason. If the words primacy or priority would be appropriate here, the moral law could be to said to be based on the responsiveness mentioned earlier, rather than the reverse (ibid., 471, cf. 472). And without forcing the analogy, Derrida suggests that it is precisely at this point that one could draw a parallel with Heidegger's notion of the call or appeal (*Ruf*, *Anspruch*) which, according to *Der Satz vom Grund*, provokes and engages language.

27. J. Derrida, "'Il faut bien manger' ou le calcul du sujet," *Cahiers Confrontation*, 20, 1989, 91-114, English transl. "'Eating Well,' or the Calculation of the Subject: An Interview with Jacques Derrida," in: E. Cadava, P. Connor, J.L. Nancy, eds., *Who comes after the subject?* (New York and London: Routledge, 1991), 96-119, 100.

28. Ibid., 109.

29. Derrida plays with the French here: *affirmation* 'is' without *fermeté* and *fermeture*, but this *without* 'is' without negativity or mere privation.

232

difference between the 'Come's' would, again, be *tonal*. This difference would be that of a breath, an accent, a timbre or gesture that
suppports none of the classifications that we know from speech act
theory, not even that of 'the performative.' For, whereas the performative is an act whose success or failure depends on the fulfilment of
certain contextual requirements, the tonal difference would 'be'
nothing but "a gesture in the word, that gesture which does not let
itself be recovered by the analysis - whether linguistic, semantic or
rhetorical - of a word" (94, 93-94). The 'Come' cannot be said to
originate in a divine, masculine or female voice, nor to direct 'itself'
(directly) to a subject already constituted and identitical to itself.
Rather, the 'Come' would be the "disaster" or "catastrophe" of all
of these sites as well as of the passages between them. In the
terminology explored (and exploited) here one could therefore call
the 'Come,' again, an apocalypse. This apocalypse would be without cause, sender, messenger or addressee. It would be an apocalypse "without apocalypse" (94, 95), without the revelatory visions
or final judgments that, at least historically, have seemed to characterize the genre. This a-apocalyptic 'Come' would only consist of
envois, i.e. dispatches or sendings, in the plural and plural in 'themselves.' And, in the light of this "immediate tonal duplicity in every
apocalyptic voice" (88, 78), the very regulative idea of a formal
(however cautiously or hypothetically reconstructed) 'unity of reason within the diversity of its voices'[30] is *ruined* in advance. What is
more, no fundamental ontology, no thought of Being as *Ereignis*,
no *legein* of the *aletheia*, no *Geschick* of the *Schicken* would ever be
capable of gathering or re-collecting these *envois* in one hand (cf. 94,
96). The motif of the sending(s), in *D'un ton apocalyptique* must
(like that of *La carte postale*) be linked to a thinking of the erring of
the destination (i.e. of *destinerrance* and the *clandestination*), which
would go "beyond the Heideggerian protocols,"[31] beyond even the
Irre des Seins, toward a thought of *la chance* as *la Neccesité*.[32]

Announcing 'itself' beyond (or, rather, before) good and evil, be
it not in any chronological, genealogical, let alone logical sense, this
'apocalypse' without apocalypse would thus be the apocalypse of all

---

30. Cf. J. Habermas, "Die Einheit der Vernunft in der Vielheit ihrer Stimme," in:
    Nachmetaphysisches Denken, Philosophische Aufsätze (Frankfurt/M: Suhr-
    kamp, 1988), 198, "The Unitiy of Reason in the Diversity of Its Voices," in:
    Postmetaphysical Thinking, Philosophical Essays, trans. W.M. Hohengarten
    (Cambridge: MIT Press, 1992), pp. 115-148.
31. "Eating Well," 106.
32. On 'chance' and *tuchè*, cf. *Du droit à la philosophie*, 46.

(past, present and future) apocalypses. No longer simply mystagogic or anagogic, it would rather seem 'an-agogic' and an-archic in its socio-political 'effects.' And yet, it would by necessity run the "risk" of being appropriated in view of a "conductive violence" or an "authoritarian 'duction'" (94,94). This danger is "unavoidable; it threatens the tone as its double" (ibid.).[33]

Thus, Derrida writes in a different context, if Kant, in the *Kritik der praktischen Vernunft*, acknowledges that *experience* never permits us to exclude the possibility that, in a particular case, a secret motive (*geheimer Triebfeder* or *Antrieb*) has been at work, then this "secret no more offers us the prospect of some decipherment, even infinite, than it allows us to hope for a rigorous decontamination between 'in conformity with duty' [*pflichtmässig*] and 'out of pure duty' [*aus reiner Pflicht*]."[34] As a consequence, Derrida continues, this 'de-contamination' is not so much impossible "by virtue of some phenomenal or empirical limit, even if indelible, but precisely because this limit is not empirical: its impossibility is linked *structurally* to the possibility of the 'out of pure duty.' Abolish the possibility of the similacrum and of external repetition, and you abolish the possibility both of the law and of duty themselves, that is, of their recurrence. Impurity is principally inherent in the purity of duty, i.e. its iterability. Flouting all possible oppositions, *there* would be the secret" (33 n.12). The 'ground' then of responsibility would be *something secret*, rather than *the* (true) secret. And the resonance between these words, "*Il y a là du secret*," (20) and the formulation *Il y a là cendre* chosen in another context, in *La dissémination* and *Feu, la cendre*, is hardly a coincidence. For no semantic content and no specific moral — or even categorical — imperative that would be "separable ... from its performative tracing" (ibid.), is revealed here.

The 'fact' that impurity is given with the purity of duty manifests itself solely in a "feeling" (Kant would say: *moralisches Gefühl*) from which we cannot "detach ourselves" and "whose linguistic or cultural conditioning is difficult to assess" (26 n.4). Only a 'feeling' would make us aware of the paradox that an act which does not go 'beyond duty' or was merely performed "out of duty" — in the

33. In "Signature, event, context," in *Limited Inc*, 15, 17, French version, 41 and 43, Derrida calls this risk a '*law*.'
34. J. Derrida, "Passions: 'An Oblique Offering,'" in: D.Wood, ed., *Derrida: A Critical Reader* (Oxford, Cambridge: Blackwell, 1992), 5-35, 33 n.12 (translation slightly modified). Hereafter cited parenthetically in the text.

234

sense (or in view) of a "restitution" or "the discharge of a debt" —
would still be "a-moral" (26 n.4, cf. 18). Such an act would fall short
of 'affirming' an "unlimited, incalculable or uncalculating giving,
without any possible reappropriation, by which one must measure
the ethicity or the morality of ethics" (26 n.4). And given this
measure — a measure, that is, beyond any possible measure — a
genuine duty, in a sense, "ought to prescribe nothing" (ibid.). In
order to remain faithful to itself, it ought not demand any acquittal
of a debt. And to the extent that no duty and no normative rule is
possible without the institution of debt, responsibility would consist in avoiding acting simply in conformity with, in virtue of or
even out of respect for duty (cf. 9).

A given ethics of discussion, Derrida notes, might not always
sufficiently "respect" this silent feeling "foreign to speech [*la pa-
role*]" (22). But it could never reduce it to something else or make it
obsolete. For the secret would continue to "*impassion*" us, even if it,
ontologically speaking, never existed as such, in the singular and
identical with itself (cf. 24). This 'passion,' Derrida claims, would
preclude all "direct intuition" (24) and to that extent be "non-
'pathological'" (14) in Kant's sense. Moreover, it would not even be
a "psycho-physical secret (...), of which Kant speaks in connection
with the transcendental schematism" (20). Neither 'conscious' nor
'unconscious,' neither 'profane' nor 'sacred' or 'mystical,' 'private'
nor 'public,' the secret would, finally, 'be' neither 'phenomenal
(izable)' nor its opposite, that is to say, 'noumenal' (20, 21). The
secret would 'exceed' the by now well-known "play of veiling/
unveiling, dissimulation/revelation" (21) and therefore no longer
determine itself in the service of some ultimate, 'promised truth,'
whether that of 'adequation' or of *aletheia*, let alone as its mere
opposite. Its "non-phenomenality," Derrida concludes, is therefore "without relation, even negative, to phenomenality" (21) and
therefore escapes the (metaphysical) overdeterminations that have
sedimented themselves in Kant's true *Geheimnis*, in Freud's *Un-
heimliche*, as well as in the "apophatic" mode of silence characteristic of so-called negative theology (20, 21).

Of course, Derrida remarks, this non-phenomenality of the secret also makes it vulnerable to abuse. One can always turn it into a
seductive power or use it to seduce. That, Derrida notes, "happens
every day" (24). However, he continues, "this very simulacrum still
bears witness to a possibility which exceeds it. It does not exceed it
in the direction of some ideal community, rather towards a solitude
without any measure common to that of an isolated subject ... or

with that of a *Jemeinigkeit* of *Dasein* whose solitude, Heidegger tells us, is still a modality of *Mitsein*" (ibid.). Precisely because it would make them possible, this secret solitude "never allows itself to be captured or covered over by the relation to the other, by being-with or by any form of 'social bond'" (ibid.). What would remain, then, would 'be' this exceeding, which cannot be entrusted to any "definite witness" or "martyr" (25). Every (moral) utterance, every action then would remain 'problematic,' or rather, "of an order other than problematicity," and this circumstance — which is also the circumvention of every stance or stasis, whether that of the 'actor' or the 'act' — should not only be considered as a tragedy (which indeed it is) but also as "a stroke of luck:" "Otherwise, why speak, why discuss?"[35]

III

What emerges from this is the necessity of revising the major premises of speech act theory as well as of the 'ethics of discussion' commonly associated with it. For without the aforementioned permanent risk of derailment and perversion, no 'call to action' and no 'call of conscience' could ever claim to be 'unconditional.' Instead of imposing itself categorically and with absolute urgency, its manifestation would, like that of the Austinian 'performative,' be guaranteed by past or present contexts of origination or by future horizons of expectation. But, Derrida insists, "the very least that can be said of unconditionality ... is that it is independant of every determinate context, even of the determination of a context in general. It announces itself only in the *opening* of context. Not that it is simply present (existent) elsewhere, outside of all context; rather it intervenes in the determination of a context from its very inception, and from an injunction, a law, a responsibility that transcends this or that determination of a given context."[36] The call, Derrida notes elsewhere, "comes from nowhere" and only thus "institutes" a response and responsibility that lies "at the root of all ulterior responsibilities (moral, juridical, political) and of every categorical imperative."[37] In order to 'be' what it 'is,' the call would have to remain at a distance from all of these determinations. Only the "irreducible opening" of all contexts would create the 'space'

35. *Limited Inc*, 120.
36. Ibid., 152.
37. "Eating Well," 110.

236

where the call would be able to *give* itself. Moreover, out of necessity — that is to say, in order to generate any 'effect' or 'respect' at all — the call can only protect its singularity and otherness by retaining an almost fictional, fabulous element and by remaining "a sheer supposition,"[38] albeit one that is not merely (or primarily) theoretical.

If, at this point, we realize that the mention and use of the expression 'unconditionality' (as well as that of 'respect' and 'as if') recalls the structure of the Kantian categorical imperative, we should be cautious in pushing this analogy too far. For, while Derrida identifies this unconditionality further as the "injunction that prescribes deconstructing,"[39] he hastens to add: "Why have I always hesitated to characterize it in Kantian terms, for example, or more generally in ethical or political terms, when that would have been so easy and would have enabled me to avoid so much criticism ...? Because such characterizations seemed to me essentially associated with philosophemes that themselves call for deconstructive questions. Through these questions *another language* and *other thoughts* seek to make their way. This language and these thoughts, which are also *new responsibilities*, arouse in me a *respect*, which, whatever the cost, I neither can nor will compromise."[40] That the *tone* of the appeal to vigilance *denotes* nothing, that it exceeds the formal structure of the Kantian categorical imperative, does not imply that the ellipsis of Enlightenment leaves us speechless or blind. And the absence of definition, rather than signaling a new 'obscurantism,' "respectfully pays hommage to a new, very new *Aufklärung*."[41] In what sense, then, does this elliptic transformation of Enlightenment into an unconditional vigilance that calls forth 'other thoughts,' 'another language' and 'new responsibilities' situate itself beyond the confines laid out by both the Kantian grounding of practical reason and its recent reconstruction in terms of a quasi-transcendental, formal pragmatics?

First of all, Derrida insists that the call can never stand alone nor give 'itself' as such, pure and simple. For even if one follows the argument of *Limited Inc* that no context is ever completely closed (or, in its turn, enclosed), this does not contradict the fact that "there are only contexts," or, more precisely, that "nothing *exists*

38. Ibid.
39. *Limited Inc*, ibid., 153.
40. Ibid., 153, italics are mine.
41. Ibid., 141.

outside context."[42] And, if the unconditional appeal consists precisely in opening up *every* given context, whether ontic or not, then it follows that its manifestation eludes not only every phenomenological or ontological description but also the transcendental deductions which Kant entrusts to the faculty of pure practical reason. If anything, the unconditional appeal 'is' an enigmatic '*otherwise than being*,' to cite a phrase of Levinas, a call which 'is' only 'there' for those whose attentiveness allows them to hear it. Therefore, the originary split of the call is *echoed* in the response or responsiveness that it provokes. For the affirmation of this appeal entails an iteration — an unconditional 'yes, yes' — which, in advance, marks and doubles (or triples etc.) even the most singular 'Hallo!' or 'here I am!' (*me voici*). And it is precisely this necessary repetition and alteration, Derrida suggests, which eventually forces us "to articulate this unconditionality with the determinate (Kant would say, hypothetical) conditions of this or that context; and this is the moment of strategies, of rhetorics, of ethics, and politics."[43] Because of this repeated intervention in given contexts, deconstruction, along with the responsibility it implies, "does not exist somewhere, pure, proper, self-identical, outside of its inscriptions in conflictual and differentiated contexts; it 'is' only what it does and what is done with it"[44] And as one cannot speak or write without thereby transforming a 'context,' the very inception of any such speech and writing *necessarily implies a politics*, "insofar as it involves determination, a certain non-'natural' relationship to others"[45] (whether human or not). For although the interrogation of the purported stability of pragmatic values and normative claims exceeds the realm of reference and truth, of science and ontology (and therefore exceeds Being *as such* or at least disrupts the *unity* of Being), it should also be acknowledged that this analysis never takes place in a vacuum, outside "pragmatically determined"[46] situations. The singular 'truth' that it unravels — in particular its insight into the structural instability or at best into the "relative," "provisional" and "finite" stability of all meaning[47] — must also "submit" itself

42. Ibid., 152.
43. Ibid.
44. Ibid.
45. Ibid., 136.
46. Ibid., 150.

"in large measure"[48] to the requirements of a given context. Thus, deconstruction must take into account the generally accepted procedures as well as the restraints of academic debate, even though its arguments are in themselves "neither false, nor nontrue ..., nor context-external or meta-contextual," but, rather, the exposition of a simili-transcendental "truth" that no longer belongs to the order of semantics. Derrida's writing, then, is composed of two seemingly contradictory gestures. It persists in 'respecting' or 'accepting' the rules of the game of which it nonetheless "exposes the deconstructability:" but, as Derrida reminds us, "without this tension ... would anything ever be done? Would anything ever be changed?"[49]

Pragrammatology would be the provisional name for the necessarily incomplete topography of the different gestures that will always already have marked the deconstructive intervention in this site of tension that marks the political. It is not always clear whether (or to what extent) this pragrammatology implies a certain shift in Derrida's earlier preoccupations: a shift, that is, away from the analysis of the general economy of *écriture* towards the particular question of the "intersection" between the 'logics' of grammatology (or iterability), on the one hand, and the so-called 'pragmatically determined situations,' on the other. Of course, Derrida argues: "Grammatology has always been a sort of pragmatics, but the discipline that bears this name today involves too many presuppositions requiring deconstruction, very much like speech act theory, to be simply homogeneous with what is announced in *De la grammatologie*. A pragrammatology (to come) would articulate in a more

47. And that "no stability is absolute, eternal, intangible, natural" is, Derrida notes, "implied" in its very concept: stability is not "immutability" and therefore always "destabilizable" (ibid., 151). The pragmatic moment — the translation of untranslatable singularities — would therefore, in turn, be imbedded in a frame of (textual) relations that make it impossible to determine the *kairos* of its moment(um). In order to circumvent the misleading conclusion that there could be a radical rupture with or escape from this law *différance*, Derrida remarks that the logics of decision can never be that of "coupure" or break, but at best that of "stricture" (J. Derrida, *Parages* [Paris: Galilée, 1986], 214). It is at this critical point that the question of *tonality* comes into play: "*tonos*, tone, first signified the tight ligament, the cord, the rope, when it is woven or braided, the cable, the strap, briefly the privileged figure of everything that is subject to *stricture*" (*D'un ton apocalyptique*, 69, italics are mine). And if the stricture of (or within) the realm of differentiality is always a *specific*, *concrete*, or *singular* tonality or, rather, tone, then this tone can, by definition, never be *pure*, *neutral* or *inaudible*, as Kant would have it.
48. *Limited Inc*, 150.
49. Ibid., 152.

239

fruitful and more rigorous manner these two discourses."[50] A pragrammatology, then, remains "to come." It is the *à venir* of deconstruction. In more than one sense. For, as the deconstructive 'logic' of iterability demonstrates, any such 'project' (if that is still the right word) will not only always be incomplete *in fact*. In a more radical sense, it is also *essentially* or *structurally* interminable, unfulfillable. The linkages or "ties" between marks and words, concepts and things, that it seeks to determine in a given context — as well as, for that matter, the "deontological" standard that 'regulates' their "discussion" — is never "*absolutely*"[51] secured by any "metacontext" or "metadiscourse." Since no adequate, let alone exhausting, conceptual or figural representation of such a pragrammatology can ever be given,[52] and since, moreover, its very description always intersects with an interpretative and institutional 'act,' one might wonder how to '*think*' *in a non-representational or aesthetic mode* the 'effects' of the said unconditionality in the realm of politics, ethics, rhetorics and strategy (terms which in Derrida's exposition all seem to be synonyms for the intervention of the 'call' or the 'Come!' in the regional domains of the 'empirical').

This politics (or economics,[53] for that matter), would need to be rethought as an "impossible and necessary compromise ... incessant daily negotiation - individual or not - sometimes microscopic, sometimes punctuated by poker - like gamble; always deprived of insurance."[54] And, if there would be a model that could clarify this inter-acting, while respecting its own rhythm without synchronizing it with the apocalyptic chorus of all times, it would be that of the *dance* or, more precisely that of *choreography*. This pragrammatological model — which for all its internal multiplicity remains in principle just one *topos* or, rather, *u-topos* among others — is anything but a sign of mere pragmatism. For, as Derrida emphasizes

50. Ibid., 159 note 16.
51. Ibid., 151.
52. As Lyotard notes in another context, a performative cannot "*represent* what it accomplishes but ... *presents it*," J.F. Lyotard, "Levinas' Logic," in: R.A. Cohen, *Face to Face with Levinas* (Albany: SUNY Press, 1986), 117-158, 172.
53. *Parages*, 214. In *Limited Inc* Derrida notes in passing, that an "economy taking account of effects of iterability" would have to call into question "the entire philosophy of the *oikos* - of the *propre*: the 'own,' 'ownership,' property' - as well as the laws that have governed it." Such an 'economy' would be "very different from 'welfare economics'" (*Limited Inc*, 76).
54. J. Derrida and C. McDonald, "Interview: Choreographies," in: *The Ear of the Other*, Otobiography, Transference, Translation, Texts and Discussions with Jacques Derrida, edited by C. McDonald (London: Lincoln, 1985), 169.

in a closely related context, it is always "in the name of a more imperative responsibility"[55] that one questions — or inverts — a traditionally defined responsibility *vis à vis* existing political and conceptual formations. All genuine responsibility would respond to a "restless excess" that disrupts all "good conscience"[56] and does not let itself be expressed in merely juridical terms. For no rule and no law could be said to be commensurate with this responsibility, which, Derrida writes, "regulates itself neither on the principle of reason nor on any sort of accountancy;" for the latter would "at best" produce a hypothetical imperative.[57]

This excess of the 'idea' of responsibility and of justice that pervades all of the passages quoted above is not that of the Kantian regulative idea that supplements the finitude of the human condition and entrusts it with a task of infinite approximation. Rather, it is closely intertwined with the 'experience' and 'experiment' of the 'undecidable' that destabilizes every (just) decision from within (or *a priori*). For a decision, Derrida writes, "can only come into being in a space that exceeds the calculable program that would destroy all responsibility by transforming it into a programmable effect of determinate causes. There can be no moral or political responsibility without this trial and this passage by way of the undecidable. Even if a decision seems to take only a second and not to be preceded by any deliberation, it its structured by this experience and experiment of the undecidable."[58] The crucial terms here — trial, passage, experience/experiment — would have to be explored in much greater detail by making numerous detours through Derrida's reading of Kafka's "Vor dem Gesetz," of Celan's exclamation of the *no passarán* and, more indirectly, of Bataille's notion of an *expérience intérieure* that does not give one time to anticipate, project, mediate or meditate. They all testify of a certain experience of the impossible, i.e. of an *aporia*.[59]

Of course, if we define the concept of experience as the designa-

55. *Du droit à la philosophie*, 35.
56. Ibid.
57. "Eating Well," 108 and ibid., 118: "responsibility is excessive or it is not a responsibility. A limited, measured, calculable, rationally distributed responsibility is already the becoming-right of responsibility; it is at times also, in the best hypothesis, the dream of every good conscience, in the worst hypothesis, of the small or grand inquisitors."
58. *Limited Inc*, "Afterword," 116.
59. Cf. Hent de Vries, "Le Schibboleth de l'éthique. Derrida avec Celan," in: M. Wetzel and J.M. Rabaté, eds., *L'éthique du don* (Paris 1992). For the parallels with G. Bataille, cf. the remarkable formulations in *L'expérience intérieure*

tion of "something that traverses and travels toward a destination for which it finds the appropriate passage," then it is certainly impossible to have an experience of this impossible: for an aporia, Derrida explains, is a 'non-road.' And yet, 'justice' (*justice* or *Gerechtigkeit*, as used, Derrida reminds us, by Pascal as well as by Levinas, by Benjamin as well as by Heidegger[60]), if anything, would be precisely this impossible 'experience' of the impossible: "A will, a desire, a demand for justice whose structure wouldn't be an experience of aporia would have no chance to be what it is, namely a call for justice. Every time that something comes to pass ..., every time that we placidly apply a good rule to a particular case, to a correctly subsumed example, according to a determinant judgment, we can be sure that law (*droit*) may find itself accounted for but certainly not justice."[61]

Justice then would be "incalculable" even though it, paradoxically, aporetically, "requires us to calculate ["*exige qu'on calcule*"] with the incalculable."[62] There would be no room here for the "condescending reticence"[63] with which Heidegger at times speaks of the *rechnen* and *planen*. Justice would prescribe — "it is just," Derrida writes — that there be law and right, both of which are never just in themselves but, rather, "the element" of an always "improbable" yet "necessary" calculation.[64] And, in order to be just, this calculation would have to pass through the abysmal experience of the incalculable.

Different examples of this insoluble paradox could be given, but in fact, Derrida writes, there is only "one potential aporetic that infinitely distributes itself."[65] In all of those cases, however, one would be obliged to 'experience' or to suffer "moments in which the

(1943): "Without night, no one would have to decide ... Decision is what is born before the worst and rises above. It is the essence of courage, of the heart, of being itself. And it is the reverse of project (it demands that one reject delay, that one decide on the spot, with everything at stake ...)" (*Inner Experience*, transl. with an introduction by L.A. Boldt [New York: SUNY Press, 1988], 26, *Oeuvres complètes* vol. V [Paris: Gallimard, 1973], 39). According to Derrida's "Force of Law. The 'Mystical Foundations of Authority'" (*Cardozo Law Review*, vol. 11, 1990, 920-1045, 967), the process of making a decision can be described as an "acting in the night of non-knowledge and non-rule."

60. "Force of Law," 927, 955.
61. Ibid., 947.
62. Ibid.
63. "Eating Well," 108.
64. "Force of Law," 947.
65. Ibid., 959.

decision between just and unjust is never insured by a rule."[66] What would be the foundation, the ground, of this requirement or demand of justice to abandon itself, to give itself (away), and to pervert itself in this very performance? Derrida writes: "If I were content to apply a just rule, without a spirit of justice and without in some way inventing the rule and the example for each case, I might be protected by law (*droit*), my action corresponding to objective law, but I would not be just. I would act, Kant would say in *conformity* with duty, but not *through* duty or *out of respect* for the law."[67] Similarly, a judge cannot pass a just judgment if he blindly follows the letter of the law and applies its principles and rules in a merely mechanical way. His decision must, up to a certain extent, 'suspend' (or even 'destroy') and 'reinvent' the law. For each case that presents itself to him will be other and therefore asks for an *epoché* followed by a decision "which no existing, coded rule can or ought to guarantee absolutely."[68] And yet, conversely, we would not call him just if he "stops short before the undecidable or if he improvises and leaves aside all rules, all principles."[69] In order not to be neutralized, a just decision would thus have to have it both ways, i.e., go through the aporia and *perform the contradiction*. No just decision — but also: no history, no communication, no discussion — would ever take place without this *tour de force*.[70]

This (indeed impossible) experience of the impossible or the un-

66. Ibid., 947.
67. Ibid., 949.
68. Ibid., 961.
69. Ibid. One could be tempted to invoke Hegel here. In the *Grundlinien der Philosophie des Rechts*, par. 12, Hegel states that it is through a certain resolve that the will is actual at all ("nur als beschliessender Wille überhaupt ist er wirklicher Wille"). Of course, this resolve, which determines the will in its singularization and individualization, is governed by a dialectical opposition in which, inevitably, one of the terms (actuality) dominates the other (potentiality or possibility). This same teleological and organic scheme can be recognized in the intriguing remark, which distinguishes the *etwas beschliessen* from a more indeterminate *sich entschliessen* that is equally constitutive of the form, the formation and the determination of the will: "Statt etwas *beschliessen*, d.h. die Unbestimmtheit, in welcher der eine sowohl als der andere Inhalt zunächst nur ein möglicher ist, aufheben, hat unsere Sprache auch den Ausdruck: *sich entschliessen*, indem die Unbestimmtheit des Willens selbst, als das Neutrale, aber unendlich Befruchtete, der Urkeim alles Daseins, in sich die Bestimmungen und Zwecke enthält und sie nur aus sich hervorbringt." (G.W.F. Hegel, *Grundlinien der Philosophie des Rechts*, Hrsg. J. Hoffmeister [Hamburg: Meiner, 1962], 36).
70. Asked by *Libération* to comment on the politics of the institution in France, some two years after the election of Mitterand, Derrida recalls that the socialist idea has always been caught in a similar 'performative contradiction.' It must at

decidable, is not that of an 'either/or.' It is not the back and forth of two conflicting or incommensurate imperatives urging us, for example, to respect at once the equality of identical cases and the uniqueness of every singular event. Furthermore, the experience of the undecidable is infinitely more complex than the experience of a 'tension' between two or more equally valid or justifiable decisions. Rather, it is the "ordeal" [*l'épreuve*] of an obligation to exceed or suspend the principles and rules of right while still somehow seriously taking them into account.[71] Without this anxious 'freedom' of being at once inside and outside the law - and only this simultaneity explains the *iterability* of the law — to be just would come down to being a moment in an 'unfolding proces' or simply 'applying a program.'[72]

We can only 'be' just to the extent that *we belong to two realms at once*. And yet, this dual status or stance, for all the resemblances with Kant's moral philosophy it evokes, also explains why no decision is justifiable on formal rational grounds only, be they those of introspection or intersubjective argumentation. For the said *double bind* precludes that the question *whether* or *how* a decision has taken place can itself ever be resolved in any decisive way. We are never in a position in which we can be sure that what presents itself as a (just) decision has not in fact followed a ruse or obeyed a

once obey and escape the economical and technological imperatives of the market: it cannot avoid the double bind of having both to satisfy and displace the competitive mechanism of modern production. And it is only in the experience and the trial of this aporia, which is not "in itself an absolute evil, a sin, an accident or a weakness," that it can be expected to create another space, another, more just, institution (*Du droit à la philosophie*, 504-505).

71. It is for that reason that neither the 'thoughtlessness' nor the 'madness' of the decision (nor that of the 'founding violence' that institutes a law for society), can be reduced to an 'existentialist' pathos à la Kierkegaard or a 'decisionism' à la Carl Schmitt, although at least the first author is never far away in this analysis. Nor are we dealing here with the so-called "*Restdezisionismus*" that Schnädelbach retraces in Apel's transcendental pragmatics (H. Schnädelbach, *Vernunft und Geschichte*, Vorträge und Abhandlungen [Frankfurt/M: Suhrkamp, 1987], 167). For Derrida does not explain the irreducibility of the 'decision' nor the violence that founds states, conventions and rules, in terms of their 'historicity' or in terms of their supposed 'empirical' conditions. Rather, he relates their manifestation to a singular 'performativity' that exceeds the theoretical framework offered by speech act theory and relies on a certain 'force' and 'enforcement' which is not only *differential*, that is to say, intertwined with other anterior 'performatives' and conventions, but ultimately based on an "irruptive" — "mystical" — "violence," which "no longer responds to the demands of theoretical rationality" as such ("Force of Law," 966).

72. Ibid., 963.

code or already transformed itself into an exemplary case of a general rule. At no point, then, can a decision claim to be "presently" or "fully" just.[73] It is this uncertainty which makes that the undecidable continues to *haunt* every 'decision,' as a *spectre* that cannot be exorcised. Even in retrospect we can never be certain that a decision, in the emphatic sense of the word, actually took place, let alone that it was just. No phenomenology, no criteriology would allow us to describe or identify its past, let alone its future occurence.

If there can never be a moment, Derrida stresses, in which we can "say *in the present* that a decision *is* just ... or that someone *is* a just man — even less, 'I *am* just,'"[74] this disrupts the entire axiomatics that governs the Kantian critique of pure practical reason and its formal-pragmatic transformation in the project of a so-called communicative ethics (*Diskursethik*). For these tie responsibility to "a whole network of connected concepts"[75] which presuppose the postulation of this very presence, not only of justice (as a regulative idea and highest good), but also of free moral agents to themselves. A deconstructed or deconstructive responsibility, however, would respond to an "interpellation,"[76] which does not originate in (nor arrive at) a subject that, philosophically speaking, is determined as free will, conscience, individual, etc. For, in the final analysis, these concepts all presuppose an "organic or atomic indivisibility,"[77] which remain "*conditions* and therefore *limitations* of responsibility, sometimes limitations in the determination of the unconditional, of the categorical imperative, itself."[78] And yet, although the other responsibility that Derrida speaks of is both "older" and "younger" than its philosophical counterparts as well as their politico-juridical implementations, it is neither "higher" nor "deeper"[79]. For, in its very diachrony and incommensurability, the other, old-new responsibility is not totally alien to its philosophical translations, but always already "inscribed" or "*engaged*"[80] in them. This 'engagement' should not be understood in terms of a logical implication or dialectical mediation. Nor does it let itself be captured by

73. Ibid.
74. Ibid., 961, 963.
75. Ibid., 955.
76. *Du droit à la philosophie*, 408.
77. "Eating Well," 107, cf. 100-101.
78. *Du droit à la philosophie*, 88.
79. Ibid., 409 and 89.
80. Ibid., 28, 89.

an essentialist and teleological organicism (as if it were inherent in language and waiting to unfold). Nor, finally, can this 'inscription' be thought as a mere empirical or pragmatic contingency (as if it overcame language by accident). For the other responsibility 'is' in a sense 'given' with language — more precisely, with the occurence of every mark — as such.

The deconstructive account of the possibility of responsibility or of 'justice' therefore obeys a peculiar *circularity* or *ellipticity*. On the one hand, there can be no justice "except to the degree that some event is possible which, as event, exceeds calculation, rules, programs, anticipations and so forth;" on the other hand, however, the inverse statement can also be made: justice is "the chance of the event."[81] In this sense, justice 'is' 'itself' the quasi-transcendental condition of possibility of all historical change. All deconstruction finds its 'force' in the 'motivation,' the 'movement' or 'impulse' [*élan*][82] that justice makes possible and which, in turn, makes justice possible.

It should be clear by now, why, in the "Afterword" of *Limited Inc*, Derrida calls the technical discussion of the performative speech act "at bottom an ethical-political one."[83] The discussion of Austin's *How to Do Things with Words* in "Signature, event, context" problematizes "the metaphysical premises" of what is said to be a "fundamentally moralistic"[84] theory of linguistic utterance. To be sure, Derrida leaves no doubt that this problematization extends far beyond the opposition of so-called Continental and Anglo-Saxon or analytic schools of thought and that the said premises also "underlie the hermeneutics of Ricoeur and the archeology of Foucault."[85] And the reception of the theory of the speech act that played such a crucial role in the linguistic turn in Critical Theory after Adorno would, on this reading, be just one more illustration of the wider significance of this same phenomenon.

One example might suffice there. When it is argued that we often cannot fulfil the counterfactual pragmatic presuppositions from which all communicative practice starts out and "in the sense of a transcendental necessity *must* begin," when it is added that in everyday life these presuppositions are *at once* implicitly affirmed

81. "Force of Law," 971.
82. Ibid., 957.
83. *Limited Inc*, 116.
84. Ibid., 39.
85. Ibid.

and denied[86], then neither the nature of this transcendental 'must' or 'necessity,' nor that of this 'performative contradiction' can be accounted for without a certain 'logic' of iterability or without a certain pragrammatology. Another structural 'force' seems to be at work here besides (or *in*) the well-known 'force of the better argument.' This other, more differential force — which, like that of the better argument and the *Verständigung* that it allows, is neither 'natural' nor based on mere 'convention' — would explain why any (for example, normative) validity claim can be made in the first place and why it always can (and indeed must) derail. The possibility of derailment, perversion, parody, or any other 'mis-understanding,' would be a structural and therefore necessary possibility, that is "a *general possibility inscribed in* the structure of positivity, of normality, of the 'standard' ... [which] must be taken into account when describing so-called ideal normality."[87] Any attempt to exclude this necessary possibility from the analysis of speech acts and to concentrate instead, "in the best Kantian tradition," on the ideal or pure conditions of their intentional fulfilment and performative success, would unwittingly 'translate' into "a politics."[88] Reiterating Hegel's critique of the Kantian concept of *Moralität*, Derrida recalls that the formalism that continues to govern speech act theory is not incompatible with a certain "intrinsic moralism" and "empiricism."[89] And, in sofar as all communicative ethics bases its reconstruction of the just procedures of the practical *Diskurs* on these very same deconstructible premises and thereby presupposes a determinable or stable (that is, formalizable) relation between intentions, rules and conventions, it as well reproduces and prolongates less the *ideal* conditions of *all* ethics but, rather, those of a given, dominant and dogmatic discourse on ethics. The so-called 'universal' or 'formal' pragmatics would not only *in fact*, but also for *essential* reasons be neither universal nor formal. Not that there would be a direct and simple correspondence between the methodological exclusion of 'parasitical' occurences and an excommunica-

---

86. J. Habermas, *Der philosophische Diskurs der Moderne* (Frankfurt a.M.: Suhrkamp, 1985), 378.
87. *Limited Inc*, 157 note, cf. 102. Cf. ibid., 57: "Once it *possible* for x to function under certain conditions (for instance, a mark in the absence or partial absence of intention), the possibility of a certain non-presence or of a certain non-actuality pertains to the structure of the functioning under consideration, and pertains to it *necessarily*."
88. Ibid., 97, 135.
89. Ibid., 97.

tion of, say, the unconscious, the marginal or the foreign.[90] But any such a speech act theory (or communicative ethics) would be forgetful of "other conditions," which, Derrida maintains, "are no less essential to ethics in general, whether of *this given* ethics or of *another* ethics."[91] These other conditions that a deconstructive reading would bring to light, might be "anethical with respect to any given ethics," but they would therefore not necessarily be "anti-ethical;" on the contrary, they would "open or recall the opening of another ethics."[92] The task of deconstruction would be to articulate the said other conditions and the opening they provoke in "another form of 'general theory,' or rather another 'discourse,' another 'logic.'"[93] This other "logic" would account, more rigorously than speech act theory, for its own intrinsic, systematic (and not merely factual) incompleteness.

In some respects, one could argue that this incompleteness is further guaranteed or even deepened by the circumstance that a deconstructed or deconstructive responsibility (or justice) is characterized by an irreducible "infinity" that is "owed to the other" or, more precisely, to "the other's coming as the singularity that is always other."[94] Derrida leaves no doubt that this infinity is not that of a regulative idea nor that of a messianic horizon, nor that of any other "eschato-teleology," whether of the "neo-Hegelian," "neo-Marxist" or "post-Marxist" type.[95] The reason he gives for this reluctance to think responsibility (and justice) in terms of a horizon and to identify their pursuit with the march toward an infinitely removed or a definite end, is not that the Kantian and messianic perspectives are each in their own singular way *totalistic*, nor that they both fail to explain how the intelligible and empirical realm can come together as, it is claimed, they should. The decisive argument here is, rather, that every horizon entails a "space" and a "period" of "*waiting*."[96] And yet, though heaven (the ultimate good) can wait, the justice demanded by responsibility cannot. Its "excessive haste" leaves no room and no time for a messianic or regulative "horizon of expectation."[97] It has no place in a future in which the

90. Cf. ibid., 134, 135, 96, 97.
91. Ibid., 122.
92. Ibid.
93. Ibid., 117.
94. "Force of law," 965.
95. Ibid., 967.
96. Ibid.
97. Ibid., 969.

antagonistic elements of the present and past would be reconciled with one stroke or brought together step by step in an asymptotic process of convergence. Justice cannot wait for the judgment of history, to cite a Levinasian topos. The modality of its singular *avenir* is that of an *à venir*, an always yet — and still — "to-come"[98] that, at any given moment, is equally close as it remains far removed and has no common measure with the present.

However, justice would be betrayed if we, for want of an appropriate language or in view of a confusedly understood 'strategy of delay,' were to resort to formulating a post-Cartesian 'provisional morality.' Given the "surplus of responsibility that summons the deconstructive gesture or that the deconstructive gesture ... calls forth [and both of these summonings are two sides of the 'same,' *double affirmation*], a waiting period is neither possible nor legitimate."[99] For the motivation for deconstruction derives its unconditional and imperative character — which, again, "is not necessarily or only Kantian" — from precisely the circumstance that it is "ceaselessly threatened." And this, Derrida holds, is "why it leaves no respite, no rest:" its exigency "can always upset, at least the institutional rhythm of every pause."[100]

When we feel, Derrida remarks in taking up the *Leitmotiv* of *D'un ton apocalyptique*, that we are no longer fully absorbed in by now all-too-familiar conceptual horizons; when we sense that we are no longer "in the running;" then this circumstance hardly means that we can "stay at the starting-line" and remain "spectators." For the fact that we are no longer part of the game and no longer naïvely move within an infinite horizon, toward the end or in the direction — under the regulation — of an idea, might well be what keeps deconstruction 'moving.' The suspense increases its intensity and "urgency"[101] and "hyperbolically raises the stakes of exacting justice."[102] Without it, the belief in certain protocols of a 'new, very new *Aufklärung*,' for example in the form of an 'ethics of discussion,' would be based on nothing but a "naïve confidence"[103] or a complacent 'good conscience.'

Justice then is "that which must not wait."[104] It belongs to the

98. Ibid.
99. "Eating Well," 117.
100. Ibid.
101. "Force of Law," 967.
102. Ibid., 955.
103. *Limited Inc*, 157 note.
104. "Force of Law," 967.

essential characteristics of a "just decision" — and only a decision, Derrida stresses, is just or unjust — that it is "required immediately,"[105] here, at this very moment. Moreover, it is demanded without mediation, absolutely, categorically. For, even if all the information about the general situation as well as the unique features of a given case were available; even if we would have *all* the time we need to collect this knowledge and even if our mastery of these facts were virtually unlimited, then still the decision itself would remain an infinitely "finite moment" and, theoretically speaking, a "precipitation" that cannot be fully justified: a genuine decision would only signal itself in the "interruption of the juridico- or ethico- or politico-cognitive deliberation that preceeds it, [and that, Derrida immediately adds] must precede it."[106] For a decision, "in its proper moment, if there is one, [must for essential reasons] be both regulated and without regulation."[107] Strictly speaking, decisions always 'are' too early or too late and never take place *on* time (nor *in* time).

Again, that the idea of justice would thus prove to be an *aporetic* notion, that it would be indeterminable and therefore "unpresentable," "cannot and should not serve as an alibi for staying out of juridico political battles."[108] And the doubleness of this command 'is' that of a *necessity* and an *ought*. For, even if we wished, we could not hope to protect the purported purity of justice by refusing to translate it into terms that are not its own. Justice must and should be "done."[109] Moreover, it is precisely when it is "left to itself" that justice as a pure idea resembles or, at least, "is very close to the bad, even the worst."[110] Not only can it "always be appropriated by the most perverse calculation."[111] In itself, if we can say so, it is no longer distinguishable from its opposite. We must (and should), therefore, "negotiate:" for, paradoxically, only the *compromise* - the translation and thereby betrayal - of justice protects it from 'the worst.'

And yet, in an uncanny, disturbing way, the possibility of 'the worst' is also the condition of 'the best,' 'the best' not being here the "lesser evil" that Lyotard, in *Le différend*, defines as the "political good" (namely a constellation that does not interdict the "occurrence" of "possible phrases" and in that sense no longer contempts

105. Ibid.
106. Ibid.
107. Ibid., 961.
108. Ibid., 971.
109. Ibid., 951.
110. Ibid., 971.
111. Ibid.

"Being")[112], but, rather, the incessant 'negotiation' of an impossible yet necessary "relation" between justice, on the one hand, and the order of law and rights, on the other.[113] This 'negotiation' should be taken "as far as possible" and its task, which is also the task of a necessary "politicization" of all discourse on justice and responsibility, is "interminable," i.e. never "total."[114] And yet, even the slightest step forward — Derrida does not hesitate to speak here of "emancipation"[115] — would affect the whole of the existing law as well as all political institutions and 'oblige' us to reinterpret and to recast their very structure. As a consequence, deconstruction could never "limit itself to a reassuring methodological reform within the confines of a given organization," nor could it, for reasons that we have made clear above, "reduce itself to an irresponsible destructive parade ... that would have the even more sure effect of leaving everything as it is and to consolidate the most immobile forces."[116]

To be sure, the displacements that deconstruction brings about could not easily be captured by the traditional programs, parades and banners (of, say, right and left) in which "the political"[117] is often framed and staged. It is for that reason, Derrida suspects, that deconstruction is regarded too partisan by some whereas for others it is too quietistic. And yet, what is at stake here, is a much more complex — double and elliptical — movement. For, in its very interrogation of the ultimate ground of institutions — in particular

---

112. Lyotard, *Le différend*, No. 197 (*The Differend*. Phrases in Dispute, translated by G. Van Den Abbeele (Minneapolis: University of Minnesota Press, 1988), 140. This would be the place to ask oneself whether there is not a *différend* between Derrida's invocation of a 'lucid vigil' and the "vigil" of which Lyotard speaks. The latter is a "feeling," "anxiety" and "joy," in short, an "expectant waiting" for *every* "occurence" (Ibid., No. 134, 135, transl., 80).

113. Cf. "Force of Law," 971. Should one want to cite Lyotard here once more, one could compare this inescapable and infinite 'negotiation' with the "politics" that is "the possibility of the différend on the occasion of the slightest linkage," a "politics" which is not "the genre that contains all the genres (...) not *a* genre" (*Le différend*, No. 192, transl., 139), but, rather, "the fact that language is not a language, but phrases, or that Being is not Being, but *There is's' [des Il y a]*."(Ibid., No. 190, transl. p. 138); a "politics," finally, that is "immediately given with a phrase as a différend to be regulated concerning the matter of the means of linking onto it" (Ibid., No. 198, transl., 141). Lyotard urges us not to confuse this "necessity" with an "obligation:" "To link is not a duty, which 'we' can be relieved of or make good upon. 'We' cannot do otherwise."

114. "Force of Law," 971.

115. Ibid.

116. *Du droit à la philosophie*, 424.

117. Ibid. Deconstructive discourse is neither on the right nor on the left side of the Kantian academic parliament. Rather, it operates as a mobile parasite which

the philosophical institution (the university) that Kant studies in *Der Streit der Fakultäten* — deconstruction does not simply resort to a superior or overlordly tone. Rather, the deconstructive interrogation re-affirms its allegiance to a new Enlightenment,[118] according to which a certain reiteration of the Kantian project will always be unavoidable. For, while this analysis demonstrates that the rigor of the Kantian architectonics is only visible through the breaches of an edifice that has become inhabitable like a *ruin* or that, more likely, was never more than a *phantasm*,[119] it remains conscious of the fact that the very question as to whether (or under what conditions) a new institutional, say academic, responsibility would be possible retains, in its generality, a classical or, more precisely, modern transcendental and critical, or Kantian, form.

The attempt to found a new institution, then, whatever the radicality of its intention, can never force a total rupture with the edifice (whether ruined or phantasmatic) that preceeds it. In order to take a step forward or beyond, the practice of this deconstruction has to *"negotiate a compromise"* with the traditional order that it seeks to displace and that offers in itself (or that offers itself as) the stepping stone from which the leap to another place can be made. Here, everything would come down to finding and using "the best [or right] lever" for change.[120] In the context of the university this would imply that the responsibility with respect to this institution should follow a paradoxical rhythm of adopting at once the most traditional and rigorous standards of academic competence *and* going as far as possible in direction of 'thinking' the groundless ground of the principle of reason. No responsible institutional politics could ever escape this "double gesture" or "double postulation."[121] Without leaving the demands of critical reason behind, it would have to push the multiplied and divided responsibility to its utmost limit *and beyond*. For the very notion of its limitation — and thereby of its being assigned to a certain time and space — would again

leaves its detractors in doubt as to whether it mediates a concordat between two parties or whether it ignites the eschatologico-apocalyptic fire that has endangered the university from its earliest beginnings, cf. ibid., 434.
118. Derrida writes: "Je suis résolument pour les Lumières d'une nouvelle *Aufklärung* universitaire," ibid., 466.
119. Cf. ibid., 409.
120. Ibid., 435-436. It is at this point that Derrida invokes Kant's use of the notion of *orientation*, in his polemic with Jacobi in "Was heisst sich im Denken orientieren?" (1786) (ibid., 437).
121. Ibid., 491.

transform it into a complacent 'good conscience.'[122] Conversely, it would be equally wrong — unjust — to identify precisely the excessiveness of the notion 'justice' as the major reason why the deconstructive displacement of the Kantian project should not be confused with an irresponsible obscurantism. For also the very insistence on its excess *alone* would reduce this responsibility to mere moralism.

It would be very difficult to *conceptualize* such a double gesture. In what sense could one read this movement as yet another *ellipsis* of Enlightenment? So far, I have been using the figure of ellipsis with reference to a *rhetorical* trope. Just as the word ellipsis can be read rhetorically as the descriptive of the suppression or omission of at least one of the linguistic elements necessary for a complete syntactic or narrative construction or composition, the ellipsis of Enlightenment was introduced as the spectral 'remainder' of a certain order and discourse of meaningfulnes which, in order to be able to speak at all, must risk loosing all determinacy. However, one might be tempted to stretch the use of ellipses a little further and stress that it also invokes another — non-rhetorical — figure that helps to circumscribe (or even visualize) the constitutive duality or polarity of tradition and renewal, universality and singularity, appropriation and distanciation, the same and the other, that characterizes the double gesture discussed above. For the term ellipsis also evokes a figure (an ellipse) that falls short of completing a certain movement and resists filling up a certain middle but instead draws a line or traces a loop — an oval figure — that no longer encircles *one* fixed focus as the purported origin or center of movement. This geometric ellipse would be a structurally incomplete 'circle' whose center has been omitted, vacuated, or split and doubled into two foci at a variable distance which orient the place of every other point in the periphery.[123]

In his essay on the principle of reason and the idea of the university, Derrida seems to broach such a model that describes how

122. Cf. ibid., 108.
123. Derrida's short text, entitled "Ellipse," which concludes and reiterates the trajectory that marks *L'écriture et la différence*, describes this iteration in the following words: "Répétée, la même ligne n'est plus tout à fait la même, la boucle n'a plus tout à fait le même centre, l'origine a joué. Quelque chose manque pour que le cercle soit parfait." Any reading would 'be' elliptical that, like this short text "Ellipse" itself, succeeds in retracing this kind of repetition, this doubling of a singular, virtual point (or *point de vue*). Derrida, *L'écriture et la différence*, 431, cf. also *Marges de la philosophie*, 202 ff. and *Psyché. Inventions de l'autre* (Paris: Galilée, 1987), 192 Cf. also J.L. Nancy, "Sens elliptique," *Revue philosophique*, 2, 1990, 325-347, 336. See also W. Hama-

the *ellipticity* of *Aufklärung* or *'thought'* can be pursued without cutting it short in a vicious *circle* of pure repetition and without paralyzing it in front of an inescapable *abyss*. Between the horns of this dilemma and beyond any speculative dialectical or hermeneutic circling back, Derrida sketches a rhythm of alternation in which both the *archaeological* and the *anarchic* extreme of all discourse keep each other in (or, rather, off) balance. Could the *formal* structure of this ellipse, as the interplay of two *foci* which are mutually exclusive and yet always already point to each other, help us to hint at the paradoxical structure of these polar constellations? The blindness of one pole would be the insight of the other (and vice versa). Both of these constitutive 'moments' could be said to oscillate in a permanent, open 'dialectic' in which none of the two *foci* implied in all utterance, is ever fully able to determine the (act of) institution and organize this dialectic around *one* center, *not even that of vigilance*. And like the ellipse, which *de*centers the circle, the apparent repetition of the given 'levers' would only draw a circle in a very peculiar, inflected or even contorted way.

'*Thought*,' Derrida argues, requires both the principle of reason and what lies beyond (or before) it. It requires a *double* gesture, an alternating movement of 'archeology' *and* 'anarchy,' of tradition *and* openness, of keeping memory *and* keeping chances. And between these two poles only the difference, only the suspension and inversion of the "breath," "accent" or "enactment" (*mise en oeuvre*) of this "thought"[124] — its *Atempause* and *Atemwende*, to cite Celan — would decide. The emphasis on one of the poles would be a *non-formalizable* gesture. This "decision of thought," Derrida continues, is "always risky, it always risks the worst,"[125] but this is the prize one has to pay if at least one does not wish to "barricade"[126] oneself and others against the future or the to-come. And yet, one step too many in the direction of a more radical principle or *archè*, one step too far beyond it, in the hope of some quasi-mystic divination of an originary '*an-archy*,' could produce or restore a

cher, "Hermeneutische Ellipsen. Schrift und Zirkel bei Schleiermacher," in: U. Nassen, ed., *Texthermeneutik*, Aktualität, Geschichte, Kritik (Paderborn, 1979), 113-148 and J. Greisch, "Le cercle et l'ellipse. Le statut de l'herméneutique de Platon à Schleiermacher," *Revue des Sciences philosophiques et théologiques*, 73, 1989, 161-184, cf. 163, 183-184.

124. *Du droit à la philosophie*, 495-496.
125. Ibid., 496.
126. Ibid.

new, more subtle and more powerful *"hierarchy"*[127] than the one that is deconstructed. Indeed, at every given point a step in either direction — or even the refusal to step — would be vulnerable to being appropriated by the forces it seeks to contest.[128] The ellipse of 'alternation' or 'polarization' is always in danger of being disrupted by a certain omission or even obliteration (by ellipsis, that is). Again, this possibility would be a necessary possibility and no mere accident. Any genuine attempt to submit the demands of formal reason to those of vigilance would be excessive to the point of bringing about its own virtual eclipse. And in precisely this sense, Enlightenment is divided in and against itself. Only an uneasy — incalculable — balance, then, would protect all thinking and institutional practice against the apocalypse or eschatology (or, what comes down to the same thing, its reification or petrification), which constantly threatens it. In order to counterbalance this ineradicable danger, it would have to "walk on two feet" supporting its body with one while the other is lifted in order to take the next step or to leap.[129]

Whereas the rhetorical ellipsis prevents the geometric — oval — elliptic figure from rounding itself off into a circle, the latter, in turn, forces upon the first a movement of repetition and change (in other words, imposes iterability) thus reinforcing its doubling (its double bind) and intensifying its uncanny and haunting character. Both of these ellipses of Enlightenment, then, imply and illuminate each other mutually and hint obliquely — elliptically — at a theoretico-ethico-political task or attentiveness that exceeds (or preceeds) philosophical reason at every instant because it is the very condition of its possibility as well as of its intrinsic incompletion.

This explains why, for all its use of vivid imagery, this analysis would still be a formalization, which in itself cannot immediately justify or translate into a determinate (for example institutional)

127. Ibid., 495.
128. It is precisely at this point, Derrida notes, that one would have to situate the serious questions about Heideggers *'politics,'* notably in the inaugural lectures of 1929 and 1933. For these texts cast their shadow on the questioning of the principle of reason, some twenty years later in *Der Satz vom Grund (Du droit à la philosophie*, 492). And even if it could be argued that Heidegger later 'shifted grounds' and displaced this whole — classical — schematics (cf. ibid., 404-405), the line drawn between science and philosophy, on the one hand, and 'thought,' on the other has in Derrida's account a different "form and function" (ibid. 29, 38) than the one found in Heidegger. It is a divided line which does not allow 'thought' to come into its own.
129. Cf. ibid., 437.

politics. For the rhythm would not so much take place *within* this formalization, but rather *with it*. It is for this reason, Derrida admits, that the deconstructive analysis, for all its political relevance, can hope at best to spell out a "negative wisdom" or, what comes down to the same thing, to provide us with "protocols of vigilance."[130]

130. Ibid., 496.

PART II:

FIGURES OF POLITICS:
PROBLEMS OF DEMOCRACY,
HUMAN RIGHTS AND FEMINISM

13. Lefort and Derrida:
The Paradoxical Status of Human Rights

1. *Introduction*

In our modern society it is a mark of good taste, and not without reason, to present oneself as a defender of human rights. Everyone seems to agree that human rights must be respected and defended at all costs. In general, there are few who would dare to claim that not all politics should take human rights as its guideline. That this gives rise to an ideological misuse of these rights, and that these "rights" are often used to legitimize a defense of Western economic and strategic interests, is something to which we are resigned, although with some reluctance. After all, human rights pertain to that horizon in which modern politics is inevitably played out, and there is a feeling that we have no other reference points at our disposal in order to realize a "just" politics.

We have no other reference points. What does this mean? What is the status of the reference to human rights? And what does it mean when we assert that human rights pertain to the "horizon" in which modern politics is inevitably played out? Starting from this latter consideration my story could take a Heideggerian turn[1]: human rights belong to our Geschick. They belong to the technological epoch that governs us. They are an expression of the domination of technology which holds sway over all forms of human culture in our era. Indeed, human rights are usually interpreted as rights of the individual and of the autonomous subject. In this sense they seem to be an inalienable part of the subject-centred tradition which, as Heidegger demonstrates, culminates in the proliferation of technology. As little as Heidegger has written about human rights, we can safely assume that he harboured the same misgivings regarding these rights as he had regarding any democracy which appeals to them.[2]

---

1. For what follows see E. Berns, "Democratie in een technische wereld," in: L. Heyde and H. Visser, *Filosofie en democratie* (Tilburg: University Press, 1990), 1-24.
2. M. Heidegger, "Der Spiegel interview with Martin Heidegger."

259

"But where danger is, grows the saving power also," writes Heidegger in his essay concerning technology.[3] Heidegger, however, did not expect this saving power to come from democracy as we know it. As a political system which defines society's ends on the basis of individual choices, democracy employs a technical conception of freedom, and hence does not escape the iron grip of technology. Heidegger seems to expect even less that the saving power would come from human rights. Human rights are often conceived as values in themselves. They are understood as a sort of extratemporal codex by which every politics can and must be measured. In this sense they seem inevitably to fall under Heidegger's critique of value[4]: to think in terms of values is to calculate in terms of utility maximization.[5,6]

In a well-known passage from Of Spirit, Derrida expresses similar reservations with respect to human rights: "...the majority of discourses which, today and for a long time to come, state their opposition to racism, to totalitarianism, to nazism, to fascism, etc., and do this in the name of spirit, and even of the freedom of (the) spirit, in the name of an axiomatic — for example, that of democracy or "human rights" — which, directly or not, comes back to this metaphysics of subjectity."[7] The axiomatic of human rights and of the Western political discourse is, Derrida argues elsewhere, in the grip of philosophemes which can and must be deconstructed.[8] It would of course be too simple, even dishonest, to reformulate Derrida's reservations regarding this axiomatic in terms of a mere dismissal of human rights. On the contrary, it seems that these reservations must be understood in the context of what Sam IJssel-

---

3. M. Heidegger, "The Question Concerning Technology," in: *Basic Writings*, 310.
4. Cf. H. Mongis, *Heidegger et la critique de la notion de valeur* (Den Haag, 1976).
5. "Value is the objectified aim which is indicated by the requirements of a representational organizing in the world which has become a picture." M. Heidegger, "Die Zeit des Weltbildes," in: *Holzwege*, 101-102.
6. The standard critique of the Heideggerian standpoint, which I have only given schematically here, is well known: the "Seinsgeschickliches Denken" lumps everything together. From the standpoint of the "Wesen" (verbal sense) of technology, all forms of society, cultural expressions, etc., are subordinate to this "Wesen." Thus, from the point of view of the history of Being, there is no intrinsic difference between collectivism and individualism (with respect to human rights), or communism and Americanism.
7. J. Derrida, *Of Spirit: Heidegger and the Question*, trans. G. Bennington and R. Bowlby (Chicago: University of Chicago Press,1989), 39-40.
8. J. Derrida, *Psychè* (Paris: Galilée, 1987), 344.

ing has called a "strategy of delay."[9] We must refrain from all too hasty judgments and interpretations. Rather, we must look for what is not explicitly articulated in the text, for the open spots, the hesitations, the places where the text, as it were, stumbles over its own words and breaks down, the stylistic idiosyncrasies, etc. These elements are not necessarily the weakness of a text; they can in fact make up its strength.[10] In an analogous way we must not be too quick to condemn or defend declarations of human rights. Rather we must wonder what precisely happens in these declarations. We must concern ourselves with the "logic" of these declarations which is perhaps not the same as their officially expressed logic.

To read, to interpret, is inevitably to pass judgment. "Judging" is always a question of justice. Indeed, interpretation always implies a certain injustice since, by definition, we do not have access to the complete context which a "correct" interpretation would permit. To a certain extent, every interpretation is violent. Consequently we always interpret too early and read too quickly. Indeed, according to Derrida we are subject to a double law: we cannot judge and yet we must judge. The problem of justice is in this sense a privileged problem for deconstruction.[11] Justice or the just society is also the problem for which the doctrine of human rights attempts to formulate an answer. Thus there are reasons enough to look into what the so-called "philosophy of deconstruction" has to tell us about (the status of) human rights.

2. Lefort and Derrida on the origin of the law

My discussion was announced under the title "Lefort and Derrida: the paradoxical status of human rights." Derrida has only rarely raised the problem directly of the status of declarations of human rights. Yet one could maintain that the problem plays a role in the background of many of his texts, in one way or another.[12] On the

9. S. IJsseling, "Jacques Derrida: een strategie van de vertraging," in: Th. de Boer & G. Widdershoven, *Hermeneutiek in discussie* (Amsterdam: Eburon, 1990), 9-15.

10. Ibidem, 13.

11. J. Derrida, "Force de loi: le 'fondement mystique de l'autorité' / Force of law: the 'mystical foundations of authority,'" *Cardozo Law Review*, volume 11 (N° 5-6), July-August 1990, 930 ff.

12. Cf. in addition to the article mentioned in the previous note, the following: "Préjugés: Devant la loi," in J. Derrida et. al., *La faculté de juger* (Paris: Ed. de minuit, 1985), 87-139; "En ce moment même dans cet ouvrage me voici," in: *Psychè* (Paris: Galilée, 1987), 159-202; "Géopsychanalyse 'and the rest of the world,'" in: idem., 327-352; "Le dernier mot de racisme," in: idem., 353-362;

other hand, the problem of human rights plays a central and unambiguous role in the political philosophy of Claude Lefort. This philosophy has rightly been called a "philosophy of (the symbolic meaning of) human rights."[13] Furthermore, Lefort gives a very obstinate definition of human rights: human rights are not a codex of trans-historic values and norms, but rather they determine, as essentially undeterminable, the generative principles of democratic society.[14] The way in which Lefort works out this idea is interesting for us because it seems to connect with some of Derrida's insights into law and justice.[15] Through Lefort's work it would then be possible to clarify what deconstruction might be able to do with the human rights problematic.

In his political philosophy, Lefort develops a notion of the political in which power can operate politically.[16] "Power," writes Lefort, "is not 'something,' not something empirically determined, but…it is indissociable from its representation…"[17] There is a symbolic dimension of the social which Lefort calls 'the political.' The social exists as identical with itself only on the basis of an internal (symbolic) articulation (one thinks, for example, of the distinction between the king and his subjects) which is effected by way of a power operation. Lefort speaks of a "symbolic" articulation in order to specify that this political-symbolic form-giving of the social may not be understood as a pure reflection of a pre-given social reality.[18] The political form-giving does not reflect a prior

"Admiration de Nelson Mandela ou le lois de la réflexion," in: idem., 453-475; "Déclaration d'indépendance," in: *Otobiographies: L'enseignement de Nietzsche et la politique du nom propre* (Paris: Galilée, 1984), 13-32; "'Il faut bien manger' ou le calcul du sujet," *Confrontations*, 20, 1989, 91-113; "Politics of Friendship," *The Journal of Philosophy*, 85, 1988, 632-644.

13. D. Loose, "Claude Lefort: een politieke filosofie van de mensenrechten," *R&R*, 18, 1989/2, 130-157.

14. For the philosophy of Claude Lefort, we are basing the discussion on the following works in particular: Claude Lefort, *L'invention démocratique* (Paris: Fayard [coll. Livre de poches], 1981); Idem, *Essais sur le politique: XIXe-XXe siècles* (Paris: Seuil, 1986). Lefort published two articles on the status of human rights: "Droits de l'homme et politique," (ID 45-86), and "Les droits de l'homme et l'état-providence" (EP 31-58). On this, see: Ph. Van Haute, "Claude Lefort: de politieke betekenis van de mensenrechten," forthcoming in *Streven*.

15. Cf. the works mentioned in note 10.

16. For this paragraph and the next, see B. Flynn, "Foucault and the body politic," *Man and World*, 20, 1987, 65-84.

17. Cl. Lefort, *Les formes de l'histoire* (Paris: Gallimard, 1978), 285.

18. Cl. Lefort, *Essais sur le politique*, 256. Lefort uses the term "symbolic" here in a sense strongly reminiscent of Lacan. It stands over against the concept of "the

social division, but rather institutes it. This symbolic articulation of the social must be imposed. It is, by definition as it were, established in a violent manner. This power operation, on the ground of which society comes into being as what it is — as simultaneously divided and identical with itself — must be represented however. Given that the 'being' itself of that social reality which comes about through an internal division is a 'being recognized', the power which brings about this internal division must be represented.

Lefort develops a topology of forms of society as a function of the place in which power is represented. This place is further defined in terms of 'mise en sens' and 'mise en scène:' "*Mise en sens* because the social space is deployed as a space of intelligibility and is articulated following a singular mode of discrimination of the real and the imaginary, the true and the false, the just and the unjust, the permitted and the forbidden, the normal and the pathological. *Mise en scène* because the space contains a quasi-representation of itself in its constitution as aristocratic, monarchic or despotic, democratic or totalitarian."[19] In Western absolute monarchies, for example, 'the body of grace' of the king was the place of social division. In the king's "body of grace," society reflects the image that it has of itself: the "body of grace" is, as it were, the externalization of society's own self-understanding. It is the place from which society sees itself, so that it can gain a grip on itself and on the fundamental decisions that define it. The legitimacy of this 'body of grace' guarantees, on the one hand, the articulation of the social in terms of rulers and subjects, and on the other hand, refers to the divine origin of every world power.[20]

As Lefort formulates it, the problem of the representation of power is inextricably bound up, although not coinciding, with the problem of the legitimation of power. Every society faces the problem of its own justification. Every society is confronted with the problem of its legitimacy. In order to establish itself as legitimate, a society will refer, for example, to an ideal of justice which

imaginary," which refers to a mere reflecting of two realities existing in themselves.

19. Cl. Lefort, *Le retrait du politique* (Paris: Galilée, 1983), 74-75. See also, for example, "La permanence du theologico-politique," in: *Essais sur le politique*, 257ff. We wonder if Lefort must not accept here a certain priority of the "mise en sens," since it seems that the quasi-representation of power will always be dependent on a specific "mise en sens."
20. Cf. E. Kantorowicz, *The King's Two Bodies: A study in medieval political theology* (Princeton: Princeton University Press, 1957).

may or may not be of divine origin. But at the same time it is clear that this justice can only become effective by virtue of a power operation.[21] Nevertheless, according to Lefort, power itself must also be represented and legitimated. For Lefort, the representation of power is constitutive of the articulation of the social. The representation, in other words, is intrinsically implied in what it represents.

Yet when the representation of power is implied in the actual articulation of the social, then this seems also to mean that the source of authority, law, and legality can ultimately be grounded only in itself. After all, every order is the result of a power operation, the representation of which constitutes, just as much as it legitimates, what is represented. Should we not then conclude, with Derrida, that the origin of authority and law presupposes a groundless violence, since there is no meta-standpoint from which the establishment of law and authority could be justified?[22] On the contrary, the justification itself institutes, on the basis of a power operation, the order that it must justify. In other words, it produces in a performative manner the conventions which define and legitimate the social order.[23] Derrida adds that it is precisely for these reasons that the law is intrinsically deconstructible.[24] He writes: "...the 'successful' foundation of a State...will produce après coup what it was destined in advance to produce, namely proper interpretive models to read in return, to give sense, necessity, and above all legitimacy, to the violence that has produced, among others, the interpretive model in question, that is, the discourse of its self-legitimation."[25] In Lefort's perspective we still must add that these "interpretive models" at the same time also determine the internal articulation of the social.

---

21. One could think here of Pascal: "Justice without force is impotent; force without justice is tyrannical ... it is necessary to put justice and force together; and, for this, to make sure that what is just be strong, or what is strong be just." Cited in Derrida, "Force de loi: le 'fondement mystique de l'autorité' / Force of law: the 'mystical foundation of authority,'" 936. See also, for example, "...if justice is not necessary law (droit) or the law, it cannot become just legitimately or de jure except by witholding force or rather by appealing to force from its first moment, from its first word," ibid, 935 et passim.
22. "Since the origin of authority, the foundation or ground, the position of the law can't by definition rest on anything but themselves, they are themselves a violence without ground," in Derrida, "Force de loi...," 943.
23. Ibidem, 968.
24. Ibidem, 942.
25. Ibidem, 993.

The subject of the performative act — or of the power operation — on the basis of which law and legitimacy come into being, is always "before the law."[26] Whenever the origin of law and legitimacy presupposes a groundless violence, then this also means that there is no "law of the law."[27] In yet other terms, every politico-juridical order implies a certain violence as an unabolishable moment of non-law within the law.[28] Consequently, the law (or legitimacy) is irrevocably transcendent for man precisely to the extent that it depends on man alone. It belongs to man, and to man alone, to give a concrete interpretation of the law, without any guarantee that this concretization is the ultimate one. Such a guaratee can never be given. The law is transcendent to the extent that it is established by virtue of a performative act which can never be given as present to the subject. This performative act has always already produced the conventions that define the social order.

It is important to notice here that it cannot be a matter of a sort of one-off act. It belongs to the structure of the founding violence, writes Derrida, to call forth its own repetition: "a foundation is a promise...Position is already iterability, a call for self-conserving repetition. Conservation, in turn, refounds, so that it can conserve what it claims to found."[29]

3. Democracy and human rights

We illustrated the problem of the representation of power on the basis of the absolute monarchies of the 18ʰh century. Lefort writes about the symbolic dispositive determined by this form of society: "the singular nature of this (symbolic) dispositive is to assure the condition of occultation without which could arise the question of an opposition between the imaginary and the real. The real, in effect, appears determinable only to the extent that it is already determined, in virtue of a speech, mythical or religious, which testifies to a knowledge the foundation of which cannot be put into play by the effective movement of understanding, technological

---

26. J. Derrida, "Préjugés: Devant la loi," in: Idem, *La faculté de juger* (Paris: Ed. de minuit, 1985), 87-139.
27. On this point see also G. Bennington, *Jacques Derrida* (Paris: Seuil, 1991), 222ff et passim.
28. Ibidem, 990. Here we cannot yet speak of "non-law" in its full sense given that the founding violence has always already taken place (and is always again taking place). In this sense it precedes the opposition between law and non-law.
29. J. Derrida, "Force de loi...," 996.

innovation, the interpretation of the visible."[30] In these societies, social determinations are understood as natural determinations. The problem of the social — the social as problem — cannot come to light because the social only appears as determinable insofar as it is already determined, namely by God. So long as the place of social division (articulation) is another place — a place outside the social — the social can never appear as a problem or, what in our perspective amounts to the same thing, the ultimate groundlessness of every social order is thus hidden from view.

Derrida describes a structure in which the law is intrinsically deconstructible because its ultimate foundation cannot be grounded.[31] In Claude Lefort's terms we could now say that as long as power is represented in another place, no experience of (and relation with)[32] the groundlessness, as we have discussed it, is possible; nor, consequently, with the deconstructibility of every order.

It is here that Lefort's considerations on declarations of human rights get their full meaning and relevance. Lefort states that the original declarations of human rights determine the generative principles of democratic society. They give form to that symbolic articulation of the social which we call "democratic." According to Lefort, these declarations can be considered as the founding deed of democratic society, because and insofar as they paradoxically inscribe, within the founding deed, the ultimate groundlessness of every legitimation and of the law.[33]

The essential function of the 18[t]h century declarations of human rights lies, for Lefort, in the fact that power, the law, and knowledge become (relatively) autonomous social spheres.[34] A few examples. Articles 10 and 11 of the declaration of human rights of 1791 stipulate that the right to one's own opinion is one of the most valuable rights of each individual. Only the legally established abuse of this freedom can or may be contested. This means for Lefort that the exchange of ideas and opinions — with the exclusion of legally

---

30. Cl. Lefort, *Les formes de l'histoire*, 293.
31. J. Derrida, ibidem, 942.
32. We leave to one side the question concerning how precisely this experience and this relation must be described. For now, we simply observe that a direct experience of the unfoundedness and deconstructability can be regarded as impossible: the law is instituted by a performative act, that has always already produced the conventions that define the social order.
33. This idea as such does not occur to Lefort. Nevertheless, we believe that our explanation permits Lefort's insights to be reformulated in this manner.
34. For what follows, see for example Lefort, *L'invention Démocratique*, 52-60.

established exceptions — escapes in principle from the political authorities. These rights, in other words, introduce a split between knowledge and power. The political power brokers can no longer set themselves up as the only legitimate source of knowledge. Articles 7, 8, and 9 of the same declaration stipulate, among other things, that no one can be punished except in conformity with a written law. The emphasis upon written law makes impossible the arbitrary manipulation of the law. The political authorities do not have free use of the law, but must reconcile themselves to the letter of the law. As soon as knowledge and power are separate in principle, the political authority can no longer claim to be in a position to autonomously determine, once and for all, the content of the law. The content and legitimacy of the law henceforth become constantly subject to discussion: "we see in its full unfurling the dimension of a (perpetual) becoming of the law."[35]

Democracy, for Lefort, is a specific "mise en forme" of society which is essentially characterized by the idea that the place of power is "empty."[36] In a democracy nobody can claim power as his essential possession. There is no single individual or group of individuals consubstantial with power, since no one has a privileged access to, or knowledge of, the one will of the people. To determine the people's will is henceforth the object of a never ending discussion. According to Lefort, this implies that in a democracy power is disincorporated. The absolute monarchies still referred to themselves as an organic unity which was represented in the king's "body of grace", but in democratic societies this place of power has become empty. No longer can any political authority make itself out to be the incarnation of the social. At the base of this symbolic mutation lies the dis-connection of the principles of power, law and knowledge. Human rights, for Lefort, lay down the generative principles of this disconnection or dissociation.

Human rights belong to the founding principles of democracy. Such principles do not exist merely as positive institutions whose factual elements can be exhaustively inventoried. The efficiency of human rights, according to Lefort, is on the contrary inherently interwoven with our attachment to them: "rights are not dissociated from the consciousness of rights."[37] Lefort nevertheless indicates that the attachment to these rights will be even better guaranteed if

---

35. Claude Lefort, *Essais sur le politique: XIXᵉ-XXᵉ siècles* (Paris: Seuil, 1986), 27.
36. Cl. Lefort, *L'invention démocratique*, 180.
37. Cl. Lefort, *L'invention démocratique*, 71.

they are proclaimed publicly, if political power presents itself as their guarantor, and if positive laws give them concrete shape. The relation between consciousness of law and institutionalization of law is therefore essentially double: the symbolic dimension of the law manifests itself on the one hand in the irreducibility of the consciousness of law to its concrete juridical objectification, and on the other hand in the instauration of a public domain in which the enactment of legislation is no longer subordinate to any transcendent authority.[38]

Human rights are laid down in written declarations.[39] It is a question of proclaimed rights. They are proclaimed as rights which man is entitled to by nature. At the same time however, these rights determine man's competence, possibly through his representatives, to lay down his own rights. In other words, man is simultaneously the subject and the object of human rights declarations.

Declarations of human rights have this paradoxical "logic" in common with declarations of independence. Jacques Derrida has devoted a chapter to this in his book **Otobiographies**.[40] He indicates that in the American declaration of independence, the American people affirm their independence through their representatives. At the same time, the people only exist on the basis of this declaration. The people who proclaim their independence do not exist apart from this declaration. As a result, here also the subject and the object of the declaration cannot be separated.

For Lefort, this paradoxical "logic" implies that the idea of a human nature on which human rights are often grounded cannot be considered in isolation. This "nature" is not some essence, given "in itself," which can be grasped intuitively. On the contrary, it concerns a "nature" which man attributes to himself in human rights declarations and, furthermore, a "nature" whose definition must constantly remain open.[41] Indeed, these declarations stipulate that no one has a privileged access to knowledge. In other words, human rights declarations do not merely produce, in a performative manner, those conventions (e.g. human nature!) which determine and legitimate democracy. Furthermore, this structure is expressed, as it were, in these declarations themselves, insofar as they make the law

38. Ibidem, 71.
39. For what follows, see especially EP 51ff. and ID 67ff.
40. J. Derrida, *Otobiographies: L'enseignement de Nietzsche et le politique du nom propre* (Paris: Galilée, 1984).
41. Cl. Lefort, *Essais sur le politique: XIXᵉ-XXᵉ siècles*, 51.

essentially dependent on an unremitting endeavour to realize it. Or to put it otherwise, declarations of human rights make possible an experience of the instituting character of every discourse with respect to the order that it institutes.[42]

Thus the so-called universality of human rights does not, according to Lefort, refer to an eternally given corpus of rights. The critique of the universality of human rights misses their essential message: "... the universality of the principle which brings the law back to an interrogation of the law."[43] Declarations of human rights, as we could now argue, place man in the most literal sense before the law. We stated already that, on the ground of human rights declarations, the symbolic dimension of the law manifests itself on the one hand in the irreducibility of the consciousness of law to its concrete juridical objectification, and on the other hand in the instauration of a public domain in which the enactment of legislation is no longer subordinate to any transcendent authority. To the extent that declarations of human rights make the law dependent on an unremitting endeavour to realize it, they place man irrevocably "before the law."[44] The law inevitably retreats, since it falls to man to bring it into being. In this way, human rights lie at the origin of an ateleological history which always remains open.[45]

4. Conclusion: deconstruction and democracy

May we conclude from this that deconstruction would be, as it were, the philosophy of democracy? Obviously not, at least not in the sense that deconstruction would offer the ultimate justification of democratic society as we know it. Deconstruction is not an ideology. But perhaps there is some intrinsic connection between deconstruction and democracy. We stated that declarations of human rights make possible an experience of the instituting character of every discourse with respect to the order that it institutes. This seems to imply that they inscribe the deconstructible structure of the law in the founding act of democracy. The possibility of a

---

42. On this point, see "Esquisse d'une génèse de l'idéologie," in: *Les formes de l'histoire*, 278-329; and also D. Loose, *Claude Lefort: een politieke filosofie van de mensenrechten*, 142ff.
43. Ibidem, 51.
44. See, on this point, Cl. Lefort, "De la démocratie," *Traces*, 1983 (N°7), 12. Here Lefort refers explicitly to the affinity between his conception of law and the Jewish tradition.
45. Cl. Lefort, *L'invention démocratique*, 69.

relation with the deconstructible structure of the law — and consequently with the ultimate groundlessness and ungroundability of every legal order — is nevertheless not an attainment. It is rather a matter of always again winning over all kinds of ideological attempts to obscure this structure.

Lefort defines ideology as an attempt to restore the dimension of an ahistoric society within an historic society.[46] Ideology manages to do this, for example, by presenting social determinations as if they were natural determinations. Yet this cannot be done in any way whatsoever, since in historical societies, the place of social division is no longer situated outside the social, as was still the case with royal absolutism for example. Consequently, the ideological "naturalization" of social determinations can no longer come about on the ground of a reference to the will of God for example. In place of this, according to Lefort, ideology attains its goal by absolutizing certain elements of the social itself such as "the People," "the rationality of History," etc.

We must however take care not to be too impulsive in calling every discourse ideological.[47] Every discourse, Lefort states, attempts to bring us into contact with the instituting or, what amounts to the same thing, with the performative act which lies at the basis of every order without ever being given in its presence. In this sense every order inevitably ignores its own unfoundability. But to the extent that this attempt is doomed to failure, discourse can also become the place in which this impossibility is experienced. Ideology, on the other hand, goes a step further. It is organized on the basis of a "principle of misrecognition" which is not inherent to discourse as such. Every discourse, we have argued, tries to bring us into contact with the instituting moment, and in this sense it is, as it were, blind to itself. But ideology, and this could possibly be a specific interpretation of (the problematic of) human rights, is set up in order to eliminate all signs that might undermine the certainties of a given order. It is set up in order to obscure all signs that might

---

46. Cl. Lefort, "Esquisse d'une génèse de l'idéologie," in: *Les formes de l'histoire*, 296. On the problem of the status of ideology, see especially Cl. Lefort, "La naissance de l'idéologie et l'humanisme," in: Ibidem, 234-277. It would of course be naive to believe that "historical" society and "democracy" would simply coincide with each other. We leave this distinction out of consideration, since it is clear at least that what Lefort says about ideology applies especially to democratic society as we have discussed it.

47. Cl. Lefort, *Les formes de l'histoire*, 297ff.

make a society, or human nature as such, foreign to itself.[48] "...The question of social space," writes Lefort in this respect, "is right away the question of its limit or of its 'outside.'"[49] Consequently, the concern for the democratic asks that we always again make room for this 'other' that breaks through our certainties and places us "before the law." Derrida calls deconstruction "an invention of the other:"[50] an ushering in of the adventure of the completely other. Perhaps this 'invention of the other' is also the concern for "the democratic."[51]

48. Perhaps the political relation must rather be understood as primarily a relation with the foreigner.
49. Ibidem, 294.
50. J. Derrida, *Psychè: Inventions de l'autre* (Paris: Galilée, 1987), especially 11-61.
51. This article was translated from Dutch by Dale Kidd.

14. Aufgeklärte oder ästhetische Subjektivität?

Der Affekt gegen das Ästhetische in der Literatur

WILLEM VAN REIJEN

Vor fast genau 180 Jahren, am 21. November 1811, erschoß Heinrich von Kleist am Berliner Wannsee, "offensichtlich ohne die geringste Irritation oder Nervosität" — "mit pistolengeübter Hand", wie der Kommentator Romantischer Briefe, Karl Heinz Bohrer anerkennend hinzufügt — zuerst seine Todesgefährtin, Henriette Vogel, und dann sich selbst.[1]

Die Ereignisse am Wannsee sind nach Bohrer ein markanter Punkt im Prozeß der "Entstehung ästhetischer Subjektivität". Mögen es damals vor allem die sozialen Begleitumstände (Kleist war Offizier, Henriette Vogel anderweitig verheiratet, zudem Mutter eines Kindes) und das kunstvolle und künstliche Arrangement der Leichen Kleists und Vogels gewesen sein, welche die Gemüter aufrührten; im nachhinein war es vor allem die Legitimation dieses Mordes und Selbstmordes, die, wie auch bei Bohrer ersichtlich noch heute, Empörung weckte.

Es klafft Bohrer zufolge ein Zwiespalt zwischen der Vernunftphilosophie der Deutschen Aufklärung, die Subjektivität bestimmt sah durch das Streben nach Authentizität und Selbsterhaltung, und der Romantik, die Subjektivität wie Kleist über "imaginative-ästhetische Kategorien bestimmte".[2]

Dieses für die Literatur der Moderne beispielhaft gewordene Konzept der romantischen und d.h. der ästhetischen Subjektivität erteilt, so Bohrer, allen Begründungsansprüchen der Aufklärungsphilosophie eine Absage und fällt damit hinter die Aufklärung zurück.[3] Das ästhetische Subjekt handelt, so stellt Bohrer tadelnd fest, nicht mehr ökonomisch-planmäßig also teleologisch, oder rational-argumentativ, also aufgeklärt; sondern in Hinblick auf ein

---

1. K.H. Bohrer, *Der romantische Brief. Die Entstehung romantischer Subjektivität*, Frankfurt a.M. 1989. S. 138.
2. A.a.O., S. 7
3. Für Habermas bedeuten die Bezeichnungen "Aufklärung" und "Moderne" in vielen Hinsichten dasselbe: rational argumentieren und legitimieren. Bohrer legt einen Schnitt zwischen "Aufklärung" und "Moderne". "Moderne" ist bei ihm das, was Habermas gerade als "postmodern" bezeichnet.

dem Zeitstrom entzogenes "Jetzt" oder eine transzendente Dimension (Liebe, Tod). Das Bewußtsein der Kontingenz des eigenen Lebens und der Lebensbedingungen sowie der Diskontinuität bestimmt Denken und Erfahrung. Das Programm der ästhetischen Subjektivität wird, so gesehen, durch agonistische Charakterzüge gekennzeichnet. Natur, Liebe und Tod als "der andere Zustand" sind final bestimmt.

Der 'Fall Kleist' ist für Bohrer von besonderer Bedeutung, weil Kleist bis zu der Kant-lektüre im Jahre 1801, die ihn in eine tiefe Krise stürzen wird, am Programm der Aufklärung festgehalten hat. Ab März 1801 gibt Kleist sich Bohrer zufolge der "Innerlichkeit" hin und "besingt sein Ich sich selbst".[4] Dieser Entwicklung entspricht die Erfahrung, von keinem Mitmenschen mehr verstanden zu werden. Ähnlich hatte sich ja auch Goethes Werther über sein Gespräch mit Albert, mit dem er über den Selbstmord diskutiert hatte, geäußert: "Und wir gingen auseinander, ohne einander verstanden zu haben. Wie denn auf dieser Welt keiner leicht den anderen versteht." Auch dieses Nicht-verstehen betrifft offenkundig nicht nur die Möglichkeit der Verständigung, sondern vor allem die Unmöglichkeit eines Einverständnisses, von dem unterstellt wurde, daß es mit Argumenten erzielt werden könnte. "Innerlichkeit" ist nicht nur der analytische Befund, sondern der moralische Vorwurf, mit dem Bohrer die Absage an die Legitimationsverpflichtung kritisiert. Das tritt besonders dann klar hervor, wenn dieser Zusammenbruch vom Dichter nicht beklagt, sondern "affirmativ enthusiastisch" gefeiert wird.[5] Kleist schließt die Möglichkeit, von anderen verstanden zu werden, aus und kündigt das Vertrauen in die Wissenschaften nach der Lektüre der Kritik der reinen Vernunft auf. "Wir können nicht entscheiden, ob das, was wir Wahrheit nennen, wahrhaft Wahrheit ist, oder ob es uns nur so scheint. Ist das letzte, so ist die Wahrheit, die wir hier sammeln, nach dem Tode nicht mehr — und alles Bestreben, ein Eigentum sich zu erwerben, das uns auch in das Grab folgt, ist vergeblich."[6] Bohrer schließt aus dieser Passage, daß Kleist den Tod als "Stufe letzter Vervollkommnung" gedacht habe. Weder war Kleist, so resümiert Bohrer, an einer vernünftigen Begründung seiner Ansich-

---

4. K.H. Bohrer, *Der romantische Brief. Die Entstehung romantischer Subjektivität*, Frankfurt a.M. 1989. S. 55-56.
5. A.a.O., S. 55
6. A.a.O., S. 88

ten gelegen, noch an einer Authentizität, die sich erst in der Interaktion und dem Streben nach Selbsterhaltung zu bewähren hätte.

Für Bohrer ist klar, daß sich die Literatur den aufklärerischen Zielsetzungen der Aufklärung unterzuordnen habe. Verweigert sie sich dieser Dienstleistung, dann wird sie romantisch, modern. Bohrer betrachtet demnach das Konzept der Aufklärung als absolut eindeutige Grundlage für den Fortschritt und für die Begründung unseres Handelns und unserer Erkenntnisse.

Das erscheint logisch genausowenig zwingend, wie die Verknüpfung des Todesmotivs mit dem Konzept der ästhetischen Subjektivität.

Diese letzte kann, aber muß nicht agonistisch gedacht werden. Paradoxal ist vor diesem Hintergrund das "Projekt" des Selbstmordes in zweierlei Hinsicht, es umfaßte zum einen die Suche nach einer Todesgefährtin (also Sozialität in Hinblick auf Vereinzelung), zum anderen den Versuch einer Legitimation der Aufgabe der verläßlichen Begründung.

Kleist ist sich nach Bohrer dieser Paradoxen durchaus bewußt gewesen und habe darauf reagiert, indem er an die Stelle der Vernunft und der Wissenschaft die Literatur gesetzt habe. Dies habe es ihm ermöglicht, das vielbeschworene "Diskontinuitätsbewußtsein", d.h. die Erfahrung eines "außer-sich-seins" (Schiller) zu entwickeln, das per definitionem agonal angelegt sei. Liebe und Selbstmord, so Bohrer, sind Substitute für den Verlust der Teleologie.[7]

Die ambivalente Einschätzung des Lebens findet sich in der Schilderung eines Schiffsausflugs auf dem Rhein, wenn ein Sturm aufkommt. Hören wir Kleist: "...Ach, es ist nichts ekelhafter, als diese Furcht vor dem Tode. Das Leben ist das einzige Eigentum, das nur dann etwas wert ist, wenn wir es nicht achten. Verächtlich ist es, wenn wir es nicht leicht fallen lassen können, und nur der kann es zu großen Zwecken nutzen, der es leicht und freudig wegwerfen könnte...eine Habe, die nichts wert ist, wenn sie uns etwas wert ist, ein Ding wie ein Widerspruch, flach und tief, öde und reich, würdig und verächtlich, vieldeutig und unergründlich..."[8]

So vieldeutig wie das Leben oder besser, seine Einschätzung - so vieldeutig ist auch die Landschaft, die hier bloß als Projektionsfläche der Stimmung erscheint. "Bald lacht, bald schreckt" die Rheinlandschaft. Der jähe Umschlag des locus amoenus in den

7. K.H. Bohrer, *Der romantische Brief. Die Entstehung romantischer Subjektivität*, Frankfurt a.M. 1989. S. 102-103.
8. A.a.O., S. 95.

locus terribilis (uns auch aus Eichendorffs Aus dem Leben eines Taugenichts vertraut) erinnert an die Ambiguität der barocken Dichtung — markiert aber auch den entscheidenden Unterschied zwischen der Romantik und dem Barock. Die Romantische Ambiguität wird getragen von der Vorstellung einer Perfektibilität (progressive Universalpoesie), d.h. einer Einheit, die symbolisch gefaßt werden kann; während im Barock die Gegensätze nicht mehr synthetisiert werden können.[9] Es ist fraglich, ob man Bohrer zustimmen kann, wenn er feststellt, daß "im Bild der Dichtung das Widersprüchliche versöhnt wird"; aber ich halte auf jeden Fall gegen Bohrer fest, daß hier keineswegs "das Projekt »Literatur« an die Stelle des Projekts »Vernunft« gesetzt wird." Auch dann, wenn man sagen muß, daß Kleist die "ideellen Motive von Kontinuität und traditioneller Selbsterhaltung ausgelöscht habe", heißt das nicht, daß diese konkrete individuelle Reaktion auf die — politisch und sozial — als korrupt erfahrene Umwelt die einzige, zwingende Antwort ist.

Diesen Schluß kann Bohrer nur ziehen, weil er die grundsätzlichen Ambiguitäten von »Literatur« und »Vernunft« (gleichermaßen teleologisch und antagonistisch zu sein) unterschlägt und dann die einseitig als problemlösend deklarierte »Vernunft« auf der pragmatischen Ebene ansiedelt. Wenn man so verfährt konkurriert die ins ästhetische abgeschobene Literatur mit der Vernunft um die Frage, wer die effizientere Lösung von Problemen ermöglicht und zieht den kürzeren.

Die Wertung des Lebens, so möchte ich pointiert behaupten, ist sowohl von der Vernunft, wie von der Literatur her gedacht in einer Ambiguität angesiedelt. Vernunft und Literatur sind grundsätzlich gleichermaßen teleologisch und agonistisch. In pragmatischer Hinsicht werden wir zur Wahl zwischen den zwei Polen dieser Alternative gezwungen; das heißt aber nicht — wie Bohrer meint — eine Entscheidung für die (moderne, d.h. agonistische) Literatur und also gegen die (teleologische) Vernunft, oder umgekehrt.

Ich möchte deswegen noch einmal hervorheben, daß auch dann, wenn Kleist sich zuletzt für den Selbstmord entschlossen hat, dies — anders als Bohrer meint — keine Wahl zwischen Vernunft und Literatur gewesen ist. Die Sicherung der Selbsterhaltung und der Kontinuität erfordert allerdings eine argumentative oder gewalttätige Lösung von Ambiguitäten. Kleist hatte die Wahl zwischen zwei Möglichkeiten. Es ist somit klar, daß eine Entscheidung Vereinseiti-

9. W. v. Reijen, *Labyrinth und Ruine*. In: W. v. Reijen (Hg.), 1992c.

gung der Ambiguität erfordert. Sofern Bohrer aber der Tatsache einer grundsätzlichen Ambiguität nicht Rechnung tragen will, lastet die Kleist zugerechnete romantische Inkonsequenz als Moment einer als ästhetisch abqualifizierten Unmoral auf dem Werk und auf der Person des Dichters. Tatsächlich aber ist die Kleist attestierte Flucht in die a-teleologische Teleologie des Todes Folge der Vereinseitigung der fundamentalen Ambiguität die eine agonale Lösung übrigens nicht weniger oder mehr zuläßt als eine konstitutive.

Das läßt sich auch an den Überlegungen über die Möglichkeit, die Wahrheit zu erkennen, nachvollziehen. Wenn Kleist, wie Bohrer meint, keine letzte Begründungsmöglichkeit gibt, dann gibt es auch keine Verantwortlichkeit, kein Recht. Aber was ist dann das Böse? Wenn es auf diese Fragen keine Antwort gibt, dann ist »Selbsterhaltung« nur noch über das Medium Literatur möglich, schließt Bohrer, denn nur hier ist das diskontinuierliche Bewußtsein nicht unglücklich.[10] Der Frage, ob die Literatur hier stellvertretend für die moderne Philosophie eine Lösung anbietet, mit der wir uns als moderne Philosophen keinesfalls zufrieden geben können, oder aber inwiefern die Auseinandersetzung zwischen den Vertretern einer modernen und einer postmodernen Philosophie Fingerzeige auf eine andere Fragestellung geben, möchte ich im folgenden nachgehen, indem ich die Beweislast, die die Philosophie von Jürgen Habermas übernimmt, einer kritischen Prüfung unterziehe und die Vorschläge Lyotards dagegen abgrenze. [11]

Die Beweislast der Philosophie

Die Frage, was die Philosophie beweisen kann und sollte, ist Gegenstand einer Auseinandersetzung zwischen Habermas, Lyotard und Rorty. Für Habermas ist klar, daß die Philosophie eine Beweislast hat. Unwiderruflich sind zwar die metaphysischen und introspektiven Sicherheiten, auf die sich die alteuropäische Philosophie stützte, erschüttert; aber das heißt keineswegs, daß man in wissenschaftlichen und praktischen Fragen auf jegliche Begründung verzichten sollte. Im Gegenteil, der Verlust verbindlicher Weltanschauungen und die damit einhergehende Pluralisierung der Lebensformen zwingt uns geradezu, neue Regeln für die Praxis der

---

10. K.H. Bohrer, *Der romantische Brief. Die Entstehung romantischer Subjektivität*, Frankfurt a.M. 1989. S. 102-103.
11. W. v. Reijen, *"Moderne versus postmoderne Philosophie"* in: W. Marotzki/H. Sünker (Hg.): *Kritische Erziehungswissenschaft*, Bielefeld, S. 9-33.

276

gewaltfreien und gerechten Konfliktlösung nicht nur zu artikulie-
ren, sondern auch zu begründen, d.h. als verpflichtend vorzustel-
len.

Schon die Theorie des kommunikativen Handelns gibt zu erkennen, daß es Habermas um eine Theorie der Rationalität geht, die
universalistische Ansprüche begründen kann. Diesen Universalisie-
rungsanspruch hat Habermas 1983 mit dem Kapitel "Diskursethik -
Notizen zu einem Begründungsprogramm" in "Moralbewußtsein
und kommunikatives Handeln" erneuert und in nachfolgenden
Veröffentlichungen unter verschiedenen Perspektiven immer wieder vorgebracht. Freilich, im Vergleich mit traditionellen Begrün-
dungsprogrammen und mit Apels Letztbegründungskonzept
macht Habermas' Begründungsvorschlag einen eher bescheidenen
Eindruck. Als Begründung gilt die Feststellung, daß kompetente
Teilnehmer im Diskurs Einverständnis über die Gültigkeit von
Handlungsnormen erzielen. Habermas unterscheidet nun zwar
zwischen theoretischer und praktischer Urteilsbildung, aber um an
seinem Begründungsanspruch festhalten zu können, sieht er sich
dazu gezwungen, zu erklären, daß praktische Urteile analog zu
theoretischen zu verstehen sind.

Diese Feststellung dient zum einen der Abgrenzung seiner eigenen Diskursethik gegen alle Formen von nicht-kognitivistischen
Theorien (der Wertskeptiker, wie Habermas sie nennt), zum anderen der Markierung seines eigenen Ansatzes. Nur über ein er-
zieltes Einverständnis läßt sich nach Habermas bewirken, worauf es
ankommt: die wechselseitige rationale Motivierung zu Handlungen.[12]

Dieses Einverständnis unterscheidet sich nach Habermas von
einem rein theoretischen, insofern es in diesem Fall "nur" um eine
gemeinsame Situationsdeutung oder dergleichen geht, während es
in jenem um mehr geht, nämlich um die Gewähr, die jemand für die
Einlösung eines Geltungsanspruchs übernimmt.

Gemeinsam, und das begründet Habermas' Annahme der Analogie zwischen theoretischen und praktischen Urteilen, ist beiden Arten von Geltungsansprüchen, daß sie diskursiv einlösbar
sind.[13]

Genau das aber ist mindestens in zweierlei Hinsicht fraglich.
Erstens wirft die Rede von der diskursiven Einlösung die Frage auf,

12. J. Habermas, *Moralbewußtsein und kommunikatives Handeln*, Frankfurt a.M.
    1983. S. 68.
13. A.a.O., S. 69.

ob es wirklich der Konsens ist, der die Begründung für eine moralische Verbindlichkeit sein kann. Zweitens fragt sich, ob moralische Überzeugungen sich rational begründen lassen müssen.

In beiden Hinsichten könnte sich zeigen, daß letzten Endes — wie Tugendhat zeigt[14] — auf das Konzept eines wie auch immer autonom gedachten Subjekts rekurriert werden muß.

Was den ersten Punkt anlangt, verweist Habermas selber auf die für sein Konsensmodell konstitutive Annahme, daß der Einzelne die Gewähr für die Einlösung von konsensuell erzielten Geltungsansprüchen übernimmt. Von dieser Übernahme kann man sich schlecht vorstellen, daß auch sie wieder im Diskurs verankert sei. Gerade in der Lebenswelt, dem Urschoß der kommunikativen Rationalität, ist die Authentizität der Mitmenschen die Gewähr dafür, daß alle relevante Information, und alle Argumente als Argumente gehandhabt werden. Nur das schafft das Vertrauen, daß die Risiken, die mit jeder Interaktion verknüpft sind, hingenommen werden können. Authentizität aber läßt sich, wie Habermas selber ausführt, so wenig wie Sinn, konsensuell oder kognitiv herstellen. Ob jemand die Gewähr dafür bietet, daß er sich an den von ihm selber propagierten Normen halten wird oder nicht, zeigt sich in der Praxis. Diese Gewähr bzw. das entsprechende Vertrauen läßt sich nicht, wie Habermas meint, als Resultat eines Diskurses verstehen. Authentizität und argumentative Diskussion sind beide gleichermaßen konstitutiv für das gelingen der gewaltfreien und gerechten Konfliktlösung. Das heißt, daß die Authentizität, die hier erfordert wird, nicht nur auf der praktischen Verständigungsebene angesiedelt ist, auch wenn sie dort erst praktisch in Erscheinung tritt. Wäre dem so, dann würde Authentizität ganz und gar als funktionalisiertes Vertrauen gefaßt und damit der Selbstdestruktion ausgesetzt werden. Gerade die Lebenswelt aber als Quelle und Kriterium für Authentizität enthält nicht-funktionalisierbare Einstellungen und Einsichten; sonst könnte sie ja nicht als Gegenkraft gegen Systeme gedacht werden. Habermas' Konzept der "entgegenkommenden Lebenwelten" ist systematisch aber nicht tragfähiger als die Idee der "Wahrheitsanalogie", wenn es um die Begründung moralischer Normen geht. Das können wir uns auch an einem anderen Topos, dem des Spannungsverhältnisses von Verwendungsregeln und Subjekt vergegenwärtigen. Habermas insistiert mit Wittgenstein darauf, daß Sprache keine Realität außerhalb ihrer Verwendungsregeln hat. Diese Annahme wendet er kritisch gegen sowohl

14. E. Tugendhat, *Probleme der Ethik*, Stuttgart 1984.

Nietzsches Abwertung der Sprache als ein "bewegliches Heer von Metonymien und Metaphern" als gegen Heideggers Überhöhung der Sprache zum metaphysischen Subjekt. ("Die Sprache spricht") Vieles mag dafür sprechen, daß es klug ist, in institutionalisierten Verhältnissen Meta-Diskursen über die Verläßlichkeit der "Sprache" aus dem Weg zu gehen; und das gilt nicht weniger für Spekulationen über Sprachmystik. Wenn man die Theorie des kommunikativen Handelns begründen will, dann sollte man tunlichst selbstrekursive Verfahren meiden.

Auch diese Theorie erhebt Gültigkeitsansprüche, die geprüft werden müssen. Um dieses Problem zu lösen, führt Habermas die aus Rawls "Theory of Justice" bekannte Vorstellung der Unparteilichkeit ein. Nach diesem Vorschlag müssen bekanntlich Teilnehmer an einem praktischen Diskurs in Unkenntnis ihrer späteren Rolle in der Gesellschaft ein ideales Normensystem erstellen.

Wir dürfen vermuten, daß Habermas, wenn er von dem quasi-transzendentalen Status seiner Begründung spricht, diese Konstruktion vor Augen stand. "Unparteilichkeit" scheint, auch in systematischer Hinsicht, eine gute Voraussetzung für die Teilnahme an einem Diskurs über strittige Normen zu sein. Nur: die kann in der Lebenswelt nicht begründet werden. Sie macht sozusagen die Verständigung und das Einverständnis in bezug auf Normen — in ständiger Konfrontation mit den Erfordernissen der "Außenwelt" (sprich: den Systemen) erst möglich und ist nicht deren Ergebnis. Sonst wäre jede mögliche Differenz zwischen einem tatsächlichen — aber gegebenfalls ungerechten — Normenkonsens und einem gerechten eingezogen. Ludwig Nagl[15] hat darauf hingewiesen, daß es Habermas' Affinität mit der Idee, daß moralische Normen in modernen Institutionen angesiedelt werden können müssen, ist, die zu einer Reduktion der Bedeutung des Subjektiven zugunsten der Institution "Diskurs" führt. Diese Begründungsproblematik läßt sich natürlich auch auf die problematische Selbstbegründung der philosophischen Reflexion abbilden. In vielen Einzelstudien zur Romantik, Hermeneutik und zu zeitgenössischen Selbstbewußtseinstheorien hat Manfred Frank das Dilemma der Begründung des Selbstbewußtseins erörtert.

Entweder, so lautet die Frage, ist der Prozeß der Selbstbegründung durch die Reflexion ein unendlicher Progreß oder ein Zirkel, oder aber er geht auf etwas Unvordenkliches, das nicht reflexiv

---

15. L. Nagl, »*Intersubjektivität*« - *ein Ausweg aus dem "starken Institutionalismus" der Hegelschen "Sittlichkeit" (unver. Ms.)*, 1986.

eingeholt werden kann, zurück. An einer Stelle seines Nachworts zu Selbstbewußtseinstheorien von Fichte bis Sartre faßt Frank seine Überlegungen folgendermaßen zusammen. "Um der begrifflichen Zugänglichkeit willen muß das Selbst als ein Verhältnis zwischen zwei Relaten gedacht werden; um aber den Zirkeln der Reflexionstheorie zu entgehen, muß diese Relation zugleich durch eine vorreflexive Vertrautheit des Selbst mit sich fundiert sein. Sie allein könnte die Identität begründen, in der sich Selbstsein — unerachtet seiner Artikulation, als Verhältnis, und mithin als Differenz — hält. Da diese Identität nicht selbst in die Reichweite (begrifflichen) Wissens fällt, kann sie nur postuliert werden als notwendige Bedingung des Gefühls, in welchem dem Selbst zwei komplementäre, scheinbar sich ausschließende Erfahrungen zugemutet werden..."[16]

Ich habe dieses Resümee etwas ausführlicher zitiert, um Franks Idee, daß das Subjekt außer als reflektierendes Bewußtsein auch als Vertraut-sein mit sich gedacht werden kann, vor einer systematischen Überlegungung zu erörtern.

Was eine rationale Begründung von Normen anlangt, sind die Argumente dafür, daß eine rationale Begründung hinreichend sei für eine praktische Verpflichtung, nicht überzeugend.

Seiner Theorie des kommunikativen Handelns legt Habermas bekanntlich ein Konzept von Rationalität zugrunde, das nicht nur instrumentelle Zweck-Mittelrationalität umfaßt, soweit wir in bezug auf die objektive Welt handeln, sondern auch eine kommunikative Rationalität, die Begründung und Legitimation von Handlungen in der sozialen Welt ermöglicht.

Es ist natürlich nicht zu bestreiten, daß wir argumentative Diskurse brauchen, um uns die Folgen der Normen, auf die wir uns festlegen wollen, zu vergegenwärtigen. Und es ist namentlich der Universalisierungssatz, den wir kennen und, was die Konsequenzen seiner Anwendung anlangt, argumentativ werten können müssen, um ihn als Grundnorm für ein normatives Prozedere akzeptieren zu können. Ebenso können wir nur mit Argumenten davon überzeugt werden, daß dieser Universalisierungssatz keine Eingriffe in konkrete Werthierarchien bedeutet, während er gleichwohl nicht wertindifferent ist. Wir verdanken namentlich Habermas' Analyse der Weberschen Vermischung von Wertinhalt und Wertmaßstab ("Tanner Lectures") nicht mehr rückgängig zu machende Einsichten. Nur: diese argumentativen Diskurse können

16. M. Frank, *Selbstbewußtseinstheorien von Fichte bis Sartre*, Frankfurt a.M. 1991. S. 500.

das "Prinzip Subjekt" nicht durch das "Prinzip Intersubjektivität" ersetzen. Darauf zielt auch Henrichs Kritik in "Konzepte", wenn er daraufhinweist, daß Selbstbeschreibungen und Fremdbeschreibungen nicht voraussetzungslos einem rationalen Diskurs unterzogen werden können. Er bezieht sich auf Kants Kritik der Indifferentisten, daß auch sie, wenn sie solches verbaliter verneinen, "über ihre Seele nachdenken" müssen. Metaphysische Voraussetzungen liegen auch dem Kampf gegen die Metaphysik zugrunde. Wir können von daher sagen, daß Habermas mehr legitimieren will als möglich und nötig ist. Das Verfahren der Konsensbildung kann legitimiert werden in Hinblick auf die Folgen, die wir uns in pragmatischer Hinsicht wünschen, wenn wir im Rahmen von Institutionen handeln. Diese Entscheidung für ein an Folgen orientiertes Verfahren kann nicht weiter rational begründet werden. Sie betrifft, um bei Tugendhat anzuschließen, eine Überzeugung und keine Norm.[17] Wir entscheiden uns für ein Verfahren, das Vorgriffe auf Wertungen und Werthierarchien im Prinzip ausschließt: wir müssen aber wohl zugeben, daß diese Entscheidung selber wie jede Prozedur eine nicht weiter rational begründbare Option für die Wertung dieses Verfahrens voraussetzt. Wir werden aber auch sehen, daß Kontrahenten von Habermas in Sachen politischer Philosophie wie Lyotard und Rorty zwar dieses Begründungsdefizit ironisch-polemisch aufgreifen, sich aber mit ihren Vorschlägen aus dem Kreis der praktischen Problemlösung verabschieden. Ihre Ansätze können auf keinen Fall in Kriterien für institutionalisiertes Handeln übersetzt werden und verhalten sich also nur negativ-kritisch zur Theorie des kommunikativen Handelns. Das heißt, positiv gesagt, daß sie die Grenzen der Reichweite der Habermasschen Theorie aufzeigen. Wenn mit der Theorie des kommunikativen Handelns ein universalistischer philosophischer Anspruch erhoben wird, ist dieser Anspruch wegen der unausgearbeiteten (und mutmaßlich nicht ausarbeitbaren) Begründungsproblematik zurückzuweisen.

Der vorerst unbefriedigende Schluß lautet denn auch, daß sich uns in Gestalt der modernen und der postmodernen Philosophie zwei nicht sogleich miteinander zu synthetisierende, Reflexionen darbieten: eine praktische und eine metaphysische oder ontologische (Lyotard). Wenn man also sagen kann, daß Habermas zuviel beweisen will, dann gilt für Lyotard, daß er nichts beweisen kann, aber nostalgisch auf den Beweis bezogen bleibt.

17. E. Tugendhat, *Probleme der Ethik*, Stuttgart 1984, S. 113.

Die Überlegungen in *"Le différend"* bauen ganz auf dem ontologischen Unterschied von Satz und "phrase" auf. "Satz" bezeichnet den diskursiven Diskurs mit übergreifenden Einheitsvorstellungen, für den bei Lyotard Habermas paradigmatisch einsteht. Lyotard weist, wie gelegentlich unterstellt wird, die demokratischen Inhalte der Habermasschen Theorie keineswegs ab. "Die Sache ist gut" heißt es, "die Argumente sind es nicht". Der Nachsatz bezieht sich eben auf die Beweisansprüche, die Habermas' Programm erhebt. Für Lyotard ist das konstitutive Moment aller Diskurse selber nicht Teil eines Diskurses, es ist eine "phrase" d.h. etwas, das noch der Verbalisierung oder Operationalisierung harrt — allerdings in dem Falle, in dem sich das ereignet, seinen ontologischen Status verliert. Was sich da ereignet, die Erfahrung des Erhabenen in der Kunst, die moralische Einsicht, die sich einstellt, wenn man (einsam) Aug" in Aug" mit dem Gesetz steht - gewiß, es sind in Metaphern gefaßte Erfahrungen. Die schliessen allerdings kontroverse argumentative Durchgänge keineswegs aus, wie u.a. die Kant-Exkurse in *"Le différend"* belegen, aber sie zeigen, daß der Anspruch, mit rationaler Begründung das rational-diskursiv nicht faßbare doch zu fassen, ins Leere läuft. Wieder anders verhält sich Rorty zu der traditionellen Beweislast der Philosophie. Von seinem Ansatz kann man sagen, daß, wer ironisch verfährt, gar nichts beweisen will.

Das Fehlen eines privilegierten Zugangs zu den eigenen Bewustseinsinhalten und -verfahren einerseits, die Aufgabe der Idee, daß es überhaupt einen Diskurs gibt, der mehr Anspruch auf Wahrheit erheben könnte als andere andererseits, führt unweigerlich zu dem Schluß, daß die philosophische Reflexion erst dann zu sich selbst kommt, wenn sie nichts mehr beweisen, sondern nur noch zeigen will.

Das heißt zusammenfassend, daß der Habermassche Diskurs normative Einsichten begründen und Handlungen legitimieren kann, sofern wir uns in einem institutionellen Rahmen bewegen - und sei es, mit Nagl gesprochen, im Rahmen der "Institution Diskurs". Was aber hier verschwindet, die Authentizität als etwas, das sich nicht auf der Ebene der Institutionen verrechnen läßt, steht bei Lyotard im Zentrum, die Einsicht, daß es etwas gibt, das konstitutiv ist für unsere moralischen Überzeugungen und Handlungen, ohne daß man dessen im Diskurs habhaft werden könnte.

Allerdings ist klar, daß eben diese Einsicht, so kritisch sie sein kann, sich nicht zur Operationalisierung in institutionalisierten Handlungskontexten hergeben kann. Sie macht allerdings auch klar, daß es ohne Beweise in diesen Kontexten nicht abgeht, schränkt aber die Ansprüche des Beweises auf die diskursiv artiku-lierbare Wirklichkeit, die nicht das Ganze ist, ein.

Dieses Operationalisierungsdefizit tritt bei Rorty noch massiver in Erscheinung, weil er überhaupt alle Hierarchisierungen, und dann hier namentlich die zwischen einem Metaniveau der Konstitu-tion und der diskursiven Realität für ein Phantom hält.

Zum Schluß wenden wir uns noch einmal der Frage nach der aufgeklärten und der ästhetischen Subjektivität zu.

Die Briefe Kleists geben klar zu erkennen, daß es einen Wider-streit zwischen seiner rational-teleologisch bestimmter Einstellung (Preussische Offizierssehre, Lebensform des Schriftstellers) und der katastrophischen Erfahrung des Ausgeschlossenseins, des Ver-trauensverlusts hinsichtlich der Wissenschaft (Kant-Krise) und der politischen Ehrlosigkeit der Zeit gibt.

Aus diesen Elementen können wir aber nicht, wie Bohrer vor-schlägt, eine Subjektivität konstruieren, der an Selbsterhaltung und Authentizität nichts gelegen war.

Das Aufgeben des Strebens nach Selbsterhaltung, so offenkundig es ist, war — so muß man vielmehr sagen — in einem Authentizitätskonzept verankert, das nun zwar nichts mit Kommu-nikation und Konsens zu tun hat (obwohl sich dieses Defizit noch ironisch in dem Versuch, eine Todesgefährtin zu beschaffen spie-gelt) aber alles mit Authentizität. Selbsterhaltung hat Kleist der Authentizität untergeordnet im Bewußtsein, daß jeder Versuch, sie kommunikabel zu machen, sie ihrer selbst entfremden muß. Daß Kleist sich zum Selbstmord entschlossen hat, läßt sich aus dieser Erfahrung der Nicht-Kommunikabilität nicht logisch ableiten. Es mag deswegen geradezu trivial erscheinen zu sagen, daß sich der Selbstmord Kleists nicht rational begründen läßt in dem Sinn, daß er sich nicht als Ergebnis eines argumentativen Verfahrens verstehen läßt; aber diese Feststellung macht klar, wo die Grenzen einer solchen Prozedur liegen, ohne daß das hieße, daß man das Leben und normative Wertungen einem agonalen Programm überant-wortet. Das kann man plausibel machen, indem man darauf ver-weist, wie sehr für Kleist die Gegensätze in der Authentizitäts-erfahrung benachbart waren. Ich erinnere an die Authentizität auf die Landschaft projizierende Beschreibung eines Tals, "das sich bald öffnet, bald schließt, bald blüht, bald öde ist, bald lacht, bald schreckt."[18]; und an die Feststellung Bohrers, daß "Katastrophe und Idyll zusammengehören."[19]

Für die subjektive Erfahrung hört sich das entsprechend so an: "Ach, es muß leer und öde und traurig sein, später zu sterben als das Herz."[20]

Diese Einsicht macht es hier ganz konkret unmöglich, die Kunst, wie Habermas das in dem Philosophischen Diskurs der Moderne tut, als genuine Verkörperung einer kommunikativen Vernunft zu betrachten. Die in der Kunst erfahrene Authentizität, kreative wie betrachtende, ist nicht Teil des in drei Hinsichten (objektiv, sozial und aufrichtig) ausdifferenzierten Weltbezugs, sondern die nur mit ihren Paradoxien beschreibbare Quelle, aus der jede rationale Artikulation eine Kommunikation erst ermöglichende Vereinseitigung darstellt.

Ein Beispiel dafür gibt Kleist übrigens in seiner Glosse "Über die allmähliche Verfertigung der Gedanken beim Reden". Kleist entwirft hier das Bild Mirabeaus, der bei seiner Ansprache an die Nationalversammlung, beim Reden, nicht nur die moralische Überlegenheit des Parlaments über die Waffengewalt entdeckt, sondern auch die demokratische Regierungsform über den Absolutismus stellt. Kleist arbeitet heraus, daß von einer planmäßigen Entwicklung dieser Ansprache keine Rede sein kann, sie speiste sich aus einer höchst ambivalenten Einstellung. Ihr Ergebnis war rational und kommunikativ — die Ausgangslage nicht.

Bert v.d.Brink und Wolfgang Herrlitz danke ich für Kritik an früheren Fassungen.

Literatur

Bohrer, K.H. (1989) Der romantische Brief. Die Entstehung romantischer Subjektivität. Frankfurt/M.

Frank, M. (1991) Selbstbewußtseinstheorien von Fichte bis Sartre. Frankfurt/M.

Frank, M. (1986) Die Unhintergehbarkeit von Individualität. Frankfurt/M.

Frank, M. (1988) Die Grenzen der Verständigung. Frankfurt/M.

18. K.H. Bohrer, *Der romantische Brief. Die Entstehung romantischer Subjektivität*, Frankfurt a.M. 1989. S. 231.
19. A.a.O., S. 235.
20. A.a.O., S. 98.

Frank, M. (1989) Einführung in die frühromantische Ästhetik. Frankfurt/M.

Habermas, J. (1983) Moralbewußtsein und kommunikatives Handeln. Frankfurt/M.

Habermas, J. (1985) Der philosophische Diskurs der Moderne. Frankfurt/M.

Henrich, D. (1987) Konzepte. Frankfurt/M.

Hörisch, J. (1988) Die Wut des Verstehens. Frankfurt/M.

Lyotard, J.-F. (1987) Der Widerstreit. München.

Nagl, L. (1986) »Intersubjektivität« — ein Ausweg aus dem 'starken Institutionalismus' der Hegelschen 'Sittlichkeit' (unver. Ms.).

Reijen, W.v. (1992a) Labyrinth und Ruine. In: W.v. Reijen (Hg.) 1992c.

Reijen, W.v. (1992b) 'Moderne versus postmoderne Philosophie:, in: W. Marotzki/H. Sünker (Hg.): Kritische Erziehungswissenschaft. Bielefeld. S. 9-33.

Reijen, W.v. (Hg.) (1992c) Allegorie und Melancholie. Frankfurt/M.

Rorty, R. (1987) Solidarität und Objektivität. Stuttgart.

Simmel, G. (1923) Philosophische Kultur. Potsdam.

Tugendhat, E. (1984) Probleme der Ethik. Stuttgart.

15. Aufklärung und die Idee des Unendlichen

H.J. ADRIAANSE

I) *Aufklärung als Einsatz der Differenz*
"Es gibt nicht eine, sondern eine Mehrzahl von Aufklärungen, die epochenweise nacheinander dem in die Welt getretenen Glauben das Wissen repräsentieren, mit dem er sich auseinanderzusetzen hat."[1] Diesem Worte Fr. Rosenzweigs zufolge ist die Differenz, die das Thema des gegenwärtigen Symposiums bildet, eine Differenz im Glauben, bzw. zwischen zwei Glaubenssystemen oder Glaubensweisen. Wenn man das Wort "Glaube" nicht gleich im religiösen Sinn versteht, sondern als allgemeine Bezeichnung für Annahmen deren Richtigkeit unentschieden ist, so dürfte damit etwas Zutreffendes ausgesprochen sein. Annahmen setzen Entscheidungen voraus; das Erkennen schwebt nicht mehr in der Unverbindlichkeit der Urteilsenthaltung; diese Freiheit - die allerdings nie vollständig ist - ist einer Gewißheit gewichen, die die Auseinandersetzung nicht scheut. Glaube ist auch in diesem allgemeinen Sinne tendentiell dogmatisch. Zugleich kommt ihm eine Art Unschuld zu, da er die eigenen Annahmen unbefangen als die richtigen geltend macht. Liest man etwa - ich beschränke mich auf die Denker vom Range und lasse die kleineren Gottheiten sowie alle Nichtphilosophen außer Betracht - was Habermas über Derrida schreibt und was Derrida Habermas erwidert, so kann man sich des Eindrucks nicht erwehren, daß hier Glaube gegen Glauben steht und daß die Bedingungen für eine sinnvolle Diskussion kaum erfüllt sind.

Nicht nur steht hier aber Glaube gegen Glauben, sondern auch, dem Worte Rosenzweigs gemäß, Wissen gegen Glauben. Das Wissen hat die Form eines Anspruchs auf Gültigkeit auch und gerade für den Gegner; es ist also eine Art Annahme die ihrer Sache noch mehr gewiß ist als der Glaube; die auch vermeint für diese Sache gute Gründe beibringen und den Gegner davon überzeugen zu können, daß dieser mit seiner Annahme unrecht hat. Das Wissen beansprucht also, die Annahme des Gegners als bloßen Glauben entlarven zu können. Beiderseits wird in der Differenz, der unser Symposium gewidmet ist, ein solches Wissen geltend gemacht.

---

1. F. Rosenzweig, *Der Stern der Erlösung* (Nijhoff Den Haag 1976), S. 108.

Beiderseits tritt man mit dem Anspruch auf den Gegner aufklären zu können und zu sollen. Die Mehrzahl von Aufklärungen, von der Rosenzweig redet, ist in diesem Fall also auf einen Zeitpunkt zusammengedrängt. Zugleich wird behauptet, einerseits etwa, daß der Aufklärung, auf die wir in der Moderne nicht verzichten können, das apokalyptische Genre entspricht, das im Stile der Offenbarung Johannis die falschen Apostel, die Lügner, "die sich Apostel nennen und es nicht sind"[2], denunziert, und andererseits, daß Aufklärung unlöslich an jenen "Fallibilismus, Universalismus und Subjektivismus" gebunden ist, deren Syndrom den normativen Gehalt der Moderne darstellt.[3] Es ist daher nicht übertrieben, das Verständnis der Aufklärung als Einsatz der Differenz zu betrachten. Das will ich im Folgenden auch versuchen.

Gibt es einen Ausgleich dieser Differenz? Läßt sich ein Schnittpunkt der strittigen Konzeptionen von Aufklärung ermitteln? Man soll über die Möglichkeit eines Ausgleichs m.E. nicht zu optimistisch urteilen. Ich neige zu der Ansicht, daß die beiden Ideen von Aufklärung sich nur im Unendlichen schneiden. Diese Ansicht will ich dem Folgenden als Vermutung zugrundelegen. Eine davon ausgehende Untersuchung ist von vornherein aussichtslos, es sei denn, daß die beiden Ideen von Aufklärung von sich her auf Unendlichkeit verweisen und ohne sie nicht angemessen verstanden werden können. Dann bestünde die Möglichkeit, daß dieser Schnittpunkt im Unendlichen doch so etwas wie einen gemeinsamen Nenner hergäbe. Ich werde die These verteidigen, daß bei beiden Denkern in der Tat eine Idee von Unendlichkeit im Spiele ist. Indessen ist sofort zu betonen, daß es mehrere Ideen von Unendlichkeit gibt und daß es keineswegs sicher ist, daß die beiden einschlägigen Ideen miteinander im Einklang sind.

Ich möchte nun so verfahren, daß ich in den zwei ersten Hauptteilen meiner Betrachtung Habermas und Derrida nacheinander auf ihr Verständnis von Aufklärung hin befrage und zwar so, daß der darin implizierte Hinweis auf das Unendliche herausgeschält werden kann. Ich möchte dabei auch einige Positionen in der Kontroverse zu Worte kommen lassen und überdies hin und wieder auf Textbeispiele Bezug nehmen; deshalb will ich das Thema Aufklä-

2. J. Derrida, "d'un ton apocalyptique adopté naguère en philosophie", in Ph. Lacoue-Labarthe & J.L. Nancy (Hrg.), *Les fins de l'homme. A partir du travail de Jacques Derrida* (Galilée Paris 1980), p. 445-479, hier S. 470.
3. J. Habermas, *Der philosophische Diskurs der Moderne. Zwölf Vorlesungen* (Suhrkamp Frankfurt 1985), S. 424.

rung nicht frontal, sondern vielmehr lateral angehen. In dem dritten Hauptteil werde ich die beiderseits implizierten Ideen von Unendlichkeit dann miteinander konfrontieren und erwägen, ob sie auf dasselbe hinauslaufen. Um dem Ergebnis gleich vorwegzunehmen: es wird negativ bzw. skeptisch ausfallen. Ich werde zu dem Schluß kommen, daß Habermas und Derrida kein positiver Begriff von Unendlichkeit gemeinsam ist, sondern nur die schlechte Unendlichkeit des Wechselspiels. Das gilt dann auch für ihre Begriffe von Aufklärung.

II) *Unendliches als Kraft des Kontrafaktischen*

In der einzigen mir bekannten Äußerung Derridas über Habermas wird die Riposte auf das Theorema von dem performativen Widerspruch gerichtet. Dieses hat bekanntlich die Funktion, den Ausweg eines konsequenten und unbegrenzten Wahrheitsrelativismus abzuschneiden, ohne sich seinerseits auf metaphysische Voraussetzungen, die ja selber fragwürdig geworden sind, stützen zu müssen. Ein solcher Widerspruch liegt vor, "wenn eine konstative Sprechhandlung 'Kp' auf nicht-kontingenten Voraussetzungen beruht, deren propositionaler Gehalt der behaupteten Aussage 'p' widerspricht." Wenn Einer etwa gegen das cartesianische "cogito ergo sum" Einspruch erheben möchte in der Form der Sprechhandlung "Ich bezweifle hiermit, daß ich existiere", so affirmiert er, indem er sie äußert, was er verneinen will.[4] Das Theorema wird von Habermas an vielen Stellen benutzt und erläutert; die hiesige Belegstelle ist willkürlich gewählt, aber für unser Thema nicht ohne Belang. Denn in seinen Vorlesungen über den philosophischen Diskurs der Moderne macht Habermas die Überwindung des von Descartes ausgegangenen subjektphilosophischen Paradigmas zum entscheidenden Problem und kritisiert er manche seiner Gegner dahingehend, daß sie trotz des gegenteiligen Scheines sich diesem Paradigma nicht entwunden hätten. Diese Kritik wird auch gegen Derrida vorgebracht, genauer gegen die von ihm entwickelte "dekonstruktivistische Auflösung des performativen Widerspruchs einer selbstreferentiellen Vernunftkritik"[5]. Darauf erwidert Derrida an der besagten Stelle, daß er glaubt gezeigt zu haben "pourquoi un performatif n'est jamais pur". Eine Performative läuft niemals richtig oder,

---

4. J. Habermas, *Moralbewusstsein und kommunikatives Handeln* (Suhrkamp Frankfurt 1983), S. 90.
5. J. Habermas, *Der philosophische Diskurs*, S. 197, 227.

anders gesagt, sie kann gar nicht auf etwas anderes hinauslaufen als auf einen Widerspruch. Einen bestimmten Widerspruch wohlgemerkt, und die Fragen, auf die es dann in Wahrheit ankommt, sind: "Welcher Widerspruch? Wie? In welchem Fall?" (Laquelle? Comment? Dans quel cas?) Nur wenn solchen Fragen nicht ausgewichen wird, kann den jeweils bestimmten Regeln und Formen Rechnung getragen werden denen eine zu kritisierende oder gar zu dekonstruierende Rationalität untersteht. Daraus ergibt sich unter anderem die Konsequenz, daß es weder Kritik, noch Diskussion, noch Kommunikation, noch Erkenntnisfortschritt, noch Vernunftgeschichte gäbe ohne diesen performativen Widerspruch. Ihn in aller Förmlichkeit und lautstark anzuzeigen genügt nicht um ihm zu entgehen. Die rein formale Anzeige ist ohne Zweifel die unfruchtbarste Wiederholung oder Bestätigung des besagten Widerspruchs.[6]

Auch wenn man dieser Konsequenz nicht ohne weiteres zustimmt, wird man, wie mir scheint, zugeben müssen, daß hier die formale Pragmatik der Habermasschen Theorie des kommunikativen Handelns kräftig herausgefordert worden ist. Blicken wir etwas näher auf die Art und Weise hin in der Habermas sich einer solchen Herausforderung zur Wehr stellt. Aufschlußreich ist dafür die Auseinandersetzung mit Derrida's Erwiderung an Searle in dem einschlägigen Kapitel seines Buches über den philosophischen Diskurs der Moderne. Sie läßt sich als eine Zusammenfassung und praktische Anwendung seines Verständnisses von Aufklärung lesen. Ein pikanter Umstand ist, daß Habermas sich bei dieser Auseinandersetzung weitgehend auf die von Jonathan Culler in dem Buch *On Deconstruction* dargebotenen Rekonstruktion der Derridaschen Erwiderung stützt und so die bestrittenen Ideen über Zitationalität und Iterabilität indirekt zu bestätigen scheint. Aber das nur nebenbei. Das erste Argument Cullers bezieht sich auf die Konventionalität gewisser Verfahrensweisen bzw. die Iterabilität gewisser Formeln. "For me to be able to make a promise in real life, there must be iterable procedures or formulas such as are used on stage." Daraus ergibt sich als Schlußfolgerung: "Serious behavior is a case of roleplaying." Habermas hält dem entgegen, daß hier vorausgesetzt wird was noch erst bewiesen werden sollte, nämlich daß sich Spielkonventionen von den Handlungsnormen, die mit der Alltagssprache einhergehen, letztlich nicht unterscheiden lassen. Diese Unterschei-

6. J. Derrida, *Mémoires pour Paul de Man* (Galilée Paris 1988), S. 226.

dung ist aber möglich mit Hilfe gewisser idealisierender Unterstellungen. Um diese handelt es sich im zweiten Argument Cullers. Der Forderung, allgemeine Kontextbedingungen für den Erfolg von Sprechhandlungen zu spezifizieren, ist faktisch nie Genüge geleistet: zu irgendeinem standardisierten Sprechakt wie etwa dem Heiratsgelübde können immer neue Kontexte hinzugedacht werden; die fragliche Spezifizierung stößt an keine natürlichen Grenzen. Habermas antwortet, daß das zwar stimmt: noch so gut analysierte Satzbedeutungen gelten nur relativ auf ein Hintergrundwissen das von den Kommunikationsteilnehmern stillschweigend ergänzt wird. Daraus folgt aber keineswegs der Bedeutungsrelativismus auf den Derrida in Habermas' Augen hinauswill. Denn "solange Sprachspiele funktionieren und das lebensweltkonstitutive Vorverständnis nicht zusammenbricht, rechnen die Beteiligten offenbar zu Recht mit den Weltzuständen, die in ihrer Sprachgemeinschaft als normal unterstellt werden." Diese Aussage mutet wie ein schroffer Positivismus an; Habermas distanziert sich jedoch ausdrücklich von dem Sprachspielpositivismus; was er gegen Derrida ins Feld führen möchte, ist die unumgängliche Bezugnahme auf die Idee eines möglichen Einverständnisses, bzw. die Idee, daß sich Fehlinterpretationen anhand eines idealerweise zu erzielenden Einverständnisses grundsätzlich müßten kritisieren lassen.

Habermas' Entgegnung umfaßt noch zwei weitere Abschnitte in denen er sich auf den fiktionalen Sprachgebrauch konzentriert. Auch hier ist das Augenmerk den Unterschied vom normalen, alltäglichen Sprachgebrauch aufrechtzuerhalten und das Trennungsmerkmal wird wiederum gefunden in der handlungskoordinierenden Kraft der illokutionären Akte. Diese Bindungskraft kann zwar gebrochen oder partiell aufgehoben werden, wenn sich die fiktionale Sprachfunktion einmischt; letztere hat aber gegenüber den expressiven, regulativen und informativen Sprachfunktionen keine Selbständigkeit. Wichtig an diesen Ausführungen ist für unseren Zusammenhang der Gedanke, daß sich das Vermögen zur Handlungskoordination durch ein "Negationspotential" auszeichnet. Gemeint ist die Problemlösungskapazität der Sprache, die - so der Vorwurf von Habermas - von Derrida und auch Rorty vernachlässigt wird zugunsten ihrer fiktionalen, welterschließenden Kapazität. Daß dem Problemlösungsvermögen der innerweltlichen Sprachpraxis tatsächlich "Negationskraft" zukomme, wird von Habermas begründet mit dem Hinweis auf "Geltungsansprüche, die über die Horizonte des jeweils bestehenden Kontextes hinauszielen" und so hält er Derrida und Rorty "die faktische Kraft des

Kontrafaktischen" vor, "die sich in den idealisierenden Voraussetzungen kommunikativen Handelns zur Geltung bringt."[7]

Was haben wir hier gehört? Von idealisierenden Voraussetzungen war hin und wieder die Rede. Ohne diese kann das reale kommunikative Handeln weder stattfinden noch verstanden werden. Es handelt sich also um Voraussetzungen, die nicht nur auf der Teilnehmerebene sondern auch auf der Beobachterebene in Anschlag zu bringen sind. Auch die Theorie des kommunikativen Handelns kann nicht umhin, idealisierende Voraussetzungen gelten zu lassen. Habermas macht daraus freilich kein Hehl. Sein Konzept der idealen Sprechsituation, in dem ja alle diese Voraussetzungen aufgenommen und neutralisiert sind, bringt das auch terminologisch ganz offen zum Ausdruck. In seinem Interview mit der New Left Review nennt er diesen Terminus sogar "etwas zu konkretistisch". Was ist mit diesem Zugeständnis aber gesagt? Der Kontext dieser Äußerung ist die Antwort auf die von dem Interviewer gestellte Frage: "Inwieweit ist der Begriff der idealen Sprechsituation als regulatives Prinzip von Wahrheit zirkulär?", wobei folgende Erläuterung gegeben wurde: "Wenn Wahrheit als jener Konsens definiert wird, der von den Sprechern in einer idealen Sprechsituation hergestellt würde – wie kann das Vorliegen einer solchen Situation selbst jemals wahrheitsgemäß festgestellt werden? (...) Unterliegt dieser Gedanke nicht derselben Kritik, die Hegel an Kants Erkenntnistheorie vorgebracht hat (...), nämlich des 'Apriori des Erkennens vor der Erkenntnis'?"[8] Ich halte das für eine sehr treffende Frage. Sie bringt zutage, daß der Begriff der idealen Sprechsituation einem Dilemma untersteht, welches beinhaltet, daß die Wahrheit der Konsenswahrheit entweder bloß ideal ist in dem Sinne, daß sie in keiner realen Sprechsituation erfüllt wird, sondern vielmehr allen realen Sprechsituationen gleichsam zugrundeliegt, oder bloß situationell ist in dem Sinne, daß sie idealisierende Voraussetzungen weder benötigt noch gestattet.

Wichtig ist nun, daß man von diesem Dilemma so oder so ins Unendliche gestoßen wird. Das zweite Horn stieße in eine Unendlichkeit, die, wenn ich richtig sehe, in etwa dem Denken Derridas entspräche: in der konkreten Gesprächsituation könnte die konsensuelle Wahrheit als konsensuelle Wahrheit nie festgestellt werden; diese Feststellung müßte wegen der Iterabilität aller der von uns in kommunikativen Akten befolgten Prozeduren und Formeln immer

7. J. Habermas, *Der philosophische Diskurs*, S. 224 ff., bes. 242.
8. J. Habermas, *Die neue Unübersichtlichkeit* (Suhrkamp 1985), S. 228 f.

291

wieder verschoben, vertagt werden. Immer wieder müßte den aktuellen oder auch bloß potentiellen, aber immerhin bestimmten Differenzen, die sich hier auftun, Rechnung getragen werden. Doch das gehört vielmehr schon zum zweiten Hauptteil unserer Betrachtung.

Habermas läßt keinen Zweifel darüber bestehen, daß er dieses Horn vermeiden will. Wenn unsere Sichtweise stimmt und hier tatsächlich ein Dilemma vorliegt, so bleibt ihm nur das erste Horn, besser gesagt: das Unendliche in das man von diesem Horn gestoßen wird, übrig. Ich kann mich nicht entsinnen, daß Habermas selbst ausführlich von dem Unendlichen redet. Wir müßten es als ein Verborgenes oder Impliziertes aus seiner Begrifflichkeit hervorholen. Welche Begriffe könnten sich dazu eignen? Ich denke etwa an Begriffe wie Utopie, Transzendenz und besonders Kraft des Kontrafaktischen. Zu allen diesen ein kurzer Hinweis. Was den zuerst genannten betrifft, erinnere ich an eine andere Stelle in dem Gespräch für das *New Left Review*. Da hebt der Interviewer die Veränderung hervor, die sich in Habermas' Behauptungen über die ideale Sprechsituation in dem letzten Jahrzehnt vollzogen hat und die er folgendermaßen formuliert: "In der *Theorie des kommunikativen Handelns* gestehen Sie den utopischen Charakter des Projekts einer idealen Kommunikationsgemeinschaft ein und weisen darauf hin, daß die prozedurale Rationalität argumentativer Begründung nicht als solche Inhalt einer Lebensform sein kann."[9] Habermas stimmt dieser Vorstellung der Tatsachen zu; nur nimmt er, wenn ich richtig sehe, gerade das Schlüsselwort "Utopie" in einem anderen Sinn als der Interviewer. Dieser meinte es, wenn ich mich nicht irre, im Sinne Adornos; in seiner Antwort zitiert Habermas eine eigene englischsprachige Äußerung in der er den Anspruch der Utopie auf Transparenz voraussetzt: "Nothing makes me more nervous than the imputation that because the theory of communicative action focusses attention on the social facticity of recognized validity claims, it proposes, or at least suggests, a rationalist utopian society. I do not regard the fully transparent society as an ideal, nor do I wish to suggest any other ideal - Marx was not the only one frightened by the vestiges of utopian socialism." Ich würde sagen: in dem Maße, worin auf völlige Transparenz verzichtet wird, erhält der Utopiebegriff Unendlichkeitsgehalt in dem hier relevanten Sinne.

Was das Wort "Transzendenz" betrifft, dessen Auftauchen m.W.

9. J. Habermas, *Die neue Unübersichtlichkeit*, S. 240.

ebenfalls eine Neuerung aus dem letzten Jahrzehnt darstellt, hier könnte vor allem auf zwei Arbeiten in dem dieses Jahr erschienenen Aufsatzband *Texte und Kontexte* hingewiesen werden. In dem einen dieser Beiträge hält Habermas der von Horkheimer vollzogenen Gleichsetzung der formalistischen Vernunft mit der instrumentellen die von Peirce durchgeführte sprachpragmatische Wendung dieses Formalismus entgegen und bemerkt dann: "Er [Peirce] begreift Wahrheit als die Einlösbarkeit eines Wahrheitsanspruchs unter den Kommunikationsbedingungen einer idealen (...) Gemeinschaft von Interpreten. Die kontrafaktische Buzugnahme auf eine solche unbegrenzte Kommunikationsgemeinschaft ersetzt das Ewigkeitsmoment oder den überzeitlichen Charakter von »Unbedingtheit« durch die Idee eines offenen, aber zielgerichteten Interpretationsprozesses, der die Grenzen des sozialen Raumes und der historischen Zeit *von innen*, aus der Perspektive einer *in der Welt* verorteten Existenz heraus transzendiert." Und eine Seite weiter: "Wer sich einer Sprache verständigungsorientiert bedient, ist einer Transzendenz von innen ausgesetzt. Darüber kann er so wenig verfügen, wie er sich durch die Intentionalität des gesprochenen Wortes zum Herrn der Struktur der Sprache macht." Am Ende dieses Gedankenganges und vor allem in dem zweiten Text, eine Replik auf Beiträge zu einer 1988 von der Theologischen Fakultät der Universität Chicago veranstalteten Konferenz, wird diese Transzendenz von innen nachdrücklich von religiöser Transzendenz unterschieden. Die Erfahrungen, die in der Religion zu Worte kommen - namentlich die Erfahrung des Trostes -, sind nur in *ihrer* Sprache, zugänglich und das ist *nicht* die Sprache der Philosophie bzw. der kommunikativen Vernunft. Philosophie in ihrer nachmetaphysischen Gestalt wird Religion weder ersetzen noch verdrängen können; zugleich aber gilt, daß sie sich der religiösen Annahme eines göttlichen Heilsversprechens enthält. "Es gehört", so behauptet er gegen Horkheimer, "zur Würde der Philosophie, unnachgiebig darauf zu beharren, daß kein Geltungsanspruch kognitiv Bestand haben kann, der nicht vor dem Forum der begründenden Rede gerechtfertigt ist."[10] Es erübrigt sich darzutun, daß dieser Begriff der Transzendenz, wie religionsrein auch immer, ohne Bezugnahme auf Unendliches nicht gedacht werden kann.

Schließlich der Ausdruck "Kraft des Kontrafaktischen". Er scheint mir in dieser Hinsicht am bedeutungsträchtigsten zu sein;

---

10. J. Habermas, *Texte und Kontexte* (Surhkamp Frankfurt 1991), S. 124f., 142f.

deshalb habe ich ihn als Titel dieses Abschnittes gewählt. Die Fundstelle wurde bereits angeführt: in den idealisierenden Voraussetzungen kommunikativen Handelns bringe sich "die faktische Kraft des Kontrafaktischen" zur Geltung und diese verschaffe das "Negationspotential" mittels dessen die Bewährung kommunikativer Sprache möglich ist. Hier wird dem Unendlichen, das ja unabdinglich im Begriff des Kontrafaktischen impliziert ist, eine Kraft beigelegt. Das Unendliche ist nicht nur eine Offenheit, wie etwa beim Utopiebegriff; auch nicht nur die sich in dieser Offenheit einzeichnende Möglichkeit einer unaufhörlichen und unverfügbaren Bewegung, wie etwa beim Begriff der Transzendenz; das Unendliche ist hier fast gedacht als etwas Wirkliches. Eine Kraft ist ja etwas Wirkliches. Habermas ist ein nachmetaphysischer Philosoph; wir sollen diesen Ausdruck nicht so auslegen wollen, alsob er das letzten Endes verleugnete. Aber Beachtung verdient die Rede von der Kraft des Kontrafaktischen immerhin. Sie nötigt uns zu erneuter Betrachtung. Wir werden im letzten Abschnitt auf sie zurückkommen müssen.

III) *Unendlichkeit im Riß des Geistes*

Fragen wir jetzt nach der Idee der Aufklärung bei Derrida. Ich möchte diese Aufgabe so in Angriff nehmen, daß ich ein Textbeispiel nehme anhand dessen diese Idee sich erläutern läßt. Dieses Verfahren scheint mir dem Stile dieses Denkens besser zu entsprechen. Nach all dem bereits Ausgeführten können wir uns über Derrida etwas kürzer fassen. Ich wähle das Beispiel aus dem 1987 erschienenen Buch *De l'esprit*, ist ja beim Problem der Aufklärung die Frage nach dem Geist eine der Hauptfragen. Das gilt nicht nur im Allgemeinen, sondern gerade auch für den Fall der uns in diesem Symposium beschäftigt. Es ist nicht ungewöhnlich Derrida als den Philosophen der Schrift zu charakterisieren und seinen Streit mit Habermas auf die Formel "Buchstabe wider Geist" zu bringen. Diese Formel könnte auch der Differenz über die Aufklärung unterstellt werden. Ich erlaube mir auf einen Satz hinzuweisen, den Hent de Vries in seiner bahnbrechenden und auch für dieses Kolloquium grundlegenden Doktorarbeit schrieb: "Aber im Ernst: es dürfte weniger fruchtbar sein, den *Geist* der *Dialektik der Aufklärung* zu explizieren wie es Habermas (mutatis mutandis) tun möchte, aber weder tut noch kann, als dem *Buchstaben* des Textes zu folgen, wie es Derrida keineswegs tun möchte, aber dennoch (mutatis mutandis) tut und auch kann."[11] Auf das Werturteil, das hier ausgesprochen wird, kommt es jetzt nicht an; nur darauf, daß Derrida sich offenbar mit einer solchen Dichotomie nicht mehr abfindet. Das Buch trägt den Untertitel *Heidegger et la question*; man darf das wohl auch so verstehen, daß die Frage nach dem Geist von Derrida keineswegs direkt und sozusagen auf eigene Rechnung in Angriff genommen wird; vielmehr wird mit der Wahl dieses Themas auch auf eine Heideggerkritik abgezielt; aber die Frage wird als solche nicht mehr abgelehnt.

Ich möchte mich bei dem Textbeispiel auf die letzten Seiten des Buches *De l'esprit* beschränken. Es ist auf diesen Seiten von dem "trait" die Rede und zwar von dem "dernier trait, le trait luimême". Es könnte hilfreich sein, das was ich darüber ausführen möchte, vorweg gleichsam bildlich darzustellen, indem ich das Ergebnis einer kleinen Recherche mitteile. In diesem Buch spielt das Thema des Übersetzens fast mehr als je die Schlüsselrolle; das hier zu Sagende scheint in das sprachliche Dreieck pneuma-spiritus-Geist, das sich übrigens nur durch Ausschluß des Hebräischen 'Ruach' als eine geschlossene Figur behaupten kann, eingefangen zu sein und in ihm wie ein seinsgeschichtlicher Strom herumzufließen. Das Fragen, das die Frömmigkeit des Denkens ist, artikuliert sich denn auch in der immer neu anhebenden Bemühung um das Übersetzen, Rückübersetzen, Berichtigen bestehender Übersetzungen usw. Kann man Besseres tun als sich gleich eingangs in die Bewegung dieses Fragens einzufügen? Ich habe in einem etwas älteren, alle Bedeutungsunterschiede möglichst präzise aufgliedernden französisch-niederländischen Wörterbuch nachgeschaut, wie das Wort "trait" übersetzt werden könnte und fand zu meiner Überraschung eine so große Fülle an Möglichkeiten, daß ich leichten Herzens davon austeilen kann. Ich nenne in Rückübersetzung ins Deutsche 21 Bedeutungen: 1) Das Ziehen, der Ruck; 2) Der Ausschlag (wie bei einer Balkenwaage); 3) Das Fortziehen (wie bei einem Zugpferd); 4) Die Vorlage (wie beim Fußballspiel); 5) Das Zugband oder der Bindfaden; 6) Der Schuß; 7) Der Pfeil oder der Wurfspieß; 8) Die Gehässigkeit oder Bösartigkeit; 9) Der Schluck oder der Schuß einer Flüssigkeit; 10) Der Strich wie beim Zeichnen; 11) Der Pinselstrich; 12) Das Anlaufen oder Schwitzen oder mit Schimmel bedeckt werden wie etwa bei Steinen oder beim Holz; 13) Der Gesichtszug; 14) Der Streich den Einer einem Anderen spielt;

11. H. de Vries, *Theologie im pianissimo & Zwischen Rationalität und Dekonstruktion. Die Aktualität der Denkfiguren Adornos und Levinas'* (Studies in Philosophical Theology 1, Kok Kampen 1989), S. 105.

15) Die Begebenheit, das Ereignis; 16) Der Einfall, der Geistes-
blitz; 17) Der Lauf wie beim Klavierspiel; 18) Der Bezug; "avoir
trait à": sich beziehen auf; 19) Der Mumm oder der Schwung; 20)
Der Sägeschnitt; 21) Die Mittelsperson, der "trait-d'union".[12] Auf-
fallend und auch belustigend ist, daß in dieser großen Bedeutungs-
fülle der von Derrida gemeinte Sinn nicht einmal enthalten ist: bei
ihm soll dem französischen "trait" das deutsche Wort "Riß" entsprechen. Man könnte einwenden, daß diese Bedeutung doch vertreten ist und zwar in der an vorletzter Stelle aufgelisteten: - Sägeschnitt. Im Folgenden wird aber klar, daß dem nicht so ist. Gemeint
wird der Riß, der die Spur der Differenz zieht; Derrida betont im
Folgenden, daß dieser Riß zwar Schmerzen bewirkt, aber keine
Teilung. Der Geist - nach ihm wird ja gefragt, und zwar mittels
einer Lektüre der Heideggerschen Auslegung eines Gedichtes von
Georg Trakl - ist vielmehr das Versammelnde. "Der Geist und als
dieser das Versammelnde", liest Derrida bei Heidegger und er
bemerkt ausdrücklich, daß das Wort 'Versammlung' die ganze Betrachtung durchzieht, beherrscht und überdeterminiert (traverse,
domine et surdétermine). Auf den letzten Seiten deutet er zwei
Denkwege an, auf denen wir die Wege, die Heidegger bei seiner
Suche nach dem Geist gegangen ist, kreuzen könnten. Es wird ein
Zwiegespräch imaginiert, in dem "uns" - "un *nous* qui peut-être
n'est pas *donné*" - die Rolle der Anfragenden zuerteilt wird und
Heidegger die Rolle des Antwortenden. Es kommt mir besonders
auf diese Antworten an; sie sind von Derrida so vorzüglich imaginiert, daß Heideggers Stimme und seine eigene - man möchte fast
sagen ineins versammelt sind; man kann sie jedenfalls noch kaum
auseinanderhalten. Ich zitiere etwas ausführlicher aus diesen Hei-
degger-Derridaschen Reden: "Mit der Behauptung, daß das Ge-
dicht von Trakl (...) weder metaphysisch noch christlich ist, sträube
ich mich nicht gegen etwas, und schon gar nicht gegen das Christen-
tum mit seiner Rede von Sündenfall, Verdammung, Verheißung,
Heil, Auferstehung, und auch nicht gegen die Rede von pneuma
und spiritus, sogar nicht, ich hatte es vergessen, von Ruach. Ich
versuche nur, bescheiden und verschwiegen, das zu denken, von
dem her (à partir de quoi) all das möglich ist. Dieses "von dem her"
ist noch nicht das was es ermöglicht. Es ist noch nicht denkbar; es
bleibt noch aus. (...) Ich habe nicht gesagt, daß die Flamme [des
Geistes] etwas anderes ist als der pneumatologische oder geistliche

---

12. Vgl. K.R. Gallas, *Nieuw Frans-Nederlands Nederlands-Frans Woordenboek*
(Thieme Zutphen o.J.), s.v. 'trait'.

Atem; ich habe gesagt, daß man erst von dieser Flamme her pneuma oder spiritus oder - da Sie darauf bestehen - Ruach denkt. Ich habe einfach gesagt: der Geist ist nicht zuerst dies oder das oder jenes." Diese imaginierte Antwort ist ein Schulbeispiel für den Schritt zurück, für die "retraite" (auf französisch), die offenbar auch ein "retrait", "re-trait", heißen kann.

Wollte man nun einwenden, daß auf diese Weise nichts mehr gedacht wird als nur das was da ist, wollte man m.a.W. den Vorwurf machen, die hier versuchte denkende Wiederholung füge nichts Neues hinzu, erfinde oder entdecke nichts, dann wäre - so die imaginierte zweite Antwort - Folgendes zu sagen: "In dem was Sie den Weg der Wiederholung nennen (...) geht das Denken, eben indem es sich auf die Möglichkeit hin bewegt die Sie zu erkennen meinen, auf das hin was ganz anders ist als was Sie zu erkennen meinen. Das ist in der Tat kein neuer Inhalt. Aber der Zugang zum Denken, der denkende Zugang zu der Möglichkeit aller pneumato-spirituellen Metaphysiken oder Religionen eröffnet etwas ganz anderes als was die Möglichkeit ermöglicht. Er eröffnet (ouvre sur) das was dem Ursprung heterogen bleibt. Was Sie vorstellen als eine schlichte ontologische und transzendentale Replik, ist ganz anders. Darum folge ich, ohne mich gegen das zu sträuben dessen früheste Möglichkeit ich zu denken versuche, ohne mich sogar anderer Worte als der der Tradition zu bedienen, dem Weg einer Wiederholung der den Weg des ganz Anderen kreuzt. Das ganz Andere macht sich kenntlich in der rigorosesten Wiederholung. Diese ist auch die schwindelerregendste und abgründlichste."

Der Text geht noch weiter; das allerletzte Wort in dieser Zwiesprache hat nicht Heidegger, sondern haben seine Gesprächspartner, also wir ("un nous qui peut-être n'est pas donné"). Wir könnten Heidegger entgegnen: "Ja, das alles ist eben genau was wir sagen. (...) Es ist die Wahrheit dessen was wir immer gesagt haben, haben sagen hören und versucht haben vernehmen zu lassen. Das Mißverständnis liegt darin, daß Sie uns besser verstehen als Sie glauben oder zu glauben vorgeben. Jedenfalls soll es von uns aus inskünftig kein Mißverständnis mehr geben; es genügt fortzufahren zu reden und die Zwiesprache zwischen dem Dichter und Ihnen, und also auch zwischen Ihnen und uns nicht zu unterbrechen. Il suffit de ne pas interrompre le colloque, même quand il est déjà très tard."[13]

So weit das Textbeispiel. Man möchte vielleicht zuerst fragen

13. J. Derrida, *De l'esprit. Heidegger et la question* (Galilée Paris 1987), S. 161-184, bes. 181ff.

wollen, ob sich hier überhaupt noch eine Idee von Aufklärung spürbar macht. Diese Frage ist m.E. entschieden zu bejahen. Wenn ich mich der Terme des Textbeispiels bedienen darf: Aufklärung besteht eben in diesem Riß des Geistes. Geist ist dann sozusagen das "Prinzip" der Aufklärung. Das Wort "Prinzip" ist zwar schief, aber doch brauchbar für den negativen Zweck, zum Ausdruck zu bringen, daß Aufklärung nicht selbst Prinzip ist. Wenn sie - was in etwa die übliche Auffassung von "Aufklärung" besagt - die Erleuchtung ist, dank derer sich die Wahrheit zeigt, so soll bedacht werden, daß sie etwas voraussetzt, das erleuchtet, das Licht gibt (wie man auf holländisch gut sagen kann). Was gibt Licht? Etwa die Flamme. Die Flamme ist deshalb ein gutes Beispiel, da man sich an ihr klar machen kann, daß das Licht-Gebende von etwas zehrt. Licht, auch das Licht der Wahrheit, gibt es nur um den Preis der Verbrennung und Einäscherung. Geist nun ist wie eine Flamme. In den vorhergehenden Kapiteln des Buches *De l'esprit* wird lange bei dieser Metapher verweilt; Derrida übernimmt sie von Heidegger und Trakl. Er zitiert den ersteren: "Doch was ist der Geist? Trakl spricht in seiner letzten Dichtung 'Grodek' von der 'heißen Flamme des Geistes'. Der Geist ist das Flammende..."[14] Das alles färbt sich nun ab auf die Klarheit, die gewöhnlich mit "Aufklärung" assoziiert wird. Von ihr ist bei Derrida allerdings auch die Rede, wenn auch ziemlich selten; es wird dann aber immer wieder zu bedenken gegeben, daß die Klarheit im Riß des Geistes eine verzehrende ist. So äußert er am Ende des ersten Kapitels die Vermutung, was uns dem Knoten der Fäden des Ungedachten näher bringen könnte, wäre "mehr Klarheit, vielleicht die doppeldeutige Klarheit der Flamme (plus de clarté, peut-être la clarté ambiguë de la flamme)".[15]

Ein anderes Bedeutungsmoment der fraglichen Idee von Aufklärung könnte man m.E. in dem Anspruch ausgedrückt finden, daß im Riß des Geistes das Mißverständnis behoben wird. Im Ereignis dieses Risses leuchtet die Wahrheit nicht nur bloß in sich auf, sondern als verständliche, als gemeinverständliche. Es soll also dank dieses Ereignisses auch möglich sein, sich zu verständigen und den gemeinsamen Befund von dem je eigenen Glauben abzuheben. (Ich beziehe mich hier auf den angeführten Satz: "le malentendu, c'est que vous nous entendez mieux que vous ne croyez ou que vous n'affectez de croire.") Zugleich wird spätestens an diesem Bedeu-

14. M. Heidegger, *Unterwegs zur Sprache* (Neske Pfullingen 1959), S. 59; zit. *De l'esprit*, S. 132.
15. J. Derrida, *De l'esprit*, S. 30.

tungsmoment deutlich, wie diese Idee der Aufklärung ins Unendliche stößt. Das Beheben des Mißverständnisses ist nicht Sache eines regelgeleiteten Eingriffes, sondern im Gegenteil des unbehinderten Geschehen-lassens. Die Zwiesprache, als der Ort dieses Geschehnisses, soll nicht eingegrenzt werden. Das genügt, sagt Derrida. Das, also das ununterbrochene, unendliche Gespräch, ist die hinreichende Bedingung der Wahrheit als solcher und als gemeinverständlicher.

Bei Derrida ist vom Unendlichen nicht nur implizit, sondern auch explizit die Rede. In der expliziten Bezeichnung sind mehrere Bedeutungsschattierungen zu erkennen. Ich werde nicht versuchen sie vollständig aufzulisten; nur möchte ich auf zwei Aspekte besonders hinweisen. Der erste ist die emphatische Verschlingung des Unendlichen mit dem Endlichen. Das ist von Derrida schon in seinen frühesten Schriften betont worden und es wird in den neueren und neuesten wiederholt: "la différance infinie est finie."[16] Das trifft selbstverständlich auch auf den von uns betrachteten Riß des Geistes zu: dieser ist ja nichts anderes als ein neues Emblem der Differänz. Der zweite Aspekt ist der sozusagen moralische. Das Unendliche, mit dem wir es in der Zwiesprache, im Umgang mit allem Geschriebenen zu tun haben, hat den Charakter einer unendlichen Verpflichtung. Hier berührt sich Derrida sogar mit Kant. Natürlich kann das Gesetz, in casu das Sittengesetz, nicht in Eindeutigkeit erörtert werden: auch beim Gesetz, gerade beim Gesetz wäre der Eindeutigkeitswille fatal und kaum besser als ein Beweis des Unernstes. Ich zitiere ein paar Sätze aus dem Aufsatz 'Préjugés. Devant la loi' in dem Kant mit Freud und Kafka zusammen-gelesen wird: "Was auf immer verschoben wird, bis zum Tode, ist der Eintritt in das Gesetz selbst, das nichts anderes ist als das was den Aufschub erheischt. Das Gesetz verbietet indem es (...) die Beziehung, den Bezug hinauszieht. Der Ursprung der Differänz, das ist eben das, dem man sich nicht nähern, das man nicht vergegenwärtigen, nicht sich vorstellen und vor allem in das man nicht eintreten soll und kann. Das ist das Gesetz des Gesetzes, der Prozeß eines Gesetzes in Ansehung dessen man nie sagen kann: 'Da ist es' oder 'da'. (...) Im Grunde ist das eine Situation in der ein Prozeß oder ein

16. J. Derrida, *Le voix et le phénomène* (PUF Paris 1967), S. 114, zit. in J. Derrida, 'Comment ne pas parler' in *Psyché. Inventions de l'autre* (Galilée Paris 1987), S. 561.

Urteil nicht in Frage kommt. Kein Entscheid, kein Rechtsspruch und das ist umso fürchterlicher."[17]

IV) *Schnittpunkt Unendlichkeit?*

Der Titel dieses Abschnittes soll metaphorisch verstanden werden. Im buchstäblichen Sinne gilt von jedem Paar Geraden, soweit ich weiß, daß sie sich spätestens im Unendlichen schneiden. Die Möglichkeit des Sichnichtschneidens gibt es hier einfach nicht. Aber diese möglichkeit sollte in meiner Betrachtung nicht von vornherein ausgeschlossen werden. Das Unendliche sollte hier nur als Schnittpunkt der beiden strittigen Ideen von Aufklärung geltend gemacht werden können, wenn es homogen wäre, d.h. wenn nicht zu befürchten stünde, daß Unendlichkeit lediglich ein übertriebener Name für Verwirrung und Unbestimmtheit wäre. Dieser Gefahr vorzubeugen haben wir auf die beiderseits implizierten Unendlichkeitsideen Rücksicht genommen. Der Gedanke war, daß wenn diese gleichsam auf dasselbe hinausliefen, die Metapher vom Schnittpunkt im Unendlichen vielleicht akzeptiert werden könnte. Im Vorangehenden haben wir die fraglichen Ideen im Umriß entwickelt; jetzt kommt es darauf an, sie miteinander zu konfrontieren und zu sehen, ob sie wirklich zueinander passen.

Zu Beginn dieser Aufgabe soll dem eventuellen Schnittpunkt aber noch eine weitere Bedingung gestellt werden. Das fragliche Unendliche soll nicht nur homogen sein, sondern auch nicht-trivial. Es soll namentlich kein bloß privativer Begriff sein, keine bloße Verneinung des Endlichen. Die gesuchte Idee des Unendlichen soll als ein Positives gedacht werden können. Geht das?

Das Musterbeispiel eines solchen Denkens in der heutigen Zeit finde ich bei Emm. Lévinas. In seinem Aufsatz 'Dieu et la philosophie' gibt er dem Präfix 'in' des Wortes 'infini' eine doppelte Bedeutung: nicht nur 'nicht' sondern auch 'in'. Die Idee des Unendlichen ist, so sagt er mit Descartes, in mir als dem der sie denkt gelegt. Damit ist aber das Unendliche selbst in mir gelegt, denn diese Idee selbst kennzeichnet sich durch eine unendliche Differenz zwischen ihrer objektiven Realität und ihrer formalen Realität, d.h. zwischen dem cogitatum und der cogitatio. Diese Idee läßt das sie denkende Ich aus den Fugen geraten. Die gewöhnliche Haltung des Denkens als einer Erfassung, wenn nicht gar Erzeugung des intentionalen

---

17. J. Derrida, "Préjugés. Devant la loi", in *La faculté de juger* (Minuit Paris 1985), S. 87-139, hier: S. 122f.

Gegenstandes weicht einer Passivität, die das Subjekt des Denkens seiner Beherrschung und Selbstgegenwart entledigt. Auf diese Weise *wirkt* das Unendliche: es bewirkt mittels seiner Idee eine Umkehrung und Umprägung der Subjektivität. Aufschlußreich ist hier besonders die Fußnote in der Lévinas sich über jene doppelte Bedeutung des Präfixes 'in' ausbreitet. Die Idee des Unendlichen ist nach Descartes, so sagt er, eine wahre Idee und nicht nur etwas das ich auffasse durch die Verneinung des Endlichen. Die Verneinung kann demnach, so Lévinas, nicht aus der Subjektivität hervorgehen, sondern nur aus der Idee des Unendlichen selbst. Und dann fügt er hinzu: "oder, wenn man so will, aus der Subjektivität *als* Idee des Unendlichen."[18]

Nun gut, bei Descartes ist 'l'infini' ein Deckname für Gott und so ist es auch bei Lévinas. Das von uns hier gesuchte positiv Unendliche, das Unendliche als *Wirkliches*, wird von ihnen beiden in dem Gottesbegriff gefunden. Was heißt aber diese Idee des Unendlichen *denken*? Ist das eine bloß intellektuelle Operation? Müßte hier das Denken nicht, wenn nicht gleich so doch allmählich verwandelt werden? Ginge es nicht in etwas Anderes über, etwa danken oder Zeugnis ablegen? Vollendet sich also das Denken der Idee des Unendlichen als eines Wirklichen, als Gott, nicht erst in der Religion? Wären wir mithin nicht auf die Religion verwiesen, wenn wir den strittigen Ideen von Aufklärung einen Schnittpunkt im Unendlichen zuerkennen möchten? Religion allerdings so wenig in einem christlichen oder gar kirchlichen Sinne wie der als Idee des Unendlichen chiffrierte Gott ein Kirchengott oder ein exklusiv christlicher Gott ist.

Die Gestalt, die die uns beschäftigende Frage jetzt annimmt, ist somit: ob nicht die Differenz zwischen Habermas und Derrida über die Aufklärung in der Dimension der Religion zum Ausgleich gebracht werden könnte. Stellen wir den beiden Herren zuerst die Gretchenfrage. Ich möchte hier ausnahmsweise Einer, und zwar Habermas, für beide antworten lassen. Die Verwandtschaft Derridas mit der jüdischen Mystik ist in seinen Augen über jeden Zweifel erhaben. Am Ende des Derrida-Kapitels in seinem Buch über den philosophischen Diskurs der Moderne zieht Habermas eine Stelle bei G. Scholem heran, die von der Spekulation eines Rabbi Mendel von Rymanow über den hebräischen Konsonanten *Aleph* handelt. Dieser stellt nichts anderes dar als den laryngalen Stimmeinsatz, der

18. E. Lévinas, "Dieu et la philosophie", in *De dieu qui vient à l'idée* (Vrin Paris 1982), S. 104ff. Meine Hervorhebung.

einem Vokal am Anfang vorausgeht. Das *Aleph*, so Scholem, "stellt also gleichsam das Element dar, aus dem jeder artikulierte Laut stammt. (...) Das *Aleph* zu hören, ist eigentlich so gut wie nichts, es stellt den Übergang zu allen vernehmbaren Sprachen dar, und gewiß läßt sich nicht von ihm sagen, daß es in sich einen spezifischen Sinn vermittelt." Und nun Habermas dazu: "Das Aleph des Rabbi Mendel ist dem tonlosen, nur schriftlich diskriminierten »a« der »différance« darin verwandt, daß in der Unbestimmtheit dieses gebrechlichen und vieldeutigen Zeichens die ganze Fülle der Verheißung konzentriert ist. Derridas grammatologisch eingekreistes Konzept einer Urschrift, deren Spuren nur umso mehr Interpretationen hervorrufen, je unkenntlicher sie werden, erneuert den mystischen Begriff der Tradition als eines *hinhaltenden* Offenbarungsgeschehens. Die religiöse Autorität behält nur so lange ihre Kraft, wie sie ihr wahres Antlitz verhüllt und dadurch die Entzifferungswut der Interpreten anstachelt. Die inständig betriebene Dekonstruktion ist die paradoxe Arbeit einer Traditionsfortsetzung, in der sich die Heilsenergie einzig durch Verausgabung erneuert." Einige Zeilen weiter führt Habermas diese Sicht auf den jüdischen Monotheismus zurück und kennzeichnet diesen solcherart, daß für uns der Zusammenhang mit dem Thema der Aufklärung fast unüberhörbar wird. "Mystische Erfahrungen konnten in jüdischen und christlichen Überlieferungen ihre Sprengkraft (...) nur entfalten, weil sie (...) auf den einen, verborgenen, die Welt transzendierenden Gott bezogen blieben. Erleuchtungen, die von dieser konzentrierenden Lichtquelle abgeschnitten sind, werden eigentümlich diffus."[19]

Die Äußerung über sich selbst findet sich in einem Gespräch das Habermas 1981 mit A.Honneth, E.Knödler-Bunte und A.Widmann 1981 geführt hat. Über die Motive seiner Arbeit sagt er da: "Ich habe ein Gedankenmotiv und eine grundlegende Intuition. Diese geht übrigens auf religiöse Traditionen, etwa der protestantischen oder der jüdischen Mystiker zurück, auch auf Schelling. Der motivbildende Gedanke ist die Versöhnung der mit sich selbst zerfallenen Moderne, die Vorstellung also, daß man ohne Preisgabe der Differenzierungen, die die Moderne (...) möglich gemacht haben, Formen des Zusammenlebens findet, in der wirklich Autonomie und Abhängigkeit in ein befriedetes Verhältnis treten (...) Diese Intuition (...) zielt auf Erfahrungen einer unversehrten Intersubjek-

---

19. J. Habermas, *Der philosophische Diskurs*, S. 216.

tivität, fragiler als alles, was bisher die Geschichte an Kommunikationsstrukturen aus sich hervorgetrieben hat…"[20]

Nun, ist es nicht überdeutlich, daß Religion, näher: die jüdisch-christliche monotheistische Religion, die Dimension darstellt, in der der Schnittpunkt der strittigen Aufklärungskonzeptionen geortet werden kann? Vielleicht ist dem in der Tat so. Auf jeden Fall kann angesichts solcher eindrucksvollen Zitate kaum bezweifelt werden, daß die jüdisch-christliche religiöse Tradition eine gemeinsame Basis ist, zu der von beiden Seiten zurückzufinden ein verheißungsvolles Unternehmen sein könnte.

Aber wir sollen hier wiederum auf die Gefahr acht geben, daß wir durch unsere Metapher vom Schnittpunkt irregeführt werden. Kann ein gemeinsamer religiöser Hintergrund ohne Mystifikation als Schnittpunkt im Unendlichen gelten? Ich habe da ernstliche Zweifel. Man müßte wenigstens folgenden zwei Tatsachen Rechnung tragen: 1) Daß zumindest für einen der zwei Kontrahenten Religion eine Lebensform ist, der die Gestalt der Aufklärung, die dem normativen Gehalt der Moderne angemessen ist, bestenfalls fremd gegenübersteht. Von seinem nachmetaphysischen Standpunkt kann er anerkennen, daß Religion "nach wie vor unersetzlich für den normalisierenden Umgang mit dem Außeralltäglichen im Alltag"[21] ist, aber er selbst bleibt ihr entschieden fern und zwar gerade um der Aufklärung willen. Weil das Denken der Idee des Unendlichen in Religion einmündet, ist es für ihn kein gangbarer Weg. Oder vielleicht richtiger: ein Weg der nicht zu Ende gegangen werden soll. Die Verwandlung des Denkens *soll* nicht zugelassen werden. 2) Wenn wir uns noch mal an das eingangs angeführte Wort F.Rosenzweigs erinnern, dann ist klar, daß sich Aufklärung in dem Konflikt zwischen Glauben und Wissen auf die Seite des letzteren schlägt. Religion ist, in welcher Gestalt auch immer, für einen wesentlichen Teil Glaubenssache. Wie sollte man sich aber die Schlichtung eines Streites zwischen zwei Wissensansprüchen von einem Glauben verhoffen können?

Diese zwei Erwägungen ergeben in meinen Augen schwer wiegende Bedenken. Der Weg, den ich in dieser Betrachtung gegangen bin, endet somit in Skepsis. Ich bin nicht sicher, daß es den fraglichen Schnittpunkt im Unendlichen in Wahrheit gibt. Man soll ernstlich mit der Möglichkeit rechnen, daß es, mit Hegel zu reden,

20. J. Habermas, *Die neue Unübersichtllichkeit*, S. 202.
21. J. Habermas, *Nachmetaphysisches Denken. Philosophische Aufsätze* (Suhrkamp Frankfurt 1988), S. 60.

eine schlechte Unendlichkeit ist, in der sich die universal-pragmatische und die poststrukturalistische Aufklärungskonzeptionen schneiden. Es könnte m.a.W. so sein, daß aller Dialog hier nur ein Schein ist, da entweder auf einer Seite oder gar auf beiden und entweder wissentlich oder unwissentlich ein Versteckspiel gespielt wird. Es könnte so sein, daß zwischen den zwei Aufklärungskonzeptionen und den philosophischen Paradigmen die sie vertreten, kein Dialog möglich ist, sondern nur, wie R.Rorty am Ende seines Artikels 'Deconstruction and Circumvention' nahelegt, eine Oszillation. "To hope for a standpoint from which we shall escape this oscillation would be to hope for just the sort of unique, total, closed vocabulary which Heidegger and Derrida rightly say we are not going to get."[22] Aber welche Möglichkeiten haben die, die einer solchen Oszillation unterworfen sind? Welche sonst als den Ernst in der Suche nach Verständigung und einen möglichst guten Gebrauch der Kraft des Kontrafaktischen?

22. R. Rorty, "Deconstruction and Circumvention", in: *Essays on Heidegger and Others* (Philosophical Papers vol. 2, Cambridge University Press 1991), S. 85-106, hier S. 105.

16. Towards a Feminist Transformation of Philosophy

HERTA NAGL-DOCEKAL

1. A research perspective that covers the entire field of philosophy

Feminist Philosophy has existed for centuries. There were f.i. the numerous studies on the "egalité des deux sexes" published between 1620 and 1740 by male as well as female authors who were influenced by Descartes,[1] and — to name but one more culminating point of this history — the essays by John Stuart Mill, Harriet Taylor Mill and Helen Taylor.[2] During the last two decades, issues related to gender differences, body politics, etc. have generated a wideranging international debate. In view of this diversity, my paper makes an attempt to clarify the essential features of the feminist approach to philosophy.

1.1 Some terminological remarks. The word "feminist" is used here in a wide sense, as meaning: "rejecting discrimination against women," and it covers the whole range of diverging concepts that have been developed in order to analyze and eradicate the subjection of women. Similarly, the expression "feminist philosophy" refers not only to one specific philosophical position. Feminist philosophers do not subscribe to any kind of orthodoxy, but they do share two basic questions: First, in which ways did philosophy in its history up to the present day contribute to supporting the framework of gender bias from which discrimination has resulted? Secondly, which theoretical means does philosophy offer both for criticizing

---

1. See L. Abensour, *La Femme et le Féminism avant la Révolution* (Paris, 1928); R. Baader, *Dames des Lettres* (Stuttgart, 1986); H. Bennent, *Galanterie und Verachtung*. Eine philosophiegeschichtliche Untersuchung zur Stellung der Frau in Gesellschaft und Kultur (Frankfurt/M.-New York, 1985); H. Schröder, "Olympe de Gouges' "Erklärung der Rechte der Frau und Bürgerin" (1791). Ein Paradigma feministisch-politischer Philosophie," in: *Feministische Philosophie*, ed. H. Nagl-Docekal (Wien/München, 1990), p. 202.
2. J.St. Mill/H. Taylor Mill, *Essays on Sex Equality*, ed. A. Rossi (Chicago, 1970); J.St. Mill/H. Taylor Mill/H. Taylor, *Die Hörigkeit der Frau*, ed. H. Schröder (Frankfurt/M., 1976).

discrimination and for rethinking gender relations in ways which preclude structures of asymmetry? It is only a matter of course, that the debate around these issues has resulted in a variety of concepts that may not only be different but also incompatible. Thus the term "feminist philosophy" refers to an entire discourse and not just to a certain set of ideas. To risk a definition, one could say: Feminist philosophy means "philosophizing guided by an interest in the liberation of women."[3]

It needs to be noted, however, that there has always been a tendency to narrow down the extension of the term. On the one hand, some feminist philosophers themselves — or rather groups of feminist philosophers — claimed that the theories they had developed were the only legitimate way of feminist thinking. On the other hand, many critics turned out to be unwilling to examine the discourse of feminist philosophy in its full complexity; instead, they chose to single out one strand of thinking which they had found particularly unconvincing, and to draw their general critical conclusions from this narrow basis. These equally reductive approaches seem to be the main reason why "feminist philosophy" still has a dubious ring in the ears of many people.

1.2 Now, just what does it mean to "philosophize guided by an interest in the liberation of women?" To this question there is first a negative answer: feminist philosophy is not an additive enterprise. Alison Jaggar has recollected in a recent interview that in the late sixties and early seventies, when women philosophers in the United States began to analyze the philosophical relevance of feminist issues, their demand was indeed to *add* the "woman question" to the register of accepted philosophical topics. It soon became clear, however, that philosophy *in toto* requires to be reconsidered under the aspect of gender.[4] Thus feminist philosophy does not claim the status of a separate topic but rather of a research perspective that covers the entire field.

Since feminist philosophy has been defined in this way, a number of sub-projects have been developed in order to meet this comprehensive claim. It is not possible, however, to give a complete account of these sub-projects here, as their range includes — to name but a few — the history of women philosophers, feminist theory of

---

3. See H. Nagl-Docekal, "Was ist Feministische Philosophie?," in: *Feministische Philosophie*, l.c., p. 7.
4. Interview with A. Jaggar and S. Benhabib, *Falter*, 27/90, p.8.

science, feminist social philosophy and ethics, as well as feminist aesthetics. The area I have selected as a paradigm case of the feminist challenge to philosophy is the critical reading of classical philosophical texts that has been performed with increasing sophistication in recent years.

2. Feminist readings of the philosophical canon

Feminist philosophers have begun to examine those concepts for which general validity — i.e. gender neutrality — has been claimed. This enterprise was not without risks: To many a critic it did and still does appear eccentric to even raise the question whether philosophical investigations concerning topics such as "Reason," "Scientific Knowledge," "Justice," "The Principles of Moral Decision," "Individuality" etc. be influenced by a significantly masculine perspective. At a closer look, however, numerous instances have become visible in which just this was the case. Carol H. Cantrell describes the risk of feminist criticism as a double-bind: "Being in a body is not a neutral fact for a woman reader... If she chooses to think of herself as a neutral body-less reader, she regards herself differently than a text regards her. If she chooses to be a 'marked' or embodied reader, she is proceeding in violation of the text's expectations."[5]

In the course of re-reading classical texts under the perspective of gender two different strands of interpretation have emerged.

2.1 Phallosophy?

One of these strands is defined by the method of genealogy. The background here is the point of view expressed f.i. in Nietzsche's aphorism: "Grad und Art der Geschlechtlichkeit eines Menschen reicht bis in den letzten Gipfel seines Geistes hinauf."[6] Within the context of contemporary philosophy authors commonly referred to as "deconstructivists" or "post-modernists" have — as is well known — radicalized the thesis that all discourse is constituted by latent power structures which need to be exposed. Feminists who were determined to unmask the patriarchal character of philosophy (and of the sciences in general) turned therefore to Foucault, Lacan, and the authors influenced by the specific concept of psychoanaly-

---

5. C.H. Cantrell, "Analogy as Destiny: Cartesian Man and the Woman Reader," *Hypatia. Special Issue "Feminism and Aesthetics,"* Summer 1990, p. 11.
6. F. Nietzsche, *Jenseits von Gut und Böse*, Aphorism No. 231.

sis developed by the latter. It seemed at first obvious, that the paradigms of thinking developed by these authors met the interests of feminism perfectly. Much attention was f.i. paid to Lacan's interpretation of early childhood according to which the moment when children begin to speak marks the point where they break away from the primary unity with their mothers and enter the realm governed by the "Law of the Father." The semiological theory arguing that the entire symbolic order is defined by "Phallo-Logo-Centrism" appeared to be in perfect accordance with feminist critique.

Another aspect of post-modern thought that became relevant in this context was that the multiple threats to survival which mankind encounters at present, as for instance the threats of a nuclear arms race and of an environmental crisis, were traced back to the traditionally male sphere of rationality ("Zweckrationalität"), while the characteristics that had commonly been attributed to women, such as emotionality and motherliness, were no longer disregarded. When Deleuze and Guattari formulated the famous demand "devenir femme" to express their vision of the changes needed, this sounded to many like the perfect summary of feminist aspirations.

From this perspective, the entire concept of philosophy as well as the other academic disciplines, appears as an enterprise of significantly masculine ways of thinking. As a consequence, the feminist alternatives that were suggested did not have the status of raising new philosophical questions, but rather of searching for ways of expression altogether different from philosophy. At this point feminist philosophy merged with the project of "écriture feminine." A number of books based on this idea have come out since the mid-seventies and have been met by great interest in many countries. Representative for this development is Luce Irigaray's "Speculum."[7]

This project has, however, also caused much criticism among feminist philosophers. Of the many objections that have been raised — mostly during the last five years — only a few can be mentioned here. One very plausible point was made by Rosi Braidotti in an article published in Vienna. She writes: "What strikes me... is the absence of real-life women from these new images of the 'feminine.'" Braidotti then reveals a paradox: The fact that the "devenir femme" is primarily addressing men implies that this very phrase cannot refer to the specific situation of women. As a consequence,

7. L. Irigaray, *Speculum de l'autre femme* (Paris, 1974).

the question arises: "Is there not a danger... that behind the glittering facade of the polymorphous dispersion of the knowing subject, a new kind of phallo-logocentrism may be taking shape? The images of the 'feminine' as the sign for creativity, fluidity... etc. would then just be a set of inter-related metaphors that bring about yet another objectification of women,"[8]

Another issue raised in this debate was whether or not it is appropriate for women today to adopt the post-modern notion of femininity. In order to prevent misunderstandings, I would like to point out that the doubts expressed here do not concern the following facts of difference: Due to the sexual division of labor which has prevailed in our culture for centuries, men and women have indeed become different — they have developed significantly distinct abilities, habits and interests. The issue raised here rather concerns the future: should women make femininity their imperative?

One of the critical considerations was: Even though traditionally feminine virtues have been re-evaluated in post-modern thinking, the basic problem of gender-dichotomy has remained unchanged. At this point I would like to make a more general remark. To human beings both the emotional as well as the rational faculties are of vital importance. Therefore, any theory proposing that men and women should develop these faculties in a mutually exclusive manner only implies a double reductionism as both sexes are being denied full development as human beings. For women the consequence is this: If they attempt to restrict themselves to feminine qualities and waver the claim to participate in the various rational discourses they implicitly consent to being patronized. When this is reflected upon more closely it becomes obvious that post-structuralism lacks the theoretical means both to analyze the oppression of women and to develop a theory of liberation politics. This shortcoming has been pointed out by several authors, f.i. by Carol Gould, Andrea Nye, and Ilona Ostner.[9]

In the course of such criticism the debate has taken a turn that may to some come as a surprise — feminist theory has begun to

8. R. Braidotti, "Patterns of Dissonance. Women and/in Philosophy," in: *Feministische Philosophie*, l.c., p.120.
9. C. Gould, "Philosophical Dichotomies and Feminist Thought: Towards a Critical Feminism," in: *Feministische Philosopie*, l.c., p. 184; A. Nye, *Feminist Theory and the Philosophies of Man* (London/New York/Sydney, 1988); I. Ostner, "Auf der Suche nach der einen Stimme. Frauenforschung im Prozeß der Selbstvergewisserung," in: *Soziologische Revue*, Sonderheft 2: Frauen. Soziologie der Geschlechterverhältnisse (München, 1987), p. 6.

dismantle the mythological image of woman. Books with titles like "Ästhetik als Kritik der Weiblichkeit" emphasize this development.[10]

The political program that has resulted from this new approach was summarized by Toril Moi: "We must aim for a society in which we have ceased to categorize logic, conceptualization and rationality as 'masculine,' not for one from which these virtues have been expelled altogether as "unfeminine.""[11]

Now, what are the consequences of this debate for a feminist critique of traditional philosophy? The various objections against deconstructivism have made it quite clear that the option of labeling the entire discipline of philosophy as "male thinking" amounts to a crass reductionism. Moreover, as feminists are renewing women's claim of reason they are also — at least indirectly — asserting the philosophical competence of women. Brigitte Weisshaupt has gone even further; to her it is not only a possibility but rather a decisive task for women to participate in the philosophical discourse. She wrote f.i.: "Frauen zur philosophischen Argumentation zu befreien ist selbst ein Desiderat heutigen Denkens von Frauen."[12] This argument leads us to the second strand of feminist critique of philosophy.

2.2 The exploration of gender-blindness

In this case, the aim is not a global dismissal of philosophy as "masculine" but a step by step investigation, examining precisely where philosophical texts that purport to be of general validity are, on the contrary, constituted by masculine bias. Research guided by this interest has produced evidence that the patriarchal structures of everyday life have in many ways influenced the thinking of male philosophers. One paradigm case is the field of ethics and philosophy of law as it has been defined in the age of Enlightenment. Feminist critique has focused on the notion of equality, which appears to be a gender-neutral concept *par excellence*. To begin with, it was pointed out, that this notion had been elaborated in the context of a theory juxtaposing the spheres of the public and the private. In this theory the public domain is accessible to men only, while women are confined to the private realm. Set against this

---

10. See A. Maiworm, *Räume, Zeiten, viele Namen. Ästhetik als Kritik der Weiblichkeit* (Weingarten, 1984).
11. T. Moi, *Sexual-Textual Politics* (London/New York, 1985), p. 160.
12. B. Weisshaupt, "Schatten über der Vernunft", in: *Feministische Philosophie*, l.c. p. 136.

background, the Enlightenment concept of law was defined primarily with regard to conflicts that may occur within the public sphere, whereas it was the very essence of privacy that it should not be regulated by the state. At this point, the ambiguity of this theory becomes obvious: while reflections on the equal rights and equal duties of all citizens are engaging a general, seemingly gender-neutral language, they are actually referring primarily to male property holders. Consequently, many aspects of family life were not discussed in terms of a philosophy of law. Thus the question of justice was not raised with regard to the domestic division of labor[13] or to women's subordination under male heads of households. As feminist critics have charged, these theoretical restrictions also supported the common attitude of concealing or even legitimating the domestic abuse of women (as well as children).[14]

In addition, there was yet another aspect of the concept of equality that has been rendered problematic by feminist critique. In analyzing classical liberalism, several authors have come to the following conclusion: the danger of androcentrism persists even where equality is defined in a way that refers explicitly to women as well as men. Feminists have begun to confront the notion that construes equality as strict identity before the law with its consequences in everyday life. Thereby they revealed that the use of this notion does not guarantee fair solutions of conflicts. As Alison Jaggar observed, "one notorious example was 'no fault' divorce settlements that divided family property equally between husband and wife, but invariably left wives in a far worse economic situation than they did husbands... this huge discrepancy in the outcome of divorce resulted from a variety of factors, including the fact that women and men typically are differently situated in the job market... In this sort of case, equality... in the treatment of the sexes appears to produce an outcome in which sexual inequality is increased."[15]

Examples like this show that in the context of feminist theory the interpretation of classical philosophical theories is rarely an end in itself. The primary concern is rather to analyze historical concepts in view of the controversial issues in our life-world as well as in contemporary legal systems. Given this concern, feminist theory

---

13. S.M. Okin, *Justice, Gender and the Family*, (New York 1989).
14. A. Jaggar, *Feminist Politics and Human Nature* (Totowa, N.J., 1983).
15. A. Jaggar, "Feminist Ethics: Some Issues for the Nineties," *Journal of Social Philosophy*, XX/1,2, Spring/Fall 1989, p. 94.

cannot confine itself to criticism but has to search for viable alternatives as well. Opinions have been divided, however, over which philosophical program is suited best to replace the androcentric notion of equality.

One pole of the current discussion is based upon the assumption that the concept of equality must be abandoned altogether. This radical strategy is motivated by the suspicion that the very idea of general principles of action implies a potential for violating legitimate claims. As it was charged, "it obscures human difference by abstracting from the particularity and uniqueness of concrete people in their specific situations." This general reflection has been specified with regard to feminist concerns. Attention was called to the fact, that men and women are hardly "similarly situated."[16] As a consequence, a number of authors have worked on a feminist ethics in which the concept of applying abstract rules is replaced by the postulate of responding directly to needs that are immediately perceived. The key terms to mark this paradigm shift are "ethics of responsibility"[17] and "ethics of care."[18]

Several authors committed to this project have linked their philosophical considerations to the findings of empirical psychology on gender difference in moral behavior. Of outstanding importance was here, of course, Carol Gilligan's book *In a Different Voice: Psychological Theory and Women's Development*,[19] but attention was also paid to other studies arriving at similar conclusions such as the book by Nel Noddings *Caring: A Feminine Approach to Ethics and Moral Education*.[20] As is well known, these psychological theories suggest a gender-related opposition of "justice perspective" and "care perspective:" while the rule-governed approach to moral dilemmas is considered significantly masculine, women have been found to emphasize individual needs, due to the specific moral issues they encounter in their life-world, notably in the context of child-raising. In the course of the extensive interdisciplinary debate that had been prompted by these publications, philosophers have

16. L.M. Finley, "Transcending Equality Theory: A Way Out of the Maternity and the Workplace Debate," *Columbia Law Review*, 86/6, October 1986.
17. L.J. Krieger, "Through a Glass Darkly: Paradigms of Equality and the Search for A Women's Jurisprudence," *Hypatia*, 2/1, 1987.
18. C. Gilligan, *In a Different Voice: Psychological Theory and Women's Development* (Cambridge, Mass., 1982).
19. See Note 18.
20. N. Noddings, *Caring: A Feminine Approach to Ethics and Moral Education* (Berkeley, 1984).

wondered whether feminist ethics could be based on these psychological observations.

But this option did not remain unchallenged. On the one hand, doubts arose as to whether there is indeed sufficient empirical support for these psychological theories; it was noted, for instance, that Gilligan's conclusions had been derived from work with only small and rather homogenous groups of women.[21] The other and main concern in this context was that a theory assigning specific moral abilities to women is bound to re-enforce the traditional pattern of gender-dichotomy, and thus to re-iterate the problems previously mentioned here. Authors like Gould[22] and Jaggar[23] have underscored, therefore, that the project of feminist ethics is not to be identified with the assumption of feminine virtues.

I would also like to mention here that Gilligan's findings may be read differently. Seyla Benhabib, herself a critic of essentialist notions of gender, has suggested that we understand Gilligan's work as contributing to a critical theory of modernity. In her view, the two approaches to moral issues that had been pointed out by Gilligan, may be seen as reflecting the binary concept of socialization which is characteristic of our tradition.[24]

Now I would like to turn to a different aspect of this debate. The concept of responsibility as we find it in feminist philosophy today is sometimes linked to Communitarianism. Some feminists have adopted the notion of an "encumbered" self which had been developed by authors like McIntyre and Sandel. Their point is not to read universalism as a typically masculine approach to moral issues, but to emphasize that all human beings, men as well as women, are members of communities which are defined by their distinctive traditions and customary expectations. The specifically feminist contribution to this discourse was to analyze the "embodiment" of women that is characteristic of our culture and the traditions which are constitutive of feminine identities.[25]

21. J. Tronto, "Beyond Gender Difference: Toward a Theory of Care," *Signs*, 12, p. 644.
22. See Note 9.
23. A. Jaggar, "Feminist Ethics: Projects, Problems, Prospects," in: *Denken der Geschlechterdifferenz*, ed. H. Nagl-Docekal and H. Pauer-Studer (Wien, 1990), p. 143.
24. S. Benhabib, "The Debate over Women and Moral Theory Revisited," in: *Feministische Philosophie*, l.c., p. 191.
25. I.M. Young, Throwing Like a Girl: A Phenomenology of Feminine Body Comportment, Motility and Spatiality, in: I.M. Young, *Throwing like a Girl*

Other feminist philosophers have joined those objecting against Communitarianism. Alison Jaggar has warned, for instance, that a theory focussing exclusively on context and emotional response faces "the danger of degenerating into a 'do what feels good' kind of subjective relativism"[26] and may well lead to a total abandonment of the idea of morality. From the feminist perspective one particularly irritating implication of Communitarianism (as well as Post-Modernism in general) is that the critique of male dominance may be dismissed as just one point of view. In order to avoid this danger, feminist theory must re-evaluate the Enlightenment claims about common humanity. Several scholars have set out recently to overcome the opposition of contextualism versus universalism and to reconcile elements of both traditions. An essential part of this program was the effort to reconstruct equality in ways that would avoid the androcentrism of the liberalist understanding of the concept. In the course of this debate constructions such as "equality of acceptance" and "equality as similarity of individual outcome" have been proposed.[27]

In support of this project, I would like to suggest an additional consideration. The post-modern critique of universalism has failed in several cases (and certainly not only in the context of feminist theory) to pay sufficient attention to the wealth of distinctions that are characteristic of classical modern philosophy. Since Descartes, Kant and the Anglo-Saxon theorists of Liberalism were perceived as belonging to one and the same tradition of thought, there resulted a tendency toward misrepresentation and even caricature of the specific features of their philosophies. My primary concern in mentioning this is not, however, to correct blurred images of past philosophical concepts. I suggest, instead, that some of the distinctions that need to be rediscovered may meet the current demand for a more complex theory. There is good reason, f.i., to re-examine the notion of formality in Kant's moral philosophy. It should be noted, to begin with, that Kant did not maintain but, on the contrary, rejected the idea that the right course of action might be discovered by consulting a list of moral rules. He viewed morality as being based on only one principle which he defined in a way which merely

and Other Essays in Feminist Philosophy and Social Theory, Bloomington – Indianapolis 1990, p. 141.
26. A. Jaggar, "Feminist Ethics: Some Issues for the Nineties," Journal of Social Philosophy, l.c., p.102.
27. Ibid., p. 96,

involves a methodological but not a substantial abstraction from particularity. The categorical imperative is formal in a sense that all it demands is to respect humanity as an end in itself. As Kant explains, one implication of this formal rule is the duty to make the ends of others, as far as possible, also "my ends." And Kant adds that this includes to endeavor, "so far as in me lies," to further others as they "seek...their own happiness."[28]

I would like to propose a feminist re-appropriation of this concept of formality since it allows to integrate the ideas both of universal moral obligation and of respecting difference. Besides, I would like to raise the suspicion that Communitarianism has got entangled in a performative self-contradiction. Its insistence on "emcumberedness" and particularism seems to be at odds with the fact that this very claim has the features of a universal rule.

3. Philosophical imaginations of femininity

In the foregoing part of my paper I have presented some examples of the feminist effort to detect male bias hidden in seemingly gender-neutral concepts. In the remaining part, I shall turn briefly to the explicit theories about sex/gender-differences which the history of philosophy confronts us with. In recent years, feminist philosophers have developed various and increasingly elaborate methods of interpretation.

One of these approaches focuses on the relation between explicit statements and hidden bias. Maybe what (male) philosophers wrote about sexuality, love, family etc. was systematically connected with the core concepts of their theories? From this perspective Seyla Benhabib has f.i. juxtaposed Hegel's reflections on Sophocles's Antigone and his notion of a dialectics of history. "Hegel...is women's grave digger... The dialectic will sweep Antigone in its onward historical march, precisely because the law of the city is public as opposed to private, rational as opposed to corporal, promulgated as opposed to intuited, human as opposed to divine."[29] Thus to Benhabib the case of Antigone reveals that Hegel's notion of history in general implies potentially deadly dichotomies.

An entirely different approach to the history of philosophical gender theory has been developed as part of the search for the

---

28. I. Kant, Groundwork of the Metaphysics of Morals (New York, 1964), p. 98.
29. S. Benhabib, Hegel, die Frauen und die Ironie, Denken der Geschlechterdifferenz, l.c., p. 37-39.

features of modernity. Feminist philosophers who were guided by this interest did no longer confine themselves to exposing the structures of gender hierarchy. The main objective has become, instead, to explore in which ways the concepts of gender difference that had been elaborated since the mid-eighteenth century offer a key to an understanding of modern life in general. Using some of Max Weber's categories in reading f.i. Rousseau, Kant, Hegel and Simmel, feminist scholars have pointed out that the image of femininity elaborated by these authors was closely related to the process of rationalization. While men were increasingly pressed to shape their identities in accordance with the principles of instrumental reason, character traits that were seen as a persistent threat to this socialization, notably traits based on emotion and sensuousness, were eliminated from the male image and were transferred to the sphere of women. Seen from this angle, the bourgeois vision of femininity (which has retained much of its influence until this very day) turns out to be a compensation for the losses accompanying the process of modernisation. Liselotte Steinbrügge therefore writes that the paradigm construing women as "sentimental" implies a critical potential: "Das weibliche Geschlecht wurde der Ort, von dem aus die Vernunft in Frage gestellt werden konnte. Das moralische Geschlecht ist die Vernunftkritik der Aufklärung."[30]

A similar interpretation was proposed by Cornelia Klinger. In analyzing the idealization of women, landscape and art that was characteristic of the century between 1750 and 1850, and in revealing the identical pattern underlying all three cases, she comes to the conclusion that the process of modernization has by no means succeeded in destroying the phenomena that were opposed to its aspirations. By contrast, Klinger sees the sentimental image of the feminine as a utopian concept: "In vielerlei Gestalt hat sich die Idee erhalten, daß der Schein des 'Anderen' irgendwie doch der Vorschein eines Besseren sein...könnte."[31]

4. Today's agenda

My comments concerning the feminist criticism of the philosoph-

---

30. L. Steinbrügge, "Vernunftkritik und Weiblichkeit in der französischen Aufklärung," in: *1789/1989 — Die Revolution hat nicht stattgefunden*, ed. A. Deuber-Mankowsky, U. Ramming and E.W. Tielsch (Tübingen, 1989), p. 77.
31. C. Klinger, "Frau-Landschaft-Kunstwerk. Gegenwelten oder Reservoire des Patriarchats?" in: *Feministische Philosophie*, l.c., p. 63.

ical canon should, by way of example, make the following clear: If the category of gender is accepted among the instruments of philosophy, this will affect large areas of the field. Even those areas traditionally claiming gender-neutrality cannot escape critical questioning of the claim's legitimacy, and thus it becomes apparent that the respective concepts of gender relations are reflected in diverse ways in a system's fundamental ideas. Thus the feminist perspective initiates a transformation of philosophy afflicting, it must be added, not only the understanding of the history of philosophy but also contemporary thought. In order to escape the gender blindness commonplace until now, gender difference must be explicitly addressed in the various areas of philosophy.

Naturally, this project requires a critical foundation capable of precluding renewed reflection in philosophy of the gender asymmetries characteristic of historical and current conceptions (in- and outside of academic discourse) as well as of living situations. The point is that the questions concerning feminine and masculine identities and the manifold relationships between the sexes must be reconsidered. (Here, at the latest, it should have become evident, that not just philosophy by, about and for women is being addressed, but that the feminist perspective exposes problems that require discussion by both sexes.)

The debate on a new conception of gender relations often deadlocks at the polarization of alterity versus equality. This development is problematic in two respects. On the one hand, it only appears that a disjunction is present; a closer look reveals that the two key words refer to argumentations that both contain plausible motifs and, additionally, that they are not mutually exclusive. On the other hand, such a polarized deadlock impedes the unfolding of additional views.

It therefore seems appropriate to first ascertain which topoi — in the current discourse — need consideration. In my opinion numerous questions (and research projects originating from these) are equally legitimate and equally necessary, and I would like to encourage their further specification. The research programs listed below are not intended to supersede one another, rather they should be pursued simultaneously.

4.1 The exploration of difference cannot be dispensed with, and especially in view of the current constellations of the sexes. Whereby one aspect should not be overlooked: women's specific experiences and unique point of view can only women themselves

317

express; neither one of the sexes can traverse the dimensions of human reality alone.

4.2 At the same time the patriarchal conditions of difference should be analyzed. One will remember that the traditional view of femininity, even where upvalued, provides for the exclusion of women from the public sphere. The demand for equality that was already developed in the older feminist movement is therefore still relevant today. Not, of course, in the sense of liberal feminism, whose goal was limited to the infusion of women into spheres traditionally dominated by men; it was already mentioned that the concept of equality must be newly defined.

4.3 In order to overcome the discrimination of women, a new proposal concerning identities is also needed. Today's agenda calls for a rethinking of the gender relations in both the intimate sense (in sexuality, love, with respect to the child) and in all other areas of life. In the process, the concept of dichotomous characters should doubtlessly become totally deflated. This concept leads, as has been seen, to a reductionism on both sides and therefore implies the constant danger of devaluation. Thus the destruction of the "feminine myth" also belongs to the elements of feminist philosophy. In the wake of such a gain in differentiation vis-à-vis the bipolar models of gender identity, the long tradition of androgynous concepts could find new actuality.

4.4 The concept of complementary gender characteristics is also problematic because it leads inevitably to heteronomy: individuals would be measured according to the "ideal woman" and the "ideal man" respectively. At this point feminist philosophy converges with the discourse on individuality. Here, the consideration that the uniqueness of individuality is created by taking on, reworking and altering the natural and historical givens is especially relevant. The biological and social givens concerning sexuality also undergo individual interpretation. Based on this thought, gender identity can be seen as no longer forced upon the individuals but rather as a matter subject to their own self-interpretation.

17. Re-figuring the Subject

ROSI BRAIDOTTI

There are no fragments where there is no whole.
Martha Rosler[1]

1. *The post-metaphysical condition*

The era commonly referred to as 'modernity,' 'modernisation,' or 'modernism' (despite the different implications and nuances of each of these terms), is marked by the changing socio-economic and discursive conditions in the status of all minorities, especially women. For a number of reasons that I have analyzed elsewhere[2], the emancipation of women and their integration into not only the labour force, but also in intellectual and political life, has become a pressing necessity in the western world. The first paradox to explore in a discussion between modernity and the feminist quest is therefore that of a historical period that needs to integrate women socially, economically and politically, thus reversing the traditional patterns of exclusion and oppression of women.

In my paper I will adopt a more theoretical approach to this question. I will argue that in this new context the women's movement has set on the agenda serious questions as to of the structures, the values and the theoretical foundations of the very system that women, like other minorities, are urged to integrate. The leading questioning line is both ethico-political and epistemological: what is the exact price to pay for 'integration'? What values shall feminist women propose to the old system? What representations of themselves will they oppose to the established ones? One can read the whole of contemporary western feminism, but also related and

1. Martha Rosler, 'In the place of the public (1983-90),' photo installation at the Decade Show, 1990, New York City.
2. Rosi Braidotti, *Patterns of Dissonance/Beelden van Leegte* (Cambridge: Polity Press, 1991/Kampen: Kok Agora, 1991).

319

equally complex cultural and political phenomena, such as women's modernist literature[3] in the light of this question.

On the discursive and theoretical level[4], modernity in the western world marks the crisis and decline of the classical system of representation of the subject, in the political, epistemological and ethical sense of the term. The established conventions about what subjectivity is and as to what it entails are radically challenged by a number of 'minorities,' who claim representation — in the political and discursive sense. In the European post-war intellectual landscape, two major schools of thought emerged on the issue of the crisis of modernity: the German critical theory school represented today by J. Habermas and the French school, of which Foucault, Deleuze, Derrida and Irigaray are leading figures. Both have repercussions for feminism, though the latter had in my opinion a larger impact.

One point these two schools have in common is that they subject the notion of the Enlightenment to serious questioning. Both argue that the notion of progress and liberation through an adequate use of reason is to be re-examined in the light of history — particularly in the light of extreme phenomena in contemporary western history, such as totalitarian political systems, genocides, colonialism and domination. The emphasis on the political need for a revision of the Enlightenment as 'myth of liberation through reason' is particularly strong in the work of Foucault and Deleuze.[5] In their perspective, faith in the self-regulating power of reason is, for us moderns, incorrect as a theoretical, political and ethical position. It must be replaced by a more radical critique of reason from within, i.e.: an analysis of its structural limitations as a theoretical and human ideal; this is a point which they share with feminism.[6] Critical theory is an ethics that takes the production of knowledge as its central concern.

The two main schools of critical thought represent also two ways of assessing the Enlightenment tradition: if I can summarize brutally

---

3. This is the line taken by Shari Benstock in *Women of the Left Bank* (University of Texas: Austin, 1986).
4. I borrow the notion of 'discourse' from Michel Foucault: *L'Ordre du Discours* (Paris: Minuit, 1977).
5. It has also been acknowledged by both: Foucault in the preface to the American edition of Deleuze's *Anti-Oedipus* and Deleuze in his masterful *Foucault* (Paris: Minuit, 1988).
6. See Jenny Lloyd, *The Man of Reason* (London, Methuen, 1984).

a debate that would require a great deal more careful attention:[7] for Habermas the problem, while criticizing scientific rationality, is to safeguard the primacy of reason as a principle, and of modernity as a project that is still open before us. For Foucault, on the other hand, the project of the Enlightenment has come to an end historically — which means that modernity requires new forms of scientific legitimation and new modes of discourse to go with it.

It is also clear that these two schools represent very different readings and conceptual re-elaborations of both Marxist and psychoanalytical theory and, even more importantly, of the connection between them. The tools of analysis they use are radically different — especially on the question of the unconscious and, therefore, of language as a symbolic structure.

I am less interested in working out the exact relationship between these two traditions of critical theory than in stressing their importance and their implications. One of them is that the feminist epistemological debate, marked by issues of gender or sexual difference and the critique of 18th century notions such as 'liberation' and 'equality' is both necessary and central to critical theory, be it of the German or French variety. Secondly, as Evelyn Fox-Keller pointed out:[8] the historical context in which feminism has emerged as theory and practice rests on structural conditions that are conducive to the revision and the extension of the meaning of reason and of scientific rationality. In other words, if the crisis of modernity consists in the decline of the rationalist paradigm, then feminist theory and practice are historically and conceptually co-extensive with, or in-built in the modernist project. I would go as far as to say, with Jardine,[9] that feminism may even provide modernity with some of its inner coherence.

In other words, I see modernity as the moment of decline of classical rationalism and the view of the subject attached to it. The century-old identification of the subject with his/her rational self is challenged by the new scientific discourses, related to changing historical conditions. The very idea of what it means to be human is thrown

---

7. For a more thorough discussion of this problem, see S. Benhabyb and D. Cornell, eds, *Feminism as critique* (Minneapolis: University of Minnesota Press, 1987).
8. Evelyn Fox-Keller, *Reflections on Gender and Science* (New Haven: Yale University Press, 1975).
9. Alice Jardine, *Gynesis* (Ithaca: Cornell University Press, 1985).

open to questoning, as Adorno and Foucault, in very different ways, never cease to tell us.

In my previous study I stated my skepticism at the very idea of a 'crisis' of the philosophical subject that takes place at the same time as the emergence of feminism as a theoretical and political force, while I also argued for the relevance of French poststructuralism for feminist theory.

I also emphasized the fact that there is little scope within the feminist framework for nihilism or cynical acceptance of the state of crisis as loss and fragmentation. On the contrary, this crisis is taken by women as the opening-up of new possibilities and potentialities. It leads women to rethink the link between identity, power and the community. It allows women to ask the question: what does it mean to be a human subject today, that is to say a civilized, socialized member of a community in a post-metaphysical world? In this era of crumbling certainties and dissolving identities, how can women assert the positivity of the difference that women can make, while recognizing the fragility of what we call 'civilization': a network of multiple differenciated, interacting subjects, functioning on a consensual basis?

This new theoretical context is a great chance for the minorities, like women, who had been historically deprived of the right to self-determination: for them, the crisis of the old schemes of subjectivity can be productive. Feminist analyses of the 'crisis,' therefore, stress its positivity, that is to say the extent to which feminist philosophy allows for alternative values to be postulated.

2. *Feminism as philosophy*

The feminist standpoint as critical philosophy rests on the assumption that what we used to call 'the universal subject of knowledge' is a falsely generalized standpoint. The discourses of science, religion, the law, and also the general assumptions that govern the production of knowledge tacitly imply a subject that is male (and also white, middle-class and heterosexual). If, in a movement of strategic mimesis, such as Irigaray[10] suggests, you replace this subject with

---

10. Luce Irigaray, *Speculum: de l'autre femme* (Paris: Minuit, 1977); *Ethique de la différence sexuelle* (Paris: Minuit, 1984).

one that is structured by other variables, such as gender or sexual difference (but also ethnicity or race), what used to be seen as 'the universal' appears as a most particular and specific approach. This particularism also explains its power of exclusion over categories of people who are deemed 'minorities,' or 'others.' What I want to argue, therefore, is that the decline of the universal in the age of modernity, therefore, marks the opportunity for the definition of a standpoint which is based on differences while not being merely relativistic.

I shall return to this point.

The notion of 'gender' outlines the conceptual framework within which feminists explained the social and discursive construction of differences between the sexes. The terms of reference for the debate on gender were fixed in the 70's, under the inspiration of Beauvoir's work and mostly in fields such as history, anthropology and sociology.

Gender is primarily an open challenge to the universalistic tendency of critical and theoretical language. This tendency consists in conflating the masculine, white point of view with the general 'human' standpoint, thereby confining the feminine to the structural position of 'other.' The corollary of this is that the mark of gender falls on women, marking them off as 'different from,' whereas the masculine is burdened with the task of carrying the universal.

In a feminist perspective, this symbolic division of labour is the mere expression of the system set up by phallo-logocentrism, which can be taken as the inner logic of patriarchy. In other words, this system whereby universal values are conflated with the masculine is neither necessary as in historically inevitable, nor is it rational as in conceptually necessary. It just *is* the powerful foundation of the patriarchal material and symbolic economy. This symbolic division of labour sets up a fundamental dissymmetry between the sexes: the price men have to pay for carrying the universal is a kind of loss of embodiment. The price women have to pay, on the other hand, is loss of subjectivity and over-emphasis of their embodied existence.

The centrality of the notion of gender can be demonstrated by the vast feminist literature existing on this subject; over the last ten years, however, feminist scholars have pointed out the need to submit to critical scrutiny the central notions, ruling concepts and methodological frameworks of gender research[11]. Considering the intrinsic polysemy of the term 'gender,' it is not surprising that recent publications have attempted to define it in a feminist perspective, either by historicizing the notion or by setting it in a narrative framework: this is the option preferred by Snitow[12] and Gallop[13]. See also the trend towards 'personal criticism' in Miller[14], Ward[15] and others. You can set these attempts at clarification of the term 'gender' alongside more epistemological works that try to analyze the implications of the term as a set of relations that allow us to think the inter-dependence of gender and other variables of oppression such as race, age, culture and life-style.

The classical approach to gender shifted in the early 1980's under the joint impact of semiotics, structuralist psychoanalysis and autonomous developments within the women's movement[16]. Central to this new approach is a shift away from the mere critique of patriarchy, to the assertion of the positivity of women's cultural traditions and range of experiences; the work of A. Rich is extremely influential in this respect[17] in that it places new emphasis and value on language and consequently representation as the site of constitution of the subject.

What remains as the constant factor, or point of consensus among the different theories of gender[18] is the critique of dualistic ways of thinking. The classical universalism, which conflates the masculine

11. Sandra Harding, *The Science Question in feminism* (Ithaca: Cornell University Press, 1986); S. Harding, M.B. Hintikka, eds, *Discovering Reality* (Boston: Reidel, 1983); S. Harding, ed., *Feminism & Methodology* (Bloomington: Indiana University Press, 1987); D. Haraway, *Simians, Cyborgs and Women* (London: Free Association Books, 1990).
12. Ann Snitow, "Gender diary," in: M. Hirsch and E. Fox-Keller, eds, *Conflicts in Feminism* (New York: Routledge, 1991).
13. Jane Gallop, *Around 1981* (New York: Routledge, 1991).
14. Nancy Miller, *Getting Personal* (New York: Routledge, 1991).
15. Nicole Jouve-Ward, *White Woman Speaks with Forked Tongue* (London, Routledge, 1991).
16. For accounts of this shift of perspectives, see C. Duchen, *Feminism in France* see also: H. Eisenstein, *Contemporary Feminist Thought* (Sydney: Allen & Unwin, 1984).
17. A. Rich, *Of Woman Born* (New York: W. Norton, 1976); *On lies, secrets and silence* (New York: Norton, 1979); *Blood, Bread and Poetry* (London: the Women's Press, 1985).
18. Rosi Braidotti, *Theories of Gender*, speech delivered at the opening of the academic year (Utrecht University, 1991).

and the white with the universal and confines the feminine to a secondary position of difference rests upon an oppositional or dualistic logic. Radical feminists, especially Irigaray argue that this dualistic mode creates binary differences only to ordain them in a hierarchical scale of power-relations.

In what I see as one of the most fruitful aspects of feminist theory, it is further argued that this conceptual scheme has served the purpose of comforting western culture in the belief in the 'natural,' that is to say inevitable and therefore historically invariable structure of its system of representation, its myths, symbols and the dominant vision of the subject.

Of great importance to this argument is the emphasis on race and ethnic specificity. This had always been present in feminist practice and in feminist thought, but it has received particular impetus of late through the work of the 'post-colonial critics,' such as Spivak, Mohanty and others[19]. Very significant is the impact of black feminist theory, which had been vocal from the start in the work of Audre Lorde, Adrienne Rich and Cherry Moraga[20], but received a new wave of interest from black scholars and writers such as Alice Walker[21], Barbara Smith[22], bell hooks[23] and many others. It had the power to invest the whole field of feminist criticism and theory, forcing a recognition of the whiteness of its concepts. Emblematic of this trend is the work of Elizabeth Spelman on S. de Beauvoir[24].

19. Gayatri Spivak, *In other Worlds* (New York: Methuen, 1987); *The post-colonial critic* (New York: Routledge, 1990); Chandra Mohanty, 'Feminist Encounters. Locating the Politics of Experience,' *Copyright*, 1, 1987; 'Under Western eyes: feminist scholarship and colonial discourse,' *Feminist Review*, 30, 1988. Trinh Minh Ha, *Woman, Native, Other* (Bloomington: Indiana University Press, 1989).
20. C. Moraga and G. Anzaldua, *This bridge called my back* (Watertown: Persephone, 1981); *Loving in the war years* (Boston: South End, 1983). A. Lorde: *Sister Outside* (Trumansberg: Crossing, 1984); Adrienne Rich, *Blood, Bread and Poetry* (London: Virago, 1983).
21. Alice Walker, *In search of our mothers' gardens* (London: The Women's Press, 1983).
22. Barbara Smith, "Towards a black feminist criticism," in E. Showalter, ed, *The new feminist criticism* (New York: Pantheon, 1985), pp. 168-185; *Home girls: a black feminist anthology* (New York: Kitchen Table, 1983).
23. bell hooks, *Feminist Theory: from margin to centre* (Boston: South End Press, 1984); *Yearning: race, gender and cultural politics*, Between the Lines (Toronto, 1990).
24. Elizabeth Spelman, *Inessential woman* (Boston: Beacon Press, 1989).

Seen in the light of these new approaches, the 'gender system' appears as a multi-layered and complex reality, which creates differences and distributes them in a hierarchical scale. Through the 80's — under the impact of post-structuralism and various forms of deconstruction — gender comes to be defined accordingly as a process[25]: gender is a material and semiotic process that defines the subject through a number of regulatory variables: sex, race, age, life style and sexual preferences etc. etc. The constitution of subjectivity is seen as the term in a process of material (institutional) and discursive (narrative) naming. The key notion here is gender as a regulative fiction, i.e. a normative activity which constructs certain categories (masculine, feminine, heterosexual, lesbian, white, brown, black etc.) in its very process.

The gender theorists of today are a new multi-faceted and transdisciplinary generation; they brought into focus the masculinity and the whiteness, as well as the class-bias of values — political as well as theoretical values — which we are trained to recognize as universal. In so doing, they have accomplished a sort of re-mixing of disciplinary positions; symptomatic of this change in intellectual climate is the position recently taken by Joan Scott. As the author of one of the most authoritative early essays on the question of gender[26], Scott had argued that 'gender' as marking a set of interrelations between variables of oppression could help us understand the intersection of sex, class, race, life-style, age as fundamental axes of differenciation. In a more recent essay[27], Scott goes further and argues for a definition of gender as marking the intersection of language with the social, i.e.: the semiotic with the material. Quoting Foucault's notion of 'discourse,' which she defends as one of the major contributions of poststructuralist thought to feminist theory[28], Scott suggests that we re-interpret 'gender' as linking the text to reality, the symbolic to the material, theory to practice in a

25. Teresa de Lauretis, *Technologies of Gender* (Bloomington: Indiana University Press, 1987); *Feminist Studies/critical Studies* (Bloomington: Indiana University Press, 1988); see also Judith Butler, *Gender Trouble* (New York: Routledge, 1990).
26. Joan Scott, "The usefulness of gender as a category of historical analysis," in: *The Politics of History* (New York: Columbia University Press, 1990).
27. J. Scott, 'Deconstructing equality versus difference," *Feminist Studies*, 14/1, 1988, pp. 33-50.
28. This point has been the object of my book-length study: *Patterns of Dissonance* (Cambridge: Polity Press, 1991); see also: N. Miller, "Subject to change" in T. de Lauretis, ed., *Feminist Studies/Critical Studies* (Bloomington: Indiana Uni-

new powerful manner. In Scott's reading feminist theory in this post-modernist phase politicizes the struggle over meaning and representation.

What has emerged in contemporary feminist thought is a radical redefinition of the text and of the textual away from the dualistic mode; the text is now approached as both a semiotic and a material structure, that is to say not an isolated item locked in a dualistic opposition to a social context and to an activity of interpretation. The text must rather be understood as a term in a process, that is to say a chain-reaction which encompasses a web of power-relations. What is at stake in the textual practice, therefore, is less the activity of interpretation than that of decoding the network of connections and effects that link the text to an entire socio-symbolic system. In other words, we are faced here with a new materialist theory of the text and of textual practice.

The new theorists emerging in the 90's rest accordingly on a vision of the subject as process; they work along the lines of a multiplicity of variables of definition of female subjectivity: race, class, age, sexual preference and life-styles count as major axes of identity. They are radically materialistic in that they stress the concrete, 'situated' conditions that structure subjectivity, but they also innovate on the classical notion of materialism, because they redefine female subjectivity in terms of a process network of simultaneous power-formations. I will argue next that a new trend seems to be emerging that emphasizes the situated, specific, embodied nature of the feminist subject, while rejecting biological or psychic essentialism. This is a new kind of female embodied materialism.

For instance, Teresa de Lauretis, basing the analysis of subjectivity on the co-extensivity of power and the process of becoming-subject borrows the foucauldian notion of 'technology of the self' to express the material foundations of this vision of the subject and, more importantly of the ways in which gender functions[29] as a variable that structures subjectivity.

versity Press, 1986); also N. Schor, "Dreaming dissymetry," in: A. Jardine and P. Smith (eds) *Men in feminism* (New York: Methuen, 1987).
29. For a definition of the 'technology of the self,' see M. Foucault, *Histoire de la sexualité*, vol, II and III (Paris: Gallimard, 1984). See also my reading of this scheme of subjectivity in *Patterns of Dissonnace*.

In other words, what lies at the heart of the redefinition of gender as the technology of the self is the notion of the politics of subjectivity. This has a two-fold sense: it refers both to the constitution of identities and to the acquisition of subjectivity, meant as forms of empowerment, or entitlements to certain practices. The French term 'assujettissement' renders both levels of this process of subjectification: it is both a material and a semiotic process that defines the subject through a number of regulative variables: sex, race, age etc. The acquisition of subjectivity is therefore a process of material (institutional) and discursive (symbolic) practices, the aim of which is both positive — because they allow for forms of empowerment — and regulative — because the forms of empowerment are the site of limitations and disciplining.

To sum up, I would say that at the beginning of the feminist 1990's a paradox has emerged: the paradox of feminist theory at the end of this century is that it is based on the very notions of 'gender' and 'sexual difference,' which it is historically bound to criticize on the basis of the new vision of subjectivity as process. Feminist thought rests on a concept that calls for deconstruction and de-essentialization in all of its aspects. More specifically, I think that the central question in feminist theory has become: how to re-assemble a vision of female subjectivity after the certainties of gender-dualism have collapsed, privileging notions of the self as process (Scott), complexity (Braidotti), inter-relatedness (Haraway), post-colonial simultaneities of oppression (Spivak, Mohanty et alia) and the multi-layered technology of the self? In other words, the social and symbolic fate of sexual polarisations is at stake here. To phrase it differently, the question now is: how to re-think the unity of the subject, without reference to humanistic beliefs, without dualistic oppositions, linking instead body and mind in a new vision of the self as having fluid boundaries? In other words: what counts as human in a post-humanist world? Can there be a feminist humanity? Can women become a collective subject?

The emphasis on the differences — of race, age, class, sexual preference — which used to be concealed by global definitions of 'the subject' leads to new questions about inter-relatedness and communication. Questions of inter-relationality, receptivity and global communication re-emerge, especially in the work of political epistemologists like Donna Haraway, to whom I shall return. The issue at stake is: how do we reconcile the radical historical specificity of women with the insistance on constructing the new figuration of humanity?

Can we speak of and act on differences as positivity, not as deviations, not as subordinated forms of being? How can we build a new kind of collectivity in differences? The challenge for post-structuralist feminism is how to struggle for an anti-relativistic specific community of historically-located semiotic -material subjects, seeking for connections and articulations in a non-ethno/gender-centered manner.

3. Rhizomatic figurations

Pursuing an argument developed more fully elsewhere[30], I would like to stress the pursue next the quest for points of intersection between the new feminist thought and contemporary poststructuralist concerns about the structures of subjectivity. My starting point is the assumption that French poststructuralism is relevant for feminism not for what it has to say about women, sexuality or the body; of rather greater importance is the redefinition of thinking and especially of the theoretical process in a creative or non-reactive manner that accompanies the poststructuralist quest for new visions of subjectivity.

As an example, I will choose Deleuze's effort to 'image' the activity of thinking differently. Deleuze shares with feminism a concern for the urgency, the necessity to re-define, re-figure and re-invent theoretical practice, and philosophy with it, in a non- molar/reactive/sedentary mode. This urgency is due to the crisis of the philosophical logos and the decline of the classical system of representation of the subject. Consequently, the challenge to which Deleuze is trying to respond is how to think about and account for changes and changing conditions: not the staticity of formulated truths, but the living process of transformation of the self.

In his determination to undo the western style of theoretical thought, Deleuze moves beyond the dualistic oppositions that conjugate the monological discourse of phallo-logocentrism.

30. See Rosi Braidotti, "Feminist deleuzian tracks, or: metaphysics and metabolism," forthcoming in K. Boundas, ed., *Gilles Deleuze: theory, text and practice* (New York: Routledge).

Deleuze stresses the extent to which in western thought the classical notion of the subject treats difference as a sub-set of the concept of identity. The subject is defined in terms of sameness, that is to say as adequation to a normative idea of a Being that remains one and the same in all its varied qualifications and attributes.

The univocity of metaphysical discourse about the subject has been reproduced by the moral discourse of metaphysics, which rests on a inherently normative image of thought[31]. Modernity is for Deleuze the moment when this image collapses, opening the way to other forms of representation.

What Deleuze aims at is the affirmation of difference in terms of a multiplicity of possible differences; difference as the positivity of differences. In turn, this leads him to redefine consciousness in terms of a multiplicity of layers of experience that does not privilege rationality as the organizing principle. In his attempt to overcome the classical idea of the subject as coinciding with his/her consciousness, Deleuze emphasizes the unconsious as a creative field. The unconscious not as the deep container of yet-unknown sources, but rather as marking the structural non-coincidence of the subject with his/her consciousness. This non-coincidence is a radical disjunction that separates the thinking subject from the normative image of thought based on the phallo-logocentric system.

The rejection of the principle of adequation to and identification with a phallogocentric image of thought lies at the heart of the nomadic vision of subjectivity that Deleuze proposes as the new, post-metaphysical *figuration* of the subject. Deleuze argues and acts upon the idea that the activity of thinking cannot and must not be reduced to reactive (Deleuze says sedentary) critique. Thinking can be critical if by critical we mean the active, assertive process of inventing new images of thought — beyond the old icon where thinking and being joined hands together under the Sphynx-like smile of the sovereign Phallus. Thinking is life lived at the highest possible power — thinking is about finding new images, new representations. Thinking is about change and transformation.

The notion of *rhizome* is Deleuze's leading figuration: it points to a redefinition of the activity of philosophy as the quest for new images of thought, better suited to a nomadic, disjuncted self. An

---

31. For a fuller exposition of these ideas, see Gilles Deleuze, *Logique du sens* (Paris: PUF, 1966) and *Nietzsche et la philosophie* (Paris: PUF 1969).

idea is an active state of very high intensity, which opens up hitherto unsuspected possibilities of life and action. For Deleuze, ideas are events, lines which point human thought towards new horizons. An idea is that which carries the affirmative power of life to a higher degree.

For Deleuze thought is made of sense and value: it is the force, or level of intensity, that fixes the value of thought, not the adequation of an idea to a pre-established normative model. Philosophy as critique of negative, reactive values is also the critique of the dogmatic image of thought; it expresses the force, the activity of the thinking process in terms of a typology of forces (Nietzsche) or an ethology (Spinoza). Deleuze's rhizomatic style brings to the fore the affective foundations of the thinking process. It is as if beyond/behind the propositional content of an idea there lay another category: the affective force, level of intensity, desire or affirmation which conveys the idea and ultimately governs its truth-value. Thinking, in other words, is to a very large extent unconscious, in that it expresses the desire to know and this desire is that which cannot be adequately expressed in language, simply because it is what sustains it as its pre-linguistic condition. With this intensive theory of the thinking process, Deleuze points to the pre-philosophical foundations of philosophy.

This impersonal style is rather 'post-personal' in that it allows for a web of connections to be drawn, not only in terms of the author's 'intentions' and the reader's 'reception,' but rather in a much wider, more complexified set of possible inter-connections that blur established, that is to say hegemonic, distinctions of class, culture, race, sexual practice and others. The image of the rhizome pops up here as a figuration for the kind of political subjectivity Deleuze is promoting.

In other words, as interlocutors in a deleuzian philosophical text, we — as post-Enlightenment thinkers — are expected to be not just traditional intellectuals and academics, but also active, interested and concerned participants in a project of research and experimentation for new ways of thinking about human subjectivity. As readers in an intensive mode, we are tranformers of intellectual energy, processors of the 'insights' Deleuze is giving us. These 'in'-sights are not to be thought of as plunging us inwards, towards a mythical 'inner' reservoir of truth. On the contrary, they are represented as propelling us along the multiple directions of extra-textual experiences. Thinking is living at a higher degree, a faster pace, a multi-directional manner.

This philosophical stance imposes not only the conventional academic requirements of passionless truth, but also the passionate engagement in the recognition of the theoretical and discursive implications of rethinking the subject. It is all a question of what kind of rhizomatic connections we can draw among ourselves, here and now, in the act of doing philosophy. This choice of a theoretical style that leaves ample room to the exploration of subjectivity follows the call for 'passionate detachment' in theory-making[32].

In the next section I will argue that Deleuze's concerns are both echoed and redesigned politically by contemporary feminist theory, taking the case of Donna Haraway as exemplary.

4. Cyborg-feminism as anti-relativism

Three notions are crucial to Donna Haraway's radical postmodernism and they all have to do with transformations in both an ethical and an epistemological sense. Firstly, the notion of feminist theory gets redefined in terms of non-taxonomical *figurations*; secondly, feminist subjectivity is reconceptualized as *cyborg* and thirdly, scientific objectivity is redefined as *situated knowledges*.

I argued earlier that in the last five years a number of feminist theorists have begun to move beyond polarized positions (for instance the opposition between the Anglo-American gender theories and the Continental 'sexual difference' theories) and to open up new perspectives in feminist thought. Donna Haraway is one of the leading figures of this new generation. If the term 'postmodernism' means anything[33], Haraway offers a convincing example of positive postmodernist situated epistemology.

32. This expression, originally coined by Laura Mulvey in film criticism, has been taken up and developed by Donna Haraway, in: "Situated knowledges: the science question in feminism and the privilege of partical perspective" and in "A cyborg manifesto: science, technology and socialist-feminism in the late twentieth century," both in *Simians, cyborgs and women* (London: Free Association Press, 1991), pp. 183-202 and 127-148.
33. For a defense of poststructuralist modernism, see Rosi Braidotti, *Patterns of Dissonance* (Cambridge: Polity Press, 1991).

Taking as her main point of reference the impact of the new technologies (micro-electronics, tele-communication and video-games including video-wars) on the condition of women in society, Haraway stresses the importance of the global village, which implies a new wave of off-shore and electronic-cottage industries, most of which employ women[34]. Reflecting on the changes that this new system of production imposes on society at large, Haraway challenges feminists to be up to the political and conceptual complexity of their times.

In her analysis, the radically new fact about the 1990's is the bio-technologies, that is to say the degree of autonomy, mastery and sophistication, reached by devices that take 'life' and 'the living organisms' as object. A great deal of this technology is optical, it has to do with increased powers of vision. Nowadays, the bio-technological gaze has penetrated into the very intimate structure of living matter, seeing the invisible and representing what used to be 'unrepresentable.' Haraway's focus is on the notion of the body as situated knowledge and the visual as location of power.

Firmly implanted in the tradition of materialism, Haraway reminds us that thinking about the subject amounts to rethinking his/her bodily roots. The body in not a biological given, but a field of inscription of socio-symbolic codes: it stands for the radical materiality of the subject. Following Foucault[35], Haraway draws our attention to the construction and manipulation of docile, knowable bodies in our present social system. She invites us to think of what new kinds of bodies are being constructed right now, i.e.: what kind of gender-system is being constructed under our very eyes.

In a foucauldian analysis, the contemporary body is a paradox: on the one hand, it is merely an empirical notion, a living organism, meant as the sum of its organic and therefore detachable parts, a complex field of integrated organs whose mode of inter-action can be studied in terms of their respective functions. This is the notion of 'the body' at work in all the bio-sciences, which is historically linked to the classical discourse on clinical anatomy[36].

---

34. An equally forceful analysis of these conditions of production is provided by Gayatri Spivak *In other worlds* (New York: Methuen, 1987).
35. Michel Foucault, *Surveiller et punir* (Paris: Gallimard, 1977).
36. I developed this point in my article "Organs without bodies," *Differences* 1/1, 1989.

On the other hand, the body cannot be reduced to the sum of its organic components: it still remains as the threshold of the transcendence of the subject, which is the cornerstone of the metaphysics of the subject. The discourse of psychoanalysis stresses this point: the body as libidinal surface, field of forces, screen of imaginary projections; site of constitution of identity.

While sharing a great deal of these premises with the French epistemologies, however, Haraway also challenges Foucault's analysis of 'bio-power' or power over the body. Supporting Jameson's idea that a postmodernist politics is made necessary by the historical collapse of the traditional left, and that it represents the left's chance to reinvent itself from within, Haraway notes that contemporary power does not work by normalized heterogeneity anymore, but rather by networking, communication and multiple interconnections. She concludes that Foucault "names a form of power at its moment of implosion. The discourse of bio-politics gives way to technobabble."[37]

Two points are noteworthy here: firstly that Haraway analyzes the contemporary scientific revolution in more radical terms than Foucault does, mostly because she bases it on first-hand knowledge about today's technology. Haraway's training in biology and sociology of science are very useful here. By comparison with her approach, Foucault's analysis of the disciplining of bodies appears already out of date (apart from being intrinsically androcentric).

Secondly, Haraway suggests a point that I think worthy of further development, namely that the foucauldian diagrams of power describe what we have already ceased to be; like all cartography, they act *a posteriori* and therefore fail to account for the situation here and now. In this respect, Haraway opposes to Foucault's strategy of bio-power, an approach based on the deconstructive genealogy of the embodied subjectivities of women. The notion of 'women's experience' and the constant reference to feminist theory — a field of which Foucault is totally ignorant — helps Haraway to draw up a sort of psycho-pathology of this end of milennium.

Whereas Foucault's analysis rests on a nineteenth century view of the production system, Haraway inscribes her analysis of the condition of women into an up-to-date analysis of the post-industrial

---

37. Haraway, "A cyborg manifesto," in: *Simians, Cyborgs and Women* (London: Free Association Books, 1990), p. 245, footnote 4.

334

system of production. Arguing that white capitalist patriarchy has turned into the informatics of domination, Haraway argues that women have been cannibalized by the new technologies, they have disappeared from the field of visible social agents. The post-industrial system makes oppositional mass politics utterly redundant: a new politics must be invented, on the basis of a more adequate understanding of how the contemporary subject functions.

More specifically, her question then becomes: what counts as human in this post-human world? How to re-think the unity of the human subject, without reference to humanistic beliefs, without dualistic oppositions, linking instead body and mind in a new flux of self? What is the view of the self that is operational in the world of the informatics of domination?

More specifically, Haraway's concern is how to re-assemble a vision of female feminist subjectivity after the old certainties have collapsed[38]. Haraway takes very seriously the point that contemporary feminism rests on the very signifier 'woman' which it must deconstruct in order to prevent its exclusionary and normative effects. Feminists in the 90's must replace naive belief in global sisterhood or more strategic alliances based on common interests, with a new kind of politics, based on temporary and mobile coalitions and therefore on *affinity*. Arguing that the insistence on victimhood as the only ground for political legitimation has done enough damage, Haraway calls for a kind of feminist politics that could embrace "partial, contradictory, permanently unclosed constructions of personal and collective selves."[39]

The central question here is the extent to which sexual difference meant as the difference that women can make to society — i.e.: not as a naturally or historically given difference, but as an open-ended project to be constructed — also allows women to think of all their other differences. Foremost among them: differences of race, class and sexual life-styles. The female subject of feminism is constructed across a multiplicity of discourses, positions, meanings, which are often in conflict with one another: therefore the signifier 'woman' is no longer sufficient as the foundational stone of the feminist project.

38. On the technology of the self, see Teresa de Lauretis, *Technologies of gender* (Bloomington: Indiana University Press, 1986).
39. Haraway, "A manifesto for cyborgs," p. 57.

This is linked to the problem of how to go beyond the particular: Can women be represented as a collective political and epistemological subject? If the universal necessitates neutrality, the question then becomes not so much how to think sexual difference as positivity (Irigaray), but rather how to avoid essentialism and biological or psychic determinism in the feminist project to redefine female subjectivity.

Haraway invites us instead to think of the community as being built on the basis of a commonly shared basis of collective figures of speech, or foundational myths. These myths, which are also purposeful tools for intervention in reality, are figurations in that they make an impact on our imagination, but they are also forms of situated knowledge. In other words, feminism is about grounding, it is about foundations.

It is in this framework that Haraway proposes a new figuration for feminist subjectivity: the *cyborg*. As a hybrid, or body-machine, the cyborg is a connection-making entity, it is a figure of inter-relationality, receptivity and global communication that deliberately blurs categorical distinctions (human/machine; nature/culture; male/female; oedipal/non-oedipal). It is a way of thinking specificity without falling into relativism. The cyborg is Haraway's representation of a generic feminist humanity, it is her answer to the question of how feminists reconcile the radical historical specificity of women with the insistance on constructing new values that can benefit humanity as a whole.

To understand how Haraway's 'cyborg-feminism' fits into the postmodernist debate, let us compare two figurations: not just two rhetorical figures of speech but also two representations of political struggle, two different ways to deal with feminist critiques of rationality. The first is Haraway's 'cyborg,' the second is Gena Corea's 'mother-machine,'[40] the artificial breeder or fertility form, which Corea criticizes in terms of 'the reproductive brothel.'

As I stated above, the first embodies a positive, friendly vision of the body-machine relationship in our high-tech world, throwing open a brand new set of innovative epistemological and ethical questions. As a political manifesto, it renews the language of political struggle,

40. Gena Corea, *The Mother Machine* (New York: Harper and Row, 1985).

moving away from the tactic of head-on confrontations, in favor of a more specific and diffuse strategy based on irony, diagonal attacks and coalitions on the basis of affinity.

Not unlike other contemporary movements of thought, the cyborg aims at reconceptualizing the human being as an embodied and yet non-unified, and therefore non-Cartesian entity.

The second image — the mother machine — embodies a negative and rather hostile view of the body-machine relation, stressing its potential for exploitation and manipulation. It therefore highlights the need for a politics of opposition. It puts into question the liberating force of scientific reason and its impact on the relationship between the sexes in our society. Haraway defends a vision of the body as machine as an image of the multiple, de-naturalized subject. On the other hand, Corea expresses in dramatic terms the fear that the body, especially the woman's, might become just a machine. In both cases, there is a powerful question mark about the future of science and technology and its repercussions on genderdifferences. These two images can be taken as two aspects of the debate in feminist epistemology about the status of rationality.

The pioneer-work of Gena Corea and others has brought to our attention the dangers and the costs of reproductive technologies for women. On the political front, the concern is shared by all. Among other things, the debate over artificial reproduction has contributed to the neo-conservative campaign in favor of the rights of the foetus and even of the embryos, thus contributing to the anti-abortionist frenzy.

Many feminist theoreticians are also concerned by the gap that these technologies open between 'real' women and particularly sterile women who seek biomedical help to reproduce — and the feminists who criticize bio-technologies. This gap is often unfairly represented by the media as a conflict of interests, between the 'real' women who seek motherhood and the bad-girls feminists who are allegedly against it.

It is important to keep in mind the fact that this debate has quite a long history in feminism: Shulamith Firestone's marxist utopia[41] of reproductive technologies as liberating women from their anatomical destiny, in the 70's struck an optimistic note that got subsequently rejected by the more ecologically-minded new generations. The work of theologians on empowering the female potential for

41. Shulamith Firestone, *The dialectics of sex* (New York: Picador, 1969).

creativity and nurturance and the eco-feminists' naturalist rejection of technology set the tone for the feminist position through the 80's. Gena Corea'a negative analysis falls in between the two.

One of the things at stake in this entire debate is how to assess the tradition of the Enlightenment, i.e.: the grand rationalist tradition that wove together, in a teleological process, reason, history and the ideal of social progress. In other words, one of the great theoretical dividing lines in feminist epistemology seems to be between those who claim that feminism is an alternative science project, capable of enlarging the scope of scientific rationality, and those who believe that meaningful change can only come by down-playing the very notion of reason.

The political implications are quite far-reaching: the modernist school (Corea) believes in the historical complicity between reason and domination, rationality and oppression. It also asserts that this complicity can be corrected by appropriating social pressure and that it is not endemic to rationality as such (Women can act as a pressure group to change science).

The other position (Haraway, postmodernism) consists in pointing out precisely the structural, implicit complicity of rationality with domination, and both of them with masculinity. The historical necessity of freeing scientific rationality from its hegemonic connotations therefore requires fundamental internal transformations that will not leave the structure of scientific thought untouched. According to this framework, one can speak of the historical decline of rationality as a scientific and human ideal.

I would add that to argue for a structural, implicit link between western reason and domination — in terms of race, class, or sex -, and to argue for the need to dismantle such a link, amounts to putting rationality back in its place. It namely presumes that rationality is not the whole of reason and that reason in turn does not sum up the totality of or even what is best in the human capacity for thinking.

Once the idea of reason as a set of God-given principles is set aside, the road is open to the deconstruction of the conceptual dichotomies on which reason rested. But what are we going to put in its place? I think that it is at this point that Haraway's approach goes beyond the oppositional logic and opens up new paths of reflection.

Are feminists closet humanists, wanting to rescue what is left of

338

rationality, needing some realist theory of discourse, or an alternative female religion? Or can they adopt a radical form of epistemology that denies access to a real world and to a final truth, attempting to approach discourse analysis in a problematic mode? What is the image of thougth — the representation of the act of thinking — which best represents the feminist theoretical *corpus*: the postmodern affinity to a cyborg, or the modernist fear of the artificial mother-machine?

To come back with all of this in mind to the two images I started with: the cyborg and the mother-machine, I would say that the opposition between them is real conceptually and less so politically. As Haraway pointed out herself, the political struggle consists in seeing the problem of scientific rationality from both the perspectives of domination and liberation. The political struggle of women for control of the reproductive technologies, in other words, does not necessarily lead to feminist rejections of science and technology.

The cyborg as an epistemological model is, in my opinion, a perfectly adequate one in so far as it breaks down the dualistic barriers between the body and its technological and technical supports. The 'mother-machine' model, on the other hand, upholds the dualistic oppositon and calls for a confrontational kind of politics that is totally inadequate in this historical time of the informatics of domination.

Moreover, the the cyborg model implies a vision of the body that is neither physical nor mechanical, nor is it just textual. The cyborg functions rather as a counter-paradigm for the bodily intersection with external reality: it is an adequate reading not only of the body, not only of machines but rather of what goes on between them. As a new functional replacement of the mind/body split, the cyborg is a post-metaphysical construct.

Metaphysics is not an abstract construction, it is a political ontology: the classical dualism body/soul is not simply a gesture of separation and of hierarchical coding, it is also a theory about their interaction, about how they hang together: it is a proposition about how we should go about thinking about the fundamental unity of the human being. What is at stake here is the definition and the political viability of materialism.

The postmodernist epistemological project is not specifically feminist, though feminism has contributed historically to creating the *a priori* conditions for the decline of the universal, rationalist

339

paradigm. The specificity of the feminist standpoint is in terms of gender-differences and gender-specific analyses, but everything in feminist theory and practice makes it capable of elaborating general theoretical frameworks.

Whereas for the modernists, a world beyond gender will be a concentration camp for women, a form of 'gendercide' (as Corea puts it) that would flatten out all differences, replacing women with artificial uteruses, Haraway warns us that, our techno-world being what it is, the future of feminist politics will depend to a large extent on how women *negotiate* the transition to high-tech motherhood. Leaving behind naturalistic nostalgia, and paranoid fears, Haraway calls for the ethics of modernity as the staring point: in the world of the informatics of domination, women must work through the issue of their implication with technology, facing up to its complexity. This is a call for the courage of living up to the historical as well as epistemological contradictions of postmodernity.

In keeping with the positive, creative approach that characterizes feminist postmodernism and differentiates it from nihilistic or nostalgic reactions to the crisis of the philosophical subject, Haraway seizes the opportunities offered by this historical context in order to redesign the parameters of a new vision of the subject, which takes gender into account but does not stop there.

The central concern here is not only the epistemological issue of scientific revolutions, but also of how fiction (the imagination) and science (logos) can be recombined in a new unity. What can be of most help in taking the leap across the postmodern void, with its corollary: the postindustrial loss of political creed: mythos or logos? The challenge is how to speak cogently of the techno-scientific world, while maintaining a certain level of mythical wander and admiration about it. We simply need new forms of literacy in order to decode today's world.

Haraway recommends that we start rethinking the world as other, as semiosis, i.e. a semiotic-material agent with which we interact so as to produce knowledge, as opposed to getting locked in a relationship of mastery and domination. Theory is corporal, bodily, literal, figurative, not metaphorical. One cannot know properly, or even begin to understand, that towards which one has no affinity. Intelligence is sympathy. One should never criticize that which one is not complicitous with; criticism turns into a nonreactive mode, a creative gesture.

340

All other differences notwithstanding — and they are considerable — I see a coalition of interests between feminist figurations of a post-human subjectivity and Deleuze's positive reaction to the decline of phallo-logocentrism, with his emphasis on rhizomatic thinking. Both stress the need to work on transforming the very image of thought and of subjectivity as an intensive, multiple and discontinuous process of inter-relations. For Haraway the feminist as cyborg is an intensive, multiple subject, rhizomatic, embodied and therefore perfectly artificial; as an artifact it is machinic, complex, capable of infinite inter-connections. And not unlike Benjamin's angel of history, it already has a foot in the next century, while keeping its satellite-eye focussed on the very past out of which it is moving, stumbling backwards towards progress.

18. Irreale Präsenz: Allegorie bei Paul de Man und Walter Benjamin

HELGA GEYER-RYAN

Der Titel meines Essays nennt nicht nur Paul de Man und Walter Benjamin, sondern ebenso George Steiner. Steiners Buch *Real Presences*[1] hat, zumindest in Deutschland, eine Literaturdebatte ausgelöst und zuvor auch in den englischen Medien Aufsehen erregt. Ich nehme die Rezeption dieses schmalen Bandes als Anzeichen für einen Prozess der Umorientierung im ideologischen Feld.

Steiners Buch ist ein frontaler Angriff auf die textuelle Praxis der Dekonstruktion. Sie richtet sich allerdings nicht gegen die philosophischen Demontagen Derridas als vielmehr gegen de Mans umfassenden Ideologieverdacht literarischer Werke. Für de Man ist Ästhetische Ideologie die Totalisierung differentieller Textualität mithilfe sprachlicher Figuren, wie sie die Rhetorik auflistet. Dadurch kommt eine Versinnlichung des abstrakten Mediums Sprache auf verschiedenen Ebenen der literarischen Kommunikation zustande. Die Versinnlichung der Sprache hat letzten Endes immer, wie verschieden die Techniken auch sein mögen, einen anthropomorphisierenden Effekt, auf den die Leser durch Einfühlung reagieren. Damit scheint Sprache nicht mehr nur zu repräsentieren mit ihrer unschliessbaren Lücke zwischen Zeichen und Bedeutung, sondern direkt Präsenz hervorzutreiben: Hinter den Bildern, die durch Mimesis und Figuralität heraufbeschworen werden, verschwindet die Konventionalität der sprachlichen Zeichen. In dieser Überblendung der symbolischen Verkettung durch eine imaginäre und räumliche Gleichzeitigkeit erfährt sich das Subjekt als mit sich selbst identisch. Es ist geborgen in einem fantastischen Wahrheitsraum, in dem Zeichen und Bedeutung, Zeichen und Referenz miteinander übereinstimmen.

Gegen diese Laterna magica der Schrift richtet sich der radikale Enthüllungsgestus de Mans. Zwar gesteht er künstlerischen Gebilden zu, die eigene Gemachtheit, ihren Mangel in der Sprache, ihre semiotische Wunde nicht zu verschweigen, aber das geht ihm nicht

---

1. George Steiner, *Real Presences. Is there anything in what we say?* (London, Boston: Faber and Faber, 1989).

weit genug. Entschlossen reisst er ihnen die Maske ästhetischer Metaphysik ganz ab.

Dass daran das Gesicht hängen bleibt, ist der Vorwurf George Steiners. Provokativ nimmt er für sich einen Wahrheitsdiskurs der Kunst in Anspruch, der heutzutage als metaphysisch und theologisch gebrandmarkt ist. Steiner geht davon aus, dass es zwischen den Diskursen von Maske und von Gesicht, von ästhetischer Dekonstruktion und von ästhetischer Erfahrung keine Vermittlung gibt. Konsequent zerfällt sein Buch in zwei Teile. Der erste ist eine wertende Analyse der Dekonstruktion. Steiner schliesst: "On its own terms and planes of argument (...) the challenge of deconstruction does seem to me irrefutable. (...) I do not, therefore, believe that an answer to its challenge (...) can be found, if it can be found at all, within linguistic or literary theory. (...) I want to ask wether a hermeneutics and a reflex of valuation (...) can be made intelligible, can be made answerable to the existential facts, if they do not imply, if they do not contain, a postulate of transcendence."[2]

In Steiners Buch gibt es keinen "quantum leap" zwischen "letter", dem ersten dekonstruktivistischen Teil, und "presence"[3], dem zweiten, transzendenten, oder wenn man so will, metaphysischen Teil, der eher phenomenologisch ist.

Ein "quantum leap" ist keine Vermittlung im dialektischen Sinn und man könnte beide Diskurse unvermittelt, heteronom, nebeneinander bestehen lassen. Dennoch glaube ich, dass Steiner eine Möglichkeit der Differenzierung zu schnell aufgibt. Nämlich den Unterschied zwischen "linguistic and literary theory".

Weil Steiner selbst nicht die letzten Endes linguistische Theorie der Literatur bei de Man kritisiert, kann er auch keine Antwort geben. Sein eigenes Bemühen um eine Begrifflichkeit der ästhetischen Erfahrung zeigt aber den energischen Vorstoss in Gebiete, die von einer rein linguistischen Semiologie, einer Semiologie, die differentiell sein muss, weil sie pur linguistisch ist, nicht mehr erfasst werden kann.

Die Ästhetik hält eine Theorie bereit, die einen möglichen Sprung zwischen der Dekonstruktion als einem Diskurs der Leere und der Literatur als einem Diskurs der Transzendenz beschreiben könnte. Das ist die Theorie des Erhabenen.

Das Erhabene ist eine Rezeptionskategorie. Sie beschreibt die Spannung in einem Subjekt, das durch eine Krisis im Verhältnis

---

2. George Steiner, *Real Presences*, S.132-134.
3. George Steiner, *Real Presences*, S.212.

zwischen Sinnlichkeit und Intellekt zur höchsten Anspannung eben dieser Kräfte aufgerufen wird. Angesichts einer vernichtenden Exzentrik von Natur, sei sie überwältigend in ihrem Andrang oder furchterregend in ihrem Ausbleiben, rettet sich das durch seine eigene Sinnlichkeit und Natürlichkeit in seinem Narzismus bedrohte Subjekt kraft seiner Vernunft vor dem Untergang und reisst selbst die besiegte Sinnlichkeit über sich selbst hinaus, um sie, wie Kant sagt, auf das Gebiet der Vernunft hin, die sittlichen Ideen, zu erweitern, und "auf das Unendliche hinaussehen zu lassen, welches für jene ein Abgrund ist"[4]. Diese Macht des Intellekts, die Kant als unser Vermögen zu moralischen Ideen umschreibt, findet ihren Ausdruck in den Positionen von Sicherheit, also im umfassendsten Sinn: unserer Kultur, angesichts bedrohlicher Natur.

Bedrohliche Natur kann auch ausbleibende Natur sein. Und hier, im schwindelerregenden Abgrund des horror vacui, zeigt sich die Konvergenz von Dekonstruktion, Allegorie, Melancholie und Erhabenem.

Die Figur der Allegorie nimmt sowohl bei Walter Benjamin als auch bei Paul de Man einen zentralen Platz ein. Beiden geht es um die essentielle Leere im sprachlichen Zeichen, wenn die Sinngarantie Gottes verfallen ist. Eine solche Einsicht müsste, in radikaler Konsequenz erfasst, beiden das weitere Sprechen verbieten. Dieser performative Widerspruch ist das zentrale Argument gegen dekonstruktivistische Aussagen.

De Man thematisiert selbst diesen Einwurf als die Aporie jedes, auch seines eigenen, Sprechakts, der genau die Verfahren wiederholen muss, die er kritisiert.

Dennoch soll eine solche Geste offener Bescheidenheit verhüllen, dass es tatsächlich die Performanz ist, die der Aussage trotz ihres widersprüchlichen Status Geltung verleiht. Dieser Sprachgestus, der seine Autorität mittels einer Rhetorik der Bescheidenheit einsetzt, wird gestützt durch die Macht des Sprechens. Durch die gewalttätige Setzung eines performativen Subjekts erfolgt der rettende Sprung aus der drohenden Vernichtung von Referenz, Bedeutung und Subjekt.

Die Theorie des Erhabenen ist deshalb wichtig, weil sie im Ver-

---

4. Immanuel Kant, *Werke in zwölf Bänden. Band X: Kritik der Urteilskraft*, hg. v. Wilhelm Weischedel (Frankfurt/Main: Suhrkamp, 1970), S.354.

gleich zur Theorie des performativen Widerspruchs — denn alle zwei behandeln das gleiche Phänomen — eine Dimension einführt, die de Man unter allen Umständen aus seiner Argumentation heraushalten muss. Es ist die Dimension des Psychischen: der Imagination und des Fantasmas, die in seiner Theorie zu Produkten einer vorgängigen Sprachmaschine werden.

Die Theorie des Erhabenen, als Teil der Ästhetik, fällt natürlich selbst unter das Verdikt ästhetischer Ideologie, wenn sie nur der Effekt der Figuralität von Sprache sein soll. Deshalb die Angriffe auf die Psychoanalyse[5], deren Theorie immer noch von einem Subjekt des Unbewussten, oder einem gespaltenen Subjekt ausgehen kann.

De Man kann die Priorität von Sprache als ästhetisches Subjekt nur deshalb aufrechterhalten, weil er von zwei Voraussetzungen ausgeht, die nicht reflektiert werden. Die erste ist die eher unterschwellige Bevorzugung der Freudschen Psychoanalyse mit Lacanscher Sprachwende.

In deren Zentrum steht der ödipuskomplex, der selbst bereits das Ergebnis der symbolischen Ordnung, also von Sprache ist. Hierdurch wird es möglich, die Sprache als Mechanismus gegenüber der Psychoanalyse zu privilegieren. Aber erst eine Psychoanalyse, die den prä-ödipalen Raum in ihren Ansatz mit hereinnimmt, wie die von Melanie Klein oder Julia Kristeva, zeigt, dass beide, Dekonstruktion und ödipale Psychoanalyse, selbst als Allegorien von Sprache als Maschine gelesen werden können.

Die zweite Voraussetzung, und sie hängt eng mit dieser ersten zusammen, ist zentral für de Mans Argumentation: dass nämlich Sprache als Figur, wie die rhetorischen Kombinationen der Zeichen genannt werden, selbst eine Metapher ist. Natürlich gibt es in der Sprache überhaupt keine Figur, es sei denn, wir denken an die Kalligramme von Apollinaire oder Benjamins Beobachtung, dass mit der Einführung der Majuskel die Allegorisierung von Abstrakta in der deutschen Sprache gefördert worden sei.

---

5. "But if her nominal presence is a mere coincidence, then we are entering an entirely different system in which such terms as desire, shame, guilt, exposure, and repression no longer have any place." (S.289)
"Far from seeing language as an instrument in the service of a psychic energy, the possibility now arises that the entire construction of drives, substitutions, repressions, and representations is the aberrant, metaphorical correlative of the absolute randomness of language, prior to any figuration or meaning." (S.299)
Paul de Man, "Excuses", in: *Allegories of Reading* (New Haven, London: Yale University Press, 1979), S. 278-301.

Wir müssen uns also fragen, warum de Man die Figuralität von Sprache als Figur nicht thematisiert und was die Funktion dieser Metapher sein könnte.

Was wird übertragen in der Metapher von Rhetorik als figürlicher Rede? Zurücktransportiert auf das linguistische Zeichen wird der ästhetische Effekt, der aber selbst gar nicht durch die Trope erzielt wird. Der ästhetische Effekt ist vielmehr das Ergebnis einer bewussten Aktualisierung der quasi-ontologischen Differenz zwischen Kunst und Realität im Rezipienten. Von der Sprache eines Textes her, und scheint er noch so literarisch in seiner rhetorischen Ausstattung zu sein, lässt sich niemals auf einen literarischen Text schliessen. Ob wir es mit Literatur zu tun haben, hängt nicht von den Tropen ab, sondern von unserer Entscheidung, einen vorliegenden Text als literarischen zu lesen. Wie die Entscheidung ausfällt, ist im Grunde willkürlich, wird aber durch die Vorgaben unserer Kultur gesteuert. Sie sind nicht ohne weiteres rückgängig zu machen, denn sie sind als Einschreibungen in unsere körperliche, inkarnierte Befindlichkeit eingelassen. Nicht nur ist Natur immer schon geschichtlich, sondern Kultur auch immer schon naturalisiert.

Der ästhetische Diskurs zeichnet sich, in Habermasschen Begriffen, durch eine "illokutive Entmächtigung" aus. Das heisst, der Leser entschliesst sich zu einer freiwilligen Suspendierung der Gültigkeitskriterien, die Sprecher voraussetzen müssen, wenn sie in verständigungsorientierte Kommunikation eintreten wollen. Das Fiktionalitätskriterium wird also tiefer angesetzt als auf der Ebene des Textes, nämlich auf der Ebene der performativen Einstellung. Die ästhetische Einstellung koppelt die Kommunikation vom unmittelbaren Bezug auf die Welt ab.

Eine solche Suspension, die bei Kant als interesseloses Wohlgefallen theoretisiert wird, ist eine Distanzfähigkeit der Umwelt, also auch der Natur, der Realität gegenüber. Kant sieht sie in allen Menschen angelegt, aber realisierbar nur unter bestimmten historischen Bedingungen, nämlich solchen, wie Technik und Wissenschaft, die tatsächlich dem Menschen die unmittelbare Eingebundenheit in Natur als bedürftiges Naturwesen lockern.

Erst in dieser Entdramatisierung des Sinnenbezugs zur Welt kann sich das Subjekt seiner eigenen Sinnlichkeit als eines allgemeinen Vermögens bewusst werden. Die Sinnlichkeit wird selbst zum Objekt der Sinnlichkeit, indem an die Stelle der Welt das Kunstobjekt tritt. Darum der Übergang von den Poetiken zu den Ästhetiken im Zeitalter der Aufklärung.[6]

Die sogenannte Figuralität der Sprache, die im literarischen Text genausogut ausbleiben kann, intensiviert die Sprache, ist aber selbst nicht der Grund für Fiktionalität oder Mimesis.

Nur um den Preis also, dass de Man nicht die Metapher der Sprachfigur befragt, kann er den *Text* privilegieren als den eigentlichen Schauplatz der ästhetischen Veranstaltung.

Mit der Verdrängung des Ästhetischen als Dimension der Sinnlichkeit und damit des Subjekts aus den Texten muss de Man auch den Körper und damit die Psychoanalyse zum Verschwinden bringen. Aber gerade die Zeichentheorie der Psychoanalyse kann uns sagen, was sich hinter der Bevorzugung der Allegorie als Zeichentheorie verbirgt. Vielleicht gibt es neben einer ästhetischen auch eine allegorische Ideologie?

Fassen wir noch einmal zusammen: De Man kann nur deshalb auf der ausschliesslich linguistischen Semiologie des literarischen Textes bestehen, weil er die Körperlichkeit von Autor und Rezipient verdrängt, für deren Anwesenheit in der literarischen Kommunikation die Metapher der sprachlichen Figur im Text steht. Erst diese Verdrängung der Sinnlichkeit reisst den Text so radikal aus seiner Verankerung in Dingen und Körpern, dass von ihm nur noch die Allegorie seiner eigenen "undecidability", seiner Unlesbarkeit, übrig bleibt.

Die Verdrängung des Körpers geschieht durch seine Kastration. Begriffe wie "mutilation", "defacement", "disfiguration", "blindness" spielen in de Mans Texten eine zentrale Rolle. Unter dem Begriff "damnatio memoriae" kennen wir diese Kastrationsrituale aus der Geschichte, wo Statuen ehemaliger Herrscher mutiliert werden, indem man ihnen Gliedmassen abschlägt, sie blendet, Nasen und Ohren verstümmelt.

In einer solchen Mutilation der Körper und vor allem des Gesichts wird die Geschichte vernichtet, deren Spuren sich in die Körper eingezeichnet haben. So wie im Stil eines Textes, seinen Figuren also, sich die Figur, der biographische und geschichtliche Körper des Autors einzeichnet und in die Interpretation die Figur des Rezipienten, so werden mit der Entkörperlichung von Texten diese selbst kastriert, ihrer Bedeutung enthoben.

6. Vgl. Helga Geyer-Ryan, "Das Paradox der Kunstautonomie. Ästhetik nach Marcuse", in: *Kritik und Utopie im Werk von Herbert Marcuse*, hg. v. Institut für Sozialforschung (Frankfurt/Main: Suhrkamp, 1992), s. 272-285.

Es ist ein Fehlschluss, dass mit dem Verlust eines Sinnzentrums, seien das Gott oder die Vernunft oder der Marxismus oder der Fortschritt der Kontrakt der Zeichen aufgehoben wäre. Vielmehr tragen Zeichen und Körper die 'einverleibten' Spuren dieser Sinnkontrakte. Wie gewalttätig darum der allegorische Blick des sinnverlassenen Melancholikers sein muss, zeigt sich an den heftigen Sprachgesten, mit denen die willkürlichen, aber doch wahlverwandten Sprachzeichen zerbrochen und neu zusammengeschweisst werden.

Der Körper der Mutter

In der Entfernung der Körperlichkeit aus der literarischen Kommunikation und der zwangsläufig anschliessenden Zerbrechung der Sprachzeichen in Signifikant und Signifikat wird im Grunde der weibliche Körper und tatsächlich der mütterliche Körper verdrängt. In der Kastration wird die Präsenz des eigenen Körpers zerstört, in den die Erinnerung an die Mutter eingeschrieben ist. Diesen Gestus repetiert de Man wie im Wiederholungszwang. Die Rückkehr des Verdrängten muss immer wieder aufs neue negiert werden. In der Disfiguration der Figuren im Text wird unaufhörlich der Gründungsgestus unserer westlichen Kultur durchgespielt, nämlich die Verwerfung des Weiblichen.

In seinem Aufsatz "Figure Foreclosed" analysiert Lyotard die judaische Religion des Bilderverbots und des nicht erinnerten Vatermords als Verwerfung der Kastration. Sie führt mit sich die Verwerfung der Figur des Weiblichen und der Mutter. Lyotard sagt: "The *Vernichtung* of the figurative is also a *Verneinung* of the maternal."[7]

Die umfassende Entsinnlichung der Kunst unter dem Verdacht der Ideologie transportiert das Vergessen, die Verneinung und die Verdrängung des Weiblichen. Dem entspricht die Allegorie in ihrer konkreten Ausstattung. Allegorien sind meistens weibliche Gestalten, denen eine fremde Bedeutung übergestülpt wird. Insofern gibt die Allegorie bildlich wieder, was der Frau im Patriarchat sowieso passiert. Ihr Körper wird zum Zeichen maskuliner Bedeutungen. Folgerichtig reduziert die Allegorie den weiblichen Körper zur weiblichen Form. Wahrscheinlich ist das einer der Gründe,

---

7. Jean-François Lyotard, "Figure Foreclosed", in: *The Lyotard Reader*, hg. v. Andrew Benjamin (Oxford: Blackwell, 1989), S.69-110, S.105.

warum Allegorien weiblich sind. Es ist die Fungibilität des weiblichen Körpers im Bereich männlicher Bedeutungsmacht.

Bei de Man tauchen Frauen nur in allegorischer, d.h. männliche Identität definierender Funktion auf: Marion als Allegorie der Zufälligkeit in "Excuses", Galathea als Allegorie der Unentscheidbarkeit von Ich und Nicht-Ich in "Self", das weibliche Portrait von Narcissus als Allegorie der Unentscheidbarkeit von Liebe, Selbstliebe und Eitelkeit und "Julie" als Allegorie der Allegorie.

Dass es überhaupt einen Bildraum gibt, aus dessen Fundus der weibliche Körper zum Material der Allegorese wird, ist bereits das Zeichen patriarchaler, also ödipaler Gewalt.

Damit geht es aber eigentlich um eine doppelte Mortifikation des weiblichen Körpers in der Allegorie. Denn ausser dieser ersten Abtötung zum Bildmaterial zeigt sich in der Lücke zwischen Bild und Bedeutung die essentielle Leere des Zeichens *und* die Leere der Existenz. Sie ist eine Folge der Trennung von der prä-ödipalen Mutter beim Eintritt in die Sprache.Das sagt das folgende Zitat: "(...) l'écriture allégorique est écriture du figurale et destruction de tout figuratif au sens stricte."[8]

Projizieren wir diese, im allegorischen Bild gleichzeitig bestehenden, Destruktionen auf eine Zeitachse der Psychographie, dann führt uns die Regression zurück durch die tödliche ödipale Bildinterpretation des Weiblichen, durch das noch nicht sexualisierte Spiegelbild, hinein in die Leere reiner Positionalität, erfahrbar später nur im Akt des Ekels.

Hier, in der allerersten Platzschaffung für ein späteres Ich, wird die allmächtige, prä-ödipale Mutter zur abjekten Mutter abgetötet. Es ist diese Doppelfigur des Mords, die in der Allegorie ihren Ausdruck findet. Darum zitiert Benjamin im *Ursprung des deutschen Trauerspiels* nicht zufällig, "die 'Egyptier' hätten 'in höltzernen Bildern Leichen begraben.'"[9]

Die Frau, als fungibles Bild, ist immer schon abgetötet, denn der patriarchale Blick macht den Körper der Frau zum Objekt, lässt ihn verstummen. Erinnerung ist gebunden an Körper- und Ding-repräsentationen, an Bilder also. Dann wäre die Heraufholung des

8. Christine Buci-Glucksmann, "Fémininité et modernité: Walter Benjamin et l'utopie féminine", in: *Walter Benjamin et Paris*, Colloque international 27-29 juin 1983, hg. v. Heinz Wisman (Paris: Les Editions du Cerf, 1986), S.418.
9. Walter Benjamin, *Ursprung des deutschen Trauerspiels*, in: *Gesammelte Schriften*, Bd.I.1, hg. v. Hermann Schweppenhäuser und Rolf Tiedemann (Frankfurt/Main: Suhrkamp, 1982), S.396.

mütterlichen Körpers aus dem prä-ödipalen Raum immer schon die Präsentation einer Leiche, die unter dem Schein verborgen läge.

Die Gewalt der Semiose

Dennoch ist der lebendige Körper der Mutter nicht völlig verschwunden. Er ist anwesend im Akt der Gewalt — "figuration" und "défiguration" als Prozess, nicht als Resultat — den jede Zeichenpraxis aufs Neue wiederholen muss, wenn sie Sinn produzieren will. Semiose ist "acting out" von Mord und Kastration im Innern der Zeichen. Je mehr Zeichen und Bedeutung auseinandergerissen und neu gefügt werden zu hermetischen Kombinationen und harten Schnitten, umso tiefer klafft der essentielle Abgrund zwischen ihnen, der sonst durch Konventionen überbrückt wird. In diesem Abgrund zeigt sich die Gewalt als Anstrengung des Sinns.

Darum ist die Allegorie, als figürliche Rede oder als Emblem, durch ihre gewalttätige, unvermittelte Fügung die Allegorie eines jeden hermeneutischen Akts.

Genauso wie bei de Man umspielt darum auch bei Benjamin eine Semantik der Gewalt die Figur der Allegorie. Breitinger wird zitiert, der die Allegorie einen *Kerker* des Begriffs nennt. Es geht um die *membra disiecta* sowohl der allegorisierten Leiber auf der barocken Bühne als auch der Sprache, die sich in den *sadistischen* Händen des Allegorikers befindet.[10] Die Allegorie *versklavt*,[11] sie *beutet aus*, in ihr wird der Sinn *auseinandergerissen*, die Sprache des Barock ist *erschüttert* von *Rebellionen* ihrer Elemente.[12]

Ganz besonders ist die Allegorie der Schauplatz, auf dem der Körper zerstückelt wird, vor allem der weibliche Körper. (Wahrscheinlich ist aber jeder Körper, der dem Zugriff von Augen und Händen als Objekt sich anbietet, automatisch weiblich konnotiert, gleichgültig, ob es sich um den konkreten Körper einer Frau oder eines Mannes handelt.) Der Rückgang hinter die Spiegelbilder führt in die Tiefe des corps morcelé, der ausgespannt ist zwischen dem Kraftfeld der abjekten, phallischen Mutter und der Anziehung des — nicht-phallischen — Vaters der persönlichen Vorzeit.

Der archaische Sog der Leere, gleichzeitig Ekel und Faszination der Verschmelzung, erscheinen in Benjamins Werk als unversöhnbares Nebeneinander von Lust und Melancholie angesichts der

---

10. Walter Benjamin, *Ursprung des deutschen Trauerspiels*, S.375/376.
11. Walter Benjamin, *Ursprung des deutschen Trauerspiels*, S.378.
12. Walter Benjamin, *Ursprung des deutschen Trauerspiels*, S.381.

Vernichtung des Subjekts und seiner Innerlichkeit. Die Reduktion des Individuums auf die Kreatur, die Puppe, den Automat, die Maschine, den Körperstumpf, die Ausweidung des Innenraums werden zutiefst genossen und ebenso tief betrauert.

Die Trauer über den Verlust von Innerlichkeit und Autonomie liegt der Interpretation der Melancholie, der Klage um den Verlust der Aura, des Erzählens, der mémoire involontaire zugrunde. Diese mimetischen Phänomene (er-)scheinen nicht mehr, weil die himmlischen Gestirne als Garanten von Transzendenz und Signifikanz aufgehört haben zu strahlen. "Das brechende Auge ist das Urphänomen des verlöschenden Scheins."[13]

Der Gott, der sich im 17. Jahrhundert versteckt und im 18. Jahrhundert stirbt, war der transzendente Garant des Sinns. Sein Tod zieht die Erosion des sittlichen Subjekts und die Entleerung des weltlichen Gehäuses unausweichlich nach sich. Das barocke Trauerspiel präfiguriert diesen Zustand der existentiellen Entleerung. "Die grossen deutschen Dramatiker des Barock waren Lutheraner. (...) Der rigorosen Sittlichkeit der bürgerlichen Lebensführung, die es lehrte, stand seine Abkehr von den 'guten Werken' gegenüber. Indem es die besondere geistliche Wunderwirkung diesen absprach, die Seele auf die Gnade des Glaubens verwies und den weltlich-staatlichen Bereich zur Probestatt eines religiös nur mittelbaren, zum Ausweis bürgerlicher Tugenden bestimmten Lebens machte, hat es im Volk zwar den strengen Pflichtgehorsam angesiedelt, in seinen Grossen aber den Trübsinn. Jeder Wert war den menschlichen Handlungen genommen. Etwas Neues entstand: eine leere Welt."[14]

Die Lust an der Zerstörung des Subjekts

Die Krise der transzendenten Heilsgewissheit zieht den Verfall des Körpers nach sich. Denn auch der Körper ist nur Körper im Lichte transzendenter Signifikanz. Ohne sie wird er zur Natur, zu beliebiger Materie, zum Ding, zur Leiche, selbst da, wo er noch lebt. Darum kann der allegorische Furor Körper, Dinge, Körperteile unterschiedslos durcheinanderwirbeln. Benjamin spricht deswegen von der Kreatur, die an die Stelle des Mitglieds der heilsgewissen Gemeinde gerückt ist. Die Leere der Kreatur repetiert auch das

---

13. Walter Benjamin, *Das Passagen-Werk. Gesammelte Schriften*, Bd.V.1 und 2, hg. v. Rolf Tiedemann, Bd.V.1, S.422.
14. Walter Benjamin, *Ursprung des deutschen Trauerspiels*, S.317.

barocke Trauerspiel unentwegt. Die Protagonisten erscheinen als Puppen, Kartenkönige, Marionetten, Miniaturen. So wie unter dem Blick des Allegorikers aus den Wortkörpern der Sinn abfliesst, sie zertrümmert und zerstückelt werden zu Silben und Buchstaben, so strömt aus den zertrümmerten und zerstückelten Bühnenkörpern das Blut ab.

Auch Benjamins eigene figürliche Sprache ist eine Rhetorik der Gewalt. Seine Metaphern, Vergleiche und Allegorien evozieren auf extrem plastische Weise Dinge und Körper, aber auch deren brutale Zerstörung. Die Allegorie ist blutig: "'l'appareil sanglant de la Destruction' ist der Hof der Allegorie."[15] Sie beherrscht und vergewaltigt: "Der allegorischen Intention ist *jede* Intimität mit den Dingen fremd. Sie berühren heisst ihr: sie vergewaltigen. Sie erkennen heisst ihr: sie durchschauen."[16]

In seiner allegorischen Rezeption der Allegorie verbindet Benjamin den Zeichenkörper mit dem Weiblichen, die Zeichenbedeutung (die allegorische Intention, die "Allegorie" tout court) mit dem Männlichen. Die Szene der Allegorese wird so zu einem Szenario sexueller Gewalt. Sie erscheint als Vielweiberei, Sadismus und Voyeurismus: "(...) der Allegoriker (...) meidet (...) keinesfalls die Willkür als drastische Bekundung von der Macht des Wissens. Die Chiffrenfülle, die derselbe in der historisch tief geprägten Kreaturwelt liegen fand, rechtfertigt Cohens Klagen über 'Verschwendung'. Sie mag dem Walten der Natur wohl ungemäss sein; die Wollust, mit welcher die Bedeutung als finsterer Sultan im Harem der Dinge herrscht, bringt sie unvergleichlich zum Ausdruck. Es ist ja dem Sadisten eigentümlich, seinen Gegenstand zu entwürdigen und darauf — oder dadurch — zu befriedigen. So tut denn auch der Allegoriker in dieser von erdichteten wie von erfahrenen Grausamkeiten trunkenen Zeit. (...) Der 'Augenaufschlag', den barocke Malerei 'zu einem Schema' ausbildet (...) verrät und entwertet die Dinge auf unaussprechliche Weise. Nicht sowohl Enthüllung als geradezu Entblössung der sinnlichen Dinge ist die Funktion der barocken Bilderschrift. Als Schrift, als Unterschrift, wie diese in Emblembüchern innig mit dem Dargestellten zusammenhängt, zerrt er dessen Wesen vors Bild."[17]

In den von Benjamin benutzten Bildern richtet sich die Aggression in letzter Instanz gegen den Körper der (phallischen) Mut-

---

15. Walter Benjamin, *Das Passagen-Werk*, S.435.
16. Walter Benjamin, *Das Passagen-Werk*, S.423.
17. Walter Benjamin, *Der Ursprung des deutschen Trauerspiels*, S.360/361.

ter, der erniedrigt und zum Bluten und Sterben gebracht werden soll. Die Essenz aller allegorischen Bilder ist das am meisten Abjekte, die Leiche. Auf den letzten vierzig Seiten des *Ursprungs des deutschen Trauerspiels* finden sich in folgender Reihenfolge die Kapitelüberschriften "Allegorische Zerstückelung", "Sprachzerstückelung", "Die Leiche als Emblem". Das ekelerregende Wesen der Leiche rührt aus der Verschmelzung und Entdifferenzierung der grundlegendsten Opposition im gesellschaftlichen Ordnungsschema, nämlich der zwischen Leben und Tod zu einer amorphen, organisch-anorganischen Masse. Nicht, dass die Leiche eine direkte Metapher für den Körper der Mutter wäre. Aber in der tiefen Abjektion, die den Menschen im Angesicht von totem Leben befällt, wird die ursprüngliche Trennungs-Angst/Lust des "mütterlichen" Körpers am stärksten erfahren.

Wir hatten gesagt, dass die Lust am Abjekten, die Zerstörung aller transzendenten und transzendentalen Garantien nur eine Seite dieser Position ist. Die andere ist Trauer und Melancholie. Die Lust an der Zerstörung muss bezahlt werden mit der Aufgabe der narzistischen Autonomie, die durch die Trennung von der Mutter eingeleitet wird. "Abjection is therefore a kind of narcissistic crisis, it is witness to the ephemeral aspect of the state called 'narcissism' (...) abjection gives narcissism its classification as 'seeming'." Aber, sagt Kristeva, "Abjection is a resurrection that has gone through death (of the ego). It is an alchemy that transforms death drive into a start of life, of new significance."[18]

Einen Weg zur Mutter zurück gibt es nicht, denn "the abject is the violence of mourning for an 'object' that has always already been lost."[19] Genauso wenig gibt es ein Zurück zu einer unhistorischen, 'natürlichen' Natur. Wo das Licht der Signifikanz abgedreht wird, herrscht kein Dunkel, keine Helle, sondern ein fahles Dämmerlicht. Das meint Benjamin mit 'dämonisch'. Ebenso fällt die Sprache nach ihrer Zerschlagung nicht in den Zustand einer tabula rasa reiner Bedeutungsfreiheit zurück. "Die Worte erweisen sich noch in ihrer Vereinzelung verhängnisvoll. Ja man ist versucht zu sagen, schon die Tatsache, dass sie, so vereinzelt, noch etwas bedeuten, gibt dem Bedeutungsrest, der ihnen verblieb, etwas Drohendes."[20]

---

18. Julia Kristeva, *Powers of Horror. An Essay on Abjection*, übers. v. Leon Roudiez (New York: Columbia University Press, 1982), S.14.
19. Julia Kristeva, *Powers of Horror*, S.15.
20. Ebd.

Die Angst ist der Blick in den Abgrund, wenn aus den Phänomenen der Sinn abfliesst. Die Allegorie und das Sublime gruppieren sich beide um die Erfahrung der schwindelerregenden Tiefe oder Leere.

Es gibt einen grossen Unterschied zwischen de Man und Benjamin. De Man will die Bilder, das Figurale, das Ästhetische gerade entlarven als ideologischen Schein über der existentiellen Leere des sprachlichen Zeichens. Deshalb müssen ihm alle Figuren zu Allegorien erstarren. De Man gelingt es am Ende des 20. Jahrhunderts nicht mehr, die zerschlagenen Figuren unter einem neuen Sinnstrahl zusammenzufügen, ihnen neue Bedeutung zu verleihen. Er verharrt heroisch im Limbo der Leere und Nicht-Entscheidbarkeit.

Benjamin dagegen will letztlich in seinem Projekt die Bilder retten gegen ihre traditionellen korrupten Bedeutungen und aus ihnen neuen revolutionären Sinn schlagen (*Das Passagenwerk*). Darum muss auch er die Figuren zerstören, die Sinnkörper zerreissen. Das tut er im Trauerspielbuch. Aber dann will er sie mit neuem Sinn auferstehen lassen. Diese Resurrektion, Sublimation oder Himmelfahrt führt er durch im Bild des Messias und des Marxistisch-Erhabenen, wie Lyotard es nennt.[21] So wie in der Erfahrung des Sublimen das (narzistische) Subjekt sich vor dem Untergang in der sinnlichen Natur durch den Aufschwung seiner Vernunft rettet, so "erwacht" der Allegoriker in "Gottes Welt", sagt Benjamin.

"Denn gerade in Visionen des Vernichtungsrauschs, in welchen alles Irdische zum Trümmerfeld zusammenstürzt, enthüllt sich weniger das Ideal der allegorischen Versenkung, denn ihre Grenze.(…) Zuletzt springt in den Todesmalen des Barock — nun erst im rückgewandten grossen Bogen und erlösend — die allegorische Betrachtung um. (…) Das löst die Ziffer des Zerstückeltsten, Erstorbensten, Zerstreutesten. (…) Das eben ist das Wesen melancholischer Versenkung, dass ihre letzten Gegenstände, in denen *des Verworfnen* sie am völligsten sich zu versichern glaubt, in Allegorien umschlagen, dass sie das Nichts, in dem sie sich darstellen, erfüllen und verleugnen, so wie die Intention zuletzt im Anblick der Gebeine nicht treu verharrt, sondern zur Auferstehung restlos überspringt."[22]

21. Vgl. *Postmodernism: ICA Documents 4*, hg. v. Lisa Appignanesi (London, 1984), zit. n. Terry Eagleton, *The Ideology of the Aesthetic* (Oxford: Blackwell, 1990), S.231.
22. Walter Benjamin, *Ursprung des deutschen Trauerspiels*, S.406.

354

Aber nicht wie im Barock soll die allegorische Form entseelt zurückbleiben, sondern gerade aus ihrem verdinglichten Bann in neuer Sinnlichkeit erwachen.

Während de Man im Anblick der Gebeine treu verharrt, springt Benjamin zur Auferstehung restlos über.

In der Rettung der Bilder geht es Benjamin um die Rettung von Körperlichkeit, Dinglichkeit, Sinnlichkeit und damit letzten Endes um die Rettung von konkreter oder vielleicht besser (wie Steiner sagt): präsenter Realität. Das geht bis in die Physis der geschriebenen Signifikanten. "Dennoch hat Schrift nichts Dienendes an sich, fällt beim Lesen nicht ab wie Schlacke. Ins Gelesene geht sie ein als dessen 'Figur'."[23] Hier ist 'Figur' keine Figur, sondern tatsächlich die Bildlichkeit des Buchstabens.

Gewalt und Souveränität

Am Anfang des Trauerspielbuchs bezieht sich Benjamin ausdrücklich auf den Souveränitätsbegriff Carl Schmitts. Schmitt sagt in seinem Buch *Politische Theologie*: "Souverän ist, wer über den Ausnahmezustand entscheidet (...) Dass der Ausnahmezustand im eminenten Sinne für die juristische Definition der Souveränität geeignet ist, hat seinen systematischen rechtslogischen Grund. Die Entscheidung über die Ausnahme ist nämlich im eminenten Sinne Entscheidung. Denn eine generelle Norm, wie sie der normal geltende Rechtssatz darstellt, kann eine absolute Ausnahme niemals erfassen und daher auch die Entscheidung, dass ein echter Ausnamefall gegeben ist, nicht restlos begründen."[24]

Nicht zufällig erscheint eine politische Machttheorie im Rahmen einer Konstruktion der Allegorie. Denn die Allegorie als Zeichentheorie versteht die Sprache der Literatur, und radikalisiert: jeden Sprechakt, als linguistischen Ausnahmezustand. Interpretationen können sich darum nicht mehr auf Verfahrensregeln oder Begründungszusammenhänge stützen. Sie können nur noch dezisionistisch gesetzt werden. Das Subjekt der Semiose, das von de Man als ästhetische Illusion aus der Sprachmaschine herauskonstruiert worden ist, kehrt zurück als Souverän der Macht.

Hiergegen richtet sich das Buch von George Steiner, das explizit eine Ethik des Lesens zu entwerfen sucht. Und gegen diese

---

23. Walter Benjamin, *Ursprung des deutschen Trauerspiels*, S.388.
24. Carl Schmitt, *Politische Theologie* (Berlin: Duncker und Humblot, 1990 [5.Aufl.]), S.11.

Möglichkeit seiner eigenen Theorie von Allegorie entwickelte Benjamin sein Verfahren der dialektischen Bilder: eine politische Ästhetik, die nicht nur ein sprechendes und schreibendes, sondern ein fühlendes und handelndes Subjekt voraussetzt.

Zwar sind Fühlen und Handeln durch das Schreiben und Sprechen gezeichnet, aber diese Metabolisierung des Symbolischen, die Verkörperlichung und die Verweltlichung der Sprache sind in einer linguistischen Semiologie oder Poetik nicht mehr zu fassen. Dass sie am Ende des 20. Jahrhunderts die Grenzen des linguistic turn für eine Theorie des Subjekts sichtbar gemacht hat, wenn auch wahrscheinlich unfreiwillig, ist das unschätzbare Verdienst der Dekonstruktion. Insofern ist sie die Allegorie des Zusammenbruchs der linguistischen Meta-Erzählung.

19. The Crisis of Oedipal Identity: Between Lacan and the Frankfurt School

PETER DEWS

At first glance it seems anomalous that the work of Jacques Lacan should have come to function as a major point of reference for feminist theory in the English-speaking world. Lacan's best-known work, dating from the inception of his *Seminar* in 1953, is characterized by an almost obsessive concern with the relation between language and subjectivity, but Lacan shies away from connecting his formal conception of language to any historical, let alone ideological, dimension of meaning. Rather, in his reformulation, psychoanalysis is focused on the simultaneous relation of dependency and non-identity between the subject and language *as such*: Lacan is unequivocal that in psychoanalysis "it is not a question of the relation of man to language as a social phenomenon."[1] To this extent, the appeal of his work for feminists derives not from its historical or sociological insights, but sheerly from it emphasis on the symbolically structured character of subjectivity in its gendered dimension, an emphasis which undermines any naturalistic conception of the opposition between the psychology of the two sexes.

At the same time, however, the political advantage which this emphasis might be considered to bring is profoundly elusive, since, in his later work at least, Lacan gives little reason to assume that such symbolic structuring might be alterable. Even those feminists most sympathetic to Lacan have found themselves struggling with the dilemma that his thought appears to establish an intrinsic relation between phallic primacy and the symbolic order. Thus, Jacqueline Rose has written: "For Lacan, to say that difference is 'phallic' difference is to expose the symbolic and arbitrary nature of its division as such. It is crucial... that refusal of the phallic term brings with it an attempt to reconstitute a form of subjectivity free of division, and hence a refusal of the notion of symbolization itself."[2] However, if refusal of the phallic term is equivalent to the absolute refusal of symbolization, then the role of the phallus can hardly be

---

1. Jacques Lacan, "La signification du phallus," in: *Écrits* (Paris: 1966), p. 688.
2. Jacqueline Rose, "Feminine Sexuality — Jacques Lacan and the école freudienne," in: *Sexuality in the Field of Vision* (London: 1986), p. 80.

considered as 'arbitrary.' Rose recognises this, for she goes on to defend her position by suggesting that: "While the objection to [the] dominant term [i.e. the phallus] must be recognised, it cannot be answered by an account which returns to a concept of the feminine as pre-given, nor by a mandatory appeal to an androcentrism in the symbolic which the phallus would simply reflect. The former relegates women outside language and history, the latter simply subordinates them to both."[3] It is difficult to understand, however, why the grounding of phallocentrism in androcentrism should subordinate women to language and history, unless this androcentrism itself is considered to be immutable. Conversely, if the symbolic role of the phallus in the unconscious formation of gender-identity is entirely detached from the question of the actual relations, including power-relations, between men and women, it is hard to perceive where the interest of pychoanalysis for feminists might lie.

In the light of these difficulties, it might appear that other intellectual traditions, both psychoanalytically informed and committed to social critique, might offer better starting-points for a feminist theorization of sexual difference. The tradition which inevitably springs to mind here is that of the Frankfurt School, which has in general been much more sensitive to the intersections between psychoanalysis and social theory than the Lacanian tradition. The earlier Frankfurt School, in particular, appreciated the need to introduce a dimension of historicity into even the most fundamental psychoanalytic categories, arguing — against Freud himself — that there can be no purely timeless unconscious, since "concrete historical components already enter early childhood experience."[4] Until recently, however, this tradition has had little to say about the specific question of women's oppression — indeed, the issue is more present, though scarcely prominent, in the work of the earlier Frankfurt School than in the contemporary critical theory of Habermas. Furthermore, although there are now the beginnings of a feminist reception of Critical Theory, particularly in North America, this reception has not — on the whole — been particularly sensitive to the psychoanalytic dimension of earlier Critical Theory, or tried to make use of it to any significant extent. Rather, its aim has

3. Ibid., p. 81.
4. Theodor Adorno, "Psychology and Sociology," *New Left Review*, 47, January-February 1967, p. 90.

been to modify the gender-insensitive universalism of Habermasian social and moral theory.[5]

On the one hand, therefore, we find the powerful influence of a form of *psychoanalytic* theory within Anglo-american feminism which appears remote from sociological and historical concerns; on the other, a tradition of *critical* theory, now being adapted and developed by feminists, which has lost the psychoanalytical emphasis on the complex internal structure of subjectivity, in its shift to an investigation of the normative structures of *inter*-subjectivity. However, a consideration of the early — now almost forgotten — phases of Lacan's thinking, opens up possibilities of at least modifying this dichotomy. For Lacan's first forays in psychoanalytic theory, prior to the inception of the *Seminar*, were by no means as hostile to historical and sociological perspectives as his later thought appears to be. Futhermore, the account of the crisis of the modern family which Lacan developed during the 1930s, and which is most fully presented in a lengthy encyclopedia article of 1938, *Les complexes familiaux,* evinces many striking similarities with the contemporaneous work of the Frankfurt School on the same issue. Against the background of these affinities, the question of why Lacan's work evolved as it did can be posed in a new way. Indeed, as we shall see, the later Lacan's apparently 'transcendental' model of a phallocentric symbolic order can itself be understood as a response to a specific *historical* crisis. Simultaneously, the possibility opens up of comparing Lacan's later work, as a response to the familial and social crisis which he diagnoses, with recent developments in psychoanalysis which attempt both to build on, and to respond to, the earlier thought of the Frankfurt School from a critical, feminist perspective — most notably the work of Jessica Benjamin.

I

Perhaps the most striking feature of *Les complexes familiaux* is the manner in which Lacan insists, against Freud himself, that the Oedipus complex represents a historically specific type of identity-formation, which emerges within the context of the patriarchal family. Lacan makes clear that marriage and the family are two distinct social institutions, and argues that the modern form of the

5. See, for example, the essays by Nancy Fraser, Iris Marion Young and Seyla Benhabib, in Seyla Benhabib and Drucilla Cornell, eds, *Feminism as Critique* (Oxford, 1987).

family, centred on the 'matrimonial' relation between the parents, should not be confused in its psychological effects with earlier familial structures, even where these seem to overlap in terms of personnel. Indeed, Lacan specifically criticizes Freud, on the grounds that he "presents this psychological element [of the Oedipus complex] as the specific form of the human family and subordinates to it all the the social variations of the family."[6] By contrast, Lacan claims, "The methodological order proposed here, both in the consideration of mental structures and of the social facts, will lead to a revision of the complex which will allow us to situate contemporary neurosis in the history of the paternalistic family, and to cast further light on it."[7]

In the account which Lacan then develops, the specific virtue of Oedipal identity-formation consists in the extreme psychological tension which is generated by the role of the father, as both "the agent of prohibition and the example of its transgression."[8] As Lacan writes, "It is... because it is invested with the power of repression that the paternal imago projects its original force into the very sublimations which are to surmount it; it is from binding together the progress of its functions in such an antinomy that the Oedipus complex derives its funcundity."[9] In other terms, the paradoxical paternal injunction, "be and do not be like me", which confronts the child in the Oedipal situation, makes possible a form of identification which fuses emulation and difference in an advanced form of individuation. As Lacan states, "If, as a result of their experience, both the psychoanalyst and the sociologist can recognize in the prohibition of the mother the concrete form of primordial obligation, they can also demonstrate a real 'opening up' of the social bond in paternalist authority and affirm that, through the functional conflict of the Oedipal situation, this authority introduces into repression a promisory ideal."[10]

Specifying this general characterization, Lacan gives three principal reasons for the superiority of Oedipal identity-formation over other corresponding processes. Firstly, because authority is incarnated in a familiar form by the nearest generation, it is more readily open to creative subversion. Secondly, because the psyche is

6. Jacques Lacan, *Les complexes familiaux* (Paris, 1984), p. 49.
7. Ibid.
8. Ibid., p. 50.
9. Ibid., pp. 66-7.
10. Ibid., p. 68.

formed not simply by the constraint of the adult but by his positive image (Lacan considers the father-son relation to be the pre-eminent example here), there occurs a "positive selection of tendencies and gifts, and a progressive realization of the ideal in the character."[11] Thirdly, the evidence of sexual life on the part of those imposing moral constraints "raises the tension of the libido to the highest degree, and increases the scope of sublimation."[12] On these grounds, Lacan has only the highest praise for the achievements of the modern family (by which he means the type of family, based on the free choice of partners, which began to emerge in Europe from the fifteenth century onwards): 'It is by realizing in the most human form the conflict of man with his most archaic anxiety, it is by offering the most loyal closed domain where he can measure himself against the profoundest figures of his destiny, it is by putting the most complete triumph over his original servitude within his grasp, that the complex of the conjugal family creates superior successes of character, happiness and creation.'[13]

By contrast with this view, Lacan is unequivocal about the 'stagnation' which is implied by non-patriarchal patterns of socialization. In such forms the repressive social instance and the social ideal are separated: Lacan cites Malinowski's account of societies in which the first of these roles is played by the maternal uncle, while the father has a more companionate relation to the child. Because of this separation, such forms are unable to rival the dialectical, sublimatory tension generated by Oedipal model. Commenting caustically on the Melanesian idylls evoked by Malinowski, Lacan remarks that "the harmony of these societies contrasts with the stereotypical quality which marks the creations of the personality, and of art and morality in such cultures."[14]

Despite his paeans to the patriarchal family, however, Lacan is extemely sensitive to the fact that this social form is caught up in a fateful historical dialectic. Up to a certain point, a positive cycle occurs, in which the "normative ideals, juridical statutes and creative inspirations" made possible by Oedipal identity-formation react back onto the family, thereby helping to concentrate even further within it the conditions of the Oedipal conflict, and "reintegrating into pschychological progress the social dialectic engendered

11. Ibid., p. 70.
12. Ibid., p. 71.
13. Ibid., p. 71.
14. Ibid., p. 66.

by this conflict."[15] However, this self-reinforcing cycle eventually reaches a crisis point, where the level of individuation achieved begins to undermine the now highly compacted conditions of Oedipal identity-formation itself. According to Lacan, the progress of culture is manifested in the increasing demands which are imposed on the ego with regard to "coherence and creative elan," with the result that "the accidents and caprices of this [Oedipal] regulation increase step by step with this same social progress which, in making the family evolve towards the conjugal form, submits it more and more to individual variations." And Lacan concludes: "This 'anomie,' which made possible the discovery of the complex, gives rise to the degenerated form in which the analysts recognizes it: a form which we could define in terms of an incomplete repression of the desire for the mother, with a reactivation of the anxiety and curiosity inherent in the birth relation; and a narcissistic debasement of the idealization of the father, which causes the emergence, in oedipal identification, of the aggressive ambivalence immanent in the primordial relation to the counterpart."[16]

Against the background of this deeply historical account of structures of subjectivity, Lacan's later thought appears in a new light. On one plausible interpretation, proposed by Mikkel Borch-Jacobsen, the later Lacan attempts to shore up the Oedipus complex by transforming it into a 'transcendental' structure constitutive of subjectivity as such, while haunted by the awareness that the Oedipal norm no longer corresponds to the socially predominant processes of identity-formation. Indeed, Lacan himself suggests in *Les complexes familiaux* that the emergence of psychoanalysis itself, in the melting-pot of turn-of-the-century Vienna, with its chaotic multiplicity of family forms, from the most traditional to the most irregular, can be explained in terms of the incipient crisis of Oedipal identity-formation. The 'true' Oedipus complex, one might say, can be recognized only privatively, though the psychoanalytic inventory of the effects of its distorted and degenerating forms.

II

Before examining in more detail Lacan's own later response to this situation, however, a useful comparative perspective on the central issues may be gained by comparing Lacan's account of the crisis of

15. Ibid., p. 67.
16. Ibid., pp. 95-96.

the bourgeois family with that of Max Horkheimer, in his classic essay on "Authority and the Family," written two years before *Les complexes familiaux*, in 1936. Unlike Lacan, Horkheimer's analysis is grounded from the normative standpoint of a possible future society devoid of institutionalized relations of force and their internalized equivalents. From this point of view, the psychic apparatus is understood as serving primarily to "interiorize, or at least to rationalize and supplement physical coercion."[17] Horkheimer does not deny the historical advance represented by the modern patriarchal family, whose emergence he dates — as does Lacan — from the 15th century: "At the beginning of the bourgeois age the father's control of his household was doubtless an indispensible condition of progress. The self-control of the individual, the disposition for work and discipline, the ability to hold firmly to certain ideas, consistency in practical life, application of reason, perseverance and pleasure in constructive activity could all be developed, in the circumstances, only under the dictation and guidance of the father whose own education had been won in the school of life."[18] However, Horkheimer argues, the function of authority can change from being progressive to regressive, relative to the goals of "self-development and happiness" which are internal to his normative standpoint.[19] As the capitalist organization of society is consolidated, the role of the family increasingly becomes that of inculcating an adaptive and submissive attitude to authority, an authority which is now reified and depersonalized, in the form of the economic system itself. Within the family, the authority of the father, based on superior physical strength and economic power, comes to embody that irrational facticity of the social in the face of which individuals would be 'irrational' to do anything other than submit.

In Horkheimer's account, the dialectic thus set in motion eventually leads to the undermining of the role of the father. Horheimer argues: "The education of authority-oriented personalities, for which the family is suited because of its own authority structure, is not a passing phenomenon but part of a relatively permanent state of affairs. Of course, the more this society enters a critical phase because of its own immanent laws, the less will the family be able to exercise its educational function... The means of protecting the

---

17. Max Horkheimer, "Authority and the Family," in *Critical Theory: Selected Essays* (New York, 1972), p. 56.
18. Ibid., p. 101.
19. Ibid., p. 71.

363

cultural totality and developing it further have increasingly come into conflict with the cultural content itself. The father as an arbitrary power no longer offers possibilities of identification, and the child instead identifies which repressive social instances."[20] The result of this direct identification with social power is the spread of the malleable narcissistic personality-type, lacking those inner capacities for self-direction which the buffer of paternal authority once provided, ostensibly well-adapted but inwardly cold and emotionless, inclined to power-worship and masochistic submission.

In considering the validity of this analysis, and its political consequences, it is instructive to compare the reasons which Lacan and Horkheimer supply for the fateful dialectic of the bourgeois family. In Horkheimer the essential mediating role is played by the capitalist economy, on the assumption that "The idealization of paternal authority, the pretense that it comes from a divine decision or the nature of things or reason proves on closer examination to be the glorification of an economically conditioned institution."[21] However, as the development of the economy moves beyond its private, entrepreneurial phase into an era characterized by increasing monopolization and bureaucratic intervention, the individual becomes increasingly dependent on processes which lie beyond his or her control, and capacities for personal initative become ever more redundant. In this context, the father is no longer able to provide a model of authority in the traditional sense, with its inextricable interweaving of rational and irrational dimensions. Rather, "The fullest possible adaptation of the subject to the reified authority of the economy is the form which reason really takes in bourgeois society."[22] The family, while not being abolished, is hollowed out, instrumentalized: the dialectic of the universal (society), the particular (the family), and the individual, as envisaged by Hegel, begins to split apart.[23]

Against the background of Horkheimer's views, it becomes apparent that there are two strands of diagnosis in Lacan's text. Lacan, too, lays considerable emphasis on the failure of the father as the crucial factor in contemporary character disorders. In his view, these disorders find their "principal determination in the personality of the father, who is always lacking in some way, absent,

20. Ibid., p. 127.
21. Ibid., p. 123.
22. Ibid., p. 83.
23. See ibid., p. 128.

364

humiliated, divided, or fake."[24] Furthermore, his description of the results of this failure converges strikingly with the Frankfurt School account of the narcissistic personality: "Like sinister godmothers installed at the cradle of the neurotic, impotence and utopianism enclose his ambition, so that he either smothers within himself the creations awaited by the world in which he appears, or misrecognizes his own impulse in the object against which he revolts."[25]

Lacan also admits that the decay of the paternal imago is in part at least the result of social and economic factors. It is a "decline conditioned by the rebounding against the individual of the extreme effects of social progress, a decline which is marked above all in our time in the collectivities which have been most tested by the effects of such progress: the concentration of economic power and political catastrophes."[26] This is comparable with Horkheimer's claim that "Property and the permanence of bourgeois society mediated the idea of one's own past and future. Today planning administration is being constituted, and the constitution of the ego is dissolving."[27] Unlike Horkheimer, however, Lacan detects another — perhaps deeper — reason for this decline, which he connects not with the suppression of individuality in mass society, but rather with the dialectic of individuation as such. In Lacan's view, Oedipal social-ization requires what he calls a "typical quality in the psychological relation between the parents,"[28] in other words, well-defined ma-ternal and paternal roles. However, in the ever more predominant "conjugal marriage", dominated by the personal choice and in-teraction of the partners, this typical quality tends to disappear. What Lacan terms the "matrimonial demands" of the modern conjugal family, generated by the very conception of marriage as a relationship between equals, one might say, leads to the "social decline of the paternal imago."[29] At this level, Lacan's diagnosis could be said to run in the opposite direction to that of Horkheimer. For the latter, the crisis of individualization occurs at the point at which the tendencies towards concentration and bureacratization of the capitalist economy begin to squeeze out the precisely the need for individual creativity, judgement and conscience. For Lacan,

24. *Les complexes familiaux*, p. 73.
25. Ibid.
26. Ibid., p. 72.
27. Max Horkheimer, "Vernunft und Selbsterhaltung" (1942), in: *Traditionelle und kritische Theorie* (Frankfurt, 1992), p. 287.
28. *Les complexes familiaux*, p. 103.
29. Ibid, p. 72.

however, working in an intellectual tradition profoundly influenced by Durkheim, it is individualization as such which poses the fundamental problem. The very "coherence and creative *élan*" which modern culture demands of individuals produces a degree of *anomie* which destroys the minimum of typicality in the relation between the parents necessary for the functioning of the Oedipus complex. Once this historical turning point is reached, then personalities characterized by a "narcissistic deviation of the libido" will begin to be formed.

Both Lacan's and Horkheimer's positions, therefore, seem to imply a certain nostalgia for the patriarchal family, although for somewhat different reasons. Horkheimer is clear that the acceptance of paternal authority should — ideally — only constitue a temporary phase of the individual's development. Normatively, Horkheimer anticipates a society in which authority, while not abolished, would be grounded in collective consent: only in this way could the internalization of coercion which he takes to be intrinsic to the formation of the psyche under past and present conditions be overcome. Lacan, however, begins from the premisses of very different philosophical anthropology. He starts from the assumption that the process of weaning, the initial traumatic break with the mother which is the precondition of independent subjectivity, is always culturally structured, and that the subject can only transcend this trauma by internalizing and repeating it. In this interpretation, castration is not a threat which *supports* paternal authority; rather, it is a phantasy through which the subject masters through repetition the trauma of separation from the mother, and thereby acts as a defense against the regressive, indeed deathly, tendencies which the maternal imago embodies. The phantasy of castration, Lacan suggests, "represents the defence which the narcissistic ego, identified with its specular double, opposes to the resurgence of anxiety which tends to overwhelm him, in the first stage of the Oedipus complex: a crisis which is caused not so much by the irruption of genital desire in the subject, as by the object which it reactualizes, namely the mother. The subject responds to the anxiety awakened by this object by reproducing the masochistic rejection through which it overcame its primordial loss, but it does so according to the structure which it has acquired, that is through an imaginary localisation of the tendency."[30] It is not difficult to

30. Ibid., p. 61.

discern here, in outline, Lacan's later account of castration as the point of transition between the imaginary and the symbolic.

III

As I have already indicated, a thought-provoking interpretation of the shift from the Lacan of *Les complexes familiaux* to the later, and better-known, Lacan has been provided by Mikkel Borch-Jacobsen, in a paper on "The Oedipus Problem." Borch-Jacobsen suggests that, in *Les complexes familiaux*, Lacan sets out to resolve a difficulty which had already troubled Freud: how can the identificatory rivalry of the Oedipus complex be resolved precisely through a *further* identification with the rival? Borch-Jacobsen argues that Lacan attempts to resolve this problem by drawing a much more rigorous distinction than Freud between the super-ego and the ego-ideal, the former forbidding rivalrous identification, and the latter encouraging a sublimatory identification. As we have already seen, for the Lacan of *Les complexes familiaux* the contemporary crisis of Oedipal identity-formation consists in the fact that this distinction is breaking down: both the "lacking" father and the arbitrarily authoritarian father fail to sustain the delicate equilibrium between idealizing identification and repression.

On Borch-Jacobsen's reading, Lacan's later work, with its strict distinction between imaginary and symbolic registers, represents an attempt to shore up a form of identity-formation which has already fallen into desuetude. The Lacanian concept of the "Name-of-the-Father," equivalent to the totem of 'primitive' societies in its function as the pole of identification which allows a symbolic resolution of the Oedipal crisis, and the concomitant distinction between the "imaginary" and the "symbolic" phallus, are in fact *normative* concepts and distinctions, vain attempts to sustain an ideal of subjectivity which no longer maps onto the actual social processes of identity-formation. As Borch-Jacobsen writes: "how is it possible to prevent the identification with the symbolic father-phallus from being confounded with the rivalrous and homosexualizing imaginary father-phallus? ...it does absolutely no good whatsoever to invoke the *rightful* difference between the two identifications, since that difference, far from being a fundamental, *a priori* structure of every society, turns out actually to be bound solely to the 'elementary structures of kinship.' Our societies, on the other hand, are defined by a general crisis of symbolic identifications — 'deficiency of the paternal function,' 'foreclosure of the name of the father,' perpetual questioning of the symbolic 'law' and 'pact,' confusion of lineage and general competition of generations, battle of the sexes, and loss of family landmarks."[31]

Borch-Jacobsen's own attitude to these social developments, however, is curiously insouciant. He believes it possible simply to "stop treating the Oedipus complex as a problem," and accept the accelerating symbolic breakdown of our societies.[32] But this response seems far too sanguine: Lacan was among the first twentieth-century thinkers to have grasped the significance of the rise of what he calls, in *Les complexes familiaux*, "an introversion of the personality through a narcissistic deviation of the libido,"[33] and in his diagnosis of the social consequences of this introversion he concurs to a considerable extent with other traditions of social critique. As a number of commentators have argued, the 'postmodern' dismantling of subjectivity and celebration of symbolic fragmentation, which view themselves as transcending such a standpoint of critique, in fact result in an even more exaggerated form of subjectivist voluntarism.[34] Unless one simply brushes aside Lacan's claim that "the promotion of the ego, consistent with the utilitiarian conception of man which reinforces it, culminates today in an ever more advanced realization of man as individual, that is to say, in an isolation of the soul ever more akin to its original dereliction," [35] the question must be posed of possible alternative patterns of identity-formation, which would be opposed to the 'deregulation' to which Borch-Jacobsen seems resigned, but which would also bridge the impossible gulf between the *pays réel* and the *pays légal* which appears to open up in later Lacanian theory.

Understandably, it is above all feminist psychoanalysts, and psychoanalytically informed feminist theorists, who have tried to address the issue of possibilities of post-Oedipal identity-formation, since Oedipal identity-formation, even if accepted as having been relatively 'successful' during a certain historical phase, suffers from an intrinsic gender disequilibrium and distortion. Indeed, it is fasci-

31. Mikkel Borch-Jacobsen, "The Oedipus Problem" (unpublished paper delivered to the Centre for Theoretical Studies in Humanities and Social Sciences, University of Essex, 25 March 1992), p. 29.
32. "The Oedipus Problem," p. 30.
33. *Les complexes familiaux*, p. 107.
34. See, for example, Charles Taylor, "Logics of Disintegration," *New Left Review* 170, July-August 1988, pp. 110-116.
35. Jacques Lacan, "Aggressivity in Psychoanalysis," in *Écrits: A Selection* (London, 1977), p. 27.

nating to observe that, in the final pages of *Les complexes familiaux*, Lacan himself describes the crisis of Oedipal identity-formation as inevitably arising from the historical suppression of the feminine principle. In a further dialectical twist, the progressive individual-ization which Oedipal socialization promotes leads to the rejection by women of their predetermined familial role. Thus, Lacan suggests, "One may perceive in the virile protest of woman the ultimate consquence of the Oedipus complex."[36] Lacan fully admits that "The origins of our culture are too connected to what we willingly describe as the adventure of the paternalist family, for it not to impose, upon all the forms whose psychic development it has enriched, a prevalence of the male principle...,"[37] and he is aware that, in the long historical run, this social and cultural bias must generate an unstable situation. The occulation of the feminine principle by the masculine ideal, as he calls it, has resulted, in contemporary society, in an "imaginary impasse of sexual polarisation," in which are "invisibly engaged" the "forms of culture, morals and the arts, struggle and thought,"[38] Significantly, it is with this thought that *Les complexes familiaux* — somewhat abruptly — concludes: contemporary feminist theoreticians working within a psycho-analytic framework can be seen to be addressing precisely that 'social antinomy' which Lacan had presciently described, and found himself unable to circumvent, in 1938.

IV

In the concluding part of this discussion, I want to take the work of Jessica Benjamin as an example of an attempt to address the issues raised in *Les complexes familiaux* from a feminist perspective. Benjamin's work is of special interest in the present context because it seeks to build on and transform the heritage of the earlier Frankfurt School, which — in her view — leads to the same 'social antinomy' which we have just found evoked in Lacan. She considers that the Horkheimer's view of individual capacities for non-conformity and critical resistance as grounded in the internalization of paternal authority fails to acknowledge the distorted form of identity produced by Oedipal socialization, which is based on an autarkic

36. *Les complexes familiaux*, p. 110-111.
37. Ibid.
38. Ibid., p. 112.

separation of the self and an instrumental relation to objects, at the cost of capacities for reciprocity and empathetic communication.[39]

The core of Benjamin's argument consists in the contention that symbolic *exclusivity* of the phallus, although not its *primacy* as the unconscious embodiment of agency and desire, is the result of an androcentric social structure.[40] Identifying with the father as bearer of the phallus allows the male child to separate from the mother, although to an excessive extent which involves a *repudiation* of femininity, while this identification is not adequately available to the female child, who nevertheless has no alternative route to independence. Benjamin's contention is that a more nurturing father and a more socially autonomous mother could provide *two* poles of idealizing identification, replacing the classical counterposition of progressive, individuating father against regressive mother.

Benjamin notes that theorists who lament the decline of the paternal imago rarely foreground the ambivalence of the father figure. Drawing on Freud's account of the genesis of the incest taboo through the overthrowing of the father of the primal horde in *Totem and Taboo*, Bejamin argues that: "Paternal authority...is a far more complex emotional web than its defenders admit: it is not merely rooted in the rational law that forbids incest and patricide, but also in the erotics of ideal love, the guilty identification with power that undermines the son's desire for freedom."[41] She suggests that it is not possible to make a hard and fast distinction between Oedipal and pre-oedipal figures, and that it is misleading to do so in order to defend the notion of the rational, progressive father. To this extent, her account seems to focus on the crucial problem for Lacan highlighted by Borch-Jacobsen: Oedipal identity-formation can only be defended as an ideal, on the normative assumption that ego-ideal and super-ego can and should be held apart, even though

39. See Jessica Benjamin, "Authority and the Family Revisited: or, A World without Fathers," *New German Critique*, No. 13, 1978, pp. 35-58.
40. In fact, this is Jessica Benjamin's implicit, rather than explicitly stated position. At a number of points in her book *The Bonds of Love* (London, 1990), she makes the argument against the Lacanian position that "In the pre-oedipal world, the father and his phallus are powerful because of their ability to stand for separation from the mother." (p. 95). At the same time, however, Benjamin also admits that "the... problem is that the symbolic level of the psyche already seems to be occupied by the phallus." (p. 124.) Her solution is to propose a symbolization of woman's desire in terms of Winnicott's notion of "holding space," which would not seek to rival or supplant the symbolism of the phallus, but rather co-exist with it. See *The Bonds of Love*, pp. 123-132.
41. *The Bonds of Love*, p. 143.

embodied in the same person. In Borch-Jacobsen's account, this has *never* been possible: "…for what mysterious reason should the hate identification with the rival *necessarily* be transformed into a respectful identification with the bearer of authority? Identification *is* precisely the reason for the rivalry and, even more essentially, for 'affective ambivalence,' so there is every reason to believe that the post-Oedipal identification should, instead, perpetuate that ambivalence."[42]

In response to this problem, Benjamin contends that the pre-Oedipal identificatory love for the father cannot simply be equated with a rivalrous, homosexual identification. Rather, "To explain what Freud called the 'short step from love to hypnotism,' from ordinary identificatory love to bondage, we must look not merely to the distinction between oedipal and pre-oedipal, but to the fate of the child's love for the father in each phase…the idealization of the pre-oedipal father is closely associated with submission when it is thwarted, unrecognized."[43] The importance of this argument is that, in Lacan's account, there is no equivalent *idealizing* identificatory love. Lacan, prior to the entry into the symbolic order brought about by the Oedipus complex, knows only the jealousy and rivalry of narcissistic identification, which — in *Les complexes familiaux* — he theorizes in terms of the child's relation to the intruding sibling. It is this rivalry which is ultimately broken by the identification with the paternal ego-ideal. Thus Lacan states: "The identification, which was formerly mimetic, has become propitiatory: the object of sado-masochistic participation detaches itself from the subject, becomes distant from it in the new ambiguity of fear and love. But, in this step towards reality, the primitive object of desire [i.e., the mother] seems to vanish."[44]

However, if one distinguishes such an idealizing paternal identification, then a reinterpretation of the roles of the sexes also becomes possible. Benjamin stresses that the result of the Oedipus complex is that the male child must abandon not only his incestuous, but also his identificatory love for the mother. This is because, even more than in the case of the father, such identificatory love is taken to be regressive. In Lacan's early theory, for example, the maternal imago is described as embodying the "the metaphysical mirage of universal harmony, the mystical abyss of affective fusion, the social

42. "The Oedipus Problem," p. 13.
43. *The Bonds of Love*, pp. 145-6.
44. *Les complexes familiaux*, p. 63.

utopia of a totalitarian guardianship, all emerging from the haunting sense of the lost paradise before birth, and the more obscure aspiration towards death."[45] Lacan is undoubtedly justified in pointing out that the interference of "primordial identifications" will mark the maternal ego ideal, and perhaps also in contending that the father presents the ego-ideal in its purest form. But Lacan himself provides no explanation for his assertion that the maternal ideal must "fail," leading to a feeling of repulsion of the part of the female child, and — by extension — in the case of the negative male Oedipus complex.[46] One might conclude that this failure, as in the paternal case, which Lacan — in part, at least — attributes to the pressure social and economic factors, derives from the general lack of recognition of the autonomy of the mother. Benjamin herself is far from suggesting that the role of the father, and indeed of the phallus, in the process of separation and individuation can be superseded, but she argues nevertheless that the possibility for separation without rupture would be opened up by a different relation to the mother. In this case, the father might also be able more readily to accept the female child's phallic identification, since this identification would not be driven by the desperation of the need to break away from an engulfing mother.

It will be apparent that the key to Benjamin's revision of the Oedipus complex, which she wishes to view as "only a step in mental life, one that leaves room for earlier and later levels of integration,"[47] consists in her conception of the identificatory love which she associates with the pre-oedipal rapprochement phase, in which the child seeks an initial balance between unity and separation. It is significant therefore, that the French psychoanalyst Julia Kristeva should also be concerned with this type of love in her attempt to break down the rigidities of the Lacanian conception of Oedipal identity-formation. Like Benjamin, Kristeva is engaged in a re-evaluation of narcissism, in an attempt to circumvent the aporia which she formulates in the observation that: "To seek to maintain, against the winds and tides of our modern civilization, the exigency of a severe father who, through his name, bestows on us separation, judgement and identity is a necessity, a more or less pious wish."[48]

45. Ibid., p. 35.
46. Cf. ibid., pp. 64-5.
47. *The Bonds of Love*, p. 177.
48. Julia Kristeva, "Freud et l'amour: le malaise dans la cure," in: *Histoires d'amour* (Paris, 1983 [paperback edition]), p. 62.

Kristeva's more detailed investigations of the character of pre-oedipal identificatory love may therefore provide a useful corroboration and substantiation of the perspective Jessica Benjamin seeks to propose.

Kristeva's essay, "Freud et l'amour: le malaise dans la cure," in her book *Histoires d'amour*, is fundamentally an attempt to retheorize the notion of narcissism, so that narcissism no longer appears as constituting an inevitable block to the achievement of individuation. Kristeva seeks to show, contrary to Lacan's account, that the emergence of the subject cannot be connected exclusively with the Oedipal crisis, with the breaking apart of the mother-child dyad through the intervention of the father. In Kristeva's account narcissism already represents an advance over an undifferentiated auto-eroticism, it implies an initial gap between self and other, before the intervention of the symbolic order, or rather before its intervention in its purely signifying aspect. Kristeva does not deny that the symbolic order is always already in place, but she suggests that there are diverse "modalities of access" to the symbolic function. In imitating and, at the same time, libidinally investing the speech of the mother, the child is already entering into an identification which constitutes an elementary form of subjectivity. However, the Other with whom the child identifies it not the purely symbolic Other of Lacanian doctrine: "Finally," Kristeva writes, "by virtue of being the pole of a loving identification, the *Other* appears not as a 'pure signifier,' but as the space of metaphorical movement itself: as the condensation of semic traits as well as the unrepresentable heterogeneity of the drives which subtends them, exceeds them and escapes them... Lacan situates idealization in the field of signifiers and of desire alone, and has detached it clearly — even brutally — both from narcissism and from the heterogeneity of the drives and their hold on the maternal container."[49]

However, for Kristeva, this initial identification does not take place with the mother figure alone. Here she agrees with Benjamin, who suggests that during the rapprochement phase the distinction between male and female identifications has not yet consolidated. Developing a suggestion of Freud, Kristeva describes an 'imaginary father,' a 'coagulation of the mother and her desire,' which allows the mother to function as lack and plenitude simultaneously, thereby making possible an initial distanciation *prior to* the entry into the Oedipal situation. The immediacy of the relation to this 'father-

49. Ibid., p. 53.

373

mother conglomerate' Kristeva suggests, has an important consequence: the term 'object' like that of 'identification' becomes *inappropriate* in this logic. A not-yet identity [of the child] is transferred, or rather is displaced, to the locus of an Other who is not yet libidinally invested as an object, but remains an Ego Ideal.'[50]

It is interesting to observe how the concerns of Benjamin, emerging from and reacting to the Frankfurt School, and those of Kristeva, similarly related to Lacanian thought, converge in this respect. This convergence should not be taken to imply an undeviating parallelism between the traditions which they oppose, however. For if one looks more closely as Horkheimer's position, then it appears that Horkheimer did not simply attribute individuation and a capacity for resistance to the role of the father, as Jessica Benjamin frequently claims. In his 1960 essay, 'Autorität und Familie in der Gegenwart' he wrote: "Earlier, the mother provided the child with a sense of security, which made it possible for him to develop a certain degree of independence. The child felt that the mother returned its love, and in a certain way drew on this fund of feeling throughout its life. The mother, who was cut off from the company of men and forced into a dependent situation, represented, despite her idealization, another principle than the reality principle..."[51] Horkheimer goes on explicitly to affirm that the sustaining of the child's relation to the mother can help to prevent too rapid an adaption to reality, at the cost of individuation.

This account might appear to be nostalgic, despite the fact that, in its emphasis, it coincides with, rather than contradicting, the tenor of Jessica Benjamin's account. The difference of orientation — bourgeois past, rather than feminist future — derives from Horkheimer's conviction that, with the increasing incorporation of women into the rationalized extra-familial world, the distinctive structure and emotional quality of the family is being destroyed: "The equality of women, their professional activity, the much quicker emancipation of the children alters the atmosphere of the home... Like existence in general, marriage is tending to become more rational, more purposive, more sober."[52] Nevertheless, Horkheimer is in general critical of the separation of the sensual and the ideal in

50. Ibid., p. 56.
51. Max Horkheimer, "Autorität und Familie in der Gegenwart," in: *Zur Kritik der instrumentellen Vernunft* (Frankfurt, 1985), p. 278.
52. Max Horkheimer, "Die Zukunft der Ehe," in: *Zur Kritik der instrumentellen Vernunft*," p. 298.

the traditional image of the mother, and in the father's attitude towards her. He argues that "under the pressure of such a family situation the individual does not learn to understand and respect his mother in her concrete existence, that is, as this particular social and sexual being... the suppressed inclination towards the mother reappears as a fanciful and sentimental susceptibility to all symbols of the dark, maternal and protective powers."[53] Thus, against Lacan's view, Horkheimer suggests that is precisely the *repression* of identificatory love which would tend to transform the imago of the mother into a focus for the longing for regressive fusion. Furthermore, Horkheimer does not assume that, on logical grounds, a social development other than the present one might not be possible, in which, instead of rationalization transforming the mother into a mere relay of social authority, the specific positive capacities which women have developed because of their historical exclusion from the public realm might contribute to the transformation of the intrumentalized structures of society: "[The woman's] whole position in the family results in an inhibiting of important psychic energies which might have been effective in shaping the world."[54]

At this point, however, it might appear plausible to object, from a Lacanian standpoint, that Horkheimer misunderstands the fundamental concepts of psychoanalytic theory, in so far as he equates "repression" with a putative suppression of the corporeal, a renunciation of drive-satisfaction (*Triebverzicht*). It is striking, for example, that, at the beginning of 'Authority and the Family,' Horkheimer quotes not Freud, but Nietzsche's *On the Genealogy of Morals*, in order to substantiate his view that "the whole psychic apparatus of members of a class society, in so far as they do not belong to the nucleus of the privileged group, serves in large measure only to interiorize or at least to rationalize and supplement physical coercion."[55] Psychoanalysis, on this view, merely explores the effects within the individual psyche of the general structures of social power. However, one might argue, this would be to misunderstand the role of unconscious phantasy in the formation of the core of the repressed. In Lacan's account, the prohibiting father functions as the support of the phantasy of castration, which allows the child to master the trauma of separation from the mother. Precisely in order for the child to achieve such separation, in order

53. "Authority and the Family," p. 121.
54. Ibid., p. 120.
55. Ibid., p. 56.

to come to *be* as a subject at all, the father's status must appear inexplicable and ungrounded, a sheer fact to be accepted, like the facts of birth and weaning themselves. Such an account would seem to suggest that the need for authority finds an ultimate anchoring point in the unconscious, and — as such — is ineradicable.

Ultimately, this dispute seems to be a matter of divergent speculative anthropologies. For Horkheimer and Adorno, in *Dialectic of Enlightenment*, subjectivity is constituted through self-sacrifice, and the nature to which the subject finds itself opposed in the process of *becoming* a subject has both the utopian and deathly features of the maternal imago, which Lacan evokes in his early account of castration. There can thus be no question of a nostalgic conception of a return to the origin in the thought of the earlier Frankfurt School. Adorno and Horkheimer state that "Novalis' definition, according to which all philosophy is homesickness, holds true only if this longing is not dissolved into the phantasm of a lost primaeval state, but represents the homeland, nature itself, as having to be wrested from myth. Homeland is the state of having escaped (*Heimat ist das Entronnensein*)."[56]

By contrast with this utopian perspective, Lacan, in *Les complexes familiaux*, refers to "these inherent properties of the human subject, the miming of its own mutilation, and the seeing of itself as other than it is."[57] Thus, in opposition to Adorno and Horkheimer, the never-completed confrontation of the subject with its original separation can only be enacted through unconscious repetition, which does not impinge on a fundamental misrecognition of the self as radically separate. There seems to be no possibility that the very acknowledgement of separation could, at the same time, be its overcoming, a recognition of self *in* the other. It should be noted that this standpoint does not entail, on Lacan's part, a denial of the possibility of post-Oedipal patterns of identity-formation. Indeed, Lacan remarks that "The Oedipus complex... cannot hold out indefinitely in forms of society where the sense of tragedy is increasingly being lost."[58] It does seem to entail, however, as this quotation implies, that, for Lacan, our contemporary culture cannot be fully adequate to the promotion of the essential function of

---

56. Max Horkheimer and Theodor Adorno, *Dialectic of Enlightenment* (London, 1979), p. 78 (translation altered).
57. *Les complexes familiaux*, pp. 93-4.
58. "Subversion du sujet et dialectique du désir dans l'inconscient freudienne," in: *Écrits*, p. 813.

castration in forming a subject which must ultimately be defined in terms of lack, and which can "only designate its being by barring everything which it signifies."[59] A psychoanalytic engagement with the relation between the Oedipus complex and the need for social authority in Lacan would therefore have to contest Lacan's claim that castration is not merely one moment of separation, but rather that "castration anxiety is like a thread which runs through all the stages of development."[60] Such a psychoanalytic critique, however, would ultimately lead to a *philosophical* interrogation of Lacan's fundamental conviction that "le *je* n'est pas un être:" that subjectivity can only be conceived as "solitude," as a "rupture of being."[61]

59. "La signification du phallus," p. 693. For the argument, from an orthodox Lacanian perspective, that the Oedipus complex is only "one cultural form" in which the fundamental function of castration is effectuated, see Moustapha Safouan, "L'Oedipe est-il universel?," in: *Études sur l'Oedipe* (Paris, 1974), pp. 115-125.

60. *Le séminaire livre XI: Les quatres concepts fondamentaux de la psychanalyse,* (Paris, 1973), p. 62.

61. The citations are from Jacques Lacan, *Le séminaire livre XX: Encore* (Paris, 1975), p. 109.

20. The Age of Paranoia

TERESA BRENNAN

Summing up the "doctrine of antiquity" in a sentence, Benjamin writes: "They alone shall possess the earth who live from the powers of the cosmos."[1] He continues:

the exclusive emphasis on an optical connection to the universe, to which astronomy very quickly led, contained a portent of what was to come. The ancients' intercourse with the cosmos had been very different: the ecstatic trance. (...) It is the dangerous error of modern man to regard this experience as unimportant and unavoidable, and to consign it to the individual as the poetic experience of starry nights. It is not; its hour strikes again and again, and then neither nations nor generations can escape it, as was made terribly clear by the last war (...) Human multitudes, gases, electrical forces were hurled into the open country, high-frequency currents coursed through the landscape, new constellations rose in the sky, aerial space and ocean depths thundered with propellers, and everywhere sacrificial shafts were dug in Mother Earth. This immense wooing of the cosmos was enacted for the first time on a planetary scale, that is, in the spirit of technology. But because the lust for profit sought satisfaction through it, technology betrayed man and turned the bridal bed into a bloodbath. The mastery of nature, so the imperialists teach, is the purpose of all technology (...) [But] technology is not the mastery of nature but of the relation between nature and man (...) In technology a physis is being organized through which mankind's contact with the cosmos takes a new and different form from that which it had in nations and families. One need recall only the velocities by virtue of which mankind is now preparing to embark on incalculable journeys into the interior of time (...).[2]

Benjamin wrote this in 1925-1926, a year before Heidegger published the treatise that was to become *Being and Time*. Like Heidegger, he thinks about the relation between technology and the mastery of nature, and between physics and metaphysics. Yet Benjamin ties technological mastery to capitalism and imperialism. He is also politically optimistic about the possible outcome of this energetic

1. Walter Benjamin, *One Way Street and Other Writings*, translated by E. Jephcott and K. Shorter (London: NLB, 1979), p. 103.
2. Ibid., pp. 103-4.

unleashing, seeing it as the source of the proletarian revolts that accompanied and followed the first world war. None the less, he left the matter of the relation between the physical cosmos and technological mastery at an allusive level. It is one that remains to be thought through. What follows will contribute to that thinking through by focusing on an argument forefronted in some feminist writing on psychoanalysis. This is the idea that psychical fantasies can both be 'transhistorical,' by which I now mean 'foundational,' yet inflated or curtailed by changing socio-historical circumstances. Still, it will be some time before it is clear how this idea illuminates the relation between technological mastery and the 'physis of the cosmos.' It will be some time because the precise nature of the psychical fantasy at issue remains to be clarified. Moreover, it will become clearer not through concentrating on the fantasies described in existing psychoanalytic theories, but through considering the desires encapsulated in consumer goods, or commodities. I shall begin with the desire for instant gratification.

The desire for instant gratification is realized in a proliferation of commodities whose common denominator may be nothing more than the desire itself. The vending machine that provides instantly upon the insertion of a coin, the fast-food establishment that promises no delay, the bank card that advertises itself as the one that does away with the need to stand in a queue, all promise the abolition of waiting time. Yet a little reflection shows that commodities cater to more than a desire for instant gratification. They are also marked by an attitude of appealing availability: the 'I'm here for you' message signified by the trolley at the airport that asks you to 'rent me,' or the advertisement that once asked you to 'fly me.' These appealing items are akin to those that promise service, such as the credit-card that delivers the object of desire to your door: "Pick up the phone; we come to you.' More than the abolition of waiting time is offered here; one will also be waited upon. And if the promise of service appeals to a desire for domination and control, it has to be noted that the illusion of control is also provided by vending machines and their ilk. The consumer makes it happen; or rather, the consumer is catered to via the fantasy of making it happen with minimal effort, even none at all. In this connection, the car is an exemplary commodity: it provides mobility without much activity to a passive director. At the same time, of course, it pollutes the surrounding environment.

As I have indicated, I want to propose that the desires encapsulated in commodities reflect an underlying foundational psychical fantasy. In other words, I am proposing that we treat the commodity as an external expression of that fantasy. But immediately, this proposition raises three problems. The first has also been indicated already; it is that the desires encapsulated in commodities do not tally exactly with any existing account of a psychical fantasy. The second problem is that of demonstrating that the fantasy expressed in commodities is in fact foundational. This problem is exacerbated by a third: namely, the problem of why it is that a foundational fantasy is externally expressed in a form which is on the socio-historical increase. For commodities, whether in the form of consumer goods, or in the form of the technologies that underlie their production, are evidently increasing.

We are not entirely in a void when it comes to considering these problems. While there is no extant account which tallies precisely with the fantasy I am assuming commodities encapsulate, a synthetic reading of certain psychoanalytic theories will provide one. In addition, that synthetic reading coheres because it makes central the fantasies Klein describes about the mother's body. This is appropriate in another way, given that it is a feminist reading of Klein, as well as of Lacan, that raises the question of the relation between transhistorical (or foundational) fantasies and socio-historical circumstances.[3] Finally, the notion that a psychical fantasy can have an increasingly macrocosmic expression is not new. Something very similar is maintained by Lacan, who writes that we are living under the sway of a paranoid social psychosis, in an 'ego's era' that began over four centuries ago.

The next section outlines a synthesis of psychoanalytic theories, based on the desires I am assuming commodities encapsulate. Specifically, it draws on Freud and Klein. A brief third section sketches Lacan's theory of the paranoid ego's era. On this basis, I return in section four to the relation between the psychical fantasy and its global enactment in a proliferation of instantly gratifying servile commodities, and speculate on the physics of the process involved.

3. This idea is elaborated in my "Controversial Discussions and Feminist Debate," in: *Freud in Exile*, edited by Edward Timms and Naomi Segal (London: Yale University Press, 1988), pp. 254-74. For another discussion that refers to the difference between psychical fantasy and social reality, see Jacqueline Rose, 'Introduction II' in: *Feminine Sexuality: Jacques Lacan and the Ecole Freudienne*, edited by Juliet Mitchell and Jacqueline Rose (London: Macmillan, 1982), pp. 27-57.

Persistently, consumer goods appeal through visual media. This, together with the desire for instant gratification these commodities encapsulate, directs us to Freud's pleasure principle. Freud's pleasure principle, more strictly his principle of Unlust, or unpleasure as he first defined it, is about a hallucinatory visual world where instant gratification is paramount. It is also about how psychical reality as distinct from 'material reality' comes into being.[4] When the longed-for object (initially the breast or mother) is not present it is hallucinated in its absence. This hallucination founds psychical reality; the breast is present in the imagination, but not present in the material here-and-now. The act of hallucination provides instant gratification, but the satisfaction it affords is only short-term. For the breast is longed for because the infant is hungry, and the hallucination cannot appease the unpleasure of the need for food. In other words unpleasure is due to the tension of need. Any need (to eat, urinate, defecate, ejaculate) increases quantitatively, and pleasure is felt when the need is relieved. A hallucinated breast does not of itself relieve the need. Indeed it ultimately leads to more unpleasure, in that it generates motor excitations it cannot dispel; the expected satisfaction that accompanies the hallucination gears the body up, but the energy amassed through this excitement cannot be relieved, any more than the original need itself.[5]

It should be clear that Freud's (un)pleasure principle is an economic or quantitative one: it is about the quantitative build-up of tension or need. In Freud's own terms, it is a matter of psychical economy, loosely based in Fechner's psycho-physics.[6] The economic or quantitative physical aspects of Freud's theory of the pleasure principle are frequently criticized. Its descriptive aspects are more generally accepted; few commentators have problems with the notion of instant gratification, or with that of visual hallucination. But if one reconsiders the desires implicit in commodities, it will be plain that while the pleasure principle accords with the desire for

4. The distinction between psychical and material reality is Freud's. It has been criticized by Laplanche and Pontalis, "Fantasy and the Origins of Sexuality," *International Journal of Psycho-Analysis*, 49, 1968, 1-18. With good reason, as will be plain in what follows.

5. See in particular the well-known seventh chapter of *The Interpretation of Dreams* in *The Standard Edition of the Complete Psychological Works of Sigmund Freud* (1953-74) (hereafter SE), Vol. V.

6. For the most thorough discussion of Freud's relation to Fechner, see H. F. Ellenberger, *The Discovery of the Unconscious: The History and Evolution of Dynamic Psychiatry* (London: Allan Lane, 1970).

instant gratification they express, and with their visual presentation in various media, it does not account for the other desires revealed in their design, namely: the desire to be waited upon; the desire to believe one is the source of agency who makes it happen; the desire to dominate and control the other who is active in providing, but whose activity is controlled by a relatively passive director, and the aggressive desire towards the other, if we take pollution as evidence of aggression.

The last-named desire evokes Klein. In her theory, the infant desires to spoil and poison the breast (and the mother) with its excrements.[7] As well as desiring to poison, the infant also desires to devour and fragment the mother's body. 'Cutting up' the mother's body is a recurrent theme in Klein's analyses of small children. She ties this cutting impulse to the drive for knowledge: the urge to get inside, grasp and in this sense understand what is hidden, and in the process destroy it.[8]

For Klein, the desires to poison, devour, dismember and to know through dismembering are prompted by two interrelated forces. The first is the strength of the death drive working within. The second is the envy of the creativeness embodied in the mother and mother's breast. While the death drive and envy motivate these fantasmatic attacks on the breast, they also lead to a fear of retaliation. The fear is that the aggressed breast will respond in kind; this fear results in what Klein terms the paranoid-schizoid position. It is paranoid because the infant projects its own aggressive desires on to the other, and the retaliation it fears (being cut up, poisoned, devoured) mirrors its own desires. It is schizoid because this paranoid projection involves a splitting both of the ego and of the other. For to deal with its dependence on the breast as the source of life, and its simultaneous fantasy that the breast is out to get it, the infant splits: there is a 'good' breast, and a 'bad' one. Yet because the badness the infant fears originates within itself, the splitting of the

7. In discussing the infant's desires in Klein's theory, I should enter a brief caveat on the notion that 'the infant' is the sole culprit when it comes to pinpointing the origin of the aggressive desires under discussion. 'The infant' is always that origin for Klein, although we will see later that the question of culpability is more complicated. But for the time being, I shall continue to write in terms of the infant.
8. For representative illustrations of these and many of the following Kleinian ideas from different periods of Klein's work, see "Early Stages of the Oedipus Conflict," in: *Love, Guilt and Reparation and Other Works, 1921-1945: The Writings of Melanie Klein*, Volume I (London: Hogarth, 1985), pp. 186-98, and "Envy and Gratitude," in: *Envy and Gratitude and Other Works 1946-1963: The Writings of Melanie Klein*, Volume III (London: Hogarth, 1980), pp. 176-235.

other presupposes and perpetuates a splitting of the ego. The ego, by depositing its own aggressive desires in the other, impoverishes itself by the splitting, and the repression or 'denial' that this entails. The ego can recover its full potential only by reclaiming that which has been cast out. This reclamation, when it occurs, can lead to depression: the recognition that the erstwhile projected badness lies within. It may also lead to reparation: the attempt to repair the damage done in fantasy.[9]

Leaving that hopeful note aside, it is important to add that the extent of the splitting, and of the poisoning, devouring, dismembering fantasies that accompany splitting, is mediated by anxiety. For Klein, anxiety derives from the death drive working within. In the last analysis, she posits that the strength of the death drive, and envy, are innate. Moreover, Klein's account of the splitting process presupposes a fantasy which has no direct correspondence with reality (the breast is not really cut up, etc.). It is a psychical fantasy, and clearly not a consequence of the infant's actual social environment nor of social events. It is also important to note that the splitting of the good and bad breast is remarkably similar to the splitting of women into two types: mother and whore. It is the splitting that constitutes the fantasy of woman, which Lacan believes is essential to the (masculine) subject's securing his sense of identity. For Lacanians, this fantasy is also meant to be transhistorical, which is why the issue of transhistoricity appeared on the feminist agenda in the first place. But as my immediate concern is with the foundational desires encapsulated in commodities, I do not intend to address here the evident ethnocentric and historical problems raised by this transhistorical claim (are women always split into two types?). Enough to say that the Kleinian account of the splitting into good and bad has the dubious advantage that it ascribes the phenomenon to any subject, masculine or feminine. There is also more warrant for assuming that this splitting and the desires that accompany it in her account are foundational, as we will see.

Thus far, we have a theory that accounts for the desire to poison, or, in commodity terms, the desire to pollute. We also have some elements of a theory that accounts for the desire to dominate and control (in so far as the desire to get inside, cut up, devour and so on

9. The most representative if difficult account of the views summarized in this paragraph is "Notes on Some Schizoid Mechanisms," in: Klein, *Writings*, volume I, pp. 1-24.

involves control and domination). It remains to tie this theory to the instant hallucinatory gratification embodied in the pleasure principle, and the desire to be waited upon from a passive though authoritative position. Here Klein's analysis of envy provides an indirect clue:

Though superficially [envy] may manifest itself as a coveting of the prestige, wealth and power which others have attained, its actual aim is creativeness. The capacity to give and preserve life is felt as the greatest gift, and therefore creativeness becomes the deepest cause for envy. The spoiling of creativity implied in envy is illustrated in Milton's *Paradise Lost,* where Satan, envious of God, decides to become the usurper of Heaven. Fallen, he and his other fallen angels build Hell as a rival to Heaven, and becomes the destructive force which attempts to destroy what God creates. This theological idea seems to come down from St. Augustine, who describes Life as a creative force opposed to Envy, a destructive force.[10]

This passage is interesting because it points out, although it does so obliquely, that envy superficially focuses on attributes or possessions, rather than the creative force which may (or may not) result in them. The passage also points out that envy will attempt to rival that which it envies, and that it will do so by constructing an alternative. More generally, Klein's analysis of envy in the essay from which the above quotation comes shows that while envious motivations are readily recognizable in destructiveness or calumny, they are less recognizable, although present, in denial. This is the form of denial which simply ignores or forgets that which is displeasing to the ego. It is present in the denial of the labour involved in creativity. We recognize it where creativity is seen as accidental, or where it is attributed to a circumstance or to a possession.

Let us add to these observations a notion that is best elaborated by Freud. This is that the infant, or small child, imagines, in a reversal of the actual state of affairs, that the mother is a dependent infant.[11] In reversing the passive experiences of childhood into active ones in his play with a cotton-reel, Freud's grandson not only masters the mother's absence and introduces himself to deathly repetition;[12] nor does he only, if simultaneously, enter the world of

---

10. Melanie Klein, "Envy and Gratitude," pp. 201-2.
11. Significantly, Freud mentions this in his discussion on "Female Sexuality," SE, XXI, 236.
12. Freud, *Beyond the Pleasure Principle*, SE, XVIII.

language through the mother's absence that forces him to call. He also makes the mother into a fantasised small child which he controls, a child which is also an inanimate thing. If the notion of the reversal of the original state of affairs is made central, rather than the incidental aside it is for Freud, it has the advantage that it reconciles otherwise diverse findings. When realities are seen in terms of their opposites, the fact of nurturance and of the means to grow becomes a threat to narcissism; it establishes the reality of dependence. From this perspective, the envy of the mother's breast is the resentment of that dependence, and the reason why nurturance, or love, or protection, or assistance, are interpreted as assertions of superiority and power. "Only saints are sufficiently detached from the deepest of the common passions to avoid the aggressive reactions to charity."[13] There is a related, if less relevant, offshoot of the reversal of the original state of affairs into its opposite, an offshoot which we might usefully term 'imitating the original', in which rivalry with the original is clearly apparent. The child imitates the mother; the commodity, harking back to this paper's point of departure, is often an imitation of the original.[14] While writing this, I went to the corner store for orange juice, and found only artificial orange drink in an orange-shaped container (with green leaves). I also took in late-night television, worst amongst it The Stepford Wives, which is all about constructing a reliable and completely controllable imitation of the original wife and mother, and Startrek II, where 'Project Genesis' shows us humans reinventing the entire process of creation.

But keeping to the main thread: the tendency to look at realities in terms of their opposites is manifest at another level, which will explain the desire to be waited upon. Originally, the infant is perforce passive, and is dependent on the mother's activity for survival. Yet it would be consistent with a fantasmatic reversal of the original state of affairs if the infant were to correlate its actual

13. J. Lacan, "Aggressivity in Psychoanalysis," in: *Écrits: A Selection*, translated by Alan Sheridan (London: Tavistock, 1977), p. 13.
14. The imitation of the original is an often implicit and sometimes explicit theme in discussions of women and technology, particularly reproductive technology. For a general representative collection on this theme, see *Reproductive Technologies*, edited by Michelle Stanworth (Cambridge: Polity Press, 1987). For discussions which bear more closely on the issues discussed here, see D. Haraway, "A Manifesto For Cyborgs: Science, Technology and Socialist Feminism in the 1980s," *Socialist Review*, 1985, 80, pp. 65-107, and R. Braidotti, "Organs without bodies," *Differences*, 1, 1, 1989, 147-61.

385

dependent reality with the fantasy of control through imagining that the mother's activity takes place at its behest. The infant does not wait upon the mother; the mother waits upon it. It is precisely this fantasy that is catered to by the commodities with which we began. But a little of reality lingers on, in the association between passivity and luxury, which recognizes that it is not the passive controller, or 'the infant,' who labours. At the same time, the labour or activity involved in fulfilling the wish is denied in so far as its intelligence is denied. In fantasy, the mental direction and design of what labour effects is appropriated, only the manual activity is left out. Thus the mental whim and control is the infant's. The work goes elsewhere.

The split occasioned by this fantasy prefigures a deeper dualism between mind and body, in which direction or agency is seen as mental and mindful, while activity, paradoxically, is viewed as something that lacks intelligence. By an ineluctable logic, the activity of women as mothers is presented as passive; in fantasy, it lacks a will of its own; it is directed. And because direction is too readily confused with a will of one's own, this denial can readily be extended to living nature overall. In this connection, it is worth noting that the oft-repeated association of women and nature can be explained not by what women and nature have in common, but by the similar fantasmatic denial imposed upon each of them. In the case of women, it is one's will that is denied. In the case of living nature, its own inherent direction is disregarded. But this is to anticipate.

As I have indicated, the fact that creativeness is not viewed as intelligent or directed activity is consistent with envy's predilection to focus on it as the possession of certain attributes, rather than as a force in itself. Creativeness is seen less as what one does, than as what one has. Or, to say a similar thing differently, the dialectics of envy conduct themselves at the level of images. What matters is the appearance of the thing, rather than the process of which it is part. To say that what is envied is the mother's possession of the breast is to work already within the terms of envy, which are those of possessions, things, appearances, discrete entities, separable and separate from an on-going process. Which brings us to the crux of the matter. While a fantasy of controlling the breast cannot survive at the level of feeling (pain or pleasure), it can survive at the literally imaginary level of hallucination. In fact, the controlling fantasy can be perpetuated through hallucinations, and this ability to perpetuate it must contribute to the addiction to the pleasure in hallucination, despite its unpleasure at other levels. In other words, by this

account, the fantasy of controlling the breast and the act of hallucination are one and the same, which means that the amazing visual
power of hallucination is tied to an omnipotent desire from the
outset.

Of course feelings of omnipotence, for Freud, are infantile in
origin, and also tied to narcissism. But while there has been some
discussion of how it is that narcissism can come into being only
through fantasy or hallucination, the other side of this issue, which
is how it is that hallucination is by nature an omnipotent or narcissistic act, has not been discussed.[15] It is one thing to concentrate on
how it is that the subject's sense of itself as a separate being is
inextricably linked to narcissism; that is to say, that it is only by the
narcissistic act of fantasizing about its own body or circumference
that it establishes its separate self. It is another to think about how
the narcissism involved is also, and simultaneously, an omnipotent
fantasy about controlling the other. For to establish itself as separate, the subject has to have something to be separate from. This
much is foreshadowed by Lacan.[16] But, by this account, the thing
the subject is separate from is the breast or mother it imagines as
available to it, subject to it, and towards whom it feels the aggressive
desires that lead in turn to paranoia. Moreover, in the omnipotent
act of hallucinating a breast it controls, the nascent subject separates
and gives priority to its own visual capacity for imagination over its
other senses. It is this visual capacity that allows one to imagine that
things are other than as they are; to focus on the distinctiveness of
entities other than oneself, rather than the senses or feelings that
connect one with those others; to believe in (and even achieve) a
situation where mental design and direction can be divorced from
bodily action.

It seems we have an account of a psychical fantasy which tallies
with the desires encapsulated in commodities. It is this fantasy that I
am positing as the original foundational fantasy. That is to say, I am
positing that the desire for instant gratification, the preference for

15. Although Borch-Jacobsen comes close when he pinpoints the core of megalo-
mania in many of the dreams Freud analysed. M. Borch-Jacobsen, *The Freudian
Subject* (London: Macmillan, 1989). Borch-Jacobsen's analysis of why narcissism is necessary, and is in fact the key to the constitution of the subject, is the
outstanding discussion of this theme. Laplanche and Pontalis's classic "Fantasy
and the Origins of Sexuality" is also important, as is J. Laplanche, *Life and
Death in Psychoanalysis*, translated by J. Mehlman (Baltimore: Johns Hopkins
University Press, 1976).
16. It is the essence of his concept of the 'objet petit a.'

visual and 'object'-oriented thinking this entails, the desire to be waited upon, the envious desire to imitate the original, the desire to control the mother, and to devour, poison, and dismember her, and to obtain knowledge by this process, are part of the original human condition. There will be more argument on why these aggressive desires are part of the human condition, and the forces that prompt the anxiety and fear that underlie them, in the concluding section. The immediate question concerns how it is that the commodities in which these desires were first discerned appear to be proliferating, as perhaps, do the desires themselves. For, as I stressed at the outset, it is one thing to say that a psychical fantasy is foundational. The socio-historical force of that fantasy, in different times and places, is another matter altogether.

As noted above, the idea that a foundational fantasy can be played out with more or less socio-historical force is implicit in Lacan's theory of a paranoid social psychosis and an ego's era. In this brief sketch of this neglected theory of Lacan's, it is useful to begin with a quotation in which Lacan, like Klein, also refers to Augustine, who, of course, is writing long before the ego's era began, which it did, according to Lacan, in the late sixteenth century. In this quotation, Lacan is discussing the individual ego as such, and the death drive:

The signs of the lasting damage this negative libido causes can be read in the face of a small child torn by the pangs of jealousy, where St. Augustine recognized original evil. "Myself have seen and known even a baby envious; it could not speak, yet it turned pale and looked bitterly on its foster brother."[17]

17. J. Lacan, "Some reflections on the ego," *International Journal of Psycho-analysis*, Vol. 34, 1953, 16. Lacan does not give a reference for the quotation from St. Augustine. It comes from the *Confessions*. The context is an argument that sin is present in infancy. When considering various possibilities, St. Augustine asks whether as an infant he sinned by endeavouring to harm "as much as possible" those larger beings, including his parents, who were not subject to him, "whenever they did not punctually obey [his] will" (non ad nutum voluntatis obtemperantibus feriendo nocere niti quantum potest ...). One sentence later comes the observation that Lacan also quotes, in part, in Latin: "vidi ego et expertus sum zelantem parvulum: nondum loquebatur et intue batur pallidus amaro aspectu conlactaneum suum." S. Aureli Augustini, *Confessionum*, edited by P. Knöll (Leipzig: Verlag von B. G. Teubner, 1989), 1/14-20, p. 8. For my purposes, it is the failure to obey punctually, in connection with envy, that is interesting.

After quoting Augustine, Lacan moves swiftly on to Hegel's master/slave dialectic, and the attempted destruction of the other consciousness that the dialectic foretells. In another context, Lacan makes it plain that that dialectic is the key to the "most formidable social hell" of the ego's paranoid era, in that the era is built on a destructive objectification of the other, together with a destructive objectification in knowledge.[18] The nature of the destructive objectification involved in the master/slave dialectic is left largely unspecified, although Lacan indicates that it means turning the other into a controllable thing.[19]

The need to control is part of the paranoia of the ego's era; it results from the subject's belief that the object, the objectified one, is out to get it, but this paranoia originates in the subject's own projected aggressive desires towards the other. None the less its paranoia makes the ego anxious, and its anxiety makes it want to control. The objectification of knowledge is also paranoid; it is knowledge based on a need for control. It is knowledge tied to a 'positivist' world view in which what is seen, or what can be tested or proved to exist, especially on the basis that it can be seen, is privileged. The objectification of knowledge helps construct a world in which only objects (or discrete entities?) are recognized, and they can only be recognized by subjects. In turn (I think) these subjects are affected, if not driven, by the objects they construct, although Lacan does not pursue this point. Lacan is more concerned with the objectification of knowledge as such; in this concern, he is at one with Heidegger, to whom Lacan frequently alludes, although Heidegger centralizes the objectification of nature as 'standing reserve', and the technocratic drive for mastery over nature, in a way that Lacan does not.[20]

In fact generally, when Lacan comes to describing how it is that the 'ego's era' comes into being, he is, aside from one brief argument, not preoccupied with its social dynamics. But it is this consideration that preoccupies the present paper. My main concerns are with how it is that a foundational fantasy goes beyond the bounds of individual dreams, and makes those dreams come true in the ego's

18. "Aggressivity in Psychoanalysis," p. 29. This and "The Function and Field of Speech and Language in Psychoanalysis," in: *Écrits: A Selection*, pp. 30-113, are the main texts in which Lacan outlines his theory of the ego's era.
19. "The Function and Field of Speech and Language in Psychoanalysis," in: *Écrits: A Selection*, p. 42.
20. M. Heidegger, *The Question Concerning Technology and Other Essays*, translated by W. Lovitt (New York: Harper and Row, 1977).

era, and how it is that gradually the ego's era spatially encompasses the world at large, as Lacan believes it does. To deal with these concerns, the nature of objectification needs to be defined more precisely than it was by Lacan, or by Heidegger. The true nature of 'objectification' is better grasped by Klein, in her analysis of the infantile desire to poison, fragment and destroy the mother's body. By this argument, these desires constitute the process of objectification. We have seen that turning the other into an object also means fragmenting it (in order partly to know it) or poisoning or in other ways attacking it, as well as making it a controllable thing. A very similar point is made by Kristeva, who, in an argument which echoes that of Mary Douglas, makes 'abjection' the foundation of objectification. Abjection is the feeling that one has of revolting (including excremental) substances that are neither inside nor outside; objectification comes from the need to exclude these substances by depositing them in the other, which brings the other, as object, into being.[21]

Some of the resonances between Klein's theory of the infant, and Lacan's theory of the ego's era should now be evident. I will assume that the links between their arguments on the role of anxiety in 'objectification' can be taken for granted. Also, as Klein's account ties the objectifying desires to the drive for knowledge, it is not difficult to leap from it to Foucault's analysis of the drive for knowledge as a drive for power, a jump that is facilitated by the similarity, or indebtedness, of Foucault's theory to Heidegger's. Yet in making the leap between the transhistorical fantasy described in the preceding section, and the processes at work in the ego's era, Klein's 'mother body' has to be correlated with living nature. It is this correlation that is the condition of recognizing that the process Klein describes is a microcosm of a large-scale assault, a psychical fantasy writ large. This correlation is also necessary to begin answering the question: what is the relation between the psychical fantasy and the socio-historical process that makes the dream of mastery over the mother/earth come true? Lacan refers to an ego's era, yet it is unclear how the historical era and the ontological ego enact the same desires and fantasies, one on a macro- (as it were),

---

21. J. Kristeva, "L'abjet d'amour," *Tel Quel*, 91, 1982, 17-32. M. Douglas, *Purity and Danger: An Analysis of Concepts of Pollution and Taboo* (London: Routledge and Kegan Paul, 1966). Douglas's cross-cultural enquiry lends further weight to the notion that what we are dealing with here is a transhistorical fantasy.

and one on a micro-scale. As I mentioned above, Lacan has only a brief argument concerning it. This argument, which concerns spatiality and the relation of spatial restrictions to psychical aggressiveness will be relevant subsequently. But it will be so only after the general relevance of spatio-temporal considerations to the questions at issue has been established. Moreover, it is only then that it will be plain how the production of commodities, or consumer goods, in which the desires embodied in the foundational fantasy were first discerned, leads to the global technocratic expansion that marks the ego's era.

Evidently, as we have every reason for supposing that the fantasy of subjecting and dismembering that on which we depend is an ancient one, then its microcosmic version predates both the technocratic acting-out of that fantasy on the large scale, and the proliferation of consumer goods which satisfy that fantasy in everyday life. Or, more accurately, as the very idea of a foundational fantasy entails the assumption that it occurs in individuals, its genesis, while it is something everyone experiences, is more individually contained. The limits on the extent to which it can be acted out are set by the available technology. It does not automatically become a corporate process.

But the question of the relation between the individual psychical fantasy and its socio-historical parallel is complicated by two other things. The first is the emphasis on the psychical fantasy of woman, which has obscured the real fantasy at issue. By the foregoing account, the ego comes into being and maintains itself partly through the fantasy that it either contains or in other ways controls the mother; this fantasy, as discussed, involves the reversal of the original state of affairs, together with the imitation of the original. When recognition of the other is unavoidable, the ego's first response is that it is not the dependent child. In patriarchal societies, the fantasised reversal of the original state is actualized in the relation between the sexes. Herein lies the importance for a man of the need to take care of the other, to be the breadwinner, a matter whose significance may lie in the distance between the extent to which he actually gives of himself, and the extent to which he relies on the other's giving him an image of himself as giving, regardless of the reality of whether he gives or not. But more to the point: the truly patriarchal society is on the decline.[22] It is easy enough to see

22. See Juliet MacCannell, *The Regime of The Brother* (London and New York, Routledge, 1991).

how in such societies, the psychical fantasy of woman could present itself as the necessary condition for containing and expressing the splitting into good and bad categories that figure in the original foundational fantasy. But by this argument, the construction of sexual identity is not the origin of the foundational fantasy. It is rather that in patriarchal societies, far more ancient psychical conflict is played out in the arena of sexual identity. It is noteworthy that the shift from a genuinely patriarchal feudal society to a sexist capitalist one is also the shift from a society with a limited technology to one that is capable of satisfying the desires in the foundational fantasy with more precision.[23]

The second, related, complicating factor involved in understanding the relation between the individual foundational fantasy and its socio-historical enactment is that the acting-out of the fantasy on the large scale also takes place over a longer time-scale. Yet it is precisely this complication that suggests how the relation between the two levels might be understood, for the key terms it introduces are those of time and space. The large-scale acting-out represents the fantasy's spatial and temporal extension. Instead of the length of an individual's lifetime, or the years of their madness, the 'ego's era' spans a few centuries. Instead of fantasies that are dreamed, there are technologies that make them come true, increasing their coverage of the earth's surface and corruption of its parameters in the process. It remains, then, to examine these connections and their physical implications at more length.

Time and space have already been implicated in the dynamics whereby the individual foundational psychical fantasy is generated. We want it now, and we want it to come to us. On the social scale, by inventing technologies that bring whatever it is we want to us, and which do so immediately, we are abolishing time and space. But paradoxically, as we have seen, this entails extending the fantasy in space, and for a reason yet to be determined, giving it more time to

---

23. It is understandable that Lacan should locate the psychical fantasy of woman as the significant one. The odd thing is that he pinpoints it in terms of feudal societies, yet he none the less sees the subject/object distinction as a sexual fantasy that has governed thought since the pre-Socratics. And when he describes the subject/object distinction as a sexual fantasy, Lacan attributes the tendency to split form from matter, and to see matter as passive, to it. See *Le Séminaire: Livre XX (Encore)* (Paris: Seuil, 1975), p. 76. This accords with the above argument on the fantasmatic denial of intelligence in the bodily activity of women as mothers.

play itself out. The only way of resolving this paradox is to suppose that as we extend the fantasy in space, and make it immediately present, we simultaneously slow down time. In turn, this means supposing that the mechanism by which we make the fantasy present and extend its spatial coverage also congeals or slows down time. What is this mechanism, and how is the paradox to be resolved?

This paradox is resolved in the case of infancy and the birth of psychical reality in this way: what prompts the hallucination is the desire that the longed-for object be present here and now. Yet if we examine Freud's account of hallucination, we find hallucination not only introduces instant gratification (in theory); in practice, it also introduces delay. In Freud's terms, the secondary process comes into being through an inhibition [*Hemmung*] of the primary process.[24] In the primary process, almost all things are possible; it is governed by the pleasure principle, and marked by hallucinatory wish-fulfilment, a lack of contradiction, the much-discussed mechanisms of condensation and displacement, and timelessness, amongst other things. The secondary process is governed by the reality principle. It is the locus of rational thought, directed motility, and planned action or agency. When it inhibits the primary process, it checks out or 'reality-tests' whether the image before it is a real perception or an imagined hallucination. In other words, it makes the psyche pause before it responds to the image it is offered. So on the one hand, hallucination inaugurates a delay; on the other hand, I would suggest that hallucination is a response to a delay, on the grounds that the wish for instant gratification must be prompted by the experience of a gap between the perception of a need and its fulfilment.[25]

In the social case, the mechanisms by which we extend the fantasy are territorial imperialism and technology. Technology constructs the commodities that satisfy the fantasy of instant gratification and

24. Freud, *The Interpretation of Dreams*, SE, V 601.
25. Of course this has consequences for real perception as well as imagined hallucination. One cannot respond immediately to the former. It has to be evaluated. Nothing visual can be taken for granted. What is more, it only becomes taken for granted at the price of establishing familiar pathways for psychical energy to follow. The more certain the pathway, the less energy is involved; the less the pathways are disrupted, the less the stress. Yet the more the pathways are fixed, the more energy, in Freud's terms, is bound: rigidity and anxiety, in the face of unfamiliar pathways, are the consequences. Two points are critical here. The first is Freud's notion that energy comes to exist in a bound, rather than freely mobile, state through checking out hallucinations. The second is that, as we will

service, but how do these constructions simultaneously slow things down? For by the parallel presented here, the commodity takes the place of the hallucination. Yet there is no need to distinguish whether the perception of a commodity is real or imagined. It exists. So how, then, can the existence of commodities demand delay, or an inhibition of the primary process, in the same way that a hallucination does?

Things might be clarified if, instead of concentrating initially on the parallel between the commodity and the hallucination, we ask what, in the socio-historical macrocosm, parallels the primary process, which means concentrating for a little on the primary process as such. The nature of the primary process is one of the most taken-for-granted yet confused areas of Freud's theory. In addition to the characteristics already noted, the primary process consists of freely mobile energy, and there are reasons for thinking Freud identified it with the "movement of life" as such. At the same time, the primary process consists of the pathways in which energy is bound, a bondage which leads to repetition, and repetition, in turn, is the hallmark of the death drive. I have analysed this confusion elsewhere.[26] Let me simply reiterate here that the bound and repetitive pathways of the primary process come into being via repression. In fact, they come into being via primal repression, which Freud distinguished from repression proper, or secondary repression. Primal repression (of some idea or ideational event) establishes a nucleus which attracts subsequent 'proper repressions' towards it.

A loose analogy connects Freud's distinction between primal repression and repression proper and a distinction drawn by Laplanche and Pontalis between primary and subsequent fantasies.[27] Given that primal repression seems to pertain to hallucination, it is appropriate to ask whether hallucinations and primal fantasies are the same thing. There is no obvious answer to this question. None the less, a distinction needs to be drawn between hallucination and fantasy, in the everyday sense of that term. A hallucination appears to be present here and now, while a conscious fantasy is the con-

see, Lacan ties anxiety to spatial constriction. The argument on bound and freely mobile energy is one that Freud attributes to Breuer, and Breuer attributes to Freud: *Studies on Hysteria*, SE, II, 194, n. 1.

26. And also elaborated on the significance of delay in hallucination between the perception of a need and its fulfilment. See Teresa Brennan, *The Interpretation of the Flesh: Freud's Theory of Femininity* (London and New York: Routledge, 1991, 1992), Chapter Six.

27. "Fantasy and the Origins of Sexuality," *International Journal of Psychoanalysis*, 49, 1968, 1-18.

templation of an event which is not occurring here and now. In addition, a hallucination is a picture on a larger scale than a daydream. If I close my eyes to daydream, the images I have seem smaller or more distanced than the images I have if I hallucinate, as everyone does in a nightmare. This difference or distance is a sensory affair; as Freud noted, hallucinations have the quality of sensory immediacy, but everyday fantasies or daydreams do not. Something else characterizes daydreams, and this something is not only memory, as daydreams encompass more than actual recollection. This something must be nothing less than the capacity for abstraction. Abstraction in any form is the removal of the subject's attention, or, for that matter, the subject's theory, from its referents in immediate felt experience. Where this distinction between hallucination and everyday or conscious fantasy leaves unconscious fantasy is unclear.

But what I want to suggest now is that the act of repressing a hallucination is basic to establishing a sense of space-time (and, perhaps, to establishing the repressed unconscious), in that it establishes a still point of reference from which the nascent ego can get its bearings. Literally, its spatio-temporal bearings. This means that the sense of perspective is a construction, as may be the sense of passing time. The idea that the sense of perspective is a construction is attested to by the fact that when sight is recovered after blindness, the sense of perspective (distance and size) does not necessarily accord with the perception of others. It is often completely out of proportion with what we know as reality. The idea that the sense of passing time is also constructed is demanded by the theory that space-time is a continuum; time is measured in terms of space, and the interval between one event and another depends on the speed it takes to cover the distance between them, and speed, in turn, depends on the potential motion or energy of the body involved.[28] But if one looks more closely at what the initial repression of hallucination involves (the process by which the hallucination becomes unconscious), it is evident that something is happening to energy in the process, and also that 'time' is measured relative to something other than the constructed space-time of which it is also part.

I suggested that a hallucination is prompted by the delay between the perception of a need and its fulfilment, and noted that Freud

---

28. There are several excellent histories of physics and the story of the shift from one dominant paradigm to another, but see in particular Jennifer Trusted, *Physics and Metaphysics* (London and New York: Routledge, 1991). For reasons of space, I cannot give an exposition of the relevant paradigm shifts here.

(although he does not postulate an initial delay) argues that the secondary process comes into being through an inhibition of the primary process, which in turn amounts to a further delay. Postulating an initial delay between the perception of a need and its fulfilment as the condition of hallucination means postulating a prior state in which perception and need coincide, or in which the delay between the need and its fulfilment was shorter. The fact that there is an intra-uterine state which is experienced before birth meets the requirements for this prior state. That is to say, if we suppose that in utero, there is no experience of a delay between perception and need, or that any delay is shorter, the intra-uterine state should constitute another pole against which the construction of space-time could be measured. This supposition will have more substance if one considers what happens to psychical energy when it is bound. Freud's argument on this (elaborated in his *Project*[29]) has to led to a debate amongst psycho-analysts as to whether the bound pathways that come into being through distinguishing between hallucination and real perception are on the side of the Life or the Death drive. The key opposed positions here, which I shall only sketch briefly, are represented by Laplanche and Lacan respectively.

Laplanche disputes Lacan's location of the ego on the side of the death drive.[30] He does so on the basis of an interpretation of Freud's assumptions about physics (which, writes Laplanche, were outdated even at the close of the nineteenth century). The essence of Laplanche's argument is that, first, the ego is a kind of giant fantasy in itself. This much he has in common with Lacan. Laplanche bases his view of the ego as a fantasy in itself on the *Project*, where Freud posits the ego as a mass of cathected neurone-pathways. Or, if we put this in terms of Freud's subsequent, less physiological vocabulary, the ego is a mass of pathways in which psychical energy is bound. It would be interesting to investigate how this bound mass tallies with Lacan's mirror-image, especially given that the mirror-stage and the nascent subject's mirror image are critical in its establishing its spatial sense, but that is beyond my scope here.

Keeping to the main thread: Laplanche also argues that Freud confused the physical principle of inertia with the principle of constancy. The former is a state in which there is no motion,

29. Freud, *Project For a Scientific Psychology (Entwurf einer Psychologie)*, SE, I, and see n. 25 above.
30. J. Laplanche, *Life and Death in Psychoanalysis*.

nothing. It is the desire to restore an earlier state of things in which the governing principle is rest. In Freud's 1920 formulation on the death drive, he termed it the Nirvana principle.[31] The principle of constancy is the desire to keep energy constant. For Freud, freely mobile energy will follow the path of least resistance, which is the path towards Nirvana. For Laplanche, while the ego is a giant fantasy, it is none the less a vital one, in that its bound pathways are the essential means for action against or towards what is necessary for sustaining life. There is no essential contradiction between its actions towards or away from life and the principle of constancy.

Where things get more complicated is that, as we have seen, the bound pathways are also tied to the death drive. This is because energy will flow along the paths that are familiar to it, and these paths might be completely inappropriate for dealing with a novel situation. The repression that brings both the pathways and the ego into being figures here; bound energy flows along pathways that are unconscious. In addition, there are two complications which reinforce the notion that the bound is on the side of the deathly. The first is that the ego is less likely to adapt and follow new pathways in a situation which arouses anxiety. Furthermore, it is precisely the protracted attachment to any fantasy (which must necessitate a bound pathway) that characterizes neurosis. Such attachments make it harder to act upon the world; they are similar in their effects to anxiety, in that they counter 'the movement of life.'[32] Hence Lacan's position.

Now it would be easy enough to take a liberal approach here, and say that, on the one hand, the ego and bound pathways are necessary: one has to deal with life's exigencies (Laplanche). On the other, if too much psychical energy is bound, if the pathways are too rigid, if anxiety is greater, then vaulting ambition overleaps itself and the result is deathly (Lacan). But this balanced solution allows one supposition to escape unchallenged. This is the notion that as freely mobile energy follows the path of least resistance, it therefore tends towards inertia. There is a related supposition, which is that an inert state is a restful one, and that any body seeking rest will seek to be inert or motionless. There is actually no reason why rest should be equated with inertia. As we have seen, the natural state (experienced in utero) could well be one of more rapid motion, and this living state could be restful in that it appears to be without the conflict contingent on delay, and is therefore 'timeless.' In other

31. Freud, *Beyond the Pleasure Principle*, SE, XVIII, 56.
32. Freud, *Inhibitions, Symptoms and Anxiety*, SE, XX, 148.

words, what leads freely mobile energy on its quest for the path of least resistance is not the notion of inertia, but the memory of a state of timeless (yet, relative to the subsequent sense of time, more rapid) motion. It is no accident that Aristotle, who argued that, while motion and time are mutually defined, motion depends on an unmoved mover, an ultimate still point, also argued that the mother's role in gestation is entirely passive. The metaphysical presupposition hidden behind the founding assumption of classical Aristotelian physics is consistent with Aristotle's denial of maternal activity. To suppose, as I have done, that in utero there is no or less delay between a perception of a need and its fulfilment is to suppose that there is a system of fleshly communication between two parties. It means that the mother is not, as Aristotle has it, a passive garden in which a tiny, active, fully formed homunculus is planted, and grows of its own accord.[33]

Of course, the spatio-temporal notion of rapidity comes into being only after the fact, that is to say after birth, and the experience of delay. The point is that, after the fact, the resultant slow plight of the ego is measured retroactively, in spatio-temporal terms, against the prior intra-uterine state. In addition, the very thing that leads freely mobile energy into conflict with the exigencies of life is the fact that it encounters a point of resistance. If there was no resistance, there is no a priori reason why freely mobile energy could not regain its prior rapid motion. Naturally, this means external as well as internal points of resistance, for it would be a travesty of what logic underlies Freud's reasoning on the ego to reduce the points of resistance the ego encounters to its own self-sustaining fantasies. The ego evidently encounters other points of resistance that would harm its chances of living (very bad weather, aggressive others, etc.), and to these it has to respond. None the less, the notion that the ego's own hallucinated responses constitute the first point of resistance will be instructive, if pursued in relation to the parallel drawn throughout this article between the desires encapsulated in commodities and those of the psyche.

Let me suppose that the construction of a commodity also binds energy in the same way that it is bound in the repression of a hallucination. That is to say, the energy is attached to an image,

33. Aristotle, *Generation of Animals*, I, 20-22. On time and motion, see *Physics*, IV, XI, 219-20, translated by Philip Wicksteed and Francis Cornford (London: Loeb/Heinemann, 1929), pp. 389-95. It should be added that the confusion between 'at rest' and 'inert' is a subsequent one. Aristotle distinguishes the two states (*Physics*, V, VI, 230) but immediately argues that 'at rest' is analogous to unchangingness.

fixing it in place. The energy attached in this way is that of living nature; it correlates with Freud's 'freely mobile energy,' although freely mobile energy knows no paths except those that tend to Nirvana. Living nature, on the other hand, has its own rhythms and paths. Yet, as we have seen, the notion that the paths of freely mobile energy and those of the life drive are not the same depends on the idea that freely mobile energy follows the path of least resistance, and this in turn depends on the existence of something that resists. The commodity provides that point of resistance, in that it encapsulates living nature in forms which remove them from the flow of life. A tree converted into a table does not enter into the production of more trees. Such conversions, which of course become more signif- icant when the commodity produced is not biodegradable, function analogously with fantasies in that they bind living substances in forms which are inert, relative to the energetic movement of life. The more of these relatively inert points there are, the slower the movement of life becomes. That is consistent with the phenomenon known as entropy. The implication here is not that nothing should be constructed (shelter etc.), any more than it means the ego should not respond to bad weather by protecting itself (seeking shelter etc.).

But the notion that points of resistance slow things down pro- vides a critical principle by which to gauge what should and should not be constructed. That gauge is: how readily can these construc- tions re-enter the movement of life? It also means we have an account of the paradox whereby the infantile fantasy takes more time to play itself out, and it is an account consistent with the idea that the fantasy simultaneously extends itself in space. It takes more 'time' to play itself out in the sense that it uses more living energy, as it systematically extends itself in the spatial conquests necessary to supply the living substances by which it sustains itself. However, it also follows from this argument that the 'time' it takes to play itself out is itself a constructed phenomenon, in that this 'time' consists of the accumulation of 'points of resistance' or commodities. Moreover this 'time' has its own direction. The construction of one commod- ity (using the term in the broadest sense[34]) fixes a relatively inert

34. A commodity varies in scale depending on the position of the consumer. From the standpoint of one consumer, it could be a small-scale consumer good. From the standpoint of another, it could be ICI. Marx's definition of the commodity, which haunts this article, should be discussed here, but lack of space prevents me from doing so.

or still point. This point (les us say it is a factory, even a town) then functions as an inert point of reference from which distances are measured and pathways built. They are built, at least in part, as a means to further the consumption of more living substances in the process of production. Of the different characteristics that mark the networks established by these means, there are two that need to be noted here. The first is that to stay in the race of efficient consumption for production and further consumption, and free-enterprise competition is always a race, these networks need to facilitate the most rapid transport of energy possible. This applies to energy of any order: the natural substances consumed in production and human labour-power. The means by which natural substance or labour is extracted and conveyed from a to b has to be speeded up. So at the level of constructed space-time, everything seems to be getting faster and faster. The second point about the networks constructed in relation to still points is that at the same time as they partake in the process whereby natural reproduction is actually slowed down, they must, like the still points themselves, have their own physical energetic effects.[35] These effects are physical both in the sense that commodities function as points of resistance to natural rhythms, so that in reality things get slower and slower. The second point is that as the networks between these points extend, creating more still points in the process, the expanding spatio-temporal construction that results has a pattern of its own.[36]

35. The notion that instruments from 'the microscope to the radio-television' have a far greater effect on us than we are aware has been put forward by Lacan (*Le Séminaire Livre XX (Encore)*, p. 76) and a similar observation is made by Benjamin, as noted at the outset.

36. At this point one has to note the argument of Niklas Luhmann, who reiterates the Parsonian point that a temporal social system can only be compared to something that is not temporal (N. Luhmann, The Differentiation of Society [New York, Columbia University Press, 1982], p. 292). He even says that it can only be compared to something that is 'immediate,' that is to say, timeless. But having had this insight, he then goes on to neglect its implications altogether. He forgets the existence of the 'immediate' something, and argues instead that a temporal system can have nothing outside itself, and thus that there is no point against which an alternative future to the one already contained within the present can be built. From the perspective of this argument, of course, that alternative point is present in the natural world. Moreover, as I imply in the text, if the 'immediate' something is the physical world, if the physical world is also spatio-temporal, from where does it gets its temœporality, if not from the

400

There is every reason for supposing that this pattern presents itself to us as temporal causality. Temporal causality is the process whereby one thing appears to lead to another across time in an apparently irreversible manner. This taken-for-granted process is of course at issue in physics, where it is regarded as something to be explained. This analysis might, incidentally, contribute to understanding the asymmetrical nature of time: the puzzle as to why time only goes one way, or why time is irreversible. For by this account, time could be understood, in theory if not in practice, as reversible, provided that all the points of resistance out of which space-time is constructed and connected were systematically undone, and if their component natural substances re-entered the natural rhythms of production, from which they were initially, physically, 'abstracted.' This understanding of time also accords with the deconstructionist idea that causality is a construction, a line of reasoning we impose on events. Except that, in this case, the causal construction really has been constructed. The fact that the construction has a fantasmatic origin makes it no less physical in its effects. In other words, to read causality as a mere illusion, which could be done away with by refusing to impose causal reasoning in theory, accords with and therefore does nothing to counter the galloping construction of causality in the physical world.

This returns me to the question of how the infantile fantasy plays itself out on the larger scale over longer time. The dynamics described in this process must be cumulative, not only in the sense that, as things get faster and faster at the level of constructed space-time, they get slower and slower in terms of the natural rhythms of reproduction. They must also be cumulative in terms of the extent to which the causality constructed presents itself to us as a historical process. 'History,' as the sense of the sequence of past events, is increasingly moulded by the extent to which a foundational psychical fantasy makes itself materially true, and by its

social world? For an excellent critique of Luhmann's 'privileging of the present' from a Derridean perspective, see Drucilla Cornell, 'Time, Deconstruction, and the Challenge to Legal Positivism: The Call for Judicial Responsibility,' Yale Journal of Law and The Humanities, 2, 2, Summer 1990, 267-97, whose argument prompted this note. The significance of time and space in social organizations generally, and the shift from modernism to 'postmodernism' in particular, is the central theme of A. Giddens, The Consequences of Modernity (Stanford: Stanford University Press, 1990).

consequent material effects on the individual psyches that entertain the fantasy. If these material effects are taken into account, the extent to which the fantasy takes hold individually, and thus, the extent to which individuals act in accord with the fantasy's constructed causal direction, might also be cumulative. At this point I return to Lacan.

When he discussed the ego's era, Lacan noted that it was accompanied by increasing aggressiveness and anxiety. He explained this in terms of the spatial constrictions of the urban environment. The more spatially constricted the environment becomes, the greater the anxiety and the greater the tendency to project this anxiety outwards in aggressiveness. Lacan's account of this process is as allusive as his account of objectification. Here again, a link needs to be made between aggressiveness, and the other dynamics of objectification revealed by the analysis of the commodity. At one level the link is self-evident. If a vending machine fails to produce, its chances of being kicked are high. At another level, it is plain that the link has to be established in spatio-temporal, physical terms. Lacan's emphasis on spatiality provides a physical pointer, which can be extended in terms of the speculative account of still points of resistance offered here. These still points are inanimate, whether they are constructed commodities or internal fantasies. What I want to suggest in concluding is that just as its own fantasies weigh heavily upon the ego, so does a subjective if subliminal sensing of what is animate or inanimate in the surrounding environment. The less animate that environment is, the slower time becomes, then the greater the ego's need to speed things up, its anxiety, its splitting, its need for control, its 'cutting-up' in its urge to know, its spoiling of living nature, and its general aggression towards the other. But of course, as with any paranoid anxiety, the ego, by these processes, only accelerates the production of the conditions that produce its fears.[37] It constructs more still points which start, or speed up, the whole show again.

The result is an increasing incapacity to tolerate delay, a greater demand for service, a more extensive need for domination, a horror of inferiority contingent on escalating envy and the constant comparisons envy demands, and an ever-rising flight away from the

---

37. There is a striking account of the paranoid's collusion in the production of the conditions it fears in Bersani's discussion of Thomas Pynchon. See Leo Bersani, *The Culture of Redemption* (Cambridge: Mass., Harvard University Press, 1990), p. 188.

active living flesh into the fantasmatic world of metaphor. It is this last that makes the sometimes obvious nature of the processes recorded here elusive.[38] The originating foundational fantasy situates the mother as a passive natural entity responding to an active agency located elsewhere. The extent to which active agency really is located elsewhere increases as the material means to control the environment increase. In other words, in that active agency is the ability to do things according to one's own direction, to impose direction, to 'make it happen', this ability must increase as the material means for accomplishing one's will also increase. To the extent that this active agency results in the imposition of a direction on the environment which goes against, rather than with, natural rhythms and their own logic, the force of the latter figures less in any calculations made about what causes what. To say the same thing differently, by this argument, the subject's sense of connection with the world is physically altered by its physical environment. And if the physical points of resistance embodied in commodities function after the manner of fantasies, closing the subject off to the movement of life, they are also visual tangible evidence of a different physical world which, however fantasmatic its origin, makes the subject more likely to see what it has made, rather than feel itself to be connected with, or part of, what had made it. The visual hallucination which denied feelings of unpleasure is now a concrete thing, and the various senses which otherwise connect the subject with the world stand back in favour of the visual sense. This visual favouritism takes us back to the optical connection with which we began.[39]

38. What confuses the issue further is, I suspect, that the accumulating physical pressure is then deflected on to women, which means both that the tendency literally to objectify women at every level should be increasing, and that one is likely to mistake the object on to, or from which, pressure is deflected as its cause. Thus, perhaps, the ludicrous projections which men direct towards women, claiming that women are really in control. On the other hand, as we have seen, the objectification of women is not, in the last analysis, a product of the psychical fantasy of woman, but of a more ancient foundational fantasy.

39. The critique of ocularcentrism is so basic to twentieth-century French critical theory that extended references seem superfluous. The key figures here, of course, are Merleau-Ponty and Foucault. There is a useful critique and review of the relevant literature in M. Jay, "In the Empire of the Gaze: Foucault and the Denigration of Vision in Twentieth-century French Thought," in: *Foucault: A Critical Reader*, edited by D. Couzens Hoy (Oxford: Basil Blackwell, 1986), pp. 175-204. Rosi Braidotti develops the critique of ocularcentrism from a feminist perspective in "*Organs Without Bodies*."

The idea that the subject's sense of perception is physically altered by its physical environment, and the correlative idea that the concrete imposition of a foundational psychical fantasy has altered that environment, also raise the possibility that different physical theories and theories of perception are more true for their times than they appear with hindsight, precisely because the times physically alter what and how we perceive.[40] If the parallel drawn here between psychical and socio-historical temporal interference is correct, if the construction of more and more commodities slows down real time while seeming to speed it up, then this means the physical reality in which we exist, the physical laws under which we live, are being and have been altered. By a socio-historical process, have we produced the chaotic physis we now discover, as if it had always been present? For if we have, we have done so by enacting a psychical fantasy which, because it relies on a divorce of mental and physical activity, reinforces the prejudice that the psychical process and its socio-historical parallel have no effect on the physical world; this prejudice in thought may be why it is difficult to get clear information from a scientist concerning the question just posed.

Pending that information, there is no reason why the process described here cannot be reversed, or at least, reversed to the extent that an awareness of the function of still or inert points of resistance means that their worst effects are avoided. In other words, we confront teleology only in the logical sense that the process described here is cumulative. Where the energy to reverse that accumulation comes from is another question, except that it comes. It is

40. Luce Irigaray argues in *Ethique de la différence sexuelle* (Paris: Minuit, 1984) that any epochal change also requires a change in how space and time are perceived. The difference between her observation and this argument is that I rigaray sees the change in space-time perception solely in subjective terms, rather than attempting to explain it as a change that is physically produced. For a good discussion of French feminist theory and spatio-temporal concerns, see Elizabeth Grosz, "Space, Time and Bodies," *On The Beach*, Sydney, 13, 1988. It should be added here that many feminist philosophers of science have suggested that the boundaries of the physical sciences and their underlying assumptions should be thrown into question; there is no reason why the physical sciences should have escaped gender-blindness, when the social sciences have not. But there is a difference between noting that the physical sciences should be questioned, or even showing that a more empathetic approach to science is possible (as does Evelyn Fox Keller, for instance in "Feminism and Science," *Signs*, Spring 1982, 589-602) and proposing an alternative, speculative, physical theory. This is not the exhortation. This is the act.

evident all around us. Perhaps Benjamin was right, and the very act of unleashing uncharted forces provides a fuel, or is it an intensity of will, that can reverse direction and revivify what is has harmed? The owl of Minerva is beginning to flutter. She might yet fly, if she can free her wings of the oil slick.[41]

41. "The Age of Paranoia" was originally published in *Paragraph*, Vol. 14, 1991. I am grateful to Oxford University Press for permission to reprint. There is a slight difference between that version and this one. Initially I described the psychical fantasy as transhistorical. This was wrong. I can only suppose that I went to an unconscious retorical extreme to sort something out. What I am actually describing is the construction of a foundational psychic fantasy. This notion is described in my *History after Lacan*, Routledge 1993; the book from which this comes.

Bio-bibliographical Information
on the Authors

H.J. Adriaanse is Professor of Philosophy of Religion and Ethics at the University of Leiden, The Netherlands. He is the author of *Zu den Sachen selbst. Versuch einer Konfrontation der Theologie Karl Barths mit der phänomenologischen Philosophie Edmund Husserls* ('s-Gravenhage: Mouton, 1974) and (together with H.A. Krop and L. Leertouwer) of *Het verschijnsel theologie. Over de wetenschappelijke status van de theologie* (Amsterdam: Boom, 1987) as well as the editor (together with H.A. Krop) of *Theologie en rationaliteit. Godsdienstwijsgerige bijdragen* (Kampen: Kok, 1988)

Geoffrey Bennington is Professor of French at the University of Sussex. He has written extensively on recent French thought and on French eighteenth-century fiction and rhetoric. He has translated work by Derrida and Lyotard into English. He is the author of *Lyotard. Writing the Event* (New York: Columbia University Press, 1988), *Dudding. Des noms de Rousseau* (Paris: Galilée, 1991), and "Derridabase" in Geoffrey Bennington and Jacques Derrida, *Derrida* (Paris: Seuil, 1991).

Rosi Braidotti is Professor and Chair of Women's Studies in the Humanities at the University of Utrecht. She is the author of *Patterns of Dissonance* (Cambridge: Polity Press, 1991), a study of women in contemporary philosophy. She has also published extensively on feminist theory in collections such as *Between Feminism and Psychoanalysis, Men in Feminism, Critical Dictionary of Feminism and Psychoanalysis,* and journals such as *Differences, Gender Studies, Hypatia, Woman's Studies International Forum, DWF, Les Cahiers du Grif,* and others. She co-ordinates an Erasmus exchange network for Women's Studies with seven European partners.

Teresa Brennan is Professor at the Universities of Cambridge and Amsterdam. She is the editor of *Between Feminism and Psycho-*

analysis (London: Routledge, 1989) and the author of *The Interpretation of the Flesh. Freud and Femininity* (London: Routledge, 1992) and *History after Lacan* (London: Routledge, 1993)

Peter Dews is Senior Lecturer in Philosophy, University of Essex, England. He is the author of *Logics of Disintegration* (Verso, 1987), and of numerous essays on contemporary European philosophy. His current research is concerned with theories of subjectivity, particularly in psychoanalysis and in German Idealism. During the Winter Semester 1992/1993 he was a Visiting Professor at the University of Konstanz.

Rodolphe Gasché is Eugenio Donato Professor of Comparative Literature at the State University of New York, at Buffalo. His publications include *Die hybride Wissenschaft* (Stuttgart: Metzler, 1973), *System und Metaphorik in der Philosophie von Georges Bataille* (Lang, 1978), and *The Tain of the Mirror: Derrida and the Philosophy of Reflection* (Harvard University Press, 1986). His forthcoming book is entitled: *Inventions of Difference: On Derrida and de Man.*

Helga Geyer-Ryan is Associate Professor of Comparative Literature at the University of Amsterdam and has taught German at the universities of Geneva and Cambridge. She has published widely on literature and feminism, popular culture and literary theory. Her major publications include *Popular Literature in the Third Reich* (1980), *Der andere Roman. Versuch über die verdrängte Aesthetik des Populären* (1983), *Literary Theory Today*, co-edited with Peter Collier (1990), and *Fables of Desire. Studies in the Ethics of Art and Gender* (forthcoming, 1993)

Beatrice Hanssen is an Assistant Professor of German at Harvard University, Cambridge, Massachusetts. She is currently working on a study of the relation between language and violence in the writings of Ingeborg Bachmann and Elfriede Jelinek.

Philippe Van Haute teaches at the Catholic University of Nijme-

407

gen. His recent publications include *Filosofie en psychoanalyse. Het imaginaire en het symbolische in het werk van Jacques Lacan* (Leuven: Peeters, 1992), and *Deconstructie en ethiek*, co-edited with S. IJsseling (Leuven, Assen: L.U.P., Van Gorcum, 1992). He is the co-editor, together with D. Loose, of Cl. Lefort, *Het demokratisch tekort. Over de noodzakelijke onbepaaldheid van de democratie* (Meppel: Boom, 1992)

Harry Kunneman is Professor of Practical Humanist Studies at the University for Humanist Studies in Utrecht. He is the author of *Der Wahrheitstrichter. Habermas und die Postmoderne* (Frankfurt/M, New York: Campus Verlag, 1991) and co-editor, together with Hent de Vries of *Die Aktualität der Diaklektik der Aufklärung. Zwischen Moderne und Postmoderne* (Frankfurt/M, New York: Campus Verlag, 1989).

Rainer Nägele is Professor of German at the Johns Hopkins University, Baltimore, Maryland. His recent books are *Text, Geschichte und Subjektivität in Hölderlins Dichtung: Unessbarer Schrift gleich* (Stuttgart: Metzler, 1985), *Reading after Freud. Essays on Goethe, Hölderlin, Habermas, Nietzsche, Brecht, Celan, and Freud* (New York: Columbia University Press, 1987), and *Theater, Theory, Speculation: Walter Benjamin and the Scenes of Modernity* (Baltimore: Johns Hopkins University Press, 1991).

Ludwig Nagl is Professor of Philosophy at the University of Vienna. His books include *Gesellschaft und Autonomie. Historisch-systematische Studien zur Entwicklung der Sozialtheorie von Hegel bis Habermas* (Vienna, 1983), *Wo steht die Analytische Philosophie heute?*, co-edited with R. Heinrich (Wien, München 1986), *Nach der Philosophie. Essays von Stanley Cavell*, co-edited with K.R. Fischer (Klagenfurt 1987), *Die Philosophen und Freud*, co-edited with H. Vetter (Wien, München, 1988), *Philosophie und Psychoanalyse*, co-edited with H. Vetter and H. Leupold-Löwenthal (Frankfurt/M 1990), *Philosophie und Semiotik*, co-edited with E. List, J. Bernard and G. Withalm (Wien, 1991), and *Charles Sander Peirce* (Frankfurt/M, New York, 1992)

Helga Nagl-Docekal is Professor of Philosophy at the University of Vienna. She has been a Visiting Professor at the universities of Utrecht, Frankfurt/M and Konstanz and is a board member of the International Association of Women Philosophers. Among her books are: *Tod des Subjekts?* (co-edited, 1987), *Feministische Philosophie* (edited, 1990), *Denken der Geschlechterdifferenz* (co-edited, 1990), and *Jenseits der Geschlechtermoral* (co-edited, 1993)

Willem van Reijen is Professor of Social and Political Philosophy at the University of Utrecht. His books include *Philosophie als Kritik* (Königstein/Ts.: Athenäum: 1984, 1986), *Walter Benjamin*, together with Norbert Bolz (Frankfurt/M: Campus Verlag, 1991), *Modernisierung. Projekt oder Paradox*, together with Hans van der Loo (München: DTV, 1992). He has co-edited *Die unvollendete Vernunft: Moderne versus Postmoderne*, together with K.O. Apel (Frankfurt/M: Suhrkamp, 1987), *Vierzig Jahre Flaschenpost. Die Dialektik der Aufklärung 1947-1987*, together with Gunzelin Schmid Noerr (Frankfurt/M: Fischer, 1987), *Die Frage nach dem Subjekt*, together with Manfred Frank (Frankfurt/M: Suhrkamp, 1988), *Allegorie und Melancholie* (Frankfurt/M: Suhrkamp, 1992), and *Bürgergesellschaft und Demokratie*, together with Bert van den Brink (forthcoming).

Jacob Rogozinsky teaches in the Philosophy Department of the University of Paris-VIII. He has been *directeur de programme* at the *Collège International de Philosophie* and is the author of several studies on Kant, Husserl, Heidegger and contemporary French philosophy (Sartre, Derrida, Deleuze and Lyotard).

Hent de Vries teaches philosophy at the University of Amsterdam. He is the author of *Theologie im pianissimo & Zwischen Rationalität und Dekonstruktion. Die Aktualität der Denkfiguren Adornos und Levinas'* (Kampen: Kok, 1989), and is the co-editor, together with Harry Kunneman, of *Die Aktualität der Dialektik der Aufklärung. Zwischen Moderne und Postmoderne* (Frankfurt/M, New York: Campus Verlag, 1989).

Elisabeth Weber is Assistant Professor of German at the University of California, Santa Barbara. She is the author of *Verfolgung und*

Trauma. Zu Emmanuel Lévinas' Autrement qu'être ou au-delà de l'essence (Viennna: Passagen, 1990), and the editor of Jacques Derrida, *Limited Inc* (Paris: Galilée, 1990) as well as of Jacques Derrida, *Points de suspension* (Paris: Galilée, 1992).

Samuel Weber is Professor of English and Comparative Literature at the University of California at Los Angeles and Director of UCLA's Paris Program in Critical Theory. He is the author of *The Legend of Freud* (Minneapolis: University of Minnesota Press, 1982), *Institution and Interpretation* (Minneapolis: University of Minnesota Press, 1987) and *Return to Freud. Jacques Lacan's Dislocation of Psychoanalysis* (Cambridge: Cambridge University Press, 1991). He has two books forthcoming: a collection of essays entitled *Mass Mediauras: Essays on Form, Technics and the Media*, and *Coming to Pass: The Writing of Walter Benjamin*.

Albrecht Wellmer is Professor of Philosophy at the Free University of Berlin. His publications include: *Zur Dialektik von Moderne und Postmoderne. Vernunftkritik nach Adorno* (Frankfurt/M: Suhrkamp, 1985), *Ethik und Dialog. Elemente des moralischen Urteilens bei Kant und in der Diskursethik* (Frankfurt/M: Suhrkamp, 1986), *Zwischenbetrachtungen. Im Prozess der Aufklärung*, edited together with Axel Honneth, Thomas McCarthy and Claus Offe (Frankfurt/M: Suhrkamp, 1989), *The Persistence of Modernity. Essays on Aesthetics, Ethics and Postmodernism* (Cambridge: Polity Press, 1991), and *Endspiele. Die unversöhnliche Moderne* (Frankfurt/M: Suhrkamp, 1993, forthcoming).

Index of Names

411